KEVIL

Brief Contents

A Note to Students from Miriam Moore   v
Thematic Table of Contents   xvii
Preface   xix

PART 1   How to Write Paragraphs and Essays   1

1   Critical Thinking, Reading, and Writing: Making Connections   3
2   Writing Basics: Audience, Purpose, Form, and Process   29
3   Finding Your Topic and Writing Your Thesis Statement: Making a Point   41
4   Supporting Your Point: Finding Details, Examples, and Facts   65
5   Drafting and Revising: The Writing Process   73

PART 2   Writing Different Kinds of Paragraphs and Essays   103

6   Narration: Writing That Tells Important Stories   105
7   Illustration: Writing That Gives Examples   128
8   Description: Writing That Creates Pictures in Words   151
9   Process Analysis: Writing That Explains How Things Happen   173
10 Classification: Writing That Sorts Things into Groups   195
11 Definition: Writing That Tells What Something Means   219
12 Comparison and Contrast: Writing That Shows Similarities and Differences   241
13 Cause and Effect: Writing That Explains Reasons or Results   267
14 Argument: Writing That Persuades   291

PART 3   The Four Most Serious Errors   323

15 The Basic Sentence   325
16 Fragments: Incomplete Sentences   337
17 Run-Ons: Two Sentences Joined Incorrectly   351
18 Problems with Subject-Verb Agreement: When Subjects and Verbs Don't Match   367
19 Verb Tense: Using Verbs to Express Different Times   379

PART 4   Other Grammar Concerns   395

20 Pronouns: Using Substitutes for Nouns   397
21 Adjectives and Adverbs: Using Descriptive Words   413
22 Misplaced and Dangling Modifiers: Avoiding Confusing Descriptions   420
23 Coordination and Subordination: Joining Sentences with Related Ideas   426
24 Parallelism: Balancing Ideas   437
25 Sentence Variety: Putting Rhythm in Your Writing   444
26 Formal English and ESL Concerns: Grammar Trouble Spots for Multilingual Students   458

PART 5   Word Use   489

27 Vocabulary and Word Choice: Using the Right Words   491
28 Commonly Confused Words: Avoiding Mistakes with Soundalike Words   502
29 Spelling: Using the Right Letters   512

PART 6   Punctuation and Capitalization   519

30 Commas ,   521
31 Apostrophes '   532
32 Quotation Marks " "   536
33 Other Punctuation ; : ( ) -- -   543
34 Capitalization: Using Capital Letters   548

APPENDIX   Understanding a Writing Prompt   553

APPENDIX   Citing Research Sources in MLA Style   555

Acknowledgments   563

Index   565

Useful Editing and Proofreading Marks   584

Eighth Edition

Real Writing with Readings

**Paragraphs and Essays for
College, Work, and Everyday Life**

Susan Anker

Miriam Moore
The University of North Georgia

bedford/st.martin's
Macmillan Learning

Boston | New York

For Bedford/St. Martin's

Vice President, Editorial, Macmillan Learning Humanities: Edwin Hill
Executive Program Director for English: Leasa Burton
Senior Program Manager: Karita F. dos Santos
Marketing Manager: Lauren Arrant
Director of Content Development, Humanities: Jane Knetzger
Advanced Developmental Editor: Kate George
Content Project Manager: Louis C. Bruno Jr.
Senior Workflow Project Manager: Jennifer Wetzel
Production Assistant: Brianna Lester
Media Project Manager: Rand Thomas
Media Editor: Adam Whitehurst
Senior Manager of Publishing Services: Andrea Cava
Project Management: Lumina Datamatics, Inc.
Composition: Lumina Datamatics, Inc.
Text Permissions Manager: Kalina Ingham
Text Permissions Researcher: Arthur Johnson/Lumina Datamatics, Inc.
Director of Rights and Permissions: Hilary Newman
Photo Researcher: Brittani Morgan/Lumina Datamatics, Inc.
Permissions Editor: Angela Boehler
Permissions Associate: Allison Ziebka
Director of Design, Content Management: Diana Blume
Text Design: Lumina Datamatics, Inc.
Cover Design: William Boardman
Cover Image: AbbieImages/Getty Images
Printing and Binding: LSC Communications

Manufactured in the United States of America.

1 2 3 4 5 6   23 22 21 20 19 18

For information, write: Bedford/St. Martin's, 75 Arlington Street, Boston, MA 02116

ISBN 978-1-319-05425-0 (Student Edition)
ISBN 978-1-319-20738-0 (Loose-Leaf Edition)

Acknowledgments

Text acknowledgments and copyrights appear at the back of the book on pages 563–64, which constitute an extension of the copyright page. Art acknowledgments and copyrights appear on the same page as the art selections they cover.

A Note to Students from Miriam Moore

Since 1991, I have taught writing, grammar, reading, and ESL in a variety of places, including two universities, an Intensive English program, two community colleges, and even a chicken-processing plant! In each place, I have tried to share my love of words with students, and I have learned by listening to their words, the rhythms of their speech, their questions, and their frustrations.

Words, and the ways we put them together, help us accomplish ordinary tasks and, as our skills improve, some incredible feats: getting a date, making a sale, convincing the boss to try a new idea, changing a law, or solving a long-standing problem. The words we use to read and write can also help us to think more creatively, more deeply, and more effectively. In the eighth edition of *Real Writing*, I want to help you see the value of language skills like reading and writing and the power of practicing them together. Sure, it takes time and attention to learn new words, understand them when you read, and master rules for combining and punctuating them accurately. But in the end, after working for these skills, you will begin to see *them* working for *you*. It will be worth the effort.

I applaud your decision to take this course, and I wish you every success.

Contents

A Note to Students from Miriam Moore   v
Thematic Table of Contents   xvii
Preface   xix

PART 1 How to Write Paragraphs and Essays   1

1 Critical Thinking, Reading, and Writing: Making Connections   3

Preparing for Success   4
STUDENT PREPAREDNESS CHECKLIST   4

Thinking Critically   7
FOUR BASICS OF CRITICAL THINKING   7

Reading Critically   10
Preview the Text   10
Read the Text: Find the Main Idea and
   Support   11
Pause to Think   13
Review and Respond   13
   A Critical Reader at Work   15
**Amanda Jacobowitz, *A Ban on Water Bottles: A
   Way to Bolster the University's Image*   15**

Writing Critically about Readings, Images, and
Problems   17
Writing about Readings?   17
   Summary   18
   Analysis   19
   Synthesis   20
   Evaluation   22

Writing Critically about Visuals   23
   Summary   23
   Analysis   25
   Synthesis   25
   Evaluation   25

Writing Critically about Problems   26

Chapter Review   27
   Reflect and Apply   28

2 Writing Basics: Audience, Purpose, Form, and Process   29

FOUR BASICS OF GOOD WRITING   29
   Understand Audience and Purpose   29
   Understand Paragraph and Essay Form   33
   Understand the Writing Process   34
   Understand Grading Criteria   38

Chapter Review   40
   Reflect and Apply   40

3 Finding Your Topic and Writing Your Thesis Statement: Making a Point   41

Understand What a Topic Is   41

Practice Narrowing a Topic   42

Practice Exploring Your Topic   45
   Freewriting   45
   Listing/Brainstorming   46
   Discussing   46
   Clustering/Mapping   47
   Reading and Researching on the Internet   48
   Keeping a Journal   48

Write Your Own Topic and Ideas   49

Understand What a Topic Sentence and a Thesis
Statement Are   49

Practice Developing a Good Topic Sentence or
Thesis Statement   54
   It Fits the Size of the Assignment   54
   It Contains a Single Main Idea   57
   It Is Specific   58
   It Is an Idea You Can Show, Explain, or
      Prove   60
   It Is a Direct Statement   61

Write Your Own Topic Sentence or Thesis
Statement   62
   Checklist: Evaluating Your Main Idea   64

Chapter Review   64
   Reflect and Apply   64

4 Supporting Your Point: Finding Details, Examples, and Facts   65

Understand What Support Is   65
   Key Features of Good Support   65
   Support in Paragraphs versus Essays   66

Practice Supporting a Main Idea   67
   Generate Support   67
   Select the Best Primary Support   68
   Add Secondary Support   69

Write Your Own Support   69
   Checklist: Evaluating Your Support   71

Chapter Review   72
   Reflect and Apply   72

5 Drafting and Revising: The Writing Process   73

Understand What a Draft Is   73

Arrange Your Ideas   73
   Use Time Order to Write about Events   74
   Use Space Order to Describe Objects, Places, or People   74
   Use Order of Importance to Emphasize a Particular Point   75

Make a Plan   76
   Outlining Paragraphs   76
   Outlining Essays   77

Practice Writing a Draft Paragraph   78
   Write a Draft Using Complete Sentences   78
   Write a Concluding Sentence   79

Practice Writing a Draft Essay   80
   Write Topic Sentences and Draft the Body of the Essay   81
   Write an Introduction   82
   Write a Conclusion   84
   Title Your Essay   86

Write Your Own Draft Paragraph or Essay   86
   Checklist: Evaluating Your Draft Paragraph   87
   Checklist: Evaluating Your Draft Essay   89

Understand What Revision Is   90
   Checklist: Revising Your Writing   90

Practice Revising for Unity, Detail, and Coherence   91
   Revise for Unity   91
   Revise for Detail and Support   93
   Revise for Coherence   95

Practice Giving and Receiving Feedback   98

Revise Your Own Paragraph   98
   Checklist: Evaluating Your Revised Paragraph   100

Revise Your Own Essay   100
   Checklist: Evaluating Your Revised Essay   102

Chapter Review   102
   Reflect and Apply   102

PART 2   Writing Different Kinds of Paragraphs and Essays   103

6 Narration: Writing That Tells Important Stories   105

Understand What Narration Is   105
   FOUR BASICS OF GOOD NARRATION   105
      First Basic: Main Idea in Narration   106
      Second Basic: Primary Support in Narration   108
      Third Basic: Secondary Support in Narration   109
      Fourth Basic: Organization in Narration   111

Evaluate Narration   114

Read and Analyze Narration   116
   Student Narration Paragraph: Jelani Lynch, *My Turnaround*   116
   Student Narration Essay: Trevor Riley-Jewell, *An Unusual Inspiration*   117
   PROFILE OF SUCCESS: Alice Adoga, Family Service Specialist   119
   Workplace Narration: Incident Descriptions (Hypothetical Example)   120
   Professional Narration Essay: Amy Tan, *Fish Cheeks*   121

Grammar for Narration   123

Write Your Own Narration (Assignments)   123
   Writing about College, Work, and Everyday Life   123
   Reading and Writing Critically   124
   Checklist: How to Write Narration   126

Chapter Review   127
   Reflect and Apply   127

7 Illustration: Writing That Gives Examples   128

Understand What Illustration Is   128
   FOUR BASICS OF GOOD ILLUSTRATION   128

First Basic: Main Idea in Illustration   129

Second Basic: Primary Support in Illustration   130

Third Basic: Secondary Support in Illustration   131

Fourth Basic: Organization in Illustration   133

Evaluate Illustration   136

Read and Analyze Illustration   137

Student Illustration Paragraph: Casandra Palmer, *Gifts from the Heart*   138

Student Illustration Essay: Sarah Bigler, *High School Is Not Preparing Us for College*   139

PROFILE OF SUCCESS: Juan C. Gonzalez, Illustration in the Real World   141

Workplace Illustration: Juan C. Gonzalez   141

Professional Illustration Essay: Andrea Whitmer, *When Poor People Have Nice Things*   143

Grammar for Illustration   146

Write Your Own Illustration (Assignments)   146

Writing about College, Work, and Everyday Life   146

Reading and Writing Critically   148

Checklist: How to Write Illustration   150

Chapter Review   150

Reflect and Apply   150

8 Description: Writing That Creates Pictures in Words   151

Understand What Description Is   151

FOUR BASICS OF GOOD DESCRIPTION   151

First Basic: Main Idea in Description   152

Second Basic: Primary Support in Description   154

Third Basic: Secondary Support in Description   155

Fourth Basic: Organization in Description   156

Evaluate Description   157

Read and Analyze Description   161

Student Description Paragraph: Alessandra Cepeda, *Bird Rescue*   161

Student Description Essay: Brian Healy, *First Day in Fallujah*   162

Workplace Description   164

PROFILE OF SUCCESS: James Roy, "Description: Malicious Wounding"   165

Professional Description Essay: Oscar Hijuelos, *Memories of New York City Snow*   166

Grammar for Description   168

Write Your Own Description (Assignments)   168

Writing about College, Work, and Everyday Life   168

Assignment Options Reading and Writing Critically   169

Checklist: How to Write Description   171

Chapter Review   172

Reflect and Apply   172

9 Process Analysis: Writing That Explains How Things Happen   173

Understand What Process Analysis Is   173

FOUR BASICS OF GOOD PROCESS ANALYSIS   173

First Basic: Main Idea in Process Analysis   174

Second Basic: Primary Support in Process Analysis   175

Third Basic: Secondary Support in Process Analysis   176

Fourth Basic: Organization in Process Analysis   177

Evaluate Process Analysis   180

Read and Analyze Process Analysis   182

Student Process Analysis Paragraph: Charlton Brown, *Buying a Car at an Auction*   182

Student Process Analysis Essay: Katie Horn, *A Beginner's Guide to Movie Night*   183

Workplace Essay: Submitting Reprint Corrections   184

PROFILE OF SUCCESS: Paola Garcia-Muniz   185

Professional Process Analysis Essay: Samantha Levine-Finley, *Isn't It Time You Hit the Books?*   187

Grammar for Process Analysis   190

Write Your Own Process Analysis (Assignments)   190

Writing about College, Work, and Everyday Life   191

Reading and Writing Critically   191

Checklist: How to Write Process Analysis   193

Chapter Review   194

Reflect and Apply   194

10 Classification: Writing That Sorts Things into Groups   195

Understand What Classification Is   195

▪▪ FOUR BASICS OF GOOD CLASSIFICATION   195

First Basic: Main Idea in Classification   196

Second Basic: Primary Support in Classification   199

Third Basic: Secondary Support in Classification   200

Fourth Basic: Organization in Classification   201

Evaluate Classification   204

Read and Analyze Classification   206

Student Classification Paragraph: Lorenza Mattazi, *All My Music*   206

Student Classification Essay: Kelly Hultgren, *Pick Up the Phone to Call, Not Text*   207

PROFILE OF SUCCESS: Lisa Currie, Mayor of Toms Brook   209

Workplace Classification: Lisa Currie, "Town Projects"   209

Professional Classification Essay: Stephanie Ericsson, *The Ways We Lie*   211

Grammar for Classification   214

Write Your Own Classification (Assignments)   215

Writing about College, Work, and Everyday Life   215

Reading and Writing Critically   216

Checklist: How to Write Classification   217

Chapter Review   218

Reflect and Apply   218

11 Definition: Writing That Tells What Something Means   219

Understand What Definition Is   219

▪▪ FOUR BASICS OF GOOD DEFINITION   219

First Basic: Main Idea in Definition   220

Second Basic: Primary Support in Definition   222

Third Basic: Secondary Support in Definition   223

Fourth Basic: Organization in Definition   226

Evaluate Definition   227

Read and Analyze Definition   228

Student Definition Paragraph: Corin Costas, *What Community Involvement Means to Me*   228

Student Definition Essay: Kevin Willey, *The Optimistic Generation*   229

PROFILE OF SUCCESS: Moses Maddox, Fellowship Specialist   232

Workplace Definition: Moses Maddox, *Email to Clients*   232

Professional Definition Essay: *Adam McCrimmon, Does My Child Have Autism or Is This "Normal" Behavior?*   234

Grammar for Definition   237

Write Your Own Definition (Assignments)   237

Writing about College, Work, and Everyday Life   237

Reading and Writing Critically   238

Checklist: How to Write Definition   240

Chapter Review   240

Reflect and Apply   240

12 Comparison and Contrast: Writing That Shows Similarities and Differences   241

Understand What Comparison and Contrast Are   241

▪▪ FOUR BASICS OF GOOD COMPARISON AND CONTRAST   241

First Basic: Main Idea in Comparison and Contrast   242

Second Basic: Primary Support in Comparison and Contrast   243

Third Basic: Secondary Support in Comparison and Contrast   246

Fourth Basic: Organization in Comparison and Contrast   246

Evaluate Comparison and Contrast   252

Read and Analyze Comparison and Contrast   253

Student Comparison/Contrast Paragraph: Said Ibrahim, *Eyeglasses versus Laser Surgery: Benefits and Drawbacks*   253

Student Comparison/Contrast Essay: Rita Rantung, *Indonesian and US School Systems*   254

PROFILE OF SUCCESS: Garth Vaz, Physician   258

Workplace Comparison and Contrast Essay: Garth Vaz, *Dyslexia and ADHD*   258

Professional Comparison/Contrast Essay: John Tierney, *Yes, Money Can Buy Happiness* . . . 260

Grammar for Comparison and Contrast 262

Write Your Own Comparison and Contrast (Assignments) 263

Writing about College, Work, and Everyday Life 263

Reading and Writing Critically 264

Checklist: How to Write Comparison and Contrast 265

Chapter Review 266

Reflect and Apply 266

13 Cause and Effect: Writing That Explains Reasons or Results 267

Understand What Cause and Effect Are 267

▪▪ FOUR BASICS OF GOOD CAUSE AND EFFECT 267

First Basic: Main Idea in Cause and Effect 268

Second Basic: Primary Support in Cause and Effect 270

Third Basic: Secondary Support in Cause and Effect 271

Fourth Basic: Organization in Cause and Effect 272

Evaluate Cause and Effect 276

Read and Analyze Cause and Effect 277

Student Cause-and-Effect Paragraph: Caitlin Prokop, *A Difficult Decision with a Positive Outcome* 278

Student Cause-and-Effect Essay: Stephanie Alaimo and Mark Koester, *The Backdraft of Technology* 279

PROFILE OF SUCCESS: Joshua Boyce, Blogger 281

Workplace Cause and Effect: Joshua Boyce, Conditioning 281

Professional Cause-and-Effect Essay: Liz Riggs, *What It's Like to Be the First Person in Your Family to Go to College* 282

Grammar for Cause and Effect 286

Write Your Own Cause and Effect (Assignments) 286

Writing about College, Work, and Everyday Life 286

Reading and Writing Critically 287

Checklist: How to Write Cause and Effect 289

Chapter Review 289

Reflect and Apply 289

14 Argument: Writing That Persuades 291

Understand What Argument Is 291

▪▪ FOUR BASICS OF GOOD ARGUMENT 291

First Basic: Main Idea in Argument 292

Second Basic: Support in Argument (Reasons and Evidence) 294

Third Basic: Consider and Respond to Different Points of View 301

Fourth Basic: Organization in Argument 302

Evaluate Argument 307

Read and Analyze Argument 308

PROFILE OF SUCCESS: Stacie Brown, Legal Assistant 309

Workplace Argument: Stacie Brown, *Billing Email* 309

Professional Argument Essay 1: Climate Change Is Not Happening, John Hawkins, *5 Scientific Reasons That Global Warming Isn't Happening* 311

Professional Argument Essay 2: Climate Change Is Happening, Brett Scheffers and James Watson, *Climate Change Is Affecting All Life on Earth—and That's Not Good News for Humanity* 314

Write Your Own Argument (Assignments) 318

Writing about College, Work, and Everyday Life 318

Reading and Writing Critically 319

Checklist: How to Write Argument 320

Chapter Review 321

Reflect and Apply 321

PART 3 **The Four Most Serious Errors** 323

15 The Basic Sentence 325

The Four Most Serious Errors 325

The Parts of Speech 326

The Basic Sentence 328

Verbs 328

Subjects 331

Completeness 333

Six Basic English Sentence Patterns 334

Chapter Review 336

Reflect and Apply 336

16 Fragments: Incomplete Sentences 337

Understand What Fragments Are 337
In the Real World, Why Is It Important to Correct Fragments? 337

Find and Correct Fragments 338
1. Fragments That Start with Prepositions 339
2. Fragments That Start with Dependent Words 340
3. Fragments That Start with –ing Verb Forms 342
4. Fragments That Start with to and a Verb 344
5. Fragments That Are Examples or Explanations 345

Edit for Fragments 346

Chapter Review 349
Reflect and Apply 350
Flowchart: Finding and Fixing Fragments 350

17 Run-Ons: Two Sentences Joined Incorrectly 351

Understand What Run-Ons Are 351
In the Real World, Why Is It Important to Correct Run-Ons? 352

Find and Correct Run-Ons 353
Add a Period 354
Add a Semicolon 354
Add a Semicolon, a Conjunctive Adverbial, and a Comma 355
Add a Comma and a Coordinating Conjunction 357
Add a Dependent Word 359
A Word That Can Cause Run-Ons: Then 362

Edit for Run-Ons 362

Chapter Review 365
Reflect and Apply 365
Flowchart: Finding and Fixing Run-Ons 366

18 Problems with Subject-Verb Agreement: When Subjects and Verbs Don't Match 367

Understand What Subject-Verb Agreement Is 367
In the Real World, Why Is It Important to Correct Errors in Subject-Verb Agreement? 368

Find and Correct Errors in Subject-Verb Agreement 368
1. The Verb Is a Form of Be, Have, or Do 368
2. Words Come between the Subject and the Verb 370
3. The Sentence Has a Compound Subject 372
4. The Subject Is an Indefinite Pronoun 372
5. The Verb Comes before the Subject 373

Edit for Subject-Verb Agreement Problems 374

Chapter Review 377
Reflect and Apply 377
Flowchart: Finding and Fixing Problems with Subject-Verb Agreement 378

19 Verb Tense: Using Verbs to Express Different Times 379

Understand What Verb Tense Is 379
In the Real World, Why Is It Important to Use the Correct Verb Tense? 379

Practice Using Correct Verbs 380
Regular Verbs 380
Irregular Verbs 382
Past Participles 387
Consistency of Verb Tense 390

Edit for Verb Problems 391

Chapter Review 393
Reflect and Apply 393
Flowchart: Finding and Fixing Verb-Tense Errors 394

PART 4 **Other Grammar Concerns** 395

20 Pronouns: Using Substitutes for Nouns 397

Understand What Pronouns Are 397

Practice Using Pronouns Correctly 397
Identify Pronouns 397
Check for Pronoun Agreement 399
Indefinite Pronouns 400
Make Pronoun Reference Clear 402
Use the Right Type of Pronoun 404
Make Pronouns Consistent in Person 409

Edit for Pronouns 409

Chapter Review   411
  Reflect and Apply   411
  Flowchart: Finding and Fixing Pronoun Problems   412

21 Adjectives and Adverbs: Using Descriptive Words   413

Understand What Adjectives and Adverbs Are   413

Use Adjectives and Adverbs Correctly   415
  Choosing between Adjectives and Adverbs   415
  Using Adjectives and Adverbs in Comparisons   416
  Using *Good, Well, Bad,* and *Badly*   417

Edit for Adjectives and Adverbs   417

Chapter Review   418
  Reflect and Apply   418
  Flowchart: Editing for Correct Usage of Adjectives and Adverbs   419

22 Misplaced and Dangling Modifiers: Avoiding Confusing Descriptions   420

Understand What Misplaced Modifiers Are   420
  Practice Correcting Misplaced Modifiers   421
  Understand What Dangling Modifiers Are   422
  Practice Correcting Dangling Modifiers   423

Edit for Misplaced and Dangling Modifiers   423

Chapter Review   424
  Reflect and Apply   424
  Flowchart: Editing for Misplaced and Dangling Modifiers   425

23 Coordination and Subordination: Joining Sentences with Related Ideas   426

Understand What Coordination Is   426

Practice Using Coordination   426
  Using Coordinating Conjunctions   426
  Using Semicolons   428

Understand What Subordination Is   430

Practice Using Subordination   431

Edit for Coordination and Subordination   434

Chapter Review   435
  Reflect and Apply   435
  Flowchart: Editing for Coordination and Subordination   436

24 Parallelism: Balancing Ideas   437

Understand What Parallelism Is   437

Practice Writing Parallel Sentences   438
  Parallelism in Pairs and Lists   438
  Parallelism in Comparisons   439
  Parallelism with Certain Paired Words   440

Edit for Parallelism   442

Chapter Review   443
  Reflect and Apply   443
  Flowchart: Editing for Parallelism   443

25 Sentence Variety: Putting Rhythm in Your Writing   444

Understand What Sentence Variety Is   444

Practice Creating Sentence Variety   445
  Start Some Sentences with Adverbs   445
  Join Ideas Using an *–ing* Verb   446
  Join Ideas Using a Past Participle   448
  Join Ideas Using an Appositive   451
  Join Ideas Using an Adjective Clause   452

Edit for Sentence Variety   455

Chapter Review   456
  Reflect and Apply   456
  Flowchart: Editing for Sentence Variety   457

26 Formal English and ESL Concerns: Grammar Trouble Spots for Multilingual Students   458

Basic Sentence Patterns   458
  Statements   458
  Negatives   461
  Questions   463
  There Is and *There Are*   464

Pronouns   465
  Confusing Subject and Object Pronouns   466
  Confusing Gender   466
  Leaving Out a Pronoun   466
  Using a Pronoun to Repeat a Subject   466
  Using Relative Pronouns   467

Verbs   467
  The Simple Tenses   467
  The Perfect Tenses   469
  The Progressive Tenses   471
  Modal (Helping) Verbs   475
  Gerunds and Infinitives   480

Articles   483
  Definite and Indefinite Articles   483
  Count and Noncount Nouns   483

Prepositions   485
  Prepositions after Adjectives   485
  Prepositions after Verbs   486

Chapter Review   488
  Reflect and Apply   488

PART 5   Word Use   489

27 Vocabulary and Word Choice: Using the Right Words   491

Understand the Importance of Building Vocabulary and Choosing Words Carefully   491
  Using Context Clues   491
  Using Word Parts   492
  Using a Dictionary   492
  Using a Thesaurus   493

Practice Avoiding Four Common Word-Choice Problems   493
  Vague and Abstract Words   494
  Slang   495
  Wordy Language   496
  Clichés   498

Edit for Word Choice   500

Chapter Review   501
  Flowchart: Editing for Word Choice   501

28 Commonly Confused Words: Avoiding Mistakes with Soundalike Words   502

Understand Why Certain Words Are Commonly Confused   502

Practice Using Commonly Confused Words Correctly   502

Edit for Commonly Confused Words   511

Chapter Review   511

29 Spelling: Using the Right Letters   512

Finding and Correcting Spelling Mistakes   512
  Use a Dictionary   512
  Use a Spell Checker—with Caution   512
  Use Proofreading Techniques   513
  Make a Personal Spelling List   513

Strategies for Becoming a Better Speller   513
  Master Commonly Confused Words   513
  Learn Six Spelling Rules   514
  Exceptions When Forming Plurals   516
  Consult a List of Commonly Misspelled Words   517

Chapter Review   518
  Reflect and Apply   518

PART 6   Punctuation and Capitalization   519

30 Commas ,   521

Understand What Commas Do   521

Practice Using Commas Correctly   521
  Commas between Items in a Series   521
  Commas between Coordinate Adjectives   522
  Commas in Compound Sentences   523
  Commas after Introductory Words   523
  Commas around Appositives and Interrupters   525
  Commas around Adjective Clauses   526
  Other Uses for Commas   528

Edit for Commas   530

Chapter Review   531

31 Apostrophes '   532

Understand What Apostrophes Do   532

Practice Using Apostrophes Correctly   532
  Apostrophes to Show Ownership   532
  Apostrophes in Contractions   533
  Apostrophes with Letters, Numbers, and Time   534

Edit for Apostrophes   535

Chapter Review   535

32 Quotation Marks " " 536

Understand What Quotation Marks Do 536

Practice Using Quotation Marks Correctly 536

Quotation Marks for Direct Quotations 536

Setting Off a Quotation within Another Quotation 538

No Quotation Marks for Indirect (Reported) Speech 539

Quotation Marks for Certain Titles 540

Edit for Quotation Marks 541

Chapter Review 542

33 Other Punctuation ; : ( ) -- - 543

Understand What Punctuation Does 543

Practice Using Punctuation Correctly 543

Semicolon ; 543

Colon : 544

Parentheses ( ) 545

Dash -- 545

Hyphen - 546

Edit for Other Punctuation Marks 546

Chapter Review 547

34 Capitalization: Using Capital Letters 548

Understand Capitalization 548

Practice Three Rules of Capitalization 548

Capitalization of Sentences 548

Capitalization of Names of Specific People, Places, Dates, and Things 549

Capitalization of Titles 551

Chapter Review 551

Reflect and Apply 552

APPENDIX **Understanding a Writing Prompt** 553

APPENDIX **Citing Research Sources in MLA Style** 555

Acknowledgments 563

Index 565

Useful Editing and Proofreading Marks 584

Thematic Contents

Education

Sarah Bigler, *High School Is Not Preparing Us for College (illustration)*

Liz Riggs, *What It's Like to Be the First Person in Your Family to Go to College (cause and effect)*

Rita Rantung, *Indonesian and U.S. School Systems (comparison and contrast)*

Humor

Amy Tan, *Fish Cheeks (narration)*

Katie Horn, *A Beginner's Guide to Movie Night (process analysis)*

Language and Communication

Kelly Hultgren, *Pick Up the Phone to Call, Not Text (classification)*

Stephanie Ericsson, *The Ways We Lie (classification)*

Personal Stories

Trevor Riley-Jewell, *An Unusual Inspiration (narration)*

Arianna Morgan, *The Time I Almost Lost My Baby Brother (narration)*

Amy Tan, *Fish Cheeks (narration)*

Oscar Hijuelos, *Memories of New York City Snow (description)*

Brian Healy, *First Day in Fallujah (description)*

Liz Riggs, *What It's Like to Be the First Person in Your Family to Go to College (cause and effect)*

Psychology: Behavior and the Mind

Brian Healy, *First Day in Fallujah (description)*

Stephanie Ericsson, *The Ways We Lie (classification)*

John Tierney, *Yes, Money Can Buy Happiness . . . (comparison and contrast)*

Adam McCrimmon, *Does My Child Have Autism or Is This "Normal" Behavior? (definition)*

Social Issues and Challenges

Amanda Jacobowitz, *A Ban on Water Bottles: A Way to Bolster the University's Image (argument)*

Andrea Whitmer, *When Poor People Have Nice Things (illustration)*

Brian Healy, *First Day in Fallujah (description)*

Stephanie Ericsson, *The Ways We Lie (classification)*

Stephanie Alaimo and Mark Koester, *The Backdraft of Technology (cause and effect)*

Liz Riggs, *What It's Like to Be the First Person in Your Family to Go to College (cause and effect)*

John Hawkins, *5 Scientific Reasons That Global Warming Isn't Happening (argument)*

Brett Scheffers and James Watson, *Climate Change Is Affecting All Life on Earth—and That's Not Good News for Humanity (argument)*

Kevin Willey, *The Optimistic Generation (definition)*

Trends

Amanda Jacobowitz, *A Ban on Water Bottles: A Way to Bolster the University's Image (argument)*

Kelly Hultgren, *Pick Up the Phone to Call, Not Text (classification)*

Stephanie Alaimo and Mark Koester, *The Backdraft of Technology (cause and effect)*

Work

Brian Healy, *First Day in Fallujah (description)*

Preface

The first aim of *Real Writing with Readings* has always been to communicate to students that good writing skills are both essential and attainable. When they have this perspective, students can start fresh, reframing the writing course for themselves not as an irrelevant hoop to jump through but as a central gateway—a potentially life-changing opportunity, worthy of their best efforts. In large and small ways, this book is designed to help students prepare for their futures. It connects the writing class to their other courses, to their real lives, and to the expectations of the larger world.

Real Writing underscores this powerful message in its initial chapter, "Critical Thinking, Reading, and Writing"; in its practical advice on writing different kinds of essays; and in its step-by-step grammar sections, which build confidence and proficiency by focusing first on the most serious errors students commonly make. A diverse collection of both student and professional readings further encourages students to see the big picture, giving them a context for what they are learning. Profiles of Success provide inspirational portraits of former students, now in the workplace, who reflect on the varied, important ways they use writing in their work. These profiles are accompanied by real samples of the kinds of writing these professionals use in the workplace.

Real Writing shares this practical, real-world approach with its companion texts—*Real Essays*, *Real Skills*, and *Real Reading and Writing*, an integrated reading and writing text. All four books put writing in a real-world context and link writing skills to students' own goals in and beyond college.

Core Features

Successful and popular features of earlier editions of *Real Writing* have been carried over to this edition, with revisions based on suggestions from many insightful instructors and students.

- **A Comprehensive Teaching and Learning Package:** *Real Writing* combines carefully curated readings, writing samples, writing assignments, grammar instruction, critical thinking coverage, and reading coverage in one convenient volume, reducing the time spent pulling together materials from various sources and allowing instructors to focus on what matters most: their students.

- **Writing Practice:** Not only does *Real Writing* feature a number of student model paragraphs and essays, workplace writing, and professional readings, it asks students to write their own paragraphs and essays in multiple assignments throughout the book. These assignments aid students in translating their writing skills to the real world, asking them to practice concepts through the lens of tasks they will need to complete in college and beyond, such as analyzing monthly expenses, evaluating instructors, and creating a résumé. Each rhetorical mode chapter also features a step-by-step writing guide and checklist that students can refer to when completing their writing assignments.

- **Profiles of Success:** These profiles feature former students who regularly use writing in their careers, highlighting their background and the ways in which they use writing beyond the classroom. These inspirational stories give students an idea of the diverse range of careers in which writing skills are valuable—from auto technician to chief of police—and how they, too, can hope to reach their career goals.

- **The Four Basics and Four Most Serious Errors:** This approach breaks the writing process down into logical steps, focusing on the four basics of each rhetorical mode as well as the four most serious errors in grammar. This lets students digest information at their own pace, helping them really understand each concept before starting a new one.

- **The Critical Reading Process:** Appearing throughout the book, this process helps students tackle readings using critical thinking skills, asking them to preview, read, pause, review, and respond to each reading. Students can use this process not only with the readings in this course, but those in all of their college courses.

New to This Edition

This edition includes carefully developed new features to help students become better readers and writers in college and beyond.

- **Expanded Reading Coverage:** Every chapter in Parts 1 and 2 contains expanded coverage and guidance for developing critical reading skills. Reflect and Apply questions at the end of the chapters throughout the book allow students to track their own progress on those skills. These features help students become stronger readers by pointing them precisely where they need to focus.

- **Expanded Critical Thinking Coverage:** Building on the basics of critical thinking developed in Chapter 1, marginal tips and the Reading and Writing Critically assignment options throughout the book give students the opportunity to practice and expand upon these vital skills.

- **Updated Readings:** This new edition features new relevant and relatable readings on topics such as climate change, children with disabilities, differences in school systems, and writing inspiration. These new pieces will allow students to hone their skills while engaging with topics that are important to them.

- **Emphasis on Situational Writing:** Real writing samples from the workplace, including a police report, a blog post, a professional and student résumé, and a program e-mail showcase the various ways in which students will use writing skills beyond the classroom, encouraging them to apply what they learn in their future college courses and in their daily lives.

- **A New Mode-Appropriate Grammar in Context Feature:** This new feature, which appears in each of the modes chapters, will allow students to practice their grammar skills within the context of real-life applications and their own writing. Research shows that students are better able to transfer skills learned in the context of their own writing to the writing they do in other courses and outside of school.

- **A New Research and MLA Appendix:** Writing research papers is an extremely important part of many college courses. With that in mind, we have added a new research and MLA appendix as a resource for students who are completing research assignments.

- **A New Interpreting a Writing Prompt Appendix:** The first step to successfully completing a writing assignment is understanding the writing prompt. This new appendix provides a step-by-step guide to approaching a writing prompt, as well as a chart that explains what a student needs to do to address specific action verbs they may come across in their prompts. This helps them understand and respond appropriately to writing prompts or tasks in other courses and contexts as well.

- **Simplified and Streamlined Chapter Openers** get students right into the action of the chapter, allowing them to focus on the skills that they are developing.

We're All In. As Always.

Bedford/St. Martin's is as passionately committed to the discipline of English as ever, working hard to provide support and services that make it easier for you to teach your course your way.

Find **community support** at the Bedford/St. Martin's English Community (community.macmillan.com), where you can follow our *Bits* blog for new teaching ideas, download titles from our professional resource series, and review projects in the pipeline.

Choose **curriculum solutions** that offer flexible custom options, combining our carefully developed print and digital resources, acclaimed works from Macmillan's trade imprints, and your own course or program materials to provide the exact resources your students need. Our approach to customization makes it possible to create a customized project uniquely suited for your students, and based on your enrollment size, return money to your department.

Rely on **outstanding service** from your Bedford/St. Martin's sales representative and editorial team. Contact us or visit macmillanlearning.com to learn more about any of the options below.

Choose from Alternative Formats of Real Writing with Readings

Bedford/St. Martin's offers a range of formats. Choose what works best for you and your students:

- *Paperback.* To order the *paperback* edition, use ISBN 978-1-319-05425-0.

- *Loose-leaf edition.* The loose-leaf edition does not have a traditional binding; its pages are loose and hole punched to provide flexibility and a low price to students. To order the *loose-leaf* edition, use ISBN 978-1-319-20738-0.

Select Value Packages

Add value to your text by packaging a Bedford/St. Martin's resource, such as *LaunchPad Solo for Readers and Writers* with *Real Writing with Readings* at a significant discount. Contact your sales representative for more information.

LaunchPad Solo for Readers and Writers allows students to work on what they need help with the most. At home or in class, students learn at their own pace, with instruction tailored to each student's unique needs. *LaunchPad Solo for Readers and Writers* features:

- **Pre-built units that support a learning arc.** Each easy-to-assign unit is comprised of a pre-test check, multimedia instruction and assessment, and a post-test that assesses what students have learned about critical reading, writing process, using sources, grammar, style, and mechanics. Dedicated units also offer help for multilingual writers.

- **Diagnostics that help establish a baseline for instruction.** Assign diagnostics to identify areas of strength and for improvement and to help students plan a course of study. Use visual reports to track performance by topic, class, and student as well as improvement over time.

- **A video introduction to many topics.** Introductions offer an overview of the unit's topic, and many include a brief, accessible video to illustrate the concepts at hand.

- **Twenty-five reading selections with comprehension quizzes.** Assign a range of classic and contemporary essays, each of which includes a label indicating Lexile level to help you scaffold instruction in critical reading.

- **Adaptive quizzing for targeted learning.** Most units include Learning-Curve, game-like adaptive quizzing that focuses on the areas in which each student needs the most help.

Order ISBN 978-1-319-22660-2 to package *LaunchPad Solo for Readers and Writers* with *Real Writing with Readings* at a significant discount. Students who rent or buy a used book can purchase access and instructors may request free access at **macmillanlearning.com/readwrite**.

Instructor Resources

You have a lot to do in your course. We want to make it easy for you to find the support you need—and to get it quickly.

The Instructor's Manual for Real Writing with Readings is available as a PDF that can be downloaded from macmillanlearning.com. Visit the instructor resources tab for *Real Writing with Readings*. In addition to chapter overviews and teaching tips, the instructor's manual includes sample syllabi, evaluation guides, activities, handouts, quizzes, and tests.

Acknowledgments

Like every edition that preceded it, this book grew out of a collaboration with teachers and students across the country and with the talented staff of Bedford/ St. Martin's. I am grateful for everyone's thoughtful contributions.

Reviewers

I would like to thank the following instructors for their many good ideas and suggestions for this edition. Their insights were invaluable.

Sandra K. Chumchal, Blinn College
Lisa Yarnell, Eastern Florida State College
Peggy Karsten, Ridgewater College
Paige Huskey, Clark State Community College
Kathleen Flynn, Glendale Community College
Linda Baillie, Eastern Florida State College
Patricia Sheehy Colella, Bunker Hill Community College
Steven Rothblatt, Fashion Institute of Design & Merchandising
Erin Severs, Mohawk Valley Community College
Debra Benedetti, Pierpont Community & Technical College
Ann Bogard, Walla Walla Community College
Denise Meyer, Western Technical College
Gina Santoro, Community College of Rhode Island
Angela Mellor, Western Technical College
Elizabeth M. Marsh, Bergen Community College

Critical Thinking, Reading, and Writing

Making Connections

If you are reading this chapter, you probably just started a college writing course, and you might not know what to expect. What will the teacher require? What will class be like? How do I get through this course—and all my courses—successfully?

Students come to college from all walks of life and with different types of experiences and backgrounds. What may be common knowledge to you about how to be a successful student may be a new idea to another student, or it could even be a strategy that one of your classmates used at one time but has forgotten. Before starting any course, it is important to recognize what your instructor expects and put yourself into a mind-set that will help create a successful college experience for you.

In this chapter, you will learn about some common expectations that college writing instructors have of their students: being prepared, thinking critically, reading carefully and critically, and writing critically about readings (also called **texts**), images, and problems. Some of these expectations may be familiar to you, and some may be new. It is important not only to be aware of these expectations, but also to know that you will not be alone as you work to achieve them. A writing class is, in fact, a writing community; in a writing class, you will collaborate with others to develop writing skills and meet your instructor's expectations. At times, you may find the experience of sharing your writing uncomfortable, but learning to work with others to brainstorm, draft, revise, and edit papers will help you become a stronger writer. By understanding your role in this community and how this community will help you grow as a writer and a student, you will be better equipped for success in this and other courses.

Preparing for Success

All students can benefit from thinking carefully about the strategies that will help them become successful in class. During the first week of class, your instructor should distribute a syllabus or some other document with expectations and policies. Not all policies and expectations will be the same because every instructor and every course is different, but most share the baseline expectations outlined here. You should be aware of these policies and expectations as you start this course because your instructor will expect you to understand and adhere to them throughout the semester.

PRACTICE 1–1   **Learn More about Your Own Preparedness**

Take a few minutes to go through the strategies below that prepare students to engage with the course. How many of these strategies do you already employ? Why have you chosen to use them? If you haven't used one of them, why not? Would you be willing to try? Why or why not?

After writing about your own preferences, interview one or two other students in the class. What did they write in their responses? Why did they make the choices they did? What does this tell you about the way different people learn and participate in a class?

Student Preparedness Checklist

Item	What it means	Do you do this?
Treat your course as seriously as you would a job.	Going to class is similar to having a job. You must do the tasks assigned to you to earn a salary at work; likewise, you must complete assignments with care to learn and earn passing marks in class. Think of your coursework as a job that can lead to bigger and better things—if you work hard and perform well.	
Come to class on time, and stay until your instructor dismisses you.	Again, attending class is like going to a job—you have to come and go on the boss's schedule, not your own. When you arrive late or leave early, you not only disrupt other students, you might miss instructions for the day's work or homework to prepare for the next class.	
Come to class prepared.	You have to do your homework or expect to fail. Even if you have never regularly done homework before and have managed to pass, you will not pass in college. Some instructors deduct points or do not accept late homework. Others may even ask you to leave class or count you as absent if you do not have your homework completed.	

Item	What it means	Do you do this?
Connect to others in class.	Students often sit in the same places for each class. Exchange names, phone numbers, and email addresses with at least one student who sits near you. That way, if you miss a class, you can find out from that person what you missed. You might also want to study with that person.	
Let your instructor know if you are going to miss class, and contact him or her about the work you missed.	Be a good communicator. Instructors can help you make up what you have missed—but only if you have made a connection and communicate in a clear, respectful way. Send an email or call your instructor to find out what you missed, and make sure you write in clear language—not texting language.	
Read the syllabus carefully and hang onto it the entire semester.	Your instructor will expect you to know what the homework is and when assignments are due: your syllabus will tell you. Always bring your syllabus to class, in case your instructor announces updates or reminders.	
Get to know your instructor.	Communication is important. If you get a low grade or do not understand something, ask in class or via email, or visit your instructor during office hours. It is up to you to take steps to clear up anything you do not understand.	
Participate in class: ask questions, answer questions, and make comments.	Do not be afraid of making a stupid comment or giving the wrong answer. That is part of the learning process. Plus, many instructors grade on participation.	
Listen and take notes.	When the instructor is talking, listen carefully, but do not try to write down every word he or she says. To figure out what you should make a note of, look at the instructor. Important points are often signaled with a hand gesture, a note on the board, or a change in the tone of the instructor's voice.	
Don't hide.	The further back in the classroom you sit or the closer you are to a back corner, the more tempting it is to let your mind wander or to stop focusing on class material. If you want to keep your mind focused on the task at hand, try to get a seat near the front of the class.	
Schedule your time wisely.	If you choose to wait until the last minute to work on a large project, you will either not be able to finish or you will do a bad job and get a bad grade. Part of being a successful student is the ability to schedule your time.	

Students who are prepared also set goals and connect coursework to their future plans. You may already know what degree you want to pursue in college and what type of job you want in the future. With these long-term goals in mind, you also need shorter-term goals—steps that help you get where you want to go. To be successful in any course, it is important to identify both long-term and short-term goals. These goals give you a reason to attend class and a tangible goal to work toward. Consider the following as you start this new semester.

PRACTICE 1-2   Looking Ahead to Degree Goals

Whether or not you have decided what you want to major in, you should still ask yourself some questions now. Which majors interest me? Which courses would I need to take to complete the major(s) that interest me? What are the required core courses that every student must take to graduate, and when should I take those courses?

Course requirements for each major are listed in the college bulletin and on the college website. It's a good idea, however, to sit down with your academic adviser as soon as possible to plan a sequence of courses. If you are like most students, you are juggling a lot of important priorities, and having a plan to reach your goals will help you achieve them.

Using these questions as a guide, write about your academic or degree goals. As you write, think about how this writing class connects to your degree plans.

What do you think you might major in?

What courses will you need for that major?

How many courses can you take next term?

What courses will fit into your schedule? (Remember, certain courses have other courses as prerequisites.)

What kinds of reading and writing assignments will be required for these courses?

Why is this class important for your degree?

PRACTICE 1-3   Looking Ahead to Career Goals

You may or may not know what your career goals are at this point. Even if you do not yet have clear goals, try answering the following questions to jump-start your thinking. Using the following questions as a guide, write about your career goals. As you write, think about how this writing course connects to your plans.

What field might I like to work in after completing my college coursework?

What kinds of additional degrees or certifications might I need to obtain to work in that field?

In this field, how is writing used? (Reports? Memos? Charts?)

In this field, how is reading used? (Computer records? Articles? Guidebooks?)

Why is this course important for your career?

Thinking Critically

College instructors expect students to think critically about course concepts and assignments. What is critical thinking?

Imagine you are the supervisor at a small, family-owned business. Recently, one of the owners hired a new employee that you are asked to train during your shift. When the shift begins, the new employee still has not shown up. In fact, she shows up fifteen minutes late. When she does finally arrive, her uniform is wrinkled and stained, and she doesn't seem in any hurry to find you or anyone else so that she can start her shift.

What do you think to yourself about this person? What assumptions have you made about her? What kind of employee will she be? Why do you think that?

Thinking critically means that you do not stop with your first impressions and assumptions. Critical thinking requires you to recognize the iceberg principle. Only about 10 percent of an iceberg is visible above the surface of the ocean; the remaining 90 percent is hidden from view. But that 90 percent has a tremendous impact on what is going on above the surface. Similarly, you may not be fully aware of what is motivating your reactions and decisions in a situation. When you think critically, you pause to explore what is hidden below the surface of what you read or see, along with your reactions to it. Such pauses help you keep an open mind, see new perspectives, find alternatives, and make better decisions.

Four Basics of Critical Thinking

1. Be alert to assumptions made by you and others.
2. Question those assumptions.
3. Consider and connect various points of view, even those different from your own.
4. Do not rush to conclusions but instead remain patient and keep an open mind.

Assumptions—ideas or opinions that we do not question and that we automatically accept as true—can get in the way of clear, critical thinking. Here are some assumptions you would probably make about the new employee:

The new employee is careless because she is late.

The new employee is sloppy because her uniform is a mess.

The new employee is unreliable because she didn't contact anyone before coming in late.

The new employee will not be a good employee because she didn't immediately apologize for her tardiness.

In college, work, and everyday life, we often hold assumptions that we are not even aware of. By identifying these assumptions, stating them, and questioning them, we stand a better chance of seeing reality and acting more effectively.

In the case of the new employee, perhaps she had not realized her shift started fifteen minutes before she arrived. Perhaps she thought she was fifteen minutes early. In that case, she would have had plenty of time to straighten her uniform, blot out the coffee stain, and introduce herself. She still should have double-checked the schedule and straightened her uniform before entering the workplace, but it's possible that some of these assumptions are entirely incorrect.

When questioning assumptions, it can help to try to get a bit of distance from them. Imagine what people with entirely different points of view might say. You might even try disagreeing with your own assumptions. Take a look at the following examples.

Questioning Assumptions

Situation	Assumption	Questions
College: I saw from the syllabus that I need to write five essays for this course.	This course may be too difficult for me.	Other students have passed this course; what makes me think I cannot? What obstacles might be getting in my way? What might be some ways around those obstacles? What have others done in this situation?
Work: Two of my coworkers just got raises.	My own raise is just around the corner.	Did my coworkers accomplish anything I did not? When were their last raises, and when was mine?
Everyday Life: My friend has been acting strangely toward me lately.	I must have done something wrong.	Is it possible it has nothing to do with me? Maybe he is going through something really difficult in his life.

Tip In every situation, try to be open to different points of view. Listen and think before responding or coming to any conclusions. Although you may not agree with other points of view, you can learn from them.

You need to be aware not only of your own assumptions but also of assumptions in what you read, see, and hear. For example, bottled-water labels and advertising might suggest directly or indirectly that bottled water is better than tap water. Think carefully about the evidence they provide to support this assumption. What other sources of information could be consulted to either support, disprove, or call into question this assumption? However confidently a claim is made, never assume it is 100 percent correct and cannot be questioned.

PRACTICE 1–4   **Thinking Critically**

What assumptions are behind each of the images below? Write down as many as you can identify. Then, write down questions about these assumptions, considering different points of view.

COURTESY OF BETH CASTRODALE

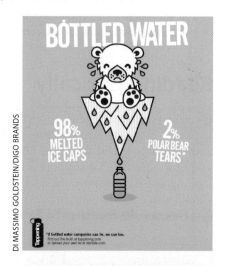

DI MASSIMO GOLDSTEIN/DIGO BRANDS

COURTESY OF BETH CASTRODALE

COURTESY OF BETH CASTRODALE

In addition to assumptions, be aware of **biases**, one-sided and sometimes prejudiced views that prevent you or others from seeing multiple perspectives. Here is just one example:

As manager, I don't hire people over fifty; after all, no one older than fifty can pick up new skills quickly.

Others could contradict this extreme statement with experiences, insights, or additional information that could show reality is more nuanced or complicated than this statement allows. The manager's bias prevents him from seeing other perspectives and possibilities.

Be on the lookout for bias in your own views and in whatever you read, see, and hear. When a statement seems one sided or extreme, ask yourself what facts or points of view might have been omitted.

Reading Critically

Instructors expect students to apply critical thinking to reading. **Critical reading** is paying close attention as you read and asking yourself questions about the author's purpose and audience, his or her main idea, the support he or she gives, and how effective that support is. It is important to think critically as you read, looking out for assumptions and biases (both the writer's and your own). You should also consider whether you agree or disagree with the points being made.

Here are the four steps of the critical reading process:

The Critical Reading Process

Preview the text.

Read the text, looking for and annotating the main idea and support.

Pause to question and interpret the text, taking notes as you read.

Review the text and your notes, and **Respond** to it.

Preview the Text

The first step in the critical reading process is **previewing**. The roots of this word can help you understand what it means: you look ("view") before ("pre") to get a general sense of what a reading is about (topic), who it is written for (audience), and why it was written (purpose). You may also be able to determine the main ideas and supporting details as you skim through a text quickly. When you preview, you also make connections with the topic and identify your purpose for reading.

To preview a reading, skim through it quickly to identify the **rhetorical context** (topic, purpose, audience). Use the following tips as a guide:

- **Source:** The source or location of publication (online magazine, newspaper, Facebook, class handout) can help you identify the writer's purpose.

- **Author:** Information about the author can help you evaluate the purpose and accuracy of the information.

- **Title:** The title or subject line can help you determine the topic and main idea.
- **Headings:** Subtitles, headings, or captions often reveal the major supporting details.
- **Marginal notes:** Definitions or comments in the margins (sidebars) often highlight key terms or major supporting details.
- **Visuals:** Charts, graphics, or photos illustrate the main idea by giving specific details.
- **Bold words:** Words or phrases in bold often show the ideas that the writer wants to emphasize.
- **Summaries:** A short summary, also called a headnote or abstract (a type of summary found in many scholarly publications), may appear at the beginning of a reading and indicate the topic, main idea, and major supporting points.

Once you have identified the rhetorical context of the text, consider your own reasons for reading: why are you reading the piece? What do you already know about the topic? What else do you need to know? Choose a guiding question—a question you think the reading might answer—to help you stay focused as you read.

Read the Text: Find the Main Idea and Support

If you have previewed a reading, you have already begun to read actively. Active readers recognize that looking at words or images on a page or screen is not the same as reading those words or images. As the name suggests, active readers act: they ask questions (using their minds, their voices, or their hands as they write or type), and they annotate—they personalize a reading by making notes and adding words or images that will help them make sense of what they are reading. After previewing a reading, active readers identify the main point and supporting details.

Main Idea and Purpose

The **main idea** of a text is the central idea the author wants to communicate. The main idea is related to the writer's **purpose**, which can be to explain, to demonstrate, to persuade, or to entertain. Writers often introduce their main idea early, so read the first few paragraphs with special care. Use these hints to help you identify the writer's main idea.

- Don't confuse the topic and the main idea. The main idea tells you what the writer says about the topic. To make sure you have identified the main idea and not just the topic, complete this sentence:

  The writer is saying that:
- A main point is often the answer to the guiding question you created when previewing the reading.
- A reading has only one main point. Make sure you identify the main idea of the entire reading, not a supporting detail. (Don't focus on only one or two paragraphs; look at the entire text.)

- A main point or thesis may be stated in a single sentence that you can find in the reading. We call this the stated main idea. When the main point is stated directly, you can double-underline it.

- A main point or thesis may not be stated directly. If a writer chooses not to state the main idea directly, we say that the main idea is implied. If there is an implied main idea, write the main point in your own words, using either the margins of the text or your notebook.

For more on main ideas, see Chapter 3.

| PRACTICE 1–5 | **Finding the Main Idea** |

Read each of the following paragraphs. Then, write the main idea in your own words.

1. Making a plan for your college studies is a good way to reach your academic goals. The first step to planning is answering this question: "What do I want to be?" If you have only a general idea—for example, "I would like to work in the health-care field"—break this large area into smaller, more specific subfields. These subfields might include working as a registered nurse, a nurse practitioner, or a physical therapist. The second step to planning is to meet with an academic adviser to talk about the classes you will need to take to get a degree or certificate in your chosen field. Then, map out the courses you will be taking over the next couple of semesters. Throughout the process, bear in mind the words of student mentor Ed Powell: "Those who fail to plan, plan to fail." A good plan boosts your chances of success in college and beyond.

2. Networking is a way businesspeople build connections with others to get ahead. Building connections in college also is well worth the effort. One way to build connections is to get to know some of your class-mates and to exchange names, phone numbers, and email addresses with them. That way, if you cannot make it to a class, you will know someone who can tell you what you missed. You can also form study groups with these other students. Another way to build connections is to get to know your instructor. Make an appointment to visit your instructor during his or her office hours. When you go, ask questions about material you are not sure you understood in class or problems you have with other course material. You and your instructor will get the most out of these sessions if you bring examples of specific assignments with which you are having trouble.

Support

Support is the details that show, explain, or prove the main idea. The author might use statistics, facts, definitions, examples, and scientific results for support. Or he or she might use memories, stories, comparisons, quotations from experts, and personal observations.

For more on support, see Chapter 4.

> **PRACTICE 1-6**   **Identifying Support**
>
> Go back to Practice 1-5 (p. 12) and underline the support for the main ideas of each passage in the practice.

Not all support that an author offers in a piece of writing is good support. When you are reading, ask yourself what information the author is including to help you understand or accept the main idea. Is the support (evidence) valid and convincing? If not, why not?

Pause to Think

Active readers also take time to pause and think during the reading process. If you race through a reading without stopping to consider what you are reading, you may not fully understand the author's point, mistaking a minor detail for the main idea or misunderstanding the author's purpose. Stop regularly as you read, and if needed, reread a sentence or paragraph. When you pause, do the following:

- Double-underline or write the main idea in the margin.
- Note the major support points by underlining them.
- Note ideas that you agree with by placing a check mark next to them (✓).
- Note ideas that you do not agree with or that surprise you with an ✗ or **!** and ideas you do not understand with a question mark (**?**).
- Note any examples of an author's or expert's assumptions or biases.
- Jot any additional notes or questions in the margin.
- Consider how parts of the reading relate to the main idea.

Review and Respond

After reading, take a few minutes to look back and review. First, make sure you can identify the main point and major supporting details of the piece.

Paraphrase

To make sure you understand the writer's point, paraphrase it. Paraphrasing means restating an idea using different language. When you have read carefully and critically, you can paraphrase what an author says, using your own words and style, to explain the writer's meaning for yourself and for others. Here are three tips to help you effectively paraphrase key points from your reading.

Tips for Effective Paraphrasing

Tip 1: Do not copy the main idea (thesis) or major supporting details (topic sentences) when you take notes.

Tip 2: Think about what the writer says for each point and imagine you are explaining that point to one of your friends. Here is one way to begin your paraphrase: "In other words, the writer is saying that . . ." Write your explanation without looking back at the original.

Tip 3: Avoid cut-and-paste paraphrases. A cut-and-paste paraphrase copies the original and then just changes one or two words. For example, here is a point from Amanda's essay (p. 15 in this chapter) followed by a cut-and-paste paraphrase. The parts that are the same are highlighted.

Original

> "Ideally, given the ban on selling water bottles, every student on campus should now take the initiative to carry a water bottle, filling it up throughout the day at the water fountains on campus. Realistically, we know this has not and will not happen."

Cut-and-paste paraphrase

> Amanda says that given the ban on selling water bottles, it would be great if every student at the college took the initiative to carry their own water bottle, filling it up as needed during the day at the water fountains on campus. But she knows that realistically this is not going to happen

Do you see how close the sentence structure and language are to the original? As a result, the cut-and-paste paraphrase is not acceptable. Now compare this to an appropriate paraphrase:

Appropriate paraphrase

> In her essay "A Ban on Water Bottles: A Way to Bolster the University's Image," Amanda Jacobowitz explains that even though her college has decided not to sell water bottles on campus, most college students are not going to respond by purchasing their own water bottles to use during the day instead.

While some of the individual words are the same in this paraphrase, the student taking these notes has not borrowed Amanda Jacobowitz's structure or longer strings of words.

Once you have identified the writer's main point, go over your guiding question, your marginal notes, and your questions—and connect with what you have read. Ask yourself, "What interested me? What did I learn? How does it fit with what I know from other sources?" When you have reviewed your reading in this way and fixed it well in your mind and memory, it is much easier to respond in class discussion and writing because to write about a reading, you need to generate and organize your ideas, draft and revise your response, and above all, use your critical thinking skills.

A Critical Reader at Work

Read the following piece. The notes in the margins show how one student applied the process of critical reading to an essay on bottled water.

Amanda Jacobowitz

A Ban on Water Bottles: A Way to Bolster the University's Image

Amanda Jacobowitz is a student at Washington University and a columnist for the university's publication *Student Life,* in which the following essay appeared.

Guiding question: What does the author think about the ban on bottled water?

Lately, I am always thirsty. Always! I could not figure out why until I realized that the bottled water I had purchased continuously throughout my day had disappeared. At first I was just confused. Where did all the water bottles go? Then I learned the simple explanation: the University banned water bottles in an effort to be environmentally friendly.

2   Ideally, given the ban on selling water bottles, every student on campus should now take the initiative to carry a water bottle, filling it up throughout the day at the water fountains on campus. Realistically, we know this has not and will not happen. As a somewhat environmentally conscious person, I have tried to bring a water bottle with me to classes, but have rarely succeeded in this effort. Instead, although I have never been too much of a soda drinker, I find myself reaching for a bottle of Coke out of pure convenience. We can't buy bottled water, but we can buy soda, juice, and other drinks, many of which come in plastic bottles. I am sure that for most people—particularly those who give very little thought to being environmentally conscientious—convenience prevails and they purchase a drink other than water. Wonderful result. The university can pride

Larger main idea (not stated directly): (1) the ban is ineffective, and (2) there are better ways to protect the environment.

Why not just drink from a water fountain? You don't have to have a bottle.

itself on being more environmentally friendly, with the fallback that its students will be less healthy!

Examples of other common forms of waste

3   Even if students are not buying unhealthy drinks, any benefit from the reduction of plastic water bottles could easily be offset by its alternatives. Students are not using their hands to drink water during meals. They are using plastic cups—cups provided by the university at every eatery on campus. Presumably no person picks up a cup, drinks their glass of water, and then saves that same cup for later in the day. That being said, how many plastic cups are used by a single student in a single day? How many cups are used by the total campus-wide population daily, yearly? This plastic-cup use must equate to an exorbitant amount of waste as well.

4   My intent is not to have the university completely roll back the water-bottle ban, nor is my intent for the university to level the playing field by banning all plastic-drink bottles. I'm simply questioning the reasons for specifically banning bottled water of all things. Why not start with soda bottles—decreasing the environmental impact, as well as the health risks? There are also many other ways to help the environment that seem to be so easily overlooked.

Examples of other ways to protect the environment

5   Have you ever noticed a patch of grass on campus that's not perfectly green? I can't say that I have. The reason: the sprinklers. Now, I admit that I harbor some animosity when it comes to the campus sprinklers; I somehow always manage to mistakenly and inadvertently walk right in their path, the spray of water generously dousing my feet. However, my real problem with the sprinklers is the waste of water they represent. Do we really need our grass to be green at all times?

6   The landscaping around our beloved Danforth University Center (Gold LEED Certified) is irrigated with the use of rainwater. There is a 50,000-gallon rainwater tank below the building to collect rain! I admit, this is pretty impressive, but what about the rest of the campus? What water is used to irrigate and keep green the rest of our 169 acres on the Danforth campus?

Town/city water, I assume

7   I understand that being environmentally conscious is difficult to do, particularly at an institutional level. I applaud the Danforth University Center and other environmental efforts the university has initiated. However, I can't help but wonder if the university's ban on the sale of water bottles is more about appearance and less about decreasing the environmental impact of our student body. The water-bottle ban has become a way to build the school's public image: we banned water bottles; we are working hard to be environmentally friendly! In reality, given the switch to plastic cups and the switch to other drinks sold in plastic bottles, is the environmental impact of the ban that significant? Now that the ban has been implemented, I certainly don't see the university retracting it. However, I hope that in the future the university focuses less on its public image and more on the environment itself when instituting such dramatic changes.

Is it really about public image? What would a university administrator say?

PRACTICE 1-7   **Making Connections**

Look back at the images on page 9. Then, review the reading by Amanda Jacobowitz. What assumptions does she make about bottled water? What evidence, if any, is provided to support these assumptions? On the basis of your observations, would you like to see bottled water not banned or banned at your college? Why or why not?

Writing Critically about Readings, Images, and Problems

In college, you will have many different kinds of writing assignments. In Chapters 2 through 5, you will learn about the process of writing paragraphs and essays. In Chapters 6 through 13, you will explore different techniques for developing an essay, such as narration and illustration. Regardless of the techniques you use, many assignments require that you write about readings, images, or problems.

Writing about Readings

Writing critically about readings is a key college skill because it shows your deep understanding of course content. When you write critically about readings, you summarize, analyze, synthesize, and evaluate, and, in doing so, you answer the following questions.

Reading and Writing Critically

Summarize

- What is important about the text?
- What is the purpose, the big picture?
- What are the main ideas and key support?

Analyze

- What elements have been used to convey the main idea?
- Do any elements raise questions? Do any key points seem missing or undeveloped?

Synthesize

- What do other sources say about the topic of the text?
- How does your own (or others') experience affect how you see the topic?
- What new point(s) might you make by bringing together all the different sources and experiences?

Evaluate

- Based on your application of summary, analysis, and synthesis, what do you think about the material you have read?
- Is the work successful? Does it achieve its purpose?
- Does the author show any biases? If so, do they make the piece more effective or less effective?

Summary

A **summary** is a condensed, or shortened, version of something—often, a longer piece of writing, a movie or television show, a situation, or an event. A summary paragraph presents the main idea, support, and organizational pattern of a longer piece of writing, stripping the information down to its essential elements. A summary is a logical final step in the reading process: it expresses what you have learned about the important features of a text, in your own words.

A summary has these features:

- a topic sentence that states the title of the selection, the author, and the main idea

- the major supporting details

- references to the author with descriptive verbs that describe what the writer says in the text

- the author's final observations or recommendations

- original language (paraphrases)

Verbs followed by a complete idea (to introduce what the writer says)

argue (that)	ask (that)	assert (that)	claim (that)
demand (that)	deny (that)	explain (that)	imply (that)
point out (that)	suggest (that)		

The following is an excerpt from the *Textbook of Basic Nursing* by Caroline Bunker Rosdahl and Mary T. Kowalski. It comes from a chapter that discusses some of the stresses that families can face, including divorce.

Adults who are facing separation from their partners—and a return to single life—may feel overwhelmed. They may become preoccupied with their own feelings, thereby limiting their ability to handle the situation effectively or to be strong for their children. The breakdown of the family system may require a restructuring of responsibilities, employment, childcare, and housing arrangements. Animosity between adults may expose children to uncontrolled emotions, arguments, anger, and depression.

Children may feel guilt and anxiety over their parents' divorce, believing the situation to be their fault. They may be unable to channel their conflicting emotions effectively. Their school performance may suffer, or they may engage in misbehavior. Even when a divorce is handled amicably, children may experience conflicts about their loyalties and may have difficulties making the transition from one household to another during visitation periods.

Experts estimate that approximately 50 percent of all children whose parents divorce will experience another major life change within three years: remarriage. The arrival of a stepparent in the home presents additional stressors for children. Adapting to new rules of behavior, adjusting to a new person's habits, and sharing parents with new family members can cause resentment and anger. When families blend children, rivalries and competition for parental attention can lead to repeated conflicts.

Now, here is a summary of the textbook excerpt. The main idea is double-underlined, and the support points are underlined.

Although divorce seriously affects the people who are splitting up, Rosdahl and Kowalski point out that the couple's children face equally difficult consequences, both immediately and in the longer term. In the short term, according to the authors, children may blame themselves for the split or feel that their loyalty to both parents is divided. The authors further assert that these negative emotions can affect children's behavior at school and elsewhere. Later on, if one or both of the parents remarry, the children may have trouble adjusting to the new family structure.

Read to Write What verbs has the writer of the summary used to introduce the main idea and support in this summary? Highlight or circle these words.

Analysis

An **analysis** breaks down the points or parts of something and considers how they work together to make an impression or convey a main idea. When writing an analysis, you often use words that show what the writer does, or what strategies the writer uses. You might also consider points or parts that seem to be missing or that raise questions in your mind.

> **Verbs followed by a noun or nouns** (to introduce what the writer **does**, or the strategies the writer **uses**)
>
> | | | | |
> |---|---|---|---|
> | analyze | classify | compare | contrast |
> | define | describe | emphasize | express |
> | evaluate | identify | illustrate | list |
> | present | narrate | | |

Here is an analysis of the excerpt from the *Textbook of Basic Nursing*. The main idea is double-underlined, and the support points are underlined.

Read to Write
Identify the verbs that show what the writing is doing in this analysis.

We all know that divorce is difficult for the people who are splitting up, but Rosdahl and Kowalski address the effects of divorce experienced by children of divorce, both right after the split and later on. The authors identify several possible results of divorce on children, including emotional and behavioral difficulties and trouble in school. They also list the stresses that remarriage can create for children.

The authors rightly emphasize the negative effects that divorce can have on children. However, I found myself wondering what a divorcing couple could do to help their children through the process. Also, how might parents and stepparents help children adjust to a remarriage? I would like to examine these questions in a future paper.

[Note how the writer raises questions about the textbook excerpt.]

Synthesis

A **synthesis** pulls together information from additional sources or experiences to make a new point. Here is a synthesis of the textbook material on divorce. Because the writer wanted to address some of the questions she raised in her analysis, she incorporated additional details from published sources and from people she interviewed. Her synthesis of this information helped her arrive at a fresh conclusion.

First source

In the *Textbook of Basic Nursing*, Rosdahl and Kowalski focus on the problems faced by children of divorce, both right after the split and later on. According to the authors, immediate problems can include emotional and behavioral difficulties and trouble in school. Later on, parents' remarriage can create additional stresses for children (92). Although the authors discuss the impact of divorce on all parties, they do not suggest ways in which parents or stepparents might help children through the process of divorce or remarriage. However, other sources, as well as original research on friends who have experienced divorce as children or adults, provide some additional insights into these questions.

Second source

A website produced by the staff at the Mayo Clinic recommends that parents come together to break the news about their divorce to their children. The website also suggests that parents keep the discussion brief and free of "ugly details." In addition, parents should emphasize that the children are in no way to blame for the divorce and that they are deeply loved. As the divorce proceeds, neither parent should speak negatively about the other parent in the child's presence or otherwise try to turn the child against the ex-spouse. Finally, the site recommends counseling for parents or their children if any problems around the divorce persist.

Authors Sharon Leigh, Maridith Jackson, and Janet Clark of the University of Missouri Extension also address the problems that can arise for children after their parents remarry. Specifically, their article describes several things that stepparents can do to make their stepchildren feel more comfortable with them and the new family situation. One strategy is to try to establish a friendship with the children before assuming the role of a parent. Later, once stepparents have assumed a more parental role, they should make sure they and their spouse stand by the same household rules and means of discipline. With time, say the authors, the stepparents might also add new traditions for holidays and other family gatherings to help build new family bonds while respecting the old ones.

To these sources, I added interviews with three friends—two who are children of divorce and one who is both a divorced parent and a stepparent. The children of divorce said that they experienced many of the same difficulties and stresses that Rosdahl and Kowalski described. Interestingly, though, they also reported that they felt guilty, even though their parents told them not to, following the advice given by the Mayo Clinic. As my friend Kris said, "For a long time after the divorce, every time my dad and I were together, he seemed distracted, like he wished I wasn't there. I felt bad that I couldn't just vanish." Dale, the stepparent I interviewed, liked the strategies suggested by Leigh, Jackson, and Clark, and he had actually tried some of these approaches with his own stepchildren. However, as Dale told me, "When you're as busy as most parents and kids are these days, you can let important things fall by the wayside—even time together. That's not good for anyone."

Thinking back on Kris's and Dale's words and everything I've learned from the other sources, I have come to conclude that divorced parents and stepparents need to make sure they build "together time" with their own children and/or stepchildren into every day. Even if this time is just a discussion over a meal or a quick bedtime story, children will remember it and appreciate it. This approach would help with some of the relationship building that Leigh, Jackson, and Clark recommend.

Read to Write
What words or phrases does the writer of this synthesis use to show that information comes from a source?

Third source

Fourth source

Fresh conclusion

It would also improve communication, help children understand that they are truly loved by *all* their parents, and assist with the process of postdivorce healing.

Tip For more information about research and MLA documentation, see the Appendix, pp. 555–561.

Works Cited

Leigh, Sharon, Maridith Jackson, and Janet A. Clark. "Foundations for a Successful Stepfamily." Updated by Kim Leon, *MOspace*, Apr. 2007. www.mospace.umsystem.edu/xmlui/bitstream/handle/10355/51356/gh6700-2007.pdf?sequence=1&isAllowed=y.

Mayo Clinic Staff. "Children and Divorce: Helping Kids after a Breakup." *Mayo Clinic,* 14 May 2011, www.mayoclinic.org/healthy-lifestyle/childrens-health/in-depth/divorce/art-20047788.

Rosdahl, Caroline Bunker, and Mary T. Kowalski. *Textbook of Basic Nursing.* 9th ed. Lippincott Williams & Wilkins, 2008.

Evaluation

An **evaluation** is the result of critical thinking: a thoughtful judgment about something based on what you have discovered through your summary, analysis, and synthesis. To evaluate something effectively, apply the questions from the Reading and Writing Critically box on page 17. You will want to refer to these questions as you work through later chapters of this book and through readings from other college courses.

Here is an evaluation of the excerpt from the *Textbook of Basic Nursing:*

In just a few paragraphs, Rosdahl and Kowalski give a good description of the effects of divorce, not only on the former spouses but also on their children. The details that the authors provide help to clearly communicate the difficulties that such children face. In the short term, these difficulties can include emotional and behavioral problems and trouble in school. In the longer term, if one or both of a child's parents remarry, the child faces the stress of dealing with a new and different family. Although the authors do not specifically address ways that parents and stepparents can ease children into divorce and/or new families, other sources—such as the websites of the University of Missouri Extension and the Mayo Clinic, as well as people I interviewed—do get into these issues. In the end, I think that Rosdahl and Kowalski present a good overview of their subject in a short piece of writing that was part of a larger discussion on family stresses.

PRACTICE 1–8   **Making Connections**

As you work through this exercise, refer to the Reading and Writing Critically box on page 17.

1. **Summary:** Summarize Amanda Jacobowitz's essay on pages 15–16.
2. **Analysis:** Whether you agree or disagree with Jacobowitz, write a paragraph analyzing the points she presents.
3. **Synthesis:** Read additional opinion pieces or blog postings about bottled water. In one paragraph, state your position on the subject according to your reading of these materials. Also, explain the range of opinions on the subject.
4. **Evaluation:** Write a paragraph that evaluates Jacobowitz's essay.

Writing Critically about Visuals

Images play a huge role in our lives today, and it is important to think critically about them just as you would about what you read or hear. Whether the image is a website, a photograph or illustration, a graphic, or an advertisement, you need to be able to "read" it. You can apply the same critical reading skills of summary, analysis, synthesis, and evaluation to read a visual.

Look carefully at the visuals on page 9. Then, consider how to read a visual using the critical thinking skills you have learned.

Summary

To summarize a visual, ask yourself what the big picture is. What is going on in the image? What is the main impression or message (the main idea)? What is the purpose? How is this purpose achieved (the support)? To answer these questions, consider some strategies used in visuals.

Dominant Elements

Artists, illustrators, and advertisers may place the most important object in the center of an image. Or, they may design visuals using a **Z pattern**, with the most important object in the top left and the second most important object in the bottom right. In English and many other languages, people read printed material from left to right and from top to bottom, and the Z pattern takes advantage of that pattern. Because of these design strategies, the main idea of a visual can often be determined by looking at the center of the image or at the top left or bottom right.

Figures and Objects

The person who creates an image has a purpose (main idea) and uses visual details to achieve (or support) that purpose. In a photograph, illustration, or painting, details about the figures and objects help create the impression the artist wants to convey. (Here, the term *figures* refers to people, animals, or other forms that can show action or emotion.) When studying any image, ask yourself the following questions:

- Are the figures from a certain period in history?
- What kind of clothes are they wearing?
- What are the expressions on their faces? How would I describe their attitudes?
- Are the figures shown realistically, or are they shown as sketches or cartoons?
- What important details about the figures does the creator of the image want me to focus on?

PUT DOWN THE PHONE AND NO ONE GETS HURT.

COURTESY OF THE NATIONAL SAFETY COUNCIL, NEBRASKA

PRACTICE 1–9   Summarizing a Visual

Focus on the public service announcement from the Nebraska Safety Council above, and answer the following questions.

1. What is the big picture? What is going on?
2. What is at the center of the ad?
3. What is the ad's purpose?
4. What are the most important details in the piece?

Analysis

To analyze a visual, focus on the parts of it (figures, objects, any text included), and ask yourself how they contribute to the message or main impression. Consider the background, the use of light and dark, and the various elements' colors, contrasts, textures, and sizes. Think also about how the designer of the image made choices to target a specific audience.

> **PRACTICE 1-10** **Analyzing a Visual**
>
> Focus on the public service announcement from the Nebraska Safety Council on page 24, and answer the following questions.
>
> 1. What elements are placed in large type? Why?
> 2. How do all the features in the ad contribute to the main impression?
> 3. Which features seem to be chosen to appeal to a specific audience?

Synthesis

To synthesize your impressions of a visual, ask yourself what the message seems to be, using your summary and analysis skills. Consider how this message relates to what else you know from experience and observation.

> **PRACTICE 1-11** **Synthesizing Your Impressions of a Visual**
>
> Focus on the public service announcement from the Nebraska Safety Council on page 24, and answer the following questions.
>
> 1. What is the ad's central message?
> 2. How does this message relate to what you already know or have heard or experienced?
> 3. How might this message be presented for other audiences?

Evaluation

To evaluate an image, ask yourself how effective it is in achieving its purpose and conveying its main idea or message. What do you think of the image, using your summary, analysis, and synthesis skills? Consider any biases or assumptions that may be working in the image.

> **PRACTICE 1-12** **Evaluating a Visual**
>
> Focus on the public service announcement from the Nebraska Safety Council on page 24, and answer the following questions.
>
> 1. What do you think about the ad, especially its visual elements?
> 2. Does the creator of the ad seem to have any biases? Why or why not?
> 3. Is the ad effective, given its purpose and the main idea it is trying to make? Why or why not?

Writing Critically about Problems

In college, at work, and in everyday life, we often need to "read" situations to make important decisions about them. This process, known as problem solving, can also involve summarizing, analyzing, synthesizing, and evaluating. Let's look at key steps in the process.

1. Summarize the problem.

    Try to describe it in a brief statement or question.

    > **Example:** My ten-year-old car needs a new transmission, which will cost at least $1,000. Should I keep the car or buy a new one?

2. Analyze the problem.

    Consider possible ways to solve it, examining any questions or assumptions you might have.

    > **Examples**
    >
    > *Assumption:* I need to have a reliable car.
    >
    > *Question:* Is this assumption truly justified?
    >
    > *Answer:* Yes. I can't get to school or work without a reliable car. I live more than fifteen miles from each location, and there is no regular public transportation to either place from my home.
    >
    > **Possible Solutions**
    > - Pay for the transmission repair.
    > - Buy a new car.

3. Synthesize information about the problem.

    Consult various information sources to get opinions about the possible solutions.

    > **Examples**
    > - My mechanic
    > - Friends who have had similar car problems
    > - Car advice from print or Web sources
    > - My past experience with car repairs and expenses

4. Evaluate the possible solutions, and make a decision.

    You might consider the advantages and disadvantages of each possible solution. Also, when you make your decision, you should be able to give reasons for your choice.

> **Examples (considering only advantages and disadvantages)**
>
> - Pay for the transmission repair.
>
>   *Advantage:* This option would be cheaper than buying a new car.
>
>   *Disadvantage:* The car might not last much longer, even with the new transmission.
>
> - Buy a new car.
>
>   *Advantage:* I will have a reliable car.
>
>   *Disadvantage:* This option is much more expensive than paying for the repair.
>
>   **Final Decision:** Pay for the transmission repair.
>
>   **Reasons:** I do not have money for a new car, and I do not want to take on more debt. Also, two mechanics told me that my car should run for three to five more years with the new transmission. At that point, I will be in a better position to buy a new car.

PRACTICE 1-13   **Solving a Problem**

Think of a problem you are facing now—in college, at work, or in your everyday life. On a separate sheet of paper, summarize the problem. Next, referring to the previous steps, write down and analyze possible solutions, considering different sources of information. Then, write down your final decision or preferred solution, giving reasons for your choice.

Chapter Review

1. What are the four basics of critical thinking?

2. What are the four major steps of the critical reading process?

3. What are the four major steps of writing critically about readings and visuals?

4. Without looking back in the chapter, define the task of synthesizing in your own words.

Reflect and Apply

1. Can you think of a time when you or someone you know did not read a document or visual critically? What happened?

2. Talk to someone who has taken courses in your major or who is working in your field. What documents or visuals will you need to be able to read for your major or your career?

3. Did the information in this chapter confirm, contradict, or complicate your expectations for college writing courses? Explain.

Writing Basics

Audience, Purpose, Form, and Process

Writing—whether in college or in the workplace—varies in form and style. Regardless of the situation, four elements are key to good writing. Keep them in mind whenever you write.

Four Basics of Good Writing

1 It reflects the writer's purpose and the needs, knowledge, and expectations of its intended audience.

2 It results from a thoughtful process.

3 It includes a clear, definite point.

4 It provides organized support that shows, explains, or proves the main idea.

This chapter addresses the first basic in detail and provides an overview of the writing process (the second basic). The chapter also gives you some typical grading criteria and shows how they are applied to assess unsatisfactory, satisfactory, and excellent paragraphs.

Chapters 3 through 5 explain the steps of the writing process in detail (the second basic). Chapter 3 focuses on finding and clarifying the main point (the third basic), and Chapter 4 shows how to find and organize strong support (the fourth basic). In Chapter 5, you will learn how to complete the writing process by drafting and revising.

Understand Audience and Purpose

Your **audience** is the person or people who will read what you write. Whenever you write, always have at least one real person in mind as a reader. Think about what that person already knows and what he or she will need to know to understand your main idea. In college, your audience is usually your instructors, but your instructors may ask you to write for a different audience, perhaps someone who is not familiar with your class and your assignments. Be careful to provide background information (also called **context**) that your reader will need in order to understand what you write.

The purpose of a piece of writing is the reason for writing it. Understanding your purpose for writing is key to writing successfully, particularly as writing tasks become more complex. In college, your purpose for writing often will be to show something; to summarize, analyze, synthesize, or evaluate something; or to make a convincing argument. Typically, your instructor will want you to demonstrate that you understand the content of the course. To understand the purpose of a particular assignment, be sure to read assignments and exam questions critically, highlighting words that tell you what your instructor wants to see in your writing.

Understanding your audience and your purpose helps you to select the most appropriate **form** and **tone** for your writing. Forms used by college writers include essays, lab reports, texts, emails, and resumes. Tone is the "voice" of your writing, formed by the words you use and the ways you use them, either formally or informally.

Audience, Purpose, Form, and Tone

Audience	Purpose	Form	Tone
College: the professor of your environmental science class	• To complete an assignment according to your professor's instructions and any research methods discussed in class • To show what you have learned about the topic	A research essay about the environmental effects of "fracking": fracturing rock layers to extract oil or natural gas	Formal
College: classmates	To generate ideas for the next essay	Graded discussion board post	Formal
College: friend	To complain about the length of an assignment	Text message	Informal or casual
Work: fellow employees	To make sure that coworkers understand important details about a new company policy about social media use at work.	An email	Formal
Everyday life: the members of your softball team	To make sure your team knows what time to show up for their game this week	A Facebook post on your recreational softball league's page informing them about a time change for this week's game	Informal

The form, tone, and content of your writing will vary depending on your audiences and purposes. Read the following three notes, which describe the same situation but are written for different audiences and purposes.

Bunker Hill CC Campus Store
250 New Rutherford Ave 4th Floor
E Building
Boston MA, 02129
(617) 241-5161
2150mgr@fheg.follett.com

==

8/28/19   5:54 PM
Store: 02150
Reg.: 804   Till: 804
Cashier: Marjan

              Balance Inquiry

Customer: Ronald
Student ID: 0396439

Award Total: 535.81
Department   Allocated Amount
Bunker Datatel
BOOKS
SUPPLIES   535.81
TECHNOLOGY   504.29
                                   504.29

...eling strange, and her face was
...her doctor's office and made an
...to stay with Marta's children in
...to watch the children until her
...other explaining why she had
...ffice, she was feeling better, and,
...ided not to wait. The nurse asked
...ptoms for the doctor to read later.
...r, Marta also wanted to make sure
...rrive a few moments late for class.
...let her know she would be coming

Thx for watching kds 4 me.

...wollen, especially around the eyes, which
...l and dry, and my face was itchy. However,

Dr. Smith,

I woke up feeling ill this morning and made an appointment with my doctor. I thought I might need to miss class, but I am now feeling better and will manage to make it to class. I am leaving the doctor's office right now and should be at school very shortly. I apologize for any inconvenience this may cause.

Sincerely,

Marta

> **PRACTICE 2–1   Comparing Marta's Notes**
>
> Read Marta's three notes, and discuss the following questions.
>
> 1. How does Marta's note to her mother differ from the one to the doctor? How does the one to the doctor differ from the one to her instructor?
>
> 2. How do the different audiences and purposes affect what the notes say (the content) and how they say it (the tone)?
>
> 3. Which note has more detail, and why?

As these examples show, we communicate with family members and friends differently than we communicate with people in authority (like doctors, instructors, or other professionals)—or we should. Marta's text to her mother is extremely informal; it not only uses incomplete sentences but also incomplete words because the two women know each other well and are used to speaking casually to each other. Because Marta's purpose is to get quick information to her mother and to reassure her, she does not need to provide a lot of details. On the other hand, Marta's note to her doctor is more formal, with complete sentences, because the relationship is more formal. Also, the note to the doctor is more detailed because the doctor will be making treatment decisions based on it. Finally, the email to the instructor is the most formal because Marta wants to maintain a strong, professional relationship with her instructor.

In college, at work, and in your everyday life, when you are speaking or writing to someone in authority for a serious purpose, use formal English; people will take you seriously.

> **PRACTICE 2–2   Writing for a Formal Audience**
>
> A student, Terri Travers, sent the following email to a friend to complain about not getting into a criminal justice course. Rewrite the email as if you were Terri and you were writing to Professor Widener. The purpose is to ask whether the professor would consider allowing you into the class given that you signed up early and have the necessary grades.
>
> To: Miles Rona
>
> Fr: Terri Travers
>
> Subject: Bummin
>
> Seriously bummin that I didn't get into Prof Widener's CJ class. U and Luis said it's the best ever, lol. Wonder why I didn't . . . I signed up early and I have the grades. Sup w/that?
>
> C ya,
>
> TT

Understand Paragraph and Essay Form

In college, professors often assign paragraphs and essays as homework assignments, course projects, or exams. Each of them has a basic structure.

Paragraph Form

A **paragraph** has three necessary parts: the topic sentence, the body, and the concluding sentence.

Paragraph Part	Purpose of the Paragraph Part
1. The **topic sentence**	states the **main idea**. The topic sentence is often the first sentence of the paragraph.
2. The **body**	supports (shows, explains, or proves) the main idea with **support sentences** that contain facts and details.
3. The **concluding sentence**	reminds readers of the main idea and often makes an observation.

Read the paragraph that follows with the paragraph parts labeled.

> Following a few basic strategies can help you take better notes, an important skill for succeeding in any course. First, start the notes for each class session on a fresh page of your course notebook, and record the date at the top of the page. Next, to improve the speed of your note taking, abbreviate certain words, especially ones your instructor uses regularly. For example, abbreviations for a business course might include *fncl* for financial, *svc* for service, and *mgt* for management. However, don't try to write down every word your instructor says. Instead, look for ways to boil down extended explanations into short phrases. For instance, imagine that a business instructor says the following: "A profit-and-loss statement is a report of an organization's revenue and expenses over a specific financial period. Often, P-and-L's are used to determine ways to boost revenue or cut costs, with the goal of increasing profitability." The note taker might write down something like, "P&L: rpt of revenue + expenses over a specific period. Used to boost rev or cut costs." Although you do not need to record every word of a lecture, listen for clues that indicate that your instructor is making a point important enough to write down. At such times, the instructor might raise his or her voice, or he or she might introduce key information with such phrases as "It's important to remember" or "Bear in mind." In addition, if the instructor has made a certain point more than once, it is a good indication that this point is important. By carefully listening to and recording information from your instructor, you are not just getting good notes to study later; you are already beginning to seal this information into your memory.

Topic sentence

Body (with support sentences)

Concluding sentence

Essay Form

An **essay** is a piece of writing that examines a topic in more depth than a paragraph. A short essay may have four or five paragraphs, totaling three hundred to six hundred words. A long essay may be many pages long, depending on what the essay needs to accomplish, such as persuading someone to do something, using research to make a point, or explaining a complex concept.

An essay has three necessary parts: the introduction, the body, and the conclusion.

Essay Part	Purpose of the Essay Part
1. The **introduction**	states the main idea, or **thesis**, generally in a single, strong statement. The introduction may be a single paragraph or multiple paragraphs.
2. The **body**	supports (shows, explains, or proves) the main idea. It generally has three or more **support paragraphs**, each containing facts and details that develop the main idea. Each support paragraph has a topic sentence that supports the thesis statement.
3. The **conclusion**	reminds readers of the main idea and makes an observation. Often, it also summarizes and reinforces the support.

Paragraph		Essay
Topic sentence	→	Thesis statement
Support sentences	→	Support paragraphs
Concluding sentence	→	Conclusion

The diagram on pages 36–37 shows how the parts of an essay correspond to the parts of a paragraph.

Understand the Writing Process

The chart that follows shows the four stages of the **writing process**. These are all the steps you need to follow to write well. The rest of the chapters in Part 1 cover every stage except editing (presented in Parts 3 through 6). You will practice each stage, see how another student completed the process, and write your own paragraph or essay. Keep in mind that you may not always go in a straight line through the four stages; instead, you might circle back to earlier steps to further improve your writing.

Some writing strategies—such as finding and exploring a topic, coming up with a main idea, and revising—are similar for both paragraphs and essays. In these cases, this book discusses the strategies for paragraphs and essays together. (See Chapters 3, 4, and 5.) However, other activities, such as supporting main ideas or drafting individual parts of paragraphs or essays, are somewhat different for the two types of writing. In those cases, this book makes greater distinctions between paragraphs and essays.

The Writing Process

Generate Ideas

Consider: What is my purpose in writing? Given this purpose, what interests me? Who will read this paper? What do they need to know?

- Find and explore your topic (Chapter 3).
- Make your point (Chapter 3).
- Support your point (Chapter 4).

Draft

Consider: How can I organize my ideas effectively and show my readers what I mean?

- Arrange your ideas, and make an outline (Chapter 5).
- Write a draft, including an introduction that will interest your readers, a strong conclusion, and a title (Chapter 5).

Revise

Consider: How can I make my draft clearer or more convincing to my readers? How do I avoid plagiarism? How do I meet the requirements of the grading rubric?

- Look for ideas that do not fit (Chapter 5).
- Look for ideas that could use more detailed support (Chapter 5).
- Connect ideas with transitional words and sentences (Chapter 5).

Edit

Consider: What errors could confuse my readers and weaken my point?

- Find and correct errors in grammar (Chapters 15–26).
- Look for errors in word use (Chapters 27 and 28), spelling (Chapter 29), and punctuation and capitalization (Chapters 30–34).

Relationship between Paragraphs and Essays

For more on the important features of writing, see the Four Basics of Good Writing on page 29.

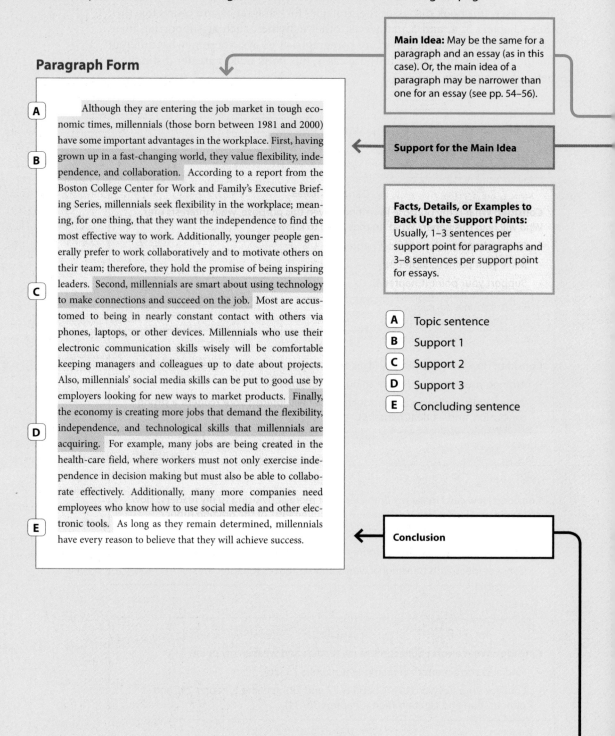

Paragraph Form

A   Although they are entering the job market in tough economic times, millennials (those born between 1981 and 2000) have some important advantages in the workplace. First, having **B** grown up in a fast-changing world, they value flexibility, independence, and collaboration. According to a report from the Boston College Center for Work and Family's Executive Briefing Series, millennials seek flexibility in the workplace; meaning, for one thing, that they want the independence to find the most effective way to work. Additionally, younger people generally prefer to work collaboratively and to motivate others on their team; therefore, they hold the promise of being inspiring leaders. Second, millennials are smart about using technology **C** to make connections and succeed on the job. Most are accustomed to being in nearly constant contact with others via phones, laptops, or other devices. Millennials who use their electronic communication skills wisely will be comfortable keeping managers and colleagues up to date about projects. Also, millennials' social media skills can be put to good use by employers looking for new ways to market products. Finally, the economy is creating more jobs that demand the flexibility, independence, and technological skills that millennials are **D** acquiring. For example, many jobs are being created in the health-care field, where workers must not only exercise independence in decision making but must also be able to collaborate effectively. Additionally, many more companies need employees who know how to use social media and other electronic tools. As long as they remain determined, millennials **E** have every reason to believe that they will achieve success.

Main Idea: May be the same for a paragraph and an essay (as in this case). Or, the main idea of a paragraph may be narrower than one for an essay (see pp. 54–56).

Support for the Main Idea

Facts, Details, or Examples to Back Up the Support Points: Usually, 1–3 sentences per support point for paragraphs and 3–8 sentences per support point for essays.

A   Topic sentence
B   Support 1
C   Support 2
D   Support 3
E   Concluding sentence

Conclusion

Essay Form

1

Fairly often, I hear older people saying that millennials (those born between 1981 and 2000) are spoiled, self-centered individuals who have much less to contribute to the workplace than previous generations did. Based on my own experiences and research, I must disagree. **Although they are entering the job market in tough economic times, millennials have some important advantages in the workplace.**

First, having grown up in a fast-changing world, they value flexibility, independence, and collaboration. Unlike their parents and grandparents, millennials never knew a world without personal computers, and the youngest of them never knew a world without the Internet or ever-changing models of smartphones. They are used to rapid change, and most of them have learned to adapt to it. Consequently, millennials, for the most part, expect workplaces to adapt to them. According to a report from the Boston College Center for Work and Family's Executive Briefing Series (EBS), millennials seek flexibility in the workplace—for example, in when and where they work. This attitude does not mean that

2

they are looking out for themselves alone. Instead, they want the independence to find the most effective and productive way to work. Additionally, according to the EBS report, millennials are more likely than older workers to reject old-fashioned business hierarchies in which managers tell lower-ranking employees what to do, and there is no give-and-take. In general, younger people prefer to work collaboratively and to do what they can to motivate others on their team; therefore, they hold the promise of being inspiring leaders.

Second, millennials are smart about using technology to make connections and succeed on the job. Most of them are accustomed to being in nearly constant contact with others via phones, laptops, or other devices. Although some people fear that such connectedness can be a distraction in the workplace, these technologies can be used productively and allow effective multitasking. For instance, over the course of a day, millennials who have learned to use their electronic communication skills wisely will be comfortable keeping managers and colleagues up to date about projects and responding to

3

questions and requests as they arise. Furthermore, most millennials are open to continuing such electronic exchanges during evenings and weekends if they feel they are collaborating with colleagues to meet an important goal. Also, many millennials are skilled in using social media to reach out to and remain connected with others; in fact, some people refer to them as "the Facebook generation." Employers can put these skills to good use as they look for new ways to market their products and find new customers.

Finally, the economy is creating more jobs that demand the flexibility, independence, and technological skills that millennials are acquiring. For example, many jobs are being created in the health-care field, where workers, such as nurses and physician assistants, must not only exercise independence in decision making but must also be able to collaborate effectively. Additionally, many more companies need employees who know how to use social media and other electronic tools for marketing purposes. Similarly, millennials with social media skills may have an advantage in finding work in the

4

marketing and advertising industries specifically. There is also always a need for independent-minded people to create new businesses and innovations. Thus, millennials can play a valuable role in helping the economy grow.

As long as they remain determined and confident, millennials have every reason to believe that they will achieve career success. According to the EBS report and other sources, meaningful, challenging work is more important to this generation than having a high salary. In the long term, workers with those types of values will always be in demand.

A	Introductory paragraph
B	Thesis statement
C	Topic sentence 1
D	Topic sentence 2
E	Support paragraphs
F	Topic sentence 3
G	Concluding paragraph

Understand Grading Criteria

Your instructor may use a **rubric**—a list of the elements on which your papers will be graded. If your instructor provides a rubric, it may be included in the course syllabus, and you should refer to it each time you write. Also, use the rubric to revise your writing.

The following sample rubric shows you some of the elements you may be graded on. As you will see, the rubric reflects the Four Basics of Good Writing (p. 29). Instructors vary in how much weight (or how many points) they assign to each element.

Sample Rubric

Element	Grading criteria	Point range
Appropriateness (First Basic)	• Did the student follow the assignment directions?	0–5
Main idea (Third Basic)	• Does the paper clearly state a strong main idea in a complete sentence?	0–10
Support (Fourth Basic)	• Is the main idea developed with specific support, including specific details and examples? • Is enough support presented to make the main idea evident to the reader? • Is all the support directly related to the main idea?	0–10
Organization (Fourth Basic)	• Is the writing logically organized? • Does the student use transitions (e.g., *also, for example, sometimes,* and *so on*) to move the reader from one point to another?	0–10
Conclusion (Fourth Basic)	• Does the conclusion remind the reader of the main point? • Does it make an observation based on the support?	0–5
Grammar (First and Second Basic)	Has the writer edited the paper so that it • is free of the four most serious errors? (See Chapters 16–19.) • has clear sentence structure? • has words that clearly express the writer's meaning in an appropriate tone? • uses correct spelling? • uses correct punctuation?	0–10

The paragraph that follows shows how rubrics are applied to a piece of writing. For a key to the correction symbols used, see the Useful Editing and Proofreading Marks chart at the back of this book.

Assignment: Write a paragraph about something you enjoy doing. Make sure you give enough details about the activity so that a reader who knows little about it will have an idea of why you enjoy it.

Paragraph

                                                        tense

In my spare time, I enjoy talking with my friend Karen. I know Karen since we

       tense   frag   ^

ten, so we have growed up together and been through many things. Like a sister.

We can talk about anything. Sometimes we talk about problems. Money problems,

            frag   frag

problems with men. When I was in a difficult relationship, for example. Now we

                                           sp   sp

both have children and we talk about how to raise them. Things are diffrent then

when we kids. Talking with a good friend helps me make good decisions and

wc   ^   frag

patience. Especially now that my son is a teenager. We also talk about fun things,

       punc

like what were going to do on the weekend, what clothes we buy. We tell each other

good jokes and make each other laugh. These conversations are as important as

talking about problems.

Read to Write
Does your instructor follow the critical reading process when marking your papers? How do you know?

Analysis of paragraph: This paragraph would receive an average grade (not an A or B), for the following reasons.

Sample Rubric

Element	Grading criteria	Point: Comment
Appropriateness	• Did the student follow the assignment directions?	5/5: Yes.
Main idea	• Does the paper clearly state a strong main idea in a complete sentence?	10/10: Yes.
Support	• Is the main idea developed with specific support, including specific details and examples? • Is there enough support to make the main idea evident to the reader? • Is all the support directly related to the main idea?	5/10: The paragraph has some support and detail, but it could use more. ➜

Element	Grading criteria	Point: Comment
Organization	• Is the writing logically organized? • Does the student use transitions (e.g., *also, for example, sometimes,* and *so on*) to move the reader from one point to another?	6/10: The student uses a few transitions (*sometimes, when, for example, now*).
Conclusion	• Does the conclusion remind the reader of the main idea? • Does it make an observation based on the support?	3/5: The conclusion relates back to the main idea, but the observation is weak.
Grammar	Has the writer edited the paper so that it • is free of the four most serious errors? (See Chapters 16–19) • has clear sentence structure? • has words that clearly express the writer's meaning in an appropriate tone? • uses correct spelling? • uses correct punctuation?	6/10: The writing has some major grammar errors. **Total Points: 35/50**

Chapter Review

1. In your own words, define *audience.*

2. In college, who is your audience likely to be?

3. What are the stages of the writing process?

4. What are four of the elements often evaluated in rubrics?

Reflect and Apply

1. Think about writing you have done for work or other courses. What were the purposes of those pieces of writing?

2. In Chapter 1, you learned that reading is a process, and in this chapter, you learned that writing is a process. How are those processes similar? How is reading involved in the writing process?

3. Have your instructors ever given you a rubric for writing assignments? Did the rubric help you understand how to complete the assignment effectively? Explain.

Finding Your Topic and Writing Your Thesis Statement

Making a Point

Good writing makes a clear, definite point. As you begin the writing process, you will find and narrow a topic so that you can develop your point.

Understand What a Topic Is

A **topic** is who or what you are writing about. It is the subject of your paragraph or essay. In many classes, you will be writing about readings or about subjects that your instructor assigns. Sometimes, however, you may be allowed to choose your own topic. A good topic for an essay is one that interests you and that fulfills the terms of your assignment. Begin to select a topic by analyzing your assignment.

- How long should the assignment be?
- How formal is the assignment?
- How much of my grade is this assignment worth?
- What freedom do I have in choosing a topic? Is there a particular topic that I am required to write on, or am I free to choose my own topic? Is there a list of banned topics?
- Does the assignment specify a particular type of paper such as a narrative, argument, or cause and effect?

Your answers will help you determine a strong topic.

Questions for finding a good topic
- Does this topic interest me? If so, why do I care about it?
- Do I know something about the topic? Do I want to know more?

- Can I get involved with some part of the topic? Is it relevant to my life in some way?
- Is the topic specific enough for the assignment (a paragraph or a short essay)?

Choose one of the following topics or one assigned by your instructor and focus on one part of it that you are familiar with. (For example, focus on one personal goal or a specific problem of working students that interests you.)

Music/group I like	Sports
Problems of working students	A personal goal
An activity/group I am involved in	A time when I took a big risk
My proudest moment	My ideal job
An issue in the news	Viral videos or memes
Relationships	

> **PRACTICE 3-1** **Finding a Good Topic**
>
> Ask the "Questions for Finding a Good Topic" about the topic you have chosen. If you answer "no" to any of them, keep looking for another topic or modify the topic. Share your topic choice with your instructor or class members.

With the general topic you have chosen in mind, read this chapter and complete all the practices. When you finish the chapter, you will have a strong and appropriate topic and a preliminary topic sentence or thesis statement, as well as some ideas for your next steps.

Practice Narrowing a Topic

If your instructor assigns a general topic, it may at first seem uninteresting, unfamiliar, or too general. It is up to you to find a good, specific topic based on the general one. Whether the topic is your own or assigned, you next need to narrow and explore it. To **narrow** a general topic, focus on the smaller parts of it until you find one that is interesting and specific.

Here are some ways to narrow a general topic.

Read to Write What is the broad topic in Amanda Jacobowitz's essay, pp. 15–16? What is her narrow topic? What are some other categories that fit in the same broad topic?

Divide It into Smaller Categories

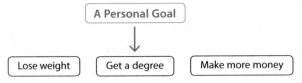

Think of Specific Examples from Your Life

General Topic	**Crime**
	Stolen identities (how does it happen?)
	When I had my wallet stolen by two kids (how? what happened?)
	The email scam that my grandmother lost money in (how did it work?)
General Topic	**Social media**
	Instagram or Snapchat (why do people feel the need to document their every move with pictures and post them online?)
	Twitter (which feeds do I follow regularly? what do I get from them?)
	Facebook (what features are fun or useful? what feels like a waste of time?)

Think of Specific Examples from Current Events

General Topic	**Job-creation ideas**
	Tax breaks for businesses
	Training of future entrepreneurs in growth areas, like solar or wind energy
	A special fund for public projects that will employ many people
General Topic	**Heroism**
	The guy who pulled a stranger from a burning car
	My aunt, who volunteers at a homeless shelter for ten hours a week

Question Your Assumptions

Questioning assumptions—an important part of critical thinking (see Chapter 1)—can be a good way to narrow a topic. First, identify any assumptions you have about your topic. Then, question them, playing "devil's advocate"; in other words, imagine what someone with a different point of view might say. For example, imagine that your general topic is the pros or cons of letting kids play video games.

Read to Write You can also question assumptions in a reading in order to find and narrow a topic for writing. Identify and question any assumptions in Amanda Jacobowitz's essay in Chapter 1, pp. 15–16.

Possible assumptions	Questions
Video game pros: Kids get rewarded with good scores for staying focused. ➔ Video games can teach some useful skills. ➔	Does staying focused on a video game mean that a kid will stay focused on homework or in class? What types of skills? How am I defining "useful"?
Video game cons: Video games make kids more violent. ➔ Video games have no real educational value. ➔	Is there really any proof for an increase in violence? What do experts say? Didn't my niece say that some video game helped her learn to read?

Next, ask yourself what assumptions and questions interest you the most. Then, focus on those interests.

When you have found a promising topic for a paragraph or essay, be sure to test it by using the Questions for Finding a Good Topic at the beginning of this chapter. You may need to narrow and test your ideas several times before you find a topic that will work for the assignment.

A topic for an essay can be a little broader than one for a paragraph because essays are longer than paragraphs and allow you to develop more ideas. But be careful: most of the extra length in an essay should come from developing ideas in more depth (giving more examples and details, explaining what you mean), not from covering a broader topic.

Read the following examples of how a general topic was narrowed to a more specific topic for an essay and an even more specific topic for a paragraph.

General topic		Narrowed essay topic		Narrowed paragraph topic
Internships	➔	How internships can help you get a job	➔	One or two important things you can learn from an internship
Social media	➔	Popularity of social media among preteens	➔	Should there be an age limit for social media use?
A personal goal	➔	Getting healthy	➔	Eating the right foods
A great vacation	➔	A family camping trip	➔	What I learned on our family camping trip to Michigan

PRACTICE 3–2 **Narrowing a General Topic**

Use one of the four methods on pages 42–44 to narrow your topic. Then, ask yourself the Questions for Finding a Good Topic on pages 41–42. Share your narrowed topic with your instructor and members of your class.

Practice Exploring Your Topic

Prewriting techniques (or **invention strategies**) can give you ideas at any time during your writing: to find a topic, to get ideas for what you want to say about it, and to support your ideas. Ask yourself these questions: what interests me about this topic? What do I know? What do I want to say? Then, use one or more of the prewriting techniques to find the answers. No one uses all these techniques; writers choose the ones that work best for them.

Prewriting Techniques

- Freewriting
- Listing/brainstorming
- Discussing
- Clustering/mapping
- Reading/researching online
- Keeping a journal

When prewriting, your goal is to come up with as many ideas as possible. Do not say, "Oh, that's stupid" or "That won't work." Just get your brain working by writing down all the possibilities.

A student, Chelsea Wilson, was assigned to write a short essay. She chose to write on the general topic of a personal goal, which she narrowed to "Getting a college degree." The following pages show how she used the first five prewriting techniques in the preceding list to explore her topic.

Freewriting

Freewriting is like having a conversation with yourself, on paper. To freewrite, just start writing everything you can think of about your topic. Write nonstop for five minutes. Do not go back and cross anything out, and do not worry about using correct grammar or spelling; just write. Here is Chelsea's freewriting:

> So I know I want to get a college degree even though sometimes
> I wonder if I ever can make it because it's so hard with work and my
> two-year-old daughter and no money and a car that needs work. I can't
> take more than two courses at a time and even then I hardly get a

Tip Scholar and writer Mina Shaughnessy said that a writer "gets below the surface of a topic." When it comes to exploring a topic, what do you think getting "below the surface" means?

Tip If you are writing on a computer, try a kind of freewriting called "invisible writing." Turn the monitor off, or adjust the screen so that you cannot see what you are typing. Then, write quickly for five minutes without stopping. After five minutes, read what you have written. You may be surprised by the ideas that you can generate this way.

Read to Write Who is the audience for your freewriting? What is your purpose in freewriting?

chance to sleep if I want to do any of the assignments or study. But I have to think I'll get a better job because this one at the restaurant is driving me nuts and doesn't pay much so I have to work a lot with a boss I can't stand and still wonder how I'm gonna pay the bills. I know life can be better if I can just manage to become a nurse. I'll make more money and can live anywhere I want because everyplace needs nurses. I won't have to work at a job where I am not respected by anyone. I want respect, I know I'm hardworking and smart and good with people and deserve better than this. So does my daughter. No one in my family has ever graduated from college even though my sister took two courses, but then she stopped. I know I can do this, I just have to make a commitment to do it and not look away.

Listing/Brainstorming

Listing (or **brainstorming**) is when you list all the ideas about your topic that you can think of. Write as many as you can in five minutes without stopping.

GETTING A COLLEGE DEGREE

want a better life for myself and my daughter

want to be a nurse and help care for people

make more money

not have to work so many hours

could live where I want in a nicer place

good future and benefits like health insurance

get respect

proud of myself, achieve, show everyone

be a professional, work in a clean place

Discussing

Many people find it helpful to discuss ideas with another person before they write. As they talk, they get more ideas and immediate feedback.

If you and your discussion partner both have writing assignments, first explore one person's topic and then explore the other's. The person whose topic is being explored is the interviewee; the other person is the interviewer. The interviewer should ask questions about anything that seems unclear and should let the interviewee know what sounds interesting. In addition, the interviewer should identify and try to question any assumptions the interviewee seems to be making (see pages 43–44). The interviewee should give thoughtful answers and keep an open mind. He or she should also take notes.

Exploring your Narrowed Topic

Use two or three prewriting techniques to explore your narrowed topic.

Clustering/Mapping

Clustering, also called **mapping**, is like listing except that you arrange your ideas visually. Start by writing your narrowed topic in the center. Then, answer the following questions around the narrowed topic: Why? What interests me? and What do I want to say? Using Chelsea's clustering that follows as a model, write three answers to these questions. Keep branching out from the ideas until you feel you have fully explored your topic. Note that when Chelsea filled in "Why?" "What interests me?" and "What do I want to say?" she had lots of reasons and ideas that she could use in her writing assignment.

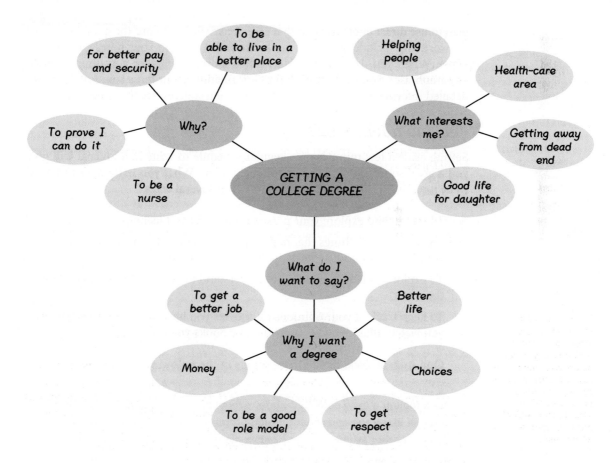

Reading and Researching on the Internet

For some assignments, you will need to do research on your topic, either online or in your college's library. (For more on research, see Chapter 15.) If you do use research to find out some basic information about your topic, take notes and use the information you find very carefully. You must be able to document where you found the information and avoid plagiarism.

Avoiding Plagiarism

Tip For more on paraphrasing, see Chapter 1, pages 13–15.

In all the writing you do, it is important to avoid plagiarism—using other people's words as your own or handing in information you gathered from another source as your own. Your instructors are aware of plagiarism and know how to look for it. Writers who plagiarize, either on purpose or by accident, risk failing a course or losing their jobs and damaging their reputations.

To avoid plagiarism, take careful notes on every source (books, interviews, television shows, websites, etc.) you might use in your writing. When recording information from sources, take notes in your own words (paraphrase), unless you plan to use direct quotations. In that case, make sure to record the quotation word for word and include quotation marks around it, both in your notes and in your paper. When you use material from other sources—whether you directly quote or paraphrase—you must give citation information about these sources. For more detailed information on citing and documenting sources, see the appendix.

Keeping a Journal

Setting aside a few minutes on a regular schedule to write in a journal will give you a great source of ideas when you need them. What you write does not need to be long or formal. You can use a journal in several ways:

- To record and explore your personal thoughts and feelings
- To comment on things that happen, to you personally or in politics, in your neighborhood, at work, in college, and so on
- To explore situations you do not understand (as you write, you may figure them out)
- To keep track of your opinions on movies you have seen, television shows you watch, music you've listened to, or books you have read.

Tip If you start keeping a journal, you might use some of the strategies described by writer Joan Didion. She says, "I write entirely to find out what I'm thinking, what I'm looking at, what I see, and what it means. What I want and what I fear."

One student, Jack, did all these things in the following journal entry.

Been feeling a little confused about school lately. Doing OK in my classes and still liking the construction tech program. But having some doubts. Elena, another student in my English class, is studying to be a solar tech in a new program at the school. She's going to learn how to install and repair solar energy systems at a facility near campus, and that's pretty cool. Solar seems kind of sci-fi, and I love sci-fi movies. But seriously I'm truly interested in the technology, and some of the skills I've been learning in construction tech would probably transfer. And maybe I'd have a better chance of getting a job in solar energy since it's a field that seems to be growing? Not sure, but something to investigate. Bottom line: I can't get this new idea out of my mind, even though I thought I was sure about construction tech. I guess I'll keep talking with Elena about the solar tech program. And maybe I should meet with one of the instructors in the program? Or visit the solar facility?

Write Your Own Topic and Ideas

You should have both your narrowed topic (from Practice 3–2) and ideas from your prewriting. Now is the time to make sure your topic and ideas about it are clear. Use the checklist that follows to make sure you have completed this step of the writing process.

CHECKLIST

Evaluating Your Narrowed Topic

- ☐ This topic interests me.
- ☐ My narrowed topic is specific.
- ☐ I can write about it in a paragraph or an essay (whichever you have been assigned).
- ☐ I have generated some things to say about this topic.

Now that you have focused your topic, you are ready to create a clear and forceful thesis statement and topic sentences.

Understand What a Topic Sentence and a Thesis Statement Are

Every good piece of writing has a **main idea**—what the writer wants to get across to the readers about the topic or the writer's position on that topic. A **topic sentence** (for a paragraph) and a **thesis statement** (for an essay) express the writer's main idea. To see the relationship between the thesis statement of an essay and the topic sentences of paragraphs that support a thesis statement, see the diagram on page 34.

Relationship between Paragraphs and Essays

For more on the important features of writing, see the Four Basics of Good Writing on page 29.

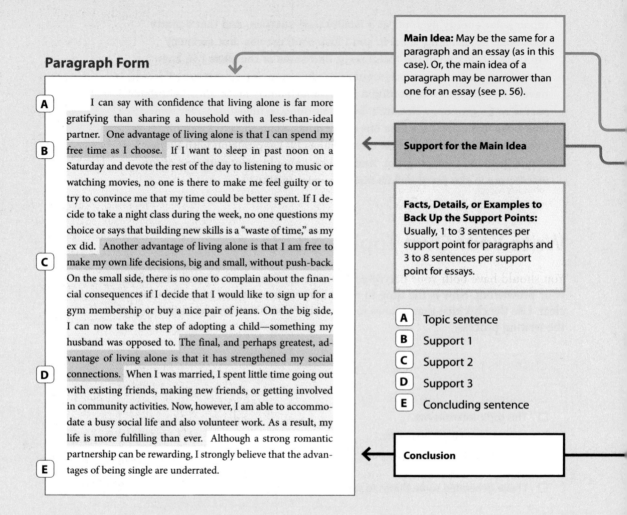

Paragraph Form

A   I can say with confidence that living alone is far more gratifying than sharing a household with a less-than-ideal partner. **B** One advantage of living alone is that I can spend my free time as I choose. If I want to sleep in past noon on a Saturday and devote the rest of the day to listening to music or watching movies, no one is there to make me feel guilty or to try to convince me that my time could be better spent. If I decide to take a night class during the week, no one questions my choice or says that building new skills is a "waste of time," as my ex did. **C** Another advantage of living alone is that I am free to make my own life decisions, big and small, without push-back. On the small side, there is no one to complain about the financial consequences if I decide that I would like to sign up for a gym membership or buy a nice pair of jeans. On the big side, I can now take the step of adopting a child—something my husband was opposed to. The final, and perhaps greatest, advantage of living alone is that it has strengthened my social **D** connections. When I was married, I spent little time going out with existing friends, making new friends, or getting involved in community activities. Now, however, I am able to accommodate a busy social life and also volunteer work. As a result, my life is more fulfilling than ever. Although a strong romantic partnership can be rewarding, I strongly believe that the advan- **E** tages of being single are underrated.

Main Idea: May be the same for a paragraph and an essay (as in this case). Or, the main idea of a paragraph may be narrower than one for an essay (see p. 56).

Support for the Main Idea

Facts, Details, or Examples to Back Up the Support Points: Usually, 1 to 3 sentences per support point for paragraphs and 3 to 8 sentences per support point for essays.

A Topic sentence
B Support 1
C Support 2
D Support 3
E Concluding sentence

Conclusion

Essay Form

1

As a young woman, I saw being single as a temporary—and undesirable—condition. When, at twenty-four, I married, I considered myself extremely lucky. That was until I spent years in an increasingly unsatisfying relationship that ultimately ended in divorce. Since the divorce, however, my life has changed for the better in many ways. **I can now say with confidence that living alone is far more gratifying than sharing a household with a less-than-ideal partner.**

One advantage of living alone is that I can spend my free time as I choose. If I want to sleep in past noon on a Saturday and devote the rest of the day to listening to music or watching movies, no one is there to make me feel guilty or to try to convince me that my time could be better spent. If I decide to take a night class during the week, no one questions my choice or says that building new skills is a "waste of time," as my ex did. Also, when I am able to take vacation days, I can spend them relaxing at home, visiting out-of-state family members, or doing something more adventurous. In other words, I can set my own agenda, all the time.

A Introductory paragraph
B Thesis statement

2

Another advantage of living alone is that I am free to make my own life decisions, big and small, without push-back. On the small side, there is no one to complain about the financial consequences if I decide that I would like to sign up for a gym membership or buy a nice pair of jeans. On the big side, I can now take the step of adopting a child—something my husband was opposed to. I realize that making all my own decisions requires personal responsibility and the ability to take some risks. But, to me, the benefits of independence far outweigh the challenges.

The final, and perhaps greatest, advantage of living alone is that it has strengthened my social connections. When I was married, I spent little time going out with existing friends, making new friends, or getting involved in community activities. If I did not spend nearly all of my free time with my husband, he would complain. Now, however, I am able to accommodate a busy social life and also volunteer work in my community. As a result, my life is more fulfilling than ever.

D Topic sentence 2
E Support paragraphs
F Topic sentence 3

3

Although a strong romantic partnership can be rewarding, I strongly believe that the advantages of being single are underrated. Consequently, I would like to offer one piece of advice to partnered people: do not feel sorry for your single friends. One day, you may join their ranks and find that you have never been happier.

A Introductory paragraph
B Thesis statement
C Topic sentence 1
D Topic sentence 2
E Support paragraphs
F Topic sentence 3
G Concluding paragraph

51

In many paragraphs, the main idea is expressed in either the first or last sentence. In essays, the thesis statement is usually one sentence (often the first or last) in an introductory paragraph that contains several other sentences related to the main idea.

A good topic sentence or thesis statement has several basic features.

Basics of a good topic sentence or thesis statement

- It fits the size of the assignment.
- It states a single main idea or position about a topic.
- It is specific.
- It is something you can show, explain, or prove.
- It is a direct statement.

Weak   Giving children chores teaches them responsibility, and in my opinion doing chores as a kid made me a better adult.

[This statement has more than one point (how chores teach responsibility and how they made the writer a better adult); it is not specific (what is "responsibility"? what does it mean to be a "better adult"?); and it is not direct (the writer says, "in my opinion").]

Good   Giving children chores teaches them the responsibilities of taking care of things and completing assigned tasks.

Being assigned chores as a child helped teach me the important adult skills of teamwork and attention to detail.

One way to write a topic sentence for a paragraph or a thesis statement for an essay is to use this basic formula as a start:

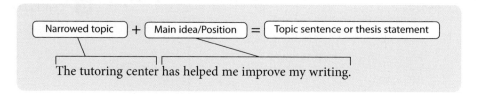

If you have trouble coming up with a main idea or position, look back over the prewriting you did. For example, when the student Chelsea Wilson looked over her prewriting about getting a college degree (see pp. 46–48), she realized that several times she had mentioned the idea of more options for employment, living places, and chances to go on and be a nurse. She could also have chosen to focus on the topic of respect or on issues relating to her young daughter, but she was most drawn to write about the idea of *options*. Here is how she stated her main idea:

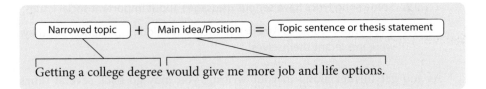

Narrowed topic + Main idea/Position = Topic sentence or thesis statement

Getting a college degree would give me more job and life options.

PRACTICE 3–4   Finding the Topic Sentence and Main Idea

Read the paragraph that follows, and underline the topic sentence. Identify the narrowed topic and the main idea.

> A recent survey reported that employers consider communication skills more critical to success than technical skills. Employees can learn technical skills on the job and practice them every day. But they need to bring well-developed communication skills to the job. They need to be able to make themselves understood to colleagues, both in speech and in writing. They need to be able to work cooperatively as part of a team. Employers cannot take time to teach communication skills, but without them an employee will have a hard time.

Read to Write Get into the habit of annotating the main idea in paragraphs and essays; the more familiar you are with strategies writers use to show their main ideas, the easier it may be to write your own.

PRACTICE 3–5   Identifying Topics and Main Ideas

In each of the following sentences, underline the topic and double-underline the main idea about the topic.

Example: Rosie the Riveter was the symbol of working women during World War II.

1. Discrimination in the workplace is alive and well.

2. The oldest child in the family is often the most independent and ambitious child.

3. Gadgets created for left-handed people are sometimes poorly designed.

4. Presidential campaigns bring out dirty politics.

5. Walking away from a mortgage has become a financial survival strategy for some homeowners.

6. The magazine *Consumer Reports* can help you decide which brands or models are the best value.

7. According to one study, dogs might be trained to detect signs of cancer on people's breath.

8. Status symbols are for insecure people.

9. Some song lyrics have serious messages about important social issues.

10. The Puritans came to America to escape religious intolerance, but they were intolerant themselves.

As you get further along in your writing, you may go back several times to revise the topic sentence or thesis statement based on what you learn as you develop your ideas. Look at how one student revised the example sentence on page 52 to make it more detailed:

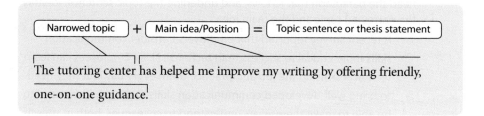

Narrowed topic + Main idea/Position = Topic sentence or thesis statement

The tutoring center has helped me improve my writing by offering friendly, one-on-one guidance.

Practice Developing a Good Topic Sentence or Thesis Statement

The explanations and practices in this section, organized according to the "basics" described previously, will help you write good topic sentences and thesis statements.

It Fits the Size of the Assignment

As you develop a topic sentence or thesis statement, think carefully about the length of the assignment.

Sometimes, a main-idea statement can be the same for a paragraph or essay.

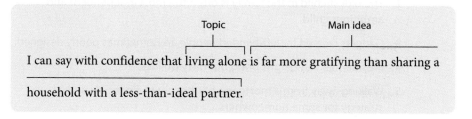

Topic   Main idea

I can say with confidence that living alone is far more gratifying than sharing a household with a less-than-ideal partner.

If the writer had been assigned a paragraph, she might follow the main idea with support sentences and a concluding sentence like those in the "paragraph" diagram on pages 50–51.

If the writer had been assigned an essay, she might develop the same support, but instead of writing single sentences to support her main idea, she would develop each support point into a paragraph. The support sentences she wrote in a paragraph might be topic sentences for support paragraphs. (For more on providing support, see Chapter 4.)

Often, however, a topic sentence for a paragraph is much narrower than a thesis statement for an essay, simply because a paragraph is shorter and allows less development of ideas.

Consider how one general topic could be narrowed into an essay topic and into an even more specific paragraph topic.

General topic	Narrowed essay topic	Narrowed paragraph topic
Internships →	How internships can help you get a job →	One or two important things you can learn from an internship

Possible thesis statement (essay)   The skills and connections you gain through a summer internship can help you get a good job after graduation.

[The essay would discuss several benefits of internships, describing the various skills they can teach and the professional connections they can offer to interns.]

Possible topic sentence (paragraph)   A summer internship is a good way to test whether a particular career is right for you.

[The paragraph would focus on one benefit of internships: they are a way to test out a career. The paragraph might go on to discuss signs that a certain type of work is or is not passing the test.]

PRACTICE 3-6   Writing Sentences to Fit the Assignment

Using the following example as a guide, write a thesis statement for the narrowed essay topic and a topic sentence for the narrowed paragraph topic.

Example:

Topic: Sports

Narrowed for an essay: Competition in school sports

Narrowed for a paragraph: User fees for school sports

Possible thesis statement (essay): *Competition in school sports has reached dangerous levels.*
Possible topic sentence (paragraph): *This year's user fees for participation in school sports are too high.*

1. **Topic:** Public service opportunities
   Narrowed for an essay: Volunteering at a homeless shelter
   Narrowed for a paragraph: My first impression of the homeless shelter
   Possible thesis statement (essay):
   Possible topic sentence (paragraph):

2. **Topic:** A personal goal
   Narrowed for an essay: Getting healthy
   Narrowed for a paragraph: Eating the right foods
   Possible thesis statement (essay):
   Possible topic sentence (paragraph):

3. **Topic:** A great vacation
   Narrowed for an essay: A family camping trip
   Narrowed for a paragraph: A lesson I learned on our family camping trip
   Possible thesis statement (essay):
   Possible topic sentence (paragraph):

Some topic sentences or thesis statements are too broad for either a short essay or a paragraph. A main idea that is too broad is impossible to show, explain, or prove within the space of a paragraph or short essay.

Too broad   Art is important.

[How could a writer possibly support such a broad concept in a paragraph or essay?]

Narrower   Art instruction for young children has surprising benefits.

A topic sentence or thesis statement that is too narrow leaves the writer with little to write about. There is little to show, explain, or prove.

Too narrow   Buy rechargeable batteries.

[OK, so now what?]

Broader   Choosing rechargeable batteries over conventional batteries is one action you can take to reduce your effect on the environment.

PRACTICE 3–7   **Writing Topic Sentences That Are Neither Too Broad nor Too Narrow**

In the following five practice items, three of the topic sentences are either too broad or too narrow, and two of them are OK. In the space to the left of each item, write "B" for too broad, "N" for too narrow, or "OK" for just right. Rewrite the three weak sentences to make them broader or narrower as needed.

Example: _B_ **Life can be tough for soldiers when they come home.**

We are not providing our returning soldiers with enough help in

readjusting to civilian life.

1. __ I take public transportation to work.

    Revision:

2. ___ Because of state and national education budget cuts, schools are having to lay off teachers and cut important programs.

    Revision:

3. __ College is challenging.

    Revision:

4. __ I would like to be successful in life.

    Revision:

5. ___ Having a positive attitude improves people's ability to function, improves their interactions with others, and reduces stress.

    Revision:

It Contains a Single Main Idea

Your topic sentence or thesis statement should focus on only one main idea. Two main ideas can split and weaken the focus of the writing.

Topic Sentence with Two Main Ideas

High schools <u>should sell healthy food instead of junk food</u>, and they <u>should start later in the morning.</u>

The two main ideas are underlined. Although both are good main ideas, together they split both the writer's and the readers' focus. The writer would need to give reasons to support each idea, and the ideas are completely different.

Topic Sentence with a Single Main Idea

High schools should sell healthy food instead of junk food.
OR
High schools should start later in the morning.

> **PRACTICE 3–8**   **Writing Sentences with a Single Main Idea**
>
> In each of the following sentences, underline the main idea(s). Put an **X** next to sentences with two main ideas.
>
> **Example:** Shopping at secondhand stores is a fun way to save money, and you can meet all kinds of interesting people as you shop. **X**

1. My younger sister, the baby of the family, was the most adventurous of my four siblings.

2. Servicing hybrid cars is a growing part of automotive technology education, and dealers cannot keep enough hybrids in stock.

3. My brother, Bobby, is incredibly creative, and he takes in stray animals.

4. Pets can actually bring families together, and they require lots of care.

5. Unless people conserve voluntarily, we will deplete our water supply.

It Is Specific

A good topic sentence or thesis statement gives readers specific information so that they know exactly what the writer's main idea is.

General   Students are often overwhelmed.

[How are students overwhelmed?]

Specific   Working college students have to learn how to juggle many responsibilities.

One way to make sure your topic sentence or thesis statement is specific is to make it a preview of what you are planning to say in the rest of the paragraph or essay. Just be certain that every point you preview is closely related to your main idea.

> **Preview:** Working college students have to learn how to juggle many responsibilities: doing a good job at work, getting to class regularly and on time, being alert in class, and doing the homework assignments.
>
> **Preview:** I have a set routine every Saturday morning that includes sleeping late, going to the gym, and shopping for food.

PRACTICE 3-9   **Writing Sentences that are Specific**

Revise each of the following sentences to make them more specific. There is no one correct answer. As you read the sentences, think about what would make them more understandable to you if you were about to read a paragraph or essay on the topic.

Example: Marriage can be a wonderful thing. Marriage to the right person can add love, companionship, and support to life.

1. My job is horrible.

2. Working with others is rewarding.

3. I am a good worker.

4. This place could use a lot of improvement.

5. My science class was challenging.

It Is an Idea You Can Show, Explain, or Prove

If a main idea is so obvious that it does not need support or if it states a simple fact, you will not have much to say about it.

Obvious	The Toyota Prius is a top-selling car.
	Many people like to take vacations in the summer.
Revised	Because of rising gas costs and concerns about the environmental impact of carbon emissions, the Toyota Prius is a top-selling car.
	The vast and incredible beauty of the Grand Canyon draws crowds of visitors each summer.
Fact	Employment of medical lab technicians is projected to increase by 14 percent between 2008 and 2018.
	Three hundred cities worldwide have bicycle-sharing programs.
Revised	Population growth and the creation of new types of medical tests mean the employment of lab technicians should increase by 14 percent between 2008 and 2018.
	Bicycle-sharing programs are popular, but funding them long-term can be challenging for cities with tight budgets.

PRACTICE 3–10 **Writing Sentences with Ideas You Can Show, Explain, or Prove**

Revise the following sentences so that they contain an idea you could show, explain, or prove.

Example: Leasing a car is popular.

Leasing a car has many advantages over buying one.

1. Texting while driving is dangerous.

2. My monthly rent is $750.

3. Health insurance rates rise every year.

4. Many people in this country work for minimum wage.

5. Technology is becoming increasingly important.

It Is a Direct Statement

A good topic sentence or thesis statement is a direct statement. Do not say you *will* make a point; just make it. Do not say "I think." Just state your point.

Weak	In my opinion, everyone should exercise.
Direct	Everyone should exercise to reduce stress, maintain a healthy weight, and feel better overall.
Weak	I think student fees are much too high.
Direct	Student fees need to be explained and justified.

PRACTICE 3-11   **Writing Direct Sentences**

Rewrite each of the following sentences to make them direct. Also, add details to make the sentences more specific.

Example: Jason's Market is the best.

Jason's Market is clean, organized, and filled with quality products.

1. I will prove that drug testing in the workplace is an invasion of privacy.

2. This school does not allow cell phones in class.

3. I strongly think I deserve a raise.

4. Nancy should be the head of the Students' Association.

5. I think my neighborhood is nice.

Write Your Own Topic Sentence or Thesis Statement

If you have worked through this chapter, you should have a good sense of how to write a topic sentence or thesis statement that includes the five features of a good one (see p. 51).

Before writing your own topic sentence or thesis statement, consider the process that Chelsea Wilson used. First, she narrowed her topic.

General Topic: *a personal goal*

Narrowed topic (for a paragraph): *why I want to get a nursing degree*

Narrowed topic (for an essay): *the many benefits of getting a college degree*

For a paragraph: *why I want to get a nursing degree*
  make more money
  get a better job
  become a respected professional
  live where I want

For an essay: *the many benefits of getting a college degree*
  get a job as a nurse
  make more money
  be a good role model for my daughter
  be proud of myself

Then, she did prewriting to get ideas about her topic.
Next, she was ready to write the statement of her main idea.

> **Topic sentence (paragraph):** *My goal is to get a nursing degree.*
>
> **Thesis statement (essay):** *My goal is to get a college degree.*

Finally, Chelsea revised this statement to make it more forceful.

> **Topic sentence:** *My goal is to become a registered nurse.*
>
> **Thesis statement:** *I am committed to getting a college degree because it will give me many good job and life options.*

You may want to change the wording of your topic sentence or thesis statement later, but following a sequence like Chelsea's should start you off with a good basic statement of your main idea.

WRITING ASSIGNMENT

Write a topic sentence or thesis statement using the narrowed topic you developed earlier in the chapter or one of the following topics (which you will have to narrow).

Community service	A holiday or family tradition
A local problem	A strong belief
Dressing for success	Bullying
Movie franchises	Exciting experiences
Saving money	Juggling many responsibilities
Interviewing for jobs	Friendship
Music	Conservation/recycling on campus
Sexual harassment	Professional athletes

After writing your topic sentence or thesis statement, complete the checklist that follows.

CHECKLIST

Evaluating Your Main Idea

☐ It is a complete sentence.

☐ It fits the assignment.

☐ It includes my topic and the main idea I want to make about it.

☐ It states a single main idea.

☐ It is specific.

☐ It is something I can show, explain, or prove.

☐ It is a direct statement.

Coming up with a good working topic sentence or thesis statement is the foundation of the writing you will do. Now that you know what you want to say, you are ready to learn more about how to show, explain, and prove your main idea to others. The next chapter, "Supporting Your Point," helps you make a strong case, consider what your readers need to know, and provide sufficient details and examples in your paragraph or essay.

Chapter Review

1. What are four questions that can help you find a good topic?

2. How can you narrow a topic that is too broad or general?

3. What are some prewriting techniques?

4. What is meant by the main idea in a piece of writing?

5. One way to write a topic sentence or a thesis statement is to include the narrowed topic and what else?

6. What are the basics of a good topic sentence or thesis statement?

Reflect and Apply

1. Think about writing you have done for work or other courses. How did you choose your topic?

2. Many students struggle with writer's block—being stuck during the process of writing. How can the invention strategies listed in this chapter help you overcome writer's block?

3. Many students see writing as a solitary activity: one person alone with a computer or a piece of paper. But as you have seen in this chapter, some prewriting techniques involve collaboration. What are the advantages of working with a partner or friend early in the writing process?

Supporting Your Point

Finding Details, Examples, and Facts

Understand What Support Is

Support is the collection of examples, facts, or evidence that shows, explains, or proves your main idea. **Primary support points** are the major ideas that back up your main idea, and **secondary support** gives details to back up your primary support.

Key Features of Good Support

Without support, you *state* the main idea, but you do not *show* the main idea. Consider these unsupported statements:

> The amount shown on my bill is incorrect.
>
> I deserve a raise.
>
> I need a vacation.

The statements may be true, but without good support, they are not convincing. If you sometimes get papers back with the comment "You need to support/develop your ideas," the suggestions in this chapter will help you.

Also, keep in mind that the same point repeated several times is not support. It is just repetition.

Repetition, Not Support	The amount shown on my bill is incorrect. You overcharged me. It didn't cost that much. The total is wrong.
Support	The amount shown on my bill is incorrect. I ordered the bacon-cheeseburger plate, which is $6.99 on the menu. On the bill, the order is correct, but the amount is $16.99.

Tip Showing involves providing visual details or other supporting observations. Explaining involves offering specific examples or illustrating aspects of the main idea. Proving involves providing specific evidence, sometimes from outside sources.

Read to Write As you read, annotate for primary and secondary support.

As you develop support for your main idea, make sure it has these three features.

Basics of good support

- It relates directly to your main idea. Remember that the purpose of support is to show, explain, or prove your main idea.

- It considers your readers and what they will need to know.

- It gives readers enough specific details, particularly through examples, so that they can see what you mean.

Support in Paragraphs versus Essays

Again, primary support points are the major ideas that back up your main idea. In paragraphs, your main idea is expressed in a topic sentence. In both paragraphs and essays, it is important to add enough details (secondary support) about the primary support to make the main idea clear to readers.

In the following paragraph, the topic sentence is underlined twice, the primary support is underlined once, and the details for each primary support point are in italics.

Read to Write What transition words signal the introduction of primary support? Of secondary support?

When I first enrolled in college, I thought that studying history was a waste of time. But after taking two world history classes, I have come to the conclusion that these courses count for far more than some credit hours in my college record. First, learning about historical events has helped me put important current events in perspective. *For instance, by studying the history of migration around the world, I have learned that immigration has been going on for hundreds of years. In addition, it is common in many countries, not just the United States. I have also learned about ways in which various societies have debated immigration, just as Americans are doing today.* Second, history courses have taught me about the power that individual people can have, even under very challenging circumstances. *I was especially inspired by the story of Toussaint L'Ouverture, a former slave who, in the 1790s, led uprisings in the French colony of Saint-Domingue, transforming it into the independent nation of Haiti. Although L'Ouverture faced difficult odds, he persisted and achieved great things.* The biggest benefit of taking history courses is that they have encouraged me to dig more deeply into subjects than I ever have before. *For a paper about the lasting influence of Anne Frank,[1] I drew on quotations from her famous diary, on biographies about her, and on essays written by noted historians. The research was fascinating, and I loved piecing together the various facts and insights to come to my own conclusions. To sum up, I have become hooked on history, and I have a feeling that the lessons it teaches me will be relevant far beyond college.*

1. Anne Frank (1929–1945): a German Jewish girl who fled to the Netherlands with her family after Adolf Hitler, leader of the Nazi Party, became chancellor of Germany. In 1944, Anne and her family were arrested by the Nazis, and she died in a concentration camp the following year.

Did you notice that the primary support points are more specific than the topic sentence, and the secondary support points are more specific than the primary support points? The primary support points, for example, include general nouns, such as "important current events" or "individual people," while the secondary support gives specific examples of each of these: immigration and Toussaint L'Ouverture.

In an essay, each primary support point, along with its supporting details, is developed into a separate paragraph. (See the diagram on pp. 50–51.) In this case, each underlined point in the previous paragraph could be turned into a topic sentence that would be supported by the italicized details. However, in preparing an essay on the preceding topic, the writer would want to add more details and examples for each primary support point. Here are some possible additions:

- **For primary support point 1:** more connections between history and current events (one idea: the rise and fall of dictators in past societies and in the modern Middle East)

- **For primary support point 2:** more examples of influential historical figures (one idea: the story of Joan of Arc, who, in the fifteenth century, led the French to victories over English armies)

- **For primary support point 3:** more examples of becoming deeply engaged in historical subjects (one idea: fascination with reprinted diaries or letters of World War II soldiers)

Read to Write Look back at the essay by Amanda Jacobowitz on pages 15–16. What are her primary support points? What are her secondary support points? How does she use proper nouns (beginning with capital letters) to provide specific supporting details?

Practice Supporting a Main Idea

Generate Support

To generate support for the main idea of a paragraph or essay, try one or more of the following strategies.

Three quick strategies for generating support

1. *Circle an important word or phrase* in your topic sentence (for a paragraph) or thesis statement (for an essay) and write about it for a few minutes. As you work, refer back to your main idea to make sure you're on the right track.

2. *Reread your topic sentence or thesis statement and write down the first thought you have.* Then, write down your next thought. Keep going.

3. *Use a prewriting technique* (freewriting, listing, discussing, clustering, and so on) while thinking about your main idea and your audience. Write for three to five minutes without stopping.

Generating Supporting Ideas

Choose one of the following sentences, or your own topic sentence, or thesis statement and use one of the three strategies to generate support just mentioned. Because you will need a good supply of ideas to support your main idea, try to find at least a dozen possible supporting ideas. Keep your answers because you will use them in later practices in this chapter.

1. Some television shows challenge my way of thinking instead of numb my mind.

2. Today there is no such thing as a "typical" college student.

3. Learning happens not only in school but throughout a person's life.

4. Practical intelligence can't be measured by grades.

5. I am an excellent candidate for the job.

Select the Best Primary Support

After you have generated possible support, review your ideas; then, select the best ones to use as primary support. Here you take control of your topic, shaping the way readers will see it and the main idea you are making about it. These ideas are yours, and you need to sell them to your audience.

The following steps can help.

1. Carefully read the ideas you have generated.

2. Select three to five primary support points that will be clearest and most convincing to your readers, providing the best examples, facts, and observations to support your main idea. If you are writing a paragraph, these points will become the primary support for your topic sentence. If you are writing an essay, they will become topic sentences of the individual paragraphs that support your thesis statement.

3. Cross out ideas that are not closely related to your main idea.

4. If you find that you have crossed out most of your ideas and do not have enough left to support your main idea, use one of the three strategies on page 67 to find more.

Tip For a diagram showing the relationship between topic sentences and support in paragraphs, and thesis statements and support in essays, see pages 50–51 in Chapter 3.

Selecting the Best Support

Refer to your response to Practice 4-1 (above). Of your possible primary support points, choose three to five that you think will best show, explain, or prove your main idea to your readers. Write down your three to five points.

Add Secondary Support

Once you have selected your best primary support points, you need to flesh them out for your readers. Do this by adding secondary support, specific examples, facts, and observations to back up your primary support points.

> **PRACTICE 4-3**   **Adding Secondary Support**
>
> Using your answers to Practice 4-2, choose three primary support points and write them in the spaces below. Then, read each of them carefully and write down at least three supporting details (secondary support) for each one. For examples of secondary support, see the example paragraph on page 66.
>
> Primary support point 1:
>
> Supporting details:
>
> Primary support point 2:
>
> Supporting details:
>
> Primary support point 3:
>
> Supporting details:

Write Your Own Support

Before developing your own support for a main idea, look at how Chelsea developed support for her paragraph.

> **Topic sentence:** *My goal is to get a nursing degree.*

First, she did some prewriting (using the listing technique) and selected the best primary support points, while eliminating those she didn't think she would use.

Primary support points

GETTING AN LPN DEGREE

nurses help people and I want to do that

jobs all over the country

good jobs with decent pay

~~good setting, clean~~

a profession, not just a job

opportunity, like RN

bigger place, more money

treated with respect

role model

pride in myself and my work, what I've done

~~good benefits~~

~~nice people to work with~~

may get paid to take more classes—chance for further professional development

~~uniform so not lots of money for clothes~~

~~I'll be something~~

Chelsea noticed that some of her notes were related to the same subject, so she arranged them into related clusters with the smaller points indented under the larger ones.

Organized list of support points

good job

    decent pay

    jobs all over the country

a profession, not just a job

    treated with respect

    opportunity for the future (like RN)

    maybe get paid to take more classes?

pride/achievement

    a job that helps people

    I would take pride in my hard work

    I'd be a role model

Then, she took the notes she made and organized them into primary support and supporting details. Notice how she changed and reorganized some of her smaller points.

Primary support: *Being an LPN is an excellent job.*

    Supporting details: *The pay is regular and averages about $40,000 a year.*

    I could afford to move to a bigger and better place with more room for my daughter and work fewer hours.

Primary support: *Nursing is a profession, not just a job.*

    Supporting details: *Nurses help care for people, an important job, giving to the world.*

    Future opportunities, like becoming an RN with more money and responsibility.

    People respect nurses.

Primary support: *Being a nurse will be a great achievement for me.*

    Supporting details: *I will have worked hard and met my goal.*

    I will respect myself and be proud of what I do.

    I will be a good role model for my daughter.

WRITING ASSIGNMENT

Develop primary support points and supporting details using your topic sentence or thesis statement from Chapter 3 or one of the following topic sentences/thesis statements.

It is important for future (name of profession) to write well.

The drinking age should/should not be lowered.

Going to college is/is not essential.

People who do not speak "proper" English are discriminated against.

Most people in the United States could/could not live without technology today.

After developing your support, complete the following checklist.

CHECKLIST

Evaluating Your Support

☐ It is directly related to my main idea.

☐ It uses examples, facts, and observations that will make sense to my readers.

☐ It includes enough specific details to show my readers exactly what I mean.

Once you have pulled together your primary support points and secondary supporting details, you are ready for the next step: drafting a paragraph or essay based on a plan. For more information, go on to the next chapter.

Chapter Review

1. What is support?

2. What are the three basics of good support?

3. What are three strategies for generating support?

4. When you have selected your primary support points, what should you then add?

Reflect and Apply

1. Think about writing you have done for work or other courses. How did you find support for those texts? How did you know when you had enough support?

2. How can reading help you in the process of generating support?

3. Karin generated support for a paragraph about the qualities of an ideal teacher. For her second support point, she wrote this:

Primary Support: A great teacher cares about her students and wants them to learn.

Secondary Support: Her students are important to her, and she is concerned about them and their progress. For example, she hopes they will do well.

Do you think Karin has provided strong secondary support for this point? Why or why not?

5

Drafting and Revising

The Writing Process

Understand What a Draft Is

A **draft** is the first whole version of all your ideas put together in a piece of writing. Do the best job you can in drafting but know that you can make changes later.

Basics of a good draft

- It has a topic sentence (for a paragraph) or a thesis statement (for an essay) that states a clear main idea.
- It has a logical organization of ideas.
- It has primary and secondary support that shows, explains, or proves the main idea.
- It has a conclusion that makes an observation about the main idea.
- It follows standard paragraph form (see p. 33) or standard essay form (see p. 34).

Two good first steps to drafting a paragraph or essay are (1) to arrange the ideas that you have generated in an order that makes sense and (2) to write out a plan for your draft. We will look at these steps next.

Arrange Your Ideas

In writing, **order** means the sequence in which you present your ideas: what comes first, what comes next, and so on. There are three common ways of ordering—arranging—your ideas: time order (also called chronological order), space order, and order of importance.

Read the paragraph examples that follow. In each paragraph, the topic sentences are underlined twice, the primary support points are underlined once, and the secondary support is in italics.

Use Time Order to Write about Events

Use **time order** (chronological order) to arrange points according to when they happened. Time order works best when you are writing about events. You can go from

- First to last or last to first
- Most recent to least recent or least recent to most recent

Example using time order

<u><u>Officer Meredith Pavlovic's traffic stop of August 23, 2011, was fairly typical of an investigation and arrest for drunk driving.</u></u> <u>First, at around 12:15 a.m. that day, she noticed that the driver of a blue Honda Civic was acting suspiciously.</u> *The car was weaving between the fast and center lanes of Interstate 93 North near exit 12. In addition, it was proceeding at approximately 45 mph in a 55 mph zone.* <u>Therefore, Officer Pavlovic took the second step of pulling the driver over for a closer investigation.</u> *The driver's license told Officer Pavlovic that the driver was twenty-six-year-old Paul Brownwell. Brownwell's red eyes, slurred speech, and alcohol-tainted breath told Officer Pavlovic that Brownwell was very drunk.* But she had to be absolutely sure. <u>Thus, as a next step, she tested his balance and blood alcohol level.</u> *The results were that Brownwell could barely get out of the car, let alone stand on one foot. Also, a Breathalyzer test showed that his blood alcohol level was 0.13, well over the legal limit of 0.08.* These results meant an arrest for Brownwell, an unfortunate outcome for him, but a lucky one for other people on the road at that time.

Read to Write
What transitions does the writer use to help readers move from one event to the next?

What kind of time order does the author use?

Use Space Order to Describe Objects, Places, or People

Use **space order** to arrange ideas so that your readers picture your topic the way you see it. Space order usually works best when you are writing about a physical object, a place, or a person's appearance. You can move from

- Top to bottom or bottom to top
- Near to far or far to near
- Left to right or right to left
- Back to front or front to back

Example using space order

I was gazing at my son's feet, in awe. There were ten toes, and they were no bigger than my fingernail. *How could something so small be moving so quickly?* Staring at those little toes squirming around as I tried to put socks on them, I had to laugh because the chubby little tree trunks that his dad and I call legs decided to get in on the action. Those full kicks that I had felt for the past several months and that had felt like someone performing kung-fu on my internal organs were now free and he clearly enjoyed that open space. Nothing, however, could prepare me for that tubby little belly. *So small, round, and smooth—yet it bounced up and down with each giggle, burp, and cry.* Two large sausage-like appendages turned into arms with long, slender fingers and fingernails that were no larger than the head of a pin, or so it appeared. But what did all that matter when the true beauty perched right atop his nonexistent neck: *that gorgeous, round head covered with brown peach fuzz, sticking up in all directions.* Add all the pieces together, and all you see is love.

What type of space order does the example use?

Use Order of Importance to Emphasize a Particular Point

Use **order of importance** to arrange points according to their significance, interest, or surprise value. Usually, save the most important point for last.

Example using order of importance

Many parents today do not realize that there is a serious problem in their own home: prescription drug abuse. Unfortunately, we live in a day and age where the answer for many different problems is a prescription drug of some type. *We are prescribed drugs for pain, illness, mental disorders, sleep disorders, and even sexual problems.* With so many different disorders or problems that need treatment today, it is likely that any household has at least two or three active prescriptions at any one time, but who is actually using and taking those pills? News reports have shown that adults do not typically think to take the same precautions with prescriptions as they would with other dangerous substances, *namely weapons like guns or knives*; however, pills are just as deadly and far more addicting. If you are not keeping your prescriptions locked up, you are not keeping your home and your children safe.

Read to Write
How many times has this writer repeated "prescription" or a related word in this paragraph? How does the repetition help the reader understand the paragraph better?

What is the writer's most important point?

Make a Plan

Tip Try using the cut-and-paste function on your computer to experiment with different ways to order support for your main idea. Doing so will give you a good sense of how your final paragraph or final essay will look.

When you have decided how to order your primary support points, it is time to make a more detailed plan for your paragraph or essay. A good, visual way to plan a draft is to arrange your ideas in an outline. An **outline** lists the topic sentence (for a paragraph) or thesis statement (for an essay), the primary support points for the topic sentence or thesis statement, and secondary supporting details for each of the support points. It provides a map of your ideas that you can follow as you write.

Outlining Paragraphs

Look at the outline Chelsea Wilson created with the support she wrote. She had already grouped together similar points and put the more specific details under the primary support (see p. 70). When she thought about how to order her ideas, the only way that made sense to her was by importance. If she had been telling the steps she would take to become a nurse, time order would have worked well. If she had been describing a setting where nurses work, space order would have been a good choice. However, because she was writing about why she wanted to get a college degree and become a nurse, she decided to arrange her reasons in order of importance. Notice that Chelsea also strengthened her topic sentence and made changes in her primary support and secondary support. At each stage, her ideas and the way she expressed them changed as she got closer to what she wanted to say.

Sample outline for a paragraph

Topic sentence: *Becoming a nurse is a goal of mine because it offers so much that I value.*

  Primary support 1: *It is a good and practical job.*

  Supporting details: *Licensed practical nurses make an average of $40,000 per year. That amount is much more than I make now. With that salary, I could move to a better place with my daughter and give her more, including more time.*

  Primary support 2: *Nursing is a profession, not just a job.*

  Supporting details: *It helps people who are sick and in need. Being an LPN offers great opportunities, like the chance to go on to become a registered nurse, with more money and responsibility. People respect nurses.*

  Primary support 3: *I will respect and be proud of myself for achieving my goal through hard work.*

  Supporting details: *I will be a good role model for my daughter. I will help her and others, but I will also be helping myself by knowing that I can accomplish good things.*

  Conclusion: *Reaching my goal is important to me and worth the work.*

Outlining Essays

The outline that follows is for a five-paragraph essay, in which three body paragraphs (built around three topic sentences) support a thesis statement. The thesis statement is included in an introductory paragraph; the fifth paragraph is the conclusion. However, essays may include more or fewer than five paragraphs, depending on the size and complexity of the topic.

This example is a "formal" outline form, with letters and numbers to distinguish between primary supporting and secondary supporting details. Some instructors require this format. If you are making an outline just for yourself, you might choose to write a less formal outline, simply indenting the secondary supporting details under the primary support rather than using numbers and letters.

Sample outline for a five-paragraph essay

Thesis statement (part of introductory paragraph 1)

    A. **Topic sentence for support point 1** (paragraph 2)

        1. Supporting detail 1 for support point 1

        2. Supporting detail 2 for support point 1 (and so on)

    B. **Topic sentence for support point 2** (paragraph 3)

        1. Supporting detail 1 for support point 2

        2. Supporting detail 2 for support point 2 (and so on)

    C. **Topic sentence for support point 3** (paragraph 4)

        1. Supporting detail 1 for support point 3

        2. Supporting detail 2 for support point 3 (and so on)

Concluding paragraph (paragraph 5)

Read to Write
Outlining is useful in both reading and writing. Practice outlining Amanda Jacobowitz's essay in Chapter 1, pages 15–16.

> **PRACTICE 5–1**   **Making an Outline**

Reread the paragraph on page 74 that illustrates time order of organization. Then, make an outline for it following the model provided.

    Topic sentence:

    Primary support 1:

      1. **Supporting detail:**

      2. **Supporting detail:**

Primary support 2:

      1. **Supporting detail:**

      2. **Supporting detail:**

Primary support 3:

      1. **Supporting detail:**

      2. **Supporting detail:**

Practice Writing a Draft Paragraph

As you write your paragraph, you will need to go through the steps in the following sections. Also, refer to the Basics of a Good Draft on page 73.

Write a Draft Using Complete Sentences

Write your draft with your outline in front of you. Be sure to include your topic sentence and express each point in a complete sentence. As you write, you may want to add support or change the order. It is okay to make changes from your outline as you write.

Read the following paragraph, annotated to show the various parts of the paragraph.

Parabens: Widely Used Chemicals Spark New Cautions ——————— Title

    Parabens, preservatives used in many cosmetics and personal- —— Topic sentence
care products, are raising concerns with more and more consumers. In
some people, parabens cause allergic reactions, but the effects of these
chemicals may be more than skin deep. After being applied to the face
or body, parabens can enter the bloodstream, where they have been
found to mimic the hormone estrogen. Because long-term exposure
to estrogen can increase the risk of breast cancer, researchers have
tried to determine whether there is any link between parabens and
breast cancer. So far, the findings have been inconclusive. One study
found parabens in the breast cancer tissue of some research subjects.
However, the study was small, and based on its results, it cannot be
said that parabens actually cause cancer. Nevertheless, some consumers ——— Support
wish to reduce their use of paraben-containing products or to avoid
them altogether. To do so, they carefully read the labels of personal-care
products, looking out for ingredients like butylparaben, ethylparaben,
methylparaben, isopropyl, and propylparaben. All these chemicals are
parabens. Consumers who do not wish to give up parabens entirely
might consider avoiding only those paraben-containing products, like
lotions and makeup, that stay on the skin for an extended period.
Products that are rinsed away quickly, like shampoos and soaps, do not
have as much time to be absorbed through the skin.

Tip For more on
topic sentences, see
Chapter 3.

    Although paragraphs typically begin with topic sentences, they may also
begin with a quote, an example, or a surprising fact or idea. The topic sentence
is then presented later in the paragraph. For examples of various introductory
techniques, see pages 82–84.

Write a Concluding Sentence

A **concluding sentence** refers back to the main idea and makes an observation
based on what you have written. The concluding sentence does not just repeat
the topic sentence.

    In the preceding paragraph, the main idea, expressed in the topic sentence, is
"Parabens, the preservatives used in many cosmetics and personal-care products,
are raising concerns with more and more consumers."

    A good conclusion might be, "Given the growing concerns about parabens
and uncertainties about their potential dangers, more research is clearly needed."
This sentence **refers back to the main idea** by repeating the words *parabens* and
concerns. It **makes an observation** by stating "more research is clearly needed."

    Concluding paragraphs for essays are discussed on pages 84–86.

PRACTICE 5-2 **Writing Concluding Sentences**

Read the following paragraphs and write a concluding sentence for each one.

1. One of the most valuable ways parents can help children is to read to them. Reading together is a good way for parents and children to relax, and it is sometimes the only "quality" time they spend together during a busy day. Reading to children develops their vocabulary. They understand more words and are likely to learn new words more easily than children who are not read to. Also, hearing the words aloud helps children's pronunciation and makes them more confident with oral language. In addition, reading at home increases children's chances of success in school because reading is required in every course in every grade.

   Possible concluding sentence:

2. Almost everyone uses certain memory devices called mnemonics. One of them is the alphabet song. If you want to remember what letter comes after *j*, you will probably sing the alphabet song in your head. Another is the "Thirty days hath September" rhyme that people use when they want to know how many days are in a certain month. Another mnemonic device is the rhyme "In 1492, Columbus sailed the ocean blue."

   Possible concluding sentence:

Practice Writing a Draft Essay

The basics of a good essay draft are all listed on page 73. In addition,

- The essay should include an introductory paragraph that draws readers in and includes the thesis statement.
- The topic sentences for the paragraphs that follow the introduction should directly support the thesis statement. In turn, each topic sentence should be backed by enough support.
- The conclusion should be a full paragraph rather than a single sentence.

Let's start by looking at topic sentences and support for them.

Write Topic Sentences and Draft the Body of the Essay

When you start to draft your essay, use your outline to write complete sentences for your primary support points. These sentences will serve as the topic sentences for the body paragraphs of your essay.

> **PRACTICE 5-3** **Writing Topic Sentences**
>
> Each thesis statement that follows has support points that could be topic sentences for the body paragraphs of an essay. For each support point, write a topic sentence.

Example

Thesis statement: My daughter is showing definite signs of becoming a teenager.

Support point: constantly texting friends

Topic sentence: *She texts friends constantly, even when they are sitting with her while I'm driving them.*

Support point: doesn't want me to know what's going on

Topic sentence: *She used to tell me everything, but now she is secretive and private.*

Support point: developing an "attitude"

Topic sentence: *The surest and most annoying sign that she is becoming a teenager is that she has developed a definite "attitude."*

Thesis statement: The Latin American influence is evident in many areas of US culture.

Support point: Spanish language used in lots of places

Topic sentence:

Support point: lots of different kinds of foods

Topic sentence:

Support point: new kinds of music and popular musicians

Topic sentence:

Drafting topic sentences for your essay is a good way to start drafting the body of the essay (the paragraphs that support each of these topic sentences). As you write support for your topic sentences, refer back to your outline, where you listed supporting details. (For an example, see Chelsea Wilson's outline on page 76.) Turn these supporting details into complete sentences, and add additional support if necessary. (Prewriting techniques can help here; see Chapter 3.) Don't let yourself get stalled if you are having trouble with one word or sentence. Just keep writing. Remember that a draft is a first try; you will have time later to improve it.

Write an Introduction

The introduction to your essay captures your readers' interest and presents the main idea. Ask yourself: how can I sell my essay to readers? You need to market your main idea.

Basics of a good introduction

- It should catch readers' attention.
- It should present the thesis statement of the essay, usually in the first or the last sentence of an introductory paragraph.
- It should give readers a clear idea of what the essay will cover.

Here are some common kinds of introductions that spark readers' interest. In each one, the introductory technique is in boldface. These introductions are not the only ways to start essays, but they should give you some useful models.

Open with a Quotation

A good, short quotation definitely gets people interested. It must lead naturally into your main idea, however, and not be there just for effect. If you start with a quotation, make sure you tell the reader who the speaker is.

> **"Never before had I truly felt such an extreme sense of estrangement and alienation,"** [a Vanderbilt student] says of his first few months. **"I quickly realized that although I may look the part, my cultural and socioeconomic backgrounds were vastly different from those of my predominantly white, affluent peers. I wanted to leave."**
>
> —*Liz Riggs, "What It's Like to Be the First Person in Your Family to Go to College"*

Give an Example or Tell a Story

People like stories, so opening an essay with a brief story or example often draws readers in.

> **The bank called today, and I told them my deposit was in the mail, even though I hadn't written a check yet.** It'd been a rough day. The baby I'm pregnant with decided to do aerobics on my lungs for two hours, our three-year-old daughter painted the living-room couch with lipstick, the IRS put me on hold for an hour, and I was late to a business meeting because I was tired.
>
> —*Stephanie Ericsson, "The Ways We Lie"*

Start with a Surprising Fact or Idea

Surprises capture people's interest. The more unexpected and surprising something is, the more likely people are to notice it.

> **In some places, towns essentially shut down in the afternoon while everyone goes home for a siesta.** Unfortunately, in the United States—more bound to our corporate lifestyles than our health—a midday nap is seen as a luxury and, in some cases, a sign of pure laziness. But before you feel guilty about that weekend snooze or falling asleep during a movie, rest assured that napping is actually good for you and a completely natural phenomena in the circadian (sleep-wake cycle) rhythm.
>
> —*Elizabeth Renter, "Napping Can Dramatically Increase Learning, Memory, Awareness, and More"*

Offer a Strong Opinion or Position

The stronger the opinion, the more likely it is that your readers will pay attention. Don't write wimpy introductions. Make your point with confidence.

> **Yes, money can buy happiness, but probably not in the way you imagined.** Spending it on yourself may not do much for your spirits, but spending it on others will make you happier, according to a report from a team of social psychologists in the new issue of *Science*.
>
> —*John Tierney, "Yes, Money Can Buy Happiness"*

Ask a Question

A question needs an answer, so if you start your introduction with a question, your readers will need to read on to get the answer.

Tip If you get stuck while writing your introductory statement, try one or more of the prewriting techniques described in Chapter 3 on pages 45–48.

> **At the end of a tour of Catskill Animal Sanctuary last year, a visitor who'd just been kissed by cows and held chickens in his lap said to me, "OK. I get it. How do I start?"**
>
> —*Kathy Stevens, "Ten Tips for Easing into Plant-Based Eating"*

PRACTICE 5–4   **Marketing Your Main Idea**

As you know from advertisements, a good writer can make just about anything sound interesting. For each of the following topics, write an introductory statement using the technique indicated. Some of these topics are purposely dull to show you that you can make an interesting statement about almost any subject if you put your mind to it.

Example

Topic: Reality TV

Technique: Question

Exactly how many recent top-selling songs have been recorded by former contestants of reality TV singing contests?

1. **Topic:** Credit cards

    Technique: Surprising fact or idea

2. **Topic:** Role of the elderly in society

    Technique: Question

3. **Topic:** Stress

    Technique: Quote (You can make up a good one.)

PRACTICE 5–5   **Identifying Strong Introductions**

In a newspaper or magazine, an online news site, an advertising flier—or anything written—find a strong introduction. Bring it to class and explain why you chose it as an example.

Write a Conclusion

When they have finished the body of their essay, some writers believe their work is done—but it isn't quite finished. Remember that people usually remember best what they see, hear, or read last. Use your concluding paragraph to drive your main idea home one final time. Make sure your conclusion has the same energy as the rest of the essay, if not more.

Basics of a good essay conclusion

- It refers back to the main idea.
- It sums up what has been covered in the essay.
- It makes a further observation or point.

In general, a good conclusion creates a sense of completion. It brings readers back to where they started, but it also shows them how far they have come.

One of the best ways to end an essay is to refer directly to something in the introduction. If you asked a question, re-ask and answer it. If you started a story, finish it. If you used a quote, use another one—maybe a quote by the same person or maybe one by another person on the same topic. Or, use some of the same words you used in your introduction. Look again at one of the introductions you read earlier and notice how the writer concluded her essay. Pay special attention to the text in boldface.

Ericsson's introduction

The bank called today, and I told them my deposit was in the mail, even though I hadn't written a check yet. It'd been a rough day. The baby I'm pregnant with decided to do aerobics on my lungs for two hours, our three-year-old daughter painted the living-room couch with lipstick, the IRS put me on hold for an hour, and I was late to a business meeting because I was tired.

— *Stephanie Ericsson, "The Ways We Lie"*

Ericsson's conclusion

Maybe if I don't tell the bank the check's in the mail I'll be less tolerant of the lies told to me every day. A country song I once heard said it all for me, "You've got to stand for something or you'll fall for anything."

— *Stephanie Ericsson, "The Ways We Lie"*

PRACTICE 5–6   **Finding Good Introductions and Conclusions**

In a newspaper or magazine or anything written, find a piece of writing that has a strong introduction and conclusion. (You may want to use what you found for Practice 5–5.) Answer the questions that follow.

1. What method of introduction is used?

2. What does the conclusion do? (Restate the main idea? Sum up the support? Make a further observation?)

3. How are the introduction and the conclusion linked?

Title Your Essay

Even if your **title** is the last part of the essay you write, it is the first thing readers read. Use your title to get your readers' attention and to tell them, in a brief way, what your paper is about. Use vivid, strong, specific words.

Basics of a good essay title

- It makes people want to read the essay.

- It hints at the main idea (thesis statement), but it does not repeat it.

One way to find a good title is to consider the type of essay you are writing. If you are writing an argument (as you will in Chapter 14), state your position in your title. If you are telling your readers how to do something (as you will in Chapter 9), try using the term *steps* or *how to* in the title. This way, your readers will know immediately not only what you are writing about but how you will discuss it.

Tip Center your title at the top of the page before the first paragraph. Do not put quotation marks around it or underline it.

> **PRACTICE 5–7**   **Titling an Essay**
>
> Reread the paragraphs from Stephanie Ericsson's essay on page 85, and write an alternate title for the essay.

Write Your Own Draft Paragraph or Essay

Before you draft your own paragraph, read Chelsea Wilson's annotated draft. It is based on her outline from page 76.

Identifying information

Title indicates main idea

Topic sentence (indented first line)

Support point 1

Chelsea Wilson
Professor Holmes
EN 099
September 7, 2012

My Career Goal

    My career goal is to become a nurse because it offers so much that I value. Being a nurse is a good and practical job. Licensed practical nurses make an average of $40,000 per year. That amount is much more than I make now working long hours at a minimum-wage job in a restaurant. Working as a nurse, I could be a better provider for my daughter. I could also spend more time with her. Also, nursing is more than just a job; it is a profession. As a nurse, I will help people who are sick, and helping people is important to me. With time, I will be able to grow within the profession, like becoming a registered nurse who makes more money and has more responsibility. Because nursing is a profession, nurses are respected. When I become a nurse, I will respect myself and be proud of myself for reaching my goal, even though I know it will take a lot of hard work. The most important thing about becoming a nurse is that it will be good for my young daughter. I will be a good role model for her. For all of these reasons, my goal is to become a nurse. Reaching this goal is important to me and worth the work.

Supporting details
Support point 2

Supporting details

Support point 3

Supporting details

Concluding sentence (refers back to main idea)

WRITING ASSIGNMENT   **Paragraph**

Write a draft paragraph using what you have developed in previous chapters or one of the following topic sentences. If you use one of the topic sentences below, you may want to revise it to fit what you want to say.

Being a good _____ requires _____.

I can find any number of ways to waste my time.

So many decisions are involved in going to college.

I thought _____ would be impossible, but it wasn't.

After writing your draft paragraph, complete the following checklist.

CHECKLIST

Evaluating Your Draft Paragraph

☐ It has a clear, confident topic sentence that states my main idea.

☐ Each primary support point is backed up with supporting details, examples, or facts.

☐ The support is arranged in a logical order.

☐ The concluding sentence reminds readers of my main idea and makes an observation.

☐ The title reinforces the main idea.

☐ All the sentences are complete, consisting of a subject and verb, and expressing a complete thought.

☐ The draft is properly formatted:
- My name, my instructor's name, the course, and the date appear in the upper left corner.
- The first sentence of the paragraph is indented, and the text is double-spaced (for easier revision).

☐ I have followed any other formatting guidelines provided by my instructor.

Before you draft your own essay, read Chelsea Wilson's annotated draft of her essay.

Chelsea Wilson
Professor Holmes
EN 099
September 14, 2012

The Benefits of Getting a College Degree

My goal is to get a college degree. I have been taking college courses for two years, and it has been difficult for me. Many times I have wondered if getting a college degree is really worth the struggle. However, there are many benefits of getting a college degree.

I can work as a nurse, something I have always wanted to do. As a nurse, I can make decent money: the average salary for a licensed practical nurse is $40,000 per year. That amount is substantially more than I make now working at a restaurant job that pays minimum wage and tips. With the economy so bad, people are tipping less. It has been hard to pay my bills, even though I work more than forty hours a week. Without a degree, I don't see how that situation will change. I have almost no time to see my daughter, who is in preschool.

I didn't get serious about getting a degree until I became a mother. Then, I realized I wanted more for my daughter than I had growing up. I also wanted to have time to raise her properly and keep her safe. She is a good girl, but she sees crime and violence around her. I want to get her away from danger, and I want to show her that there are better ways to live. Getting a college degree will help me do that.

The most important benefit of getting a college degree is that it will show me that I can achieve something hard. My life is moving in a good direction, and I am proud of myself. My daughter will be proud of me, too. I want to be a good role model for her as she grows up.

Because of these benefits, I want to get a college degree. It will give me the chance to earn a better living, it will give my daughter and me a better life, and I will be proud of myself.

Identifying information

Title indicates main idea

Introduction

Thesis statement
Topic sentence/ Support point 1

Supporting details

Topic sentence/ Support point 2

Supporting details

Topic sentence/ Support point 3

Supporting details

Conclusion

WRITING ASSIGNMENT   **Essay**

Write a draft essay using what you have developed in previous chapters or one of the following thesis statements. If you choose one of the thesis statements that follow, you may want to modify it to fit what you want to say.

Being successful at _____ requires _____.

Doing _____ gave me a great deal of pride in myself.

Training for _____ requires a lot of discipline.

Some of the differences between men and women create misunderstandings.

After you have finished writing your draft essay, complete the following checklist.

CHECKLIST

Evaluating Your Draft Essay

- ☐ A clear, confident thesis statement states my main idea.
- ☐ The primary support points are now topic sentences that support the main idea.
- ☐ Each topic sentence is part of a paragraph, and the other sentences in the paragraph support the topic sentence.
- ☐ The support is arranged in a logical order.
- ☐ The introduction will interest readers.
- ☐ The conclusion reinforces my main idea and makes an additional observation.
- ☐ The title reinforces the main idea.
- ☐ All the sentences are complete, consisting of a subject and verb, and expressing a complete thought.
- ☐ The draft is properly formatted:
  - My name, my instructor's name, the course, and the date appear in the upper left corner.
  - The first sentence of each paragraph is indented, and the text is double-spaced (for easier revision).
  - The pages are numbered.
- ☐ I have followed any other formatting guidelines provided by my instructor.

Give yourself some time away from your draft, at least a few hours and preferably a day or two. Taking a break will allow you to return to your writing later with a fresher eye and more energy for revision, resulting in a better piece of writing—and a better grade. After your break, you will be ready to take the next step: revising your draft.

Understand What Revision Is

When you finish a draft, you probably wish that you were at the end: you don't want to have to look at it again. But a draft is just the first whole version, a rough cut; it is not the best you can do to represent yourself and your ideas. After taking a break, you need to look at the draft with fresh eyes to revise and edit it.

Revising is making your ideas clearer, stronger, and more convincing. When revising, you are evaluating how well you have made your point. **Editing** is finding and correcting problems with grammar, word usage, punctuation, and capitalization. When editing, you are evaluating the words, phrases, and sentences you have used.

Most writers find it difficult to revise and edit well if they try to do both at once. It is easier to solve idea-level problems first (by revising) and then to correct smaller, word-level ones (by editing). This chapter focuses on revising. For editing help, use Chapters 15 through 34.

Read to Write
For more on reading critically, see Chapter 1.

Tips for revising your writing

- Wait a few hours or, if possible, a couple of days before starting to revise.

- Read your draft aloud and listen for places where the writing seems weak or unclear.

- Read critically and ask yourself questions, as if you were reading through someone else's eyes.

- Write notes about changes to make. For small things, like adding a transition (pp. 95–96), you can make the change on the draft. For other things, like adding or getting rid of an idea or reordering your support points, make a note in the margin.

- Get help from a tutor at the writing center, or get feedback from a friend (see the following section for information on peer review).

Even the best writers do not get everything right the first time. So, if you finish reading your draft and have not found anything that could be better, you are not reading carefully enough or are not asking the right questions. Use the following checklist to help you make your writing better.

CHECKLIST

Revising Your Writing

☐ If someone else just read my topic sentence or thesis statement, what would he or she think the paper is about? Would the main point make a lasting impression? What would I need to do to make it more interesting?

☐ Does each support point really relate to my main idea? What more could I say about the topic so that someone else will see it my way? Is any of what I have written weak? If so, should I delete it?

☐ What about the way the ideas are arranged? Should I change the order so that the writing makes more sense or has a stronger effect on a reader?

☐ What about the ending? Does it just droop and fade away? How could I make it better?

☐ If someone knew nothing about the topic or disagreed with my position before reading my paragraph or essay, would what I have written be enough for him or her to understand the material or be convinced by my argument?

Practice Revising for Unity, Detail, and Coherence

You may need to read what you have written several times before deciding what changes would improve it. Remember to consider your audience and your purpose and to focus on three areas: unity, detail, and coherence.

Revise for Unity

Unity in writing means that all the points you make are related to your main idea; they are *unified* in support of it. As you draft a paragraph or an essay, you may detour from your main idea without even being aware of it, as the writer of the following paragraph did with the underlined sentences. The diagram after the paragraph shows what happens when readers read the paragraph. The main idea of the paragraph has been double-underlined.

If you want to drive like an elderly person, use a cell phone while driving. A group of researchers from the University of Utah tested the reaction times of two groups of people—those between the ages of sixty-five to seventy-four and those who were eighteen to twenty-five—in a variety of driving tasks. All tasks were done with hands-free cell phones. That part of the study surprised me because I thought the main problem was using only one hand to drive. I hardly ever drive with two hands, even when I'm not talking to anyone. Among other results, braking time for both groups slowed by 18 percent. A related result is that the number of rear-end collisions doubled. The study determined that the younger drivers were paying as much—or more—attention to their phone conversations as they were to what was going on around them on the road. The elderly drivers also experienced longer reaction times and more accidents, pushing most of them into the category of dangerous driver. This study makes a good case for turning off the phone when you buckle up.

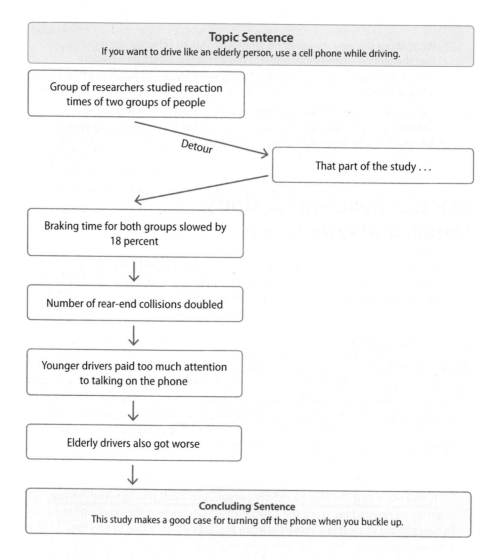

Detours weaken your writing because readers' focus is shifted from your main idea. As you revise, check to make sure your paragraph or essay has unity.

PRACTICE 5-8 Revising for Unity

Each of the following paragraphs contains a sentence that detours from the main idea. First, double-underline the main idea. Then, underline the detour in each paragraph.

Example: "**Education is one of the few things people are willing to pay for and not get.**" When we buy something expensive, we make sure we take it home and use it. For example, we wouldn't think of spending a couple of hundred dollars on a new coat and shoes only to hide them away in a closet never to be worn. And we certainly wouldn't pay for those items and then decide to leave them at the store. <u>I once left a bag with three new shirts in it at the cash register, and I never got it back.</u> People pay a lot for education, but sometimes they look for ways to leave the "purchase" behind. They cheat themselves by not attending class, not paying attention, not studying, or not doing assignments. At the end of the term, they have a grade but didn't get what they paid for: education and knowledge. They have wasted money, just as if they had bought an expensive sound system and had never taken it out of the box.

1. One way to manage time is to keep a print or electronic calendar or schedule. It should have an hour-by-hour breakdown of the day and evening, with space for you to write next to the time. As appointments or responsibilities come up, add them on the right day and time. Before the end of the day, consult your calendar to see what's going on the next day. For example, tomorrow I have to meet Kara at noon, and if I forget, she will be furious with me. Once you are in the habit of using a calendar, you will see that it frees your mind because you are not always trying to think about what you're supposed to do, where you're supposed to be, or what you might have forgotten.

2. As you use a calendar to manage your time, think about how long certain activities will take. A common mistake is to underestimate the time needed to do something, even something simple. For example, when you are planning the time needed to get money from the cash machine, remember that a line of people may be ahead of you. Last week, in the line I met a woman I went to high school with. When you are estimating time for a more complex activity, such as reading a chapter in a textbook, block out more time than you think you will need. If you finish in less time than you have allotted, so much the better.

Revise for Detail and Support

When you revise a paper, look carefully at the support you have developed. Will readers have enough information to understand and be convinced by the main idea?

In the margin or between the lines of your draft (which should be double-spaced), note ideas that seem weak or unclear. As you revise, build up your support by adding more details.

> **PRACTICE 5-9**   **Revising for Detail and Support**

Read the following paragraphs, double-underline the main idea, and add at least three additional support points or supporting details. Write them in the spaces provided under each paragraph and indicate where they should go in the paragraph by writing in a caret (^) and the number.

Example: <u>Sojourner Truth was a brave woman who helped educate people about the evils of slavery.</u> She was a slave herself in New York 1. 2 After she had a religious vision, she traveled from place to place ^ ^ giving speeches about how terrible it was to be a slave. 3 But even after the Emancipation Proclamation was signed in 1863, slave owners did not follow the laws. Sojourner Truth was active in the Civil War, nursing soldiers and continuing to give speeches. She was active in the fight for racial equality until her death in 1883.

1. *and was not allowed to learn to read or write*

2. *Sojourner Truth ran away from her owner because of his cruelty.*

3. *Although she was beaten for her beliefs, she continued her work and was part of the force that caused Abraham Lincoln to sign the Emancipation Proclamation freeing the slaves.*

1. Sports fans can turn from normal people into destructive maniacs. After big wins, a team's fans sometimes riot. Police have to be brought in. Even in school sports, parents of the players can become violent. People get so involved watching the game that they lose control of themselves and are dangerous.

   1.

   2.

   3.

2. If a friend is going through a hard time, try to be as supportive as you can. For one thing, ask if you can help out with any errands or chores. Also, find a time when you can get together in a quiet, calm place. Here, the two of you can talk about the friend's difficulties or just spend time visiting. Let the friend decide how the time is spent. Just knowing that you are there for him or her will mean a lot.

   1.

   2.

   3.

Revise for Coherence

Coherence in writing means that all your support connects to form a whole. In other words, you have provided enough "glue" for readers to see how one point leads to another.

A good way to improve coherence is to use **transitions**—words, phrases, and sentences that connect your ideas so that your writing moves smoothly from one point to the next. The table on page 96 shows some common transitions and what they are used for.

Here are two paragraphs: one that does not use transitions and one that does. Read them and notice how much easier the second paragraph is to follow because of the underlined transitions.

No transitions

It is not difficult to get organized—it takes discipline to stay organized. All you need to do is follow a few simple ideas. You must decide what your priorities are and do these tasks first. You should ask yourself every day: what is the most important task I have to accomplish? Make the time to do it. To be organized, you need a personal system for keeping track of things. Making lists, keeping records, and using a schedule help you remember what tasks you need to do. It is a good idea not to let belongings and obligations stack up. Get rid of possessions you do not need, put items away every time you are done using them, and do not take on more responsibilities than you can handle. Getting organized is not a mystery; it is just good sense.

Transitions added

It is not difficult to get organized—<u>although</u> it takes discipline to stay organized. All you need to do is follow a few simple ideas. You must decide what your priorities are and do these tasks first. <u>For example</u>, you should ask yourself every day: what is the most important task I have to accomplish? <u>Then</u>, make the time to do it. To be organized, you <u>also</u> need a personal system for keeping track of things. Making lists, keeping records, and using a schedule help you remember what tasks you need to do. <u>Finally</u>, it is a good idea not to let belongings and obligations stack up. Get rid of possessions you do not need, put items away every time you are done using them, and do not take on more responsibilities than you can handle. Getting organized is not a mystery; it is just good sense.

Common Transitional Words and Phrases

Indicating space

above	below	near	to the right
across	beside	next to	to the side
at the bottom	beyond	opposite	under
at the top	farther/further	over	where
behind	inside	to the left	

Indicating time

after	eventually	meanwhile	soon
as	finally	next	then
at last	first	now	when
before	last	second	while
during	later	since	

Indicating importance

above all	in fact	more important	most important
best	in particular	most	worst
especially			

Signaling examples

for example	for instance	for one thing	one reason

Signaling additions

additionally	and	as well as	in addition
also	another	furthermore	moreover

Signaling contrast

although	however	nevertheless	still
but	in contrast	on the other hand	yet
even though	instead		

Signaling causes or results

as a result	finally	so	therefore
because			

PRACTICE 5–10   **Adding Transitions**

Read the following paragraphs. In each blank, add a transition that would smoothly connect the ideas. In each case, there is more than one correct answer.

Example

LifeGem, a Chicago company, has announced that it can turn cremated human ashes into high-quality diamonds. _After_ cremation, the ashes are heated to convert their carbon to graphite. _Then_, a lab wraps the graphite around a tiny diamond piece and again heats it and pressurizes it. _After_ about a week of crystallizing, the result is a diamond. _Because of_ the time and labor involved, this process can cost as much as $20,000. _Although_ the idea is very creative, many people will think it is also very weird.

1. Frida Kahlo (1907–1954) is one of Mexico's most famous artists. From an early age, she had an eye for color and detail. _____ , it was not until she was seriously injured in a traffic accident that she devoted herself to painting. _____ her recovery, she went to work on what would become the first of many self-portraits. _____ , she married the famous muralist Diego Rivera. _____ Rivera was unfaithful to Kahlo, their marriage was difficult. _____ , Kahlo continued to develop as an artist and produce great work. Rivera may have summed up Kahlo's paintings the best, describing them as "acid and tender, hard as steel and delicate and fine as a butterfly's wing, lovable as a beautiful smile, and profound and cruel as the bitterness of life."

2. Many fast-food restaurants are adding healthier foods to their menus. _____ , several kinds of salads are now on most menus. These salads offer fresh vegetables and roasted, rather than fried, chicken. _____ , be careful of the dressings, which can be very high in calories. ___ , avoid the huge soft drinks that have large amounts of sugar. _____ , skip the French fries. They are high in fat and calories and do not have much nutritional value.

Another way to give your writing coherence is to repeat a **key word**—a word that is directly related to your main idea. For example, in the paragraphs on page 95, the writer repeats the word *organized* several times. Repetition of a key word is a good way to keep your readers focused on your main idea but make sure you don't overdo it.

Practice Giving and Receiving Feedback

Part of learning to be a successful writer is learning how to become a part of a writing community. Most composition classes will use a process called peer review at some point. During **peer review**, class members read your paper and respond with thoughtful feedback to help you see how your ideas appear to a reader. To create a successful peer review experience, keep the following in mind:

Read to Write
When you are participating in peer review, you read your classmates' work. What is the purpose for your reading in this case?

- Know what questions you want to ask your peer. Try to avoid simple yes or no questions because they may not give you enough information to move forward in your writing process.

- Have your classmates identify your main idea and major support first. Then ask what sections are unclear and where additional information is needed.

- Don't feel shy about asking for help. If you don't understand something or you are having trouble with something, ask about it during the peer review process. Your peers may have the same writing assignment that you do, so they may be able to explain it to you in a way that makes more sense. If not, you may feel better knowing someone else is also confused, and the two of you can ask for clarification from the instructor.

- When responding to another person's paper, avoid being overly harsh and critical with your word choices. The purpose is to give helpful feedback in a constructive manner. However, you should also avoid being too general or too positive. Telling other writers that "everything looks good" doesn't help them improve their paper.

- Most importantly, when you receive feedback on your paper or your ideas, try to think about them objectively. It is up to you what ideas you choose to use or how you want to revise or approach your assignment. Peer review is a process meant to help you and give you an additional set of eyes.

By keeping these factors in mind, you can make the peer review process beneficial for all involved and help create a supportive writing community within the classroom and beyond.

Revise Your Own Paragraph

On pages 86–87, you read Chelsea's draft paragraph. Reread that now as if it were your own, asking yourself the questions in the Checklist for Revising Your Writing on pages 90–91. Work either by yourself or with a partner or small group to answer the questions about Chelsea's draft. Then, read Chelsea's revised paragraph below, and compare the changes you suggested with those that she made. Make notes on the similarities and differences to discuss with the rest of the class.

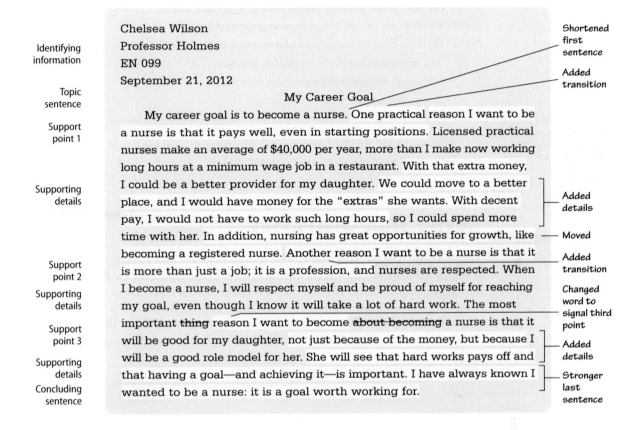

Identifying information

Topic sentence

Support point 1

Supporting details

Support point 2

Supporting details

Support point 3

Supporting details

Concluding sentence

Chelsea Wilson
Professor Holmes
EN 099
September 21, 2012

My Career Goal

My career goal is to become a nurse. One practical reason I want to be a nurse is that it pays well, even in starting positions. Licensed practical nurses make an average of $40,000 per year, more than I make now working long hours at a minimum wage job in a restaurant. With that extra money, I could be a better provider for my daughter. We could move to a better place, and I would have money for the "extras" she wants. With decent pay, I would not have to work such long hours, so I could spend more time with her. In addition, nursing has great opportunities for growth, like becoming a registered nurse. Another reason I want to be a nurse is that it is more than just a job; it is a profession, and nurses are respected. When I become a nurse, I will respect myself and be proud of myself for reaching my goal, even though I know it will take a lot of hard work. The most important ~~thing~~ reason I want to become ~~about becoming~~ a nurse is that it will be good for my daughter, not just because of the money, but because I will be a good role model for her. She will see that hard works pays off and that having a goal—and achieving it—is important. I have always known I wanted to be a nurse: it is a goal worth working for.

Shortened first sentence

Added transition

Added details

Moved

Added transition

Changed word to signal third point

Added details

Stronger last sentence

PRACTICE 5–11   **Revising a Paragraph**

1. What major changes did you suggest for Chelsea's draft in response to the Checklist for Revising Your Writing?

2. Did Chelsea make any of the suggested changes? Which ones?

3. Did Chelsea make any changes that were not suggested? Which ones? Were they good changes?

WRITING ASSIGNMENT   **Paragraph**

Revise the draft paragraph you wrote on page 87. After revising your draft, complete the following checklist.

CHECKLIST

Evaluating Your Revised Paragraph

☐ My topic sentence is confident, and my main idea is clear.

☐ My ideas are detailed, specific, and organized logically.

☐ My ideas flow smoothly from one to the next.

☐ This paragraph fulfills the original assignment.

☐ I am ready to turn in this paragraph for a grade.

☐ This paragraph is the best I can do.

After you have finished revising your paragraph, you are ready to edit it. See the Important Note about editing on page 102.

Revise Your Own Essay

Earlier in the chapter, you read Chelsea's draft essay (p. 88). Reread that now as if it were your own, asking yourself the questions in the Checklist for Revising Your Writing on pages 90–91. Work either by yourself or with a partner or a small group to answer the questions about Chelsea's draft. Then, read Chelsea's revised essay that follows and compare the changes you suggested with those that she made. Make notes on the similarities and differences to discuss with the rest of the class.

Identifying information

Title, centered

First line indented

Details

Thesis statement

Topic sentence/ Support point 1

Chelsea Wilson

Professor Holmes

EN 099

September 28, 2012

The Benefits of Getting a College Degree

I have been taking college courses for two years, and it has been difficult for me. I have a full-time job, a young daughter, and a car that breaks down often. Many times as I have sat, late at night, struggling to stay awake to do homework or to study, I have wondered if getting a college degree is really worth the struggle. That is when I remind myself why getting a degree is so important: it will benefit every aspect of my life.

One benefit of getting a degree is that I can work as a nurse, something I have always wanted to do. Even as a child, I enjoyed helping my mother care for my grandmother or take care of my younger

— Added details

— Added transition

Supporting
details

brothers and sisters when they were sick. I enjoy helping others, and nursing will allow me to do so while making good money. The average salary for a licensed practical nurse is $40,000 per year, substantially more than I make now working at a restaurant. Without a degree, I don't see how that situation will change. Meanwhile, I have almost no time to spend with my daughter.

Added
transitions

Topic
sentence/
Support
point 2

Another benefit of getting a college degree is that it will allow me to be a better mother. In fact, I didn't get serious about getting a degree until I became a mother. Then, I realized I wanted more for my daughter than I had had: a safer place to live, a bigger apartment, some nice clothes, and birthday presents. I also wanted to have time to raise her properly and keep her safe. She is a good girl, but she sees crime and violence around her. I want to get her away from danger, and I want to show her that there are better ways to live. The job opportunities I will have with a college degree will enable me to do those things.

Supporting
details

Topic
sentence/
Support
point 3

The most important benefit of getting a college degree is that it will show me that I can achieve something hard. In the past, I have often given up and taken the easy way, which has led to nothing good. The easy way has led to a hard life. Now, however, working toward a goal has moved my life in a good direction. I have confidence and self-respect. I can honestly say that I am proud of myself, and my daughter will be proud of me, too. I will be a good role model as she grows up, not only for her but also for her friends. She will go to college, just like her mother.

Added
details

Supporting
details

Conclusion

So why am I working so hard to get a degree? I am doing it because I see in that degree the kind of life I want to live on this earth and the kind of human being I want to be. Achieving that vision is worth all the struggles.

Conclusion
strengthened
with an
observation

PRACTICE 5-12   **Revising an Essay**

1. What major changes did you suggest for Chelsea's draft in response to the questions in the Checklist for Revising Your Writing?

2. Did Chelsea make any of the suggested changes? Which ones?

3. Did Chelsea make any changes that were not suggested? Which ones? Were they good changes?

WRITING ASSIGNMENT   **Essay**

Revise the draft essay you wrote earlier in the chapter. After revising your draft, complete the following checklist.

> **CHECKLIST**
>
> **Evaluating Your Revised Essay**
> ☐ My thesis statement is confident, and my main idea is clear.
> ☐ My ideas are detailed, specific, and organized logically.
> ☐ My ideas flow smoothly from one to the next.
> ☐ This essay fulfills the original assignment.
> ☐ I am ready to turn in this essay for a grade.
> ☐ This essay is the best I can do.

Important note: After you have revised your writing to make the ideas clear and strong, you need to edit it to eliminate any distracting or confusing errors in grammar, word use, punctuation, and capitalization. When you are ready to edit your writing, turn to Part 3, the beginning of the editing chapters.

Chapter Review

1. What is a draft?
2. List the basic features of a good draft paragraph or essay.
3. What are three ways to order ideas?
4. What is an outline and why is it helpful to writers?
5. What are five strategies for starting an essay?
6. What are three features of a strong conclusion?
7. What are two features of an essay title?
8. What is revising?
9. What is peer review?
10. What are three areas to focus on in revision?
11. Define unity and coherence.
12. What are two strategies for improving coherence?
13. What is the difference between revising and editing?

Reflect and Apply

1. Have you ever received good feedback on your writing before? When? What made the feedback helpful to you?
2. Have you ever procrastinated on a writing assignment? What happens if you do not leave yourself enough time to revise and edit your work?
3. Interview students who have been successful in your major. What strategies have they used for successful drafting, revising, and editing?

Part 2
Writing Different Kinds of Paragraphs and Essays

6 Narration 105
7 Illustration 128
8 Description 151
9 Process Analysis 173
10 Classification 195
11 Definition 219
12 Comparison and Contrast 241
13 Cause and Effect 267
14 Argument 291

FOXLINE/GETTY IMAGES

Narration

Writing That Tells Important Stories

Understand What Narration Is

Narration is writing that tells the story of an event or an experience.

> ### **Four Basics** of Good Narration
>
> **1** It reveals something of importance to the writer (the main idea).
>
> **2** It includes all the major events of the story (primary support).
>
> **3** It brings the story to life with details about the major events (secondary support).
>
> **4** It presents the events in a clear order, usually according to when they happened (logical organization).

Read to Write As you read the narrative essays in this chapter and elsewhere, annotate the four basics of good narration with numbers or highlighters of different colors.

In the following paragraph, the numbers and colors correspond to the Four Basics of Good Narration.

1 Last year, a writing assignment I hated produced the best writing I have done. **2** When my English teacher told us that our assignment would be to do a few hours of community service and write about it, I was furious. **3** I am a single mother, I work full-time, and I am going to school—isn't that enough? **2** The next day, I spoke to my teacher during her office hours and told her that I was already so busy I could hardly make time for homework, never mind housework. My own life was too full to help with anyone else's life. **3** She said that she understood perfectly and that the majority of her students had lives as full as mine. Then, she explained that the service assignment was just for four hours and that other students had enjoyed both doing the assignment and writing about their experiences. She said they

4 Events in time order

were all surprised and that I would be, too. **2** After talking with her, I decided to accept my fate. The next week, I went to the Community Service Club and was set up to spend a few hours at an adult day-care center near where I live. A few weeks later, I went to the Creative Care Center in Cocoa Beach, not knowing what to expect. **3** I found friendly, approachable people who had so many stories to tell about their long, full lives. **2** The next thing I knew, I was taking notes because I was interested in these people: **3** their marriages, life during the Depression, the wars they fought in, their children, their joys and sorrows. I felt as if I was experiencing everything they lived while they shared their history with me. **2** When it came time to write about my experience, I had more than enough to write about: **3** I wrote the stories of the many wonderful elderly people I had talked with. **2** I got an A on the paper, and beyond that accomplishment, I made friends whom I will visit on my own, not because of an assignment but because I value them.

You can use narration in many practical situations.

College	In a lab course, you are asked to tell what happened in an experiment.
Work	Something goes wrong at work, and you are asked to explain to your boss—in writing—what happened.
Everyday life	In a letter of complaint about service you received, you need to tell what happened that upset you.

In college, the word *narration* probably will not appear in writing assignments. Instead, an assignment might ask you to *describe* the events, *report* what happened, or *retell* what happened. Words or phrases that call for an *account of events* are situations that require narration.

For more information on how to analyze a writing assignment prompt, see the Appendix, page 553.

First Basic: Main Idea in Narration

In narration, the **main idea** is what is important about the story—to you and to your readers. To help you discover the main idea for your own narration, complete the following sentence:

Read to Write To identify the main idea in a narrative you are reading, complete the following sentence: The writer told this story to show that…

Main idea in narration	**What is important to me about the experience is that . . .**

The topic sentence (paragraph) or thesis statement (essay) usually includes the topic and the main idea the writer wants to make about the topic. Let's look at a topic sentence first.

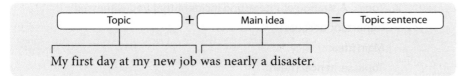

My first day at my new job was nearly a disaster.

Remember that a topic for an essay can be a little broader than one for a paragraph.

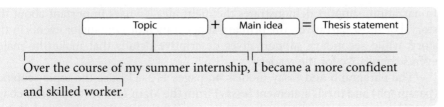

Over the course of my summer internship, I became a more confident and skilled worker.

Tip Sometimes, the same main idea can be used for a paragraph and an essay, but the essay must develop this idea in more detail. (See pp. 112–113.)

Whereas the topic sentence is focused on just one workday, the thesis statement considers a season-long internship.

PRACTICE 6-1   Writing a Main Idea

Look at the example narration paragraph on page 105. Fill in the diagram with the paragraph's topic sentence.

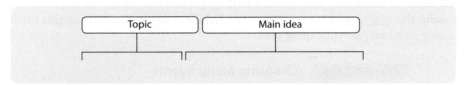

PRACTICE 6-2   Deciding on a Main Idea

For each of the following topics, write a main idea for a narration. Then, write a sentence that includes your topic and your main idea. This sentence would be your topic sentence (paragraph) or thesis statement (essay).

Example:

Topic: A fight I had with my sister

Important because: it taught me something

Main idea: learned it is better to stay cool

Topic sentence/Thesis: After a horrible fight with my sister, I learned the value of staying calm

1. Topic: A powerful, funny, or embarrassing experience
    Important because:
    Main idea:
    Topic sentence/Thesis:

2. Topic: A strange or interesting incident that you witnessed

Important because:

Main idea:

Topic sentence/Thesis:

Second Basic: Primary Support in Narration

In narration, support demonstrates the main idea—what's important about the story. For most narratives, the primary support includes the major events in the story, while secondary support gives descriptive details that make the major events come alive for the reader.

The paragraph and essay models on pages 112–113 use the topic sentence (paragraph) and thesis statement (essay) from the Main Idea section of this chapter. (The thesis statement has been revised slightly.) Both models include the support used in all narration writing—major events (primary support) backed up by details about the events (secondary support). In the essay model, however, the major support points (events) are topic sentences for individual paragraphs.

Choosing Major Events

When you tell a story to a friend, you can include events that are not essential to the story. In contrast, when you are writing a narration, you need to give more careful thought to which events you will include, selecting only those that most clearly demonstrate your main idea.

Tip In an essay, the major events may form the topic sentences of paragraphs. The details supporting the major events then make up the body of these paragraphs.

PRACTICE 6–3 **Choosing Major Events**

Choose two items from Practice 2, and write down the topic sentence or thesis statement you came up with for each. Then, for each topic sentence/thesis statement, write three events that would help you show your main idea.

Example:

Topic: A fight I had with my sister

Topic sentence/Thesis: After a horrible fight with my sister, I learned the value of staying calm.

Events: We disagreed about who was going to have the family party. She made me so mad that I started yelling at her, and I got nasty. I hung up on her, and now we're not talking.

Think Critically What happens if the events you choose to tell are not directly related to your main idea? How do those events affect your readers?

1. Topic: A powerful, funny, or embarrassing experience

Topic sentence/Thesis:

Events:

2. Topic: A strange or interesting incident that you witnessed

Topic sentence/Thesis:

Events:

Third Basic: Secondary Support in Narration

When you write a narration, include examples and details that will make each event easier to visualize and understand. While a major event may be general, the descriptive details that support it are more specific and often appeal to a reader's senses: sight, touch, taste, sound, or smell. Read the following paragraph from Amy Tan's essay, "Fish Cheeks." (The full essay appears on pp. 121–122.) The first sentence introduces the major event ("a strange menu"), and the rest of the paragraph provides sensory details:

> On Christmas Eve, I saw that my mother had outdone herself in creating a strange menu. She was pulling black veins out of the backs of fleshy prawns. The kitchen was littered with appalling mounds of raw food: a slimy rock cod with bulging eyes that pleaded not to be thrown into a pan of hot oil. Tofu, which looked like stacked wedges of rubbery white sponges. A bowl soaking dried fungus back to life. A plate of squid, their backs crisscrossed with knife markings so they resembled bicycle tires.

To emphasize how different this meal is from a traditional American meal, Tan could have just listed the menu items: prawns, rock cod, tofu, fungus, and squid. But readers accustomed to turkey and dressing might not be able to imagine these Chinese foods. So Tan gives us sensory details; she helps us see and feel the food. For example, the prawns are "fleshy," and there are "black veins" that must be removed from them. Even if you have never eaten prawns, you can visualize this menu item more effectively because of her description.

Another strategy for adding descriptive details in narration is to use dialogue. Dialogue occurs when you quote what a person said in a conversation, allowing readers to "hear" a speaker's voice. For example, look at what one student wrote about encouragement from a coach after a particularly difficult loss:

> Back in the locker room, Coach Ormand didn't tell us what we did wrong. Instead, he encouraged us to keep trying.

While these sentences give the reader important information, they don't provide a lot of detail; they don't show the reader how the coach encouraged his team. Look at this revision to the paragraph. Why is this version more effective?

> Back in the locker room, Coach Ormand didn't tell us what we did wrong. Instead, he huddled us together and said, "Gentlemen, you lost today. But you are not losers. What I saw today tells me you are winners. If you keep playing with as much heart as you did today, pretty soon the scoreboard is going to show what I already know: you are winners."

> "Coach," I answered, "I don't feel like a winner."
>
> "Maybe not. But it's not what you feel that makes you a winner. It's what you do when you walk out of here," he replied.

Notice the following features of dialogue:

- The dialogue is introduced by the word *said* and a comma.
- There are quotation marks at the beginning and at the end of the spoken lines.
- The quoted dialogue begins with a capital letter.
- A change in speaker is signaled by a new paragraph.

The word *said* is part of a signal phrase, words that let the reader know a quote is coming. Other verbs may also be used in signal phrases, including *ask, demand, claim, suggest, explain, yell,* or *whisper.* Writers often, but not always, use signal phrases in dialogue.

PRACTICE 6–4 **Giving Details about the Events**

Write down the topic sentence or thesis statement for each item from Practice 3. Then, write the major events in the spaces provided. Give a detail about each event.

Example:

Topic sentence/Thesis: After a horrible fight with my sister, I learned the value of staying calm.

Event: We disagreed about who was going to have the family party.

> **Detail:** Even though we both work, she said, "I'm just too busy—you will just have to do it." Her voice was bossy and demanding.

Event: She made me so mad, I started yelling at her, and I got nasty.

> **Detail:** I brought up times in the past when she had tried to pass responsibilities off on me, and I told her I was sick of being the one who did everything.

Event: I hung up on her, and now we are not talking.

> **Detail:** I was so mad I threw my phone into the wall, shattering my screen and putting a dent in the paint. I was mad, but I shouldn't have

lost my cool. After three days of not talking to her and hearing only the sound of her voicemail instead of her quirky, high-pitched laugh, I knew it was time to apologize.

1. Topic sentence/Thesis:

    Event:

        Detail:

    Event:

        Detail:

    Event:

        Detail:

2. Topic sentence/Thesis:

    Event:

        Detail:

    Event:

        Detail:

    Event:

        Detail:

Tip For more on time order, see page 74.

Transitions move readers from one event to the next.

Fourth Basic: Organization in Narration

Narration usually presents events in the order in which they happened, which is referred to as time (chronological) order. As shown in the paragraph and essay models on pages 112–113, a narration starts at the beginning of the story and describes events as they unfolded.

Common Transitions in Narration

after	eventually	meanwhile	since
as	finally	next	soon
at last	first	now	then
before	last	once	when
during	later	second	while

Paragraphs versus Essays in Narration

For more on the important features of narration, see the Four Basics of Good Narration on page 105.

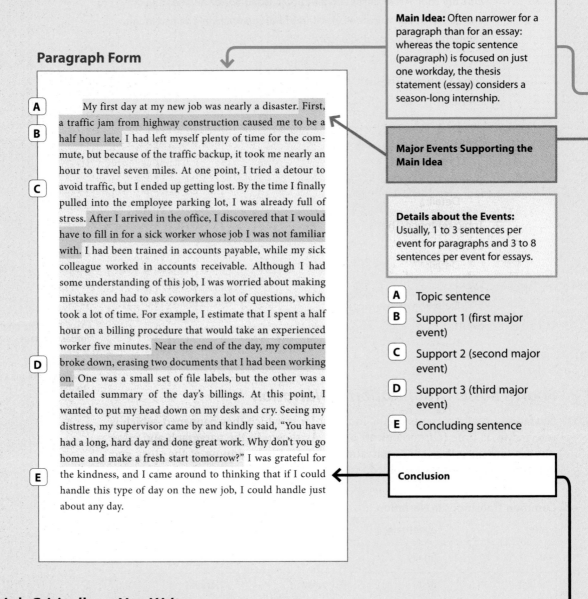

Paragraph Form

A My first day at my new job was nearly a disaster. First, **B** a traffic jam from highway construction caused me to be a half hour late. I had left myself plenty of time for the commute, but because of the traffic backup, it took me nearly an hour to travel seven miles. At one point, I tried a detour to **C** avoid traffic, but I ended up getting lost. By the time I finally pulled into the employee parking lot, I was already full of stress. After I arrived in the office, I discovered that I would have to fill in for a sick worker whose job I was not familiar with. I had been trained in accounts payable, while my sick colleague worked in accounts receivable. Although I had some understanding of this job, I was worried about making mistakes and had to ask coworkers a lot of questions, which took a lot of time. For example, I estimate that I spent a half hour on a billing procedure that would take an experienced worker five minutes. Near the end of the day, my computer **D** broke down, erasing two documents that I had been working on. One was a small set of file labels, but the other was a detailed summary of the day's billings. At this point, I wanted to put my head down on my desk and cry. Seeing my distress, my supervisor came by and kindly said, "You have had a long, hard day and done great work. Why don't you go home and make a fresh start tomorrow?" I was grateful for **E** the kindness, and I came around to thinking that if I could handle this type of day on the new job, I could handle just about any day.

Main Idea: Often narrower for a paragraph than for an essay: whereas the topic sentence (paragraph) is focused on just one workday, the thesis statement (essay) considers a season-long internship.

Major Events Supporting the Main Idea

Details about the Events: Usually, 1 to 3 sentences per event for paragraphs and 3 to 8 sentences per event for essays.

A Topic sentence

B Support 1 (first major event)

C Support 2 (second major event)

D Support 3 (third major event)

E Concluding sentence

Conclusion

Think Critically as You Write

Ask Yourself

- Have I made my point clearly?
- Have I provided enough detail to bring each major event to life?
- Have I organized my ideas and details logically so readers can follow the story?

Essay Form

1

Several of my friends question whether summer internships are really worthwhile, especially if the pay is low or nonexistent. However, the right internship definitely pays off professionally in the long run even if it doesn't financially in the short run. The proof is in my own summer marketing internship, which made me a far more confident and skilled worker.

A

B

During the first two weeks of the internship, I received thorough training in every part of my job. For example, my immediate supervisor spent three full days going over everything I would need to do to help with e-mail campaigns, online marketing efforts, and other promotions. She even had me draft a promotional e-mail for a new product and gave me feedback about how to make the message clearer and more appealing. I also spent a lot of time with other staffers, who taught me everything from how to use the photocopier and printers to how to pull together marketing and sales materials for executive meetings. Most impressive, the president of the company took some time out of a busy afternoon to answer my questions about

C

2

how he got started in his career and what he sees as the keys to success in the marketing field. As I explained to a friend, I got a real "insider's view" of the company and its leadership.

Next, I got hands-on experience with listening to customers and addressing their needs. Specifically, I sat in on meetings with new clients and listened to them describe products and services they would like the company's help in promoting. They also discussed the message they would like to get across about their businesses. After the meetings, I sat in on brainstorming sessions with other staffers in which we came up with as many ideas as we could about campaigns to address the clients' needs. At first, I didn't think anyone would care about my ideas, but others listened to them respectfully and even ended up including some of them in the marketing plans that were sent back to the clients. I learned later that some of my ideas would be included in the actual promotional campaigns.

D

By summer's end, I had advanced my skills so much that I was asked to return next summer. My

E

3

supervisor told me that she was pleased not only with all I had learned about marketing but also with the responsibility I took for every aspect of my job. I did not roll my eyes about having to make photocopies or help at the reception desk, nor did I seem intimidated by bigger, more meaningful tasks. Although I'm not guaranteed a full-time job at the company after graduation, I think my chances are good. Even if I don't end up working there long term, I am grateful for how the job has helped me grow.

In the end, the greatest benefit of the internship might be the confidence it gave me. I have learned that no matter how challenging the task before me—at work or in real life—I can succeed at it by getting the right information and input on anything unfamiliar, working effectively with others, and truly dedicating myself to doing my best. My time this past summer was definitely well spent.

F

A Introductory paragraph

B Thesis statement

C Topic sentence 1 (first major event)

D Topic sentence 2 (second major event)

E Topic sentence 3 (third major event)

F Concluding paragraph

Tip For more on using and punctuating sentences with transition words, see Chapter 23.

| PRACTICE 6–5 | **Using Transitions in Narration** |

Read the paragraph that follows, and fill in the blanks with time transitions.

Some historians believe that as many as four hundred women disguised themselves as men so that they could serve in the U.S. Civil War (1861–1865). One of the best known of these women was Sarah Emma Edmonds. _____ the war began, Edmonds, an opponent of slavery, felt driven to join the Union Army, which fought for the free states. _____ President Abraham Lincoln asked for army volunteers, she disguised herself as a man, took the name Frank Thompson, and enlisted in the infantry. _____ her military service, Edmonds worked as a male nurse and a messenger. _____ serving as a nurse, she learned that the Union general needed someone to spy on the Confederates. _____ extensive training, Edmonds took on this duty and, disguised as a slave, went behind enemy lines. Here, she learned about the Confederates' military strengths and weaknesses. _____, she returned to the Union side and went back to work as a nurse. In 1863, Edmonds left the army after developing malaria. She was worried that hospital workers would discover that she was a woman. As a result of her departure, "Frank Thompson" was listed as a deserter. In later years, Edmonds, under her real name, worked to get a veteran's pension and to get the desertion charge removed from her record. _____, in 1884, a special act of Congress granted her both of these wishes.

Evaluate Narration

To become a more successful writer, it is important not only to understand the Four Basics of Good Narration but to read and evaluate examples as well. In this section, you will have the opportunity to use a sample rubric to analyze or evaluate the samples of narrative writing provided. By using this rubric, you will gain a better understanding of how the components of good narration work together to create a successful paragraph or essay. Additionally, reading examples of narration will help you write your own.

Read the following sample narration paragraph. Using the Four Basics of Good Narration and the sample grading rubric, decide what grade this paragraph would earn. Explain your answer.

Assignment: Write a paragraph about one moment that made a significant difference in your week. You should use clear transitions to indicate the passage of time, and you should use enough detail to bring the story to life for your reader.

As I was driving to work the other day, I noticed that it was starting to rain. Normally, that would not be a problem, but on this day it was. I had no windshield wipers. They had broken the previous week and I had not had enough money to fix them yet. Although the rain never became overly heavy, it was enough to be annoying. Perhaps I should consider putting in new wipers when I get home. Without good windshield wipers, I am putting both myself and others in danger in poor weather.

Analysis of Sample Paragraph:

Sample rubric

Element	Grading criteria	Point: Comment
Appropriateness	• Did the student follow the assignment directions?	___/5:
Main idea	• Does the paper clearly state a strong main idea in a complete sentence?	___/10:
Support	• Is the main idea developed with specific support, including specific details and examples? • Is there enough support to make the main idea evident to the reader? • Is all the support directly related to the main idea?	___/10:
Organization	• Is the writing logically organized? • Does the student use transitions (*also, for example, sometimes,* and so on) to move the reader from one point to another?	___/10:
Conclusion	• Does the conclusion remind the reader of the main idea? • Does it make an observation based on the support?	___/5:
Grammar	• Is the writing free of the Four Most Serious Errors? (See Chapters 16–19.) • Is the sentence structure clear? • Does the student choose words that clearly express his or her meaning? • Are the words spelled correctly? • Is the punctuation correct?	___/10: *The paper is free from the common errors but is not descriptive.*
		TOTAL POINTS: ___/50

Read and Analyze Narration

The first two examples of narrative writing here come from students Jelani Lynch and Trevor Riley-Jewell. In the third example, a Profile of Success, Alice Adoga shows how she uses narration in her field of social work. The final example is a narration essay by Amy Tan, a professional writer. As you read these selections, pay attention to the vocabulary and the questions in the margin. They will help you read critically.

Student Narration Paragraph

Jelani Lynch

My Turnaround

Predict What will Jelani's paragraph explain?

Before my big turnaround, my life was headed in the wrong direction. I grew up in the city and had a typical sad story: broken home, not much money, gangs, and drugs. In this world, few positive male role models are available. I played the game "Street Life": running the streets, stealing bikes, robbing people, carrying a gun, and selling drugs. The men in my neighborhood did not have regular jobs; they got their money outside the system. No one except my mother thought school was worth much. I had a history of poor school performance, a combination of not showing up and not doing any work when I did. My pattern of failure in that area was pretty strong. When I was seventeen, though, things got really bad. I was arrested for possession of crack cocaine. I was kicked out of school for good. During this time, I realized that my life was not going the way I wanted it to be. I was headed nowhere, except a life of crime, violence, and possibly early death. I knew that way of life, because I was surrounded by people who had chosen that direction. I did not want to go there anymore. When I made that decision, my life started to change. First, I met Shawn Brown, a man who had had the same kind of life I did. He got out of that life, though, by graduating from high school and college and getting a good job. He has a house, a wife, and children, along with great clothes. Shawn became my role model, showing me that with honesty, integrity, and hard work I could live a much better life. Since meeting Shawn, I have turned my life around. I started taking school seriously and graduated from high school, something I thought I would never do. Working with Shawn, I have read books and learned I enjoy writing. I have met the mayor of Boston and got a summer job at the State House. I have been part of an educational video and had many opportunities to meet and work with people who are successful. Now, I am a mentor with Diamond Educators, and I work with other young, urban males to give them a role model and help them make good choices. Now, I have a bright future with goals and plans. I have turned my life around and know I will be a success.

Reflect Have you ever made a decision that changed your life?

Summarize How did meeting Shawn change Jelani's life?

Read to Write: Annotate

1. Underline the topic sentence.

2. Number the major events.

3. Circle the transitions.

Think Critically

1. What is important about the story?

2. Does Jelani's paragraph follow the Four Basics of Good Narration (p. 105)? Be ready to give specific reasons for your answer.

Student Narration Essay

Trevor Riley-Jewell

An Unusual Inspiration

Trevor Riley-Jewell is studying cybersecurity at Lord Fairfax Community College in Virginia, where he serves as president of the Cyber Advocates Club and team captain for the Cyber Competition Team, among many other activities. He plans to transfer to George Mason University. This essay began as a journal entry discussing inspirational people.

I've always found it strange to think about "my inspiration." I don't find that one singular person in my life stands out as inspirational; rather, I find that several people have been inspirational in small ways. My mother, sister, biological father, ex-stepdad, distant family, friends, and neighbors have all shown me something that has given me a little insight. Usually people think of positive actions that others have done to inspire them, but I draw on both the positive and the negative. Inspiration, for me, is a life lesson learned, especially when I am not the main character of an event that transpired.

2   I once had a neighbor named Betty. Betty was in her eighties and was quite a character. She would do some downright strange things. For example, she would walk into her open backyard completely nude and water her garden while singing old songs, play her grand piano at 3 a.m. with all the windows in her house open, chase squirrels around the front yard, slam her front door for hours on end for fun, and so much more. She obviously wasn't "all there," but she was friendly when I talked to her, and she had a pleasant enough demeanor when approached.

3   One day she asked me to help her move some furniture in her house. Being the fourteen-year-old guy next door, I willingly obliged. When I walked through

the door, I realized her house was a train-wreck: ripped sofas, broken chairs, unhinged cupboards, sinking floors, a horrible smell, etc. As I helped her move her recliner, which was blocking the front door, she said something in one of her lucid moments that I recall. She asked me why I came over to help her; in that moment, she was obviously fully aware of how her house—and she—looked. I told her that I just wanted to be of help, and I didn't mind the house or the situation.

4   She then said something like this: "I'm glad you decided to help me; I know that I am a bit off my rocker at times, and no one wants to talk to me. At least I know I'm not completely crazy, seeing as you are here helping me." Later on, she told me that her late husband had loved the piano and that he used to feed the squirrels. She talked about how he would slam the front door when he got back from work, how he reupholstered the sofa that I saw ripped in the living room. Her husband had been deceased for over twenty years.

5   At first I thought that it was all just the delusional ramblings of my neighbor, but I thought about it more that night when I was lying in bed trying to sleep. The way she worded her sentence was very particular and made me realize something. "She knows she isn't 100 percent there, but she is thankful that it didn't bother me enough to keep me from helping her," I thought. "She looks delusional based on the stuff that she does, but a lot of her actions have to do with her dead husband; she misses him." Her broken mind was trying to remember him by recreating the sounds and actions from the time when he was still alive. No longer did I remember her as an unstable old lady, but as a poor soul who lost half of herself—and then got lost in her own lonely abyss.

6   Betty has inspired me in two ways. First, I hope to at least remember someone special to me by the time I get to her age, as I have a horrible memory even now. Second, she taught me that even though people judge others, there is often a logical reason behind their actions, not just insanity or mental illness. I have drawn inspiration from people like Betty. They teach me something, directly or indirectly, and if it's important to me, then I will remember it. That's my version of inspiration.

Read to Write: Annotate

1. Double underline the main idea.
2. Underline the main events in the story.
3. Highlight or circle each example of dialogue.

Think Critically

1. What details does Riley-Jewell provide to support his narrative? Which senses do these details appeal to?
2. Does this essay demonstrate the Four Basics of Good Narration? Why or why not?

Profile of Success
Narration in the Real World

COURTESY OF ALICE ADOGA

Alice Adoga
Family Service
Specialist

Background: In January 2007, I moved from West Africa, Nigeria, to the United States at the age of eighteen to live with my stepmom and three siblings. Before my departure from Nigeria, I knew my life was going to change a great deal. However, I had no idea what these changes would be. In the fall of 2007, I was admitted into the twelfth grade at Franklin High School after taking many Standards of Learning Tests. (Also referred to as SOLs, Standards of Learning Tests are exams that students in Virginia are required to pass in order to take courses at a specific grade level.) Many were surprised that I could speak English or even articulate well. Not only did I have to deal with cultural differences, I also had to adjust to the educational system of this country. In my English classes, I was lacking in grammar, and I had difficulties writing research papers. I was always self-conscious about my writing and panicked when asked to write a paper. After graduating from high school in 2008, I decided to further my education at Paul D. Camp Community College (PDCCC). While at PDCCC, I had to take developmental English, and I struggled through most English classes during my freshman year in college. I worked very closely with all my English teachers and professors in high school and college. I also had several tutors assist me with my papers. Although my grammar has improved, I am still learning how to be a better writer today.

I have always had a passion for education. I believe that knowledge is power. The many challenges I faced all these years have sparked my zeal to continue my academic journey no matter what it takes. I am currently seeking my master's degree online at Liberty University in Human Services Counseling with concentration in crisis response and trauma.

Degrees/Colleges: A.S., Paul D. Camp Community College; B.S. Psychology, George Mason University

Employer: City of Franklin, Department of Social Services

Writing at work: My writing at work is an objective narrative of reports from mandated reporters and clients' documentation during intake assessment or investigations. My job requires accurate documentation of interactions with clients during interviews and any interactions carried out with child victims and anyone involved. Reports made to our agency need to be documented in the Online Automated Structured Information System (OASIS). Part of my job is to write out accurately what has been reported to me during interviews to help give the reader a better picture of what took place during the incident. After interviews with a client, I write a descriptive narrative of what was said to me without inclusion of personal thoughts or opinions.

119

Workplace Narration

Incident Descriptions (Hypothetical Example)

Caller, Ms. Joyce Baton, stated that she knows that Courtney Moses is leaving her seven-year-old daughter, Lilian Moses, at home alone in the evening several nights of the week and all day during the weekends without any food. Also, the apartment has been without power for the past three weeks. Caller informed this worker that she noted several times over the past month that Lilian has come over to their house after school and near dinnertime to see their daughter, Melody Baton. Caller informed this worker that Lilian and her daughter Melody go to the same school and ride the same bus to and from school. Whenever she stops by their house, Lilian asks if she can join Melody for dinner because "Mom doesn't have anything for me to eat." Ms. Baton stated that her daughter and Lilian "hang out" after school, and sometimes Lilian stays over for dinner. Ms. Baton says she always makes Lilian call her mother to get permission, and she has even talked with Ms. Moses about Lilian's frequent dinner requests. Ms. Baton reports that Ms. Moses does not mind that Lilian stays over and profusely thanks her for letting Lilian eat dinner with them. When this first began, Ms. Baton thought Lilian just didn't like what was being offered at home. However, Ms. Baton said she recently began to notice that Lilian "wolfs her food down" when she eats and is always finished earlier than her family. Lilian has told Ms. Baton on a few occasions, "we don't have any food left."

2   Ms. Baton stated that Melody is in the same class as Lilian. Melody told her that Lilian did not have food in her lunch bag several times last week. She also told her that Lilian asks other kids for food at school and on the bus. Ms. Baton has been to the Moses's home but has not been comfortable talking with Ms. Moses about the lack of food. Ms. Baton is concerned because her daughter has come home every day this week and reported that Lilian was begging for food. She has begun putting extra sandwiches and fruit in her daughter's lunch to share with Lilian. Ms. Baton informed this worker that she saw Lilian and her daughter get on the bus this morning. They use the same bus stop. Lilian is currently at All Kings Elementary School. The address is 1539 Lakeview Drive, Franklin, Virginia 23851. Ms. Baton stated that she wants to remain anonymous because no one knows she is calling us. She believes Ms. Moses knows about Lilian's behavior.

Read to Write: Annotate

1. What is your main impression of what is happening in the Moses home?

2. Underline the primary details that support the main impression.

3. Double underline or circle any secondary details that help tell the story and give more information to the reader.

Think Critically

1. Who is the intended audience for this report?

2. What is the purpose of the report?

3. How is this report different in style and tone from the narratives of Tan (p. 121) or Riley-Jewell (p. 117)? Why do you think this is the case?

Professional Narration Essay

Amy Tan

Fish Cheeks

Amy Tan was born in Oakland, California, in 1952, several years after her mother and father emigrated from China. She studied at San Jose City College and later San Jose State University, receiving a B.A. with a double major in English and linguistics. In 1973, she earned an M.A. in linguistics from San Jose State University. In 1989, Tan published her first novel, *The Joy Luck Club*, which was nominated for the National Book Award and the National Book Critics Circle Award. Tan's other books include *The Kitchen God's Wife* (1991), *The Hundred Secret Senses* (1995), *Saving Fish from Drowning* (2005), and *The Valley of Amazement* (2013). Her short stories and essays have been published in the *Atlantic, Grand Street, Harper's, The New Yorker,* and other publications.

In the following essay, which was originally published in *Seventeen* (a magazine for girls ages 13–19), Tan uses narration to describe an experience that taught her an important lesson.

I fell in love with the minister's son the winter I turned fourteen. He was not Chinese, but as white as Mary in the manger. For Christmas I prayed for this blond-haired boy, Robert, and a slim new American nose.

2   When I found out that my parents had invited the minister's family over for Christmas dinner, I cried. What would Robert think of our shabby Chinese Christmas? What would he think of our noisy Chinese relatives who lacked proper American manners? What terrible disappointment would he feel upon seeing not a roasted turkey and sweet potatoes but Chinese food?

3   On Christmas Eve I saw that my mother had outdone herself in creating a strange menu. She was pulling black veins out of the backs of fleshy prawns. The kitchen was littered with appalling mounds of raw food: a slimy rock cod with bulging eyes that pleaded not to be thrown into a pan of hot oil. Tofu, which looked like stacked wedges of rubbery white sponges. A bowl soaking dried fungus back to life. A plate of squid, their backs crisscrossed with knife markings so they resembled bicycle tires.

4   And then they arrived—the minister's family and all my relatives in a clamor of doorbells and rumpled Christmas packages. Robert grunted hello, and I pretended he was not worthy of existence.

Predict Based on the second paragraph, what do you think will happen?

appalling: horrifying

Reflect Name an event during which you tried to make a good impression on someone.

clamor: noise

murmured: spoke in low tones

5   Dinner threw me into despair. My relatives licked the ends of their chopsticks and reached across the table, dipping them into the dozen or so plates of food. Robert and his family waited patiently for platters to be passed to them. My relatives murmured with pleasure when my mother brought out the whole steamed fish. Robert grimaced. Then my father poked his chopsticks just below the fish eye and plucked out the soft meat. "Amy, your favorite," he said, offering me the tender fish cheek. I wanted to disappear.

6   At the end of the meal, my father leaned back and belched loudly, thanking my mother for her fine cooking. "It's a polite Chinese custom to show you are satisfied," explained my father to our astonished guests. Robert was looking down at his plate with a reddened face. The minister managed to muster up a quiet burp. I was stunned into silence for the rest of the night.

Reflect Have you ever felt different on the outside than you did on the inside?

7   After everyone had gone, my mother said to me, "You want to be the same as American girls on the outside." She handed me an early gift. It was a miniskirt in beige tweed. "But inside you must always be Chinese. You must be proud you are different. Your only shame is to have shame."

8   And even though I didn't agree with her then, I knew that she understood how much I had suffered during the evening's dinner. It wasn't until many years later—long after I had gotten over my crush on Robert—that I was able to fully appreciate her lesson and the true purpose behind our particular menu. For Christmas Eve that year, she had chosen all my favorite foods.

Read to Write: Annotate

1. What is Tan's main idea?

2. Underline the major events in the story.

3. Circle all the transition words and time references that Tan uses to help readers follow the story.

Think Critically

1. What is Tan's purpose for writing?

2. Does she achieve it?

3. The essay was originally published in *Seventeen* magazine. How does this information help you understand Tan's intended audience and her choice of details?

4. Paraphrase the lesson Tan's mother taught her after the dinner.

Respond

1. Have you ever been embarrassed by your family or by others close to you? Write about the experience, and describe what you learned from it.

2. Write about a time when you felt different from other people. How did you react at the time? Have your feelings about the situation changed since then? If so, how?

3. Write about an experience that was uncomfortable at the time but funny later. Explain how you came to see humor in the situation.

Grammar for Narration

Because narration describes events as they unfold over time, it is important to pay attention to verb tenses when you are editing a narrative paragraph or essay. Be consistent in your use of tenses, and make sure the tenses fit the logic and order of the events in the narrative. Take a look at these sentences from Amy Tan's essay:

Sentence	Tense	Explanation
I <u>fell</u> in love with the minister's son the winter I <u>turned</u> fourteen.	Simple past	Use simple past for major events in the story.
When I found out that my parents <u>had invited</u> the minister's family over for Christmas dinner, I cried.	Past perfect	Use past perfect for events that occurred before the major events in the story.
Robert <u>was looking</u> down at his plate with a reddened face.	Past progressive	Use past progressive for actions that were in progress during the major events.

For more information about verb tenses and verb endings, see Chapter 19.

Write Your Own Narration

In this section, you will write your own narrative essay based on one of the following assignments. For help, refer to the "How to Write Narration" checklist on page 126.

Assignment Options: Writing about College, Work, and Everyday Life

Write a narration paragraph or essay on one of the following topics or on one of your own choice.

College
- Tell the story of how a teacher, coach, or other mentor made a difference in your life.
- Write an essay telling the story of how you overcame a challenge during your school experiences.
- Interview a college graduate working in your field. Tell that person's story, focusing on how he or she achieved success.

Work
- Write about a situation or incident that made you decide to leave a job.
- Imagine a successful day or a frustrating day at your current or previous job. Then, tell the story of that day, including examples of successes.
- Write your own work history, guided by a statement that you would like to make about this history or your work style. Here is one example: "Being a people person has helped me in every job I have ever had." You might imagine that you are interviewing with a potential employer.

Everyday life
- Write about an experience that triggered a strong emotion: happiness, sadness, fear, anger, regret.
- Find a campus community service club that offers short-term assignments. Take an assignment and write about your experience.
- Tell the story of a community issue that interests you. One example is plans to create a bike lane on a major road. Discuss how the issue arose, and describe key developments. Research details by visiting a local newspaper's website.

Assignment Options: Reading and Writing Critically

Complete one of the following assignments, which ask you to apply the critical thinking, reading, and writing skills discussed in Chapter 1.

Writing Critically about Readings

Tip For a reminder of how to summarize, analyze, synthesize, and evaluate, see the Reading and Writing Critically box on page 17.

Both Alice Adoga's "Incident Descriptions" (p. 120) and James Roy's "Police Report" (p. 164) require the writer to carefully tell a specific story, recording only the facts. Review both of these pieces. Then, follow these steps:

1. **Summarize** Briefly summarize the works, listing major events.
2. **Analyze** Identify the intended audience for each piece, and consider how the details used reflect the purpose and audience. List any types of examples or details the authors could have added to their reports. Also, write down any questions that the pieces raise for you.

3. **Synthesize** Using examples from either Adoga's or Roy's stories and from your own experience, write about an observation in your own life. Choose an event that was significant and write about it clearly and with detail.

4. **Evaluate** Which piece do you find more effective? Why? To write your evaluation, look back on your responses to step 2.

Writing about Images

Study the photograph below, and complete the following steps.

DAN BANNISTER/GETTY IMAGES

1. **Read the image** Ask yourself: What is the setting of the photo? What details does the photographer focus on? What seems to be the photo's message? (For more information on reading images, see Chapter 1.)

2. **Write a narration** Write a narration paragraph or essay about what has happened (or is happening) in the photograph. Be as creative as you like, but be sure to include details and reactions from step 1. As you write, consider a possible purpose and audience for your essay.

Writing to Solve a Problem

Read or review the discussion of problem solving in Chapter 1 (pp. 26–27). Then, consider the following problem:

> You have learned that a generous scholarship is available for low-income, first-generation college students. You really need the money to cover day-care expenses while you are taking classes (in fact, you had thought you would have to stop going to college for a while). Many people have been applying. Part of the application is to write about yourself and why you deserve the scholarship.

Tip Such scholarships really do exist. Go on-line or to the college financial aid office to find out about them. If you are pleased with what you have written for this assignment, you could use it as part of your application.

Assignment: Write a paragraph or essay that tells your story and why you should be considered for the scholarship. Think about how you can make your story stand out. You might start with the following sentence:

Even though you will be reading applications from many first-generation college students, my story is a little different because...

CHECKLIST

How to Write Narration

Steps	Details
☐ Narrow and explore your topic. See Chapter 3.	• Make the topic more specific. • Prewrite to get ideas about the narrowed topic.
☐ Write a topic sentence (paragraph) or thesis statement (essay). See Chapter 3.	• State what is most important to you about the topic and what you want your readers to understand.
☐ Support your point. See Chapter 4.	• Come up with examples and details to explain your main idea to readers.
☐ Write a draft. See Chapter 5.	• Make a plan that puts events or examples in a logical order. • Include a topic sentence (paragraph) or thesis statement (essay) and all the supporting events, examples, and details.
☐ Revise your draft. See Chapter 5.	• Make sure it has *all* the Four Basics of Good Narration. • Make sure you include transitions to move readers smoothly from one event or example to the next.
☐ Edit your revised draft. See Parts 3 through 6.	• Correct errors in grammar, spelling, word use, and punctuation.

Chapter Review

1. What is narration?

2. List the Four Basics of Good Narration.

3. The topic sentence in a narration paragraph or the thesis statement in a narration essay usually includes what two things?

4. What type of organization do writers of narration usually use?

5. List five common transitions for this type of organization.

Reflect and Apply

1. Have you ever written or read narration before? How does that experience confirm, contradict, or complicate what you have learned in this chapter?

2. Interview someone studying in your major or working in your career. What situations require reading or writing narration in your major or career?

3. What was the most difficult about your writing for this chapter? What do you want to do differently next time?

4. What part of your writing for this chapter was most successful? What do you need to remember for next time?

7

Illustration

Writing That Gives Examples

Understand What Illustration Is

Illustration is writing that uses examples to support a point.

> **Four Basics** of Good Illustration
>
> **1** It has a point to communicate to readers.
> **2** It gives specific examples that show, explain, or prove the point.
> **3** It gives details to support the examples.
> **4** It is organized with transitions to guide readers through the examples.

In the following paragraph, the numbers and colors correspond to the Four Basics of Good Illustration.

4 Organized with transitions

1 Many people would like to serve their communities or help with causes that they believe in, but they do not have much time and do not know what to do. Now, the Internet provides people with ways to help that do not take much time or money. **2** Websites now make it convenient to donate online. With a few clicks, an organization of your choice can receive your donation or money from a sponsoring advertiser. For example, if you are interested in helping rescue unwanted and abandoned animals, you can go to www.theanimalrescuesite.com. **3** When you click as instructed, a sponsoring advertiser will make a donation to help provide food and care for the 27 million animals in shelters. Also, a portion of any money you spend in the site's online store will go to providing animal care. **2** If you want to help fight world hunger, go to The Hunger Site's website **3** and click daily to have sponsor fees directed to hungry people in more than seventy countries via the Mercy Corps, Feeding America, and Millennium Promise. Each year, hundreds of millions of cups of food are distributed to one billion hungry people around the world. **2** Other examples of click-to-give sites are The Child Health Site, The Literacy Site, and The Breast Cancer Site. **3** Like the animal-rescue and hunger sites, these other sites have click-to-give links, online stores that direct a percentage of sales income to charity, and links to help you learn about causes you are interested in. One hundred percent of the sponsors' donations go to the charities, and you can give with a click every single day. Since I have found out about these sites, I go to at least one of them every day. **1** I have learned a lot about various problems, and every day I feel as if I have helped a little.

It is hard to explain anything without using examples, so you use illustration in almost every communication situation.

College	An exam question asks you to explain and give examples of a concept.
Work	Your boss asks you to tell her what office equipment needs to be replaced and why.
Everyday life	You complain to your landlord that the building superintendent is not doing his job. The landlord asks for examples.

In college, the words *illustration* and *illustrate* may not appear in writing assignments. Instead, you might be asked to *give examples* of a topic or to be *specific about* a topic. Regardless of an assignment's wording, to be clear and effective, most types of writing require specific examples. Include them whenever they help you make your point.

For more information on analyzing writing assignment prompts, see the Appendix, page 553.

Read to Write
To identify the main idea when you are reading an illustration essay, complete the following sentence: The writer is giving these examples to show that …

First Basic: Main Idea in Illustration

In illustration, the **main idea** is the message you want your readers to receive and understand. To help you discover your main idea, complete the following sentence:

Main idea in illustration	What I want readers to know about this topic is that . . .

The topic sentence (in a paragraph) or thesis statement (in an essay) usually includes the topic and the main idea the writer wants to make about the topic. Let's look at a topic sentence first.

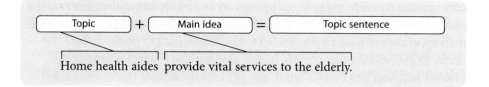

Home health aides provide vital services to the elderly.

Remember that a thesis statement for an essay can be a little broader than a paragraph topic.

Tip Sometimes, the same main idea can be used for a paragraph and an essay, but the essay must develop this point in more detail. (See pp. 134–135.)

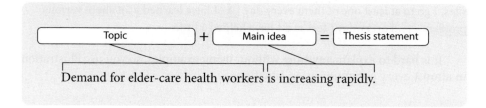

Demand for elder-care health workers is increasing rapidly.

Whereas the topic sentence is focused on just home health aides, the thesis statement considers elder-care careers in general.

PRACTICE 7–1   Forming a Main Idea

Each of the items in this practice is a narrowed topic. Think about each of them, and write a main idea about each topic in the space provided.

Example: The words to songs I like *relate closely to experiences I have had.*

1. A few moments alone

2. A course I am taking

3. The busiest time at work

4. Being a parent of a newborn baby

5. Working with people from other countries

Second Basic: Primary Support in Illustration

The paragraph and essay models on pages 134–135 use the topic sentence (paragraph) and thesis statement (essay) from the Main Idea section of this chapter. Both models include the support used in all illustration writing: examples backed up by details about the examples. In the essay model, however, the major support points (examples) are topic sentences for individual paragraphs.

To generate good detailed examples, use one or more of the prewriting techniques discussed in Chapter 3. First, write down all the examples that come into your mind. Then, review your examples, and choose the ones that will best communicate your point to your readers.

PRACTICE 7–2   **Supporting Your Main Idea with Examples**

Read the following main ideas, and give three examples you might use to support each one.

Example: My boss's cheapness is unprofessional.

makes us bring in our own calculators

makes us use old, rusted paper clips

will not replace burned-out lightbulbs

1. My (friend, sister, brother, husband, wife—choose one) has some admirable traits.

2. This weekend is particularly busy.

Third Basic: Secondary Support in Illustration

Effective examples in illustration are supported by specific details, which may include sensory details and dialogue (see Chapter 6). In addition, writers of illustration may use **proper nouns** to help readers visualize the examples. A proper noun is a name, and it is always capitalized. A proper noun is always more specific than a general noun. For example, in her essay, "When Poor People Have Nice Things" (p. 143), Andrea Whitmer makes the following point:

> Now, I could understand it if I had a Lamborghini or two in my garage.

Whitmer could have said *expensive car* in this sentence. But *expensive car* might mean different things to different readers. Instead, Whitmer uses the proper noun *Lamborghini* to emphasize her point: a *Lamborghini* is one of the most expensive luxury vehicles in the world.

Read to Write As you read illustration paragraphs and essays in this chapter, put a check mark next to examples with proper nouns. How do these nouns support the writer's point?

PRACTICE 7–3   **Giving Details about the Examples**

In the spaces provided, copy your main ideas and examples from Practice 2. Then, for each example, write a detail that further shows, explains, or proves what you mean.

Example:

Main idea: My boss's cheapness is unprofessional.

Example: makes us bring in our own calculators

   Detail: Some people do not have a calculator and must use their iPhones.

Example: makes us use old, rusted paper clips

   Detail: They leave rust marks on important documents.

Example: will not replace burned-out lightbulbs

   Detail: The dim light leads to more errors.

1. Main idea:

    Example:

        Detail:

    Example:

        Detail:

    Example:

        Detail:

2. Main idea

    Example:

        Detail:

    Example:

        Detail:

    Example:

        Detail:

Fourth Basic: Organization in Illustration

Illustration often uses **order of importance**, saving the most powerful example for last. This strategy is used in the paragraph and essay models on pages 134–135. Or, if the examples are given according to when they happened, it might be organized by **time order**.

Transitions in illustration let readers know that you are introducing an example or moving from one example to another.

Tip For more on order of importance and time order, see pages 74–75.

Think Critically
Why do writers save the most important point for last?

Common Transitions in Illustration

also	for example	the most/the least
another	for instance	one example/another example
finally	for one thing/ for another	
first, second, and so on	in addition	

PRACTICE 7–4 **Using Transitions in Illustration**

Read the paragraph that follows, and fill in the blanks with transitions.

Greek myths include many heroes, such as the great warriors Achilles and Heracles. _____, the myths describe several monsters that tested the heroes' strength. _____ of these frightening creatures was the Hydra, a water serpent with many heads. When a warrior cut off one of these heads, two or more would sprout up in its place. _____ of these mythical monsters was the Gorgons, three sisters who had snakes for hair. Any person who looked into the Gorgons' eyes would turn to stone. _____ terrifying monster was Cerberus, a three-headed dog with snapping jaws. He guarded the gates to the underworld, keeping the living from entering and the dead from leaving. Fortunately, some heroes' cleverness equaled the monsters' hideousness. _____, Heracles discovered that by applying a torch to the wounds of the Hydra, he could prevent the creature from growing more heads. ___, Orpheus, a famous mythical musician, soothed Cerberus by plucking the strings of a lyre. In this way, Orpheus got past the beast and entered the underworld, from which he hoped to rescue his wife.

Paragraphs versus Essays in Illustration

For more on the important features of illustration, see the Four Basics of Good Illustration on page 128.

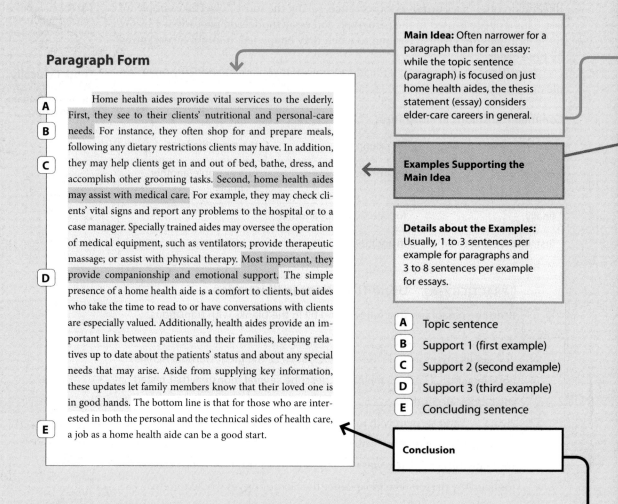

Paragraph Form

A **B** **C** Home health aides provide vital services to the elderly. First, they see to their clients' nutritional and personal-care needs. For instance, they often shop for and prepare meals, following any dietary restrictions clients may have. In addition, they may help clients get in and out of bed, bathe, dress, and accomplish other grooming tasks. Second, home health aides may assist with medical care. For example, they may check clients' vital signs and report any problems to the hospital or to a case manager. Specially trained aides may oversee the operation of medical equipment, such as ventilators; provide therapeutic massage; or assist with physical therapy. **D** Most important, they provide companionship and emotional support. The simple presence of a home health aide is a comfort to clients, but aides who take the time to read to or have conversations with clients are especially valued. Additionally, health aides provide an important link between patients and their families, keeping relatives up to date about the patients' status and about any special needs that may arise. Aside from supplying key information, these updates let family members know that their loved one is in good hands. **E** The bottom line is that for those who are interested in both the personal and the technical sides of health care, a job as a home health aide can be a good start.

Main Idea: Often narrower for a paragraph than for an essay: while the topic sentence (paragraph) is focused on just home health aides, the thesis statement (essay) considers elder-care careers in general.

Examples Supporting the Main Idea

Details about the Examples: Usually, 1 to 3 sentences per example for paragraphs and 3 to 8 sentences per example for essays.

A Topic sentence
B Support 1 (first example)
C Support 2 (second example)
D Support 3 (third example)
E Concluding sentence

Conclusion

Think Critically as You Write Illustration

Ask Yourself

- Does each of my current examples clearly illustrate the main idea?
- Do I have enough examples? If my paragraph or essay feels "thin," might I find relevant new examples to enrich it? (For more on generating ideas, see pp. 67–69.)
- Do I provide transitions to guide my readers?

Essay Form

1

During these difficult economic times, many students are looking to pursue careers in expanding fields with good long-term prospects. One field that they should seriously consider is elder care. Because the U.S. population is aging, demand for workers who specialize in the health of the elderly is increasing rapidly.

One set of workers in great demand consists of physical therapists, who help elderly patients improve their mobility and retain their independence. Some of these therapists are based at hospitals or nursing facilities, others at clinics or private offices. Regardless of where they work, they provide a variety of services to elderly patients, from helping stroke sufferers relearn how to walk and perform other daily activities to showing others how to live a more active life. Physical therapists can also help patients injured in falls reduce their reliance on painkillers, which can become less effective over time and in certain cases even addictive. According to the U.S. Department of Labor, employment of physical therapists will grow by 30 percent

2

over the next ten years, largely because of the increasing number of elderly Americans.

Also in demand are nutritionists who specialize in older people's dietary needs. These professionals may plan meals and provide nutrition advice for hospitals, nursing homes, and other institutions, or they may counsel individual patients on how to eat more healthfully or on how to prepare meals that meet certain dietary restrictions. For instance, elderly patients suffering from heart disease may need to eat foods that are low in salt and saturated fat. Other patients might have to avoid foods that interfere with the absorption of certain medications. Although the market for nutritionists is not expected to grow as quickly as that for physical therapists, it is projected to increase steadily as the population continues to age.

The highest-demand workers are those who provide at-home health care to the elderly. One subset of these workers consists of home nurses, who often provide follow-up care after patients are released from a hospital or other medical facility. These nurses help

3

patients transition from an institutional setting while making sure they continue to receive high-quality care. For instance, they track patients' vital signs, administer and monitor medications, and carry out specific tasks required to manage particular diseases. Another subset of home health workers is made up of home health aides, who assist nurses and other professionals with medical care, see to clients' nutritional and personal-care needs, and provide companionship and emotional support. Both home health aides and nurses provide an important link between patients and their families, keeping relatives up to date about the patients' status and about any special needs that may arise. In addition to supplying key information, these updates let family members know that their loved one is in good hands. Because of home health-care workers' vital role in serving the expanding elderly population, their employment is expected to grow significantly: on average, 30 to 40 percent over the next ten years.

4

Given the growing demand for elder-care workers, people pursuing these professions stand an excellent chance of getting jobs with good long-term outlooks. Based on what I have learned about these professions, the best candidates are those who have a strong interest in health or medicine, a willingness to work hard to get the necessary qualifications, and, perhaps most important, an ability to connect with and truly care for others.

A Introductory paragraph
B Thesis statement
C Topic sentence 1 (first example)
D Topic sentence 2 (second example)
E Topic sentence 3 (third example)
F Concluding paragraph

Evaluate Illustration

To become a more successful writer, it is important not only to understand the Four Basics of Good Illustration but to read and evaluate examples as well. In this section, you will have the opportunity to use a sample rubric to analyze or evaluate the samples of illustration provided. By using this rubric, you will gain a better understanding of how the components of good illustration work together to create a successful paragraph or essay. Additionally, reading examples of illustration will help you write your own.

Read the following sample illustration paragraph. Using the Four Basics of Good Illustration (p. 128) and the sample grading rubric, decide what grade this paragraph would earn. Explain your answer.

Assignment: Write a paragraph explaining why any one particular extracurricular activity is important.

When I mention "marching band," it's pretty clear that most of my readers have already tuned out. In fact, I think that a lot of people reading this may not even consider it a true activity because it does not involve physical exercise, like any number of sporting activities; intense intellectual thought, as a chess or math team may require; or even individual performance, as you may see in theater. But to feel this way is to overlook activities like choir and band that not only keep students involved and out of trouble but also help them learn leadership and teamwork skills that they may not find in other activities. As a member of a large group, every member of that group is always counting on them, so while it seems like it may be a "safety" activity where one can hide, I believe it is a significant and important activity.

Analysis of Sample Paragraph:

Sample rubric

Element	Grading criteria	Point: Comment
Appropriateness	• Did the student follow the assignment directions?	___/5:
Main idea	• Does the paper clearly state a strong main idea in a complete sentence?	___/10:

Element	Grading criteria	Point: Comment
Support	• Is the main idea developed with specific support, including specific details and examples? • Is there enough support to make the main idea evident to the reader? • Is all the support directly related to the main idea?	___/10:
Organization	• Is the writing logically organized? • Does the student use transitions (*also, for example, sometimes*, and so on) to move the reader from one point to another?	___/10:
Conclusion	• Does the conclusion remind the reader of the main idea? • Does it make an observation based on the support?	___/5:
Grammar	• Is the writing free of the Four Most Serious Errors? (See Chapters 16–19.) • Is the sentence structure clear? • Does the student choose words that clearly express his or her meaning? • Are the words spelled correctly? • Is the punctuation correct?	___/10:
		TOTAL POINTS: ___/50

Read and Analyze Illustration

Reading examples of illustration will help you write your own. First, two pieces of student work, a paragraph and an essay, are featured as examples. Next, the Profile of Success is paired with writing from the real world. In this profile, Juan C. Gonzalez shows how he uses illustration in his work as an automobile technician. The final example is an illustration essay by Andrea Whitmer, a professional writer. As you read these selections, pay attention to the vocabulary, and answer the questions in the margin. They will help you read critically.

Predict After reading the title, what do you think the paragraph will be about?

Reflect Have you ever received a gift that made you laugh or cry?

Student Illustration Paragraph

Casandra Palmer

Gifts from the Heart

In our home, gift exchanges have always been meaningful items to us. We do not just give things so that everyone has lots of presents. Each item has a purpose, such as a need or something that someone has desired for a long time. Some things have been given that may have made the other person laugh or cry. I remember one Christmas, our daughter Hannah had her boyfriend, who looked a lot like Harry Potter, join us. We wanted to include him, but we did not know him well, so it was hard to know what to give him. We decided to get Hannah a Harry Potter poster and crossed out the name Harry Potter. In place of Harry Potter, we put her boyfriend's name. Everyone thought it was funny, and we were all laughing, including Hannah's boyfriend. It was a personal gift that he knew we had thought about. For some reason, Hannah did not think it was so funny, but she will still remember it. Another meaningful gift came from watching the movie *Titanic* with my other daughter, Tabitha. We both cried hard and hugged each other. She surprised me by giving me a necklace that resembled the gem known as "Heart of the Ocean." I was so touched that she gave me something to remind me of the experience we shared. These special moments have left lasting impressions on my heart.

Read to Write: Annotate

1. Double-underline the topic sentence.

2. Underline the examples that support the main idea.

3. Circle the transitions.

Think Critically

1. Does the paragraph use the Four Basics of Good Illustration (p. 128)? Why or why not?

2. Does the paragraph use a particular kind of organization, like time, space, or importance? Does that choice help the paragraph's effectiveness or not?

3. What suggestions would you make for this student to help her revise the paragraph?

Student Illustration Essay

Sarah Bigler

High School Is Not Preparing Us for College

Sarah Bigler is an Engagement Coordinator at One Love Foundation. She formerly worked as the editor of *The Daily Eastern News* and holds a B.A. in Political Science from Eastern Illinois University and a M.S. in International Public Policy from the University College London.

W hen I first got to college, I heard the same thing over and over again from professors in all of my general education classes.

2   "How do you not know this?" "What are they teaching you in high school?"

3   As a freshman, I would sort of shrug and didn't have an answer for them. I remembered analyzing a lot of literature, and I vaguely remember triangles in math and dates from history. As a senior, I totally understand my professors' point. I even feel bad for them now.

4   The problem everyone misses is that there's a gap in high school teaching and college teaching. High school is supposed to prepare you for college; it doesn't. It prepares you for getting into college and for little else.

5   My high school teachers used to warn us whenever we felt they were being unfairly strict that college professors wouldn't compromise with us and that we had no idea what we were in for. I don't know why they were trying to scare us, but that wasn't true. I'm a transfer student, and neither of the schools I've been to have lived up to the terrifying hype.

6   They also told us that high school was preparation for the type of study we'd experience in college. That's definitely not true. High school was all about learning for the myriad tests the government requires. It was about passing the SAT and ACT and getting a high enough GPA to apply to the particular college you wanted.

7   Basically, high school was just about getting through. It was a way station between grade school and college.

8   It wasn't about learning and knowledge; it was about memorization of facts. I look back and wonder the same thing my professors do, because it seems nothing I learned back then has an impact on my day-to-day life now.

9   The public school system is failing us. They teach without explaining why something is important. They don't instill a sense that education is an important factor in our lives. They teach us names and dates and numbers without showing us how they will affect our decisions and ability to get good jobs in the future.

10   Take writing for an example. The way grammar is taught is tedious and mind-numbing, especially when there are just random sentences lined up on a page and covered in red markings. Every high school student complains about

having to take grammar and learn all of the awful exceptions to every grammar and spelling rule in the English language.

11   But every job that requires a college degree in America will expect a good level of writing competence. Even mathematicians and scientists have to be able to write cover letters for their resumes, research grant proposals, and reports for their bosses.

12   No one bothered to explain that in my high school English class, and no type of writing outside of a grocery list requires someone to line up random sentences in order.

13   But in college, the emphasis is on learning and thinking. I've had dozens of teachers emphasize critical thinking in their classes, and advisers, counselors, professors, and parents suddenly want students to think for themselves. It's a huge change from high school, where students are expected to follow rules and lessons blindly.

14   Sometimes the instinct to just get by has been so embedded in students that they don't even make a serious effort in their chosen majors. These are the classes that students are supposed to feel passionately about and that they assumedly want to use for the rest of their lives.

15   To use my grammar example again, I've even seen evidence of students majoring in English and journalism who do not take grammar seriously. I'm wondering why they chose those majors if they don't care about making their writing more clear and professional.

16   High school should be a time to prepare for college and for the real world. The teenage years are the beginning of finding out who each person is and what he or she wants to do with his or her life. High schools should be promoting individuality and should be providing a more college-like atmosphere, instead of just herding teenagers through.

Reflect Does your experience with grammar match Bigler's? Think about your chosen field or the career you would like to have. How is writing used in that field?

Reflect How does your experience in this class confirm or contradict Bigler's claims?

Read to Write How could Bigler improve or expand her example in paragraph 15?

Read to Write: Annotate

1. Double-underline the topic sentence.
2. Underline the examples that Bigler uses to support her point.

Think Critically

1. Does Bigler use enough examples to make her point clear?
2. Does Bigler's essay follow the Four Basics of Good Illustration (p. 128)? Explain your answer.

Profile of Success
Juan C. Gonzalez
Illustration in the Real World

Background   I grew up in Amarillo, Texas, in a family of ten children. For most of my life, going to college never even occurred to me. I was a marginal student, on the slow track in school. I expected to either join the military or to work with the Rock Island Railroad, as my father did for thirty-seven years.

However, my circumstances changed when I was a sophomore in high school. That year, my father lost both of his legs in a railroad accident at work. As I sat with him through his long stay in the hospital, I realized that I wanted a different future. I knew then that I had to go to college, but I didn't know how I could accomplish that seemingly impossible goal.

Timing is often miraculous. Soon after making the decision to pursue higher education, I was approached by a TRiO/Upward Bound counselor who asked me to consider participating in the program. I jumped at the opportunity. The TRiO/Student Support Services program gave me the support, encouragement, and skills I needed for college work, and I will always be deeply grateful for their help.

Writing at work   Most of the writing I do at work is in creating lectures and presentations for a variety of different audiences, reviewing and revising statements of school policy, and writing and updating various reports on student life at the school. I work closely with graduate students, and much of our communication is oral—shared exchanges of ideas during class and meetings. However, in those meetings I take minutes of what occurs so that I have accurate records. I maintain active correspondence with students, with administrators in other areas of the college, and with faculty. I also spend a good amount of time writing e-mail messages to people at the university, in the community, and to colleagues around the country.

How Gonzalez uses illustration   In reports to the administration and in presentations to parents, trustees, and students, I have to give detailed examples of the work that our faculty and I achieve in our academic department.

JUAN GONZALEZ

Juan Gonzalez

Vice Chancellor for Student Affairs, University of California, San Diego

minutes: notes of what is said during a meeting

Workplace Illustration

The following is from an address Gonzalez gave to a group of new students.

1   As new students, you are embarking on an incredibly exciting and challenging time, a time of expanding knowledge, relationships, viewpoints, and achievements. In my role as vice president, I am constantly striving to match that energy level so

Reflect   How does Gonzalez consider his audience in his speech?

embarking: beginning

Read to Write
How does Gonzalez
use illustration in the
opening paragraph?

diligently: with care,
effort, and focus

Reflect What is
the motto or driving
force of the Student
Affairs Division at your
school? How could you
find out?

encapsulates: shows
clearly in a brief way

gauge: a way of
measuring something

collaborative: marked
by groups or people to
work together

integrated: linked or
blended

that we can offer the highest level of service on this very diverse campus. I frequently marvel at college students who seem to have an unlimited amount of energy that allows them to attend classes, read and study, maintain a social life, run for political office, pursue a hobby, play an intramural sport, volunteer for a worthy cause, hold down a job. We in the Division of Student Affairs strongly encourage activities outside the classroom that enrich the academic experience, as we recognize that a university education is enhanced through involvement in our campus community.

2   Last November, a group of Student Affairs staff, students, and faculty began work on creating a strategic plan for the division. They have been laboring diligently on this document, and I am excited to share with you the fruit of that labor: our newly developed Student Affairs Strategic Plan, which has as its motto "Student Affairs: Where Life and Learning Intersect."

3   This phrase encapsulates the driving force behind the Division of Student Affairs. We exist, in essence, to help students succeed and grow, and we believe that growth and success must be measured in many ways. Academic success is one gauge of how well students are performing, but there are a variety of indicators other than grades. Those who take the most from their college experience are those who recognize that learning happens both inside and outside the classroom.

4   In fact, I recently had our units count the services they offer that are collaborative efforts with the academic side of the family, and a rough survey yielded 140 programs. This idea of integrated learning carries through most of what we do, whether it is a program to recruit the best students from around Texas like the Honors Colloquium, the increasingly popular "Academic Community Centers" for studying and advising on site in the residence halls, Summer Orientation, or the professor-led Freshman Reading Round-Up book discussions.

Our Vision Statement

aspire: hope or desire,
have as a goal

5   Our vision statement lights the path we are following to where we aspire to be:

Reflect Why does
Gonzalez quote the
vision statement? Does
your college have
a vision statement?
Where can you find it?

The Division of Student Affairs at the University of Texas at Austin seeks to become the premier organization of its kind. We envision a network of programs and services that excels in meeting students' out-of-classroom needs, complementing their academic experiences, and building community on a diverse campus. In doing so, we will contribute to developing citizens and leaders who will thrive in and enrich an increasingly complex world.

Our Mission

Reflect What is the
difference between a
vision and a mission?

6   Our mission, or the explanation of what we do, is described this way:

facilitate: help

foster: encourage or
support

The Division of Student Affairs facilitates students' discovery of self and the world in which they live. We enhance students' educational experiences through programs and services that support academic success. We provide for fundamental needs, including shelter, nourishment, and a sense of security. We create environments that foster physical, emotional, and psychological wellness, and advance healthy lifestyles. Student Affairs builds communities, both real and virtual, that encourage inclusiveness, invite communication, and add to the cultural richness of the institution. We focus on personal development, including career decision making, problem solving, and group dynamics, challenging students to work both independently and as part of a team.

7   The work group that wrote the strategic plan also composed a defining phrase to encapsulate Student Affairs: "Our passion is complete learning." These, I hope you will agree, are stirring words. We take our responsibility for providing an environment that is inclusive and promotes a healthy lifestyle seriously. We are committed to supporting you as you achieve your goals at this university.

Reflect What is "complete learning"? How do the vision and mission statements above show "complete learning"?

Read to Write: Annotate

1. What is Gonzalez illustrating? Underline or highlight his examples.

2. Circle all transitions that Gonzalez uses.

Think Critically

1. Gonzalez does not use as many transitions as other writers in this chapter. Why not? Recall that Gonzalez first wrote this as a speech. How is a speech different from an essay?

2. Who is the audience for Gonzalez's illustration? What is his purpose?

3. Carefully reread the Four Basics of Good Illustration (p. 128) and decide whether you think Gonzalez's essay is a good example of illustration. Make notes to support your opinion.

Professional Illustration Essay

Andrea Whitmer

When Poor People Have Nice Things

Andrea Whitmer is a web developer and blogger. Most of her writing attempts to help others—mothers in particular—find the humor in everyday situations. She also hopes to share her hard-earned wisdom with others so that they can learn from and, possibly, not make some of the same choices she did. This essay first appeared on her blog, *So Over This*, in June of 2012.

Predict What will Whitmer's essay be about?

There's a graphic circulating on some of my friends' Facebook profiles that really gets on my nerves. I told myself I wouldn't write about it, but I saw it again last night, and I just can't help myself. The graphic says, "Maybe someday I'll be able to afford an iPhone like the person in front of me at the grocery store. The one paying with FOOD STAMPS!"

indignant: a feeling or expressing of extreme disgust or anger

Read to Write
Why does Whitmer use "blah blah blah" instead of finishing the sentence?

Read to Write
What is Whitmer's profession? Why does she mention it here?

Reflect Has there ever been a time in your own life where you had to make a difficult financial decision? What factors did you consider before making that decision?

scrounging: attempt to gather something by looking carefully or asking for the help of others.

Reflect When you read about Whitmer's experience, what is your first assumption? Why?

Reflect Have any of Whitmer's examples affected your initial assumption?

Read to Write
What does Whitmer suggest by using the letters X, Y, and Z here instead of specific examples?

Reflect Has there ever been a time when someone has judged you without knowing you? Or have you judged someone else and found out you were incorrect?

2   Anytime that picture (or something similar) is posted, it gets about fifty "likes" and a long string of comments from indignant people who have personally witnessed a poor person owning something of value. The rage is evident—how dare someone on food stamps have a smartphone! Why should they even be allowed to have a phone at all? Our tax dollars blah blah blah blah . . .

3   Here's the thing: we can all think of at least one person who games the system. After working as a therapist for almost seven years, I can think of quite a few. But no one knows the life situation of every single person on the planet, no matter how much they think they do.

4   A good friend of mine got fired from her job just days after her husband was laid off. Both of them had iPhones on his parents' plan, which cost them $50 a month total. Now what makes the most sense—breaking that contract at hundreds of dollars, or scrounging up the $50 a month in hopes that one or both of them would find another job soon? They didn't have to sign up for assistance—they were both lucky to get jobs before their emergency fund was drained—but if they had, they would have been in the grocery checkout line with iPhones in their pockets.

I Speak from Experience

5   The only assistance I've ever personally used was Medicaid for my son at two different times during his life. But I will tell you—during both of those times, I had cable television. I had Internet access at home. This last time, I had an iPhone (gasp!). I also owned several items that could have been pawned or sold for a decent amount of money.

6   Was I living it up? No. Not even close. But as someone with two college degrees and tons of ambition, I also never planned to continue collecting that assistance forever. Why should I empty my house of all the things I bought with my own money, only to have to buy them again when the crisis was over? That really doesn't make sense.

7   Now, I could understand it if I had a Lamborghini or two in my garage. But when you're used to a fairly middle-class existence and something happens to you (no matter what it is), you assume that your situation will improve at some point. It's not like the poverty police come take all your stuff in the middle of the night. You still own all the things you did before. If you had nice clothes, you'll still have nice clothes. If your cousin bought you an expensive handbag last Christmas, you'll still have that handbag. No one drops off a tattered, dirty wardrobe for you to put on before you leave your house.

I Know What You're Thinking

8   I can just hear the comments now. "Well, I know someone who did X and Y," or "I saw a lady buy Z at the mall." I know. I've seen it too. That's not the point.

9   The point is, some people are in situations that we know nothing about. Some people own nice things from a better time in their lives and choose to keep those things during a setback. And some people make choices after becoming poor that we wouldn't personally make. Talking smack about those people on Facebook isn't doing anything to eradicate poverty or to change the fact that there is widespread abuse of our current system.

10   If you get upset when you see a poor person with nice things like smart-phones, all I ask is that you consider this:

Maybe they just got laid off last month and they already owned the iPhone.

Maybe a family member pays the phone bill.

Maybe they're picking up groceries for a disabled neighbor with the neighbor's food stamp card.

Maybe the phone was a gift and it's on a prepaid plan.

Maybe you should worry less about what someone else has and more about yourself.

11   To many people, I could be considered "poor" right now (even though my bills are paid and I'm saving money). And guess what? I own several nice things. Some of you will judge me for that, and there's nothing I can do about it. But I will continue to be disgusted when people criticize another person's choices, especially when they can't possibly know the full set of circumstances.

Evaluate Based on Whitmer's observations, do you think we have become too comfortable making judgments based only on appearance?

Read to Write: Annotate

1. Underline the examples Whitmer provides to support her main idea.

2. Circle Whitmer's transitions. What sort of organization is she using?

3. Highlight each question that Whitmer asks. Why do you think she asks these questions?

Think Critically

1. In your own words, state Whitmer's main idea.

2. Do you think Whitmer has successfully supported her idea? Why or why not?

3. In the last sentence of paragraph 9, Whitmer makes an assumption that there is "widespread abuse of our current system." What do you make of Whitmer's claim? Is there sufficient evidence to support it?

4. Does this essay demonstrate all of the Four Basics of Good Illustration (p. 128)? Explain.

Respond

1. Write about a time when someone made a snap judgment about you. This could be because of where you work, how you speak, or how you dress. How did you find out about it? How did it make you feel? How close to being accurate was it? Why do you think that person made those assumptions?

2. With social networking and its primary focus on images and short text, it has become easier than ever to publicly humiliate or bully others. Do you think that social networking has created more bullying and caused more harm than there was before media like Facebook, Instagram, Twitter, and other platforms existed?

3. In your opinion, why is it important to question our assumptions about other people? How can that benefit both ourselves and other people?

Grammar for Illustration

Several of the illustration essays in this chapter use lists of examples. We can format a list by making each item a separate paragraph, as Whitmer does with her list of suggestions on page 145. Or we might choose to format a list with bullets, as the items in the checklist on page 150 illustrate. Finally, we can put the items in a list within a single sentence. In that case, we must separate each item in the list with commas, as Juan Gonzalez has done in this sentence:

> I frequently marvel at college students who seem to have an unlimited amount of energy that allows them to attend classes, read and study, maintain a social life, run for political office, pursue a hobby, play an intramural sport, volunteer for a worthy cause, hold down a job.

For more on the uses of commas, see Chapter 30.

Write Your Own Illustration

In this section, you will write your own illustration based on one of the following assignments. For help, refer to the How to Write Illustration checklist on page 150.

Assignment Options: Writing about College, Work, and Everyday Life

Write an illustration paragraph, essay, or other document (as described below) on one of the following topics or on one of your own choice.

College

- Choose a concept from another course you are taking and illustrate it for students who have not taken the course.
- If you are still deciding on a degree program or major, identify at least two areas of study that interest you. To get some ideas, you might refer to a course catalog. Also, consider visiting a counselor at your college's guidance office or career center. The counselor might be able to recommend some study programs to you based on your goals and interests. Next, write about the areas of study that appeal to you the most, giving examples of what you would learn and explaining how each of your choices matches your goals and interests.

- Produce a one- or two-page newsletter for other students in your class on one of the following topics. Make sure to describe each club, opportunity, or event in enough detail for readers. Also, include contact information, as well as hours and locations for events and club meetings.

  - Student clubs
  - Volunteer opportunities
  - Upcoming campus events (such as lectures, movies, and sports events)
  - Upcoming events in the larger community

Work

- What is the best or worst job you have ever had? Give examples of what made it the best or worst job.
- Think about people who work behind the scenes at your school or workplace. Write an essay that shows how jobs we don't always notice are critical for success, and give examples of these jobs. Give enough details about each job to make it clear why that job is important.
- Think of the job you would most like to have after graduation. Then, write a list of your skills—both current and those you will be building in college—that are relevant to the job. To identify skills you will be building through your degree program, you might refer to a course catalog. To identify relevant work skills, consider your past or present jobs as well as internships or other work experiences you would like to have before graduation. Finally, write a cover letter explaining why you are the best candidate for your ideal job. Be sure to provide several examples of your skills, referring to the list that you prepared.

Everyday life

- Write about stresses in your life or things that you like about your life. Give plenty of details for each example.
- Give examples of memories that have stayed with you for a long time. For each memory, provide enough details so that readers will be able to share your experience.
- Identify at least three public improvements you think would benefit a significant number of people in your community, such as the addition of sidewalks in residential areas to encourage exercise. These improvements should not include changes, such as the creation of a boat dock on a local lake, that would benefit only a small portion of the community. Then, in a letter to the editor of your local paper, describe each suggested improvement in detail, and explain why it would be an asset to the community.

Tip Check with your school's career center for more tips and advice on cover letters.

Assignment Options: Reading and Writing Critically

Complete one of the following assignments, which ask you to apply the critical thinking, reading, and writing skills discussed in Chapter 1.

Tip For a reminder of how to summarize, analyze, synthesize, and evaluate, see the Reading and Writing Critically box on page 17.

Writing Critically about Readings

Both Andrea Whitmer's *When Poor People Have Nice Things* (pp. 143–145) and Joshua Boyce's *Conditioning* (pp. 281–282) illustrate the assumptions that people make about others around them on a daily basis. Read or review both of these pieces, and then follow these steps:

1. **Summarize** Briefly summarize the works, listing major examples.

2. **Analyze** What questions do the essays raise for you? Are there any other issues you wish they had covered?

3. **Synthesize** Using examples from both Whitmer's and Boyce's essays and from your own experience, discuss why we make these assumptions about others or how it feels to have others make assumptions about you.

4. **Evaluate** Which essay, Whitmer's or Boyce's, do you think is more effective? Why? Does the writers' use of clear examples get their points across? Why or why not? In writing your evaluation, you might look back on your responses to step 2.

Writing about Images

Study the infographic on page 149, and complete the following steps.

1. **Read the image** Ask yourself: What is the main idea in this graphic? Who is the intended audience? What evidence of credibility or reliability do you see in the infographic? (For more information on reading images, see Chapter 1.)

2. **Write an illustration** This infographic illustrates an important point about the role of food in our diet. Explore the connection between another health condition and diet. Write an essay illustrating how diet can help patients manage the health condition; alternatively, create your own infographic to illustrate what you have learned.

Writing to Solve a Problem

Read or review the discussion of problem solving in Chapter 1 (pp. 26–27). Then, consider the following problem.

> Your college is increasing its tuition by $500 next year, and you do not think that you can continue. You have done well so far, and you really want to get a college degree.

OBESITY EPIDEMIC Design Elements > 10

GOOD CALORIES VS. BAD CALORIES

Whole Grain Breads | Bran Cereals | Fresh Fruit | Green Vegetables

Sweets & Desserts | Sugared Cereals | Sugary Drinks | Refined Breads

Good Calories

Bad Calories

GOOD Calories

BAD Calories

KATHYKONKLE/GETTY IMAGES

Assignment Rather than just giving up and dropping out next year, as many students do, working in a small group or on your own, make a list of resources you could consult to help you, and explain how they might help. You might want to start with the following sentence:

> Before dropping out of school for financial reasons, students should consult _____ because _____.

For a paragraph: Name your best resource, and give examples of how this person or office might help you.

For an essay: Name your three best resources, and give examples of how they might help you.

CHECKLIST

How to Write Illustration

Steps	Details
☐ Narrow and explore your topic. See Chapter 3.	• Make the topic more specific. • Prewrite to get ideas about the narrowed topic.
☐ Write a topic sentence (paragraph) or thesis statement (essay). See Chapter 3.	• State what you want your readers to understand about your topic.
☐ Support your point. See Chapter 4.	• Come up with examples and details to show, explain, or prove your main idea to readers.
☐ Write a draft. See Chapter 5.	• Make a plan that puts examples in a logical order. • Include a topic sentence (paragraph) or thesis statement (essay) and all the supporting examples and details.
☐ Revise your draft. See Chapter 5.	• Make sure it has *all* the Four Basics of Good Illustration. • Make sure you include transitions to move readers smoothly from one example to the next.
☐ Edit your revised draft. See Parts 3 through 6.	• Correct errors in grammar, spelling, word use, and punctuation.

Chapter Review

1. What is illustration?
2. What are the Four Basics of Good Illustration?
3. How can writers make their examples clear to a reader?
4. How is illustration usually organized?

Reflect and Apply

1. Have you ever written or read illustration before? How does that experience confirm, contradict, or complicate what you have learned in this chapter?
2. Interview someone studying your major or working in your career. What situations require reading or writing illustration in your major or career?
3. What was most difficult about your writing for this chapter? What do you want to do differently next time?
4. What part of your writing for this chapter was most successful? What do you need to remember for next time?

8

Description

Writing That Creates Pictures in Words

Understand What Description Is

Description is writing that creates a clear and vivid impression of a person, place, or thing, often by appealing to the physical senses.

> **Four Basics** of Good Description
>
> **1** It creates a main impression—an overall effect, feeling, or image—about the topic.
>
> **2** It uses specific examples to support the main impression.
>
> **3** It supports those examples with details that appeal to the five senses: sight, hearing, smell, taste, and touch.
>
> **4** It arranges examples and details logically, by space, time, or order of importance.

In the following student paragraph, the numbers and colors correspond to the Four Basics of Good Description.

1 Nojoqui Falls is a special place to me because its beauty provides a break from human worries. **2** At the start of the trail leading to the falls, the smell and sound of oak trees and pine trees help visitors feel they are up for the journey. **3** The sun hitting the trees makes the air fresh with a leafy aroma. Overhead, the wind blows through the leaves, making a soft noise. **2** Closer to the waterfall, the shade from the trees creates a shielding blanket. **3** When the sun comes out, it fills the place with light, showing the vapor coming out of the trees and plants. **2** To the left of the trail are rocks that are positioned perfectly for viewing the waterfall.

4 Spatial arrangement of details

3 Water splashes as it hits the rocks. 2 The waterfall itself is beautiful, like a transparent, sparkling window of diamonds. 3 The water is so clear that objects on the other side are visible. It appears like a never-ending stream of water that splashes onto the rocks. 1 The total effect of these sights, sounds, and smells is a setting where daily cares can be set aside for a while.

—Liliana Ramirez, student

Being able to describe something or someone accurately and in detail is important in many situations.

College	On a physical therapy test, you describe the symptoms you observed in a patient.
Work	You write a memo to your boss describing the disorganization in the company supply closet.
Everyday life	You describe something you lost to the lost-and-found clerk at a store.

In college assignments, the word *describe* may mean *tell about* or *report*. When an assignment asks you to actually describe a person, place, or thing, however, you will need to use the kinds of specific descriptive details discussed later in this chapter.

For more information about understanding writing assignment prompts, see the Appendix, page 553.

Think Critically
Some students believe that description only occurs in creative writing, not academic writing. How would you respond to that statement?

First Basic: Main Idea in Description

In description, the **main idea** is the main impression you want to create for your readers. To help you discover your main idea, complete the following sentence:

Read to Write
To identify the main idea when you are reading a description, complete this sentence: The writer is describing the topic to show that. . . .

| Main idea in description | **What is most interesting, vivid, and important to me about this topic is that . . .** |

If you do not have a main impression about your topic, think about why it is important and how it smells, sounds, looks, tastes, or feels.

PRACTICE 8–1   Finding a Main Impression

For the following general topics, jot down impressions that appeal to you, and circle the one you would use as a main impression. Base your choice on what is most interesting, vivid, and important to you.

Example:

Topic: A vandalized car

Impressions: wrecked, smashed, damaged, battered

Think Critically
Who might be the audience for these descriptions? The purpose?

1. **Topic:** A fireworks display

   Impressions:

2. **Topic:** A football player
   Impressions:

3. **Topic:** The room you are in
   Impressions:

The topic sentence (paragraph) or thesis statement (essay) in description usually contains both your narrowed topic and your main impression. Here is a topic sentence for a description paragraph:

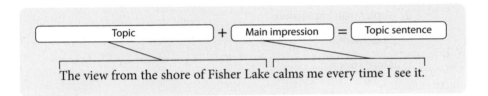

Remember that a topic for an essay can be a little broader than one for a paragraph.

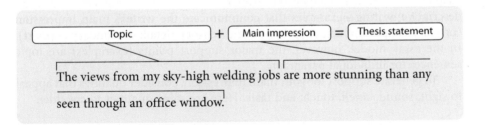

Whereas the topic sentence is focused on just one location and view, the thesis statement sets up descriptions of different views from different sites.

To be effective, your topic sentence or thesis statement should be a complete, specific sentence. You can make it specific by adding details that appeal to the senses.

Tip Sometimes, the same main idea can be used for a paragraph and an essay, but the essay must develop this point in more detail. (See pp. 158–159.)

> **PRACTICE 8–2**   **Writing a Statement of Your Main Impression**

For two of the items from Practice 1, write the topic and your main impression. Then, write a statement of your main impression. Finally, revise the statement to make the main impression sharper and more specific.

Example:

Topic/main impression: A vandalized car/battered

Statement: The vandalized car on the side of the highway was battered.

More specific: The shell of a car on the side of the road was dented all

over, apparently from a bat or club, and surrounded by broken glass.

1. Topic/main impression:

   Statement:

   More specific:

2. Topic/main impression:

   Statement:

   More specific:

Second Basic: Primary Support in Description

The paragraph and essay models on pages 158–159 use the topic sentence (paragraph) and thesis statement (essay) from the Main Idea section of this chapter. Both models include the primary and secondary support used in all descriptive writing—examples that communicate the writer's main impression (primary support), backed up by specific sensory details (secondary support). In the essay model, however, the major support points (examples) are topic sentences for individual paragraphs.

   To generate support for your main impression, consider qualities that appeal to sight, sound, smell, touch, and taste. Here are some qualities to consider.

Sight	Sound	Smell
Colors?	Loud/soft?	Sweet/sour?
Shapes?	Piercing/soothing?	Sharp/mild?
Sizes?	Continuous/off and on?	Good? (Like what?)
Patterns?	Pleasant/unpleasant? (How?)	Bad? (Rotten?)
Shiny/dull?		New? (New what? Leather? Plastic?)
Does it look like anything else?	Does it sound like anything else?	Old?
		Does it smell like anything else?

Taste	Touch
Good? (What does "good" taste like?)	Hard/soft?
Bad? (What does "bad" taste like?)	Liquid/solid?
Bitter/sugary? Metallic?	Rough/smooth?
Burning? Spicy?	Hot/cold?
Does it taste like anything else?	Dry/oily?
	Textures?
	Does it feel like anything else?

Tip When writing descriptions, consider this advice from writer Rhys Alexander: "Detail makes the difference between boring and terrific writing. It's the difference between a pencil sketch and a lush oil painting. As a writer, words are your paint. Use all the colors."

PRACTICE 8-3   Finding Details to Support a Main Impression

Read the following statements, and write four sensory details you might use to support the main impression.

Example: The physical sensations of a day at the beach are as vivid as the visual ones.

a. softness of the sand

b. push and splash of waves

c. chill of the water

d. smoothness of worn stones and beach glass

1. My favorite meal smells as good as it tastes.

2. The new office building has a contemporary look.

3. A classroom during an exam echoes with the "sounds of silence."

Third Basic: Secondary Support in Description

The examples and sensory qualities you choose to support the main impression in description should be backed up with enough detail to make them come alive for your reader. You can do this by introducing additional adjectives (describing words) that appeal to the reader's senses. You can also expand your support by adding comparisons, using words such as "like," "similar to," "just as," or "as if."

In his essay, "Memories of New York City Snow" (pp. 166–168), Oscar Hijuelos describes his father and godfather "posing in a snow-covered meadow in Central Park." After describing their clothing, Hijuelos uses a comparison with "as if" to help readers visualize the men standing in the snow.

They stand on a field of whiteness, the two men seemingly afloat in midair, **as if** they were being held aloft by the magical substance itself.

Fourth Basic: Organization in Description

Description can use any of the orders of organization—**time**, **space**, or **importance**—depending on your purpose. If you are writing to create a main impression of an event (for example, a description of fireworks), you might use time order. If you are describing what someone or something looks like, you might use space order, the strategy used in the paragraph model on page 158. If one detail about your topic is stronger than the others, you could use order of importance and leave that detail for last. This approach is taken in the essay model on page 159.

Order	Sequence
Time	first to last/last to first, most recent to least recent/least recent to most recent
Space	top to bottom/bottom to top, right to left/left to right, near to far/far to near
Importance	end with detail that will make the strongest impression

Use **transitions** to move your readers from one sensory detail to the next. Usually, transitions should match your order of organization.

Common Transitions in Description

Time			
as	finally	next	then
at last	first	now	when
before/after	last	second	while
during	later	since	
eventually	meanwhile	soon	
Space			
above	beneath	inside	over
across	beside	near	to the left/right
at the bottom/top	beyond	next to	to the side
behind	farther/further	on top of	under/underneath
below	in front of	opposite	where
Importance			
especially	more/even more	most vivid	
in particular	most	strongest	

PRACTICE 8-4   **Using Transitions in Description**

Read the paragraph that follows, and fill in the blanks with transitions.

> I saw the kitchen at Morley's Place on my first day assisting the town restaurant inspector. _____, Morley's was empty of customers, which made sense for 3 p.m. on a Tuesday. _____ my boss and I saw the kitchen, we hoped the restaurant would stay empty. _____ from the kitchen entrance was the food-prep counter that was covered with a faint layer of grime. _____ the counter were three food bins. __ I aimed my flashlight into one bin, numerous roaches scuttled away from the light. _____ the counter, a fan whirred loudly in an open window. _____ the stove, we discovered a mousetrap holding a shriveled, long-dead mouse. Because of the violations, the health department closed Morley's Place.

Evaluate Description

To become a more successful writer, it is important not only to understand the Four Basics of Good Description but to read and evaluate examples as well. In this section, you will have the opportunity to use a sample rubric to analyze or evaluate the samples of descriptive writing provided. By using this rubric, you will gain a better understanding of how the components of good description work together to create a successful paragraph or essay. Additionally, reading examples of description will help you write your own.

Tip For more on these orders of organization, see pages 73–75.

Read the following sample description paragraph. Using the Four Basics of Good Description and the sample grading rubric, decide what grade this paragraph would earn. Explain your answer.

> **Assignment:** Identify one moment in your life that remains clear and vivid in your mind. In no more than a paragraph, use the five senses to share that experience with the reader. Your goal is to be so descriptive that readers feel as though they are experiencing it with you.

> **The day I graduated from high school was very important to me. When I arrived at the football field to line up, I began to notice how hot it was. Unfortunately, there wasn't any wind. I looked around and noticed that all of my friends were grouped together and talking about all of the parties that they would attend later that day. Finally, I heard the music start, and I began to line up to make my way down the aisle and take my seat. It was truly a wonderful day.**

Paragraphs versus Essays in Description

For more on the important features of description, see the Four Basics of Good Description on page 151.

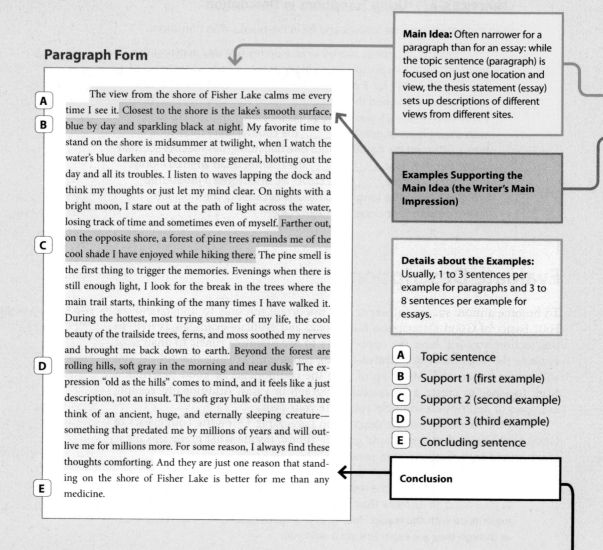

Paragraph Form

A   The view from the shore of Fisher Lake calms me every time I see it. Closest to the shore is the lake's smooth surface,
B   blue by day and sparkling black at night. My favorite time to stand on the shore is midsummer at twilight, when I watch the water's blue darken and become more general, blotting out the day and all its troubles. I listen to waves lapping the dock and think my thoughts or just let my mind clear. On nights with a bright moon, I stare out at the path of light across the water, losing track of time and sometimes even of myself. Farther out,
C   on the opposite shore, a forest of pine trees reminds me of the cool shade I have enjoyed while hiking there. The pine smell is the first thing to trigger the memories. Evenings when there is still enough light, I look for the break in the trees where the main trail starts, thinking of the many times I have walked it. During the hottest, most trying summer of my life, the cool beauty of the trailside trees, ferns, and moss soothed my nerves and brought me back down to earth. Beyond the forest are
D   rolling hills, soft gray in the morning and near dusk. The expression "old as the hills" comes to mind, and it feels like a just description, not an insult. The soft gray hulk of them makes me think of an ancient, huge, and eternally sleeping creature—something that predated me by millions of years and will outlive me for millions more. For some reason, I always find these thoughts comforting. And they are just one reason that stand-
E   ing on the shore of Fisher Lake is better for me than any medicine.

Main Idea: Often narrower for a paragraph than for an essay: while the topic sentence (paragraph) is focused on just one location and view, the thesis statement (essay) sets up descriptions of different views from different sites.

Examples Supporting the Main Idea (the Writer's Main Impression)

Details about the Examples: Usually, 1 to 3 sentences per example for paragraphs and 3 to 8 sentences per example for essays.

A   Topic sentence
B   Support 1 (first example)
C   Support 2 (second example)
D   Support 3 (third example)
E   Concluding sentence

Conclusion

Think Critically As You Write Description

Ask Yourself

- Have I included enough examples and details to get across my main impression and to bring my subject to life?
- Do the examples and details appeal to more than one of the senses (sight, hearing, smell, taste, and touch)?
- Have I arranged my examples and details logically, with transitions that help the reader follow the paragraph or essay?

Essay Form

1

I have worked in many places, from a basement-level machine shop to a cubicle in a tenth-floor insurance office. Now that I am in the construction industry, I want to sing the praises of one employment benefit that does not get enough attention: the views from my sky-high welding jobs have been more stunning than any seen through an office window.

From a platform at my latest job, on a high-rise, the streets below look like scenes from a miniature village. The cars and trucks—even the rushing people—remind me of my nephews' motorized toys. Sometimes, the breeze carries up to me one of the few reminders that what I see is real: the smell of sausage or roasting chestnuts from street vendors, the honking of taxis or the scream of sirens, the dizzying clouds of diesel smoke. Once, the streets below me were taken over for a fair, and during my lunch break, I sat on a beam and watched the scene below. I spotted the usual things—packs of people strolling by concession stands or game tents, and bands playing to crowds at different ends of the fair. As I finished my lunch, I saw two

2

small flames near the edge of one band stage, nothing burning, nothing to fear. It was, I soon realized, an acrobat carrying two torches. I watched her climb high and walk a rope, juggling the torches as the crowd looked up and I looked down, fascinated.

Even more impressive are the sights from an oil rig. Two years ago, I worked on a rig in Prudhoe Bay, Alaska, right at the water's edge. In the long days of summer, I loved to watch the changing light in the sky and on the water: bright to darker blue as the hours passed, and at day's end, a dying gold. At the greatest heights I could see white dots of ships far out at sea, and looking inland, I might spot musk ox or bears roaming in the distance. In the long winter dark, we worked by spotlights, which blotted the views below. But I still remember one time near nightfall when the spotlights suddenly flashed off. As my eyes adjusted, a crowd of caribou emerged below like ghosts. They snuffled the snow for food, oblivious to us.

To me, the most amazing views are those from bridges high over rivers. In 2006, I had the

3

privilege of briefly working on one of the tallest bridge-observatories in the world, over the Penobscot River in Maine. As many tourists now do, I reached the height of the observatory's top deck, 437 feet. Unlike them, however, my visits were routine and labor-intensive, giving me little time to appreciate the beauty all around me. But on clear days, during breaks and at the end of our shift, my coworkers and I would admire the wide, sapphire-colored river as it flowed to Penobscot Bay. Looking south, we would track the Maine coast's winding to the Camden Hills. Looking east, we would spot Acadia National Park, the famous Mount Desert Island offshore in the mist. Each sight made up a panoramic view that I will never forget.

My line of work roots me in no one place, and it has a generous share of discomforts and dangers. But there are many reasons I would never trade it for another, and one of the biggest is the height from which it lets me see the world. For stretches of time, I feel nearly super human.

A Introductory paragraph
B Thesis statement
C Topic sentence 1 (first example)
D Topic sentence 2 (second example)
E Topic sentence 3 (third example)
F Concluding paragraph

Analysis of Sample Paragraph:

Sample rubric

Element	Grading criteria	Point: Comment
Appropriateness	• Did the student follow the assignment directions?	_/5:
Main idea	• Does the paper clearly state a strong main idea in a complete sentence?	_/10:
Support	• Is the main idea developed with specific support, including specific details and examples? • Is there enough support to make the main idea evident to the reader? • Is all the support directly related to the main idea?	_/10:
Organization	• Is the writing logically organized? • Does the student use transitions (*also, for example, sometimes,* and so on) to move the reader from one point to another?	_/10:
Conclusion	• Does the conclusion remind the reader of the main idea? • Does it make an observation based on the support?	_/5:
Grammar	• Is the writing free of the four most serious errors? (See Chapters 16–19.) • Is the sentence structure clear? • Does the student choose words that clearly express his or her meaning? • Are the words spelled correctly? • Is the punctuation correct?	_/10:
		TOTAL POINTS: _/50

Read and Analyze Description

Reading examples of description will help you write your own. The first two examples are by students; one is a shorter paragraph, and the second is a longer essay. In the third example, the Profile of Success, college police Chief James Roy shows how he uses description in a crime scene report. Last is an example of a professional description essay by Oscar Hijuelos. As you read, pay attention to the vocabulary, and answer the questions in the margin. They will help you read critically.

Student Description Paragraph

Alessandra Cepeda

Bird Rescue

When the owner opened the empty storage unit, we could not believe that any living creature could have survived under such horrible conditions. The inside was complete darkness, with no windows and no ventilation. The air hit us with the smell of rot and decay. A flashlight revealed three birds, quiet and huddled in the back corner. They were quivering and looked sickly. Two of the birds had injured wings, hanging from them uselessly at odd angles, obviously broken. They were exotic birds that should have had bright and colorful feathers, but the floor of the unit was covered in the feathers they had molted. We entered slowly and retrieved the abused birds. I cried at how such beautiful and helpless creatures had been mistreated. We adopted two of them, and our Samantha is now eight years old, with beautiful green feathers topped off with a brilliant blue and red head. She talks, flies, and is a wonderful pet who is dearly loved and, I admit, very spoiled. She deserves it after such a rough start to her life.

Read to Write
What effect does the author's addition of "I admit" have for the reader?

Read to Write: Annotate

1. Double-underline the topic sentence.
2. Underline the sensory details (sight, sound, smell, taste, texture) that create the main impression.

Think Critically

1. What main impression does the writer create?
2. Does the paragraph have the Four Basics of Good Description (p. 151)? Why or why not?

Student Description Essay

Brian Healy

First Day in Fallujah

Brian Healy served in Iraq and later pursued a degree in business management at Florida Community College. His descriptive essay shows readers what it is like to be in a war zone, and for this reason, some of the images he presents may be disturbing.

Although a typical writing process includes submitting a piece to several rounds of revision, Healy decided to "revise this essay as little as possible." He says, "I felt that given the topic, I should go with what I first wrote so that it would show more dirty truth than be polished to perfection." He values the role of emotion in writing and exhorts others not to "write for the sake of writing, [but to] write because you are passionate about it."

Predict What type of experience will Healy be describing?

wasteland: an area that is uncultivated and barren or devastated by natural disasters or war
squandered: wasted; not used to good advantage

Read to Write
What specific sounds, sights, and feelings does Healy use when describing transportation? Why does he want the reader to be able to feel like they are sharing this experience with him?

Reflect Have you ever had an experience where you were anxious about something because you did not know what was about to happen? What did it feel like? Use your five senses to describe.

The year was 2004, and I was a young, 21-year-old U.S. Marine corporal on my second tour of Iraq. I had been in the country for five months and was not enjoying it any more than I had the first time. From the first time I set foot in Iraq, I perceived it as a foul-smelling wasteland where my youth and, as I would soon find out, my innocence were being squandered. I had been in a number of firefights, roadside bomb attacks, and mortar and rocket attacks; therefore, I had thought I had seen it all. So when the word came down that my battalion was going to Fallujah to drive through the center of the city, I was as naïve as a child on the first day of school. The lesson of that first day would be taught with blood, sweat, and tears, learned through pain and suffering, and never forgotten.

2   At 2:00 in the morning on November 10, the voice of my commander pierced the night: "Mount up!" Upon hearing these words, I boarded the Amtrak transport. I heard a loud "clank, clank," the sound of metal hitting metal as the ramp closed and sealed us in. Sitting shoulder to shoulder, we had no more room to move than sardines in a pitch-dark can. The diesel fumes choked our lungs and burned our throats. There was a sudden jolt as the metal beast began to move, and with each bump and each turn, I was thrown from side to side inside the beast's belly with only the invisible bodies of my comrades to steady myself. I thought back to my childhood, to a time of carefree youth. I thought how my father would tell me how I was the cleanest of his sons. I chuckled as I thought, "If only he could see me now, covered in sweat and dirt and five days away from my last shower."

3   I was violently jerked back into the present with three thunderous explosions on the right side of the Amtrak vehicle. We continued to move faster and faster with more intensity and urgency than before. My heart was racing, pounding as if it were trying to escape from my chest when we came to a screeching halt.

4   With the same clank that sealed us in, the ramp dropped and released us from our can. I ran out of the Amtrak nearly tripping on the ramp. There was no moon, no streetlight, nothing to pierce the blanket of night. Therefore,

seeing was almost completely out of the question. However, what was visible was a scene that I will never forget. The massive craters from our bombs made it seem as if we were running on the surface of the moon. More disturbing were the dead bodies of those enemies hit with the bombs. Their bodies were strewn about in a frenzied manner: a leg or arm here, torso there, a head severed from its body. Trying to avoid stepping on them was impossible. Amid all this and the natural "fog of war," we managed to get our bearings and move toward our objective. We were able to take the entrance to a government complex located at the center of the city, and we did so in fine style. "Not so tough," we all thought. We would not have to wait long until we would find out how insanely foolish we were.

5   As the sun began to rise, there were no morning prayers, no loudspeakers, and no noise at all. This, of course, was odd since we had become accustomed to the sounds of Iraq in the morning. However, this silence did not last long and was shattered as the enemy released hell's wrath upon us. The enemy was relentless in its initial assault but was unable to gain the advantage and was slowly pushed back.

6   As the day dragged on, the enemy fought us in an endless cycle of attack and retreat. There was no time to relax as rocket-propelled grenades whistled by our heads time and time again. Snipers' bullets skipped off the surface of the roof we were on. While some bullets tore through packs, radios, boots, and clothing, a lucky few found their mark and ripped through flesh like a hot knife through butter.

7   Suddenly, there was a deafening crack as three 82-millimeter mortars rained upon us, throwing me to the ground. The dust blacked out the sun and choked my lungs. I began to rise only to be thrown back down by a rocket-propelled grenade whizzing just overhead, narrowly missing my face. At this point, it seemed clear to me that there was no end to this enemy. In the windows, out the doorways, through alleyways, and down streets, they would run. We would kill one and another would pop up in his stead, as if some factory just out of sight was producing more and more men to fight us.

8   As the sun fell behind the horizon, the battle, which had so suddenly started, ended just as swiftly. The enemy, like moths to light, were nowhere to be seen. The rifles of the Marines, which were so active that day, were silent now. We were puzzled as to why it was so quiet. My ears were still ringing from that day's events when the order came down to hole up for the night. There was no sleep for me that night; the events of the day made sure of that. I sat there that cold November night not really thinking of anything. I just sat in a trance, listening to small firefights of the battle that were still raging: a blast of machine gun fire, tracer rounds, and air strikes. Artillery flying through the air gave the appearance of a laser light show. Explosions rattling the earth lit my comrades' faces. As I looked over at them, I did not see my friends from earlier in the day; instead, I was looking at old men who were wondering what the next day would bring. I wondered if I would survive the next day.

9   The battle for Fallujah would rage on for another three weeks. The Marines of the First Battalion Eighth Marine Regiment would continue to fight with courage and honor. As each day of the battle passed, I witnessed new horrors and acts of bravery, of which normal men are not capable. However, none of those days would have the impact on me that that first day did.

Read to Write
How does Healy create suspense and prepare the reader for what comes next?

fog of war: a term describing the general uncertainty that soldiers experience during military operations

relentless: steady; persistent; unyielding

Read to Write
Healy takes a lot of time to describe the evening, the day, and the afternoon. Why does he do this? What may be about to happen?

Reflect Healy says that his friends had become "old men" in one day. How did that happen? What caused it?

tracer rounds: ammunition containing a substance that causes bullets or rounds to leave a trail

Reflect What effect does this essay have on you?

Reflect Have you ever had an experience that made you feel frightened or overwhelmed? What did you do to work through that situation or try to deal with it?

Summarize What particular ideas went through Healey's mind as he found himself in the middle of the firefight?

10   The battle is over, but for the men who were there, it will never end. It is fought every day in their heads and in voices of friends long gone, all the while listening to the screams and taunts of people who know nothing of war but would call these men terrorists.

Read to Write: Annotate

1. Underline the sensory details. Do these details appeal to sight, sound, smell, touch, or taste?

2. Circle any transitional words or phrases Healy uses.

3. Double underline any comparisons Healy uses.

Think Critically

1. What is the main idea of Healy's essay?

2. Is Healy's paper organized by space, time, or importance?

3. Who is Healy's intended audience? How do you know?

4. Healy said that he wanted to "show more dirty truth" than present an essay that is "polished to perfection." Did he accomplish this purpose? Explain.

5. Does this essay have the Four Basics of Good Description? Explain.

Workplace Description

The following report is a hypothetical example similar to the descriptive reports Roy writes on a regular basis. The people and places mentioned in the report are not real people or places.

Description: Malicious Wounding

At 03:20 a.m. I responded to a call that reported a fight and gunshots. When I arrived in the area, several people in the roadway pointed across a field to a mobile home on Yancey Drive. A woman, Ginny Pyle, was walking around a car in front of the mobile home and shouting. Two men, later identified as Jerry Smythe and his father Willie Smythe, were sitting on the porch of the mobile home, and two other men were on the ground. I approached them and saw Gary Pyle Sr. on top of his son, Gary Pyle Jr., holding him down on the ground. Pyle Sr. yelled, "Arrest him! He's drunk and out of control." Pyle Jr. was bleeding from his nose and had small bloody scrapes on his arms. A strong odor of alcohol was on his breath, and he exhibited blood shot eyes, slurred speech, and unsteady balance. Deputy White arrested Pyle Jr. for being drunk in public.

When I walked back to the mobile home, Jerry Smythe said, "I've been shot." I noticed two bloody wounds above and below his right knee. Smythe claimed he was sleeping on his couch when Pyle Jr. shot him through the window of the

Profile of Success
Description in the Real World

COURTESY OF JAMES ROY

Background   I joined the Marine Corps immediately after graduating from High School and served for four very eventful years. Since joining the Marines I had the pleasure of traveling to many parts of Europe, Africa, Asia, and South America. At the age of thirty-five I was offered a position as a deputy sheriff in my hometown; a choice I gladly accepted. My success in law enforcement led to numerous promotions from patrol supervisor to investigator and I now serve as a chief of police at a community college.

College   Lord Fairfax Community College

Employer   Lord Fairfax Community College Police Department

Writing at work   I learned very quickly how important writing is to my position as a law enforcement officer. Our reports are used in criminal and civil cases that many times have serious, long-lasting, and often life-changing outcomes for victims, suspects, and witnesses. These reports must be written accurately and articulately to convey the facts and circumstances of the case for the courts and prosecutors to do their job. Learning to write well has given me the confidence to present cases before judges, juries, and the public.

James Roy
Chief of Police
Lord Fairfax Community College

front door of his mobile home. The front door window was approximately 10 inches by 10 inches and was broken, with most of the broken glass lying on the inside of the doorway. Blood was mingled with broken glass on the porch.

I spoke with Pyle Jr., who was handcuffed and sitting in the back of Deputy White's patrol vehicle. I read him his Miranda rights and then asked, "Where is the gun?" Pyle Jr. laughed and said, "You'll never find it." Deputy White transported Pyle Jr. to the county jail, and Jerry Smythe was transported to the hospital at 03:30 a.m. Detective Gomez arrived on location at 04:14 a.m. to process the scene.

Read to Write: Annotate

1. Underline the supporting details in this paragraph. What senses do these details appeal to?

2. Circle the transitions Roy has used. How is the piece organized?

Think Critically

1. What is your main impression of the scene and of the incident?

2. What is Roy's purpose? Who is the intended audience?

3. Unlike other descriptive pieces in this chapter, Roy's description does not use comparisons. Given his audience and purpose, why do you think this might be the case?

Professional Description Essay

Oscar Hijuelos

Memories of New York City Snow

Oscar Hijuelos, the son of Cuban immigrants, was born in New York City in 1951. After receiving undergraduate and master's degrees from the City University of New York, he took a job at an advertising firm and wrote fiction at night. Since then, he has published numerous novels. His first, *The Mambo Kings Play Songs of Love* (1989), was awarded the Pulitzer Prize for fiction, making Hijuelos the first Hispanic writer to receive this honor. His most recent novels include *A Simple Habana Melody* (2002), *Dark Dude* (2008), and *Beautiful Maria of My Soul* (2010). Hijuelos has also published a memoir, *Thoughts without Cigarettes* (2011).

> **Predict** Why might snow be significant to the author's father and godfather?

The following essay was taken from the anthology *Metropolis Found* (2003). In it, Hijuelos describes a New York City winter from the perspective of new immigrants, noting the emotions that the season inspired in them.

> **Circa:** [taken] around

> **Oriente Province:** a former province of Cuba, in the eastern part of the country

For immigrants of my parents' generation, who had first come to New York City from the much warmer climate of Cuba in the mid-1940s, the very existence of snow was a source of fascination. A black-and-white photograph that I have always loved, circa 1948, its surface cracked like that of a thawing ice-covered pond, features my father, Pascual, and my godfather, Horacio, fresh up from Oriente Province, posing in a snow-covered meadow in Central Park. Decked out in long coats, scarves, and black-rimmed hats, they are holding, in their be-gloved hands, a huge chunk of hardened snow. Trees and their straggly witch's hair branches, glimmering with ice and frost, recede into the distance behind them. They stand on a field of whiteness, the two men seemingly afloat in midair, as if they were being held aloft by the magical substance itself.

2 That they bothered to have this photograph taken—I suppose to send back to family in Cuba—has always been a source of enchantment for me. That something so common to winters in New York would strike them as an object of exotic admiration has always spoken volumes about the newness—and innocence—of their immigrants' experience. How thrilling it all must have seemed to them, for their New York was so very different from the small town surrounded by farms in eastern Cuba that they hailed from. Their New York was a fanciful and bustling city of endless sidewalks and unimaginably high buildings; of great bridges and twisting outdoor elevated train trestles; of walkup tenement houses with myste-riously dark basements, and subways that burrowed through an underworld of girded tunnels; of dancehalls, burlesque houses, and palatial department stores with their complement of Christmas Salvation Army Santa Clauses on every street corner. Delightful and perilous, their New York was a city of incredibly loud noises, of police and air raid sirens and factory whistles and subway rum-ble; a city where people sometimes shushed you for speaking Spanish in a public

> **girded:** reinforced
> **burlesque houses:** theaters that offer live, often humorous performances and/or striptease acts
> **palatial:** palace-like
> **perilous:** dangerous

place, or could be unforgiving if you did not speak English well or seemed to be of a different ethnic background. (My father was once nearly hit by a garbage can that had been thrown off the rooftop of a building as he was walking along La Salle Street in upper Manhattan.)

3   Even so, New York represented the future. The city meant jobs and money. Newly arrived, an aunt of mine went to work for Pan Am; another aunt, as a Macy's saleslady. My own mother, speaking nary a word of English, did a stint in the garment district as a seamstress. During the war some family friends, like my godfather, were eventually drafted, while others ended up as factory laborers. Landing a job at the Biltmore Men's Bar, my father joined the hotel and restaurant workers' union, paid his first weekly dues, and came home one day with a brand-new white chef's toque in hand. Just about everybody found work, often for low pay and ridiculously long hours. And while the men of that generation worked a lot of overtime, or a second job, they always had their day or two off. Dressed to the hilt, they'd leave their uptown neighborhoods and make an excursion to another part of the city—perhaps to one of the grand movie palaces of Times Square or to beautiful Central Park, as my father and godfather and their ladies had once done, in the aftermath of a snowfall.

4   Snow, such as it can only fall in New York City, was not just about the cold and wintry differences that mark the weather of the north. It was about a purity that would descend upon the grayness of its streets like a heaven of silence, the city's complexity and bustle abruptly subdued. But as beautiful as it could be, it was also something that provoked nostalgia; I am certain that my father would miss Cuba on some bitterly cold days. I remember that whenever we were out on a walk and it began to snow, my father would stop and look up at the sky, with wonderment—what he was seeing I don't know. Perhaps that's why to this day my own associations with a New York City snowfall have a mystical connotation, as if the presence of snow really meant that some kind of inaccessible divinity had settled his breath upon us.

nary: not even

stint: brief job

Read to Write
What main impression do these descriptions of the city create?

toque: hat

Reflect What types of weather do you associate with particular feelings or moods?

nostalgia: a longing for something from the past

connotation: meaning or association

inaccessible divinity: unreachable god

Read to Write: Annotate

1. Underline the sensory details. Do these details appeal to the readers' sight, sound, smell, touch, or taste?

2. Circle the transitions.

3. Put a check mark by all descriptions that include proper nouns. How does use of these nouns help the writer create an impression?

Think Critically

1. Does the essay create a clear picture of New York City in the winter? Why or why not?

2. Why is the last sentence in paragraph 2 in parentheses? What is the writer suggesting about New York in this comment?

Respond

1. Describe a place that is important to you or associated with significant memories. It might be a city, a favorite park, a friend's or relative's home, or a vacation spot.

2. Describe an outdoor scene from your favorite season. You might work from a personal photograph taken during that season.

3. Describe a person who has played a major role in your life. Try to include sensory details that go beyond the person's appearance. For instance, you might describe the sight of his or her usual surroundings, the sound of his or her voice, or the texture of a favorite piece of clothing.

Grammar for Description

One way to appeal to a reader's senses is to use descriptive adjectives. Adjectives are words that describe or modify nouns: adjectives can specify age, size, color, condition, appearance, and many other features. In addition, writers can make adjectives more specific by using adverbs: words that modify adjectives and often end in -ly. In the following sentence from Oscar Hijuelos's essay, the adjectives are italicized, and the adverbs are underlined.

> Their New York was a *fanciful* and *bustling* city of *endless* sidewalks and <u>unimaginably</u> *high* buildings; of *great* bridges and *twisting outdoor elevated* train trestles; of *walkup* tenement houses with <u>mysteriously</u> *dark* basements, and subways that burrowed through an underworld of *girded* tunnels; of dance-halls, *burlesque* houses, and *palatial* department stores with their complement of Christmas Salvation Army Santa Clauses on every street corner.

For more on adjectives and adverbs, see Chapter 21.

Write Your Own Description

In this section, you will write your own description based on one of the following assignments. For help, refer to the How to Write Description checklist on page 171.

Assignment Options: Writing about College, Work, and Everyday Life

Write a description paragraph or essay on one of the following topics or on one of your own choice.

College
- Describe the sights, sounds, smells, and tastes in the cafeteria or another popular spot on campus.
- Find a place where you can get a good view of your campus (for instance, a window on an upper floor of one of the buildings). Then, describe the scene using space order (p. 158).
- Think about a person who has made you feel at home or welcome on campus. Describe that person with specific examples and details to show why he or she made such an impression on you.

Work
- Describe your workplace, including as many sensory details as you can.
- Describe your boss or a colleague you work with closely. First, think of the main impression you get from this person. Then, choose details that would make your impression clear to readers.
- Have you ever worked with anyone who creates a mess in their office environment? If so, describe the person's workspace and/or messes in detail.

Everyday life
- Describe a favorite photograph, using as many details as possible. For a good example of a photograph description, see the first paragraph of Oscar Hijuelos's essay (p. 166).
- Describe a holiday celebration from your past, including as many sensory details as possible. Think back on the people who attended, the food served, the decorations, and so on.
- Visit an organization that serves your community, such as an animal shelter or a food pantry. During your visit, take notes about what you see. Later, write a detailed description of the scene.

Assignment Options Reading and Writing Critically

Complete one of the following assignments that ask you to apply the critical thinking, reading, and writing skills discussed in Chapter 1.

Writing Critically about Readings

Both Oscar Hijuelos's "Memories of New York City Snow" (p. 166) and Amy Tan's "Fish Cheeks" (p. 121) describe scenes from the past. Read or review both of these pieces, and then follow these steps:

1. **Summarize** Briefly summarize the works, listing major examples and details.
2. **Analyze** Tan uses humor to make her point, whereas Hijuelos's essay is more serious. Why do you think the authors might have chosen these different approaches?

Tip For a reminder of how to summarize, analyze, synthesize, and evaluate, see the Reading and Writing Critically box on page 17.

3. **Synthesize** Using examples from both Tan's and Hijuelos's essays and from your own experience, discuss the types of details that make certain things in our lives (such as an event or a photograph) so memorable.

4. **Evaluate** Which essay, Tan's or Hijuelos's, do you think is more effective? Why? In writing your evaluation, you might look back on your responses to step 2.

Writing about Images

Study the photographs below, and complete the following steps.

1. **Read each image** Ask yourself: what part of the photograph draws your attention the most, and why? What main impression does each picture create, and what details contribute to this impression? (For more information on reading images, see Chapter 1.)

2. **Write a description** Would you prefer the view from a home office or from a traditional office? Write a paragraph or essay that describes each photograph and explains the main impression it gives, or describe the view from your current workspace.

Writing to Solve a Problem

Read or review the discussion of problem solving in Chapter 1 (pp. 26–27). Then, consider the following problem:

An abandoned house on your street is a safety hazard for the children in the neighborhood. Although you and some of your neighbors have called the local board of health, nothing has been done. Finally, you and your neighbors decide to write to the mayor.

Assignment Working in a small group or on your own, write to the mayor describing why this house is a safety hazard. Thoroughly describe the house (outside and inside). Imagine a place that is not just ugly; it must also pose safety problems to children. You might start with the following sentence:

Not only is the abandoned house at 45 Main Street an eyesore, but it is also....

For a paragraph: Describe in detail one room on the first floor of the house or just the exterior you can see from the street.

For an essay: Describe in detail at least three rooms in the house or the exterior you can see if you walk entirely around the house.

CHECKLIST

How to Write Description

Steps	Details
☐ Narrow and explore your topic. See Chapter 3.	• Make the topic more specific. • Prewrite to get ideas about the narrowed topic.
☐ Write a topic sentence (paragraph) or thesis statement (essay). See Chapter 3.	• State what is most interesting, vivid, and important about your topic.
☐ Support your point. See Chapter 4.	• Come up with examples and details that create a main impression about your topic.
☐ Write a draft. See Chapter 5.	• Make a plan that puts examples in a logical order. • Include a topic sentence (paragraph) or thesis statement (essay) and all the supporting examples and details.
☐ Revise your draft. See Chapter 5.	• Make sure it has *all* the Four Basics of Good Description. • Make sure you include transitions to move readers smoothly from one detail to the next.
☐ Edit your revised draft. See Parts 3 through 6.	• Correct errors in grammar, spelling, word use, and punctuation.

Chapter Review

1. What is description?

2. What are the Four Basics of Good Description?

3. The topic sentence in a description paragraph or the thesis statement in a description essay includes what two elements?

4. How can writers make a description come alive for readers?

Reflect and Apply

1. Have you ever written or read description before? How does that experience confirm, contradict, or complicate what you have learned in this chapter?

2. Interview someone studying in your major or working in your career. What situations require reading or writing description in your major or career? For what purposes and audiences do people in this area write?

3. What was most difficult about your writing for this chapter? What do you want to do differently next time?

4. What was most successful about your writing for this chapter? What do you need to remember for next time?

9

Process Analysis
Writing That Explains How Things Happen

Understand What Process Analysis Is

Process analysis either explains how to do something (so that your readers can do it) or explains how something works (so that your readers can understand it).

> **Four Basics** of Good Process Analysis
>
> **1** It tells readers what process the writer wants them to know about and makes a point about it.
>
> **2** It presents the essential steps in the process.
>
> **3** It explains the steps in detail.
>
> **4** It presents the steps in a logical order (usually time order).

In the following paragraph, the numbers and colors correspond to the Four Basics of Good Process Analysis.

The poet Dana Gioia once said, "Art delights, instructs, consoles. It educates our emotions." **1** Closely observing paintings, sculpture, and other forms of visual art is a great way to have the type of experience that Gioia describes, and following a few basic steps will help you get the most from the experience. **2** First, choose an art exhibit that interests you. **3** You can find listings for exhibits on local museums' websites or in the arts section of a newspaper. Links on the websites or articles in a newspaper may give you more information about the exhibits, the

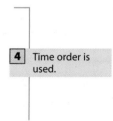 **4** Time order is used.

173

artists featured in them, and the types of work to be displayed. [2] Second, go to the museum with an open mind and, ideally, with a friend. [3] While moving through the exhibit, take time to examine each work carefully. As you do so, ask yourself questions: what is my eye most drawn to, and why? What questions does this work raise for me, and how does it make me feel? How would I describe it to someone over the phone? Ask your friend the same questions, and consider the responses. You might also consult an exhibit brochure for information about the featured artists and their works. [2] Finally, keep your exploration going after you have left the museum. [3] Go out for coffee or a meal with your friend. Trade more of your thoughts and ideas about the artwork, and discuss your overall impressions. If you are especially interested in any of the artists or their works, you might look for additional information or images on the Internet, or you might consult books at the library. Throughout the whole experience, put aside the common belief that only artists or cultural experts "get" art. The artist Eugène Delacroix described paintings as "a bridge between the soul of the artist and that of the spectator." Trust your ability to cross that bridge and come to new understandings.

You use process analysis in many situations:

College	In a science course, you explain photosynthesis.
Work	You write instructions to explain how to operate something (the copier, the fax machine).
Everyday life	You write out instructions for chores that must be completed while you are out of town.

In college, a writing assignment may ask you to *describe the process of doing something*, but you might also be asked to *describe the stages of something* or *explain how something works*. Whenever you need to identify and explain the steps or stages of anything, you will use process analysis.

For more information on understanding writing assignment prompts, see the Appendix, page 553.

First Basic: Main Idea in Process Analysis

A process analysis can have two purposes: to explain or to instruct. An **explanatory process analysis** explains how something works *so that readers can understand*. For example, a text that explains the circulatory system is an explanatory process analysis. An **instructional process analysis**, on the other hand, explains how to do something *so that readers can actually try the process themselves*. For example, a nursing textbook that explains how to take and record vital signs uses instructional process analysis to teach students to perform this task.

Regardless of the purpose, the main point in a process analysis is what the writer wants the readers to know about the process—its significance, expected results—or encouragement to try the process for themselves. To help you discover the main idea for your process analysis, complete the following sentence:

Main idea in   **What I want readers to know about this process is that . . .**
process analysis

Here is an example of a topic sentence for a paragraph:

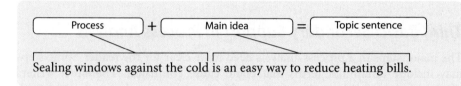

Sealing windows against the cold is an easy way to reduce heating bills.

Remember that the topic for an essay can be a little broader than one for a paragraph.

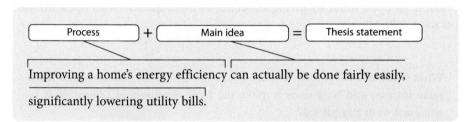

Improving a home's energy efficiency can actually be done fairly easily, significantly lowering utility bills.

Whereas the topic sentence focuses on just one method to improve energy efficiency, the thesis statement sets up a discussion of multiple methods.

Second Basic: Primary Support in Process Analysis

The paragraph and essay models on pages 178–179 use the topic sentence (paragraph) and thesis statement (essay) from the Main Idea section of this chapter. Both models include the support used in all writing about processes: the steps in the process (primary support) backed up by details about these steps (secondary support). In the essay model, however, the major support points (steps) are topic sentences for individual paragraphs.

When you are planning primary support, consider your audience and purpose to make sure you have included all the important steps. While some steps may seem too obvious to mention, readers who are not familiar with the process may not know what to do. Be careful to include all the information that a reader needs to understand or complete the process.

Read to Write To identify the main point when you are reading a process analysis, complete the following sentence: The most important thing about this process is that…

Tip Sometimes, the same main idea can be used for a paragraph and an essay, but the essay must develop this point in more detail. (See pp. 178–179.)

Think Critically To include all the necessary steps, writers must put themselves in the position of a reader. As you begin listing the steps, imagine someone you know who is not familiar with this process. Ask yourself: where is this person most likely to get confused during the process? Then make sure you have included all the necessary information to avoid this confusion.

> **PRACTICE 9–1** **Finding and Choosing the Essential Steps**
>
> For each of the following topics, write the essential steps in the order you would perform them.
>
> 1. Making (your favorite food) is simple.
>
> 2. I think I could teach anyone how to . . . .
>
> 3. Operating a . . . is . . . .

Third Basic: Secondary Support in Process Analysis

The major steps in a process analysis need to be clear for the reader. Some steps may include unfamiliar terms that could cause confusion. Therefore, writers often include definitions, descriptions of tools and materials, or examples with each step so that readers can follow the process easily. For example, the second step in the paragraph on page 174 tells readers to "go to the museum with an open mind." What does it mean to have an open mind at the museum? The writer explains an open mind by giving examples of three questions an open-minded person might ask:

What is my eye most drawn to, and why? What questions does this work raise for me, and how does it make me feel? How would I describe it to someone over the phone?

Tip If you have written a narration paragraph already, you will notice that narration and process analysis are alike in that they both usually present events or steps in time order—the order in which they occur. The difference is that narration reports what happened, whereas process analysis describes how to do something or how something works.

> **PRACTICE 9–2** **Adding Details to Essential Steps**
>
> Choose one of the topics from Practice 9–1. In the spaces that follow, first copy down that topic and the steps you wrote for it in Practice 9–1. Then, add a detail to each of the steps.
>
> Topic:
>
> Step 1:
>
>   Detail:
>
> Step 2:
>
>   Detail:

Step 3:

    Detail:

Step 4:

    Detail:

Fourth Basic: Organization in Process Analysis

Process analysis is usually organized by **time order** because it explains the steps of the process in the order in which they occur. This is the strategy used in the paragraph and essay models on pages 178–179.

    Transitions move readers smoothly from one step to the next.

Tip For more on time order, see page 74.

Common Transitions in Process Analysis

after	eventually	meanwhile	since
as	finally	next	soon
at last	first	now	then
before	last	once	when
during	later	second	while

Tip For more on using and punctuating these transitions, see Chapter 23.

> **PRACTICE 9–3**   **Using Transitions in Process Analysis**
>
> Read the paragraph that follows, and fill in the blanks with transitions.
>
>   Scientists have discovered that, like something from a zombie movie, a mind-controlling fungus attacks certain carpenter ants. _____, as if following the fungus's orders, the ants help their invader reproduce. The process begins when an ant is infected. _____, the ant begins to act strangely. For instance, instead of staying in its home high in the trees, it drops to the forest floor. _____ wandering, it searches for a cool, moist place. _____ the zombie-ant finds the right place, it clamps its jaws to a leaf and dies. _____, the fungus within the ant grows until it bursts from the insect's head, and more ants are infected. By studying this process, researchers may find better ways to control the spread of carpenter ants.

Paragraphs versus Essays in Process Analysis

For more on the important features of process analysis, see the Four Basics of Good Process Analysis on page 173.

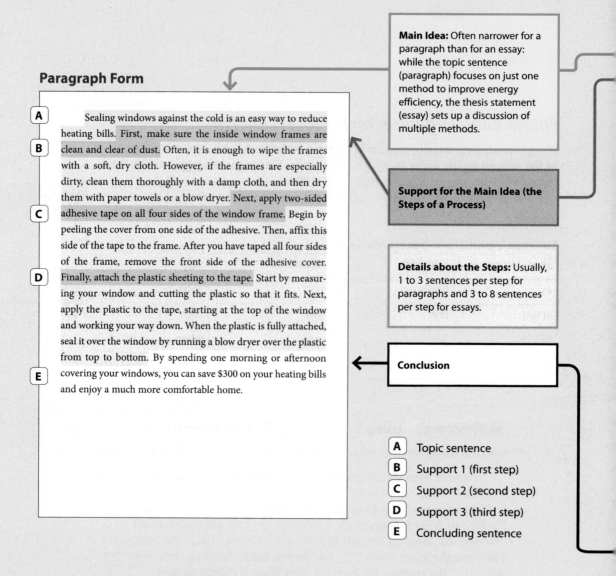

Paragraph Form

A   Sealing windows against the cold is an easy way to reduce heating bills. **B** First, make sure the inside window frames are clean and clear of dust. Often, it is enough to wipe the frames with a soft, dry cloth. However, if the frames are especially dirty, clean them thoroughly with a damp cloth, and then dry them with paper towels or a blow dryer. Next, apply two-sided **C** adhesive tape on all four sides of the window frame. Begin by peeling the cover from one side of the adhesive. Then, affix this side of the tape to the frame. After you have taped all four sides of the frame, remove the front side of the adhesive cover. **D** Finally, attach the plastic sheeting to the tape. Start by measuring your window and cutting the plastic so that it fits. Next, apply the plastic to the tape, starting at the top of the window and working your way down. When the plastic is fully attached, seal it over the window by running a blow dryer over the plastic from top to bottom. By spending one morning or afternoon **E** covering your windows, you can save $300 on your heating bills and enjoy a much more comfortable home.

Main Idea: Often narrower for a paragraph than for an essay: while the topic sentence (paragraph) focuses on just one method to improve energy efficiency, the thesis statement (essay) sets up a discussion of multiple methods.

Support for the Main Idea (the Steps of a Process)

Details about the Steps: Usually, 1 to 3 sentences per step for paragraphs and 3 to 8 sentences per step for essays.

Conclusion

A Topic sentence
B Support 1 (first step)
C Support 2 (second step)
D Support 3 (third step)
E Concluding sentence

Think Critically As You Write Process Analysis

Ask Yourself

- Have I included all the steps necessary for others to complete or understand the process?
- Have I organized the steps in chronological order and included appropriate transitions?

Essay Form

1

Many people are intimidated by the work necessary to make their homes more energy efficient, and they do not see it as a do-it-yourself job. **However, improving a home's energy efficiency can actually be done fairly easily, significantly lowering utility bills.** **A**

First, seal air leaks around windows and doors. To seal air leaks around windows, apply caulk between window frames and walls. Also, if you have old-fashioned windows that are not weather-proof, cover them with plastic before the cold temperatures set in. This process involves affixing two-sided adhesive tape to the window frames and then attaching plastic sheeting, which is sealed with the use of a blow dryer. Next, look for drafty spots around doors. Many air leaks at the top or sides of doors can be sealed with adhesive-backed foam strips. Leaks under doors can be stopped with foam draft guards. Alternatively, a rolled-up blanket, rug, or towel can keep the cold from coming in. All of these measures can save up to $600 per season on heating bills. **B**

Second, install water-saving showerheads and faucet aerators. These fixtures are inexpensive and are

2

available in most hardware stores. Also, they are easy to install. First, unscrew the old shower or faucet head. Then, follow the package instructions for affixing the new showerhead or aerator. In some cases, you might have to use pipe tape or a rubber washer to ensure a good seal. After this step, run the water to make sure there are no leaks. If you find any leaks, use pliers to tighten the seal. In time, you will discover that the new showerheads and aerators will cut your water usage and the cost of water heating by up to 50 percent. **C**

Finally, look for other places where energy efficiency could be increased. One simple improvement is to replace traditional light bulbs with compact fluorescent bulbs, which use up to 80 percent less energy. Also, make sure your insulation is as good as it can be. Many utilities now offer free assessments of home insulation, identifying places where it is missing or inadequate. In some cases, any necessary insulation improvements may be subsidized by the utilities or by government agencies. It is well worth considering such improvements, which, in the case of poorly **D**

3

insulated homes, can save thousands of dollars a year, quickly covering any costs. Although some people prefer to have professionals blow insulating foam into their walls, it is not difficult to add insulation to attics, where a large amount of heat can be lost during cold months.

Taking even one of these steps can make a significant financial difference in your life and also reduce your impact on the environment. My advice, though, is to improve your home's energy efficiency as much as possible, even if it means doing just a little at a time. The long-term payoff is too big to pass up. **E**

A Thesis statement
B Topic sentence 1 (first step)
C Topic sentence 2 (second step)
D Topic sentence 3 (third step)
E Concluding paragraph

Evaluate Process Analysis

To become a more successful writer, it is important not only to understand the Four Basics of Good Process Analysis but to read and evaluate examples as well. In this section, you will have the opportunity to use a sample rubric to analyze or evaluate the samples of process analysis writing provided. By using this rubric, you will gain a better understanding of how the components of good process analysis work together to create a successful paragraph or essay. Additionally, reading examples of process analysis will help you write your own.

Read the following sample process analysis paragraph. Using the Four Basics of Good Process Analysis and the sample grading rubric, decide what grade this paragraph would earn. Explain your answer.

Assignment Please write a paragraph about how to take better notes when reading and studying. You should make sure that your instructions are careful and deliberate: what steps should be taken, what is involved in each step, and in what order a student should proceed.

Learning to take effective notes in class can be very easy once a student understands what they need to do. Too often, a student will start taking notes as they read. This becomes a problem because the student does not know what the main idea or most significant ideas of the reading are because they have not read the entire assignment yet. In order to avoid extra work or overly lengthy notes it is best to preview the reading: look at the title, any subheadings, and any bold or italicized words. After previewing, read the entire article from start to finish. Once you have completed those two steps, highlight or underline. In this way, your notes will be clearer and easier to read. It is also less likely they will contain too much extra information.

Analysis of Sample Paragraph

Sample rubric

Element	Grading criteria	Point: Comment
Appropriateness	• Did the student follow the assignment directions?	_/5:
Main Idea	• Does the paper clearly state a strong main idea in a complete sentence?	__/10:
Support	• Is the main idea developed with specific support, including specific details and examples? • Is there enough support to make the main idea evident to the reader? • Is all the support directly related to the main idea?	_/10:
Organization	• Is the writing logically organized? • Does the student use transitions (*also, for example, sometimes,* and so on) to move the reader from one point to another?	_/10:
Conclusion	• Does the conclusion remind the reader of the main idea? • Does it make an observation based on the support?	_/5:
Grammar	• Is the writing free of the four most serious errors? (See Chapters 16–19.) • Is the sentence structure clear? • Does the student choose words that clearly express his or her meaning? • Are the words spelled correctly? • Is the punctuation correct?	__/10:
		TOTAL POINTS: __/50

Read and Analyze Process Analysis

Reading examples of process analysis will help you write your own. The first two examples of process analysis are a paragraph from a student writer and a student essay. In the Profile of Success, editorial assistant Paola Garcia-Muniz explains steps for submitting reprint corrections for a textbook, and the final example is a professional essay by Samantha Levine-Finley. As you read, pay attention to the vocabulary and the questions in the margin. They will help you read critically.

Student Process Analysis Paragraph

Charlton Brown

Buying a Car at an Auction

Predict What preparation do you think Brown will say buyers need before attending a car auction?

legitimate: lawful; genuine; real

savvy: knowledgeable; well informed

thorough: complete; detailed

Summarize What steps are necessary to buy a car at auction?

Buying a car at an auction is a good way to get a cheap car, but buyers need to be prepared. First, decide what kind of vehicle you want to buy. Then, find a local auction. Scams are common, though, so be careful. Three top sites that are legitimate are Gov-Auctions.org, Carauctioninc.com, and Seizecars.com. When you have found an auction and a vehicle you are interested in, become a savvy buyer. Make sure you know the car's actual market value. You can find this out from Edmunds, Kelly Blue Book, or NADA (the National Automobile Dealers Association). Because bidding can become like a competition, decide on the highest bid you will make, and stick to that. Do not get drawn into the competition. On the day of the auction, get to the auction early so that you can look at the actual cars. If you do not know about cars yourself, bring someone who does with you to the auction so that he or she can examine the car. Next, begin your thorough examination. Check the exterior; especially look for any signs that the car has been in an accident. Also, check the windshield because many states will not give an inspection sticker to cars with any damage to the windshield. Check the interior and try the brakes. Start the engine and listen to how it sounds. Check the heat and air conditioning, the CD player, and all other functions. As a final check before the bidding, look at the car's engine and transmission. Finally, get ready to place your bid, and remember, do not go beyond the amount you settled on earlier. Good luck!

Read to Write: Annotate

1. Double-underline the topic sentence.
2. Underline the major steps.
3. Circle the words that signal when Brown moves from one step to the next.

Think Critically

1. Paraphrase Brown's main point.

2. Does Brown's paragraph follow the Four Basics of Good Process Analysis (p. 173)? Why or why not?

Student Process Analysis Essay

Katie Horn

A Beginner's Guide to Movie Night

Katie Horn is a community college graduate currently pursuing a BA in professional writing. She is the lead tutor at a college writing center, where she helps students develop the skills they need to communicate effectively in academics and in the workplace. Horn loves taking on new challenges in writing, both in fiction and nonfiction, and enjoys the imagination and creativity of storytelling as well as sharing ideas and information in nonfiction writing.

Going to the movies presents many choices, from which theater and which snacks to which seats. The possibilities can be overwhelming, but by following a few simple steps, you can enjoy the ultimate movie experience.

2   The first thing to consider is which theater to visit. Be careful to choose a location that spells its name "theater" and not "theatre." Theatres are places full of hoity-toity people in uncomfortable shoes watching foreign films (for the cultural experience, not just the nudity). Theaters, on the other hand, offer thrilling action sequences and heart-wrenching love stories on forty-foot screens. Beyond that, any establishment that is nearby, offers stadium seating, and has an Ice machine should work.

3   Next, you must select a movie from the films currently available at the theater you have chosen. Most theaters will have at least one action movie, one sappy romantic movie, and one family-friendly movie. If you are on a date, keep in mind that the potential for future dates hinges on your movie selection. For those hoping to indulge in mid-movie snuggling, a film from the romance or suspense genre is likely to encourage couples to get a little closer together—albeit for quite different reasons. If these are sold out, you may choose to view a comedy, which can be very useful in assessing if your date has a sense of humor.

4   The next step is to purchase movie munchies. Traditionally speaking, popcorn is the ultimate movie snack and, therefore, must be included in every movie menu. Popcorn can be supplemented by beverages and candies, including classics like Goobers and Junior Mints and newfangled treats such as chocolate-covered cookie dough bites and Sour Skittles. The alternative to purchasing candy at the theater is to smuggle it in, which requires skills carefully honed over a lifetime of movie going. Beginners should practice their smuggling techniques during the winter, when large

Predict What process will Horn describe? Who might be interested in this topic?

Read to Write What does Horn's description of theatres tell you about her audience and purpose? What specific words help you answer this question?

Reflect What other factors determine your choice of a movie? Do you think that Horn should have included these, too?

Reflect What do you think of Horn's advice? Is the last line meant to be taken literally? Why or why not?

coats and awkward bulges arouse less suspicion. With a little practice, anyone can successfully sneak a bag of M&M's into the movies. Over time, you may develop the skills of hiding snacks in skimpier clothing or managing more impressive snacks, such as ice cream or fried mozzarella sticks.

5   Once snacks are in hand, the next step is to select a seat. Begin with a quick scan of the patrons who have already been seated. It is important to avoid small children (who are messy), people with cell phones (which will buzz during the movie), and tall people (because they block the screen). Having avoided these hazards, head toward the back of the theater, avoiding the social stigma that comes with sitting in the front. The back rows should be surveyed for spilled soda and stray candies—getting stuck in a half-chewed gumdrop ruins the movie experience. Then test the seat to determine the viewing angle. While the center seats of each row generally offer prime views, moviegoers with small bladders may prefer easier access to the bathrooms.

6   After choosing a seat, settle in and watch the previews. As other patrons trickle in and fill the remaining seats, the wise moviegoer will protect nearby seats from tall people and anyone who has an obnoxious laugh. You can accomplish this with outright lies, such as "this seat is saved," or with more subtle methods, such as balancing jackets or purses across the seats. As a last resort, you can make yourself unappealing to potential neighbors by using the seatbacks as a footrest, chewing open-mouthed, and laughing noisily—annoying behaviors that must be halted as soon as the movie begins.

7   Once these skills have been mastered, anyone can be a successful moviegoer. Some may even move on to become movie buffs, which is a noble aspiration indeed. It takes hard work, dozens of movies, and gallons of popcorn, but eventually these valiant film aficionados will bask in the glow of their movie buff success. As for the rest of us, we will still be sneaking around with licorice in our shoes.

Read to Write
Why does Horn put some comments in parentheses in this paragraph?

Read to Write
Do Horn's examples in this paragraph confirm or change your understanding of her target audience?

Reflect Horn has mentioned two behaviors some consider wrong: breaking rules and lying. Do you think these are acceptable in this context?

aspiration: goal or hope

valiant: courageous

aficionados: experts

Read to Write: Annotate

1. Underline the steps in Horn's process.

2. Circle all the transition words Horn uses to move readers through the process. Pay attention to the punctuation she uses with her transition words.

3. Note any proper nouns (names with capital letters) Horn uses. How do these words help her readers follow the steps?

Think Critically

1. What is Horn's thesis? Paraphrase it.

2. What is Horn's tone in this essay? Is she completely serious? How do you know?

3. Does this essay include all of the Four Basics of Good Process Analysis? Explain.

For more information on citations, please see the **Appendix: Citing Research Sources In MLA Style** at the end of the book.

Workplace Essay: Submitting Reprint Corrections

PLEASE, submit corrections as soon as you are made aware of them. Do NOT wait until a reprint is called for your title; titles often come up for reprint on just 24-hour notice, and then it is too late to make the corrections.

Profile of Success
Workplace Process Analysis

Paola Garcia-Muniz
Editorial Assistant

PAOLA GARCIA-MUNIZ

Bio When it comes to my family, we are truly a salad bowl. I have a mother and a father, a stepmother, a brother, a stepsister, and a brilliant younger half-sister. Although we aren't perfect and not every moment has been colorful, they have pushed me, challenged me, and loved me unconditionally all the way through my life. They are a huge part of who and where I am today. Leaving them and my home island of Puerto Rico to attend Fairfield University in Connecticut was the hardest decision of my life. Regardless of the sacrifices I've made, they were there cheering me on as I completed a bachelor's in Creative Writing with a minor in psychology. I graduated believing that my dream was to became a trade publishing editor or a well-known writer myself, and then I stepped foot into the Macmillan Learning offices in Boston. Having spent more than thirteen years of my life in a classroom as a student and having the teacher's perspective from my step-mother, who teaches elementary school back home, I wasn't surprised when I fell in love with educational publishing.

Degree BA, Fairfield University

Employer Macmillan Learning

Writing at work My daily life in publishing is all about writing. I send and answer emails throughout the day, communicating with professors, editors, and authors about different aspects of our textbooks.

Professionalism in email writing is a key skill. I also edit manuscript pages for our titles in development, which means I have to think about how students will respond to each example, sentence, or chapter. Editing manuscript means I make sure the writing and its placement is clear and accessible.

At the beginning, even though I am fluent in both English and Spanish, I often doubted myself and my writing because English is still my second language. However, as time went by and more emails were drafted, pages edited, corrections made, suggestions received, and compliments appreciated, I understood that my dual-language skills are a gift rather than an obstacle. They allow me to look at words and interpret them for two different communities. I am working for those native English speakers and making sure that their native language lives up to its potential, as well as checking that it is accessible to those non-English speakers who are trying to grasp the language or strengthen their understanding of it.

Once I am outside of the office walls I text, help edit my siblings' and friends' school papers, and work on my own personal writing. In other words, the only part of my day that does not involve writing—or reading other people's writing— is when I am sound asleep; even then, I may dream about writing, too!

Workplace Process Analysis

Reprints include changes to any of the following:
- Interior Text
- Covers
- Custom Titles
- Card Inserts
- Access Cards

A **compositor** is the person who takes the original manuscript files of a book and converts them into the designed book that will go to the printer.

A **Development Editor** is the person who works with both the author(s) of a book and with his or her publishing colleagues to help craft a book project from start to finish. He or she not only edits content, but also provides feedback on ideas, structure, etc. and serves as the project manager to keep each book on track for publication.

Make sure that the following are clearly marked on every page:

- Author
- Title
- Edition
- Split/Version
- ISBN

The preferred method for transmitting reprints is via PDF files, which should be emailed to the Assistant Content Project Manager and the Senior Managing Editor.

Ideally, these PDFs should be pulled from the PDF book files and marked up using Adobe editing tools.

Please DO NOT submit handwritten corrections, as the compositor a) has trouble finding these and b) cannot always read the handwriting. Handwritten corrections can cause delays with the printing of the books. Although authors sometimes submit handwritten corrections, the Development Editor should incorporate these into electronic mark ups.

Your correction MUST show the whole page where the correction occurs. It MUST be from the correct version (i.e., full versus brief). And it MUST be from the final version of the document. If there was a large reprint correction made (for example, due to an update of the MLA, Chicago, or APA formatting styles), please track down these final pages, because often content and reflow has drastically changed. If PDF book files cannot be located, the book pages may be scanned, but mark-up should be done electronically.

Multiple pages of corrections can be submitted as a single PDF file, but please remove any unneeded pages (don't submit PDFs of an entire chapter if only three pages in that chapter have corrections; send only the three corrected pages). For special reprints like updates to the MLA, Chicago, or APA formatting styles, where entire chapters are being overhauled, it is okay to submit the entire chapter without removing extraneous pages.

Color matters if it's relevant to the correction.

The editorial department should retrieve updated files for authors through the Electronic File Requests spreadsheet. The most updated files (including reprint corrections) can be found in the Digital Asset Management system.

Email corrected PDFs to the Senior Managing Editor.

For corrections that apply to multiple versions that may vary in pagination, trim size, or content, please create a separate PDF for each version.

The phrase "trim size" refers to the dimensions (length and width) of a printed book.

Labeling the different versions:

For versions with identical book files, it is okay to submit one PDF file that clearly lists titles, versions, and version ISBNs that need to be corrected.

For versions that do not have identical book files (i.e., pagination, content, etc. varies between files) distinct PDF files are needed for each version with corrections.

Read to Write: Annotate

1. Double-underline the main idea.
2. Underline the steps in the process (primary support).

Think Critically

1. Who is the intended audience for this piece? How do you know?
2. What text features (underlines, bullets, bold, capitalization) has Garcia-Muniz used? Why? Would these features be appropriate in all types of writing? Explain.
3. How are these instructions organized?
4. Does this piece demonstrate the Four Basics of Good Process Analysis? Explain.

Professional Process Analysis Essay

Samantha Levine-Finley

Isn't It Time You Hit the Books?

The author of the essay "Isn't It Time You Hit the Books?," Samantha Levine-Finley, has worked as a reporter for several publications, including the *Houston Chronicle*, where she covered topics relating to national politics, and *U.S. News & World Report*, where she contributed to the "Education" and "Nation & World" sections. This article was originally published in *U.S. News & World Report*'s "America's Best Colleges" 2008.

It was freshman year, and Angie Trevino thought she'd ace her microeconomics class at the University of Oklahoma. An older student had told her she could skip the lectures—the required discussion sessions would cover all the course material. So Trevino gladly slept in on lecture days and faithfully attended the discussions. "I was doing fairly well—I got high grades on tests and quizzes. I went in and took the final and thought I did great," she says. When she ended up with a B, she was shocked. "It was because my professor didn't see my face in the lecture," she says. "It was a rude awakening."

2   Now a graduating senior, Trevino, 22, realizes she got bum advice. "In high school, I was so monitored to go to class, it was hard to miss," she says. "In college, you are responsible for your own actions and can't blame problems on someone else. It doesn't work like that."

3   Disappointing grades are just one hint that the approach many students took during high school won't work in college. The answer for new students is to step up their academic game. So, in addition to a "things to do" list, here are a few "things to be" that can help your transition to college.

4   *Be there.* "You will get an experience in the classroom that you will not get from a book," says Gavin Sands, 22, a graduating senior from Elon University in

Predict Read the first two sentences and then stop. What do you think will happen?

Read to Write Why does the author include quotes? How do these quotes help you understand the intended audience for this piece?

mete: give

North Carolina. Skipping class may seem tempting, especially those introductory classes that can have several hundred students in them. The professors are unlikely to take attendance or even learn most students' names. But Trevino says class is great for meeting people, feeling connected to campus, and getting those crucial snippets of advice that professors mete out to help with exams.

5   *Be willing to talk to teachers.* Stress, confusion, and a low grade here or there are all part of college. Talking to a professor or adviser can keep those problems from spiraling. But talking up takes moxie. "If you are shy, it might be intimidating, but you have to put yourself out there," says Heath Thompson, 19, a sophomore at the University of Oklahoma. Sands thought "professors were going to be crazy, ridiculous, intense academic scholars, and I would be racing to keep up with them. But when I got here, I was amazed that they were real people and approachable."

6   You won't be wasting anyone's time. Professors are usually required to maintain a certain number of office hours per week to see students, says Alice Lanning, who teaches a freshman-year experience class, also at Oklahoma. The problem is when "students don't take advantage of these office hours until the end of the semester, and the grades are scary." Her advice? Visit each professor at least once during the first month of school. "Ask what the professor is looking for and how to get the most out of class," Lanning says. That's especially critical because you'll have fewer exams and graded papers than in high school, so rebounding from a bad grade is tough.

7   Trevino recalled a time when she had a family problem and needed an extension on a project in her business communications class. She had already talked with the professor several times about career and academic issues. When the problem came up, Trevino says, the professor's reaction blew her away. "He gave me an extension because he felt that he knew me and could trust me."

8   *Be a syllabus-ologist.* The syllabus can be your salvation. Professors hand out these precious pages at the start of each semester. The syllabus outlines the material required for the class, all assignments, and the dates that papers are due and exams are held. "You have to keep track of things because there is not going to be anyone handing you a reminder note before you leave for home or writing everything on the board," says Sands. Her solution: go through each syllabus immediately, highlight all the quizzes, tests, and assignments, and put them in a day planner. "If you know you have three big projects due around the same time," she says, "you can think about it early on."

9   *Be deep.* College-level assignments require a questioning attitude, analytical abilities, and a level of organization beyond anything you came across in high school. College-level writing assignments also demand higher-order thinking. Independent and creative thinking is key. Sands says she was baffled at first in a class that focused on how to ask questions and do research. "I couldn't understand why you would ask a question you couldn't find an answer to," she says. "But that wasn't the point. It was to find something that hasn't been asked a million times before. I struggled with that for weeks." As for writing the papers themselves, Ian Brasg, 18, a sophomore at Princeton, accidentally learned many ways to annoy professors. "Random, fancy-sounding adjectives may not make a paper better," he says. And in a paper about the philosopher Descartes, Brasg's

moxie: courage, nerve

Reflect Have you visited an instructor during office hours? What happened?

Reflect Why is it important to talk to professors early?

Reflect How have you used your syllabus for this class?

Reflect How have teachers evaluated you based on your writing?

Descartes: French philosopher and mathematician René Descartes (1596–1650), who has been called the "Father of Modern Philosophy"

grade suffered because he inconsistently capitalized certain words. "To the professor, it showed a lack of preparation," he says.

10   One sure way to stay on track with college papers is to give yourself enough time to write a couple of drafts before you hand them in. Some professors require students to rewrite their papers so they can see where they're doing well and where they need to do more work. It gets ugly, but it helps. "There is a point when the students will hate me, and I will hate them because we are handing things back and forth," says Carol Zoref, a writing instructor at Sarah Lawrence College. "And then this amazing thing happens: they all get much better at it. They have a kind of fearlessness. If they can put themselves through that, there will be a big payoff."

11   *Be a good manager.* The important thing is to manage your day and not waste time. Pay attention to how your time is spent and manage it to fit your preferences and habits and your various responsibilities. Time management methods vary according to the individual.

12   If time management methods differ among students, so do study styles. Sands stays organized using three-ring binders with dividers, loose-leaf paper, and pencil pouches in the front (high-tech approaches work, too). Trevino cheats her brain by writing due dates for assignments as earlier than they really are. Finding your own way to work, but also time for fun, is key, Thompson says. "You can't study every day of the week, and you can't play video games every day of the week," he says. "Balancing things is the most important part."

13   *Be cool.* Colleges know that students, especially those who were successful in high school, might resist seeking help, says Steven Lestition, dean of Mathey College, one of five residential colleges at Princeton. Get over it! "If nobody had that problem, the resources wouldn't be there," Trevino says. "If you are embarrassed or shy about getting help, weigh your options. Are you more worried about hurting your pride or your grade point average?"

14   Tip: all-nighters should be rare; same with end-of-semester cram sessions. Plugging away as assignments come in is the best way to get the most out of college.

Read to Write
What strategies does Levine-Finley use to develop secondary support for her steps?

Reflect What resources are available to help student writers at your school? Have you used them? Why or why not?

Read to Write
How does the final tip connect to the steps Levine-Finley has already presented?

Read to Write: Annotate

1. Underline the major steps in this process.

2. Circle the name of each person interviewed and quoted for this essay. Pay attention to the way that quotes are introduced and punctuated.

Think Critically

1. What is Levine-Finley's thesis?

2. Are the steps in this process in chronological order? Why or why not?

3. What words or examples help you understand who Levine-Finley's audience is?

4. Does this essay follow the Four Basics of Good Process Analysis (p. 173)? Why or why not?

Respond

1. Interview instructors, advisers, and experienced students from your college to find out what steps they believe are essential to success. Then, write an essay that describes the process of success at your school, using quotes from your interviews.

2. In paragraph 10, Levine-Finley suggests that there is a big "payoff" for working through the hard process of revising writing. What is something else that requires a lot of work but offers a big payoff? Write an essay that describes this process.

3. Levine-Finley recommends visiting professors during office hours, but many students—especially new students—are nervous about doing this. Talk to several instructors to discover tips for successfully talking with professors, and then write an essay that explains how to visit and talk to teachers in your school.

Grammar for Process Analysis

Like many other writers, Levine-Finley includes quotations from others to help support the steps in her process. Those quoted include students, professors, and a dean (an academic official who oversees a department within a college or university). Notice how Levine-Finley introduces one of the students:

> "You will get an experience in the classroom that you will not get from a book," says Gavin Sands, 22, a graduating senior from Elon University in North Carolina.

Pay attention to the commas in this sentence: there is a comma after the quotation (before the signal phrase), and there are commas after the student's name and the student's age. We use commas to mark extra information in a sentence. Specifically, we use commas to mark an **appositive**.

An **appositive** follows a noun and gives an explanation of the noun (or renames the noun). In this sentence, the appositive "graduating senior" explains who Gavin Sands is. When Levine-Finley uses the appositive, she is showing her readers *why* she is quoting Gavin Sands: he is a graduating senior, so he has a lot of experience with studying.

For more about appositives and commas, see Chapter 30.

Write Your Own Process Analysis

In this section, you will write your own process analysis based on one of the following assignments. For help, refer to the How to Write Process Analysis checklist on pages 193–194.

Assignment Options: Writing about College, Work, and Everyday Life

Write a process analysis paragraph or essay on one of the following topics or on one of your own choice.

College
- Describe the process of preparing for an exam.
- Attend a tutoring session at your college's writing center. Afterward, describe the process: what specific things did the tutor do to help you? Also, explain what you learned from the process.
- Interview a student who has been selected for a scholarship or internship. Write an essay that explains how to find, apply, and win a scholarship or internship.

Work
- Describe how to make a positive impression at a job interview.
- Think of a challenging task you had to accomplish at work. What steps did you go through to complete it?
- Identify a job that you would like to have after graduation. Then, investigate the process of getting this job, including the courses you need to take, any exams or certifications that are required, the search stage, and the interview. To gather information, visit the website of your college's career center. Better yet, make an appointment to speak with a career counselor. After you have completed your research, describe the process in writing.

Everyday life
- Describe the process of making something, such as a favorite meal, a set of shelves, or a sweater.
- Think of a challenging process that you have completed successfully, such as fixing a leak under the sink, applying for a loan, or finding a good deal on a car or an apartment. Describe the steps specifically enough so that someone else could complete the process just as successfully.
- Take part in a community activity, such as a fund-raising event for a charity, a neighborhood cleanup, or food preparation at a homeless shelter. Then, describe the process you went through.

Assignment Options: Reading and Writing Critically

Complete one of the following assignments that asks you to apply the critical thinking, reading, and writing skills discussed in Chapter 1.

Writing Critically about Readings

Both Sarah Bigler's essay "High School Is Not Preparing Us for College" (pp. 139–140) and Samantha Levine-Finley's "Isn't It Time You Hit the Books" (pp. 187–189) address problems encountered by students entering college after completing high school. Read or review both of these pieces, and then follow these steps:

Tip For a reminder of how to summarize, analyze, synthesize, and evaluate, see the Reading and Writing Critically box on page 17.

1. **Summarize** Briefly summarize the works, listing the major support points in each one.

2. **Analyze** Are there any other steps or details that the authors might have included?

3. **Synthesize** Using examples from both Bigler's and Levine-Finley's writings and from your own experience, discuss what steps high school teachers, parents, and administrators could take to help prepare graduates for college success.

4. **Evaluate** Which piece, Bigler's or Levine-Finley's, do you think is more effective? Why?

Writing about Images

Study this infographic, and complete the following steps.

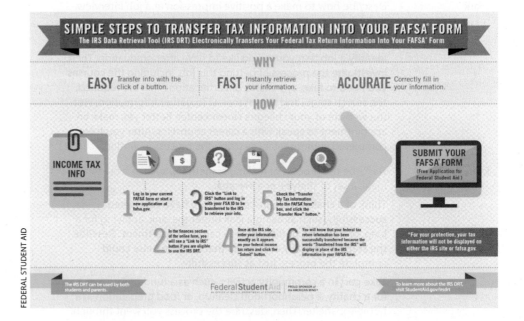

1. **Read the images** Ask yourself: What is the "thesis" in this infographic? How is this main idea presented to viewers? What are the major steps in the process? Do you think that the infographic successfully supports the main idea? (For more information on reading images, see Chapter 1.) Is it as simple to read and comprehend this visual process as it would be if there were detailed written instructions? Why or why not?

2. **Write a process analysis** Write a paragraph or essay that describes the process shown in this infographic.

Writing to Solve a Problem

Read or review the discussion of problem solving in Chapter 1 (pp. 26–28). Then, consider the following problem.

Midway through a course you are taking, your instructor asks the class to tell her how she could improve the course. You have not been happy with the class because the instructor is always late, comes in seeming rushed and tense, and ends up releasing class late because of material she forgot to cover. During class, she uses PowerPoint slides and reads to the class from them, seldom adding new information. Then, after handing out an assignment for students to work on, she returns to her desk to grade papers. You are afraid to ask questions about the lecture or assignment because the instructor does not seem overly helpful. You want to tell the instructor how the course could be better, but you do not want to offend her.

Assignment Working in a small group or on your own, write to your instructor about how she could improve the course. Think of how the class could be structured differently so that you could learn more. Begin with how the class could start. Then, describe how the rest of the class period could proceed, suggesting specific activities if you can. State your suggestions in positive terms. For example, instead of telling the instructor what *not* to do, make suggestions using phrases like *you could, we could,* or *the class could.* Be sure to use formal English. You might start in this way:

Several simple changes might improve our learning. At the start of each class. . .

At the end, remember to thank your instructor for asking for students' suggestions.

CHECKLIST

How to Write Process Analysis

Steps	Details
☐ Narrow and explore your topic See Chapter 3.	• Make the topic more specific. • Prewrite to get ideas about the narrowed topic and how you will explain the steps to your audience. • Make sure your topic can be covered in the space given.
☐ Write a topic sentence (paragraph) or thesis statement (essay) See Chapter 3.	• Decide what you want readers to know about the process you are describing. →

Steps	Details
☐ Support your point See Chapter 4.	• Include the steps in the process, and explain the steps in detail.
☐ Write a draft See Chapter 5.	• Make a plan that puts the steps in a logical order (often chronological). • Include a topic sentence (paragraph) or thesis statement (essay) and all the supporting details about each step.
☐ Revise your draft See Chapter 5.	• Make sure it has *all* the Four Basics of Good Process Analysis. • Read to make sure all the steps are present. • Make sure you include transitions to move readers smoothly from one step to the next.
☐ Edit your revised draft See Parts 3 through 6.	• Correct errors in grammar, spelling, word use, and punctuation.

Chapter Review

1. What is process analysis?

2. What are two purposes for process analysis?

3. What are the Four Basics of Good Process Analysis?

Reflect and Apply

1. When have you written or read process analysis before? What makes reading or writing process analysis difficult?

2. Interview someone studying in your major or working in your career. What situations require reading or writing process analysis in your major or career?

3. What challenged you the most when writing for this chapter? What do you want to do differently next time?

4. What worked well in your writing for this chapter? What do you need to remember for next time?

10

Classification
Writing That Sorts Things into Groups

Understand What Classification Is

Classification is writing that organizes, or sorts, people or items into categories. It uses an **organizing principle**: *how* the people or items are sorted. The organizing principle is directly related to the purpose for classifying. For example, you might sort clean laundry (your purpose) using one of the following organizing principles: by ownership (yours, your roommate's) or by where it goes (the bedroom, the bathroom).

> **Four Basics** of Good Classification
>
> **1** It makes sense of a group of people or items by organizing them into categories according to a single organizing principle.
>
> **2** It sets up logical and comprehensive categories.
>
> **3** It gives detailed explanations or examples with details of what fits into each category.
>
> **4** It organizes information by time, space, or importance, depending on its purpose.

In the following paragraph, the numbers and colors correspond to the Four Basics of Good Classification.

1 In researching careers I might pursue, I have learned that there are three major types of workers, each having different strengths and preferences. **2** The first type of worker is a big-picture person, who likes to look toward the future and think of new businesses, products, and services. **3** Big-picture people might also identify ways to make their workplaces more successful and productive. Often, they

4 Examples organized by order of emphasis

hold leadership positions, achieving their goals by assigning specific projects and tasks to others. Big-picture people may be drawn to starting their own businesses, or they might manage or become a consultant for an existing business. **2** The second type of worker is a detail person who focuses on the smaller picture, whether it be a floor plan in a construction project, a spreadsheet showing a business's revenue and expenses, or data from a scientific experiment. **3** Detail people take pride in understanding all the ins and outs of a task and doing everything carefully and well. Some detail people prefer to work with their hands, doing such things as carpentry or electrical wiring. Others prefer office jobs, such as accounting or clerical work. Detail people may also be drawn to technical careers, such as scientific research or engineering. **2** The third type of worker is a people person, who gets a lot of satisfaction from reaching out to others and helping them meet their needs. **3** A people person has good social skills and likes to get out in the world to use them. Therefore, this type of worker is unlikely to be happy sitting behind a desk. A successful people person often shares qualities of the other types of workers; for example, he or she may show leadership potential. In addition, his or her job may require careful attention to detail. Good jobs for a people person include teaching, sales, nursing, and other health-care positions. Having evaluated my own strengths and preferences, I believe that I am equal parts big-picture person and people person. I am happy to see that I have many career options.

You use classification anytime you want to organize people or items.

College	In a health class, you are asked to group foods into the correct category based on the food pyramid.
Work	For a sales presentation, you classify the kinds of products your company produces.
Everyday life	You classify your typical monthly expenses to make a budget.

In college, writing assignments probably will not use the word *classification*. Instead, you might be asked to *describe the types of something* or *explain the types or kinds of something*. You might also be asked, *How is something organized?* or *What are the parts of something?* These are the words and phrases that signal that you need to sort things into categories.

For more information on understanding writing assignment prompts, see the Appendix, page 553.

First Basic: Main Idea in Classification

The **main idea** in classification uses a single **organizing principle** to sort items in a way that serves your purpose. The categories should help you achieve your purpose.

To help you discover the organizing principle for your classification, complete the following sentences:

> | Main idea in classification | **My purpose for classifying my topic is to explain that . . .** |
> | | **It would make most sense to my readers if I sorted this topic by . . .** |

Read to Write
To identify the main idea when you are reading a classification essay, complete this sentence: This writer has organized (the topic) by to show that . . .

Sometimes, it helps to think of classification in diagram form. Here is a diagram of the paragraph on pages 195–196.

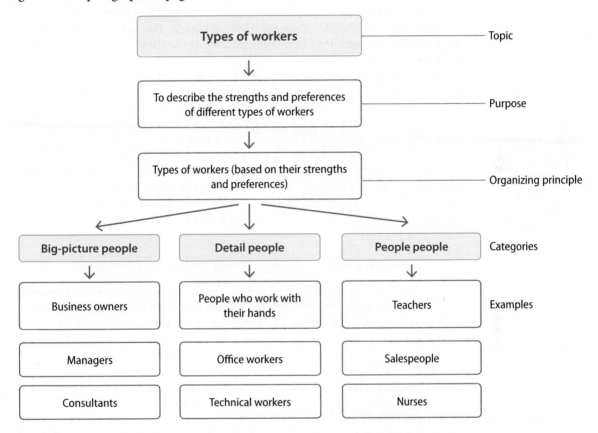

In classification, the main idea may or may not state the organizing principle directly. Look at the following examples:

        Topic   Organizing principle

The columns of ancient Greek buildings can be classified into three major types.

        Topic   Categories (indicating the organizing principle)

The most impressive structures in ancient Greece were stadiums, theaters, and temples.

In the first example, the organizing principle is the type of column, which, is determined by the date of development and the major structural features. While the words *date* and *features* are not mentioned directly, each category is defined by these principles.

In the second example, the structures of ancient Greece are divided into types according to the purpose of the structure (sports, performances, or worship). The words *type of building* and *purpose* are not stated directly. Instead, the categories themselves—stadiums, theaters, and temples—and the details given about each one make the organizing principle clear.

The first sentence is the topic sentence for the paragraph that appears on page 202. The second example is the thesis statement for the essay on page 203. The thesis is broader than the topic sentence: the latter focuses on just one part of Greek buildings (the columns), while the thesis considers the entire structure.

The organizing principle in classification should logically support the purpose of the paper. For example, it makes sense to classify Greek structures according to their function in ancient Greek society if the purpose of the paper is to show the cultural accomplishments of that civilization. Similarly, a writer organizing a restaurant guide for newcomers to the city might either use cost or type of cuisine as a logical organizing principle. There are many other ways to classify restaurants—by the pay that kitchen staff receive, for example—but those principles would not logically support the purpose of the paper. When you are writing or reading classification, ask yourself if there are other ways of classifying the topic and, if so, whether the organizing principle selected makes sense for the purpose of the text.

Think Critically
Some students confuse a category (fast-food restaurants) with an example (Wendy's). What is the difference between a category and an example? Which one is more specific?

PRACTICE 10–1   **Using a Single Organizing Principle**

For each topic that follows, one of the categories does not fit the same organizing principle as the rest. Circle the letter of the category that does not fit, and, in the space provided, write the organizing principle that the rest follow.

Example:

Topic: Sports

Categories:

a. Sports played on fields   b. Sports played on courts   c. Sports played by both men and women   d. Sports played on ice

Organizing principle: *location/playing surface*

1. Topic: Movies

    Categories:

    a. Oscar winners   b. Romantic   c. Science Fiction   d. Action/
                           comedies   Adventure

    Organizing principle:

2. Topic: Jobs

    Categories:

    a. Weekly   b. Hourly   c. Monthly   d. Summer

    Organizing principle:

3. Topic: Classes

    Categories:

    a. Face-to-face   b. Science   c. Online   d. Hybrid

    Organizing principle:

Second Basic: Primary Support in Classification

The major supporting details in classification are the categories that the writer sets up, and as you learned in the first basic, the categories must follow an organizing principle that logically supports the purpose of the paper. As you select your categories, make sure you can answer these questions:

Tip Sometimes, the same main idea can be used for a paragraph and an essay, but the essay must develop this point in more detail. (See pp. 202–203.)

- *Do all of the categories match the organizing principle logically?* Make sure all of your categories relate to the same organizing principle. If, for example, you plan to classify types of devices according to size, you might include desktop, laptop, tablet, and handheld and wearable devices, but you would not also include cheap imitations, which is a category logically related to quality or cost, not size.

- *Have you included all the categories that could be covered by your organizing principle?* Returning to the classification of electronic devices by size, if you stop at just three categories (desktop, laptop, and tablet), you have left out a significant number of other members of the group. Your classification should cover all or nearly all of the possible examples of the topic.

- *Do you have enough information to develop each category equally?* When you select your organizing principle and set up your categories, make sure that you have enough information to address all categories with the same level of detail. If you have never used wearable electronics, for example, you might want to reconsider your classification of devices or plan to do some research before you begin writing.

PRACTICE 10–2   **Choosing Categories**

In the items that follow, you are given a topic and a purpose for sorting. For each item, list three categories that serve your purpose. (There are more than three correct categories for each item.)

Example:

Topic: Pieces of paper in my wallet

Purpose for sorting: To get rid of what I do not need

Categories:

a. *Things I need to keep in my wallet*

b. *Things I can throw away*

c. *Things I need to keep, but not in my wallet*

1. Topic: College courses

   Purpose for sorting: To decide what I will register for

   Categories:

2. Topic: Stuff in my notebook

   Purpose for sorting: To organize my schoolwork

   Categories:

3. Topic: Wedding guests

   Purpose for sorting: To arrange seating at tables

   Categories:

4. Topic: Tools for home repair

   Purpose for sorting: To make them easy to find when needed

   Categories:

Third Basic: Secondary Support in Classification

Tip For more on writing description, see Chapter 8.

Within each category, a writer may choose different ways to provide secondary support. In the essay on page 203, for example, the major supporting details are stadiums, theaters, and temples, and the writer has chosen to use a ***description*** of each type of structure as secondary support.

A writer may choose to **define** each category. A **definition** explains what something is or what it means. The writer of the sample paragraph on page 195, for example, gives a definition for each type of worker in his classification:

- *Big-picture people* = those who like to look to the future and think of new businesses, products, and services
- *Detail people* = those who focus on the smaller picture
- *People people* = those who get satisfaction from reaching out to others and meeting their needs

Tip For more on writing definition, see Chapter 11.

Writers may also *illustrate* each category with examples. Most classification essays use some form of illustration. For example, Stephanie Ericsson offers several examples of lies in her essay, "The Ways We Lie" (pp. 211–214).

Tip For more on writing illustration, see Chapter 7.

Fourth Basic: Organization in Classification

Classification can be organized in different ways (**time order**, **space order**, or **order of importance or emphasis**), depending on its purpose.

Tip For more on the orders of organization, see pages 73–75.

Purpose	Likely Organization
To explain changes or events over time	time
To describe the arrangement of people/items in physical space	space
To discuss parts of an issue or problem, or types of people or things	importance
To focus on a specific feature of groups	emphasis

In the essay model on page 203, order of emphasis is used to highlight the beauty of the structures.

As you write your classification, use **transitions** to move your readers smoothly from one category to another.

Common Transitions in Classification

another	for instance
another kind	last
first, second, third, and so on	one example/another example
for example	

Paragraphs versus Essays in Classification

For more on the important features of classification, see the Four Basics of Good Classification on page 195.

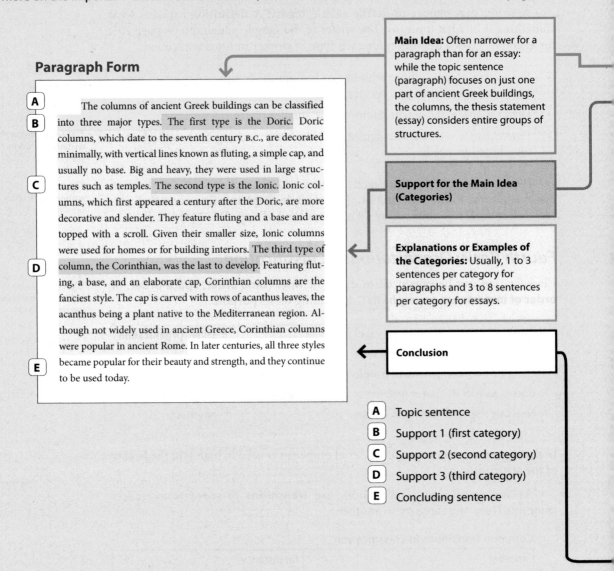

Paragraph Form

A   The columns of ancient Greek buildings can be classified
B into three major types. The first type is the Doric. Doric
columns, which date to the seventh century B.C., are decorated
minimally, with vertical lines known as fluting, a simple cap, and
usually no base. Big and heavy, they were used in large struc-
C tures such as temples. The second type is the Ionic. Ionic columns, which first appeared a century after the Doric, are more
decorative and slender. They feature fluting and a base and are
topped with a scroll. Given their smaller size, Ionic columns
were used for homes or for building interiors. The third type of
D column, the Corinthian, was the last to develop. Featuring fluting, a base, and an elaborate cap, Corinthian columns are the
fanciest style. The cap is carved with rows of acanthus leaves, the
acanthus being a plant native to the Mediterranean region. Although not widely used in ancient Greece, Corinthian columns
were popular in ancient Rome. In later centuries, all three styles
became popular for their beauty and strength, and they continue
E to be used today.

Main Idea: Often narrower for a paragraph than for an essay: while the topic sentence (paragraph) focuses on just one part of ancient Greek buildings, the columns, the thesis statement (essay) considers entire groups of structures.

Support for the Main Idea (Categories)

Explanations or Examples of the Categories: Usually, 1 to 3 sentences per category for paragraphs and 3 to 8 sentences per category for essays.

Conclusion

A Topic sentence
B Support 1 (first category)
C Support 2 (second category)
D Support 3 (third category)
E Concluding sentence

Think Critically As You Write Classification

Ask Yourself

- Is my organizing principle clear (even if my main idea doesn't state it directly)?
- Do the categories that make up the support for my main idea match my organizing principle?
  If not, does it make sense to rethink the categories, the organizing principle, or both?
- Are all the explanations or examples for each category relevant?

Essay Form

1

Ancient Greek civilization produced a wealth of architectural wonders that were both beautiful and lasting. The most impressive structures were stadiums, theaters, and temples. **A**

The stadiums were designed to hold thousands of spectators. These open-air spaces were set into hillsides so that the seating, often stone benches, would rise up from the central space, giving all spectators a decent view. One of the most famous stadiums, built in Delphi in the fifth century B.C., seated audiences of about seven thousand people. Many stadiums featured ornamental details such as dramatic arches, and some of the more sophisticated examples included heated bathhouses with heated floors. Most often, the stadiums hosted sporting events, such as foot races. A common racing distance was the "stade," equaling one length of the stadium. **B**

Another type of structure, the theater, was also a popular public gathering place. Like stadiums, the theaters were open-air sites that were set into hillsides. But instead of sports, they featured plays, musical **C**

2

performances, poetry readings, and other cultural events. In the typical Greek theater, a central performance area was surrounded by semicircular seating, which was often broken into different sections. Wooden, and later stone, stages were set up in the central area, and in front of the stage was a space used for singing and dancing. This space was known as the "orchestra." Among the most famous ancient Greek theaters is the one at Epidaurus, built in the fourth century B.C. and seating up to fourteen thousand people. Performances still take place there.

The most beautiful structures were the temples, with their grand entrances and large open spaces. Temples were rectangular in shape, and their outer walls as well as some interior spaces were supported by columns. Their main structures were typically made of limestone or marble, while their roofs might be constructed of terra-cotta or marble tiles. Temples were created to serve as "homes" for particular gods or goddesses, who were represented by statues. People left food or other offerings to these gods or goddesses **D**

3

to stay in their good graces, and communities often held festivals and other celebrations in their honor. Temples tended to be built in either the Doric or Ionic style, with Doric temples featuring simple, heavy columns and Ionic temples featuring slightly more ornate columns. The most famous temple, in the Doric style, is the Parthenon in Athens.

Turning to the present day, many modern stadiums, theaters, and columned civic buildings show the influence of ancient Greek buildings. Recognizing the lasting strength and beauty of these old structures, architects and designers continue to return to them for inspiration. I predict that this inspiration will last at least a thousand more years. **E**

A Introductory paragraph
B Topic sentence 1 (first category)
C Topic sentence 2 (second category)
D Topic sentence 3 (third category)
E Concluding paragraph

203

> **PRACTICE 10-3**   **Using Transitions in Classification**

Read the paragraph that follows, and fill in the blanks with transitions.
You are not limited to the ones listed in the preceding box.

> Every day, I get three kinds of email: work, personal, and junk. The
> _____ of email, work, I have to read carefully and promptly. Sometimes,
> the messages are important ones directed to me, but mostly they are group
> messages about meetings, policies, or procedures. _____,
> it seems as if the procedure for leaving the building during a fire alarm is
> always changing. _____ of email, personal, is from
> friends or my mother. These I read when I get a chance, but I read them
> quickly and delete any that are jokes or messages that have to be sent to
> ten friends for good luck. _____ of email is the most
> common and most annoying: junk. I get at least thirty junk emails a day,
> advertising all kinds of things that I do not want, such as life insurance or
> baby products. Even when I reply asking that the company stop sending me
> these messages, they keep coming. Sometimes, I wish email did not exist.

Evaluate Classification

Read the sample classification paragraph below. Using the Four Basics of Good
Classification and the sample grading rubric, decide what grade this paragraph
would earn. Explain your answer.

> **Assignment**   Write a paragraph that classifies the types of classes a student
> usually has to pass to earn a degree in a particular field.

> As a student, we are required to take a lot of classes. Some of them
> are interesting, and some are not. Usually, in the first year or two
> there are some basic courses. These include math, history, science,
> and writing. Sometimes there are some other types of courses you
> can take, like psychology or music, but not always. These classes don't
> really relate to a particular major. When everyone has to take them.
> Then, when you finish those basic courses you can finally take classes
> about material that interests you. For instance, I want to be a math
> teacher. To take classes about education and how to teach. I would
> also get to take classes about how to teach math. These courses are
> more important to me because they are useful for my career.

Analysis of Sample Paragraph:

Sample rubric

Element	Grading criteria	Point: Comment
Appropriateness	• Did the student follow the assignment directions?	_/5:
Main Idea	• Does the paper clearly state a strong main idea in a complete sentence?	_/10:
Support	• Is the main idea developed with specific support, including specific details and examples? • Is there enough support to make the main idea evident to the reader? • Is all the support directly related to the main idea?	_/10:
Organization	• Is the writing logically organized? • Does the student use transitions (*also, for example, sometimes*, and so on) to move the reader from one point to another?	_/10:
Conclusion	• Does the conclusion remind the reader of the main idea?	_/5:
Grammar	• Is the writing free of the four most serious errors? (See Chapters 16–19.) • Is the sentence structure clear? • Does the student choose words that clearly express his or her meaning? • Are the words spelled correctly? • Is the punctuation correct?	_/10:
		TOTAL POINTS: __/50

Read and Analyze Classification

Reading examples of classification will help you write your own. In the first example, Lorenza Mattazi uses classification to talk about her experiences with music. In the next example, student Kelly Hultgren classifies the various types of texters. The Profile of Success highlights Professor and Mayor Lisa Currie's methods of classification. Finally, in the last essay, professional writer Stephanie Ericsson lists the number of ways in which we lie.

As you read these pieces, pay attention to the vocabulary and the questions in the margin. They will help you read critically.

Student Classification Paragraph

Lorenza Mattazi

All My Music

From the time I was young, I have always loved music, all kinds of music. My first experience of music was the opera that both of my parents always had playing in our house. I learned to understand the drama and emotion of operas. My parents both spoke Italian, and they told me the stories of the operas and translated the words sung in Italian to English so that I could understand. Because hearing opera made my parents happy, and they taught me about it, I loved it, too. Many of my friends think I am weird when I say I love opera, but to me it is very emotional and beautiful. When I was in my early teens, I found rock music and listened to it no matter what I was doing. I like the music with words that tell a story that I can relate to. In that way, rock can be like opera, with stories that everyone can relate to, about love, heartbreak, happiness, and pain. The best rock has powerful guitars and bass, and a good, strong drumbeat. I love it when I can feel the bass in my chest. Rock has good energy and power. Now, I love rap music, too, not the rap with words that are violent or disrespectful of women, but the rest. The words are poetry, and the energy is so high that I feel as if I just have to move my body to the beat. That rhythm is so steady. I have even written some good rap, which my friends say is really good. Maybe I will try to get it published, even on something like Helium, or I could start a blog. I will always love music because it is a good way to communicate feelings and stories, and it makes people feel good.

Read to Write: Annotate

1. Double-underline the topic sentence.

2. Number Mattazi's categories.

3. Circle the transitions.

Think Critically

1. Does the paragraph have the Four Basics of Good Classification (p. 195)? Why or why not?

2. Does the paragraph have adequate secondary support (description, definition, or illustration)? Explain.

3. What kind of organization does Mattazi use? Is this organization effective? Why or why not?

Student Classification Essay

Kelly Hultgren

Pick Up the Phone to Call, Not Text

Kelly Hultgren studied journalism, communication, and anthropology at the University of Arizona. Hultgren got her start contributing articles to the *Arizona Daily Wildcat,* the student newspaper in which the following essay first appeared, and now works as a reporter and project manager for Jean Chatzky.

"So, I met this guy last week and I thought he really liked me, because he was texting me all the time, and then suddenly he started taking longer to respond. I think he's not interested anymore. You better believe I am not texting him until he texts me first. I can't believe he led me on like that."

2   Does that sound familiar? That's because you've probably heard someone say it or have said it yourself. Perhaps not word for word, but please raise your hand if you've ever made assumptions at the beginning of a relationship, based solely on texts. My hand just hit the ceiling.

3   Once upon a time, people pursuing potential mates evaluated each other on personality, looks, lifestyle, and how the person felt he or she was being treated. People always will base their opinions on the categories listed above, but now, a more relevant and scrutinized trait is a person's texting habits. People, especially we college students, rely on texting to get to know someone. Both men and women are equally guilty of this. We are all busy, and texting is quick and convenient and facilitates communication throughout the day. I've used those arguments too. But instead of spending three hours on Facebook or watching TV, pick up the damn phone, call, and meet in person.

4   For budding relationships, texting is used not only as a screening device but also as a deal-breaker. It sounds absolutely ridiculous because it is. From simply looking to get some action to embarking on a long-lasting romantic journey, cellular discourse is now crucial in the process. Take my starting quote, for example. The hypothetical girl first assumed the hypothetical guy liked her and then assumed he didn't based only on his texting frequency. What if the poor guy was having phone issues

Predict Who is speaking? What will the essay categorize?

Read to Write Why does the author ask readers to raise their hands? What does this tell you about her audience?

scrutinized: closely observed or studied

facilitates: makes something easier

hypothetical: theoretical; supposed or imagined

or was working? You're just getting started; don't expect him to drop the whole world just to send back a response to your simple "hey" text message.

5   This example addresses some aspects of texting: you don't know what the person is physically doing, and you cannot tell the person's mood (emoticons do not count). Therefore, one of every student's favorite forms of interaction is inherently deceiving. At the start of a relationship, why do we communicate and subsequently put so much emphasis on texting, when it's not a reliable way to get to know someone?

6   As I mentioned before, texting can be a deal-breaker. Let's classify some different types of texters and how they can create problems.

7   First up, we have Lazy Texters. Lazy Texters often initiate the conversation and then leave the responsibility of carrying on the conversation with the other person, rarely asking questions and usually responding with one-word answers.

8   Then we have the Minimalists. Minimalists make their texts short and concise, and they often take longer to respond. They are also notorious for ignoring people, but you would never know this, because you didn't call. This leads us to another bittersweet characteristic of texting: you really don't know if someone has seen your text or not (unless your messaging service include read receipts; then, your cover is blown).

9   The next type is the Stage Five Clinger, who will constantly blow up your phone wanting to know what you're doing, where you're going, and where you live. This texter sometimes sends text after text, even when you're not responding. Creepy.

10   A less creepy yet still consistent type of texter is the Text-a-holic. They are constantly texting, and they experience separation anxiety when away from their phones. The use of texting to get acquainted with someone is really just a small portion of humanity's increasing problem of becoming socially inept. I said socially inept, not social-networking inept, as in not being able to communicate with someone face to face.

11   The next time you meet someone and get that warm and fuzzy feeling in your tummy, break through the technological barricade and get to know the person in person. And, please refrain from sending the emoticon with hearts for its eyes.

Read to Write: Annotate

1. Double-underline the thesis statement.

2. Underline the categories (major support) that Hultgren sets up.

3. Circle the transitions.

Think Critically

1. What is Hultgren's organizing principle? Are all her categories relevant?

2. Does Hultgren provide enough secondary support for each category?

3. What kind of organization does Hultgren use? Would you recommend a different arrangement? Why or why not?

---

inherently: by its very nature

subsequently: afterward

Reflect Have you ever made an incorrect assumption about a texter based on his or her message or a lack of response to one of your own texts?

Reflect Which of Hultgren's categories makes the most sense to you? Why?

Read to Write The author has capitalized the name of each category. Why? What effect does this choice have on readers?

inept: clumsy or lacking in skill

Reflect Do you agree that society is becoming more socially inept? Why or why not?

Reflect Do you plan to take any of Hultgren's advice? Why or why not?

Profile of Success
Classification in the Real World

Background   Reading and writing have been and are the bedrock of my life. With a BA in English/writing from George Mason University, I became a journalist with beats that included local government, health, education, and feature stories for several different daily and weekly newspapers in western Virginia. While serving as both an editor/reporter, I learned the importance of background reading prior to writing, the value of concise writing under deadlines, and the magnitude of editing, the most significant aspect of writing. I left the newspaper when elected to the local school board and later earned a MS in Education from Shenandoah University. I currently teach English as Another Language courses at Lord Fairfax Community College and work as the adviser for international students. In this position, I must communicate via the written word with students, colleagues, and governments that represent the various student backgrounds as well as teach nonnative speakers of English the many rhetorical styles of both reading and writing in English.

Also, I am an active member of local government. I was first elected to the town council in 1992 and served on the council until my election to the school board in 2002. As a member of the town council, and later as a member of the school board, I read volumes of information on a weekly basis—local, state, and national documents. This comprehensive reading prepared me for weekly meetings and reports.

Writing at Work   Now, as mayor, I communicate via email and through hard copies with various county and state elected officials, service agencies, and local businesses. I also produce the town's bimonthly newsletter.

Writing is a daily aspect of the job, writing that must be concise and comprehensive at the same time. Background reading—approached carefully—is also critical now because social media inundates us daily with a deluge of reading materials. Finally, editing skills play as great a role in my current position as mayor as they did in my role as journalist.

Lisa Currie
Mayor of Toms Brook, VA

Workplace Classification

Thank you for taking the time to meet with the town planner and myself. We learned a great deal about project funding and the types of funding available. After careful consideration of resources and project immediacy, we classify the town's proposals into three specific projects: soil and water erosion projects, town wall and sidewalks, and curb and guttering projects.

2   The first project that requires attention is the problem with water runoff and soil erosion. Currently, the town's storm water overflow, or dry bed, allows rainwater to move from west to east and flow into the town's creek, which feeds into the Shenandoah River and then the Chesapeake Bay, a protected water source. Over

the years, the dry gully that cuts under Main Street and across several properties on the eastern side of town has filled with soil and sediment. This soil and sediment, combined with debris from careless property owners, has changed the depth and shape of the gully, distorting the storm water flow to the creek. Now, shifted from its normal path, rainwater overflows the bed, crosses the creek bank, and threatens homeowners' properties while eroding the bank of the creek, altering the natural flow of the creek. This erosion, in turn, threatens the creek bank's stability as well as property on both sides of the creek. Besides engineering and legal expertise, this project requires input from soil and water erosion professionals. The erosion issue needs attention before the sidewalk and town wall renovations.

3   Another project requiring our attention is the maintenance and repair of the town wall. The blue stone town wall dates back to the late 1930s, a Civilian Conservation Corp (CCC) project, and once existed on both the western and eastern borders of the town. Today, only remnants of the wall remain. When the main thoroughfare was widened in the early 1950s, much of the wall was either removed or replaced with concrete; over the last seventy years, the concrete has weakened, cracked and been damaged. The deteriorating wall is no longer secure, and if the wall collapses, the sidewalk that extends the length of the eastern side, from the northern to the southern end, would follow. Considering the eastern wall's proximity to the sidewalk, any repairs made to the wall impact the sidewalk's condition. Because the wall ranges in height from several inches to several feet above the ground, the restorations require engineering expertise. Since the sidewalk passes over the town's dry run, the town's dry run requires attention prior to sidewalk and wall repairs. These two aspects need attention prior to the curb and guttering.

4   The final project requiring our attention is the replacement of the curb and guttering that run the length of Main Street. The pockmarked guttering remains a byproduct of years of weather and daily abuse by vehicles. Debris and refuse collect in these areas creating unsafe conditions. The broken and damaged curbs are the result of a lack of maintenance; again, an unsightly decay that creates unsafe conditions. In our meeting, we discussed these repairs as part of the overall maintenance of the road, which is budgeted and planned for the future. After the new asphalt is laid down, the town will again be bordered by the brightly painted curbs.

5   Funding these projects provides the town with the resources it needs to provide for the safety and wellbeing of its citizens. Considering the town's limited budget, the town welcomes the assistance of transportation grants and transportation expertise. The town has multiple projects to address, which must be completed in a systematic method for best results.

Read to Write: Annotate

1. Double-underline the main idea of Currie's letter.

2. Underline the names of the categories that Currie has set up.

3. Circle the key transitions she uses.

Think Critically

1. What is Currie's purpose? Who is her audience?

2. Why does Currie provide information about her town's history within her categories?

3. Does the letter have the Four Basics of Classification (p. 195)? Explain.

Professional Classification Essay

Stephanie Ericsson

The Ways We Lie

Stephanie Ericsson was born in 1953 and raised in San Francisco. She has lived in a variety of places, including New York, Los Angeles, London, Mexico, the Spanish island of Ibiza, and Minnesota, where she currently resides. Ericsson's life took a major turn when her husband died suddenly; she was two months pregnant at the time. She began a journal to help her cope with the grief and loss, and she later used her writing to help others with similar struggles. An excerpt from her journal appeared in the *Utne Reader*, and her writings were later published in a book titled *Companion through the Darkness: Inner Dialogues on Grief* (1993).

In "The Ways We Lie," which also appeared in the *Utne Reader* and is taken from her follow-up work, *Companion into the Dawn: Inner Dialogues on Loving* (1994), Ericsson continues her search for truth by examining and classifying our daily lives.

The bank called today, and I told them my deposit was in the mail, even though I hadn't written a check yet. It'd been a rough day. The baby I'm pregnant with decided to do aerobics on my lungs for two hours, our three-year-old daughter painted the living-room couch with lipstick, the IRS put me on hold for an hour, and I was late to a business meeting because I was tired.

2   I told my client that the traffic had been bad. When my partner came home, his haggard face told me his day hadn't gone any better than mine, so when he asked, "How was your day?" I said, "Oh, fine," knowing that one more straw might break his back. A friend called and wanted to take me to lunch. I said I was busy. Four lies in the course of a day, none of which I felt the least bit guilty about.

3   We lie. We all do. We exaggerate, we minimize, we avoid confrontation, we spare people's feelings, we conveniently forget, we keep secrets, we justify lying to the big-guy institutions. Like most people, I indulge in small falsehoods and still think of myself as an honest person. Sure I lie, but it doesn't hurt anything. Or does it?

4   I once tried going a whole week without telling a lie, and it was paralyzing. I discovered that telling the truth all the time is nearly impossible. It means living with some serious consequences: the bank charges me $60 in overdraft fees, my partner keels over when I tell him about my travails, my client fires me for telling

Read to Write
As you read this essay, pay attention to Ericsson's categories. What do you think her organizing principle is?

haggard: drawn, worn out

indulge: to become involved in (usually something negative)

keelsover: falls over

travails: painful efforts, tribulations

Reflect Can a person tell the truth all the time? Why or why not?

hedging: avoiding the question

Reflect Do you agree that there "must be some merit to lying"? Why or why not?

Read to Write
Ericsson asks a question at the end of paragraph 3, and she answers it in paragraph 3. What is her answer?

Read to Write
What is the purpose of the word but in the middle of this paragraph?

pittance: a small amount

facades: masks

Reflect When have you seen people lying through facades? Does social media encourage facades?

plethora: excess

her I didn't feel like being on time, and my friend takes it personally when I say I'm not hungry. There must be some merit to lying.

5   But if I justify lying, what makes me any different from slick politicians or the corporate robbers who raided the S&L industry? Saying it's OK to lie one way and not another is hedging. I cannot seem to escape the voice deep inside me that tells me: when someone lies, someone loses.

6   What far-reaching consequences will I, or others, pay as a result of my lie? Will someone's trust be destroyed? Will someone else pay *my* penance because I ducked out? We must consider the *meaning of our actions*. Deception, lies, capital crimes, and misdemeanors all carry meanings. *Webster's* definition of *lie* is specific:

1. a false statement or action especially made with the intent to deceive;

2. anything that gives or is meant to give a false impression.

7   A definition like this implies that there are many, many ways to tell a lie. Here are just a few.

The White Lie

8   The white lie assumes that the truth will cause more damage than a simple, harmless untruth. Telling a friend he looks great when he looks like hell can be based on a decision that the friend needs a compliment more than a frank opinion. But, in effect, it is the liar deciding what is best for the lied to. Ultimately, it is a vote of no confidence. It is an act of subtle arrogance for anyone to decide what is best for someone else.

9   Yet not all circumstances are quite so cut and dried. Take, for instance, the sergeant in Vietnam who knew one of his men was killed in action but listed him as missing so that the man's family would receive indefinite compensation instead of the lump-sum pittance the military gives widows and children. His intent was honorable. Yet for twenty years this family kept their hopes alive, unable to move on to a new life.

Facades

10   We all put up facades to one degree or another. When I put on a suit to go to see a client, I feel as though I am putting on another face, obeying the expectation that serious businesspeople wear suits rather than sweatpants. But I'm a writer. Normally, I get up, get the kid off to school, and sit at my computer in my pajamas until four in the afternoon. When I answer the phone, the caller thinks I'm wearing a suit (although the UPS man knows better).

11   But facades can be destructive because they are used to seduce others into an illusion. For instance, I recently realized that a former friend was a liar. He presented himself with all the right looks and the right words and offered lots of new consciousness theories, fabulous books to read, and fascinating insights. Then I did some business with him, and the time came for him to pay me. He turned out to be all talk and no walk. I heard a plethora of reasonable excuses, including in-depth descriptions of

the big break around the corner. In six months of work, I saw less than a hundred bucks. When I confronted him, he raised both eyebrows and tried to convince me that I'd heard him wrong, that he'd made no commitment to me. A simple investigation into his past revealed a crowded graveyard of disenchanted former friends.

Ignoring the Plain Facts

12   In the sixties, the Catholic Church in Massachusetts began hearing complaints that Father James Porter was sexually molesting children. Rather than relieving him of his duties, the ecclesiastical authorities simply moved him from one parish to another between 1960 and 1967, actually providing him with a fresh supply of unsuspecting families and innocent children to abuse. After treatment in 1967 for pedophilia, he went back to work, this time in Minnesota. The new diocese was aware of Father Porter's obsession with children, but they needed priests and recklessly believed treatment had cured him. More children were abused until he was relieved of his duties a year later. By his own admission, Porter may have abused as many as a hundred children.

13   Ignoring the facts may not in and of itself be a form of lying, but consider the context of this situation. If a lie is *a false action done with the intent to deceive*, then the Catholic Church's conscious covering for Porter created irreparable consequences. The church became a coperpetrator with Porter.

Stereotypes and Clichés

14   Stereotype and cliché serve a purpose as a form of shorthand. Our need for vast amounts of information in nanoseconds has made the stereotype vital to modern communication. Unfortunately, it often shuts down original thinking, giving those hungry for truth a candy bar of misinformation instead of a balanced meal. The stereotype explains a situation with just enough truth to seem unquestionable.

15   All the *isms*—racism, sexism, ageism, et al.—are founded on and fueled by the stereotype and the cliché, which are lies of exaggeration, omission, and ignorance. They are always dangerous. They take a single tree and make it a landscape. They destroy curiosity. They close minds and separate people. The single mother on welfare is assumed to be cheating. Any black male could tell you how much of his identity is obliterated daily by stereotypes. Fat people, ugly people, beautiful people, old people, large-breasted women, short men, the mentally ill, and the homeless all could tell you how much more they are like us than we want to think. I once admitted to a group of people that I had a mouth like a truck driver. Much to my surprise, a man stood up and said, "I'm a truck driver, and I never cuss." Needless to say, I was humbled.

Out-and-Out Lies

16   Of all the ways to lie, I like this one the best, probably because I get tired of trying to figure out the real meanings behind things. At least I can trust the bald-faced lie. I once asked my five-year-old nephew, "Who broke the fence?" (I had seen him do it.) He answered, "The murderers." Who could argue?

ecclesiastical: relating to a church

pedophilia: sexual abuse of children

diocese: a district or churches under the guidance of a bishop

Reflect Do you agree that this example is a lie? Why or why not?

Reflect Is there a difference between being wrong and lying? Explain.

Read to Write Pause just as you start the "Out-and-Out Lies" section. How do you think Ericsson might define such lies?

refute: to deny

sleight: a skillful trick

pious: religious

embellish: to decorate

shrouds: covers, conceals

Read to Write Why does Ericsson ask so many questions in this paragraph?

reticent: reserved, silent, reluctant

Reflect Think back on your answer to the question on page 212 about whether lying ever has any merit. Have your views on this issue changed? Why or why not?

17   At least when this sort of lie is told it can be easily confronted. As the person who is lied to, I know where I stand. The bald-faced lie doesn't toy with my perceptions—it argues with them. It doesn't try to refashion reality; it tries to refute it. *Read my lips . . .* No sleight of hand. No guessing. If this were the only form of lying, there would be no such thing as floating anxiety or the adult-children of alcoholics movement.

18   These are only a few of the ways we lie. Or are lied to. As I said earlier, it's not easy to entirely eliminate lies from our lives. No matter how pious we may try to be, we will still embellish, hedge, and omit to lubricate the daily machinery of living. But there is a world of difference between telling functional lies and living a lie. Martin Buber once said, "The lie is the spirit committing treason against itself." Our acceptance of lies becomes a cultural cancer that eventually shrouds and reorders reality until moral garbage becomes as invisible to us as water is to a fish.

19   How much do we tolerate before we become sick and tired of being sick and tired? When will we stand up and declare our *right* to trust? When do we stop accepting that the real truth is in the fine print? Whose lips do we read this year when we vote for president? When will we stop being so reticent about making judgments? When do we stop turning over our personal power and responsibility to liars?

20   Maybe if I don't tell the bank the check's in the mail I'll be less tolerant of the lies told to me every day. A country song I once heard said it all for me: "You've got to stand for something or you'll fall for anything."

Read to Write: Annotate

1. Double-underline the thesis statement. Paraphrase this in your own words.

2. Number Ericsson's categories. Has she included all possible categories?

3. Underline all the places Ericsson asks questions. What is the purpose of her questions?

Think Critically

1. Do you agree with these categories? If not, which ones don't seem to be labeled appropriately? Should she create a new category for some of the examples?

2. How does Ericsson organize her essay?

3. What is Ericsson's attitude toward lying? What examples in the essay support your answer?

Grammar for Classification

Study this sentence from the third paragraph of Ericsson's essay.

> "We exaggerate, we minimize, we avoid confrontation, we spare people's feelings, we conveniently forget, we keep secrets, we justify lying to the big-guy institutions."

What do the underlined phrases have in common? In a list, all the words must have the same grammatical structure. This is called **parallel structure**. In this case, each item in the list contains the subject "we" and a verb in the present tense. For more information on parallel structure, see Chapter 24.

Write Your Own Classification

In this section, you will write your own classification based on one of the following assignments. For help, refer to the How to Write Classification checklist on page 217.

Assignment Options: Writing about College, Work, and Everyday Life

Write a classification paragraph or essay on one of the following topics or on one of your own choice.

College
- Classify the types of resources available in your college's library, giving examples of things in each category. If you don't have time to visit the library, spend time looking at its website. (Some library websites include virtual tours.)
- Classify the course requirements for your program into different categories, such as easy, challenging, and very challenging. Your purpose could be to help a future student in the program understand what to expect.
- Classify the types of students at your college, giving explanations and examples for each category. You might classify students by such things as their interests, their level of dedication to school, and their backgrounds. Be sure to use only one organizing principle.

Work
- Classify the different types of bosses or employees, giving explanations and examples for each category.
- Classify the types of skills you need in your current job or a job you held in the past. Give explanations and examples for each category of skill.
- Look back at the paragraph on pages 195–196 that illustrates the Four Basics of Good Classification. Based on your own experiences, think of at least two other ways in which workers might be classified. In writing about your classification, give examples of the types of jobs these workers would like and dislike.

Everyday life
- Using Lorenza Mattazi's paragraph as a guide (see p. 206), classify the types of music you enjoy.
- Write about the types of challenges you face in your everyday life, giving explanations and examples for each category.
- Find out about social-service volunteer opportunities in your community. Write about the types of opportunities that are available. Or research an organization that interests you, and write about the kinds of things it does.

Assignment Options: Reading and writing critically

Complete one of the following assignments that asks you to apply the critical thinking, reading, and writing skills discussed in Chapter 1.

Writing Critically about Readings

Tip For a reminder of how to summarize, analyze, synthesize, and evaluate, see the Reading and Writing Critically box on page 17.

Both Stephanie Ericsson's "The Ways We Lie" (pp. 211–214) and Kelly Hultgren's "Pick Up the Phone to Call, Not Text" (pp. 207–208) describe certain behaviors (lying or stretching the truth in certain circumstances and refusing to call a person and speak to them). Read or review both of these essays, and then follow these steps:

1. **Summarize** Briefly summarize the works, listing examples they include.

2. **Analyze** Are there any other examples or details that the authors might have provided? Are their classifications complete? Do they achieve the authors' purposes?

3. **Synthesize** Using examples from both Ericsson's and Hultgren's essays and from your own experience, discuss trends that can hurt or destroy relationships in our society.

4. **Evaluate** Which piece, Ericsson's or Hultgren's, do you think is more effective? Why? In writing your evaluation, you might look back on your responses to step 2.

Writing about Images

Study the visual below, and complete the following steps.

OZGUR DONMAZ/GETTY IMAGES

1. **Read the image** Ask yourself: what purpose does the visual serve? What do the expressions and gestures in each frame say about the woman? (For more information on reading images, see Chapter 1.)

2. **Write a classification** Write a paragraph or essay classifying the messages we can express with body language, especially in the classroom or the workplace. You might include or expand on the expressions and gestures represented in the visual.

Writing to Solve a Problem

Read or review the discussion of problem solving in Chapter 1 (pp. 26–27). Then, consider the following problem.

> **You need a car loan. The loan officer gives you an application that asks for your monthly income and expenses. Because you find yourself short on money every month, you realize that you need to see how you spend your money. You decide to make a monthly budget that categorizes the kinds of expenses you have.**

Assignment Working with a group or on your own, break your monthly expenses into categories, thinking of everything that you spend money on. Then, review the expenses carefully to see which ones might be reduced. Next, write a classification paragraph or essay for the loan officer that classifies your monthly expenses, with examples, and ends with one or two suggestions about how you might reduce your monthly spending. You might start with this sentence:

My monthly expenses fall into (_number_) basic categories: _____, _____, and _____.

CHECKLIST

How to Write Classification

Steps	Details
☐ Narrow and explore your topic. See Chapter 3.	• Make the topic more specific. • Prewrite to get ideas about the narrowed topic.
☐ Write a topic sentence (paragraph) or thesis statement (essay). See Chapter 3.	• State your topic and your organizing principle or categories. ➡

Steps	Details
☐ Support your point. See Chapter 4.	• Come up with explanations/examples to support each category.
☐ Write a draft. See Chapter 5.	• Make a plan that puts the categories in a logical order. • Include a topic sentence (paragraph) or thesis statement (essay) and all the supporting categories with explanations and examples.
☐ Revise your draft. See Chapter 5.	• Make sure it has *all* the Four Basics of Good Classification. • Make sure you include transitions to move readers smoothly from one category to the next.
☐ Edit your revised draft. See Parts 3 through 6.	• Correct errors in grammar, spelling, word use, and punctuation.

Chapter Review

1. What is classification?

2. What is an organizing principle?

3. What are the Four Basics of Good Classification?

4. What are three ways to give secondary support in classification?

Reflect and Apply

1. When have you written or read classification before? What makes reading or writing classification difficult?

2. Interview someone studying in your major or working in your career. What situations require reading or writing classification in your major or career?

3. What challenged you the most when writing for this chapter? What do you want to do differently next time?

4. What worked well in your writing for this chapter? What do you need to remember for next time?

11

Definition
Writing That Tells What Something Means

Understand What Definition Is

Four Basics of Good Definition

1 It makes a point by defining a concept.

2 It presents characteristics or key features of the concept.

3 It uses examples and details to illustrate the key features.

4 It arranges key features and examples in a logical order.

In the following paragraph, the numbers and colors correspond to the Four Basics of Good Definition.

A **2** stereotype is a conventional idea or image that is simplistic—and often wrong, particularly when it is applied to people or groups of people. **1** Stereotypes can prevent us from seeing people as they really are because stereotypes blind us with preconceived notions about what a certain type of person is like. **3** For example, I had a stereotyped notion of Native Americans until I met my friend Daniel, a Chippewa Indian. **1** I thought all Indians wore feathers and beads, had long black hair, and avoided all contact with non-Native Americans because they resented their land being taken away. Daniel, however, wears jeans and T-shirts, and we talk about everything—even our different ancestries. After meeting him, I understood that my stereotype of Native Americans was completely wrong. **2** Not only was it wrong, but it set up an us–them concept in my mind that made me feel that I, as a non-Native American, would never have anything in common with Native Americans. My stereotype would not have allowed me to see any Native

4 Logical Organization

219

American as an individual: I would have seen him or her as part of a group that I thought was all alike and all different from me. From now on, I won't assume that any individual fits my stereotype; I will try to see that person as I would like them to see me: as myself, not a stereotyped image.

You can use definition in many practical situations.

Think Critically
What is the difference between illustration and definition? While many writers use illustration as part of the definition, giving examples is not the same as defining.

College	On a math exam, you are asked to define *exponential notation*.
Work	On a performance evaluation for work, you define *positive attitude* before giving examples of how a coworker demonstrates it.
Everyday life	In a relationship, you define for your partner what you mean by *commitment* or *communication*.

In college, writing assignments may include the word *define,* but they might also use phrases such as *explain the meaning of a concept* and *discuss the meaning of a term*. In these cases, use the strategies discussed in this chapter to complete the assignment.

For more information on understanding writing prompts, see the Appendix, page 553.

First Basic: Main Idea in Definition

In definition, the **main idea** usually defines a term or concept. The main idea is related to your purpose: to help your readers understand the term or concept as you are using it.

When you write your definition, do not just copy the dictionary definition; write it in your own words as you want your readers to understand it. To help you, you might first complete the following sentence:

Read to Write
To find the main idea when you are reading definition, complete the following sentence: The author is saying that this term means…

Main idea in definition   **I want readers to understand that this term means . . .**

Then, based on your response, write a topic sentence (paragraph) or thesis statement (essay). These main idea statements can take the following forms.

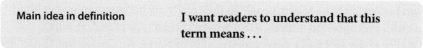

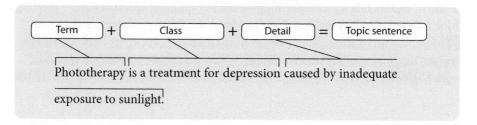

Phototherapy is a treatment for depression caused by inadequate exposure to sunlight.

In this example, "Class" is the larger group the term belongs to. Main-idea statements do not have to include a class, however. For example:

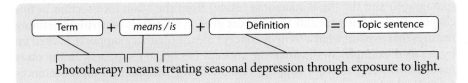

Now, look at this thesis statement about a related topic.

Tip Sometimes, the same main idea can be used for a paragraph and an essay, but the essay must develop this point in more detail. (See pp. 224–225.)

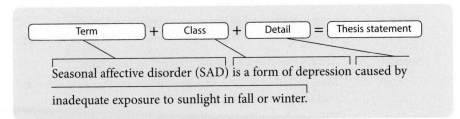

The thesis statement is broader in scope than the topic sentences because it sets up a discussion of the larger subject of seasonal affective disorder. In contrast, the topic sentences consider one particular treatment for this disorder (phototherapy).

PRACTICE 11–1   Writing a Statement of Your Definition

For each of the following terms, write a definition statement using the pattern indicated in brackets. You may need to use a dictionary.

Example:

Cirrhosis [term + class + detail]:

Cirrhosis is a liver disease often caused by alcohol abuse.

1. Stress [term + class + detail]:

2. Vacation [term + *means /is* + definition]:

3. Confidence [term + class + detail]:

4. Conservation [term + *means /is* + definition]:

5. Marriage [term + *means /is* + definition]:

Second Basic: Primary Support in Definition

The paragraph and essay models on pages 224–225 use one topic sentence (paragraph) and the thesis statement (essay) from the Main Idea section in this chapter. Both models include the support used in all definition writing: defining features that explain what a term or concept means (primary support), backed up by detailed examples to illustrate the concept (secondary support). In the essay model, however, the major support ideas (defining features) are topic sentences for individual paragraphs.

Look at the following examples:

Thesis	Science fiction (sci-fi) is a genre or type of writing that speculates about how a scientific concept could affect humanity.
Support	Always involves a scientific concept or principle
	Must include a setting, situation, or technology that is not a part of our current experience
	Explores how humans will react and adapt to this concept or setting
Thesis	Any prospective roommate needs to know that I am an introvert.
Support	I need time alone with privacy.
	I am not comfortable with loud social events like parties; I will need a place to get away.
	I disconnect from social media every now and then.

PRACTICE 11-2   Selecting Key Features for the Definitionn

List three examples or pieces of information you could use to explain each of the following definitions.

Example:

Insomnia means sleeplessness.

a.   hard to fall asleep

b.   wake up in the middle of the night

c.   wake up without feeling rested in the morning

1. A good workout is essential to self-care.

2. A real friend is not just someone for the fun times.

3. A family is a group you always belong to, no matter what.

4. Beauty is an important element in life that a viewer needs to be always looking for, even in unlikely places.

Third Basic: Secondary Support in Definition

Strong definition provides detailed examples to explain and illustrate the key features of the concept or term you are defining. Study the following examples:

Thesis	Science fiction (sci-fi) is a genre or type of writing that speculates about how a scientific concept could affect humanity.
Support	Always involves a scientific concept or principle
	• Example: C. S. Lewis's novel *Out of the Silent Planet* explores the concept of long-distance space travel.
	Must include a setting, situation, or technology that is not a part of our current experience
	• The novel is set on Malacandra, on Mars.
	Explores how humans will react and adapt to this concept or setting
	• The novel explores the effects of human conquest of other planets and races, painting a negative picture of the human ambition to conquer the galaxies.
Thesis	Any prospective roommate needs to know that I am an introvert.
Support	I need time alone with privacy.
	• I have to have a bedroom with a lock on it. I study alone for hours at a time.
	I am not comfortable with loud social events like parties; I will need a place to get away.
	• At parties, I may leave for 15 minutes or so in order to let my brain calm down.
	• Long stretches of loud music and talk give me a migraine.
	I disconnect from social media every now and then.
	• I do not answer or look at texts, emails, snapchats, or messages while I am talking with someone face to face.

Paragraphs versus Essays in Definition

For more on the important features of definition, see the Four Basics of Good Definition on page 219.

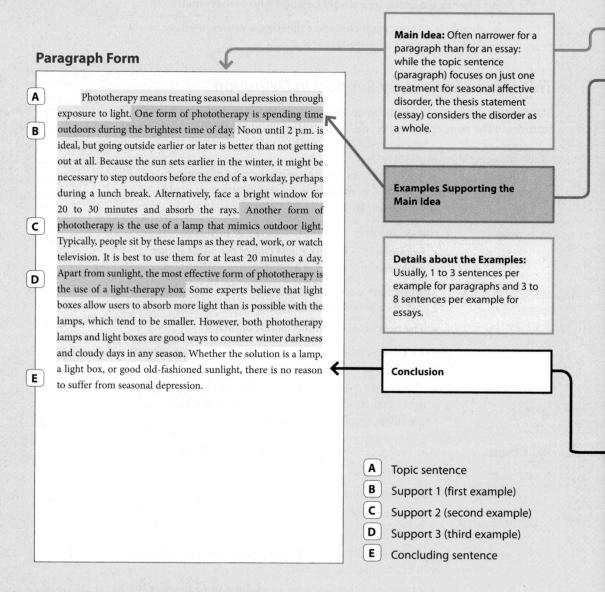

Paragraph Form

A   Phototherapy means treating seasonal depression through exposure to light. One form of phototherapy is spending time **B** outdoors during the brightest time of day. Noon until 2 p.m. is ideal, but going outside earlier or later is better than not getting out at all. Because the sun sets earlier in the winter, it might be necessary to step outdoors before the end of a workday, perhaps during a lunch break. Alternatively, face a bright window for 20 to 30 minutes and absorb the rays. Another form of **C** phototherapy is the use of a lamp that mimics outdoor light. Typically, people sit by these lamps as they read, work, or watch television. It is best to use them for at least 20 minutes a day. **D** Apart from sunlight, the most effective form of phototherapy is the use of a light-therapy box. Some experts believe that light boxes allow users to absorb more light than is possible with the lamps, which tend to be smaller. However, both phototherapy lamps and light boxes are good ways to counter winter darkness and cloudy days in any season. Whether the solution is a lamp, a light box, or good old-fashioned sunlight, there is no reason **E** to suffer from seasonal depression.

Main Idea: Often narrower for a paragraph than for an essay: while the topic sentence (paragraph) focuses on just one treatment for seasonal affective disorder, the thesis statement (essay) considers the disorder as a whole.

Examples Supporting the Main Idea

Details about the Examples: Usually, 1 to 3 sentences per example for paragraphs and 3 to 8 sentences per example for essays.

Conclusion

A   Topic sentence

B   Support 1 (first example)

C   Support 2 (second example)

D   Support 3 (third example)

E   Concluding sentence

Think Critically As You Write Definition

Ask Yourself

- Have I considered different points of view on this term or concept?
- Have I included the most important features to define the term?
- Would someone who is unfamiliar with this term or concept understand it based on my definition and my supporting details and examples?

Essay Form

1

Seasonal affective disorder (SAD) is a form of depression caused by inadequate exposure to sunlight in fall or winter. It can seriously affect the daily life of those who suffer from it. **[A]**

One characteristic of SAD is sleepiness and a lack of energy. SAD sufferers may find that they are sleeping longer yet are still drowsy during the day, especially during the afternoon. Connected to the drowsiness may be moodiness and an inability to concentrate. The latter effect can result in poorer performance at work and at other tasks. Those affected by SAD may also find that they move more slowly than usual and that all types of physical activity are more challenging than they used to be. All these difficulties can be a source of frustration, sometimes worsening the depression. Another characteristic of SAD is loss of interest in work, hobbies, and other activities. To some extent, these symptoms may be connected to a lack of energy. Often, however, the feelings run deeper than that. Activities that once lifted one's spirits may have the opposite effect. For instance, a mother who at one time never **[B]** **[C]**

2

missed her child's soccer games might now see attending them as a burden. Someone who was once a top performer at work may find that it is all he or she can do to show up in the morning. Such changes in one's outlook can contribute to a feeling of hopelessness.

The most serious symptom of SAD is withdrawal from interactions with others. SAD sufferers may find that they are no longer interested in going out with friends, and they may turn down requests to get together for movies, meals, or social events. They may even withdraw from family members, engaging less frequently in conversations or even spending time alone in their room. Furthermore, they may postpone or cancel activities, such as vacation trips, that might require them to interact with family for hours at a time. Withdrawal symptoms may also extend to the workplace, with SAD sufferers becoming less vocal at meetings or avoiding lunches or conversations with colleagues. Concern that family members or coworkers may be noticing such personality changes can cause or worsen anxiety in those with SAD. **[D]**

3

Because the symptoms and effects of SAD can be so significant, it is important to address them as soon as possible. Fortunately, there are many good therapies for the condition, from drug treatment to greater exposure to sunlight, whether real or simulated through special lamps or light boxes. Often, such treatments have SAD sufferers feeling better quickly. **[E]**

[A] Thesis statement
[B] Topic sentence 1 (first characteristic)
[C] Topic sentence 2 (second characteristic)
[D] Topic sentence 3 (third characteristic)
[E] Concluding paragraph

PRACTICE 11-3   **Selecting Examples and Details for the Definition**

Choose one of the thesis statements and defining features from Practice 2. Give one or two examples or details to explain or illustrate each feature.

Fourth Basic: Organization in Definition

Tip For more on order of importance, see page 75.

The characteristics and examples in definition are often organized by **order of importance**, meaning that the example that will have the most effect on readers is saved for last. This strategy is used in the paragraph and essay models on pages 224–225.

Transitions in definition move readers from one example to the next. Here are some transitions you might use in definition, although many others are possible, too.

Common Transitions in Definition

alternately	first, second, third, and so on
another; one/another	for example
another kind	for instance

PRACTICE 11-4   **Using Transitions in Definition**

Read the paragraph that follows, and fill in the blanks with transitions. You are not limited to the ones listed in the preceding box.

Each year, *Business Week* publishes a list of the most family-friendly companies to work for. The magazine uses several factors to define the organizations as family-friendly. ___ factor is whether the company has flextime, allowing employees to schedule work hours that better fit family needs. _____, a parent might choose to work from 6:30 a.m. to 2:30 p.m. to be able to spend time with children. _____, a parent might split his or her job with a colleague, so each person thus has more time for child care. _____ factor is whether family leave programs are encouraged. In addition to maternity leaves, _____, does the company encourage paternity leaves and leaves for care of elderly parents? Increasingly, companies are trying to become more family-friendly to attract and keep good employees.

Evaluate Definition

Read the following sample definition paragraph. Using the Four Basics of Good Definition and the sample grading rubric, decide what grade this paragraph would earn. Explain your answer.

Assignment Define one important trait that you would look for in a best friend.

Finding a best friend isn't always easy because it's important to make sure to know the person well. When I first meet a person and begin to spend time with them, I want to make sure that we have enough in common to be good friends. If we can't agree on places to go or what to do, then that may mean that we do not really share enough interests to spend a lot of time together. For example, I am passionate about football, basketball, and baseball. What if I always want to go to sporting events and the other person always wants to go to a movie? That makes it hard for us to hang out because we just don't find the same things entertaining. Therefore, if we are not spending a lot of time together, then we probably are not a great fit as best friends.

Analysis of Sample Paragraph:

Sample rubric

Element	Grading criteria	Point: Comment
Appropriateness	• Did the student follow the assignment directions?	_/5:
Main idea	• Does the paper clearly state a strong main idea in a complete sentence?	__/10:
Support	• Is the main idea developed with specific support, including specific details and examples? • Is there enough support to make the main idea evident to the reader? • Is all the support directly related to the main idea?	__/10:
Organization	• Is the writing logically organized according to a basic principle (order of importance)? • Does the student use transitions (*also, for example, sometimes,* and so on) to move the reader from one point to another?	_/10:

→

Element	Grading criteria	Point: Comment
Conclusion	• Does the conclusion remind the reader of the main idea?	_ /5:
Grammar	• Is the writing free of the four most serious errors? (See Chapters 16–19.) • Is the sentence structure clear? • Does the student choose words that clearly express his or her meaning? • Are the words spelled correctly? • Is the punctuation correct?	__ /10:
		TOTAL POINTS: __ /50

Read and Analyze Definition

Reading examples of definition will help you write your own. The first example is a student paragraph by Corin Costas about a community service group in which he is involved. A student essay by Kevin Willey looks at the defining characteristics of a generation. In the Profile of Success, Moses Maddox describes how he uses definition in his career. Finally, a professional essay by Adam McCrimmon defines autism to help parents understand when they need to have a child evaluated. As you read these pieces, pay attention to the vocabulary and the questions in the margin. They will help you read critically.

Student Definition Paragraph

Corin Costas

What Community Involvement Means to Me

S.H.O.C.W.A.V.E.S. is a student organization at Bunker Hill Community College. S.H.O.C.W.A.V.E.S. stands for Students Helping Our Community with Activities, and its mission is to get students involved with the community—to become part of it by actively working in it in positive ways. Each year, S.H.O.C.W.A.V.E.S. is assigned a budget by the Student Activities Office, and it spends that budget in activities that help the community in a variety of ways. Some of the money is spent, for example, in fund-raising events for community causes. We have money to plan and launch a fund-raiser, which raises far more than we spend. In the process, other students and members of the community also become involved in the helping effort. We get to know lots of people, and we usually have a lot of fun—all while helping others. Recently, we have worked as part of the Charles River Cleanup, the Walk for Hunger, collecting toys for sick and needy children, and Light One Little Candle. While S.H.O.C.W.A.V.E.S.'s mission is to help the community, it also benefits its members. Working in the community, I have learned so many valuable skills, and I always have something I care about to write about for my classes. I have learned about budgeting, advertising, organizing, and managing. I have also developed my creativity by coming up with new ways to do things. I have networked with many people, including people who are important in the business world. S.H.O.C.W.A.V.E.S. has greatly improved my life and my chances for future success.

Read to Write: Annotate

1. Double-underline the topic sentence.
2. Underline the examples of what S.H.O.C.W.A.V.E.S. does for the community.
3. Double-underline the sentence that makes a final observation about the topic.

Think Critically

1. Does this paragraph follow the Four Basics of Good Definition (p. 219)? Why or why not?
2. Has the author provided enough examples for readers to understand what the organization is? Would you recommend that the author add any more details?

Student Definition Essay

Kevin Willey

The Optimistic Generation

Kevin Willey wrote this essay while he was a senior mechanical engineering major at the University of Maine. He graduated in May 2011, and, after looking for some time and contacting many companies, he landed a job in his field. In "The Optimistic Generation," Willey offers a defining trait of his generation that is perhaps different from what most people think of when they hear his age group called "the Millennials."

The media are quick to name and define each generation of Americans, from the Baby Boomers to Generation X to Generation Y, also known as the Millennials. Already, there is Generation Z, to refer to children born after the early 1990s. My friends and I are Millennials, those people born between the mid-1970s to the early 1990s. When people try to sum up what we Millennials are like, they say that we are immature, impatient, restless, and distracted by constant technological interaction, and other negative descriptions. Instead, it is more accurate to say that we are optimistic. The *Merriam-Webster Dictionary Online* defines *optimism* as "an inclination to put the most favorable construction upon actions and events or to anticipate the best possible outcome" ("Optimism"). This optimism is a characteristic that will serve us and others well.

2   One area we are optimistic about is our job prospects. As we enter young adulthood, the economy took a nosedive, and many of us are unable to find the jobs we thought would be there for us when we graduated. Many of us have large student loans to repay, and we need to find good work. Instead of jobs waiting for us, and companies ready to put us to work, we find too many people looking and not enough positions open: the older generation is not retiring fast enough, and many companies have cut thousands of jobs or sent jobs overseas, to be done by lower-paid workers. Many of us are settling for the kinds of jobs we had during high school. As a group, however, we are not bitter or angry. We believe that the future will be better. The Pew Research Center recently published a report about Millennials, describing us as "confident" and "upbeat and open to change" (Pew Res. Center 1). The report goes on to say: "Millennials have not escaped the current economic downturn. But even though they're not happy with their current economic circumstances, they remain highly optimistic about their financial future" (20).

3   I am optimistic that our connectedness will help us, too. We do not have to make an effort to network because we already keep in frequent touch through all kinds of social and business groups online. We also like working in groups, and businesses operate to a large degree on good teamwork. The Pew report also describes us as more open to technology and social media than previous generations (25), and that experience has helped us adapt to new things, since technology is always changing. This openness to change is part of our optimism. We believe that the world will always be changing and improving, and we are ready. We do not fight change; we welcome it. Bring it on.

4   Our world has many other major threats, such as wars, global warming, and poverty. Here in the United States, we have not only a bad economy but a Congress that cannot seem to work together and as a result is unproductive. The U.S. divorce rate is high, and the gap between the richest and the poorest just keeps growing. Prices are rising on necessities such as food, gasoline, and heating oil. And the cost of housing means that my friends and I, if we are lucky enough to get jobs, will need many roommates in our tiny apartments to help us keep up

with the rent. Others will live with their parents, if they can. But our optimism here, too, helps us: we know it will get better.

5   A 2011 report in *Time* magazine focused on optimism as a positive characteristic. Optimism allows us to get through bad times such as these because we believe in a better future (Sharot 39). We do not give up. This belief that the situation will improve gives us the initiative to try to solve the problems facing us. Author Tali Sharot says, "To make progress, we need to be able to imagine alternative realities—better ones—and we need to believe that we can achieve them. Such faith helps motivate us to pursue our goals" (42).

Reflect Is there a danger in the ability to "imagine alternate realities"? Explain.

6   As I go out to find a job, I know I might not get exactly the position I want or the one that I thought a college degree would give me. My friends and I will not have it easy. But as a group, we have real and durable optimism. That characteristic will serve us well, and our generation, the Millennials, have a lot to contribute to the world.

Summarize How are Millenials optimistic? How will optimism help them going forward?

Works Cited

"Optimism." *Merriam-Webster Dictionary Online.* Merriam-Webster Dictionary. 10 Apr. 2011. www.merriam-webster.com/dictionary/optimism.

Pew Research Center. "Millennials: A Portrait of Generation Next." 24 Feb. 2010. pewresearch.org/millennials/. 4 Apr. 2011.

Sharot, Tali. "The Optimism Bias." *Time* 28 May 2011: 39–46.

Read to Write: Annotate

1. Double-underline the main idea of the essay.

2. Underline the defining features of the "optimistic generation."

3. Circle the transitions used by the author.

Think Critically

1. The writer uses source material to help illustrate the defining characteristics. Are these sources effective? Could the author have made his point without including the source material? Explain.

2. How is this essay organized?

3. Does this essay use the Four Basics of Good Definition (page 219)? Why or why not?

Profile of Success
Definition in the Real World

COURTESY OF MOSES MADDOX

Moses Maddox

Fellowship Specialist at
The Mission Continues

Background When I was pursuing my degree, I struggled with writing. It wasn't that I didn't enjoy writing, but with my program being in social sciences I had concentrations in sociology, political science, and history, and I also pursued a minor in philosophy because, well, why not? The struggle with having four different focuses was that all four subjects had different tones in writing. When writing a paper in history, you had to present facts and analysis of those facts, and there was little room for personality or creativity beyond the presentation of those facts. In philosophy, one had to be careful of what one was writing so that one didn't commit any logical fallacies. In philosophy, it will take you four pages to write something that would be one page in history because you have to be careful that the reader understands your premise before you get to your point. It was a tough learning experience to get a "C" on a history paper because I "didn't write a history paper." That happened a lot.

What I learned through experiences like that was to understand my audience. Sometimes people just want the facts and your presentation of those facts; however, in my current position, if I just presented facts, it would impact how seriously a person would take this program. I have also learned how to find my voice through my writing. I was encouraged by my professors to experiment, to look at writing as my true expression of self. People will forget what you've said, but what you write can last forever. I was taught to write so that if someone one hundred years from now read something I'd written, they would get a sense of who I am, as though I was able to communicate with a person in the future. Writing is that powerful.

Degrees/Colleges BA Social Sciences with Philosophy Minor from California State University, San Marcos; AA Arts & Humanities, Social & Behavioral Sciences, Sociology from Palomar College, San Marcos, CA

Writing at work What I do at The Mission Continues is manage returning post-9/11 veterans as they navigate through their six-month fellowships. A fellowship with The Mission Continues resembles more of an executive internship

Workplace Definition: Moses Maddox, Email to Clients

The following is an email Moses sent out to his clients at The Mission Continues.

Hello Fellows,

2   First: amazing work! Thanks to each and every single one of you for getting me your written assignments on time. Your candid responses have let me know that you are taking this seriously and have given me a look into the impact you all want to make. All of your goals are achievable, and all of your fears can be overcome!

3   In Month 2, we talk more about overcoming fear and identifying allies. In a few minutes, I will share some tips and tricks to get the most out of Month 2. First, I want to recap the two main terms I went over with all of you in Month 1:

4   **Eudaimonia:** Gotta love the work that goes into "well-being" or "being well." My goal for all of you is to find your joy and be well.

candid: truthful and straightforward

where Fellows pick the nonprofit organization they want to serve, but as they pick that organization, it has to fulfill some sort of qualitative and quantitative goals. That means that they have to fulfill a professional goal, a continued education goal, or a continued service goal, and they have to generate data. What Fellows accomplish throughout their fellowships serves as resume fodder for many of them, who have a ton of leadership experience from the military but do not necessarily have the relevant work experience to be marketable in the civilian job market.

Veterans are really good at the "how" part of life. If you give military members a job to do, they will do it and do it well. However, if you ask them why they are doing the job, many don't know the answer. My position is to facilitate our curriculum, when we focus on personal and professional development through goal setting, finding allies, identifying role models, identifying driving force, and creating personal mission statements. The overarching goal is for our veterans to be in a place where they can go out into the world and understand what they are

looking for in a career and understand how their military experience applies to the nonmilitary world. We feel that service is a vehicle through a successful transition, and my job is to hold the Fellows accountable for the goals that they set and push them to explore their inner selves so that they can move on and find joy in their lives.

As such, writing is a huge part of my job. Although the writing is mainly conversational in tone, creating the correct message is important. Things such as punctuation are important because there is a difference between "You're doing a great job." and "You're doing a great job!" It is part of the job to remain positive, as well as approachable, in all of my interactions. In covering rather deep philosophical conversations, if one approaches the topic in a completely academic tone, then people will check out. If one approaches it in a conversational tone, people are more receptive. One email—in fact, one sentence—can mean the difference between a successful fellowship or someone giving up completely. So focusing on writing is one of the key competencies of my work.

5 **10,000 Hours:** Malcolm Gladwell stated that it takes 10,000 hours of deliberate practice to become an expert at something. The actual research suggests that it takes ten years. I think most of us have agreed that achieving 10,000 hours of deliberate practice helps you master the basics. We have also agreed that for many of you, due to your time in the military, you have devoted more than 10,000 hours of your life to service, and your fellowships add to your tally.

6 **Month 2:** Month 2 is less intimidating, but just as deep. Here are the terms that I enjoyed researching and the stuff we will talk about over the month.

7 **Mental Rehearsal:** The best way to face your fears is to think about them, visualize the worst-case scenario, and then in your visualization, come up with a way to solve your worst-case scenario. In philosophy, we call this a thought experiment. Einstein famously used thought experimentation during his development of the theory of special relativity. Long story short, with enough practice, mental rehearsal can be a great tool.

8   **Finding Allies:** You will read (or have already read) an excerpt from Reid Hoffman from his book *The Start-Up of You*. The summary I attached is basically a CliffsNotes version of the book. Also, *How to Win Friends and Influence People* was mentioned, and I included the entire book mainly because it is such an amazing and enlightening read.

no person is an island: people need others to live well; no one should be isolated.

9   Remember that no person is an island, so when you are thinking about your allies, the reading states that "allies can be friends, spouses, colleagues, family, supervisors, mentors," which I agree with. However, don't pick your spouse as an ally just because he or she is there. Choose allies that share your goals, offer something of their own, and are willing to be helped. Also remember that an ally is:

- Someone you consult regularly for advice.
- Someone with whom you share opportunities and collaborate.

Cheers,
Mo

Read to Write: Annotate

1. Double-underline the topic sentence.
2. Underline the terms Maddox defines in his email and paraphrase the definitions.

Think Critically

1. Maddox notes that "allies can be friends, spouses, colleagues, family, supervisors, mentors"; however, he also warns his readers about choosing someone just because they are close in proximity. Why do you think he does this? What does he want his readers to do as they choose an ally?

2. Maddox notes that he is always aware of his audience and how they will perceive his work. Who do you think he is writing to in this email? What clues do you see that help you identify that reader?

Professional Definition Essay

Adam McCrimmon

Since 2009, Adam McCrimmon has been an Associate Professor in the School and Applied Child Psychology program in the Werklund School of Education at the University of Calgary, where he also received his doctorate. As a psychologist and educator, he teaches graduate courses and conducts research on the diagnosis and response to autism spectrum disorder (ASD).

Does My Child Have Autism or Is This "Normal" Behavior?

Raising a child is often one of the most challenging and joyous events in a person's life. Watching your child grow and develop is a source of delight. However, some parents become concerned when their child appears to develop differently than others. At times, parents may worry about the possibility of autism spectrum disorder, or ASD.

2   As an associate professor and registered psychologist in the Werklund School of Education at the University of Calgary, I specialize in diagnostic assessment of ASD for individuals from toddlerhood to adulthood. Many families speak to me of their concerns (or others' concerns) for their child and wonder about the possibility of ASD. I have found that informing parents of the symptoms of ASD can help them decide if their worries are warranted. As well, many parents are unaware of how the disorder is currently characterized and therefore struggle to understand if an assessment may benefit their child.

Individual Symptoms are Unique

3   ASD is, according to the description used by most clinicians in North America, a "neurodevelopmental disorder"—meaning it becomes apparent during a child's early development and results in difficulties with their personal, social, academic or occupational functioning. Those with ASD typically demonstrate symptoms by two to three years of age. However, many will display signs earlier in development and ASD can be reliably diagnosed around eighteen months of age.

4   Individuals must demonstrate challenges in two domains of functioning: 1) social communication and 2) restricted and/or repetitive patterns of behavior. Importantly, individuals with ASD are seen to fall on a "spectrum," meaning that they can experience a range of difficulties within each domain. This means that each individual's specific symptoms will be unique.

Social Communication Challenges

5   Within the social communication domain, children may demonstrate a delay in speech development—either by using no single words by eighteen months or no two- to three-word phrases by thirty-three months of age. They may fail to direct others' attention (e.g., by pointing or eye contact), follow another's point or respond to their name. Sometimes they lack or have limited skill with pretend play. Other signs could include reduced interest in playing with peers, not showing or bringing objects to others to share an interest, smiling infrequently at others or failing to gesture to express their needs—for example by nodding or raising their arms to be picked up.

6   Many children who receive an ASD diagnosis do not imitate others' behaviors. For example, they might not wave back to someone who waves at them. Or they struggle to understand others' language or show a limited range of facial expressions.

7   Sometimes they use others' hands as a tool—for example, using a parent's hand to point at pictures in a book rather than pointing themselves. And they may echo others' words rather than using their own language to express needs or wants.

Read to Write
Who is McCrimmon's intended audience? How can you tell?

warranted: justified, reasonable

Read to Write
How does the writer introduce the definition of "neurodevelopmental disorder" for his readers? What does it mean?

Reflect What are the two key features required for a diagnosis of autism?

Reflect The writer provides several examples of social communication challenges here. Based on what he said in paragraph 4, does a child need to demonstrate all of these in order to be diagnosed with ASD?

Read to Write
Notice the use of apostrophes in paragraph 7. Why does the apostrophe follow the "s" in the first sentence? For more on apostrophes, see Chapter 31.

Repetitive Patterns of Behavior

aversion: a strong dislike

8   Regarding restricted/repetitive patterns of behavior, some children show a strong preference for, or aversion to, sensory stimuli. For example, a child may crave visual input by staring at a fan for a long period of time. Or they may be overly distressed by typical household noises, haircuts, or being touched.

sensory stimuli: things that cause a response from one of the five senses

9   Children often become attached to specific objects—such as a block or a notebook that they must carry around with them—yet show little interest in toys. They can become intensely interested in things like door knobs or toilet seats or become obsessed with a familiar cartoon character or toy.

Read to Write
What is the purpose of the parentheses in paragraph 10?

10   They may repetitively wave their arms or hands, rock or spin when excited. Some children repeat actions over and over, such as turning a light switch on and off. Some focus on small parts of an object (the wheel of a toy car) rather than the entire object (the car). Others may insistently line objects up—such as toys or family members' shoes—and become distressed if the objects are moved. They may be aggressive toward others or may injure themselves. They often crave predictability and struggle when their routines are disrupted.

Early Identification is Key

sufficient: enough, adequate

11   Importantly, no single symptom is necessary or sufficient for a diagnosis. However, more symptoms do increase the potential for a diagnosis. As well, many children display symptoms consistent with ASD yet grow out of them naturally and do not receive a diagnosis. Experienced clinicians take typical child development into account when determining if a diagnosis is warranted.

Reflect Paraphrase the first sentence of paragraph 11. Why is this information particularly important for parents?

12   If you are concerned that your child may have ASD, an important first step is to speak with your doctor or pediatrician. Autism Canada is an excellent resource that provides information on assessment and intervention opportunities. Assessment often involves teams of professionals working together to identify a child's fit with the symptoms of ASD and typically includes observation of the child in different settings, interviews with parents and completion of assessment tasks to evaluate a child's development.

Reflect Based on your reading of this article, what would you advise a friend who is concerned about a child's development?

13   Early identification is key. This recognition enables children and their families to access interventions and supports that have their greatest impact during early childhood.

Read to Write: Annotate

1. Double-underline the thesis statement.

2. Circle the transitions or repeated words used to introduce examples.

Think Critically

1. What is the writer's purpose in this essay? Does he achieve it? Explain.

2. In paragraph 2, the author presents his credentials, or qualifications that establish his expertise. Given his purpose and audience, why is it important for him to present these credentials?

3. Look at the last sentence of the essay. Is the writer's tone optimistic or pessimistic? How does his tone support his purpose?

Respond

1. McCrimmon defines the word *spectrum* in this essay. What is a spectrum? How is a spectrum different from a binary (either/or) trait? What are some examples of human traits that fall along a spectrum rather than a binary difference?

2. The title contrasts autism with "normal behavior," and the author's analysis shows that it can be very difficult to separate the two. Why is it so very difficult to define what "normal" means when it comes to behavior and development? Are there other words that might be more helpful?

Grammar for Definition

Because definitions describe situations or concepts that are true all the time, we often use simple present tense to write them. It is important to pay attention to subject–verb agreement in the simple present tense. Look at the following example from McCrimmon's essay. The subjects are underlined once, and the verbs are underlined twice.

> Importantly, no single symptom is necessary or sufficient for a diagnosis. However, more symptoms do increase the potential for a diagnosis. As well, many children display symptoms consistent with ASD yet grow out of them naturally and do not receive a diagnosis. Experienced clinicians take typical child development into account when determining if a diagnosis is warranted.

In the present tense, a singular subject requires a singular verb, and a plural subject requires a plural verb. For more on subject-verb agreement, see Chapter 18.

Write Your Own Definition

In this section, you will write your own definition based on one of the following assignments. For help, refer to the How to Write Definition checklist on page 240.

Assignment Options: Writing about college, work, and everyday life

Write a definition paragraph or essay on one of the following topics or on one of your own choice.

College	• How would you define effective study habits and noneffective study habits? Give examples to explain your definitions.
	• Identify a difficult or technical term from a class you are taking. Then, define the term, and give examples of different ways in which it might be used.
	• Define *learning,* not only in terms of school but in terms of all the ways in which it can occur. You might start by writing down the different types of learning that go on both in school and in other settings. Then, (1) write a main idea that defines learning in a broader way, and (2) support your definition with the examples you came up with.
Work	• Define a satisfying job, giving explanations and examples.
	• If you have ever held a job that used unusual or interesting terminology, write about some of the terms used, what they meant, and their function on the job.
	• How do members of your profession refer to themselves or to outsiders? Write an essay that defines one of these terms.
Everyday life	• What does it mean to be a good friend or parent? Provide a definition, giving explanations and examples.
	• Write an essay defining a term that describes a problem in your community, such as *addiction, road rage, poverty, discrimination,* or *xenophobia.* Provide explanations and examples.
	• Ask three (or more) people to tell you what they think *community service* means. Take notes on their responses, and then write a paragraph or an essay combining their definitions with your own.

Assignment Options Reading and writing critically

Complete one of the following assignments that asks you to apply the critical thinking, reading, and writing skills discussed in Chapter 1.

Writing Critically about Readings

Both Kelly Hultgren's essay, "Pick up the Phone to Call, Not Text" (p. 207) and Stephanie Alaimo and Mark Koester's "The Backdraft of Technology" (p. 279) define potential hazards of technology in society. While these essays are primarily classification and cause/effect, both define concepts through evidence and examples. Read or review both of these essays, and then follow these steps:

1. **Summarize** Briefly summarize the works, listing examples they include.
2. **Analyze** What questions do the essays raise for you?

3. **Synthesize** Using examples from both essays and from your own experience, describe how you draw the line between acceptable and unacceptable behavior in your life.

4. **Evaluate** Which essay do you think is more effective? Why? In writing your evaluation, look back on your responses to step 2.

Tip For a reminder of how to summarize, analyze, synthesize, and evaluate, see the Reading and Writing Critically box on page 17.

Writing about Images

Study the photograph, and complete the following steps.

1. **Read the image** Describe the setting and participants in this photo. What draws your attention? Why?

2. **Write a definition** Many companies and organizations promote *workplace wellness* or *work/life balance* programs. Using your reflections in number 1 above as a starting point, write a definition of one of these two terms. List the key features of the term, as well as examples and details.

ANDRESR/GETTY IMAGES

Writing to Solve a Problem

Read or review the discussion of problem solving in Chapter 1 (pp. 26–27). Then, consider the following problem.

> A recent survey asked business managers what skills or traits they value most in employees. The top five responses were (1) motivation, (2) interpersonal skills, (3) initiative, (4) communication skills, and (5) maturity.
>
> You have a job interview next week, and you want to be able to present yourself well. Before you can do that, though, you need to have a better understanding of the five skills and traits noted above and what examples you might be able to give to demonstrate that you have them.

Assignment Working in a group or on your own, come up with definitions of three of the five terms, and think of some examples of how the skills or traits could be used at work. Then, do one of the following assignments. You might begin with the following sentence:

I am a person who is (or has) . . .

For a paragraph: Choose one of the terms, and give examples of how you have demonstrated the trait.

For an essay: Write about how you have demonstrated the three traits.

CHECKLIST

How to Write Definition

Steps	Details
☐ Narrow and explore your topic. See Chapter 3.	• Make the topic more specific. • Prewrite to get ideas about the narrowed topic.
☐ Write a topic sentence (paragraph) or thesis statement (essay). See Chapter 3.	• State the term that you are focusing on, and provide a definition for it.
☐ Support your point. See Chapter 4.	• Come up with examples and details to explain your definition.
☐ Write a draft. See Chapter 5.	• Make a plan that puts the examples in a logical order. • Include a topic sentence (paragraph) or thesis statement (essay) and all the supporting examples and details.
☐ Revise your draft. See Chapter 5.	• Make sure it has *all* the Four Basics of Good Definition. • Make sure you include transitions to move readers smoothly from one example to the next.
☐ Edit your revised draft. See Parts 3 through 6.	• Correct errors in grammar, spelling, word use, and punctuation.

Chapter Review

1. What is a definition?
2 What are the Four Basics of Good Definition?
3. What is one way to develop secondary support in a definition essay?

Reflect and Apply

1. How is a definition essay different from a dictionary definition? How is it similar?
2. Interview someone from your major or career. What situations require reading or writing definition in your major or future profession?
3. What would happen if someone read or wrote definition carelessly?
4. What will you do differently the next time you read or write a definition?

12

Comparison and Contrast
Writing That Shows Similarities and Differences

Understand What Comparison and Contrast Are

Comparison is writing that shows the similarities among subjects—people, ideas, situations, or items; **contrast** shows the differences. In conversation, people often use the word *compare* to mean either compare or contrast, but as you work through this chapter, the terms will be separated.

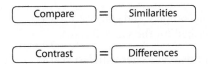

Compare = Similarities

Contrast = Differences

Four Basics of Good Comparison and Contrast

1 It compares and/or contrasts for a purpose—to help readers make a decision, to help them understand the subjects, or to show the writer's understanding of the subjects.

2 It presents several parallel, important points of comparison/contrast.

3 It develops points of comparison/contrast fairly, with supporting details for both subjects.

4 It arranges points in a logical order.

In the following paragraph, written for a biology course, the numbers and colors correspond to the Four Basics of Good Comparison and Contrast.

Tip This paragraph uses point-by-point organization. For more information, see page 246.

4 Points arranged in a logical order

1 Although frogs and toads are closely related, they differ in appearance, habitat, and behavior. **2** The first major difference is in the creatures' physical characteristics. **3** Whereas most frogs have smooth, slimy skin that helps them move through water, toads tend to have rough, bumpy skin suited to drier surroundings. Also, whereas frogs have long, muscular hind legs that help them leap away from predators or toward food, most toads have shorter legs and, therefore, less ability to move quickly. **3** Another physical characteristic of frogs and toads is their bulging eyes, which help them see in different directions. This ability is important because neither creature can turn its head to look for food or spot a predator. However, frogs' eyes may protrude more than toads'. **2** The second major difference between frogs and toads is their choice of habitat. **3** Frogs tend to live in or near ponds, lakes, or other sources of water. In contrast, toads live mostly in drier areas, such as gardens, forests, and fields. But, like frogs, they lay their eggs in water. **2** The third major difference between frogs and toads concerns their behavior. **3** Whereas frogs may be active during the day or at night, most toads keep a low profile until nighttime. Some biologists believe that it is nature's way of making up for toads' inability to escape from danger as quickly as frogs can. At night, toads are less likely to be spotted by predators. Finally, although both frogs and toads tend to live by themselves, toads, unlike frogs, may form groups while they are hibernating. Both creatures can teach us a lot about how animals adapt to their environments, and studying them is a lot of fun.

College	In a pharmacy course, you compare and contrast the side effects of two drugs prescribed for the same illness.
Work	You are asked to contrast this year's sales with last year's.
Everyday life	At the supermarket, you contrast brands of the same food to decide which to buy.

In college, writing assignments may include the words *compare and contrast,* but they might also use phrases such as *discuss similarities and differences, how is X like (or unlike) Y?,* or *what do X and Y have in common?* Also, assignments may use only the word *compare.*

For more information on understanding writing assignment prompts, see the Appendix, page 553.

First Basic: Main Idea in Comparison and Contrast

The **main idea** should state the subjects you want to compare or contrast and help you achieve your purpose.

To help you discover your main idea, complete the following sentence:

Main idea in comparison and contrast	**I am comparing/contrasting subject X and subject Y to show that …**

Read to Write
To find the main idea when you are reading comparison and contrast, complete this sentence: The writer compared/contrasted these subjects to show that . . .

Then, write a topic sentence (paragraph) or thesis statement (essay) that identifies the subjects and states the main idea you want to make about them. Here is an example of a topic sentence for a paragraph:

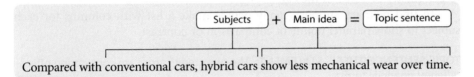

Compared with conventional cars, hybrid cars show less mechanical wear over time.

[Purpose: to help readers understand mechanical differences between conventional cars and hybrids.]

Remember that the topic for an essay can be a little broader than one for a paragraph.

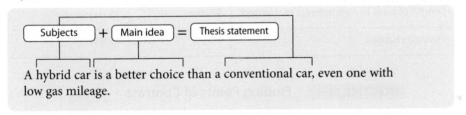

A hybrid car is a better choice than a conventional car, even one with low gas mileage.

[Purpose: to help readers decide which type of car to buy.]

Whereas the topic sentence focuses on the mechanical advantages of hybrid cars, the thesis statement sets up a broader discussion of these cars' benefits.

Tip Sometimes, the same main idea can be used for a paragraph and an essay, but the essay must develop this point in more detail. (See pp. 250–251.)

Second Basic: Primary Support in Comparison and Contrast

The paragraph and essay models on pages 250–251 use the topic sentence (paragraph) and thesis statement (essay) from the Main Idea section in this chapter. Both models include the support used in all comparison and contrast writing: points of comparison/contrast (primary support) backed up by details (secondary support). In the essay model, however, the points of comparison/contrast are topic sentences for individual paragraphs.

A **point of comparison or contrast** is an aspect or feature that is relevant to both subjects. For example, if you are comparing two automobiles, points of comparison or contrast could include gas mileage, speed capabilities, and interior comfort. The specific details would explain these three features for both subjects. In the paragraph contrasting frogs and toads (p. 242), the points of comparison/contrast are *appearance, habitat,* and *behavior.*

The points of comparison and/or contrast that you choose should relate directly to the purpose of the essay. For example, if your purpose in contrasting two automobiles is to recommend one over the other, you should not include the companies' celebrity spokespersons as a point of contrast; while the companies may have different approaches to advertising, those differences are not relevant to the quality or value of the car.

To find primary support, many people make a list with columns for each subject to show parallel points of comparison or contrast.

TOPIC SENTENCE/THESIS STATEMENT: The two credit cards I am considering offer different financial terms.

Points of Contrast	Big card	Mega card
Annual fee	none	$35
Cash advance fee	$1 per advance	$1.50 per advance
Length of time before interest is charged	30 days	25 days
Finance charges	15.5%	17.9%

PRACTICE 12–1   **Finding Points of Contrast**

Each of the following items lists some points of contrast. Fill in the blanks with more points and examples, and then write a topic sentence.

Example:

Contrast hair lengths

Points of Contrast	Long hair	Short hair
Drying Time	takes a long time to dry	dries quickly
Styling	can be worn a lot of ways	only one way to wear it
Cuts	does not need to be cut often	needs to be cut every five weeks
Maintenance	gets tangled, needs brushing	low maintenance

Topic Sentence: Short and long hairstyles offer different options for busy college students.

1. Contrast high school and college

Points of Contrast	High school	College
Schedules	selected by school	selected by student
		purchased by student
Types of Assignments		

Topic Sentence:

2. Contrast sports

Points of Contrast	Baseball	Soccer
Scoring Points	Runs	Goals
Equipment Used		

Topic Sentence:

PRACTICE 12–2   Finding Points of Comparison

Each of the following items lists some points of comparison. Add more points of comparison, and then write a topic sentence.

1. Compare high school and college

Points of Comparison	High school	College
Grades	Determined by tests, homework, papers, presentations, and projects.	Determined by tests, homework, papers, presentations, and projects.

Topic Sentence:

2. Compare sports

Points of Comparison	Baseball	Soccer
Individual or team?	team sport	team sport

Topic Sentence:

Third Basic: Secondary Support in Comparison and Contrast

In the sample essay on page 250, the writer mentions three points of contrast between hybrid and conventional cars: benefits such as tax breaks, long-term savings, and environment impacts. The writer's purpose is to show why he is buying a hybrid vehicle; in order to accomplish this purpose, the writer provides evidence—details, examples, descriptions, and facts. The writer should also be careful to provide details fairly and equally between both subjects. Giving extensive information about the gas mileage in a hybrid vehicle, for example, without providing similar data about the conventional car does not help the reader assess the importance of these numbers.

Fourth Basic: Organization in Comparison and Contrast

Comparison/contrast can be organized in one of two ways: a **point-by-point** organization presents one point of comparison or contrast between the subjects and then moves to the next point. (See the essay model on p. 251.) A **whole-to-whole** organization presents all the points of comparison or contrast for one subject and then all the points for the next subject. (See the paragraph model on p. 250.)

When you are writing, consider which organization will best explain the similarities or differences to your readers. Whichever organization you choose, stay with it throughout your writing.

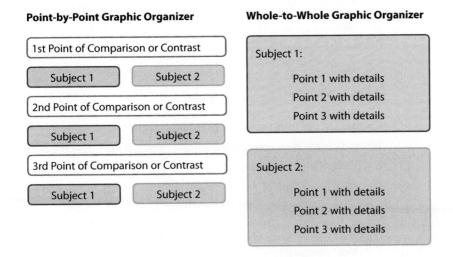

Point-by-Point Graphic Organizer

1st Point of Comparison or Contrast

Subject 1   Subject 2

2nd Point of Comparison or Contrast

Subject 1   Subject 2

3rd Point of Comparison or Contrast

Subject 1   Subject 2

Whole-to-Whole Graphic Organizer

Subject 1:

Point 1 with details
Point 2 with details
Point 3 with details

Subject 2:

Point 1 with details
Point 2 with details
Point 3 with details

PRACTICE 12–3   **Organizing a Comparison/Contrast**

The first outline that follows is for a comparison paper using a whole-to-whole organization. Reorganize the ideas and create a new outline (outline 2) using a point-by-point organization. The first blank has been filled in for you. The third outline is for a contrast paper using a point-by-point organization. The fourth outline is for a contrast paper using a whole-to-whole organization. Complete the third and fourth outlines with points of contrast and details.

1. Comparison paper using whole-to-whole organization

   Main idea: My daughter is a lot like I was at her age.

   a. Me
       Not interested in school
       Good at sports
       Hard on myself

   b. My daughter
       Does well in school but doesn't study much or do more than the
         minimum
       Plays in a different sport each season
       When she thinks she has made a mistake, she gets upset with
         herself

2. Comparison paper using point-by-point organization

   Main idea: My daughter is a lot like I was at her age.

   a.   Interest in school

   Me:

   My daughter:

   b.   Me:

   My daughter:

   c.   Me:

   My daughter:

3. Contrast paper using point-by-point organization

   Main idea: My new computer is a great improvement over my old one.

   a.   Weight and portability

   New computer:

   Old computer:

   b.   Speed

   New computer:

   Old computer:

   c.   Cost

   New computer:

   Old computer:

4. Contrast paper using whole-to-whole organization

   Main idea: My new phone is a great improvement over my old one.

   a.   New phone

   b.   Old phone

In a point-by-point comparison/contrast essay, writers often organize points by **order of importance**, meaning that the most important point is saved for last. This strategy is used in the essay model on page 251.

Transitions in comparison/contrast move readers from one subject to another and from one point of comparison or contrast to the next.

Common Transitions in Comparison and Contrast

	Adjective + Noun	Conjunctive Adverbials	Subordinating Conjunctions	Prepositions
Comparison	one similarity another similarity both subjects	similarly likewise in the same way	just as	like similar to
Contrast	one difference another difference the most important difference	on the other hand in contrast however	while although whereas	unlike different from

PRACTICE 12–4   **Using Transitions in Comparison and Contrast**

Read the paragraph that follows, and fill in the blanks with transitions.
You are not limited to the ones listed in the preceding box.

Modern coffee shops share many similarities with the coffeehouses that opened hundreds of years ago in the Middle East and Europe. _____ is that the coffeehouses of history, like modern cafés, were popular places to socialize. In sixteenth-century Constantinople (now Istanbul, Turkey) and in seventeenth- and eighteenth-century London, customers shared stories, information, and opinions about current events, politics, and personal matters. The knowledge shared at London coffeehouses led customers to call these places "Penny Universities," a penny being the price of admission. _____ is that the old coffeehouses, like today's coffee shops, were often places of business. However, although most of today's coffee-shop customers work quietly on their laptops, customers of the old shops openly, and sometimes loudly, discussed business and sealed deals. In fact, for more than seventy years, traders for the London Stock Exchange operated out of coffeehouses. _____ similarity between the old coffeehouses and modern coffee shops is that they both increased the demand for coffee and places to drink it. In 1652, a former servant from western Turkey opened the first coffeehouse in London. As a result of its popularity, many more coffeehouses soon sprouted up all over the city, and within a hundred years there were more than five hundred coffeehouses in London. _____, in recent years the popularity of Starbucks, and its shops, spread rapidly throughout the United States.

Paragraphs versus Essays in Comparison and Contrast

For more on the important features of comparison and contrast, see the Four Basics of Good Comparison and Contrast on page 241.

Main Idea: Often, narrower for a paragraph than for an essay: while the topic sentence (paragraph) focuses on the mechanical advantages of hybrid cars, the thesis statement (essay) sets up a broader discussion of these cars' benefits.

Paragraph Form

A   Compared with conventional cars, hybrid cars show less mechanical wear over time. **B** In conventional vehicles, braking and idling place continual stress on the engine and brakes. When braking, drivers of such vehicles rely completely on the friction of the brake pads to come to a stop. As a result, brakes wear down over time, sometimes rather quickly. Additionally, these vehicles burn gas even while idling, making the engine use unnecessary energy and fuel. **C** In contrast, hybrid cars are designed to reduce brake and engine wear. Say that a hybrid driver is moving from a sixty-mile-per-hour stretch of highway to a twenty-five-mile-per-hour off-ramp. When he or she brakes, the hybrid's motor goes into reverse, slowing the car and allowing the driver to place less strain on the brakes. Then, as the driver enters stop-and-start traffic in town, the electric motor takes over from the gas engine, improving energy efficiency during idling and reducing engine wear. **D** These mechanical benefits of hybrids can lead to lower maintenance costs, a significant improvement over conventional cars.

Support for the Main Idea (Points of Comparison/Contrast)

Details about Each Point of Comparison/Contrast: Usually, 1 to 3 sentences per point for paragraphs and 3 to 8 sentences per point for essays.

Conclusion

A   Topic sentence

B   Support 1 (first point of comparison/contrast))

C   Support 2 (second point of comparison/contrast)

D   Concluding sentence

Think Critically As You Write Comparison and Contrast

Ask Yourself

- Do I have a clear purpose for my comparison or contrast?
- Do I have points of comparison or contrast that support my purpose?
- Have I provided adequate details about both subjects to support my points of comparison or contrast?

Essay Form

1

They are too expensive. For the past two years, while trying to keep my dying 1999 Chevy on the road, these words have popped into my head every time I have thought about purchasing a hybrid car. But now that I have done some research, I am finally convinced: a hybrid car is a better choice than a conventional car, even one with low gas mileage.

A

The first advantage of hybrid cars over conventional cars is that buyers can get tax breaks and other hybrid-specific benefits. Although federal tax credits for hybrid purchasers expired in 2010, several states, including Colorado, Louisiana, Maryland, and New Mexico, continue to offer such credits. Also, in Arizona, Florida, and several other states, hybrid drivers are allowed to use the less congested high-occupancy vehicle (HOV) lanes even if the driver is the only person on board. Additional benefits for hybrid drivers include longer warranties than those offered for conventional cars and, in some states and cities, rebates, reduced licensing fees, and free parking.

B

2

None of these benefits are offered to drivers of conventional cars.

The second advantage of hybrid cars over conventional cars is that they save money over the long term. In addition to using less fuel, hybrids show less mechanical wear over time, reducing maintenance costs. When braking, drivers of conventional cars rely completely on the friction of the brake pads to come to a stop. As a result, brakes wear down over time, sometimes rather quickly. Additionally, these vehicles burn gas even while idling, making the engine use unnecessary energy and fuel. In contrast, when hybrid drivers hit the brakes, the car's motor goes into reverse, slowing the car and allowing the driver to place less strain on the brakes. Then, as the driver enters stop-and-start traffic in town, the electric motor takes over from the gas engine, improving energy efficiency during idling and reducing engine wear.

C

The most important benefit of hybrid cars over conventional cars is that they have a lower impact on the environment. Experts estimate that each gallon of

D

3

gas burned by conventional motor vehicles produces 28 pounds of carbon dioxide (CO_2), a greenhouse gas that is a major contributor to global warming. Because hybrid cars use about half as much gas as conventional vehicles, they reduce pollution and greenhouse gases by at least 50 percent. Some experts estimate that they reduce such emissions by as much as 80 percent. The National Resources Defense Council says that if hybrid vehicles are widely adopted, annual reductions in emissions could reach 450 million metric tons by the year 2050. This reduction would be equal to taking 82.5 million cars off the road.

Although hybrid cars are more expensive than conventional cars, they are well worth it. From an economic standpoint, they save on fuel and maintenance costs. But, to me, the best reason for buying a hybrid are ethical: by switching to such a vehicle, I will help reduce my toll on the environment. So goodbye, 1999 Chevy, and hello, Toyota Prius!

E

A Introductory paragraph

B Topic sentence 1 (first point of comparison/contrast)

C Topic sentence 2 (second point of comparison/contrast)

D Topic sentence 3 (third point of comparison/contrast)

E Concluding paragraph

Evaluate Comparison and Contrast

Read the following sample comparison and contrast paragraph. Using the Four Basics of Good Comparison and Contrast and the sample grading rubric, decide what grade this paragraph would earn. Explain your answer.

Assignment Describe one significant difference between your classes in high school and those you are enrolled in at college.

> **High school and college are completely different in many ways. When I was in high school, I didn't have a lot of choices about what courses I wanted to take and I didn't really need to think about what classes I was taking because it didn't really apply to my future or job or anything. When I got to college I found out that everything was different. Although a lot of classes were required. Some of them were choices that I got to make on my own. The biggest change is the amount of homework, time I have to spend on it all.**

Analysis of Sample Paragraph:

Sample Rubric

Element	Grading criteria	Point: Comment
Appropriateness	• Did the student follow the assignment directions?	_/5:
Main idea	• Does the paper clearly state a strong main idea in a complete sentence? • Do the two topics have enough in common to be compared and contrasted?	_/10:
Support	• Is the main idea developed with specific support, including specific details and examples? • Is there enough support to make the main idea evident to the reader? • Is all the support directly related to the main idea?	_/10:
Organization	• Is the writing in order of importance? • Is it apparent that the writer is using point-by-point or whole-to-whole as their organizational pattern?	_/10:

Element	Grading criteria	Point: Comment
Conclusion	• Does the conclusion remind the reader of the main idea? • Does it make an observation based on the support?	_/5:
Grammar	• Is the writing free of the four most serious errors? (See Chapters 16–19.) • Is the sentence structure clear? • Does the student choose words that clearly express his or her meaning? • Are the words spelled correctly? • Is the punctuation correct?	_/10:
		TOTAL POINTS: ___ /50

Read and Analyze Comparison and Contrast

Reading examples of comparison and contrast will help you write your own. The first example is a paragraph by a student writer, followed by an essay by a student writer. Following these, there is a comparison and contrast explanation written by a physician. Finally, John Tierney's essay is an example of professional comparison and contrast. As you read, pay attention to vocabulary and answer the questions in the margin. These will help you think critically and apply the reading to your own writing.

Student Comparison/Contrast Paragraph

Said Ibrahim

Eyeglasses versus Laser Surgery: Benefits and Drawbacks

Although both eyeglasses and laser surgery can successfully address vision problems, each approach has particular benefits and drawbacks. Whereas one pair of eyeglasses is reasonably priced in comparison with laser surgery, eyeglass prescriptions often change over time, requiring regular lens replacements. As a result, over the wearer's lifetime, costs of eyeglasses can exceed $15,000. On the positive side, an accurate lens prescription results in clear vision with few or no side effects. Furthermore, glasses of just the right shape or color can be a great fashion accent. In contrast to eyeglasses, laser vision correction often has to be done only once. Consequently, although the costs average $2,500 per eye, the patient can save thousands of dollars over the following years. On the downside, some recipients of laser surgery report difficulties seeing at night, dry eyes, or infections. Fortunately, these problems are fairly rare. The final advantage of laser surgery applies to those who are happy to forgo the fashion benefits of eyeglasses. Most laser-surgery patients no longer have to wear any glasses other than sunglasses until later in life. At that point, they may need reading glasses. All in all, we are fortunate to live in a time when there are many good options for vision correction. Choosing the right one is a matter of carefully weighing the pros and cons of each approach.

forgo: go without

Read to Write: Annotate

1. Double-underline the topic sentence.

2. Underline and number each point of contrast in the sample paragraph. Give each parallel point the same number.

3. Circle the transitions Ibrahim uses to guide readers through the paragraph.

Think Critically

1. Is the purpose of the paragraph to help readers make a decision, to help them understand the subjects better, or both?

2. Which organization (point-by-point or whole-to-whole) does Ibrahim use? Is this organization effective?

3. Does Ibrahim accomplish his purpose? Explain.

Student Comparison/Contrast Essay

Rita Rantung

Indonesian and U.S. School Systems

Rita Rantung was born in Kawangkoan (North Sulawesi), Indonesia, where she graduated from high school in 1992. After marrying an American citizen, she moved to the United States in 2001 and began homeschooling her children. In 2017, she went back to school, taking an English class at Lord Fairfax Community College. She hopes to study computer science in future semesters.

Indonesia is not as famous as the United States; in fact, for many, it is nonexistent. Nevertheless, it is still a great country to live in, and definitely, it is worth visiting. There you will find Borobudur, the largest Buddhist temple in the world, which was once considered as one of the world's seven wonders and is still a popular tourist site today. Indonesia is also the largest archipelago in the world, consisting of more than 13,000 big and small islands, bringing about the richness and diversity of its culture and language. Like America, Indonesia has been shaped by trials and triumphs that lead the nation to its distinct cultural and ideological foundation. Simply put, America's culture and dominant ideology give its citizens a lot more freedom of expression compared to Indonesia's. The distinct ideological foundation of each country inevitably affects the course of actions, goals, and objectives of each national education system.

archipelago: a group of islands

ideology: a system of values and beliefs

2   In Indonesia, starting with grade 4, a classroom appoints a student chairman and a vice chairman to manage the class responsibilities, including keeping the room clean and reporting to teachers. Students will remain in the same classroom with the same classmates during school hours for the entire school year, and the teachers rotate from classroom to classroom. Each classroom has its own class master, a teacher, who is assigned to put together the end of semester grading. School is in session six days a week, Monday to Saturday, and the school year starts sometime in mid-July and ends in the first week of June the year after. This gives students about a month of school break in addition to national and religious holidays.

Reflect How is the description of an Indonesian classroom different from your own school experiences?

3   In Indonesia, schools receive only some government support. In fact, Indonesia provides its students with only necessary things to facilitate their education. Transportation to elementary, secondary, and high school, for example, is up to the students. In cities, private cars or paid public transportation such as bus, taxi, becak (cycle rickshaw), or ojek (motorcycle taxi) may be used, but students in villages are left with almost no choice for their transportation. Cars and motorcycles are rare commodities in a lot of villages, so a bendy (buggy and horse pulling), the most economical option available for transport, is the favorite choice of transportation to and from school. Still, even the economical option requires a fee, and for that reason, students are likely to walk miles and miles, sometimes 8 to 10 miles one way, to school. In schools, the classrooms are furnished only with essential furniture, such as long benches paired with long desks for students, a small wooden desk and a chair for teacher, and a blackboard. A classroom usually has about twenty students, and two or three students will share a bench and a desk.

4   The relationship aspect between students and teachers in Indonesia is based on its hierarchical culture. Although there are some relaxed and easygoing teachers, for the most part, students are expected to respect the teachers and to submit without question. To some degree, teachers are allowed to give physical disciplinary actions when students misbehave, arrive late for school, or miss homework (at least that's what happened about twenty-five years ago, when I was in school). Conversations between students and teachers are limited to school subjects and almost never personal matters. Students are very intimidated by a teacher's presence; in fact, it is a common practice to hide and avoid being seen when students see teachers outside of school.

Read to Write What is the focus of the details in this paragraph?

5   Finally, the curriculum in Indonesia is centralized and headed by the Ministry of Education and Culture. All over the country, students in the same grade level study the same materials. By the time students are in high school, they cover up to

Read to Write What is the point of contrast addressed in this paragraph?

fourteen subjects in a week, including religion, national moral education, economy, and English, among other things. The compulsory attendance is from seven to fifteen years of age, yet this rule has never been enforced, for there is no such thing as a truancy officer in Indonesia. According to UNESCO's International Bureau of Education, Indonesia has two objectives for the national educational system. First, the nation wants to develop its citizens, whose values are based on the five principles of the state ideology: belief in one God, just and civilized humanity, the unity of Indonesia, democracy, and social justice for all. Second, it points out that the education system aims to support the Indonesian society, people, and state. Furthermore, it says that the Indonesian educational system maintains its cultural background, but at the same time, it strives to generate knowledge, skills, and scientific progress for the nation to move along with the development of the twenty-first century.

6   In the United States, on the other hand, students move from room to room to attend their classes while teachers remain in the same classroom; as a result, the responsibility to maintain the cleanliness of classrooms falls to the teachers and janitor, not students. The school day is five days a week, Monday to Friday. The school year starts sometime in the first week of September and ends in the middle of June, giving students about two-and-a-half months of long summer break along with winter and spring breaks.

7   U.S. schools are filled with conveniences that can help students soar in their education if they are willing to put in the work. Besides free public education through twelfth grade and school bus transportation, cheap but healthy cafeteria foods are also available. In almost all schools, students have their own desk and chair, and in some schools, especially at the high school level, they even have lockers. Gym rooms, computer and technology rooms, and labs with modern equipment are all within reach for most school districts. Perhaps these facilities show that the United States realizes how important it is to invest in the educational field, as it is one of the pillars of a great nation.

8   According to Thomas Lee, a graduate of the US public school system, the relationship between students and teachers in the U.S. public schools is somewhat relaxed; unfortunately, he adds, this relaxed relationship can be abused and taken advantage of by students who in turn communicate disrespectfully toward their teachers. Moreover, Lee says that the consequences toward student misconduct are generally minimal; teachers can assign after-school detention or send students to the principal's office, but no serious and physical disciplinary actions are allowed.

9   In America, although national Common Core has been implemented, the educational system is still decentralized. To a large extent, each state is given the right to determine its own curriculum. For example, the Virginia Department of Education expected students K-12 in Virginia to cover at least nine subjects, including English, mathematics, science, history/social science, technology, fine arts, foreign language, health and physical education, and driver education. But in Pennsylvania, the code indicates that K-12 students have to cover six core subjects (English, mathematics, science, social studies, art or humanities or both, and health and physical education) plus five more approved additional courses, including foreign languages, vocational education, and industrial arts, computer science, and consumer education, among other things. The United States also

---

truancy officer:
a school official who investigates students who do not attend school regularly

Read to Write
How does Rantung show that she is moving to a new subject?

Reflect Do you agree with Rantung's description of schools in the United States? Why or why not?

gives parents permission to home educate their children if they choose to do so; however, the homeschooling regulations can be different from one state to another. Another thing that varies from state to state is the compulsory attendance, but overall, it ranges from five to eighteen years of age. Unlike Indonesia, religious education is viewed as a personal subject in the United States; it is up to parents to attend to their children's spiritual education if they choose to do so.

10   Naturally, being a third world country, Indonesia looks up to America's great educational system, yet it does not forget—nor does it want to forget—its roots and identity as a nation. The educational systems of these two nations can be likened to two parenting styles: authoritarian and permissive. Indonesia leans toward the authoritarian style, while America tends toward the permissive. But in reality, implementing either style is easier said than done. Both the Indonesian and American governments consistently look for ways to improve their educational systems to first suit the needs of the nations and, at the same time, to engage in this competitive and ever-changing world.

Read to Write
What is the purpose of Rantung's contrast?

Works Cited

International Bureau of Education. "Indonesia Goals and Objectives of Education." UNESCO, http://www.ibe.unesco.org/curriculum/Asia%20Networkpdf/ndrepid.pdf. Accessed 4 Mar. 2018.

Pennsylvania State Board of Education. "State Academic Standards." www.stateboard.education.pa.gov/Regulations/AcademicStandards/Pages/default.aspx. Accessed 4 Mar. 2018.

Rulistia, Novia D. "Parents Take Education by the Horns." *The Jakarta Post*, 29 Sept. 2011, www.thejakartapost.com/news/2011/09/29/parents-take-education-horns.html.

United States, Virginia Department of Education. "Testing and Standard of Learning (SOL)." http://www.doe.virginia.gov/testing/sol/standards_docs/.

Read to Write: Annotate

1. Double-underline the thesis statement.
2. Label and number the points of contrast.
3. Circle or highlight transition words.

Think Critically

1. What organization does Rantung use? Is it effective? Why or why not?
2. Does Rantung provide sufficient details to support her point? Explain.
3. What is the purpose of the comparison? Do all the details included reflect this purpose? Explain.

Profile of Success:
Garth Vaz, physician

Comparison and Contrast in the Real World

Background   I was born in Jamaica, and at school, everyone thought I was lazy because I couldn't read. I knew I worked hard but didn't understand why I had such trouble reading. When it came time to go to high school, I dropped out and moved to Brooklyn, New York. Shortly thereafter, I was drafted and served as a medic in the military, where I got my GED. After completing my service, I went to Central Florida Community College and transferred to the University of Florida. I dropped out eventually and worked for a few years as an orderly.

I was accepted at the University of Florida Medical School but flunked out, at which point I finally discovered that my reading and writing problems were caused not by laziness but by dyslexia. I petitioned the school to return and passed my courses with the help of a note-taking service. But I failed the medical boards twice before I was allowed accommodation for dyslexia.

Today I am a doctor working at a community health clinic that, in addition to other medical services, provides care for migrant workers and their families. I also travel and speak extensively on learning behaviors, especially dyslexia and attention-deficit/hyperactivity disorder (ADHD).

Writing at work   For work, I write patient reports, speeches, and papers for publication. As a dyslexic, writing is still very difficult for me, though I have learned how to compensate for the difficulty. Because I still make lots of spelling errors, I have to read very carefully and reread anything I write to correct the mistakes.

Garth Vaz
Physician
Community Health Centers
of South Central Texas

Workplace Comparison and Contrast Essay:
Dyslexia and ADHD

Reflect What do you know about dyslexia? ADHD?

The following is excerpted from an article that Dr. Vaz published on the subject of dyslexia.

Read to Write Notice how many words begin with the prefix "mis" in this paragraph. What does this prefix mean?

diligent: being careful, with effort and focus

For decades, dyslexics have been one of the most misunderstood groups in our society. Misconceptions and misdiagnoses abound, as when dyslexics are mislabeled stupid, retarded, or lazy and placed among the mentally deficient. Many dyslexics have been placed in special education programs along with the slow learners. Later, after appropriate remediation, these same students have gone on to become educators, lawyers, and doctors. It is therefore of great importance that we be aware of the sensitive nature of dealing with these prize products of our society, our dyslexic students. We must be diligent in our efforts to help them in their struggle for success.

2   Such misdiagnoses are due to the lack of understanding of dyslexia and conditions such as attention-deficit/hyperactivity disorder (ADHD), childhood depressive disorder (CDD), central auditory processing deficit (CAPD), and many others that share some similarities with common symptoms of dyslexia. I will now list, in brief, some of the differences in behaviors that characterize ADHD and dyslexia in children, particularly children in the elementary school classroom.

3   A young person with ADHD cannot easily sit still, certainly a problem in the classroom. He or she often leaves his assigned seat, running around and attempting to climb on shelves, desks, and the like. When told firmly to remain in his seat, the child will try to obey but will squirm and fidget almost constantly, clearly in a state of agitation. He acts as if he is driven by a motor.

4   A child with ADHD often talks excessively and is unable to wait to be called on: instead, he blurts out answers and responses. He seems to just butt into games and conversations, not observing social norms that require a give-and-take among group members. Such behavior often alienates other children and frustrates teachers and others who try to maintain control. Other children may shun the child with ADHD. This ostracism, in turn, results in further negative effects, such as low self-esteem and greater isolation.

5   In contrast, a young person with dyslexia can sit still but has trouble organizing objects, belongings, and letters. She may mix up sounds, saying, for example, "plain" for "plan" or "seal" for "soul." She may have a stutter, furthering the frustration and embarrassment she already feels.

6   A dyslexic child typically reads poorly, confusing the order of letters, for example, in words such as "saw" and "was." Also, she may confuse words that have similar shapes or start and end with the same letters, as in "form" and "from" or the words cited in the last paragraph. While a dyslexic's reading is labored, her handwriting and spelling are usually worse. All of these symptoms of dyslexia, while quite different, often result in the same ostracism and loss of self-esteem. These problems then cause other behavior problems that are similar to those shown in children with ADHD and a number of other conditions. This explains why certain conditions are often confused. In addition, many children indeed have more than one condition. For example, over 40 percent of children with dyslexia have ADHD as well.

7   Unfortunately, because of budgeting restrictions, dyslexics are sometimes placed among the wrong group for remediation. In order for any intervention to succeed, it must be tailored specifically for the dyslexic. There are many improved techniques now being used successfully in reading remediation that are based on the Orton-Gillingham method. Arlene Sonday and the Scottish Rite Hospital have such programs on the market, and many other good ones can be located on the Internet.

8   There are many successful dyslexics in our society, some contemporary and others in the past. Albert Einstein, Benjamin Franklin, and General George Patton are a few who have made history. Athletes Caitlyn Jenner and Nolan Ryan and entertainers Whoopi Goldberg, Tom Cruise, and Steven Spielberg are among

Read to Write
This excerpt is only part of a larger article. Do you think the entire article is a comparison and contrast? Why or why not?

Reflect What details does the author provide to describe ADHD? Does this describe you or someone you know?

norms: standards or expectations

alienate: separate or cause to be isolated

shun: avoid

ostracism: being excluded from a group

Read to Write
Why does the author here use the pronoun "she" in paragraph 5?

labored: slow, with great effort

Reflect What details does the author provide to describe dyslexia? Does this describe you or someone you know?

ostracism: being excluded or left out of a group

Reflect What is Vaz's tone in the final paragraph? How does his tone reflect his purpose?

our contemporaries. Identifying with the successful dyslexic offers some hope to parents and children alike. The book *Succeeding with LD* is a collection of stories of successful dyslexics. The book was authored by Jill Lauren and published by Free Spirit Publishers. Each of these stories could make a book by itself but is short enough for the dyslexic to enjoy reading.

Read to Write: Annotate

1. Double-underline Vaz's thesis.
2. Circle the transition words that he includes.

Think Critically

1. Why doesn't Vaz discuss ADHD in the first or final paragraph?
2. What is his purpose?
3. Why is Vaz so interested in dyslexia?
4. What organization does Vaz use, point-by-point or whole-to-whole?

Professional Comparison/Contrast Essay

John Tierney

Yes, Money Can Buy Happiness . . .

John Tierney is a columnist for the Science Times section of the *New York Times.* He has also written for many other science publications such as *Discovery, Hippocrates,* and *Science 86.* According to his biography, "he's using TierneyLab to check out new research and rethink conventional wisdom about science and society. The Lab's work is guided by two founding principles: just because an idea appeals to a lot of people doesn't mean it's wrong. But that's a good working theory."

This essay originally appeared in his TierneyLab column in the *New York Times* in 2008. Tierney no longer writes this blog.

Predict What two things are being contrasted in this essay?

correlated: to be related in some sense

Yes, money can buy happiness, but probably not in the way you imagined. Spending it on yourself may not do much for your spirits, but spending it on others will make you happier, according to a report from a team of social psychologists in the new issue of *Science.*

2   The researchers confirmed the joys of giving in three separate ways. First, by surveying a national sample of more than six hundred Americans, they found that spending more on gifts and charity correlated with greater happiness, whereas spending more money on oneself did not. Second, by tracking sixteen workers

before and after they received profit-sharing bonuses, the researchers found that the workers who gave more of the money to others ended up happier than the ones who spent more of it on themselves. In fact, how the bonus was spent was a better predictor of happiness than the size of the bonus.

3   The final bit of evidence came from an experiment in which forty-six students were given either $5 or $20 to spend by the end of the day. The ones who were instructed to spend the money on others—they bought toys for siblings, treated friends to meals and made donations to the homeless—were happier at the end of the day than the ones who were instructed to spend the money on themselves.

4   "These experimental results," the researchers conclude, "provide direct support for our causal argument that spending money on others promotes happiness more than spending money on oneself." The social psychologists—Elizabeth Dunn and Lara Aknin of the University of British Columbia, Vancouver, and Michael Norton of Harvard Business School—also conclude that "how people choose to spend their money is at least as important as how much money they make."

5   I asked Dr. Dunn if she had any advice on how much to spend on others. Her reply:

> I think even minor changes in spending habits can make a difference. In our experiment with college students, we found that spending just $5 prosocially had a substantial effect on happiness at the end of the day. But I wouldn't say that there's some fixed amount that everyone should spend on others. Rather, the best bet might be for people to think about whether they can push themselves to devote just a little more of their money to helping others.

6   But why wouldn't people be doing that already? Because most people don't realize the personal benefits of charity, according to Dr. Dunn and her colleagues. When the researchers surveyed another group of students, they found that most of the respondents predicted that personal spending would make them happier than spending the money on other people.

7   Perhaps that will change as word of these experiments circulates—although that prospect raises another question, which I put to Dr. Dunn: if people started giving away money chiefly in the hope of making themselves happier, as opposed to wanting to help others, would they still derive the same happiness from it?

8   "This is a fascinating question," she replied. "I certainly hope that telling people about the emotional benefits of prosocial spending doesn't completely erase these benefits; I would hate to be responsible for the downfall of joyful prosocial behavior."

9   Do you have any theories on the joys of giving? Any reports of your own experiments? Or any questions you'd like to ask the researchers? Dr. Dunn, in keeping with the results of her experiments, has generously offered to provide some answers free of charge.

Summarize What are the three pieces of evidence that giving money away brings joy?

prosocially: good for society

Reflect Do you think giving money away makes you happy? Why or why not?

Read to Write What do the final questions tell you about Tierney's intended audience?

Read to Write: Annotate

1. Double-underline the thesis statement.
2. Underline the points of contrast in this essay.
3. Circle the transitions.

Think Critically

1. What type of organization does this essay use (point-by-point or whole-to-whole)?
2. Why do you suppose each group of people had different outcomes from spending money?
3. Why is it that even though spending money on others makes people happier, more people don't give to charity?

Respond

1. The main idea of the article involves our intent: whether we spend money on others or ourselves, we feel differently about the experience. Why do you suppose the students instructed to spend money on others felt better than those who spent it on themselves?
2. In paragraph 7, Tierney asks Dr. Dunn if people would still feel happy when spending money on others if they knew that it would make them happier. What do you think? Explain your answer.

Grammar for Comparison and Contrast

Writers of contrast often use the comparative form of adjectives to emphasize differences between two subjects. Notice the comparative forms in the following sentences from Tierney's essay.

Second, by tracking sixteen workers before and after they received profit-sharing bonuses, the researchers found that the workers who gave more of the money to others ended up *happier than* the ones who spent more of it on themselves. In fact, how the bonus was spent was a *better* predictor of happiness *than* the size of the bonus.

The comparative form of adjectives requires the addition of *-er* (for most one and two-syllable adjectives) or the word *more* (for adjectives of three or more syllables), along with the word *than*. For more on these forms, see Chapter 21.

Write Your Own Comparison and Contrast

In this section, you will write your own comparison and contrast based on one of the following assignments. For help, refer to the How to Write Comparison and Contrast checklist on page 265.

Assignment Options: Writing about college, work, and everyday life

Write a comparison/contrast paragraph or essay on one of the following topics or on one of your own choice.

College
- Describe similarities and differences between high school and college (or two colleges you have attended), and give examples.
- Compare two approaches you have used to study, such as studying in a group and studying on your own using notes or other aids. Explain whether you prefer one approach over the other or like to use both methods.
- If you are still deciding on a major area of study, see if you can sit in on a class or two in programs that interest you. Then, compare and contrast the classes. If this process helped you decide on a program, explain the reasons for your choice.

Work
- Compare a job you liked with one you did not like, and give reasons for your views.
- Have you had experience working for both a bad supervisor and a good one? If so, compare and contrast their behaviors, and explain why you preferred one supervisor to another.
- Work styles tend to differ from employee to employee. For instance, some like to work in teams, whereas others prefer to complete tasks on their own. Some like specific directions on how to do things, whereas others want more freedom. Contrast your own work style with someone else's whose approach and preferences are quite different from yours.

Everyday life
- Compare your life now with the way you would like it to be in five years.
- Have your experiences changed how you see your surroundings? If so, discuss your experiences, and give examples.
- Participate in a cleanup effort in your community, and then compare and contrast how the area looked before the cleanup with how it looked afterward.

Assignment Options: Reading and writing critically

Tip For a reminder of how to summarize, analyze, synthesize, and evaluate, see the Reading and Writing Critically box on page 17.

Complete one of the following assignments that asks you to apply the critical thinking, reading, and writing skills discussed in Chapter 1.

Writing Criticaly about Readings

Both Amy Tan's "Fish Cheeks" (p. 121) and Liz Riggs "What It's Like to Be the First Person in Your Family to Go to College" (p. 282) present an unfamiliar scene or a time that the writer felt concerned about fitting in. Read or review both of these pieces, and then follow these steps:

1. **Summarize** Briefly summarize the works, listing major events.

2. **Analyze** What questions do the pieces raise for you?

3. **Synthesize** Sometimes we approach new experiences tentatively, as in Riggs's piece, and other times we are embarrassed by them, as in Tan's. Using examples from these writings and from your own experience, discuss which types of changes are positive, which types are negative, and why.

4. **Evaluate** Which piece did you connect with more, and why? In writing your evaluation, you might look back on your responses to step 2.

Writing about Images

Study the photographs below, and complete the following steps.

1. **Read the images** Ask yourself: What details are you drawn to in each photograph? What differences do you notice as you move from the earlier classrooms to the modern classroom? (For more on reading images, see Chapter 1.)

2. **Write a comparison and contrast** Write a paragraph or essay about the ways college classrooms, students, and teaching methods have changed

over the years. You might want to address how changes in classrooms represent larger changes in society and culture. Also, answer this question: how do you think classrooms will be different in another ten years? In writing your comparison/contrast, include the details and differences you identified in step 1. You might also talk to students who attended college at different times.

Writing to Solve a Problem

Read or review the discussion of problem solving in Chapter 1 (pp. 26–27). Then, consider the following problem:

You need a new smartphone, and you want the best one for your money. Before ordering, you do some research.

Assignment Consult a website that rates smartphones, such as www.pcworld. com. Identify three features covered by the ratings, and make notes about why each feature is important to you. Then, choose a model based on these features. Finally, write a contrast paragraph or essay that explains your decision and contrasts your choice versus another model. Make sure to support your choice based on the three features you considered.

CHECKLIST

How to Write Comparison and Contrast

Steps	Details
☐ Narrow and explore your topic. See Chapter 3.	• Make the topic more specific. • Prewrite to get ideas about the narrowed topic.
☐ Write a topic sentence (paragraph) or thesis statement (essay). See Chapter 3.	• State the main idea you want to make in your comparison/contrast.
☐ Support your point. See Chapter 4.	• Come up with points of comparison/contrast and with details about each one.
☐ Write a draft. See Chapter 5.	• Make a plan that sets up a point-by-point or whole-to-whole comparison/contrast. • Include a topic sentence (paragraph) or thesis statement (essay) and all the support points. →

Steps	Details
☐ Revise your draft. See Chapter 5.	• Make sure it has *all* the Four Basics of Good Comparison and Contrast. • Make sure you include transitions to move readers smoothly from one subject or comparison/contrast point to the next.
☐ Edit your revised draft. See Parts 3 through 6.	• Correct errors in grammar, spelling, word use, and punctuation.

Chapter Review

1. What are the Four Basics of Good Comparison and Contrast?

2. The topic sentence (paragraph) or thesis statement (essay) in comparison/contrast should include what two parts?

3. What are the two ways to organize comparison/contrast?

4. In your own words, explain the two ways of organizing comparison/contrast.

Reflect and Apply

1. Have you written a comparison and contrast essay before this class? If so, how was your experience in this class similar? What was new or different?

2. Interview someone from your major or career. What situations require reading or writing comparison and contrast in your major or future profession?

3. Did you get feedback on your writing for this chapter? If so, what parts of the feedback were most helpful?

4. What will you do differently the next time you read or write a comparison and contrast essay?

13

Cause and Effect

Writing That Explains Reasons or Results

Understand What Cause and Effect Are

A **cause** is what made an event happen. An **effect** is what happens as a result of the event.

Four Basics of Good Cause and Effect

1 The main point reflects the writer's purpose: to explain causes, effects, or both.

2 If the purpose is to explain causes, the writing presents real causes; if the purpose is to explain effects, the writing presents real effects.

3 It provides details and examples that support and explain the causes and/or effects.

4 It can be organized in different ways—order of importance, space order, or time order—depending on its purpose.

In the following paragraph, the numbers and colors correspond to the Four Basics of Good Cause and Effect.

Followers of college football recognize several outstanding programs, including Notre Dame, Michigan, Ohio State, and Florida State. However, in the past decade, one school in particular has dominated the college football rankings, with championships in 2009, 2011, 2012, 2015, and 2017: the University of Alabama, known as the Crimson Tide. **1** What has led to Alabama's dominance? **2** First, there is a tradition of winning at Alabama, **3** which has had seventeen national titles in its history, with six under the legendary Paul "Bear" Bryant in the 1960s and 1970s, and five under current coach Nick Saban. **2** That tradition of winning has

4 Causes arranged by order of importance

led to outstanding recruiting: Alabama has brought some of the best talent in the country to the university. The 2017 recruiting class was ranked first in the country by 247Sports. **3** The ability to recruit well means that Alabama's teams have depth: they can substitute outstanding players throughout the game, bringing fresh energy to the field. **2** Another reason for Alabama's success is the financial investment they have made in the team. **3** According the NCAA, Alabama spent just under $1 million in 2012–2013 on recruiting, and coach Nick Saban is one of the highest paid coaches in college football, earning about $7 million annually. Coach Saban does not coach alone: the university employs up to fourteen assistant coaches as well. **2** But perhaps more important than the tradition and the money spent, Alabama has a winning philosophy embraced by all the coaches: develop a solid defense and treat every opponent with respect. **3** In a recent broadcast on ESPN, former Alabama quarterback Greg McElroy noted that Coach Saban and his staff expect the same preparation each week, both for the lowest-ranked opponent and for the championship game. **1** With tradition, financial support, strong coaching, and a solid team philosophy, Alabama should continue winning for years to come.

You use cause and effect in many situations.

College	In a nutrition course, you are asked to identify the consequences (effects) of poor nutrition.
Work	Sales are down in your department or branch, and you have to explain the causes.
Everyday life	You explain to your child why a certain behavior is not acceptable by warning him or her about the negative effects of that behavior.

In college, writing assignments might include the words *discuss the causes (or effects) of,* but they might also use phrases such as *explain the results of, discuss the impact of,* and *how did X affect Y?* In all these cases, use the strategies discussed in this chapter.

For more information on how to understand writing assignment prompts, see the Appendix, page 553.

First Basic: Main Idea in Cause and Effect

The **main idea** introduces causes, effects, or both. To help you discover your main idea, complete the following sentence:

Read to Write
You can also use these sentences to identify the main idea when you are reading cause-and-effect analysis.

Main idea in cause and effect	(This topic) causes (or caused) . . .
	(This topic) resulted in (or results in) . . .

Here is an example of a topic sentence for a paragraph:

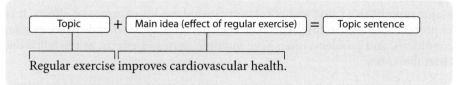

Regular exercise improves cardiovascular health.

Remember that the main idea for an essay can be a little broader than one for a paragraph.

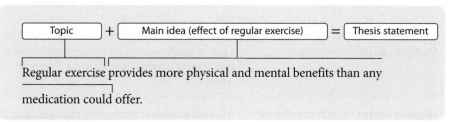

Regular exercise provides more physical and mental benefits than any medication could offer.

Tip If the writer wanted to explore causes, he or she might look into the factors that motivate people to exercise.

Tip Sometimes, the same main idea can be used for a paragraph and an essay, but the essay must develop this point in more detail. (See pp. 274–275.)

Whereas the topic sentence focuses on just one major benefit of regular exercise, the thesis statement considers multiple benefits.

PRACTICE 13-1   **Stating Your Main Idea**

For each of the following topics, make notes about possible causes and effects on a separate sheet of paper. Then, in each of the spaces below, write a sentence that states a main idea. First, look at the following example.

Example:

Topic: Bankruptcy

Main idea: Although many different kinds of people declare bankruptcy each year, the causes of bankruptcy are often the same.

1. Topic: A fire in someone's home
   Main idea:

2. Topic: An A in this course
   Main idea:

3. Topic: Waking up late in the morning
   Main idea:

Second Basic: Primary Support in Cause and Effect

Major support in a cause and effect essay includes a list of causes or effects. It is important to think carefully when you are determining causes and effects; events, conditions, and problems often have multiple causes or effects, as the following chart illustrates.

One cause → one effect	Thunderstorm → game was cancelled
One cause → multiple effects	Hurricane → flooding, loss of electricity, loss of homes and buildings, higher insurance, etc.
Multiple causes → one effect	Lack of exercise, consumption of junk food and sweets, stress, sleeplessness → weight gain
Multiple causes → multiple effects	Injuries, academic probation, changes in coaching staff, heat wave → 0–6 record, NCAA investigation, coach fired
Cause → effect → effect → effect	Lost cell phone → missed a key business call → didn't get a contract → didn't get the promotion

As you choose causes or effects, make sure you avoid two common **logical fallacies**, or mistakes in reasoning.

The **post hoc fallacy** comes from a Latin phrase, *post hoc ergo propter hoc*, that literally means "after this, therefore because of this." We make this mistake when we look at two events and assume that the one that occurred first caused the second one. Superstitions, for example, illustrate the post hoc fallacy. Imagine a student whose teacher asks why she did not pass a test. The student responds, "Well, a black cat crossed in front of me on the way to school—and I just had bad luck." While the student may have seen a black cat crossing on the way to school, there is no logical reason to believe that the cat caused the student's problems on the test.

Think Critically
Many superstitions reflect the post hoc fallacy. Can you think of some examples of superstitions that are based on post hoc thinking? How might you explain the problem to someone who is basing behavior on a superstition?

PRACTICE 13–2   **Identifying Post Hoc Mistakes**

Evaluate each of the statements of cause below. Are any of them examples of the post hoc fallacy? Explain.

1. John spent the past two weeks partying and getting in shape for football try-outs; he didn't even open his books. That's why he failed the test today.

2. John forgot to wear his lucky shirt to class. That's why he failed the test.

3. The professor forgot to return John's homework last week. That's why he failed the test today.

4. John injured his knees during a workout a few weeks ago. That's why he failed the test.

The **slippery slope fallacy** occurs when someone suggests certain effects will occur following an action or event, but there is no logical basis for that belief. For example, a student who receives an F grade on a daily homework assignment might plead with her instructor this way: "If I get an F on this assignment, I will never be able to transfer to the university, graduate, or get a good job." Because homework counts for only 5 percent of the grade for this class, the student has presented an illogical effect; in other words, she is going down a slippery slope. A single homework assignment cannot lead to all the negative outcomes she suggested. *Post hoc thinking* leads to illogical cause statements; *slippery slope thinking* leads to illogical effect statements.

Think Critically
It is often easier to see logical fallacies in someone else's words than in our own. Why is this true?

> **PRACTICE 13-3** **Recognizing Slippery Slope Statements**
>
> Study the following statements. Determine if the writer has committed a slippery slope fallacy in any of them.
>
> 1. I cannot believe I just ate that slice of pizza. There is no way I will be able to fit into my prom dress.
>
> 2. I should not have eaten that slice of pizza; I will probably have heartburn later tonight.
>
> 3. I should not have eaten that slice of pizza; it had mushrooms on it, and they always give me a headache.
>
> 4. I should not have eaten that slice of pizza. Who knows what kinds of preservatives it has? I'm going to get cancer.

Third Basic: Secondary Support in Cause and Effect

Once you have identified the causes or effects of an event or action, provide details that will help your reader understand these causes or effects. Details may include examples, descriptions, statistics, definitions, or expert opinions.

The paragraph and essay models on pages 274–275 use the topic sentence (paragraph) and the thesis statement (essay) from the Main Idea section of this chapter. Both models include the support used in all cause-effect writing:

statements of cause or effect (primary support) backed up by detailed explanations or examples (secondary support). In the essay plan, however, the major support points (statements of cause/effect) are topic sentences for individual paragraphs.

> **PRACTICE 13-4**   **Giving Examples and Details**
>
> Write down two causes or two effects for two of the three topics from Practice 13-1. Then, give an example or detail that explains each cause or effect.
>
> **Example:**
>
> **Topic: Bankruptcy**
>
> **Cause 1:** Overspending
>
>   **Example/Detail:** bought a leather jacket I liked and charged it
>
> **Cause 2:** Poor budgeting
>
>   **Example/Detail:** not tracking monthly expenses versus income
>
> 1. Topic: A fire in someone's home
>   Cause/Effect 1:
>   Example/Detail:
>   Cause/Effect 2:
>   Example/Detail:
>
> 2. Topic: An A in this course
>   Cause/Effect 1:
>   Example/Detail:
>   Cause/Effect 2:
>   Example/Detail:
>
> 3. Topic: Waking up late in the morning
>   Cause/Effect 1:
>   Example/Detail:
>   Cause/Effect 2:
>   Example/Detail:

Fourth Basic: Organization in Cause and Effect

Cause and effect can be organized in a variety of ways, depending on your purpose.

Main Idea	Purpose	Organization
The Women's Marches of 2017 and 2018 brought attention to the needs and struggles of women across the United States.	To explain the effects of the protests	Order of importance, saving the most important effect for last
A desire to be respectful of the environment led Women's March protesters to recycle posters and clean up protest sites.	To demonstrate that the protest respected the environment	Space order
The Women's March in Washington, DC inspired other protests throughout the country.	To describe the spread of the protest movement over time	Time order

Tip For more on the different orders of organization, see pages 73–75.

NOTE: If you are explaining both causes and effects, you would present the causes first and the effects later.

Use transitions to move readers smoothly from one cause to another, from one effect to another, or from causes to effects. Because cause and effect can use any method of organization depending on your purpose, the following list shows just a few of the transitions you might use.

Common Transitions in Cause and Effect

	Conjunctive Adverbials	Subordinating Conjunctions	Adjective + Noun	Prepositions
Cause		because since	a primary cause a serious cause the most important cause one cause	because of due to as a result of
Effect	therefore as a result consequently		a long-term or short-term effect a primary effect a serious effect one effect the most important effect	

For more information on using and punctuating these transitions, see Chapters 17 and 23.

Paragraphs versus Essays in Cause and Effect

For more on the important features of cause and effect, see the Four Basics of Good Cause and Effect on page 267.

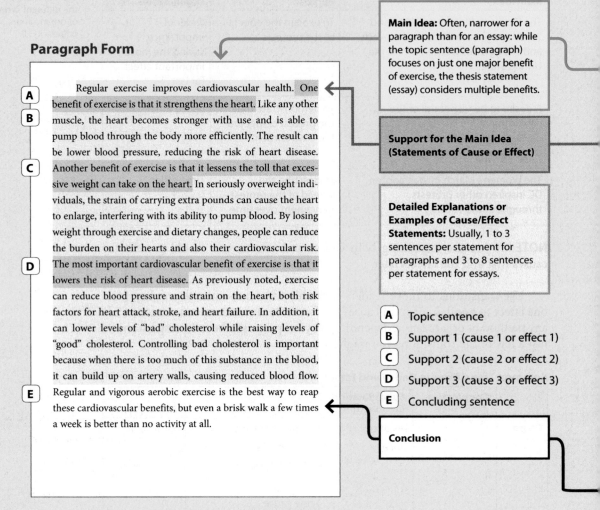

Paragraph Form

A Regular exercise improves cardiovascular health. One benefit of exercise is that it strengthens the heart. **B** Like any other muscle, the heart becomes stronger with use and is able to pump blood through the body more efficiently. The result can be lower blood pressure, reducing the risk of heart disease. **C** Another benefit of exercise is that it lessens the toll that excessive weight can take on the heart. In seriously overweight individuals, the strain of carrying extra pounds can cause the heart to enlarge, interfering with its ability to pump blood. By losing weight through exercise and dietary changes, people can reduce the burden on their hearts and also their cardiovascular risk. **D** The most important cardiovascular benefit of exercise is that it lowers the risk of heart disease. As previously noted, exercise can reduce blood pressure and strain on the heart, both risk factors for heart attack, stroke, and heart failure. In addition, it can lower levels of "bad" cholesterol while raising levels of "good" cholesterol. Controlling bad cholesterol is important because when there is too much of this substance in the blood, it can build up on artery walls, causing reduced blood flow. **E** Regular and vigorous aerobic exercise is the best way to reap these cardiovascular benefits, but even a brisk walk a few times a week is better than no activity at all.

Main Idea: Often, narrower for a paragraph than for an essay: while the topic sentence (paragraph) focuses on just one major benefit of exercise, the thesis statement (essay) considers multiple benefits.

Support for the Main Idea (Statements of Cause or Effect)

Detailed Explanations or Examples of Cause/Effect Statements: Usually, 1 to 3 sentences per statement for paragraphs and 3 to 8 sentences per statement for essays.

A Topic sentence
B Support 1 (cause 1 or effect 1)
C Support 2 (cause 2 or effect 2)
D Support 3 (cause 3 or effect 3)
E Concluding sentence

Conclusion

Think Critically As You Write Cause and Effect

Ask Yourself

- Have I examined a variety of possible causes and/or effects related to my topic? (If not, research them, and consider revising your main idea and support based on what you learn.)
- Am I certain that my causes are real causes and my effects real effects? (For help with answering this question, see p. 271.)
- Have I provided supporting evidence for the causes or effects?

Essay Form

1

Most people know how hard it is to start and stick with an exercise program. However, there is a good reason to build a significant amount of physical activity into every week: regular exercise provides more physical and mental benefits than any medication could offer.

First, exercise helps people achieve and maintain a healthy weight. A nutritious diet that is not excessive in calories has a greater effect on weight loss than exercise does. However, regular exercise—ideally, interspersed throughout the day—can make an important contribution. For instance, people trying to lose weight might walk to work or to other destinations instead of driving. Or, they might take the stairs to their office instead of the elevator. If they go to the gym at the end of the day, so much the better. Added up, all these efforts can make a difference.

Second, exercise boosts mood and energy levels. For example, exercise causes the body to release endorphins, chemicals that give us a sense of well-being, even happiness. Accordingly, exercise can help reduce

2

stress and combat depression. In addition, because exercise can make people look and feel more fit, it can improve their self-esteem. Finally, by improving strength and endurance, exercise gives individuals more energy to go about their lives.

The most important benefit of exercise is that it can help prevent disease. For example, exercise can improve the body's use of insulin and, as noted earlier, help people maintain a healthy weight. Therefore, it can help prevent or control diabetes. Additionally, exercise can lower the risk of heart attacks, strokes, and heart failure. For instance, exercise strengthens the heart muscle, helping it pump blood more efficiently and reducing high blood pressure, a heart disease risk factor. Also, exercise can lower levels of "bad" cholesterol while raising levels of "good" cholesterol. Controlling levels of bad cholesterol is important because when there is too much of this substance in the blood, it can build up in the walls of arteries, possibly blocking blood flow. Finally, some research suggests that

3

regular exercise can reduce the risk of certain cancers, including breast, colon, and lung cancer.

In my own life, exercise has made a huge difference. Before starting a regular exercise program, I was close to needing prescription medications to lower my blood pressure and cholesterol. Thanks to regular physical activity, however, both my blood pressure and cholesterol levels are now in the normal range, and I have never felt better. Every bit of time spent at the gym or exchanging a ride in an elevator for a walk up the stairs has been well worth it.

A Introductory paragraph

B Thesis statement

C Topic sentence 1 (cause 1 or effect 1)

D Topic sentence 2 (cause 2 or effect 2)

E Topic sentence 3 (cause 3 or effect 3)

F Concluding paragraph

275

PRACTICE 13-5   **Using Transitions in Cause and Effect**

Read the paragraph that follows, and fill in the blanks with transitions.

Recently, neuroscientists, who have long been skeptical about meditation, confirm that it has numerous positive outcomes. _____ ___ is that people who meditate can maintain their focus and attention longer than people who do not. This ability to stay "on task" was demonstrated among students who had been practicing meditation for several weeks. They reported more effective studying and learning because they were able to pay attention. _____ positive outcome was the ability to relax on command. Many people lead busy, stressful lives with multiple pressures on them—family responsibilities, work duties, financial worries, and uncertainties about the future. While meditating, people learned how to reduce their heart rates and blood pressure so that they could relax more easily in all kinds of situations. _____ outcome was a thickening of the brain's cortex. Meditators' cortexes were uniformly thicker than non-meditators'. Because the cortex enables memorization and the production of new ideas, this last outcome is especially exciting, particularly in fighting Alzheimer's disease and other dementias.

Evaluate Cause and Effect

Read the following sample cause-and-effect paragraph. Using the Four Basics of Good Cause and Effect and the sample grading rubric, decide what grade this paragraph would earn. Explain your answer.

Assignment   Write a paragraph that identifies one reason (cause) that may have resulted in a poor grade on a test (effect).

> **Failing grades on a test can have any number of causes. For example, lack of sleep. Sleep is important to help a student perform well on tests. If tired may cause the student to not pay attention or read questions. Tired may also cause misunderstanding. When you know you have a test coming, you need to make sure that you have more than enough rest in order to focus.**

Analysis of Sample Paragraph:

Sample Rubric

Element	Grading criteria	Point: Comment
Appropriateness	• Did the student follow the assignment directions?	_/5:
Main idea	• Does the paper clearly state a strong main idea in a complete sentence?	_/10:
Support	• Is the main idea developed with specific support, including specific details and examples? • Is there enough support to make the main idea evident to the reader? • Is all the support directly related to the main idea?	_/10:
Organization	• Does the writer clearly demonstrate how one behavior causes the end result? • Does the student use transitions (*also, for example, sometimes,* and so on) to move the reader from one point to another?	_/10:
Conclusion	• Does the conclusion remind the reader of the main idea?	_/5:
Grammar	• Is the writing free of the four most serious errors? (See Chapters 16–19.) • Is the sentence structure clear? • Does the student choose words that clearly express his or her meaning? • Are the words spelled correctly? • Is the punctuation correct?	_/10:
		TOTAL POINTS: __/50

Read and Analyze Cause and Effect

Reading examples of cause and effect will help you write your own. The first example is a student cause-and-effect paragraph, followed by a student essay written about the effects of modern technology. The Profile of Success and workplace cause-and-effect essay are by blogger Joshua Boyce, and the final essay is by professional writer Liz Riggs.

Student Cause-and-Effect Paragraph

Caitlin Prokop

A Difficult Decision with a Positive Outcome

When my mother made the decision to move back to New York, I made the choice to move in with my dad so that I could finish high school. This decision affected me in a positive way because I graduated with my friends, built a better relationship with my father, and had the chance to go to college without leaving home. Graduating with my friends was important to me because I have known most of them since we were in kindergarten. It was a journey through childhood that we had shared, and I wanted to finish it with them. Accomplishing the goal of graduating from high school with my close friends, those who accompanied me through school, made me a stronger and more confident person. Another good outcome of my difficult decision was the relationship I built with my dad. We never saw eye to eye when I lived with both of my parents. For example, we stopped talking for five months because I always sided against him with my mom. Living together for the past five years has made us closer, and I cherish that closeness we have developed. Every Thursday is our day, a day when we talk to each other about what is going on in our lives, so that we will never again have a distant relationship. A third good outcome of my decision is that I can go to Brevard Community College, which is right down the street. In high school, I had thought that I would want to go away to college, but then I realized that I would miss my home. By staying here, I have the opportunity to attend a wonderful college that is preparing me for transferring to a four-year college and finding a good career. I have done some research and believe I would like to become a police officer, a nurse, or a teacher. Through the school, I can do volunteer work in each of these areas. Right now, I am leaning toward becoming a teacher, based on my volunteer work in a kindergarten class. There, I can explore what grades I want to teach. In every way, I believe that my difficult decision was the right one, giving me many opportunities that I would not have had if I had moved to a new and unfamiliar place.

Read to Write: Annotate

1. Double-underline the topic sentence.

2. Circle the transitions Prokop uses to move readers from one point to the next.

Think Critically

1. Does the paragraph address causes, effects, or both? Are the causes or effects logical and well-supported?

2. Does Prokop's paragraph include the Four Basics of Good Cause and Effect? Why or why not?

3. Have you made a difficult decision that turned out to be a good one? Why and how?

Student Cause-and-Effect Essay

Stephanie Alaimo and Mark Koester

The Backdraft of Technology

Stephanie Alaimo and Mark Koester both graduated from DePaul University of Chicago. Alaimo was a Spanish major who volunteered as an English tutor. She is now studying sociology at the University of California, San Diego. Koester majored in philosophy and taught English in Hangzhou, China, after graduation. He is now developing software in China as an entrepreneur.

Read to Write
Do Alaimo and Koester present causes, effects, or both in their essay? Keep track of them while you read.

You have picked up the bread and the milk and the day's miscellaneous foodstuffs at your local grocery store. The lines at the traditional, human-operated checkouts are a shocking two customers deep. Who wants to wait? Who would wait when we have society's newest upgrade in not having to wait: the self-checkout?

2 Welcome to the automated grocery store. "Please scan your next item," a repetitively chilling, mechanical voice orders you.

3 If you have yet to see it at your nearest grocer, a new technological advance has been reached. Instead of waiting for some minimally waged, minimally educated, and, most likely, immigrant cashier to scan and bag your groceries for you, you can now do it yourself. In a consumer-driven, hyperactive, "I want" world, an increase in speed is easily accepted thoughtlessly. We're too busy. But, in gaining efficiency and ease, a number of jobs have been lost, particularly at the entry level, and a moment of personal, human engagement with actual people has vanished.

4 It seems easy enough to forget about the consequences when you are rushed and your belly is grumbling. The previously utilized checkout lanes at local grocery stores and super, mega, we-have-everything stores are now routinely left unattended during the peak hours. In these moments, your options are using the self-checkout or waiting for a real human being. Often in a hurried moment we choose the easiest, fastest, and least mentally involved option without much consideration.

5 We forget to consider that with the aid of the self-checkout, at least two jobs have been lost. As a result, a human cashier and grocery bagger are now waiting in the unemployment line. Furthermore, self-checkout machines are probably not manufactured in the United States, thus shipping more jobs overseas. And sadly, the job openings are now shrinking by putting consumers to work. The wages from these jobs are stockpiled by those least in need—corporations and those who own them.

6 The mechanization of the service industry has been occurring throughout our lifetimes. Gas stations were once full-service. Human bank tellers, instead of

Predict Before reading the rest of the paper, consider what you may already know about this topic. What are some of the reasons Alaimo and Koester may use to support their thesis?

Read to Write
What pronouns do the authors use in paragraphs 4 and 5? Why do you think they chose to use these pronouns?

Read to Write
What specific information do Alaimo and Koester supply about self-checkouts? Are they a cause of the problem of unemployment or an effect? How could the authors strengthen paragraphs 5 and 6?

ATMs, handled simple cash withdrawals. And did you know that you can now order a pizza for delivery online without even talking to a person?

7   Sure, these new robots and computers reduce work, which could potentially be a really good thing. But these mechanizations have only increased profit margins for large corporations and have reduced the need to hire employees. Jobs are lost along with the means of providing for one's self and family.

8   For those who find the loss of grocery store labor to be meaningless and, quite frankly, beyond impacting their future lives as accountants or lawyers, it does not seem to be entirely implausible that almost any job or task could become entirely technologically mechanized and your elitist job market nuked.

9   We are a society trapped in a precarious fork in the road. We can either eliminate the time and toil of the human workload and still allow people to have jobs and maintain the same standard of living, though working less, or we can eliminate human work in terms of actual human jobs and make the situation of the lower classes more tenuous. Is it our goal to reduce the overall time that individuals spend laboring? Or is it our goal to increase corporate profits at the loss of many livelihoods?

10   At present, corporations and their executives put consumers to work, cut the cost of labor through the use of technology such as self-checkouts and ATMs, and profit tremendously. But a host of workers are now scrambling to find a way to subsist. To choose the self-checkout simply as a convenience cannot be morally justified unless these jobs remain.

11   The choices we make on a daily basis affect the whole of our society. Choosing convenience often translates to eliminating actual jobs that provide livelihoods and opportunities to many. Think before you simply follow the next technological innovation. Maybe it could be you in their soon-to-be-jobless shoes. Say "No!" to self-checkout.

mechanization: changing from work done by hand to work done by machines

Reflect Have you seen negative publicity about self-checkouts? Has it made you consider whether you choose to use them, or did you ignore it? Explain your answer.

Reflect Do you think the authors are exaggerating the consequences of mechanization? Why or why not?

subsist: to exist or survive at a basic level.

Summarize Briefly restate the main ideas of this essay.

Read to Write: Annotate

1. Double-underline the thesis of the essay.

2. Underline the effects introduced by the writers.

3. The authors use strong and emotional language throughout the essay. Circle or highlight the words you find most powerful. Why did they choose these words?

Think Critically

1. Do the authors use enough examples and detail to demonstrate the causes and effects in the essay?

2. Are the effects mentioned reasonable? Explain.

3. Does this essay follow the Four Basics of Good Cause and Effect (p. 267)?

4. If you were reviewing this essay for class, what suggestions would you make for improving it?

Profile of Success
Cause and Effect in the Real World

Background   I grew up in poverty and graduated from high school not knowing how to read, write, or do any math beyond simple arithmetic. This occurred because I was wrongfully placed in special education at an early age. Upon completion of high school, I attended Job Corps. There I learned how to weld and moved to Vicksburg, Mississippi. Shortly after moving, I met Dr. Nettle, a local minister. He taught me how to read and encouraged me to pursue my GED.

After getting my GED, I enrolled full time at a two-year college where I graduated with honors. Then I attended a four-year institution and received my B.S. degree in exercise science. Currently, I am a fitness trainer and blogger. My blog, "Slim Chance Motivation," is aimed at inspiring others to dream and pursue their goals no matter what the odds are.

Degrees/Colleges   A.A. Degree/Hinds Community College; B.S./Mississippi College

Writing at work   This blog post reveals the harmful effect of wrong conditioning and challenges people to make steps to recondition their mind.

Joshua Boyce
Blogger

Workplace Cause and Effect: Conditioning

"If you make a man feel that he is inferior, you do not have to compel him to accept an inferior status, for he will seek it himself. If you make a man think that he is justly an outcast, you do not have to order him to the back door. He will go without being told; and if there is no back door, his very nature will demand one."
                                                              —Dr. Carter G. Woodson

Dr. Woodson's quote paints a good picture of the effect of conditioning. In athletics, conditioning is important. It is the combination of physical and mental training with the right nutritional plan. The right conditioning program makes a difference between experiencing the sweet taste of victory or the bitterness of defeat and the same applies to people and their goals.

2   I was conditioned to accept failure, and this mindset wreaked havoc in my life for many years. This became even more evident when I was in Job Corp. No matter how many welding processes or techniques I learned, I still had this strong internal feeling that I was going to fail. My conditioning was preventing me from believing in my ability to weld even though I had all the proof that suggested differently.

3   There are still many enslaved by this conditioning. It leads to the acceptance of going to prison instead of college or trade school. It forces you into submission to a mindless, backbreaking job. It causes fear in doing the most simple of tasks.

I have been, and I have watched too many individuals, held down by this conditioning.

4   I was reconditioned to think otherwise by two important factors. **(1) People**—Mr. Beard, my Job Corp welding instructor, saw my ability to weld and often helped me to shake the doubts. **(2) Interpretation**—With the help of Mr. Beard, I was able to understand and accept that it was not luck but my ability to perform a task well that was producing the result. With people and good discernment, I was able to decrease the doubts and increase my confidence.

5   In the end, it is still a battle, one you cannot win on your own. I needed help, and you will also. So to make a slim chance a chance, I had to be reconditioned, and so will you.

Read to Write: Annotate

1. Double-underline the main idea of the article.

2. Underline the causes or effects mentioned by Boyce.

3. Circle each time the writer uses *conditioning* or a related word. Why does he repeat this word so often? How does repetition help the reader?

Think Critically

1. What is Boyce's purpose?

2. What supporting details does Boyce give to illustrate the causes and effects he identifies? Are these details adequate? Explain.

3. Does this piece demonstrate the Four Basics of Good Cause and Effect (p. 267)?

Professional Cause-and-Effect Essay

Liz Riggs

What It's Like to Be the First Person in Your Family to Go to College

Liz Riggs is a writer and teacher who lives in Nashville, Tennessee. Her work has appeared in *The Atlantic*, *The Huffington Post*, and *Relevant* magazine, to name just a few. This piece first appeared in *The Atlantic* in January 2014.

Read to Write
As you read the article, try to identify potential causes and effects for the way Harry felt during his time at school.

Read to Write
Why does the author use *so-called*? What does this suggest about the author's opinion of the description of Harry's high school?

When Harry arrived at Vanderbilt University in 2008, he became the first person in his family to attend college. His parents were immigrants from Nicaragua, and he had attended a so-called "academically and economically disadvantaged" high school on the north side of Miami. Even after completing a rigorous IB [international baccalaureate] program as a high-school student and receiving a scholarship, he arrived on campus feeling like an outsider.

2   "Never before had I truly felt such an extreme sense of estrangement and alienation," he says of his first few months. "I quickly realized that although I may look the part, my cultural and socioeconomic backgrounds were vastly different from those of my predominantly white, affluent peers. I wanted to leave."

3   Harry opted to stay at Vanderbilt, but he found acclimating to the school's cultural climate to be extremely difficult. His scholarship covered books, tuition, and housing, but it didn't cover little costs like dorm move-in needs and travel costs home for breaks—expenses his classmates could typically afford that exacerbated his feelings of alienation. Eventually, he found refuge in the school's theater department and student government.

4   "There were very few Latinos that I could connect with," he says. "[But], I got very involved in extra-curricular activities in hopes of meeting people. . . . It was in each of these organizations that I met older students that informally mentored me. . . . I would ask questions shamelessly and learn about their experiences."

5   Harry's difficult adjustment is just one example of the many obstacles first-generation and minority students confront each year that don't typically plague their second- and third-generation peers. Extensive studies show that low-income and first-generation students are more likely to be academically behind, sometimes several years in core subjects. They're more likely to live at home or off-campus. They're less likely to have gained AP [advanced placement] credit and more likely to have to take uncredited remedial courses. And they're more likely to face serious financial hurdles.

6   These challenges are sometimes so formidable that studies say that only 8 percent of low-income (many of whom are first-generation) students will graduate college by age 25. Social integration is only one piece of the puzzle for these students, and for Harry—like many other students—combating this transition can be easier with the help of older peers, teachers and professors who act as mentors. While the definition of "mentor" varies, there are both informal and formal structures that have the potential to influence first-generation college: persistence and graduation. Armed with this understanding, many secondary and postsecondary institutions have created programming to better support and mentor first-generation students.

7   In Chicago, The Noble Network of Charter Schools collects extensive data on their alumni to determine what students need in order to persist and graduate from college. Last year, nine of the campuses graduated seniors and each of these nine schools has a college counselor and an alumni coordinator—allowing students to have extensive support through the college application, matriculation, and transition process.

8   "It's very intentionally called college counseling," Matt Niksch, Noble's Chief College Officer, tells me. "They're not kids anymore, [and] a lot of it is about helping young adults determine the right choice for them."

---

rigorous: academically challenging, strict

estrangement: physical or emotional separation or distance

alienation: isolation or separation from a group

affluent: wealthy

acclimating: adjusting or adapting to

exacerbated: made worse

Reflect Have you ever found yourself in a situation where you felt you didn't belong or understand what was going on around you?

remedial: intended to correct or improve skills, usually not for credit

Reflect What specific causes are identified in the previous paragraph that explain why first-generation students may have difficulty when they begin their college education? What challenges have you faced?

matriculation: enrollment in a college or university

Reflect Do you think you or students you know would benefit from the types of mentoring and counseling these schools provided? Explain.

Reflect In the previous paragraphs, the author identifies many causes of student success or lack of success. Have you ever found yourself in one of these situations? What did you do about it?

9   Noble schools look to a college's institutional minority graduation rate as a predictor of student success, but even these statistics can't always foresee what different students will face.

10   Caroline Kelly, a college counselor at Noble's Pritzker College Prep, categorizes the challenges into "different buckets. One is financial, one is motivation, one is family, one is academics, and one is social integration."

11   Many first-generation students, like Harry, struggle socially when they arrive on a college campus only to find that they have trouble identifying with their wealthier peers, or they feel a distinct "otherness" that they didn't experience in high school. Others adjust socially but find themselves paying for their education for the first time in their lives.

12   "In high school your education was given to you for free in most cases," says Mac, a current junior at the University of Illinois at Urbana-Champaign. Mac is an alumnus of a traditional public school on the Southside of Chicago, where he participated in OneGoal, a teacher-led college persistence program for low-income students that provides school-based support for students over the course of three years. OneGoal teachers begin work with students during their junior year of high school and bridge the gap between high school and college with a curriculum that continues into each student's first-year of college.

13   "College becomes a major expense. I have to focus a lot more on how I will pay for school before attending school each semester," he says. He has had support from the program since his junior year in high school, when OneGoal teachers helped him prepare for standardized tests, research and apply for schools, and apply for financial aid. His OneGoal teacher even drove him to college on move-in day. "Before OneGoal I don't feel that college was even on my radar," he says.

14   "There's just a huge financial gap," says Thomas Dickson, the Director of Teacher Recruitment for OneGoal.

15   Since its official launch in 2007, 82 percent of OneGoal's high school graduates have enrolled in college, and of those who have enrolled, 78 percent are persisting in college or have graduated with a college degree.

Reflect Out of all the causes Riggs identifies, which do you believe is the biggest hurdle for first-generation college students and why?

Read to Write Why do some paragraphs only include one sentence?

16   OneGoal has many look-alike organizations in other cities, some of which are school-based (KIPP Through College, Achievement First's Alumni Program) and others that are independent companies such as College Forward—a non-profit college-coaching organization—based in Texas that boasts 78 percent of their students as still enrolled or graduated, or InsideTrack, a for-profit coaching organization aimed at increasing college enrollment and graduation rates.

17   Despite the influx of programs on high-school and college campuses, many programs still lag in hard graduation numbers.

18   "Our four-year college graduation numbers are not even close to where we want them to be," Angela Montagna, Noble's Director of External Affairs, says. Noble says 88 percent of their students make it from their first to their second year, but don't always make it to graduation.

19   Though there isn't significant research that measures all mentoring relationships and their effects on college persistence, there is some research showing the positive effects of mentoring relationships on young kids. Colleges across the country are implementing mentoring initiatives for first-generation college students in attempts to combat the staggeringly low graduation rates.

20   And, while a degree is the ultimate goal for many parents, teachers, and students, there are other results that are perhaps more important for first-generation college students, Noble's Matt Niksch says.

21   "A lot of [students] talk about college as the goal. But we also don't want them to forget that really the goal is: we want them to have happy, successful, choice-filled lives."

Summarize What is the author's main idea in this article?

Read to Write: Annotate

1. Double-underline the thesis statement.

2. Underline the causes and/or effects Riggs introduces.

3. Highlight quotes from students or college employees. How do these quotes support the causes or effects in the essay?

Think Critically

1. Does this essay present causes, effects, or both? Explain how you came to your conclusion.

2. How does Riggs use statistics to support the causes and effects she presents? Explain.

3. Does this essay follow the Four Basics of Good Cause and Effect (p. 267)? Why or why not?

Respond

1. At the beginning of her essay, Riggs writes about situations that may cause students to feel uncomfortable or alienated at college because of their backgrounds. Write about a time when your past created an uncomfortable situation and how you managed to work through it.

2. In paragraph 10, Caroline Kelly identifies some causes of difficulty as a student enters college: finances, motivation, family, academics, and social integration. Which of these causes can be controlled by a student? In other words, to be successful, students can change the effect that some of these have on their life: Which would those be?

3. In paragraph 19, Riggs presents some research that shows how mentoring can have a positive effect on both children and college students. Why do you think that is?

Grammar for Cause and Effect

Look at the following sentences from Riggs's essay:

> **Though** there isn't significant research that measures all mentoring rela-
> tionships and their effects on college persistence, there is some research
> showing the positive effects of mentoring relationships on young kids.

> And, **while** a degree is the ultimate goal for many parents, teachers, and
> students, there are other results that are perhaps more important for
> first-generation college students, Noble's Matt Niksch says.

Did you notice how both of these sentences have a contrast word (*though, while*)
at the beginning? Using a contrast word like these allows Riggs to acknowledge an
important idea (*there isn't much research, a degree is the focus of many*) but emphasize
a different idea (*research showing the positive effects of mentoring, other important
results of a college education*). The contrast words here are subordinating conjunctions (dependent words), and they introduce dependent clauses. These clauses are
followed by commas. For more information on dependent clauses, see Chapter 23.

Write Your Own Cause and Effect

In this section, you will write your own cause-and-effect paragraph or essay
based on one of the following assignments. For help, refer to the How to Write
Cause and Effect checklist on page 289.

Assignment Options: Writing about College, Work, and Everyday Life

Write a cause-and-effect paragraph or essay on one of the following topics or on
one of your own choice.

College
- Write about the causes, effects, or both of not studying for an exam.
- If you have chosen a major or program of study, explain the factors behind your decision. How do you think this choice will shape your future?
- Why do some people stay in college, while others drop out? Interview one or two college graduates about the factors behind their decision to stay in school. Also, ask them how staying in school and graduating has affected their lives. Then, write about the causes and effects they describe.

Work	• Write about the causes, effects, or both of stress at work.

Work
- Write about the causes, effects, or both of stress at work.
- Identify a friend or acquaintance who has been successful at work. Write about the factors behind this person's success.
- Write about the causes, effects, or both of miscommunication in the workplace.

Everyday life
- Think of a possession that has great personal meaning for you. Then, write about why you value the possession, and give examples of its importance in your life.
- Try to fill in this blank: "_____ changed my life." Your response can be an event, an interaction with a particular person, or anything significant to you. It can be something positive or negative. After you fill in the blank, explain how and why this event, interaction, or time had so much significance.
- Arrange to spend a few hours at a local soup kitchen or food pantry, or on another volunteer opportunity that interests you. (You can use a search engine to find volunteer opportunities in your area.) Write about how the experience affected you.

Assignment Options: Reading and Writing Critically

Complete one of the following assignments that asks you to apply the critical thinking, reading, and writing skills discussed in Chapter 1.

Writing Critically about Readings

Jelani Lynch's "My Turnaround" (p. 116), Caitlin Prokop's "A Difficult Decision with a Positive Outcome" (p. 278), and Liz Riggs's "What It's Like to Be the First Person in Your Family to Go to College" (p. 282) talk about taking control of one's life. Read or review these pieces, and then follow these steps:

1. **Summarize** Briefly summarize the works, listing major examples.
2. **Analyze** What questions do these pieces raise for you? Are there any other issues you wish they had covered?
3. **Synthesize** Using examples from Lynch's, Prokop's, and Riggs's writings and from your own experience, discuss different ways—big and small—in which people can take control of their lives.
4. **Evaluate** Which of the pieces had the deepest effect on you? Why? In writing your evaluation, you might look back on your responses to step 2.

Tip For a reminder of how to summarize, analyze, synthesize, and evaluate, see the Reading and Writing Critically box on page 17.

Writing about Images

Study the following infographic, and then answer the following questions.

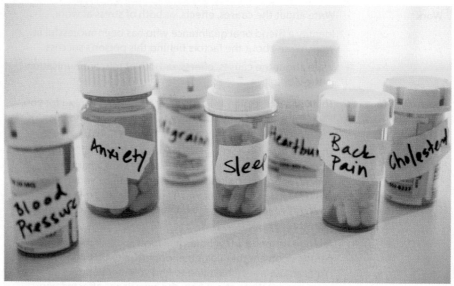

JAMIE GRILL/GETTY IMAGES

1. **Read the images** What strikes you as important about this image? What situations might cause someone to have these medications on hand? What might the results of long-term use of these medications be? (For more information on reading images, see Chapter 1.)

2. **Write a cause-and-effect paragraph or essay** Using your notes from question 1 above as well as your own experience, write a paragraph or essay describing causes or effects of a highly stressful life.

Writing to Solve a Problem

Read or review the discussion of problem solving in Chapter 1 (pp. 26–27). Then, consider the following problem.

> **You have learned of a cheating ring at school that uses cell phones to give test answers to students taking the test. A few students in your math class, who are also friends of yours, think that this scheme is a great idea and are planning to cheat on a test you will be taking next week. You decide not to participate, partly because you fear getting caught, but also because you think that cheating is wrong. Now you want to convince your friends not to cheat, because you don't want them to get caught and possibly kicked out of school. How do you make your case?**

Assignment Working in a group or on your own, list the various effects of cheating—both immediate and long term—you could use to convince your friends. Then, write a cause-and-effect paragraph or essay that identifies and explains some possible effects of cheating. You might start with this sentence:

Cheating on tests or papers is not worth the risks.

CHECKLIST

How to Write Cause and Effect

Steps	Details
☐ Narrow and explore your topic. See Chapter 3.	• Make the topic more specific. • Prewrite to get ideas about the narrowed topic.
☐ Write a topic sentence (paragraph) or thesis statement (essay). See Chapter 3.	• State your subject and the causes, effects, or both that your paper will explore.
☐ Support your point. See Chapter 4.	• Come up with explanations or examples of the causes, effects, or both.
☐ Write a draft. See Chapter 5.	• Make a plan that puts the support points in a logical order. • Include a topic sentence (paragraph) or thesis statement (essay) and all the supporting explanations and examples.
☐ Revise your draft. See Chapter 5.	• Make sure it has *all* the Four Basics of Good Cause and Effect. • Make sure you include transitions to move readers smoothly from one cause and effect to the next.
☐ Edit your revised draft. See Parts 3 through 6.	• Correct errors in grammar, spelling, word use, and punctuation.

Chapter Review

1. What is a cause? An effect?

2. What are the Four Basics of Good Cause and Effect?

3. What is the post hoc fallacy?

4. What is the slippery slope fallacy?

Reflect and Apply

1. Have you written or read cause-and-effect analysis before? What makes reading or writing cause-and-effect analysis difficult?

2. Interview someone studying your major or working in your career. What situations require reading or writing cause-and-effect analysis in your major or career?

3. Have you ever seen or heard someone commit a post hoc or slippery slope fallacy? When? What happened as a result?

4. What worked well in your writing for this chapter? What do you need to remember for next time?

14

Argument
Writing That Persuades

Understand What Argument Is

Argument is writing that takes a position on an issue and gives supporting evidence to persuade someone else to accept, or at least consider, the position. Argument is also used to convince someone to take (or not take) an action.

> **Four Basics** of Good Argument
>
> **1** It takes a strong and definite position.
> **2** It gives good reasons and supporting evidence to defend the position.
> **3** It considers opposing views thoughtfully.
> **4** It organizes support logically.

In the following paragraph, the numbers and colors correspond to the Four Basics of Good Argument.

1 Even though I write this blog post on an 88-degree day, I am truly glad that I stopped using my air conditioner, and I urge you to follow my lead. **2** For one thing, going without air conditioning can save a significant amount of money. Last summer, this strategy cut my electricity costs by nearly $2,000, and I am on my way to achieving even higher savings this summer. For another thing, living without air conditioning reduces humans' effect on the environment. Agricultural researcher Stan Cox estimates that air conditioning creates 300 million tons of carbon dioxide (CO_2) emissions each year. This amount, he says, is the equivalent of every U.S.

4 Logical Organization

household buying an additional car and driving it 7,000 miles annually. Because CO_2 is one of the greenhouse gases responsible for trapping heat in our atmosphere, reducing CO_2 emissions is essential to curbing climate change. The final reason for going without air conditioning is that it is actually pretty comfortable. The key to staying cool is keeping the blinds down on south-facing windows during the day. It is also a good idea to open windows throughout the home for cross-ventilation while turning on ceiling fans to improve air circulation. **3** Although some people argue that using fans is just as bad as switching on the air conditioner, fans use far less electricity. In closing, let me make you a promise: the sooner you give up air conditioning, the sooner you will get comfortable with the change—and the sooner you and the planet will reap the rewards.

Knowing how to make a good argument is one of the most useful skills you can develop.

College	You argue for or against make-up exams for students who do not do well the first time.
Work	You need to leave work an hour early one day a week for twelve weeks to take a course. You persuade your boss to allow you to do so.
Everyday life	You try to negotiate a better price on an item you want to buy.

In college, writing assignments might include questions or statements such as the following: *Do you agree or disagree with this point? Defend or refute this idea or proposal. Is this idea or proposal fair and just?* In all these cases, use the strategies discussed in this chapter.

For more information on understanding writing assignment prompts, see the Appendix, page 553.

First Basic: Main Idea in Argument

Read to Write To find the main point when you are reading an argument, look for "should" or "should not" statements.

Your **main idea** in argument is the position you take on the issue (or topic) about which you are writing. In formal discussions of argument, the main idea is called a **claim.** When you are free to choose an issue, choose something that matters to you. When you are assigned an issue, try to find some part of it that matters to you. You might try starting with a "should" or "should not" sentence:

Main idea in argument	**College football players should/should not be paid.**

If you have trouble seeing how an issue matters or finding a claim, talk about it with a partner or write down ideas about it using the following tips.

Tips for Building Enthusiasm and Finding a Claim

- Talk to others to understand what different positions on the issue might be.
- Imagine yourself arguing your position with someone who disagrees.
- Imagine that your whole grade rests on persuading your instructor to agree with your position.
- Imagine how this issue could affect you or your family personally.
- Imagine that you are representing a large group of people who care about the issue very much and whose lives will be forever changed by it. It is up to you to win their case.

In argument, the topic sentence (in a paragraph) or thesis statement (in an essay) usually includes the issue/topic and your position about it. Here is an example of a topic sentence for a paragraph:

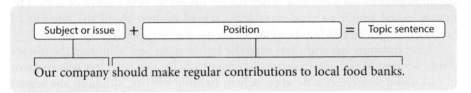

| Subject or issue | + | Position | = | Topic sentence |

Our company should make regular contributions to local food banks.

Remember that the main idea for an essay can be a little broader than one for a paragraph.

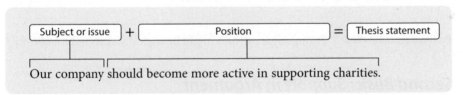

| Subject or issue | + | Position | = | Thesis statement |

Our company should become more active in supporting charities.

> **Tip** Sometimes, the same main idea can be used for a paragraph and an essay, but the essay must develop this point in more detail. (See pp. 304–305.)

Whereas the topic sentence focuses on just one type of charitable organization, the thesis statement sets up a discussion of different ways to help different charities.

> ### PRACTICE 14–1   Writing a Statement of Your Position
>
> Write a statement of your position for each item.
>
> **Example:**
>
> **Issue:** Prisoners' rights
>
> **Position statement:** *Prisoners should not have more rights and privileges*
>
> *than law-abiding citizens.*

1. Issue: Lab testing on animals

   Position statement:

2. Issue: Using cell phones in the classroom

   Position statement:

3. Issue: Athletes' salaries

   Position statement:

4. Issue: Treadmill desks

   Position statement:

5. Issue: GMOs

   Position statement:

Jess, a college student working on sharpening her reading and writing skills, used these skills while working on an argument paper for her English class. She got an idea for the paper while waiting to start her shift at a local restaurant. Scrolling through the newsfeed on her phone, she saw a link to an article about the city's plan to tax soda and other sugary drinks to help reduce obesity. The money raised would be used to educate schoolchildren about the benefits of healthy eating. The article was written by a nurse from a local hospital.

After finishing her shift, Jess read the article again and identified the nurse's claim: we should tax sugary drinks in order to reduce obesity. Jess was in favor of just about any reasonable approach to fighting obesity, although she wasn't sure that a tax on soda and other sugary beverages would work. Jess thought this would be a good topic for a paper, but she needed to do some careful thinking before writing. Jess made a note of her preliminary claim, and she set aside some time to think about the issue more carefully later.

Preliminary main idea   Taxing sugary drinks might be a good way to reduce obesity.

Second Basic: Support in Argument (Reasons and Evidence)

When you write an argument, you must think critically about your reasons as well as the ideas of those who disagree with you. We learned in Chapter 1 that critical thinking is a careful and reasoned approach to making decisions, solving problems, and understanding complex issues. In order to write about the issue of a soda tax, Jess needed to think critically about the issue. Jess followed these three steps to develop support for her argument.

Thinking Critically about Support in Arguments

1. Identify reasons and question the assumptions behind those reasons.

2. Recognize different types of evidence.

3. Evaluate the evidence.

Identify Reasons and Question Assumptions

First, Jess needed to find reasons for her position. She decided to record her thinking in a notebook, so she made a chart with three columns. Jess read the article again, and she identified two main reasons for the author's claim. She wrote those in the first column. Next, she tried to identify some of the **assumptions** (unquestioned ideas or opinions) behind the author's point. She put those assumptions in the second column. Finally, she questioned each of the writer's assumptions, trying to put herself in the shoes of someone opposed to beverage taxes. She noted her questions in the third column.

Tip Consider this advice from actor Alan Alda:

"Begin challenging your own assumptions. Your assumptions are your windows on the world. Scrub them off every once in a while, or the light won't come in."

The author's reasons	The author's assumptions	Questions about the author's assumptions
"We have a problem with obesity. Since 2010, obesity in our city has risen from 26 percent to 33 percent. At the same time, sales of soda and sweet tea in 16-ounce containers and higher have increased by 10 percent"	Sugary drinks, like soda, energy drinks, and sweetened tea, are making people fat.	But why target sugary drinks instead of other junk food? Aren't French fries just as bad for the waistline as soda is?
"We need to discourage people from drinking so much soda. A tax of 20 to 25 cents per drink would reduce consumption of these beverages."	People won't buy as many sodas if they cost more and will therefore gain less weight.	Really? It's easy for me to say that this tax would work because I'm not a big fan of these drinks. But if they taxed coffee, the taxes would have to be pretty big to break my four-cup-a-day habit. And what if people are eating food that causes them to gain weight; how much difference would cutting out sugary drinks really make?
The tax revenues would benefit the public through an education program.	Children are more likely to make healthy eating choices if they are provided with information on good nutrition.	Is there evidence that providing this kind of information makes a difference?

After considering the author's ideas, Jess decided to explore her own reasons for supporting the tax. Once again, Jess made a chart with three columns. She listed her reasons, the assumptions behind them, and questions about those assumptions.

My reasons	The assumptions behind my reasons	Questions about my assumptions
If we reduce obesity, medical expenses will go down.	Obesity causes medical problems that cost a lot of money.	Is there evidence that obesity increases medical costs? What kinds of costs?
The tax will also help reduce obesity by paying for education in our schools.	If we teach children about healthy eating, they will develop good habits.	Sometimes I do things even if I know they aren't healthy. How do I know an education program will make a difference?

Recognize Different Types of Evidence

The questions in the third column of each chart could help Jess find and evaluate evidence. She knew her own **opinions**, which are beliefs that cannot be proved or disproved, would not be sufficiently convincing evidence. In order to support her position on the sugar tax, she would need to gather the following types of evidence, which are used most often to support arguments:

Think Critically Can you find an example of a misuse of statistics, either in social media or on television?

- **Facts: Statements or observations that can be proved.** One type of fact is statistics, or real numbers taken from carefully designed studies of an issue. The article Jess read included statistics, such as the increased percentage of obesity in the city.

  CAUTION: Be sure to check the context and source of any statistical data. For example, if a source says that 75 percent of college students surveyed do not support a tax on soda, you need to know how many students were surveyed and where those students came from. If 7 out of 10 students, all identified as above-average soda drinkers, said they did not support the tax, how useful is this information? How representative is this sample? Ask who paid for the study. If a group of companies who sell sugary drinks provided this statistic, you should look for other sources of information that do not have an investment in the soft drink market.

- **Examples: Specific information or experiences that support a position.** Examples can come from a writer's reading and research, or they may be drawn from the writer's own life. Jess had a high-school friend who loved to get 32-ounce sodas after school every day, and he had a problem with weight. She considered using her friend as an example in the paper.

Think Critically
Stereotypes can be a form of overgeneralization. Can you explain why? Why are stereotypes dangerous?

  CAUTION: Do not overgeneralize based on one or two examples. **Overgeneralizing** means drawing a conclusion based on only a few examples. Jess cannot conclude that sodas cause obesity based on one example.

- **Expert Opinions: The opinions of people considered knowledgeable about a topic because of their *credentials* (education, work, experience, or research).**

    CAUTION: It is important to investigate expert opinions carefully. For example, an economics professor might be very knowledgeable about the possible benefits and drawbacks of beverage taxes. He or she probably would not be the best source of information on the health effects of soda.

- **Predictions: Forecasts of the possible outcomes of events or actions.** These forecasts should be the informed or educated views of experts, not the best guesses of nonexperts.

Tip When looking for evidence about assumptions, always seek the most reliable sources of information.

PRACTICE 14–2   **Identifying Types of Evidence**

Jess talked to a librarian who helped her find sources that could provide evidence about her topic. The following chart shows the evidence that Jess pulled together to address her assumptions and her questions about them. Determine which kind of evidence Jess found: fact, example, expert opinion, or prediction. The first one has been done for you.

Assumptions / questions to investigate	Evidence in response to assumptions and questions
To what degree do sugary drinks contribute to obesity?	**Example:** According to the Centers for Disease Control and Prevention, about half of all Americans get a major portion of their daily calories from sweetened beverages.
	Type of evidence: fact
	1. In the *Journal of Pediatrics*, Robert Murray reported that one-fourth of US teenagers drink as many as four cans of soda or fruit drinks a day, each one containing about 150 calories. That translates to a total of 600 calories a day, the equivalent of an additional meal.
	Type of evidence:
	2. Kerry Neville, a registered dietician, says, "Sugary foods and beverages do not cause obesity—no single food does. Although it sounds simplistic, obesity is a consequence of eating too many calories and expending too few."
	Type of evidence: ➡

Do sugary drinks deserve to be targeted more than other dietary factors that can contribute to obesity?	3. My brother, his wife, and their three kids are all big soda drinkers, and they are all overweight. They also eat lots of junk food, however, so it is hard to tell how much the soda is to blame for their weight.
	Type of evidence:
	4. The Center for Science in the Public Interest says that sugary beverages are more likely to cause weight gain than solid foods are. After eating solid food, people tend to reduce their consumption of other calorie sources. Unlike solid foods, however, sugary beverages do not make people feel full.
	Therefore, they may add on calories to satisfy their hunger.
	Type of evidence:
To what degree would taxes on sugary drinks discourage people from buying these beverages and reduce obesity?	5. Several researchers say that the taxes would have to be pretty significant to affect consumer behavior. The average national tax on a 12-ounce bottle of soda is five cents, and that has not provided enough discouragement.
	Type of evidence:
	6. In the *New England Journal of Medicine*, Kelly D. Brownell says that a penny-per-ounce tax on sugary beverages could reduce consumption of these beverages by more than 10 percent.
	Type of evidence:
Would the taxes have any other benefits?	7. Kelly D. Brownell says that by reducing the consumption of sugary beverages, the taxes could help cut public expenditures on obesity. Each year, about $79 billion goes toward the health-care costs of overweight and obese individuals. Approximately half of these costs are paid by taxpayers.
	Type of evidence:
	8. Brownell also believes that the tax revenues could/should be used for programs to prevent childhood obesity.
	Type of evidence:

PRACTICE 14-3   **Deepening the Search for Evidence**

Come up with at least one other question that could be raised about the sugary drinks tax issue. Then, list the type(s) of evidence (such as personal examples, an expert opinion from a scientific study, or a prediction from a business leader) that could help answer the question.

Question(s):

Type(s) of evidence:

Evaluate the Evidence

As Jess reviewed her sources, she thought critically about the evidence. According to her instructor, good supporting evidence is accurate, **relevant** (closely related to the subject), and **credible** (trustworthy); also, whenever possible, it should come from an unbiased source. A source that is **biased** does not review both sides fairly. For example, a referee who only calls penalties on one team (even though both are committing the same fouls) might be accused of bias; he did not treat both teams fairly and equally.

To test the strength of her evidence, Jess asked these questions:

Tip Having an opinion (and expressing it) does not make someone biased. Why not?

- Are my facts and examples accurate? How do I know?
- Are my facts, examples, expert opinions, and predictions relevant, or do they distract my reader?
- Is the evidence from a credible source? Is it a recognized organization? Does the author have relevant credentials? Does anything about it seem suspicious? Does the evidence include vague sources ("everyone knows" or "people say")?
- Does the source present evidence fairly, or does it appear to be biased toward one side?

PRACTICE 14-4   **Reviewing the Evidence**

For each of the following positions, one piece of evidence is weak: it does not support the position. Circle the letter of the weak evidence, and, in the space provided, state why it is weak.

Example:

Position: Advertisements should not use skinny models.

Reason: Skinny should not be promoted as ideal.

a.   Three friends of mine became anorexic trying to get skinny.
b.   Everyone knows that most people are not that thin.

c. A survey of girls shows that they think that they should be as thin as models.

d. People can endanger their health trying to fit the skinny "ideal" promoted in advertisements.

Not strong evidence because *"everyone knows" is not strong evidence; everyone obviously doesn't know that.*

1. Position: People who own guns should not be allowed to keep them at home.

   Reason: It is dangerous to keep a gun in the house.

   a. Guns can go off by accident.

   b. Keeping guns at home has been found to increase the risk of home suicides and adolescent suicides.

   c. Just last week, a story in the newspaper told about a man who, in a fit of rage, took his gun out of the drawer and shot his wife.

   d. Guns can be purchased easily.

   Not strong evidence because

2. Position: Schoolchildren in the United States should go to school all year.

   Reason: Year-round schooling promotes better learning.

   a. All my friends have agreed that we would like to end the long summer break.

   b. A survey of teachers across the country showed that children's learning improved when they had multiple shorter vacations rather than entire summers off.

   c. Many children are bored and restless after three weeks of vacation and would be better off returning to school.

   d. Test scores improved when a school system in Colorado went to year-round school sessions.

   Not strong evidence because

3. Position: The "three strikes and you're out" law that forces judges to send people to jail after three convictions should be revised.

   Reason: Basing decisions about sentencing on numbers alone is neither reasonable nor fair.

   a. A week ago, a man who stole a slice of pizza was sentenced to eight to ten years in prison because it was his third conviction.

   b. The law makes prison overcrowding even worse.

    c.   Judges always give the longest sentence possible anyway.

    d.   The law too often results in people getting major prison sentences for minor crimes.

Not strong evidence because

Third Basic: Consider and Respond to Different Points of View

In the process of investigating her assumptions, Jess not only gathered good support; she also encountered some opposing views. In an argument, we call an opposing view a **counterclaim**; reasons that support counterclaims are called **counterarguments**. A counterclaim Jess found in her reading is that the city should not tax sugary beverages.

Critical thinkers consider counterarguments carefully and respectfully. If they believe that a counterargument makes sense, they will make a **concession**: they will agree that some of the evidence presented by the other side is accurate or important. A concession often includes one of the following expressions:

> It is true that…
> Granted…

A concession shows that a writer has thought carefully about both sides of the issue. Another way writers show they have considered both sides of the issue is to introduce a counterargument and then offer a **rebuttal**, which is a response to the counterargument. A rebuttal points out problems with the arguments of the other side. A rebuttal always responds to a counterargument, and it often begins with one of these expressions: *but, however,* or *nevertheless.*

Jess found an opposing view from Dr. Richard Adamson of the American Beverage Association. When Jess reviewed his evidence, she thought he might be biased because he represents the interests of the beverage industry. Jess decided that as long as she mentioned his affiliation with the beverage industry, his point might be worth including as a counterargument in her paper. In the following example, you will see how Jess introduced Adamson's counterargument (underlined), offered a concession (bold), and then provided a rebuttal (italics).

> <u>Some people who are opposed to taxing sugary beverages, such as Dr. Richard Adamson of the American Beverage Association, argue that it is unfair to blame one product for our expanding waistlines.</u> **It is true that overconsumption of soda and other sweetened beverages is just one cause of obesity.** *Nevertheless, targeting this one cause could play a vital, lasting role in a larger campaign to bring this major health crisis under control.*

Jess discovered some counterarguments by reading what others had written on her topic. Another way to find counterarguments is to consider your audience. For this assignment, Jess needed to identify a specific audience for the paper and then consider what questions her readers would ask, what objections they might have, and what kind of evidence they would find convincing.

PRACTICE 14–5   **Consider the Audience**

Select one of the following target audiences. Determine what objections they would have to the tax on sugary sodas. Would the evidence Jess has gathered (see Practice 14–2, p. 297) address their concerns? Why or why not?

1. Parents of children and teens

2. Soda company employees

3. College students

4. Restaurant owners

After reviewing the evidence from both sides (the second and third basics), you may need to refine the initial position. Here is how Jess revised her preliminary main idea.

Revised main idea	To help address the obesity crisis, states should place significant taxes on sugary beverages.

Notice the removal of the word *might* that was part of the original main idea. Having done some research, Jess now believes strongly that the taxes are a good idea—as long as they are high enough to make a significant dent in consumption.

Fourth Basic: Organization in Argument

Before writing an argument, create a simple outline stating the main idea and the major support points—the reasons for the position expressed in the main idea and your consideration of the opposing side. The reasons are based on the evidence you gathered. Your simple outline will help you organize a draft of your paper.

Jess's rough outline

Claim: To help address the obesity crisis, states should place significant taxes on sugary beverages.

Support/reasons:

    I.   *Sugary drinks are a major contributor to obesity.*

    II. *As long as they are significant, taxes on these drinks could reduce consumption.*

    III. *The taxes could fund programs targeting childhood obesity.*

Most arguments are organized by **order of importance**, starting with the least important evidence and saving the most convincing reason and evidence for last.

Use **transitions** to move your readers smoothly from one supporting reason to another. Here are some of the transitions you might use in your argument.

Tip For more on order of importance, see page 75.

Common Transitions in Argument

above all	more important
also	most important
best of all	one fact/another fact
especially	one reason/another reason
for example	one thing/another thing
in addition	remember
in fact	the first (second, third) point
in particular	worst of all
in the first (second, third) place	

Jess used order of importance to organize her argument in favor of taxes on sugary drinks. Notice that she did not incorporate all the evidence from the chart on pages 297–298. Instead, she chose the evidence she believed offered the strongest support for her main point. She also included an opposing view. As you read the first draft of her essay below, pay attention to the transition words she used. (The transitions have been highlighted in bold.)

To help address the obesity crisis, states should place significant taxes on sugary beverages, such as soda, sweetened tea and fruit juices, and energy drinks. These drinks are a good target for taxation because they are a major contributor to obesity. According to the Centers for Disease Control and Prevention, about half of all Americans get a major portion of their daily calories from sweetened beverages.

In addition, the Journal of Pediatrics reports that one-fourth of U.S. teenagers get as many as 600 calories a day from soda or fruit drinks. This consumption is the equivalent of an additional meal.

Another reason to tax sugary drinks is that such taxation could reduce consumption. However, it is important that these taxes be significant, because taxes of just a few additional pennies per can or bottle probably wouldn't deter consumers. According to Kelly D. Brownell, director of the Rudd Center for Food Policy and Obesity, a penny-per-ounce tax on sugary beverages could cut consumption of these beverages by more than 10 percent. It could also reduce the estimated $79 billion of taxpayer money spent each year on health care for overweight and obese individuals.

Paragraphs versus Essays in Argument

For more on the important features of argument, see the Four Basics of Good Argument on page 291.

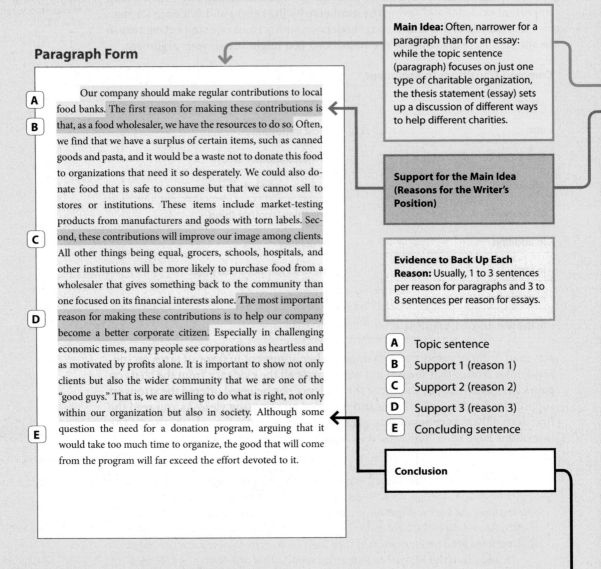

Paragraph Form

A Our company should make regular contributions to local food banks. B The first reason for making these contributions is that, as a food wholesaler, we have the resources to do so. Often, we find that we have a surplus of certain items, such as canned goods and pasta, and it would be a waste not to donate this food to organizations that need it so desperately. We could also donate food that is safe to consume but that we cannot sell to stores or institutions. These items include market-testing products from manufacturers and goods with torn labels. C Second, these contributions will improve our image among clients. All other things being equal, grocers, schools, hospitals, and other institutions will be more likely to purchase food from a wholesaler that gives something back to the community than one focused on its financial interests alone. D The most important reason for making these contributions is to help our company become a better corporate citizen. Especially in challenging economic times, many people see corporations as heartless and as motivated by profits alone. It is important to show not only clients but also the wider community that we are one of the "good guys." That is, we are willing to do what is right, not only within our organization but also in society. E Although some question the need for a donation program, arguing that it would take too much time to organize, the good that will come from the program will far exceed the effort devoted to it.

Main Idea: Often, narrower for a paragraph than for an essay: while the topic sentence (paragraph) focuses on just one type of charitable organization, the thesis statement (essay) sets up a discussion of different ways to help different charities.

Support for the Main Idea (Reasons for the Writer's Position)

Evidence to Back Up Each Reason: Usually, 1 to 3 sentences per reason for paragraphs and 3 to 8 sentences per reason for essays.

A Topic sentence
B Support 1 (reason 1)
C Support 2 (reason 2)
D Support 3 (reason 3)
E Concluding sentence

Conclusion

Think Critically As You Write Argument

Ask Yourself

- Have I questioned the assumptions behind my main idea?
- Have I looked for evidence to respond to these questions and to develop support for my argument?
- Have I evaluated this evidence before including it in my paper?
- Have I considered opposing points of view?

Essay Form

1

At the last executive meeting, we discussed several possible ways to improve our company's marketing and advertising and to increase employee morale. Since attending the meeting, I have become convinced that one effort would help in those areas and more: our company should become more active in supporting charities.

First, giving time and money to community organizations is a good way to promote our organization. This approach has worked well for several of our competitors. For example, Lanse Industries is well known for sponsoring Little League teams throughout the city. Its name is on the back of each uniform, and banners promoting Lanse's new products appear on the ball fields. Lanse gets free promotion of these efforts through articles in the local papers, and according to one company source quoted in the *Hillsburg Gazette*, Lanse's good works in the community have boosted its sales by 5 to 10 percent. Another competitor, Great Deals, has employees serve meals at soup kitchens over the holidays and at least once during the spring or summer. It, too, has gotten great publicity from these efforts, including a spot on a local televi-

2

sion news show. It is time for our company to start reaping these kinds of benefits.

Second, activities like group volunteering will help employees feel more connected to one another and to their community. Kay Rodriguez, a manager at Great Deals' and a good friend of mine, organized the company's group volunteering efforts at the soup kitchens, and she cannot say enough good things about the results. Aside from providing meals to the needy, the volunteering has boosted the morale of Great Deals employees because they understand that they are supporting an important cause in their community. Kay has also noticed that as employees work together at the soup kitchens, they form closer bonds. She says, "Some of these people work on different floors and rarely get to see each other during the work week. Or they just do not have time to talk. But while they work together on the volunteering, I see real connections forming." I know that some members of our executive committee might think it would be too time-consuming to organize companywide volunteering efforts. Kay assures me, however, that this is not

3

the case and that the rewards of such efforts far exceed the costs in time.

The most important reason for supporting charities is that it is the right thing to do. As a successful business that depends on the local community for a large share of revenue and employees, I believe we owe that community something in return. If our home city does not thrive, how can we? By giving time and money to local organizations, we provide a real service to people, and we present our company as a good and caring neighbor instead of a faceless corporation that could not care less if local citizens went hungry, had trash and graffiti in their parks, or couldn't afford sports teams for their kids. We could make our community proud to have us around.

I realize that our main goal is to run a profitable and growing business. I do not believe, however, that this aim must exclude doing good in the community. In fact, I see these two goals moving side by side and hand in hand. When companies give back to local citizens, their businesses benefit, the community benefits, and everyone is pleased by the results.

A Introductory paragraph

B Thesis statement

C Topic sentence 1 (reason 1)

D Topic sentence 2 (reason 2)

E Topic sentence 3 (reason 3)

F Concluding paragraph

The most important reason to tax sugary drinks is that the money from such taxes could be used to prevent future cases of obesity. As Brownell notes, the taxes could fund antiobesity programs aimed at educating children about healthy diets and encouraging them to exercise. Some people who are opposed to taxing sugary beverages, such as Dr. Richard Adamson of the American Beverage Association, argue that it is unfair to blame one product for our expanding waistlines. It is true that overconsumption of soda and other sweetened beverages is just one cause of obesity. Nevertheless, targeting this one cause could play a vital, lasting role in a larger campaign to bring this major health crisis under control.

PRACTICE 14–6   Using Transitions in Argument

The following argument essay encourages students to get involved in service work during college. It was written by Jorge Roque, an Iraq War veteran and Miami-Dade College student who is vice president of a service fraternity.

After reading Jorge's essay, fill in the blanks with transitions. You are not limited to the ones listed in the box on page 303.

Even for the busiest student, getting involved in service organizations is worth the time and effort it takes. At one point, after I had returned from Iraq, I was homeless and experienced post-traumatic stress disorder. I was referred to Veteran Love, a nonprofit organization that helps disabled ex-soldiers: it helped me when I needed it most. When I was back on track, I knew that I wanted to help others. I was working and going to school with little extra time, but getting involved has been important in ways I had not expected.

_____ you meet many new people and form a new and larger network of friends and colleagues. You also learn new skills, like organization, project management, communication, teamwork, and public speaking. The practical experience I have now is more than I could have gotten from a class, and I have met people who want to help me in my career.

_____ you help other people and learn about them. You feel as if you have something valuable to give. You also feel part of something larger than yourself. So often, students are not connected to meaningful community work: service work helps you while you help others.

_____ service work makes you feel better about yourself and your abilities. What I am doing is important and real, and I feel better than I ever have because of my service involvement. If you get involved with community service of any kind, you will become addicted to it. You get more than you could ever give.

Evaluate Argument

To become a more successful writer, it is important not only to understand the Four Basics of Good Argument but also to read and evaluate examples. In this section, you will have the opportunity to use a sample rubric to analyze or evaluate the samples of argument writing provided. By using this rubric, you will gain a better understanding of how the components of good argument work together to create a successful paragraph or essay.

Read the following sample argument paragraph. Using the Four Basics of Good Argument and the sample grading rubric, decide what grade this paragraph would earn. Explain your answer.

Assignment Concealed carry laws are becoming increasingly controversial, especially when people feel as though their rights are being restricted or that they are in danger. Write a paragraph that takes a position on the question: Should students be allowed to carry a concealed weapon on a college campus? Support your argument with specific examples and evidence.

College students should be allowed to carry concealed weapons on campus if they are legally permitted to do so. To have a firearm legally, people are required to apply for a FOID card (Firearms Owner Identification) and subject themselves to a background check. This process is meant to ensure that the people who are allowed to carry these weapons have no history of violence or mental illness that may create future problems. Although there has not been a security issue at my own campus, I would like to know that I have the option to protect myself if a situation like this occurred. In addition, the legal age for owning specific firearms is eighteen or twenty-one, depending on what type of gun a person chooses to carry. I am safer with a weapon than without.

Analysis of Sample Paragraph:

Sample Rubric

Element	Grading criteria	Point: Comment
Appropriateness	• Did the student follow the assignment directions?	__/5:
Main idea	• Does the paper clearly state a strong main idea in a complete sentence?	__/10: ➜

Support	• Is the main idea developed with specific support, including specific details and examples? • Is there enough support to make the main idea evident to the reader? • Is all the support directly related to the main idea? • Is there a counterargument present at some point?	___/10:
Organization	• Is the writing logically organized? • Does the student use transitions (*also, for example, sometimes,* and so on) to move the reader from one point to another?	___/10:
Conclusion	• Does the conclusion remind the reader of the main idea? • Does it make an observation based on the support?	___/5:
Grammar	• Is the writing free of the four most serious errors? (See Chapters 16–19.) • Is the sentence structure clear? • Does the student choose words that clearly express his or her meaning? • Are the words spelled correctly? • Is the punctuation correct?	___/10:
		TOTAL POINTS: ___/50

Read and Analyze Argument

In this section, the Profile of Success illustrates how Stacie Brown uses argument in her job in a legal office. Next, two professional articles present different positions in the debate surrounding climate change. The first one makes the claim that climate change is not a problem and is not occurring at present. The second article argues that climate change is a very real threat to animals, plants, and humans. Both articles present a clear position and evidence to support that position. Both of the professional pieces originally appeared online, and both provided hyperlinks for readers to investigate their evidence. In this book, the links are provided as footnotes. As you read these selections, pay attention to the vocabulary and the questions in the margin. They will help you read critically.

Profile of Success
Argument in the Real World

Stacie Brown
Legal Assistant

Background I grew up in an exceptionally small town (population 99) where it was easy for me to excel in high school—and I did—because all the teachers would know why I didn't do well if I didn't. After my dad died during my senior year of high school, though, school was just something I had to finish.

After high school, I couldn't settle on anything because everything seemed useless or pointless. Hoping to find my way, I enrolled in Blinn College for the first time. I ended up dropping two classes and failing the other two, one of which was English 1301. A few years later, I enrolled in a veterinary technician course, but I soon decided that also wasn't for me.

I started dating my husband a while after that and soon became pregnant. Twenty-five years old, no career plan, no college degree, baby on the way—I knew I had to get my act together. With support from family and friends, I enrolled in college for the third time.

While at Blinn College, a few encouraging teachers helped me to realize my potential, and I started writing again. (I had put the pen down after my dad died.) Indeed, I graduated Blinn College with honors. My long-term goal is to become a novelist.

After getting my associate's degree, I started my career in the administrative field as a legal assistant, and I get to use my writing and editing skills every day to communicate with clients, attorneys, courts, and other business entities. I am now situated to pursue my passion. My career has taught me that everyone has at least one remarkable story. It's up to me to write it.

Degrees/Colleges Associate of Applied Science, Blinn College

Writing at Work I write business emails, letters, memos, legal pleadings, and other legal documents. Working with clients often involves discussing uncomfortable or difficult topics. Addressing issues related to billing are necessary not only for a business to succeed but also for building a strong, successful attorney-client relationship. Many times, an attorney needs to communicate with not only a client but also the client's family member—and family members can be quite inexorable. One must respond in a firm but tactful manner.

inexorable: hard to stop or manage

Workplace Argument

The following is an example of an email pertaining to billing.

Dear John Doe:

1 We recently sent your most recent invoice (November 2017) to the address we have in our file: 555 No Name Street, Anywhere, Texas 55555. It was returned to us as "not deliverable as addressed, unable to forward." As a result, I am emailing your November 2017 invoice, which is attached. If the mailing address we

have on file is incorrect, please notify our office immediately of your correct mailing address.

2   Additionally, when we last spoke about payment arrangements, you agreed to send a money order once you received your tax return, which you indicated would be in ten to twelve days. It has been six months since that phone conversation, and our office has yet to receive payment of any kind. As you are aware, our office policy dictates that attorneys may not continue work for a client for which there is no money left in the Trust account. This means that any pending or future issues related to your case will not be considered until your balance is paid in full.

3   If you believe there has been an error in receiving payment, please contact our office to discuss. Otherwise, please consider this email a formal demand for payment in full. If your payment is not received within fifteen days from the date of this email, our office will have no choice but to begin formal collection actions. These actions will, of course, increase the amount owed to this office. I sincerely hope this will not be necessary.

Thank you,

Stacie

Stacie Brown

Legal Assistant

Law Firm

555 No Name Street

Anywhere, Texas 55555

Phone: 555.555.5555

Fax: 555.555.5556

Email: emailaddress@domain.net

Read to Write: Annotate

1. Double-underline the thesis statement.

2. Circle the transitions that introduce the different reasons supporting the argument.

3. Underline the parts of the email that present each supporting reason for the argument.

Think Critically

1. Does this workplace sample follow the Four Basics of Good Argument (p. 291)? Why or why not?

2. What is the tone of the email? What words help you identify the tone?

Professional Argument Essay 1: Climate Change Is Not Happening

John Hawkins

5 Scientific Reasons That Global Warming Isn't Happening

John Hawkins is a well-known writer and political commentator. Not only does Hawkins write for publications such as *The Huffington Post*, *Washington Examiner*, and *The Hill*, he also makes numerous regular appearances on ABC News, MSNBC, and C-Span. Throughout his career, he has spent a great deal of time interviewing and working with conservatives. He is the founder of the Rightroots group, an organization that raises money to fund conservative political candidates nationwide. This piece first appeared on TownHall.com on February 18, 2014.

How did global warming discussions end up hinging on what's happening with polar bears, unverifiable predictions of what will happen in a hundred years, and whether people are "climate deniers" or "global warming cultists"? If this is a scientific topic, why aren't we spending more time discussing the science involved? Why aren't we talking about the evidence and the actual data involved? Why aren't we looking at the predictions that were made and seeing if they match up to the results? If this is such an open and shut case, why are so many people who care about science skeptical? Many Americans have long since thought that the best scientific evidence available suggested that man wasn't causing any sort of global warming. However, now, we can go even further and suggest that the planet isn't warming at all.

2   There hasn't been any global warming since 1997: if nothing changes in the next year, we're going to have kids who graduate from high school who will have never seen any "global warming" during their lifetimes. That's right; the temperature of the planet has essentially been flat for seventeen years.[1] This isn't a controversial assertion either. Even the former director of the Climate Research Unit (CRU) of the University of East Anglia, Phil Jones, admits that it's true. Since the planet was cooling from 1940 to 1975[2] and the upswing in temperature afterward only lasted twenty-two years, a seventeen-year pause is a big deal. It also begs an obvious question: How can we be experiencing global warming if there's no actual "global warming"?

unverifiable: cannot be proven or shown to be true

Read to Write
What are the author's credentials for writing about this topic? How does knowledge of those credentials affect you as a reader?

assertion: a positive statement, often without support

Read to Write As you read this essay, identify what specific evidence the writer uses to support the main argument.

Read to Write Why does Hawkins ask so many questions in the first paragraph?

Reflect How could you test Hawkins's evidence in this paragraph?

[1] http://rightwingnews.com/climate-change/report-no-statistical-global-warming-in-17-years/
[2] http://rightwingnews.com/uncategorized/10-questions-for-al-gore-and-the-global-warming-crowd/

consensus: general agreement

Read to Write
Why does Hawkins use quotation marks around certain words in this paragraph? How do readers interpret these words?

3   There is no scientific consensus that global warming is occurring and caused by man: questions are not decided by "consensus." In fact, many scientific theories that were once widely believed to be true were made irrelevant by new evidence. Just to name one of many, many examples, in the early seventies, scientists believed global cooling was occurring. However, once the planet started to warm up, they changed their minds. Yet, the primary "scientific" argument for global warming is that there is a "scientific consensus" that it's occurring. Setting aside the fact that's not a scientific argument, even if that ever was true (and it really wasn't[3]), it's certainly not true anymore. Over 31,000 scientists have signed on to a petition saying humans aren't causing global warming.[4] More than one thousand scientists signed on to another report saying there is no global warming at all.[5] There are tens of thousands of well-educated, mainstream scientists who do not agree that global warming is occurring at all, and people who share their opinion are taking a position grounded in science.

mainstream: the dominant tendency

4   Arctic ice is up 50 percent since 2012:[6] the loss of Arctic ice has been a big talking point for people who believe global warming is occurring. Some people have even predicted that all of the Arctic ice would melt by now because of global warming. Yet, Arctic ice is up 50 percent since 2012. How much Arctic ice really matters is an open question since the very limited evidence we have suggests that a few decades ago, there was less ice than there is today,[7] but the same people who thought the drop in ice was noteworthy should at least agree that the increase is important as well.

Read to Write
What significance does the amount of Arctic ice have on the planet? How could you evaluate Hawkins's evidence?

5   Climate models showing global warming have been wrong over and over: these future projections of what global warming will do to the planet have been based on climate models. Essentially, scientists make assumptions about how much of an impact different factors will have; they guess how much of a change there will be and then they project changes over time. Unfortunately, almost all of these models showing huge temperature gains have turned out to be wrong.[8]

Read to Write What is Hawkins's reason in this paragraph? What evidence supports it?

6   Former NASA scientist Dr. Roy Spencer says that climate models used by government agencies to create policies "have failed miserably." Spencer analyzed ninety climate models against surface temperature and satellite temperature data, and found that more than 95 percent of the models "have over-forecast the warming trend since 1979, whether we use their own surface temperature dataset (HadCRUT4) or our satellite dataset of lower tropospheric temperatures (UAH)."

troposphere: lowest layer of the earth's atmosphere

---

[3] https://wattsupwiththat.com/2013/05/17/to-john-cook-it-isnt-hate-its-pity-pity-for-having-such-a-weak-argument-you-are-forced-to-fabricate-in-epic-proportions/
[4] http://www.petitionproject.org/
[5] http://rightwingnews.com/climate-change/blockbuster-new-report-1000-scientists-agree-there-is-no-man-caused-global-warming/
[6] http://www.breitbart.com/national-security/2013/12/17/cryosat-satellite%20-findings-arctic-ice-increase/
[7] https://wattsupwiththat.com/2012/03/01/nasa-and-multi-year-arctic-ice-and-historical-context/
[8] http://dailycaller.com/2014/02/11/report-95-percent-of-global-warming-models-are-wrong/#ixzz2t4gPo8iJ

7 There's an old saying in programming that goes, "Garbage in, garbage out." In other words, if the assumptions and data you put into the models are faulty, then the results will be worthless. If the climate models that show a dire impact because of global warming aren't reliable—and they're not—then the long-term projections they make are meaningless.

8 Predictions about the impact of global warming have already been proven wrong: the debate over global warming has been going on long enough that we've had time to see whether some of the predictions people made about it have panned out in the real world. For example, Al Gore predicted all the Arctic ice would be gone by 2013.[9] In 2005, the *Independent* ran an article saying that the Arctic had entered a death spiral.[10]

9 Scientists fear that the Arctic has now entered an irreversible phase of warming that which will accelerate the loss of the polar sea ice that has helped to keep the climate stable for thousands of years. . . . The greatest fear is that the Arctic has reached a "tipping point" beyond which nothing can reverse the continual loss of sea ice and with it the massive land glaciers of Greenland, which will raise sea levels dramatically. Of course, the highway is still there.

10 Meanwhile, Arctic ice is up 50 percent since 2012. James Hansen of NASA fame predicted that the West Side Highway in New York would be under water by now because of global warming.[11]

11 If the climate models and the predictions about global warming aren't even close to being correct, wouldn't it be more scientific to reject hasty action based on faulty data so that we can further study the issue and find out what's really going on?

Read to Write Summarize what the author means by "garbage in, garbage out." How does this statement support his argument in paragraphs 5 and 6?

Read to Write What is a "tipping point"?

Read to Write The author begins and ends with questions. What is the effect of these questions on a reader?

Read to Write: Annotate

1. Double-underline the thesis statement.

2. Underline the reasons for the claim.

3. Circle each question mark. Why does the writer include these questions?

Think Critically

1. Briefly summarize the article, including the claim and reasons in your own words.

2. Does the author consider counterarguments? What are they?

3. What is the author's tone? Give an example to support your answer.

4. Explore some of the supporting links provided by the author. How would you assess the quality of his sources?

[9] http://www.thegatewaypundit.com/2013/12/boy-was-al-gore-wrong-satellite-data-shows-arctic-sea-ice-coverage-up-50-percent/

[10] http://rightwingnews.com/john-hawkins/10-global-warming-doomsday-predictions/

[11] https://wattsupwiththat.com/2009/10/22/a-little-known-but-failed-20-year-old-climate-change-prediction-by-dr-james-hansen/

Respond

1. According to the author, what are the definitions of *global warming* and *global cooling* (see paragraph 3)? What evidence does the author provide to support his claims that either one is or is not happening currently? Is enough evidence provided to support those claims?

2. In paragraph 9, Hawkins writes about Arctic ice and the claim that global warming and climate change has created an inevitable tipping point for our planet. Do you agree or disagree with this claim? Explain your answer.

Professional Argument Essay 2: Climate Change Is Happening

Brett Scheffers and James Watson

Climate Change Is Affecting All Life on Earth – and That's Not Good News for Humanity

Brett Scheffers is an Assistant Professor in the Department of Wildlife Ecology and Conservation at the University of Florida. He has studied in Canada, Singapore, and the United States, and he has worked in Australia and the United States.

James Watson is an Associate Professor Fellow at University of Queensland. He is also the director of the Science and Research Initiative at the Wildlife Conservation Society. He earned his doctorate from Oxford University, and he has worked in both the United States and Australia.

Read to Write
Based on the title and first paragraph, what evidence will the authors use to support the reality of climate change?

parlance: way of speaking

cryptic: mysterious and hard to understand

Read to Write The authors use illustration to provide evidence. How many examples are given? Are these examples effective?

More than a dozen authors from different universities and nongovernmental organizations around the world have concluded, based on an analysis of hundreds of studies, that almost every aspect of life on Earth has been affected by climate change.

2   In more scientific parlance, we found in a paper published in *Science*[12] that genes, species and ecosystems now show clear signs of impact. These responses to climate change include species' genome (genetics), their shapes, colors and sizes (morphology), their abundance, where they live and how they interact with each other (distribution). The influence of climate change can now be detected on the smallest, most cryptic processes all the way up to entire communities and ecosystems.

3   Some species are already beginning to adapt. The color of some animals, such as butterflies, is changing[13] because dark-colored butterflies heat up faster than light-colored butterflies, which have an edge in warmer temperatures.

[12] http://science.sciencemag.org/content/354/6313/aaf7671
[13] https://www.nature.com/articles/ncomms4874

Salamanders in eastern North America and cold-water fish are shrinking in size[14] because being small is more favorable when it is hot than when it is cold. In fact, there are now dozens of examples globally of cold-loving species contracting and warm-loving species expanding their ranges in response to changes in climate.[15]

4   All of these changes may seem small, even trivial, but when every species is affected in different ways these changes add up quickly and entire ecosystem collapse is possible. This is not theoretical: scientists have observed that the cold-loving kelp forests of southern Australia, Japan, and the northwest coast of the United States have not only collapsed from warming[16] but their reestablishment has been halted by replacement species better adapted to warmer waters.

Flood of Insights from Ancient Flea Eggs

5   Researchers are using many techniques, including one called resurrection ecology, to understand how species are responding to changes in climate by comparing the past to current traits of species.[17] And a small and seemingly insignificant organism is leading the way.

6   One hundred years ago, a water flea (genus Daphnia), a small creature the size of a pencil tip, swam in a cold lake of the upper northeastern United States looking for a mate. This small female crustacean later laid a dozen or so eggs in hopes of doing what Mother Nature intended—that she reproduce.

7   Her eggs are unusual in that they have a tough, hardened coat that protects them from lethal conditions such as extreme cold and droughts. These eggs have evolved to remain viable for extraordinary periods of time and so they lay on the bottom of the lake awaiting the perfect conditions to hatch.

8   Now fast forward a century: a researcher interested in climate change has dug up these eggs, now buried under layers of sediment that accumulated over the many years. She takes them to her lab and amazingly, they hatch, allowing her to show one thing: that individuals from the past are of a different architecture than those living in a much hotter world today. There is evidence for responses at every level from genetics to physiology and up through to community level.

9   By combining numerous research techniques in the field and in the lab, we now have a definitive look at the breadth of climate change impacts for this animal group. Importantly, this example offers the most comprehensive evidence of how climate change can affect all processes that govern life on Earth.

From Genetics to Dusty Books

10   The study of water fleas and resurrection ecology is just one of many ways that thousands of geneticists, evolutionary scientists, ecologists, and biogeographers around the world are assessing if—and how—species are responding to current

Read to Write
How do the authors address potential objections from the audience?

kelp: a type of seaweed

ecology: the study of the interactions between organisms and their environment

crustacean: an aquatic animal similar to crabs or lobsters

viable: able to survive or work effectively

Read to Write
Summarize the evidence from the water flea example. How does it show the effects of warming?

definitive: concluded with authority or certainty

[14] http://www.nature.com/news/salamander-shrinkage-linked-to-climate-change-1.14936
[15] https://www.nature.com/articles/nclimate1958
[16] http://science.sciencemag.org/content/353/6295/169
[17] palgrave.nature.com/nclimate/journal/v5/n7/full/nclimate2628.html

climate change. Other state-of-the-art tools include drills that can sample gases trapped several miles beneath the Antarctic ice sheet to document past climates and sophisticated submarines and hot air balloons that measure the current climate.

sampling: technique for collecting representative examples
physiology: study of the parts of organisms and their functions
morphology: the form of organisms

11   Researchers are also using modern genetic sampling to understand how climate change is influencing the genes of species, while resurrection ecology helps us understand changes in physiology. Traditional approaches such as studying museum specimens are effective for documenting changes in species morphology over time.

12   Some rely on unique geological and physical features of the landscape to assess climate change responses. For example, dark sand beaches are hotter than light sand beaches because black color absorbs large amounts of solar radiation. This means that sea turtles breeding on dark sand beaches are more likely to be female because of a process called temperature dependent sex determination. So with higher temperatures, climate change will have an overall feminizing effect on sea turtles[18] worldwide.

Read to Write
What is the evidence provided in paragraph 13?

13   Wiping the dust off of many historical natural history volumes from the forefathers and foremothers of natural history, who first documented species distributions in the late 1800s and early 1900s, also provides invaluable insights by comparing historical species distributions to present-day distributions. For example, Joseph Grinnell's extensive field surveys in early 1900s California led to the study of how the range of birds there shifted based on elevation.[19] In mountains around the world, there is overwhelming evidence[20] that all forms of life, such as mammals, birds, butterflies and trees, are moving up toward cooler elevations as the climate warms.

How this Spills Over onto Humanity

Read to Write How do the authors answer these two questions?

14   So what lessons can be taken from a climate-stricken nature and why should we care?

Read to Write What facts do the authors give? Can these facts be verified?

15   This global response occurred with just a 1 (one) degree Celsius increase in temperature since preindustrial times. Yet the most sensible forecasts suggest we will see at least an increase of up to an additional two to three degrees Celsius over the next fifty to one hundred years unless greenhouse gas emissions are rapidly cut.

Read to Write How will changes to other species affect humans?

yield: the amount of something produced

16   All of this spells big trouble for humans because there is now evidence that the same disruptions documented in nature are also occurring in the resources that we rely on such as crops, livestock, timber, and fisheries. This is because these systems that humans rely on are governed by the same ecological principles that govern the natural world. Examples include reduced crop and fruit yields,[21] increased consumption of crops and timber by pests,[22] and shifts in the distribution

[18] https://www.nature.com/articles/nclimate2236
[19] http://onlinelibrary.wiley.com/doi/10.1890/12-0928.1/abstract
[20] http://science.sciencemag.org/content/333/6045/1024
[21] http://link.springer.com/article/10.1007/s10584-009-9581-7
[22] http://www.nature.com/nclimate/journal/v3/n11/full/nclimate1990.html

of fisheries.[23] Other potential results include the decline of plant-pollinator networks and pollination services[24] from bees.

17   Further impacts on our health could stem from declines in natural systems such as coral reefs and mangroves, which provide natural defense to storm surges, expanding or new disease vectors and a redistribution of suitable farmland. All of this means an increasingly unpredictable future for humans.

vectors: an organism that transmits diseases

18   This research has strong implications for global climate change agreements,[25] which aim to keep total warming to 1.5C. If humanity wants our natural systems to keep delivering the nature-based services we rely so heavily on, now is not the time for nations like the United States to step away from global climate change commitments.[26] Indeed, if this research tells us anything it is absolutely necessary for all nations to up their efforts.

Read to Write
What do the authors want the United States to do?

19   Humans need to do what nature is trying to do: recognize that change is upon us and adapt our behavior in ways that limit serious, long-term consequences.

Read to Write
Paraphrase the final sentence.

Read to Write: Annotate

1. Double-underline the thesis statement.

2. Highlight or circle the key examples used as evidence in the article.

Think Critically

1. What is the main idea of this article?

2. What counterarguments do you see in this article?

3. Do you think the evidence provided by the authors is strong?

4. Explore some of the supporting links provided by the authors. How would you assess the quality of their sources?

Respond

1. What do humans do that cause climate change? Do you think we would alter our behavior to save the planet? Explain your answer.

2. The authors present several techniques used to evaluate the effects of climate change on different species. Are these techniques clear to you? What questions do you have about them? Explain your answer.

---

[23] http://icesjms.oxfordjournals.org/content/early/2014/03/27/icesjms.fsu002
[24] http://www.pnas.org/content/110/12/4656.abstract
[25] http://www.cop21.gouv.fr/en/
[26] https://theconversation.com/what-president-trump-means-for-the-future-of-energy-and-climate-68045

Write Your Own Argument

In this section, you will write your own argument based on one of the following assignments. For help, refer to the How to Write Argument checklist on pages 320–321.

Assignment Options: Writing about College, Work, and Everyday Life

Write an argument paragraph or essay on one of the following topics or on one of your own choice.

College
- Take a position on a controversial issue on your campus. If you need help coming up with topics, you might consult the campus newspaper.

- Argue for or against the use of standardized tests or placement tests. Make sure to research different positions on the tests to support your argument and address opposing views. Many schools use placement tests for incoming students to determine what courses they are prepared to take. If your school has one, think about what it tests and how it affects your schedule or the courses you have to take. One website you might consult is standardizedtests.procon.org.

- Within the past few years, the media have started to discuss student loans and how they often cause a college student to enter the workforce deeply in debt. Does it cost too much to attend college? Is there a way, other than student loans, for a potential student to be able to afford a college education? Take one clear position on the issue and support that position with evidence.

Work
- Argue for a change in company policy such as a new chain of command, clearer job descriptions, or more transparency in the hiring process.

- Argue for something that you would like to get at work, such as a promotion, a raise, or a flexible schedule. Explain why you deserve what you are asking for, and give specific examples.

- Argue for an improvement in your workplace, such as the addition of a bike rack, new chairs in the break room, or a place to swap books or magazines. Make sure your request is reasonable in cost and will be beneficial to a significant number of employees.

Everyday life
- Take a position on a controversial issue in your community.
- Choose a community organization that you belong to, and write about why it is important. Try to persuade your readers to join.

- Oscar Wilde (1854–1900), a famous Irish writer, once commented, "Most people are other people. Their thoughts are someone else's opinions, their lives a mimicry, their passions a quotation." Write an argument that supports or opposes Wilde's views, giving reasons and examples for your position.

mimicry: an imitation of something else

Assignment Options: Reading and Writing Critically

Complete one of the following assignments that asks you to apply the critical thinking, reading, and writing skills discussed in Chapter 1.

Writing Critically about Readings

Stephanie Ericsson's article titled "The Ways We Lie" (p. 211) and John Tierney's essay, "Yes, Money Can Buy Happiness" (p. 260) both take a strong position on an issue. That position can be expressed either implicitly (it requires you to use clues in the paper to determine the position) or explicitly (it is clearly identified). Read or review these pieces, and then follow these steps:

Tip For a reminder of how to summarize, analyze, synthesize, and evaluate, see the Reading and Writing Critically box on page 17.

1. **Summarize** Briefly summarize the two works, listing major examples and details.

2. **Analyze** What features of argument do you see in each essay?

3. **Synthesize** Using examples from one or both of the two essays and from your own experience, describe the features that make an argument successful and convincing. Think of features beyond those in the Four Basics of Good Argument.

4. **Evaluate** In your opinion, are strongly focused arguments or subtler arguments more effective? Or do both types of writing have a place? Explain your answer.

Writing about Images

The following image illustrates the concept of climate change as it affects animals, not just humans.

Study the photograph, and complete the following steps on the next page.

SMETEK/GETTY IMAGES

1. **Read the image** Ask yourself: What details are you drawn to, and why? What emotions or reactions does the melting glacier or stranded animals bring about in you? (For more information on reading images, see Chapter 1.)

2. **Write an argument** Write a paragraph or essay in which you respond to this image and discuss the argument you think it is making. How effective do you find the visual argument? Is it a good way to convey the effects of climate change? Why or why not? Include the details and reactions from step 1.

Writing to Solve a Problem

Read or review the discussion of problem solving in Chapter 1 (pp. 26–27). Then, consider the following problem.

> **Your friend/child/relative has just turned sixteen and is planning to drop out of high school. He has always done poorly, and if he drops out, he can increase his hours at the restaurant where he works. You think that this idea is terrible for many reasons.**

Assignment In a group or on your own, come up with various reasons in support of your decision. Consider, too, your friend's/child's/relative's possible objections to your argument, and account for them. Then, write an argument paragraph or essay to persuade him to complete high school. Give at least three solid reasons, and support your reasons with good evidence or examples. You might start with the following sentence:

> **There are so many important reasons to stay in school and get your high school diploma.**

CHECKLIST

How to Write Argument

Steps	Details
☐ Narrow and explore your topic. See Chapter 3.	• Make the topic more specific. • Prewrite to get ideas about the narrowed topic.
☐ Write a topic sentence (paragraph) or thesis statement (essay). See Chapter 3.	• State your position on your topic.
☐ Support your point. See Chapter 4.	• Come up with reasons and evidence to back up your position.

☐ Write a draft. See Chapter 5.	• Make a plan that puts the reasons in a logical order. • Include a topic sentence (paragraph) or thesis statement (essay) and all the reasons and supporting evidence.
☐ Revise your draft. See Chapter 5.	• Make sure it has *all* the Four Basics of Good Argument. • Make sure you include transitions to move readers smoothly from one reason to the next.
☐ Edit your revised draft. See Parts 3 through 6.	• Correct errors in grammar, spelling, word use, and punctuation.

Chapter Review

1. What is an argument?

2. What are the Four Basics of Good Argument?

3. What is a claim?

4. What three types of information make good evidence?

5. What are three steps for thinking critically about support in arguments?

6. Why do you need to be aware of opposing views (counterarguments)?

7. What are two ways of responding to counterarguments?

Reflect and Apply

1. When have you written or read argument in the past? What happened?

2. Why do you need to consider your audience when you are preparing to write an argument? What can happen if you don't consider the audience?

3. Interview someone who has taken advanced courses in your major or who is working in your chosen profession. What sorts of arguments has that person read or written? What is the purpose of argument in this major or profession?

4. Review your writing from this chapter, including the feedback you received on your drafts. What worked well? What do you need to improve?

Part 3

The Four Most Serious Errors

15 The Basic Sentence 325

16 Fragments 337

17 Run-Ons 351

18 Problems with Subject-Verb Agreement 367

19 Verb Tense 379

The Basic Sentence

The Four Most Serious Errors

This part of the book focuses first on the four grammar errors that people most often notice.

The Four Most Serious Errors

1. Fragments (Chapter 16)
2. Run-ons (Chapter 17)
3. Problems with subject-verb agreement (Chapter 18)
4. Problems with verb tense (Chapter 19)

If you can edit your writing to correct these four errors, your grades will improve.

This chapter reviews the basic sentence elements you will need to understand to find and fix the four most serious errors.

The building blocks of sentences are words. But a sentence requires more than a group of words put together in any order. Consider the following version of the first sentence in this paragraph. Is it an accurate and effective sentence?

Of are blocks sentences building words the.

In this chapter, you will learn how to classify words and use them to build simple sentences.

The Parts of Speech

There are seven basic parts of speech:

1. **Noun:** names a person, place, thing, or idea (for information on making nouns plural, see pp. 517–518). Nouns may be preceded by articles (the words *a*, *an*, and *the*) or quantifiers (words like *one, two, many,* or *a few*). A **noun phrase** is a group of words that includes a noun, or a word that functions as a noun, and any surrounding articles and modifiers. In the following example, the noun phrases are in italics, and the nouns are bold.

> For **Christmas**, I prayed for *this blond-haired **boy**, **Robert***, and *a slim new American **nose*** (Tan 121).

2. **Pronoun:** replaces a noun in a sentence. *He, she, it, we,* and *they* are pronouns. In the following example, the pronoun is bold.

> **He** was not Chinese, but as white as Mary in the manger (Tan 121).

3. **Verb:** tells what action the subject does or links a subject to another word that describes it. In the following examples, the verbs are bold.

> For Christmas, I **prayed** for this blond-haired boy, Robert, and a slim new American nose (Tan 121).

[The verb *prayed* tells us what the subject—*I*—did].

> He **was** not Chinese, but as white as Mary in the manger (Tan 121).

[The verb *was* links the subject, *he,* to the describing word *Chinese*. In this case, the link is negative.]

4. **Adjective:** describes a noun or a pronoun (can also be a participle, a verb that functions as an adjective). In the example below, the adjectives are bold.

> For Christmas, I prayed for this **blond-haired** boy, Robert, and a **slim new American** nose (Tan 121).

[The adjective *blond-haired* describes the noun *boy,* while the adjectives *slim, new,* and *American* describe the noun *nose.*]

5. **Adverb:** describes an adjective, a verb, or another adverb. Adverbs often end in -*ly*. In the following examples, the adverbs are bold.

I was **violently** jerked back into the present with three thunderous explosions on the right side of the Amtrak vehicle (Healy 162).

[The adverb *violently* describes the verb *was jerked*.]

Delightful and perilous, their New York was a city of **incredibly** loud noises, of police and air raid sirens and factory whistles and subway rumble… (Hijuelos 166).

[The adverb *incredibly* describes the adjective *loud*.]

6. **Preposition:** connects a noun, pronoun, or verb with information about it. *Across, around, at, in, of, on,* and *out* are prepositions (see the list of common prepositions, below). In the following example, the preposition is bold.

He was not Chinese, but as white as Mary **in** the manger (Tan 121).

[The preposition *in* connects a noun, *Mary*, with a place, *in*.]

 Language note: Prepositions are used differently in other languages; as a result, words like *in* and *on* can be tricky for people whose native language is not English. Keep these definitions and examples in mind:

1. ***in* = inside of** (*in* the box, *in* the classroom); on a nonspecific day in a month, season, or year (*in* September, *in* spring, *in* 2014); for any time within a limited period of time (*in* three weeks, *in* two years, *in* six days); indicating a general location (*in* the United States, *in* London)

2. ***on* = resting on top of something** (*on* the table, *on* my head); indicating a more specific location (*on* this side of the street, *on* the next page, *on* Elm Avenue); on a specific day (*on* December 25, *on* Thursday)

Common Prepositions

about	before	from	out	up
above	behind	in	outside	upon
across	below	inside	over	with
after	beneath	into	past	within
against	beside	like	since	without
along	by	near	through	
among	down	next to	to	
around	during	of	toward	
at	except	off	under	
because of	for	on	until	

Tip For more on coordinating conjunctions, see pages 428–429. For more on subordinating conjunctions (dependent words), see pages 433–434.

7. **Conjunction:** connects words to each other. An easy way to remember the seven common conjunctions is to connect them in your mind to **FANBOYS:** *for, and, nor, but, or, yet,* and *so.* In the example below, the conjunction is bold.

> Amid all this **and** the natural "fog of war," <u>we</u> <u>managed</u> to get our bearings and move toward our objective (Healy 163).

The Basic Sentence

A sentence is the basic unit of written communication. A sentence must contain at least one **independent clause**. A **clause** is a group of words with a subject and a verb. A clause is **independent** if it is complete; in other words, it doesn't depend on any other sentences to make sense. To make sure that each sentence contains an independent clause, writers look for three required elements:

- A **verb**
- A **subject**
- **Completeness**

Verbs

Every sentence has a **main verb**, the word or words that tell what the subject does or that link the subject to another word that describes it. The main verb of a sentence indicates the time of the events or descriptions in the sentence (past, present, future) and the nature of the events or descriptions (in progress or completed). In addition, the main verb can help writers find the subject of the sentence. Thus, when analyzing a sentence, writers often look for the main verb first. There are three kinds of verbs: *action verbs, linking verbs,* and *auxiliary (helping) verbs.*

Action Verbs

An **action verb** tells what action the subject performs.

To find the main action verb in a sentence, ask yourself: **What action occurs in this sentence?**

| Action verbs | The diesel <u>fumes</u> <u>choked</u> our lungs and <u>burned</u> our throats (Healy 162). |

Linking Verbs

A **linking verb** connects (links) the subject to another word (or group of words) that describes the subject. Linking verbs show no action. The most common linking verb is *be* (*am, is, are,* and so on). Other linking verbs, such as *seem* and *become,* can usually be replaced by a form of the verb *be,* and the sentence will still make sense.

To find linking verbs, ask yourself: **What word joins the subject and the words that describe it?** You can also ask yourself about time in the sentence: **Which word shows if the description was true in the past, present, or future?**

Linking verbs	Their <u>New York</u> <u><u>was</u></u> a fanciful and bustling city of endless sidewalks and unimaginably high buildings (Hijuelos 166).
	<u>Tofu</u> … <u><u>looked</u></u> like stacked wedges of rubbery white sponges (Tan 121). (<u>Tofu</u> <u><u>was</u></u> like stacked wedges).

Some words can be used as either action verbs or linking verbs, depending on how the verb is used in a particular sentence.

Action verb	<u>Justine</u> <u><u>smelled</u></u> the flowers.
Linking verb	The <u>flowers</u> <u><u>smelled</u></u> wonderful. (The <u>flowers</u> <u><u>are</u></u> wonderful).

Common Linking Verbs

Forms of *be*	Forms of *seem* and *become*	Forms of sense verbs
am	seem, seems, seemed	look, looks, looked
are	become, becomes, became	appear, appears, appeared
is		smell, smells, smelled
was		taste, tastes, tasted
were		feel, feels, felt

 Language note: The verb *be* cannot be left out of sentences in English, although there are languages that allow sentences without it.

Incorrect	<u>Tonya</u> well now.
Correct	<u>Tonya</u> **is** well now.

Auxiliary (Helping) Verbs

An **auxiliary** (or **helping**) **verb** joins the main verb in a sentence to form the **complete verb** (also known as a verb phrase—**the main verb and all of its auxiliary verbs**). The auxiliary verb is often a form of the verb *be, have,* or *do.* Modal verbs such as *can, could,* or *would* are also auxiliary verbs. A sentence may have more than one auxiliary verb along with the main verb.

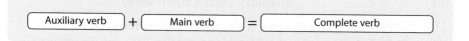

Auxiliary verb + Main verb = Complete verb

In the following examples, complete verbs are double-underlined.

> Yes, money **can** buy happiness, but probably not in the way you imagined. Spending it on yourself **may** not do much for your spirits, but spending it on others **will** make you happier, according to a report from a team of social psychologists in the new issue of *Science* (Tierney 260).

Common Auxiliary Verbs

Forms of *be*	Forms of *have*	Forms of *do*	Modal verbs
am	have	do	can
are	has	does	could
been	had	did	may
being			might
is			must
was			should
were			will
			would

Before you begin Practice 15–1, look at these examples to see how action, linking, and auxiliary verbs are different.

Action verb	Kara graduated last year.
	[The verb *graduated* is an action that Kara performed.]
Linking verb	Kara is a graduate.
	[The verb *is* links Kara to the word that describes her: *graduate*. No action is performed.]
Auxiliary verb	Kara is graduating next spring.
	[The auxiliary verb *is* combines with *graduating* to make the complete verb *is graduating*, which tells what action the subject is taking.]

PRACTICE 15–1   **Identifying the verb (action, linking, or auxiliary verb + main verb)**

The following sentences are adapted from Caitlin Prokop's paragraph, "A Difficult Decision with a Positive Outcome" (p. 278). In each sentence, double-underline the verb. Then, identify each verb as an action verb, a linking verb, or a helping verb + a main verb.

Action verb
Example: My mother <u>made</u> the decision to move back to New York.

1. This decision affected me in a positive way.

2. I graduated with my friends, built a better relationship with my father, and had the chance to go to college without leaving home.

3. Graduating with my friends was important to me.

4. I have known most of them since we were in kindergarten.

5. Another good outcome of my difficult decision was the relationship with my dad.

6. Living together for the past five years has made us closer.

7. I cherish that closeness we have developed.

8. I would like to become a police officer, a nurse, or a teacher.

9. Through the school, I can do volunteer work in each of these areas.

10. Right now, I am leaning toward becoming a teacher, based on my volunteer work in a kindergarten class.

Subjects

The **subject** of a sentence (or of a clause) is the person, place, or thing that does the action of the sentence or that is described in the sentence. The subject of a sentence is usually a noun or a pronoun. For a list of common pronouns, see page 400.

To find the subject, first identify the verb. Then create a question, using the verb to fill in the blank: who or what _____?

Person as subject   <u>Human bank tellers</u>… <u>handled</u> simple cash withdrawals (Alaimo and Koester 279).
[The verb is *handled. Who* handled? *Human bank tellers.*]

Thing as subject   But these <u>mechanizations</u> <u>have</u> only <u>increased</u> profit margins for large corporations.
[The verb is *have increased. What* have increased? *Mechanizations.*]

A **compound subject** consists of two or more subjects joined by *and, or,* or *nor.*

Two subjects   Sure, these new <u>robots and computers</u> <u>reduce</u> work… (Alaimo and Koester 280).

Several subjects   <u>Essays</u>, <u>drafts</u>, <u>homework</u>, and <u>presentations</u> <u>will contribute</u> to your grade.

The subject of a sentence is *never* in a **prepositional phrase**, a word group that begins with a preposition and ends with a noun or pronoun, called the **object of a preposition**.

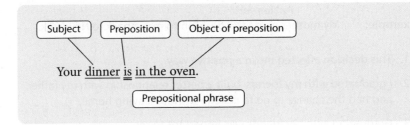

Preposition	Object	Prepositional phrase
from	the bakery	from the bakery
to	the next corner	to the next corner
under	the table	under the table

See if you can identify the subject of the following sentence:

One of my best friends races cars.

Although you might think that the word *friends* is the subject, it isn't. *One* is the subject. The word *friends* cannot be the subject because it is in the prepositional phrase *of my best friends*. When you are looking for the subject of a sentence, cross out the prepositional phrases.

Prepositional Phrase Crossed Out

<u>One</u> of the students <u><u>won</u></u> the science prize.
The <u>rules</u> about the dress code <u><u>are</u></u> very specific.

 Language note: The subject cannot be left out of sentences in English, even if the subject is obvious from the context. Many other languages do not require a stated subject when the verb or the context makes the subject clear.

PRACTICE 15–2   **Identifying Subjects and Prepositional Phrases**

The following sentences are adapted from the essay "Climate Change is Happening" by Brett Scheffers and James Watson. In each sentence, cross out any prepositional phrases, and underline the subject of the sentence.

Example: The <u>influence</u> of climate change can now be detected on the smallest, most cryptic processes.

1. The color of some animals, such as butterflies, is changing.

2. All of these changes may seem small, even trivial.

3. The cold-loving kelp forests of southern Australia, Japan, and the northwest coast of the United States have collapsed from warming.

4. A small creature about the size of a pencil tip swam in a cold lake of the upper northeastern United States looking for a mate.

5. The eggs of this creature are unusual.

6. A researcher with an interest in the effects of climate change has dug up these eggs.

7. Individuals from the past are of a different architecture than those living today.

8. The study of water fleas and resurrection ecology is just one of many ways that thousands of geneticists, evolutionary scientists, ecologists, and biogeographers are assessing responses to current climate change.

9. Extensive field surveys in early 1900s California led to the study shifts in bird ranges according to elevation.

10. Further impacts on our health could stem from declines in natural systems such as coral reefs and mangroves.

Completeness

A sentence (or an independent clause) is complete when it makes sense by itself, without additional words. An incomplete thought will leave readers confused and wondering what is going on.

Incomplete thought	because my alarm did not go off
Complete thought	I <u>was</u> late because my alarm did not go off.
Incomplete thought	the people who won the lottery
Complete thought	The <u>people</u> who won the lottery <u>were</u> old.

To determine whether a thought is complete, ask yourself: **Do I have to ask a question to understand?**

Incomplete thought	When told firmly to remain in his seat. [You would have to ask a question to understand, so it is not a complete thought.]
Complete thought	When told firmly to remain in his seat, the <u>child</u> <u>will</u> <u>try</u> to obey but <u>will squirm</u> and <u>fidget</u> almost constantly, clearly in a state of agitation (Vaz 259).

Six Basic English Sentence Patterns

In English, there are six basic sentence patterns, some of which you have just worked through in this chapter. Although there are other patterns, they build on these six.

1. **Subject-Verb (S-V).** This pattern is the most basic one, as you have already seen.

   S   V
   <u>Babies</u> <u>cry</u>.

2. **Subject-Linking Verb-Noun (S-LV-N)**

   S LV   N
   <u>They</u> <u>are</u> children.

3. **Subject-Linking Verb-Adjective (S-LV-ADJ)**

   S   LV ADJ
   <u>Parents</u> <u>are</u> tired.

4. **Subject-Verb-Adverb (S-V-ADV)**

   S   V   ADV
   <u>They</u> <u>sleep</u> poorly.

5. **Subject-Verb-Direct Object (S-V-DO).** A *direct object* directly receives the action of the verb.

   S   V DO
   <u>Teachers</u> <u>give</u> tests.   [The *tests* are given.]

6. **Subject-Verb-Direct Object-Indirect Object.** An *indirect object* does not directly receive the action of the verb.

   S   V DO   IO
   <u>Teachers</u> <u>give</u> tests to students.   [The *tests* are given; the *students* are not.]

   This pattern can also have the indirect object before the direct object.

   S   V IO   DO
   <u>Teachers</u> <u>give</u> students tests.

> **PRACTICE 15–3**   **Identifying Basic Sentence Patterns**
>
> Identify the subject, complete verb, and sentence pattern for each of the following sentences, adapted from John Tierney's essay "Yes, Money Can Buy Happiness" (Chapter 12). Remember to cross out any prepositional phrases before you identify the subject.
>
> **Example:**   The <u>researchers</u> <u>surveyed</u> a national sample of more than six hundred Americans. *Pattern 5, S-V-DO*

1. Money can buy happiness.

2. The researchers confirmed the joys of giving in three separate ways.

3. The workers gave more money to others.

4. They made donations to the homeless.

5. These workers were happier at the end of the day.

6. Most people don't realize the personal benefits of charity.

7. Perhaps that fact will change.

8. This is a fascinating question.

9. The researchers surveyed another group of students.

10. Dr. Dunn has generously offered some answers free of charge.

> **PRACTICE 15–4**   **Analyzing Clauses for Subjects, Verbs, and Completeness**

In this essay, underline the subject of each sentence, and double-underline the verb. Correct five incomplete thoughts.

Space travel fascinates my grandpa Bill. He watches every space movie at least a dozen times. Before 1996, he never even thought about the moon, Mars, or beyond. He was too old to be an astronaut. Now, however, he is on board a satellite. It analyzes particles in the atmosphere. He has the company of millions of other people. And me, too. Truthfully, only our names travel to Mars or beyond. We are happy with that.

In 1996, the Planetary Society flew the names of members into space. Using the Mars *Pathfinder*. At first, individuals signed a paper. Then, Planetary Society members put the signatures into electronic form. Now, people submit names on the Internet. By filling out a form. The names go on a microchip. One spacecraft to the moon had more than a million names on board. Some people have placed their names on a space-craft going past Pluto and out of our solar system. Their names are on a CD. Which could survive for billions of years.

Grandpa and I feel good about our journey into space. In a way, we will travel to places only dreamed about. After signing up, we received colorful certificates to print out. To tell about our mission. My certificate hangs on my wall. My grandpa and I travel proudly into space.

Chapter Review

1. What are the seven parts of speech?

2. What is a clause?

3. What are three things a sentence (independent clause) must have?

4. What is a prepositional phrase? Give an example.

5. What is the difference between action verbs, linking verbs, and auxiliary verbs?

Reflect and Apply

1. What grammar concepts in this chapter were new to you?

2. Analyze a paragraph from your own writing: find subjects and verbs, check your sentences for completeness, and identify the sentence patterns you have used. What problems or patterns do you notice?

3. How can an understanding of grammar concepts help you edit your writing?

4. What concepts from this chapter are not yet clear to you?

16

Fragments
Incomplete Sentences

Understand What Fragments Are

A **fragment** is a group of words that is punctuated like a sentence but is missing one of the three required elements of an independent clause: a *subject*, a *verb*, or *completeness*. As the name suggests, a fragment is a piece of a sentence, not a complete sentence.

Sentence	I was hungry, so I ate some cold pizza and drank a soda.
	[Complete sentence.]
Fragment	I was hungry, so I ate some cold pizza. *And drank a soda.*
	[The first sentence in the above example is a complete sentence. *And drank a soda* contains a verb (*drank*) but no subject, so it is a fragment.]

Language note: Remember that any idea that ends with a period should include an independent clause: a subject, a verb, and a complete thought. As a quick review, a subject is the person, place, or thing that acts or is described in the sentence. A verb tells what the subject does, links the subject to another word that describes it, or "helps" another verb form a complete verb.

In the Real World, Why Is It Important to Correct Fragments?

People outside of the English classroom notice fragments and consider them major mistakes. You may be wondering why a fragment is viewed as a significant problem in writing; after all, in ordinary conversation people can use fragments without causing any problems:

Mallory: Why didn't you do the homework assignment?
Ben: Because I didn't understand it. [This group of words by itself is a fragment.]
Mallory: You could have called me to get help.
Ben: Nah—didn't want to. I knew I would get it later. [The first group of words is a fragment; it does not contain a subject.]

The standards for college and professional writing, however, are different from the rules we follow in conversation. Fragments may confuse a reader, and they may suggest that a writer is careless or sloppy. In fact, academic readers may not take a piece of writing seriously if it contains fragments and other major sentence errors. Let's look at a situation where using fragments carelessly might cause trouble for a writer.

Situation: Justina is interested in starting a blog to establish an online presence and attract potential employers. Here is part of an email that Justina sent to a popular blogger:

> I am getting in touch with you about starting a blog on dress design. Because I have heard about the success you have had with your fashion blog. For a long time, I have designed and sewn many dresses for myself and my friends, and I have a good sense of style. On my blog, I would like to share sewing tips and patterns based on my dress designs. Which should appeal to many readers. I would like to ask your opinion about many things. Especially about how to write clear, interesting blog posts. I have to admit that my dream would be for my blog to catch the eye of a major fashion house looking for talent. To come up with new looks for its dress line. Could we set up a time to talk in person?

Read to Write

What are your thoughts about Justina's email?

Does Justina present herself professionally in her email?

How could grammar and spelling mistakes in an email potentially affect Justina's future as a blogger?

What can Justina do to improve her email?

Find and Correct Fragments

To find fragments in your own writing, look for the five trouble spots in this chapter. They often signal fragments.

When you find a fragment in your own writing, you can usually correct it in one of two ways.

Basic Ways to Correct a Fragment

- Add what is missing (a subject, a verb, or both).
- Attach the fragment to the sentence before or after it.

PRACTICE 16–1   **Finding Fragments**

Find and underline the four fragments in Justina's email.

1. *Fragments That Start with Prepositions*

Whenever a preposition starts what you think is a sentence, check for a subject, a verb, and a complete thought. If the group of words is missing any of these three elements, it is a fragment.

Tip Remember that the subject of a sentence is *never* in a prepositional phrase (see p. 331).

Tip In the examples in this chapter, subjects are underlined once, and verbs are underlined twice.

Fragment	I <u>pounded</u> as hard as I could. *Against the door.*
	[*Against the door* lacks both a subject and a verb.]

Correct a fragment that starts with a preposition by connecting it to the sentence either before or after it. If you connect such a fragment to the sentence after it, put a comma after the fragment to join it to the next sentence.

Complete sentence	I <u>pounded</u> as hard as I could against the door.

Common Prepositions

about	before	for	on	until
above	behind	from	out	up
across	below	in	outside	upon
after	beneath	inside	over	with
against	beside	into	past	within
along	between	like	since	without
among	by	near	through	
around	down	next to	to	
at	during	of	toward	
because of	except	off	under	

 Language note: Remember that the subject of the sentence is never in a prepositional phrase. Watch out for sentences that begin with prepositional phrases but do not have a subject:

Incorrect   Without a book or internet access means you cannot do the homework.

[There is no subject for the verb *means*].

Correct   Without a book or internet access, you cannot do the homework.

2. Fragments That Start with Dependent Words

A **dependent word** (also called a **subordinating conjunction**) is the first word in a dependent clause. A dependent clause has a subject and a verb, like all clauses do, but a dependent clause can never express a complete thought by itself. Instead, it depends on another clause (an independent clause) to make sense.

Sentence with a dependent word	We <u>arrived</u> late *because* <u>the bus was delayed.</u>
	[*Because* is a dependent word introducing the dependent clause *because the bus was delayed.*]

When writers begin a sentence with a dependent clause, they must always attach that clause to an independent clause. Otherwise, they will have a fragment.

Fragment	*Since I moved.* <u>I</u> <u>have eaten</u> out every day.
	[*Since I moved* has a subject (*I*) and a verb (*moved*), but it does not express a complete thought.]
Corrected	Since I moved, <u>I</u> <u>have</u> eaten out every day.

Whenever you see a dependent word at the beginning of a sentence, check for a subject, a verb, and another clause (a complete thought).

Writing Note In Chapters 6 through 14 you learned about using transition words in different kinds of writing. One type of transition word is a subordinating conjunction. Subordinating conjunctions are dependent words (see the chart). Be careful when you are creating transitions in your writing: if you use a subordinating conjunction, you must make sure that the sentence also contains an independent clause.

Common Dependent Words

after	if/if only	until
although	now that	what (whatever)
as/as if/as though	once	when (whenever)
as long as/as soon as	since	where (wherever)
because	so that	whether
before	that	which
even if/even though	though	while
how	unless	who/whose

When a word group starts with *who, whose,* or *which,* it is not a complete sentence unless it is a question.

Fragment	That <u>woman</u> <u>is</u> the police officer. *Who gave me a ticket last week.*
Question	<u>Who</u> <u>gave</u> you a ticket last week?
Fragment	<u>He</u> <u>is</u> the goalie. *Whose team is terrible this season.*
Question	*Whose* team <u>are</u> <u>you</u> on?
Fragment	<u>Sherlene</u> <u>went</u> to the HiHo Club. *Which serves alcohol.*
Question	*Which* <u>club</u> <u>serves</u> alcohol?

Correct a fragment that starts with a dependent word by connecting it to the sentence before or after it. If the dependent clause is joined to the sentence after it, put a comma after the dependent clause.

Corrected sentence	That <u>woman</u> <u><u>is</u></u> the police officer who gave me a ticket last week.
Corrected sentence	He <u><u>is</u></u> the goalie whose team is terrible this season.
Corrected sentence	<u>Sherlene</u> <u><u>went</u></u> to the HiHo Club, which serves alcohol.

Tip For more on commas with dependent clauses, see Chapters 23 and 30.

> **PRACTICE 16–2   Correcting Fragments that Start with Prepositions or Dependent Words**
>
> In the following items, circle any prepositions or dependent words that start a word group. Then, correct each fragment by connecting it to the sentence before or after it.
>
> **Example:** The fire at the Triangle Waist Company in New York City
>
> marked a turning point. (In) U.S. labor history.

1. Before the fire occurred, on March 25, 1911. Labor activists had raised complaints against the company, a maker of women's blouses.

2. The activists demanded shorter hours and better wages. For the company's overworked and underpaid sewing-machine operators.

3. The owners refused these requests, however. Because they placed profits over their employees' welfare.

4. When activists demanded better safety measures, such as sprinkler systems. The owners again refused to do anything.

5. On the day of the fire. A scrap bin on the eighth floor of the blouse factory ignited by accident.

6. Although workers threw buckets of water on the flames. Their efforts could not keep the fire from spreading to other floors.

7. Without access to safe or unlocked exits. Many workers died in the smoke and flames or jumped to their deaths.

8. One hundred and forty-six workers had lost their lives. By the end of this tragic day.

9. After news of the tragedy spread. The public reacted with outrage and greater demands for better working conditions.

10. Within a few years of the fire. Legislatures in New York and other states passed laws to improve workplace safety and worker rights.

> **PRACTICE 16–3** **Correcting Fragments that Start with Prepositions or Dependent Words**

Read the following paragraph, and circle the twelve fragments that start with prepositions or dependent words. Then, correct the fragments.

Staying focused at an office job can be difficult. Because of these jobs' many distractions. After making just a few changes. Workers will find that they are less distracted and more productive. A good first step is to clear away clutter, such as old files. From their desktop screen. Once that screen is cleared. It is helpful to make a list of the most important tasks for the day. It is best for workers to do brain-demanding tasks when they are at their best. Which is often the start of the day. Workers can take on simpler tasks, like filing. When they are feeling less energetic. While they are doing something especially challenging. Workers might want to disconnect themselves from the Internet and turn off their personal cell phones. Although it is tempting to look at social media sites and answer emails and phone calls immediately. They are among the worst workplace distractions. Since social media is particularly distracting. It is important to avoid it while at work. Because it is not an appropriate work activity. Some people set a special electronic folder. For personal emails. They check this folder only while they are on break or between tasks. Finally, it is important for workers to remember the importance of breaks. Which recharge the mind and improve its focus.

3. Fragments That Start with -ing Verb Forms

An -*ing* **verb form** is the form of a verb that ends in -*ing*: *walking, writing, running*. Sometimes, an -*ing* verb form is used at the beginning of a complete sentence.

Sentence	Walking is good exercise.

[The -*ing* verb form *walking* is the subject; *is* is the verb. The sentence expresses a complete thought. In this sentence, *walking* is a gerund; in other words, it is the -ing form of a verb used as a noun. We know that *walking* is used as a noun here because we can replace it with a pronoun: Is *walking* good exercise? Yes, *it* is.]

Sometimes, an -*ing* verb form introduces a fragment. When an -*ing* verb form starts what you think is a sentence, stop and check for a subject, a verb, and a complete thought.

Fragment	I ran as fast as I could. *Hoping to get there on time.*

[*Hoping to get there on time* lacks a subject, and it does not express a complete thought.]

Correct a fragment that starts with an -*ing* verb form either by adding whatever sentence elements are missing (usually a subject and a helping verb) or by connecting the fragment to the sentence before or after it. You will usually need to put a comma before or after the fragment to join it to the complete sentence.

> **PRACTICE 16–4**   **Correcting Fragments that Start with -*ing* Verb Forms**
>
> Circle any -*ing* verb that appears at the beginning of a word group in the paragraph. Then, read the word group to see if it has a subject and a verb and expresses a complete thought. Not *all* the word groups that start with an -*ing* verb are fragments, so read carefully. In the space provided, record the numbers of the word groups that are fragments. Then, correct each fragment either by adding the missing sentence elements or by connecting it to the sentence before or after it.

Which word groups are fragments? _____

(1) People sometimes travel long distances in unusual ways trying to set new world records. (2) Walking is one unusual way to set records. (3) In 1931, Plennie Wingo set out on an ambitious journey. (4) Walking backward around the world. (5) Wearing sunglasses with rearview mirrors, he started his trip early one morning. (6) After eight thousand miles, Wingo's journey was interrupted by a war in Pakistan. (7) Ending his ambitious journey. (8) Hans Mullikan spent more than two years in the late 1970s traveling to the White House by crawling from Texas to Washington, D.C. (9) Taking time out to earn money as a logger

and a Baptist minister. (10) Alvin Straight, suffering from poor eyesight, traveled

across the Midwest on a lawn mower. (11) Looking for his long-lost brother.

4. Fragments that Start with to and a Verb

When what you think is a sentence begins with *to* and a verb (called the *infinitive* form of the verb), you need to make sure it is not a fragment.

Fragment	Each day, I <u>check</u> freecycle.org. *To see if it has anything I need.*

Corrected	Each day, I <u>check</u> freecycle.org to see if it has anything I need.

If a word group begins with *to* and a verb, it must have another verb; if not, it is not a complete sentence. When you see a word group that begins with *to* and a verb, first check to see if there is another verb. If there is no other verb, the word group is a fragment.

Sentence	<u>To run</u> a complete marathon <u>was</u> my goal.
	[*To run* is the subject; *was* is the verb.]
Fragment	<u>Cheri got</u> underneath the car. *To change the oil.*
	[No other verb appears in the word group that begins with *to change*.]

To correct a fragment that starts with *to* and a verb, join it to the sentence before or after it, or add the missing sentence elements.

PRACTICE 16–5   **Correcting Fragments that Start with *to* and a Verb**

Circle any *to*-plus-verb combination that appears at the beginning of a sentence in the paragraph. Then, read the word group to see if it has a subject and a verb and expresses a complete thought. Not *all* the word groups that start with *to* and a verb are fragments, so read carefully. In the space provided, record the numbers of the word groups that are fragments. Then, correct each fragment either by adding the missing sentence elements or by connecting it to the sentence before or after it.

Which word groups are fragments? _____

(1) For people older than twenty-five, each hour spent watching television lowers life expectancy by nearly twenty-two minutes. (2) This finding is the result of Australian researchers' efforts. (3) To investigate the health effects of television viewing. (4) To put it another way, watching an hour of television is about the same as smoking two cigarettes. (5) The problem is that most people are inactive

while watching television. (6) They are not doing anything, like walking or

playing sports. (7) To strengthen their heart and maintain a healthy weight.

(8) Fortunately, it is possible. (9) To counteract some of television's negative health

effects. (10) To increase their life expectancy by three years. (11) People need

to exercise just fifteen minutes a day. (12) To accomplish this goal, they might

exchange a ride in an elevator for a climb up the stairs. (13) Or they might walk

around the block during a lunch break at work.

5. *Fragments that Are Examples or Explanations*

As you edit your writing, pay special attention to groups of words that are examples or explanations of information you presented in the previous sentence. They may be fragments.

Fragment	More and more <u>people</u> <u>are reporting</u> food allergies. *For example, allergies to nuts or milk.*
Fragment	My <u>body</u> <u>reacts</u> to wheat-containing foods. *Such as bread or pasta.*
	[*For example, allergies to nuts or milk* and *Such as bread or pasta* are not complete thoughts.]

This last type of fragment is harder to recognize because there is no single word or kind of word to look for. The following words may signal a fragment, but fragments that are examples or explanations do not always start with these words.

especially	for example	like	such as

When a group of words gives an example or an explanation connected to the previous sentence, stop to check it for a subject, a verb, and a complete thought.

Fragment	<u>I</u> <u>have found</u> great things at freecycle.org. *Like a nearly new computer.*
Fragment	<u>Freecycle.org</u> <u>is</u> a good site. *Especially for household items.*
Fragment	<u>It</u> <u>lists</u> many gently used appliances. *Such as DVD players.*
	[*Like a nearly new computer, Especially for household items,* and *Such as DVD players* are not complete thoughts.]

Tip *Such as* and *like* do not often begin complete sentences.

Correct a fragment that starts with an example or an explanation by connecting it to the sentence before or after it. Sometimes, you can add whatever sentence elements are missing (a subject, a verb, or both) instead. When you connect the fragment to a sentence, you may need to change some punctuation. For example, fragments that are examples are often set off by a comma.

> **PRACTICE 16–6** **Correcting Fragments that Are Examples or Explanations**
>
> Circle word groups that are examples or explanations. Then, read the word group to see if it has a subject and verb and expresses a complete thought. In the space provided, record the numbers of the word groups that are fragments. Then, correct each fragment either by adding the missing sentence elements or by connecting it to the sentence before or after it.
>
> Which word groups are fragments? _____
>
> (1) Being a smart consumer can be difficult. (2) Especially when making a major purchase. (3) At car dealerships, for example, important information is often in small type. (4) Like finance charges or preparation charges.
>
> (5) Advertisements also put negative information in small type. (6) Such as a drug's side effects. (7) Credit-card offers often use tiny, hard-to-read print for the terms of the card. (8) Like interest charges and late fees, which can really add up. (9) Phone service charges can also be hidden in small print. (10) Like limits on text messaging and other functions. (11) Especially now, as businesses try to make it seem as if you are getting a good deal, it is important to read any offer carefully.

Edit for Fragments

Use the chart on page 350, Finding and Fixing Fragments, to help you complete the practices in this section and edit your own writing.

PRACTICE 16–7   **Correcting Various Fragments**

In the following items, circle each word group that is a fragment. Then, correct fragments by connecting them to the previous or next sentence or by adding the missing sentence elements.

Example: (With the high cost of producing video games,) ~~Game~~ game

publishers are turning to a new source of revenue.

1. To add to their income. Publishers are placing advertisements in their games.

2. Sometimes, the ads show a character using a product. For example, drinking a specific brand of soda to earn health points.

3. One character, a race-car driver, drove his ad-covered car. Across the finish line.

4. When a warrior character picked up a sword decorated with an athletic-shoe logo. Some players complained.

5. Worrying that ads are distracting. Some publishers are trying to limit the number of ads per game.

6. But most players do not seem to mind seeing ads in video games. If there are not too many of them.

7. These players are used to seeing ads in all kinds of places. Like grocery carts and restroom walls.

8. For video game publishers. The goal is making a profit, but most publishers also care about the product.

9. To strike a balance between profitable advertising and high game quality. That is what publishers want.

10. Doing market research. Will help publishers find that balance.

PRACTICE 16–8   **Editing Paragraphs for Fragments**

Find and correct the ten fragments in the following paragraphs.

In her essay, "When Poor People Have Nice Things," Andrea Whitmer uses multiple examples to make a point: we shouldn't judge peowwple's choices. Especially when we don't know the situation or context. Whitmer begins by describing an angry Facebook post. Criticizing someone who had an iPhone but paid for groceries with food stamps. Whitmer doesn't think we should assume this person is "gaming the system." To suggest an alternative explanation. She gives an example of a friend who had lost a job. While temporarily unemployed, the friend kept her iPhone.

I can appreciate Whitmer's argument. In fact, I have been on the receiving end of some glares and rude remarks. Because I was getting government aid. My second child was born with some health problems, so I decided not to return to work for several months. To care for her special needs. During that time, my husband's income fell, and we needed help. For about 6 months, we accepted food coupons through the WIC (Women, Infants, and Children) program. These coupons allowed us to get milk, cereal, and sources of protein. Like peanut butter or dried beans for free.

The first time I used the coupons, I felt very awkward. Standing in line at the store. I gave the clerk my coupons, and she frowned. Then she sighed heavily before entering my coupon codes. After a few minutes. The man behind me said, "How long is this going to take?" And then he noticed that my baby daughter was wearing clothes from the Baby Gap. Which are expensive. The man rolled his eyes and said, "I guess we know what's most important to you." My eyes filled with tears, and I could not answer him. I wanted to tell him that the clothes were a gift from friends at my office. I would never have purchased them myself. As I was leaving the store. I heard the clerk say, "Some people shouldn't be allowed to be parents."

PRACTICE 16–9   **Editing Fragments and Using Formal English**

Your friend wants to send this thank-you note to an employer who interviewed her for a job. She knows that the note has problems and has asked for your help. Correct the fragments in the note. Then, suggest ways the author can improve the style and the level of formality in the letter.

Dear Ms. Hernandez,

Thank you so much for taking the time. To meet with me this past Wednesday. I am more psyched than ever about the administrative assistant position at Fields Corporation. Learning more about the stuff I would need to do. Was very cool. Also, I enjoyed meeting you and the other managers. With my strong organizational skills, professional experience, and friendly personality. I'm sure that I would be awesome for the job. Because I'm totally jazzed about the position. I hope you will keep me in mind. Please let me know if you need any other info. Like references or a writing sample.

Thank U much,

Sincerely,

Terri Hammons

PRACTICE 16–10   **Editing Justina's email**

Look back at Justina's email on page 338. You may have already underlined the fragments in her email; if not, do so now. Next, using what you have learned in this chapter, correct each fragment in the email.

Chapter Review

1. A *sentence* is a group of words that has an independent clause. What are the three elements required in an independent clause?

2. What is a fragment?

3. What are five trouble spots that signal possible fragments?

4. What are the two basic ways to correct fragments?

Reflect and Apply

1. Has your instructor in this course (or previous instructors) pointed out problems with fragments in your writing? If so, how have you tried to fix the problem?

2. Writers may have trouble finding fragments in their own work; when they review their work, they may not look at individual sentences in isolation. They are reading entire paragraphs. If you have identified fragments as a problem in your writing, try this editing technique. After revising for content and organization, separate the sentences in your essay so that you can look at them individually. You can do this by hitting *enter* after each period that you see. Then read each sentence, beginning at the end of the paragraph or essay and going backward until you reach the first sentence. Make sure each sentence has all the required elements of an independent clause. Once you have corrected any fragments you find, delete the line breaks between each sentence.

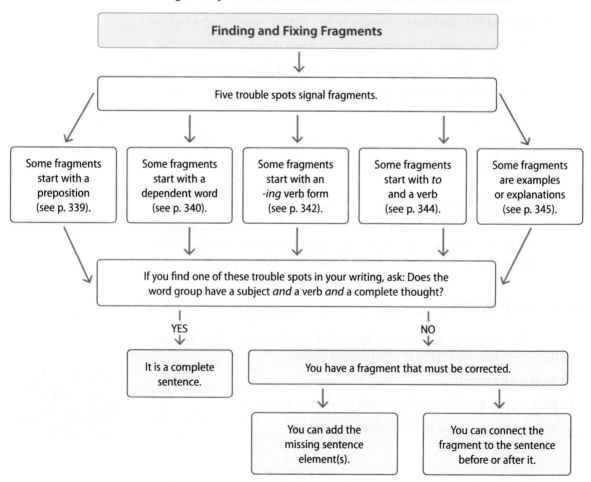

Finding and Fixing Fragments

Five trouble spots signal fragments.

| Some fragments start with a preposition (see p. 339). | Some fragments start with a dependent word (see p. 340). | Some fragments start with an *-ing* verb form (see p. 342). | Some fragments start with *to* and a verb (see p. 344). | Some fragments are examples or explanations (see p. 345). |

If you find one of these trouble spots in your writing, ask: Does the word group have a subject *and* a verb *and* a complete thought?

YES → It is a complete sentence.

NO → You have a fragment that must be corrected.

You can add the missing sentence element(s).

You can connect the fragment to the sentence before or after it.

17

Run-Ons

Two Sentences Joined Incorrectly

Understand What Run-Ons Are

In Chapter 15, you learned that an independent clause is a group of words with a subject and a verb that expresses a complete thought. Sometimes, two independent clauses can be joined to form one larger sentence. In the example below, brackets indicate independent clauses.

[The <u>college</u> <u>offers</u> financial aid], and [<u>it</u> <u>encourages</u> students to apply].

[I once tried going a whole week without telling a lie], and [it was paralyzing] (Ericsson 211).

[Harry opted to stay at Vanderbilt], but [he found acclimating to the school's cultural climate to be extremely difficult] (Riggs 283).

A **run-on** is two complete sentences (independent clauses) joined incorrectly as one sentence. There are two kinds of run-ons: **fused sentences** and **comma splices**.

A **fused sentence** is two complete sentences joined without a coordinating conjunction (*for, and, nor, but, or, yet, so*) or any punctuation.

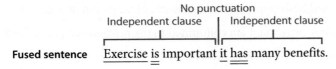

No punctuation
Independent clause | Independent clause

Fused sentence   Exercise is important it has many benefits.

A **comma splice** occurs when two complete sentences are joined by only a comma.

Tip To find and correct run-ons, you need to be able to identify a complete sentence. For a review, see Chapter 15.

Tip In the examples throughout this chapter, subjects are underlined once, and verbs are underlined twice.

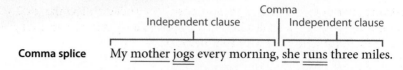

Comma
Independent clause | Independent clause

Comma splice   My mother jogs every morning, she runs three miles.

When you join two sentences, use the proper punctuation.

Corrections   Exercise is important; it has many benefits.

My mother jogs every morning; she runs 3 miles.

💬 **Language note:** Punctuation rules for commas, periods, and semicolons vary in academic writing in different countries, even if the primary language for writing in that country is English.

In the Real World, Why Is It Important to Correct Run-Ons?

People outside the English classroom notice run-ons and consider them major mistakes.

Situation: Naomi is applying to a special program for returning students at Cambridge College. Here is one of the essay questions on the application, followed by a paragraph from Naomi's answer.

Statement of Purpose: In two hundred words or less, describe your intellectual and professional goals and how a Cambridge College education will assist you in achieving them.

For many years, I did not take control of my life, I just drifted without any goals. I realized one day as I met with my daughter's guidance counselor that I hoped my daughter would not turn out like me. From that moment, I decided to do something to help myself and others. I set a goal of becoming a teacher. To begin on that path, I took a math course at night school, then I took another in science. I passed both courses with hard work, I know I can do well in the Cambridge College program. I am committed to the professional goal I finally found it has given new purpose to my whole life.

Read to Write

What are your thoughts about Naomi's essay?

If you were a college official looking at applications, how would you perceive Naomi as a potential student? Why?

What kind of error is Naomi making most often? How does it affect the text? In other words, can you still easily read and comprehend what she wants to say? Is it harder to understand certain ideas or thoughts?

How would you correct Naomi's essay?

Find and Correct Run-Ons

To find run-ons, focus on each sentence in your writing, one at a time, looking for fused sentences and comma splices. Pay special attention to sentences longer than two lines. By spending this extra time, your writing will improve.

> **PRACTICE 17–1** **Finding Run-Ons**
>
> Find and underline the four run-ons in Naomi's writing on page 352.

Once you have found a run-on, there are five ways to correct it. Each method represents a sentence pattern that you can use to improve your writing.

How to Correct Run-Ons

IC = independent clause

DC = dependent clause

ca = conjunctive adverb

cc = coordinating conjunction

sc = subordinating conjunction

S = subject

V = verb

Strategy	Example	Pattern
Add a period.	He I saw the man. he did not see me.	IC. IC. (S + V. S + V.)
Add a semicolon.	I saw the man; he did not see me.	IC; IC. (S + V; S + V.)
Add a semicolon, a conjunctive adverb, and a comma.	however, I saw the man; he did not see me.	IC; ca, IC. (S + V; ca, S + V.)
Add a comma and a coordinating conjunction.	but I saw the man, he did not see me.	IC, cc IC. (S +V, cc S + V.) ➔

Add a subordinating conjunction (dependent word).	$\overset{\text{when}}{\text{The man did not see me I saw him.}}$ When I saw the man, he did not see me.	IC DC. DC, IC. (S + V + sc + S + V.) (sc + S + V, S + V.)

Notice that the corrections are the same for both fused sentences and comma splices. Some students mistakenly believe that they can correct a fused sentence by adding a comma. Adding a comma, however, does not correct the fused sentence; it creates a comma splice. Use one of the strategies in the chart to correct a comma splice. Let's look at these strategies in more detail.

Add a Period

You can correct run-ons by adding a period to make two separate sentences. After adding the period, capitalize the letter that begins the new sentence. Reread your two sentences to make sure they each contain a subject, a verb, and a complete thought.

Pattern 1: IC. IC.

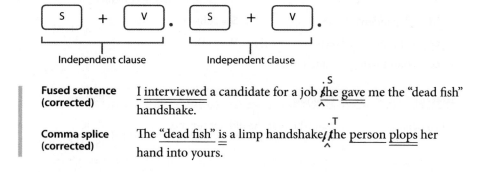

Fused sentence (corrected)	I interviewed a candidate for a job $\overset{. S}{\text{she}}$ gave me the "dead fish" handshake.
Comma splice (corrected)	The "dead fish" is a limp handshake $\overset{. T}{\text{the}}$ person plops her hand into yours.

Add a Semicolon

A second way to correct run-ons is to use a semicolon (;) to join the two sentences. Use a semicolon only when the two sentences express closely related ideas, and the words on each side of the semicolon can stand alone as a complete sentence. Do not capitalize the word that follows a semicolon unless it is the name of a specific person, place, or thing that is usually capitalized—for example, Mary, New York, or the Eiffel Tower.

Pattern 2: IC; IC.

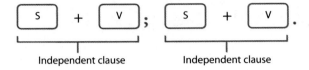

Independent clause   Independent clause

Fused sentence (corrected)	Slouching creates a terrible impression it makes a person seem uninterested, bored, or lacking in self-confidence.
Comma splice (corrected)	It is important in an interview to hold your head up it is just as important to sit up straight.

Pattern 2 is an example of coordination: using two independent clauses in a single sentence. For more on coordination, see Chapter 23.

Add a Semicolon, a Conjunctive Adverbial, and a Comma

A third way to correct run-ons is to add a semicolon followed by a **conjunctive adverbial** and a comma.

Common Conjunctive Adverbials

consequently	instead	nevertheless	then
finally	likewise	otherwise	therefore
furthermore	meanwhile	similarly	in fact
however	moreover	still	for example
indeed			

Pattern 3: IC; ca, IC.

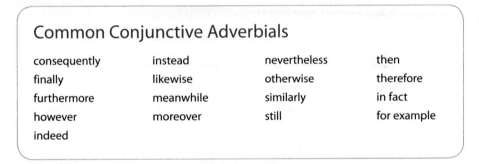

Independent clause   Conjunctive adverbial   Independent clause

Comma splice	I stopped by the market, it was closed.
Fused sentence	Sharon is a neighbor she is my friend.

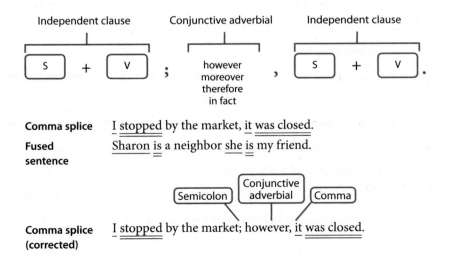

Comma splice (corrected)	I stopped by the market; however, it was closed.

Tip Like Pattern 2, Pattern 3 is an example of coordination.

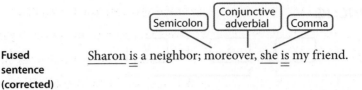

Fused sentence (corrected)   Sharon is a neighbor; moreover, she is my friend.

PRACTICE 17-2   Correcting Run-Ons by Adding a Period or a Semicolon

For each of the following items, indicate in the space to the left whether it is a fused sentence ("FS") or a comma splice ("CS"). Then, correct the error by adding a period or a semicolon. Capitalize the letters as necessary to make two sentences.

Example: _**FS**_ Being a farmer can mean dealing with all types of challenges one of the biggest ones comes from the sky.

1. _CS_ Farmers have been trying to keep hungry birds out of their crops for centuries. the first scarecrow was invented for this reason.

2. _CS_ Some farmers have used a variety of chemicals, other farmers have tried noise, such as small cannons.

3. _CS_ Recently, a group of berry farmers tried something new, they brought in bigger birds called falcons.

4. _FS_ Small birds such as starlings love munching on berries. Each year, they destroy thousands of dollars' worth of farmers' berry crops.

5. _FS_ Because these starlings are frightened of falcons, they fly away when they see these birds of prey in the fields. they need to get to where they feel safe.

6. _CS_ Using falcons to protect their crops saves farmers money, it does not damage the environment either.

7. _FS_ A falconer, or a person who raises and trains falcons, keeps an eye on the birds during the day. he makes sure they only chase away the starlings instead of killing them.

8. _CS_ Falcons are used for protection in other places as well, they are used in vineyards to keep pests from eating the grapes.

9. <u>fs</u> In recent years, the falcons have also been used in landfills to scatter birds, and other wildlife, some have even been used at large air-ports to keep flocks of birds out of the flight path of landing airplanes.

10. <u>fs</u> Although a falconer's services are not cheap, they cost less than some other methods that farmers have tried, for example, putting nets over a berry field can often cost more than $200,000.

Add a Comma and a Coordinating Conjunction

A fourth way to correct run-ons is to add a comma and a **coordinating conjunction**: a link that joins independent clauses to form one sentence. The seven coordinating conjunctions are *and, but, for, nor, or, so,* and *yet.* Some people remember these words by thinking of **FANBOYS:** *for, and, nor, but, or, yet, so.*

To correct a fused sentence this way, add a comma and a coordinating conjunction. A comma splice already has a comma, so just add a coordinating conjunction that makes sense in the sentence.

Pattern 4: IC, cc IC.

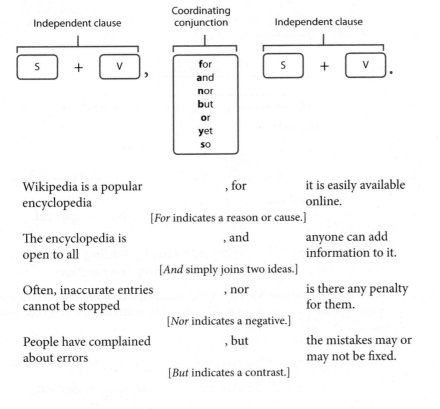

Wikipedia is a popular encyclopedia   , for   it is easily available online.

[*For* indicates a reason or cause.]

The encyclopedia is open to all   , and   anyone can add information to it.

[*And* simply joins two ideas.]

Often, inaccurate entries cannot be stopped   , nor   is there any penalty for them.

[*Nor* indicates a negative.]

People have complained about errors   , but   the mistakes may or may not be fixed.

[*But* indicates a contrast.]

Some people delete information	, or	they add their own interpretations.

[*Or* indicates alternatives.]

Many people know that Wikipedia is flawed	, yet	they continue to use it.

[*Yet* indicates a contrast or possibility.]

Wikipedia now has trustees	, so	perhaps it will be monitored more closely.

[*So* indicates a result.]

Be careful to choose the conjunction that fits the sentence logically.

<table>
<tr><td>**Fused sentence**</td><td>Nekeisha was qualified for the job she hurt her chances by mumbling.</td></tr>
<tr><td>**Illogical correction**</td><td>Nekeisha was qualified for the job, and she hurt her chances by mumbling.</td></tr>
<tr><td>**Logical correction**</td><td>Nekeisha was qualified for the job, but she hurt her chances by mumbling.</td></tr>
</table>

> **Tip** Notice that the comma does not follow the conjunction. The comma follows the word before the conjunction.

Coordinating conjunctions need to connect two independent clauses. They are not used to join a dependent and an independent clause.

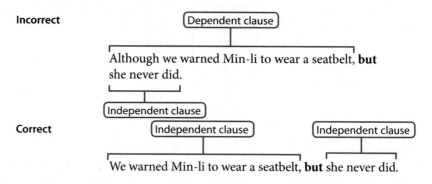

Incorrect

Dependent clause

Although we warned Min-li to wear a seatbelt, **but** she never did.

Independent clause

Correct

Independent clause   Independent clause

We warned Min-li to wear a seatbelt, **but** she never did.

PRACTICE 17–3   Correcting Run-Ons by Adding a Comma and/or a Coordinating Conjunction

Correct each of the following run-ons by adding a comma, if necessary, and an appropriate coordinating conjunction. First, underline the subjects, and double-underline the verbs.

Example:

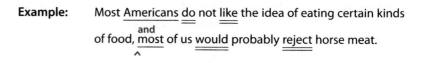

Most Americans do not like the idea of eating certain kinds
and
of food, most of us would probably reject horse meat.

1. In most cultures, popular foods depend on availability and tradition people tend to eat old familiar favorites.

2. Sushi shocked many Americans thirty years ago, today some young people in the United States have grown up eating raw fish.

3. In many societies, certain foods are allowed to age this process adds flavor.

4. Icelanders bury eggs in the ground to rot for months, these aged eggs are considered a special treat.

5. As an American, you might not like such eggs the thought of eating them might even revolt you.

6. In general, aged foods have a strong taste, the flavor is unpleasant to someone unaccustomed to those foods.

7. Many Koreans love to eat kimchee, a spicy aged cabbage, Americans often find the taste odd and the smell overpowering.

8. Herders in Kyrgyzstan drink kumiss this beverage is made of aged horse's milk.

9. Americans on a visit to Kyrgyzstan consider themselves brave for tasting kumiss, local children drink it regularly.

10. We think of familiar foods as normal, favorite American foods might horrify people in other parts of the world.

Add a Dependent Word

A fifth way to correct run-ons is to make one of the complete sentences a dependent clause by adding a dependent word (a **subordinating conjunction** or a **relative pronoun**), such as *after, because, before, even though, if, that, though, unless, when, who,* and *which.* (For a more complete list of these words, see the chart on page 360.) Choose the dependent word that best expresses the relationship between the two clauses.

Turn an independent clause into a dependent one when it is less important than the other clause, explains the other clause, or provides background information, as in the following sentence:

When I get to the train station, I will call Josh.

The italicized clause is dependent (subordinate) because it just explains when the most important part of the sentence—calling Josh—will happen. It begins with the dependent word *when*.

Because a dependent clause is not a complete sentence (it has a subject and a verb but does not express a complete thought), it can be joined to a sentence without creating a run-on. When the dependent clause is the second clause in a sentence, you usually do not need to put a comma before it unless it is showing contrast.

Two sentences

Halloween <u>was</u> originally a religious holiday. <u>People</u> <u>worshipped</u> the saints.

Dependent clause: no comma needed

Halloween <u>was</u> originally a religious holiday *when <u>people</u> <u>worshipped</u> the saints.*

Dependent clause showing contrast: comma needed

Many <u>holidays</u> <u>have</u> religious origins, *although some <u>celebrations</u> <u>have</u> <u>moved</u> away from their religious roots.*

Pattern 5, Option 1: IC DC.

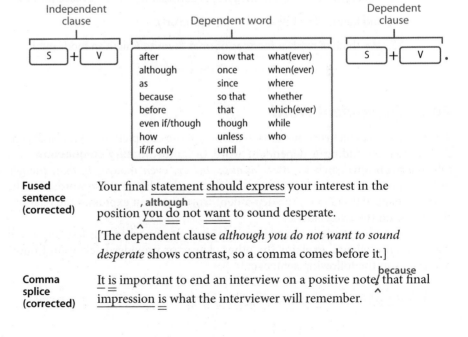

Fused sentence (corrected)	Your final <u>statement</u> <u>should express</u> your interest in the , although position <u>you</u> <u>do</u> not <u>want</u> to sound desperate.

[The dependent clause *although you do not want to sound desperate* shows contrast, so a comma comes before it.]

Comma splice (corrected)	<u>It</u> <u>is</u> important to end an interview on a positive note̸ because <u>that</u> final <u>impression</u> <u>is</u> what the interviewer will remember.

You can also put the dependent clause first. When the dependent clause comes first, be sure to put a comma after it.

Pattern 5, Option 2: DC, IC.

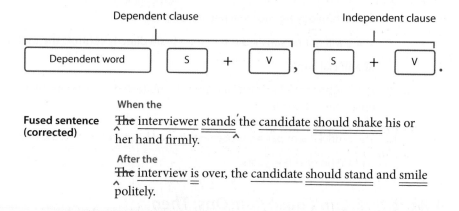

Fused sentence (corrected)

When the
~~The~~ interviewer stands the candidate should shake his or her hand firmly.

After the
~~The~~ interview is over, the candidate should stand and smile politely.

PRACTICE 17–4   Correcting Run-Ons by Adding a Dependent Word

Correct run-ons by adding a dependent word to make a dependent clause. First, underline the subjects, and double-underline the verbs. Although these run-ons can be corrected in different ways, in this exercise, correct by adding dependent words. You may want to refer to the graphic on page 360.

Example:
When many
~~Many~~ soldiers returned from Iraq and Afghanistan missing arms or legs, demand for better artificial limbs increased.

1. Computer chips were widely used artificial limbs remained largely unchanged for decades.

2. Computer chips now control many artificial limbs, these limbs have more capabilities than those of the past.

3. The i-LIMB artificial hand picks up electrical signals from nearby arm muscles the amputee can move individual fingers of the hand.

4. Lighter-weight materials were introduced artificial limbs were not as easy to move as they are today.

5. Now, the C-Leg artificial leg is popular it is lightweight, flexible, and technically advanced.

6. A C-Leg user wants to jog, bike, or drive instead of walk he or she can program the leg for the necessary speed and motion.

7. Major advances have been made in artificial limbs, researchers believe the technology has not reached its full potential.

8. Many will not be satisfied the human brain directly controls the motion of artificial limbs.

9. A thought-controlled artificial arm is being tested on patients, that time may not be far off.

10. The artificial arm passes those tests it may be introduced to the market within the next few years.

A Word that Can Cause Run-Ons: Then

Many run-ons are caused by the word *then*. You can use *then* to join two sentences, but if you add it without the correct punctuation or added words, your sentence will be a run-on. Often, writers use just a comma before *then*, but that makes a comma splice.

Comma splice   I picked up my laundry, then I went home.

Some of the methods you have just practiced can be used to correct errors caused by *then*. These methods are shown in the following examples.

I picked up my laundry. Then I went home.

I picked up my laundry; then I went home.

I picked up my laundry, and then I went home.

I picked up my laundry; before then I went home.
[dependent word *before* added to make a dependent clause]

Edit for Run-Ons

Use the chart on page 366, Finding and Fixing Run-Ons, to help you complete the practices in this section and edit your own writing.

PRACTICE 17–5   **Correcting Various Run-Ons**

In the following items, correct any run-ons. Use each method of correcting such errors—adding a period; adding a semicolon; adding a semicolon, a conjunctive adverb, and a comma; adding a comma and a coordinating conjunction; or adding a dependent word—at least once.

Example: Although some
~~Some~~ people doubt the existence of climate change, few
^ can deny that the weather has become more extreme and
dangerous.

1. Nearly fourteen hundred tornadoes tore through the United States in 2017, hundreds of people lost their lives.

2. That same year, parts of the United States experienced severe flooding droughts in California cost farmers upward of $600 million.

3. Some cities are taking steps to adapt to environmental changes, they are focusing on the biggest threats.

4. Global temperatures are rising, sea levels are also rising—a threat to coastal regions.

5. As a result, some coastal cities are planning to build protective walls, others are raising roadbeds.

6. Extreme heat is another major problem, urban planners are studying different ways to address it.

7. New York City is painting some rooftops white, light and heat will be reflected away from the city.

8. In Chicago, landscapers are planting heat-tolerant trees, these trees should help cool the environment and reduce flooding during heavy rains.

9. All of these efforts are encouraging most parts of the United States are doing little or nothing to plan for ongoing environmental changes.

10. One study reports that only fourteen states are undertaking such planning the threats of severe weather remain.

PRACTICE 17–6   **Editing Paragraphs for Run-Ons**

Find and correct the run-ons you underlined in Naomi's paragraph in Practice 1.

PRACTICE 17–7   **Editing Paragraphs for Run-Ons**

The following student assignment contains five run-on sentences. Find and correct each one.

    In her essay "The Ways We Lie," Stephanie Ericsson discusses types of lies, and she argues that each type carries negative consequences, even if the lie seems innocent or common. One of the types of lies she discusses is stereotype or cliché this is of course when someone judges someone else without getting to know that person fully. I understand Ericsson's point when she calls a stereotype a lie; stereotypes do a lot of damage. My brother, for example, is a high school dropout. People always assume that he is not intelligent or that he won't understand instructions. The truth is that he is much smarter than the average high school graduate he dropped out because of peer pressure and social problems, not academic issues. I agree with Ericsson when she points out just how bad stereotypes are, "They are always dangerous" (201). On the other hand, I am not sure that a stereotype is a lie. When a person forms an opinion without enough information, I don't think that person intends to mislead anyone; he is just being stupid. Stereotyping proves a person is not thinking, it doesn't mean a person is deceptive.

PRACTICE 17–8   **Editing Run-Ons and Using Formal English**

Tip For more advice on using formal English, see Chapter 26. For advice on choosing appropriate words, see Chapter 27.

Your brother has been overcharged for an MP3 player he ordered online, and he is about to send this email to the seller's customer-service department. Help him by correcting the run-ons. Then, edit the informal English.

    I'm writing 2U cuz I was seriously ripped off for the Star 3 MP3 player I ordered from your website last week. U listed the price as $50 $150 was charged to my credit card. Check out any competitors' sites, U will see that no one expects people 2 cough up that much cash for the Star model, the prices are never higher than $65. I overpaid big bucks on this, I want my money back as soon as possible.

Seriously bummin',

Chris Langley

Chapter Review

1. What is an independent clause?

2. What is a fused sentence?

3. What is a comma splice?

4. What are the five ways to correct run-ons?

5. What word in the middle of a sentence may signal a run-on?

6. What are the seven coordinating conjunctions?

Reflect and Apply

1. Has your instructor in this course (or previous instructors) pointed out problems with run-on sentences in your writing? If so, how have you tried to fix the problem?

2. Why do comma splices and fused sentences cause such problems for readers? What would happen, for example, if you tried to read an entire paragraph that contained no periods?

3. Why do comma splices and fused sentences cause such problems for writers? If you read your work aloud, can you hear a comma splice or fused sentence? Explain.

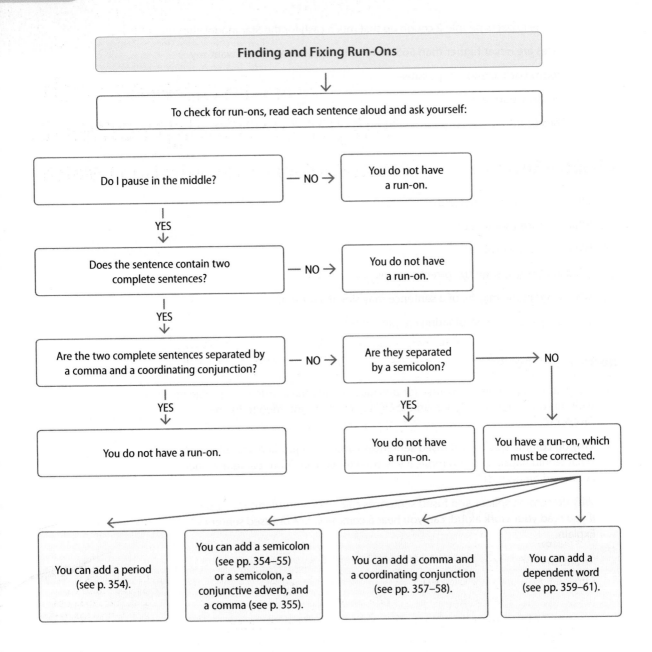

Finding and Fixing Run-Ons

To check for run-ons, read each sentence aloud and ask yourself:

Do I pause in the middle? — NO → You do not have a run-on.

YES

Does the sentence contain two complete sentences? — NO → You do not have a run-on.

YES

Are the two complete sentences separated by a comma and a coordinating conjunction? — NO → Are they separated by a semicolon? → NO

YES

You do not have a run-on.

YES

You do not have a run-on.

You have a run-on, which must be corrected.

You can add a period (see p. 354).

You can add a semicolon (see pp. 354–55) or a semicolon, a conjunctive adverb, and a comma (see p. 355).

You can add a comma and a coordinating conjunction (see pp. 357–58).

You can add a dependent word (see pp. 359–61).

18

Problems with Subject-Verb Agreement
When Subjects and Verbs Don't Match

Understand What Subject-Verb Agreement Is

In any sentence, the **subject and the verb must match—or agree**—in number. If the subject is singular (one person, place, or thing), the verb must also be singular. If the subject is plural (more than one), the verb must also be plural.

Singular	The <u>skydiver</u> <u><u>jumps</u></u> out of the airplane.
Plural	The <u>skydivers</u> <u><u>jump</u></u> out of the airplane.

Regular Verbs, Present Tense

	Singular		Plural
First person	I walk.	} no -s	We walk.
Second person	You walk.		You walk.
Third person	He (she, it) walks.	} all end in -s	They walk.
	Joe walks.		Joe and Alice walk.
	The student walks.		The students walk.

Tip In the examples throughout this chapter, subjects are underlined, and verbs are double-underlined.

Regular verbs (with forms that follow standard English patterns) have two forms in the present tense: one that ends in -s and one that has no ending. The third-person subjects—*he, she, it*—and singular nouns always use the form that ends in -s. First-person subjects (*I*), second-person subjects (*you*), and plural subjects use the form with no ending.

In the Real World, Why Is It Important to Correct Errors in Subject-Verb Agreement?

People outside the English classroom notice subject-verb agreement errors and consider them major mistakes.

Situation: Regina Toms wrote the following brief report about a company employee whom she was sending to the employee assistance program. These programs help workers with various problems, such as alcoholism or mental illness, that may affect their job performance.

Mr. X, who has been a model employee of the company for five years,

have recently behaved in ways that is inappropriate. For example, last week he

was rude when a colleague asked him a question. He has been late to work

several times and has missed work more often than usual. When I spoke to

him about his behavior and asked if he have problems, he admitted that he had

been drinking more than usual. I would like him to speak to someone who

understand more about this than I do.

Read to Write

Did you immediately notice Regina's errors in subject-verb agreement in her report? Which ones were most obvious? Which ones did you miss?

How does a problem with subject-verb agreement affect the reader's understanding of the material?

Find and Correct Errors in Subject-Verb Agreement

To find problems with subject-verb agreement in your own writing, look for five trouble spots that often signal these problems.

1. The Verb Is a Form of Be, Have, or Do

The verbs *be, have,* and *do* do not follow the rules for forming singular and plural forms; they are **irregular verbs**.

These verbs cause problems for writers who in conversation use the same form in all cases: *He do the cleaning; they do the cleaning.* People also sometimes use the word *be* instead of the correct form of *be: She be on vacation.*

Forms of the Verb *Be*

Present tense	Singular	Plural
First person	I am	we are
Second person	you are	you are
Third person	she, he, it is	they are
	the student is	the students are

Past tense		
First person	I was	we were
Second person	you were	you were
Third person	she, he, it was	they were
	the student was	the students were

Forms of the Verb *Have*, Present Tense

	Singular	Plural
First person	I have	we have
Second person	you have	you have
Third person	she, he, it has	they have
	the student has	the students have

Forms of the Verb *Do*, Present Tense

	Singular	Plural
First person	I do	we do
Second person	you do	you do
Third person	she, he, it does	they do
	the student does	the students do

In college and at work, use the forms of the verbs *be, have,* and *do* as shown in the charts on page 369.

>   *are*
> They ~~is~~ sick today.
>
>   *has*
> Joan ~~have~~ the best jewelry.
>
>   *does*
> Carlos ~~do~~ the laundry every Wednesday.

> **PRACTICE 18–1**   **Identifying Problems with Subject-Verb Agreement**
>
> Find and underline the four problems with subject-verb agreement in Regina Toms's report on page 368.

2. Words Come between the Subject and the Verb

When the subject and verb are not directly next to each other, it is more difficult to find them to make sure they agree. Most often, either a prepositional phrase or a dependent clause comes between the subject and the verb.

Prepositional Phrase between the Subject and the Verb

Tip For a list of common prepositions, see page 339.

A **prepositional phrase** starts with a preposition and ends with a noun or pronoun: I took my bag *of books* and threw it *across the room.*

     The subject of a sentence is never in a prepositional phrase. When you are looking for the subject of a sentence, you can cross out any prepositional phrases.

A <u>volunteer</u> ~~in the Peace Corps~~ (serve/<u>serves</u>) two years.

<u>Those</u> ~~with ASD~~ typically <u>demonstrate</u> symptoms by two to three years of age (McCrimmon 235)

> **Language note:** In some languages, a subject may be followed by a subject pronoun; however, in English, this is not allowed:
>
> **Incorrect**   The cities near major airports they often host large conferences and concerts.
>
>   [The subject is *cities*; the word *they* should not be added.]
>
> **Correct**   The cities near major airports often host large conferences.

Dependent Clause between the Subject and the Verb

A **dependent clause** has a subject and a verb, but it does not express a complete thought. When a dependent clause comes between the subject and the verb, it usually starts with the word *who, whose, whom, that,* or *which.*

The subject of a sentence is never in a dependent clause. When you are looking for the subject of a sentence, you can cross out any dependent clauses.

The coins ~~that I found last week~~ (seem/seems) valuable.

Many children ~~who receive an ASD diagnosis~~ do not imitate others' behaviors (McCrimmon 235).

> **PRACTICE 18–2**   **Making Subjects and Verbs Agree When They Are Separated by a Dependent Clause**

In each of the following sentences, cross out any dependent clauses. Then, correct any problems with subject-verb agreement. If the subject and the verb agree, write "OK" next to the sentence.

Example: My cousins, ~~who immigrated to this country from Ecuador,~~ have
~~has~~ jobs in a fast-food restaurant.
^

1. The restaurant that hired my cousins are not treating them fairly.

2. People who work in the kitchen has to report to work at 7:00 A.M.

3. The boss who supervises the morning shift tells the workers not to punch in until 9:00 A.M.

4. The benefits that full-time workers earn have not been offered to my cousins.

5. Ramón, whose hand was injured slicing potatoes, need to have physical therapy.

6. No one who works with him has helped him file for worker's compensation.

7. The doctors who cleaned his wound and put in his stitches at the hospital expects him to pay for the medical treatment.

8. The managers who run the restaurant insists that he is not eligible for medical coverage.

9. My cousins, whose English is not yet perfect, feels unable to leave their jobs.

10. The restaurant that treats them so badly offers the only opportunity for them to earn a living.

3. The Sentence Has a Compound Subject

Tip Whenever you see a compound subject joined by *and,* try replacing it in your mind with *they.*

A **compound subject** is two (or more) subjects joined by *and, or,* or *nor.*

And/Or Rule: If two subjects are joined by *and,* use a plural verb. If two subjects are joined by *or* (or *nor*), they are considered separate, and the verb should agree with whatever subject it is closer to.

Plural subject = Plural verb

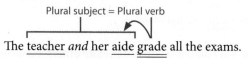

The teacher *and* her aide grade all the exams.

Subject *or* Singular subject = Singular verb

Either the teacher *or* her aide grades all the exams.

Subject *or* Plural subject = Plural verb

The teacher *or* her aides grade all the exams.

Subject *nor* Plural subject = Plural verb

Neither the teacher *nor* her aides grade all the exams.

4. The Subject Is an Indefinite Pronoun

An **indefinite pronoun** replaces a general person, place, or thing or a general group of people, places, or things. Indefinite pronouns are often singular, although there are some exceptions, as shown in the following chart.

Singular	Everyone wants the semester to end.
Plural	Many want the semester to end.
Singular	Either of the meals is good.

Often, an indefinite pronoun is followed by a prepositional phrase or a dependent clause. Remember that the verb of a sentence must agree with the subject of the sentence, and the subject of a sentence is *never in a prepositional phrase or dependent clause.* To choose the correct verb, cross out the prepositional phrase or dependent clause.

Everyone in all the classes (want/wants) the term to end.

Several who have to take the math exam (is/are) studying together.

Indefinite Pronouns

Always singular			May be singular or plural
another	everybody	no one	all
anybody	everyone	nothing	any
anyone	everything	one (of)	none
anything	much	somebody	some
each (of)*	neither (of)*	someone	
either (of)*	nobody	something	

*When one of these words is the subject, mentally replace it with *one*. *One* is singular and takes a singular verb.

> Each of the students has/have a laptop.
> One (of the students) has a laptop.
> The correct answer is *has*.

5. *The Verb Comes before the Subject*

In most sentences, the subject comes before the verb. Two kinds of sentences often reverse the usual subject-verb order: questions and sentences that begin with *here* or *there*. In these two types of sentences, check carefully for errors in subject-verb agreement.

Questions

In questions, the verb or part of the verb comes before the subject. To find the subject and verb, you can turn the question around as if you were going to answer it.

> Where is the bookstore?/The bookstore is . . .
>
> Are you excited?/You are excited.

Note: Sometimes the verb in a sentence appears before the subject even in sentences that are not questions:

> Most inspiring of all were her speeches on freedom.

Sentences that Begin with Here or There

When a sentence begins with *here* or *there,* the subject often follows the verb. Turn the sentence around to find the subject and verb.

> Here is your key to the apartment./Your key to the apartment is here.
>
> *There* are four keys on the table./Four keys are on the table.

Read to Write

Sentences where the subject follows the verb are called inverted sentences. Where do you think writers are likely to use inversion? Why?

> **PRACTICE 18–3**   **Correcting a Sentence When the Verb Comes Before the Subject**

Correct any problem with subject-verb agreement in the following sentences. If a sentence is already correct, write "OK" next to it.

                            does
Example: What electives ~~do~~ the school offer?

1. What are the best reason to study music?

2. There is several good reasons.

3. There is evidence that music helps students with math.

4. What is your favorite musical instrument?

5. Here is a guitar, a saxophone, and a piano.

6. There is very few people with natural musical ability.

7. What time of day does you usually practice?

8. There is no particular time.

9. What musician does you admire most?

10. Here are some information about the importance of regular practice.

Edit for Subject-Verb Agreement Problems

Use the chart on page 378, "Finding and Fixing Problems with Subject-Verb Agreement," to help you complete the practices in this section and edit your own writing.

> **PRACTICE 18–4**   **Correcting Various Subject-Verb Agreement Problems**

In the following sentences, identify any verb that does not agree with its subject. Then, correct the sentence using the correct form of the verb.

                                                      wake
Example: Some twenty-somethings in Washington, D.C., ~~wakes~~ before dawn to read the news.

1. They does so not out of interest in current events.

2. Instead, their jobs in government and business requires them to read and summarize the latest information related to these jobs.

3. Each of their bosses need this information early in the morning to be prepared for the day.

4. For example, a politician who introduces new legislation want to know the public's reaction as soon as possible.

5. Learning of new complaints about such legislation by 8 A.M. give the politician time to shape a thoughtful response for a 10 A.M. news conference.

6. What is the benefits of the reading-and-summarizing job?

7. There is several, according to the young people who do such work.

8. Information and power goes together, some of them say.

9. A reputation for being in-the-know help them rise through the ranks at their workplaces.

10. Also, they has a chance to build skills and connections that can lead to other jobs.

PRACTICE 18–5   Editing Paragraphs for Subject-Verb Agreement

Find and correct six problems with subject-verb agreement in the following paragraphs.

In her essay, "Isn't It Time You Hit the Books?," Samantha Levine-Finley offers advice for students who want to improve grades and succeed in their college studies. Almost all students can benefit from some of her advice, including suggestions that students attend class regularly and make good use of the syllabus. But there is some students who cannot relate to all of the steps that Levine-Finley recommend: students who are also working parents. For example, Levine-Finley urges students to visit their instructors during their office hours. But students who also have to punch a time clock or drive an afternoon carpool does not always have the luxury of getting to the professor's office during his or her scheduled office hours. Most instructors will accommodate a working parent's schedule, but even with that flexibility, students may need to take off work to attend a conference with the instructor. Other students with responsibility for childcare sometimes has to bring an infant or toddler with them to an appointment. Anyone who has tried to hold a serious conversation with a small child nearby knows that time is limited in these situations. A baby that is crying for attention make it difficult for a parent trying to understand an assignment. Finally, Levine-Findley recommends that students become good time managers. Well, a student who is a parent and employee at the same time probably know already how to manage time; it's the only way that student could function with such different roles. Perhaps students who is also parents and workers most need help finding time to relax, rest, and re-energize.

PRACTICE 18-6   **Editing Subject-Verb Agreement Errors and Using Formal English**

Tip For more advice on using formal English, see Chapter 26. For advice on choosing appropriate words, see Chapter 27.

A friend of yours has been turned down for a course because of high enrollment, even though she registered early. She knows that her email to the instructor teaching the course has a few problems in it. Help her by correcting any subject-verb agreement errors. Then, edit the informal English in the email.

Hey Prof Connors,

I am emailing you to make sure you gets the email I sent before about registering for your Business Writing course this semester. IMHO, it is one of the best classes this college offers. I does not miss the deadline; I signed up on the first day, in fact. I plans to graduate with a degree in business and economics, so your class is important to me. Could you please check yur class roster to see if I was somehow skipped or missed? I would sure appreciate it a ton, LOL. Plz let me know what you finds out. If I cannot get into your class this semester, I will have to rearrange my schedule so that I can

takes it next semester instead. I look forward to taking your class and learn-

ing all about business writing. You rocks, prof.

Sincerely,

Cameron Taylor

PRACTICE 18–7   **Editing Regina's Report**

Look back at Regina Toms's report on page 368. You may have already underlined the subject-verb agreement errors; if not, do so now. Next, using
what you have learned in this chapter, correct each error.

Chapter Review

1. What is subject-verb agreement?

2. What are five trouble spots that cause problems for subject-verb agreement?

Reflect and Apply

1. Has your instructor for this course (or a previous instructor) pointed out
   problems with subject-verb agreement in your writing? If so, what strategies are
   you using to address those problems?

2. Keep a record of subject-verb agreement errors in your own writing. Which of
   the five trouble spots mentioned in this chapter seems to cause a problem
   for you?

3. Read Regina Toms's report on page 368 aloud, without corrections. Can you
   hear the subject-verb agreement problems? How can your voice and your ears
   help you edit your work?

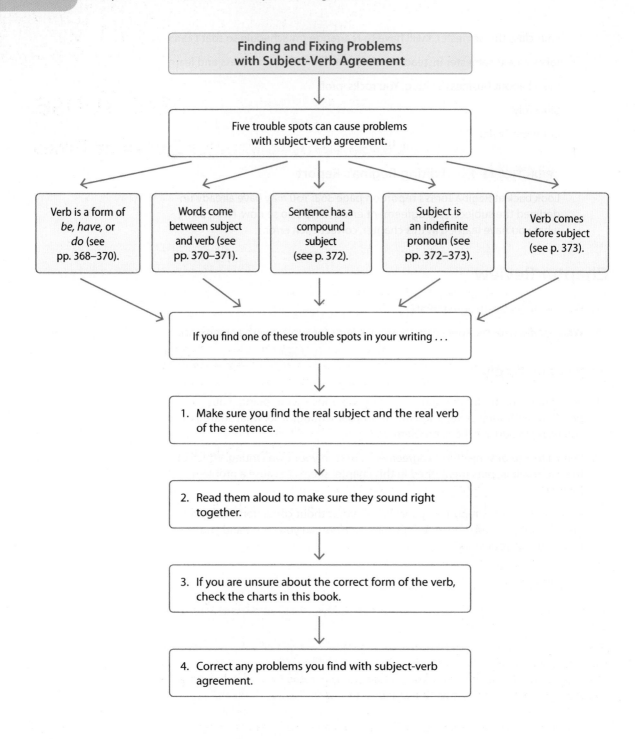

Finding and Fixing Problems with Subject-Verb Agreement

Five trouble spots can cause problems with subject-verb agreement.

Verb is a form of *be, have,* or *do* (see pp. 368–370).

Words come between subject and verb (see pp. 370–371).

Sentence has a compound subject (see p. 372).

Subject is an indefinite pronoun (see pp. 372–373).

Verb comes before subject (see p. 373).

If you find one of these trouble spots in your writing . . .

1. Make sure you find the real subject and the real verb of the sentence.

2. Read them aloud to make sure they sound right together.

3. If you are unsure about the correct form of the verb, check the charts in this book.

4. Correct any problems you find with subject-verb agreement.

Verb Tense

Using Verbs to Express Different Times

Understand What Verb Tense Is

Verb tense tells *when* an action happened or will happen: in the past, in the present, or in the future. Verb tenses also indicate if an action is complete or ongoing (linguists call this information a verb's **aspect**). Verbs change their **base form** or use the helping verbs *have, be,* or *will* to indicate different tenses.

Present tense	Every high school <u>student</u> <u>complains</u> about having to take grammar and learn all of the awful exceptions to every grammar and spelling rule in the English language (Bigler 139).
Past tense	<u>Dinner</u> <u>threw</u> me into despair (Tan 122).
Future tense	But <u>I</u> <u>will continue</u> to be disgusted when people criticize another person's choices (Whitmer 145).

In the Real World, Why Is It Important to Use the Correct Verb Tense?

People outside the English classroom notice written errors in verb tense and consider them major mistakes.

Situation: Cal is a summer intern in the systems division of a large company. He would like to get a part-time job there during the school year because he is studying computer science and knows that the experience would help him get a job after graduation. He sends this email to his supervisor.

I have work hard since coming to Technotron and learn many new things.

Mr. Joseph tell me that he like my work and that I shown good motivation and teamwork. As he know, I spended many hours working on a special project for him. I would like to continue my work here beyond the summer. Therefore, I hope that you will consider me for future employment.

Sincerely,

Cal Troppo

Read to Write

What are your thoughts about Cal's email?

Does Cal present himself professionally in this email?

How could verb errors affect Cal's potential career or how he is perceived as an applicant for a job?

What can Cal do to improve his email? Rewrite it so it has no verb errors.

Would you recommend any other changes? Explain.

Tip To find and correct problems with verbs, you need to be able to identify subjects and verbs. For a review, see Chapter 15.

Tip A complete verb, also known as a verb phrase, is made up of the main verb and all of its helping verbs.

Practice Using Correct Verbs

This section will teach you about verb tenses and give you practice with using them. You should also pay attention to the verb tenses in your reading. Select paragraphs from your reading, circle the verbs, and think about the way the tenses are used. You can also read the paragraph out loud, focusing on pronouncing and hearing yourself say the verb forms correctly.

> **PRACTICE 19–1** Identifying Verb Errors

Find and underline the seven verb errors in Cal's email.

Regular Verbs

Most verbs in English are **regular verbs** that follow standard rules about what endings to use to express time.

Present Tense Endings: -S and No Ending

Tip For more about making verbs match subjects, see Chapter 18.

The **present tense** is used for habits, situations that do not change, and actions that happen all the time. Regular verbs in the present tense either end in -*s* or have no ending added.

-s ending	No ending
jumps	jump
walks	walk
lives	live

Use the *-s* ending when the subject is *he, she, it,* or the name of one person or thing. Use no ending for all other subjects.

Regular Verbs in the Present Tense

	Singular	Plural
First person	I jump.	We jump.
Second person	You jump.	You jump.
Third person	She (he, it) jumps.	They jump.
	The child jumps.	The children jump.

Tip In the examples throughout this chapter, subjects are underlined, and verbs are double-underlined.

 Language note: Do not confuse the simple present tense with the **present progressive,** which is used with a form of the helping verb *be* to describe actions that are in progress right now.

Simple present	I eat a banana every day.
Present progressive	I am eating a banana.

One Regular Past Tense Ending: -Ed

The **past tense** is used for actions that began and ended in the past. An *-ed* ending is needed on all regular verbs in the past tense.

	Present tense	Past tense
First person	I avoid her.	I avoided her.
Second person	You help me.	You helped me.
Third person	He walks quickly.	He walked quickly.

Tip If a verb already ends in *-e*, just add *-d*: *dance/danced.* If a verb ends in a consonant and *-y,* the *-y* changes to *-i* when *-ed* is added: *spy/spied; try/tried.* If the verb ends in a vowel and *-y,* just add *-ed*: *play/played; enjoy/enjoyed.*

One Regular Past Participle Ending: -Ed

The **past participle** is a verb form that is used with an auxiliary verb, such as *have* or *be.* For all regular verbs, the past participle form is the same as the past tense form: it uses an *-ed* ending. (To learn about when past participles are used, see pp. 387–390.)

Past tense	Past participle
My kids <u>watched</u> cartoons.	They <u>have watched</u> cartoons before.
George <u>visited</u> his cousins.	He <u>has visited</u> them every year.

Irregular Verbs

Irregular verbs do not follow the simple rules of regular verbs, which have just two present tense endings (*-s* or *-es*) and two past tense endings (*-d* or *-ed*). Irregular verbs show past tense with a change in spelling, although some irregular verbs, such as *cost, hit,* and *put,* do not change their spelling. The most common irregular verbs are *be* and *have* (see "Irregular Verbs" chart). As you write and edit, use the following chart to make sure you use the correct form of irregular verbs.

Note: What is called "present tense" in the chart that follows is sometimes called the "base form of the verb."

Irregular Verbs

Present tense (base form of verb)	Past tense	Past participle (used with helping verb)
be (am/are/is)	was /were	been
become	became	become
begin	began	begun
bite	bit	bitten
blow	blew	blown
break	broke	broken
bring	brought	brought
build	built	built
buy	bought	bought
catch	caught	caught
choose	chose	chosen
come	came	come
cost	cost	cost
dive	dived, dove	dived
do	did	done
draw	drew	drawn
drink	drank	drunk
drive	drove	driven
eat	ate	eaten

Present tense (base form of verb)	Past tense	Past participle (used with helping verb)
fall	fell	fallen
feed	fed	fed
feel	felt	felt
fight	fought	fought
find	found	found
fly	flew	flown
forget	forgot	forgotten
get	got	gotten
give	gave	given
go	went	gone
grow	grew	grown
have/has	had	had
hear	heard	heard
hide	hid	hidden
hit	hit	hit
hold	held	held
hurt	hurt	hurt
keep	kept	kept
know	knew	known
lay	laid	laid
lead	led	led
leave	left	left
let	let	let
lie	lay	lain
light	lit	lit
lose	lost	lost
make	made	made
mean	meant	meant
meet	met	met
pay	paid	paid
put	put	put
quit	quit	quit
read	read	read
ride	rode	ridden
ring	rang	rung
rise	rose	risen
run	ran	run

→

Present tense (base form of verb)	Past tense	Past participle (used with helping verb)
say	said	said
see	saw	seen
seek	sought	sought
sell	sold	sold
send	sent	sent
shake	shook	shaken
show	showed	shown
shrink	shrank	shrunk
shut	shut	shut
sing	sang	sung
sink	sank	sunk
sit	sat	sat
sleep	slept	slept
speak	spoke	spoken
spend	spent	spent
stand	stood	stood
steal	stole	stolen
stick	stuck	stuck
sting	stung	stung
strike	struck	struck, stricken
swim	swam	swum
take	took	taken
teach	taught	taught
tear	tore	torn
tell	told	told
think	thought	thought
throw	threw	thrown
understand	understood	understood
wake	woke	woken
wear	wore	worn
win	won	won
write	wrote	written

Present Tense of Be *and* Have

The present tense of the verbs *be* and *have* is irregular, as shown in the following chart.

Present Tense of *Be* and *Have*

Be		Have	
I am	we are	I have	we have
you are	you are	you have	you have
he, she, it is	they are	he, she, it has	they have
the editor is	the editors are	the editor has	the editors have
Beth is	Beth and Christina are	Beth has	Beth and Christina have

Past Tense of Be

The past tense of the verb *be* is tricky because it has two forms: *was* and *were*.

Past Tense of *Be*

	Singular	Plural
First person	I was	we were
Second person	you were	you were
Third person	she, he, it was	they were
	the student was	the students were

 Language note: Some languages have different forms for singular and plural *you*, but English does not. Use *were* as the past tense of *be* when the subject is *you*, no matter how many people you are speaking to.

PRACTICE 19–2   **Using Irregular Verbs in the Past Tense**

In the following paragraph, replace any incorrect present tense verbs with the correct past tense of the verb. If you are unsure of the past tense forms of irregular verbs, refer to the chart on pages 382–84.

(1) For years, Homer and Langley Collyer are known for their strange living conditions. (2) Neighbors who passed by the brothers' New York City townhouse see huge piles of trash through the windows. (3) At night, Langley roamed the streets in search of more junk. (4) In March 1947, an anonymous caller tells the police that someone had died in the Collyers' home. (5) In response, officers break through a second-floor window and tunneled through mounds of newspapers, old umbrellas, and other junk. (6) Eventually, they find the body of Homer Collyer, who seemed to have died of starvation. (7) But where was Langley? (8) In efforts to locate him, workers spend days removing trash from the house—more than one hundred tons' worth in total. (9) They bring a strange variety of items to the curb, including medical equipment, bowling balls, fourteen pianos, and the frame of a Model T car. (10) In early April, a worker finally discovered Langley's body. (11) It lies just 10 feet from where Homer had been found. (12) Apparently, Langley died while bringing food to his disabled brother. (13) As he tunneled ahead, a pile of trash falls on him and crushed him. (14) This trash was part of a booby trap that Langley had created to stop intruders. (15) Not long after the brothers' deaths, the city demolished their former home. (16) In 1965, community leaders do something that might have surprised Homer and Langley: where the trash-filled home once stands, workers created a neat and peaceful park. (17) In the 1990s, this green space becomes the Collyer Brothers Park.

For irregular verbs, the past participle is often different from the past tense.

	Past tense	Past participle
Regular verb	I walked home.	I have walked home before.
Irregular verb	I drove home.	I have driven home before.

It is difficult to predict how irregular verbs form the past participle. Until you are familiar with them, find them in the chart on pages 382–84.

Past Participles

A **past participle**, by itself, cannot be the main verb of a sentence. When a past participle is combined with a form of the auxiliary verb *have*, however, it can be used to make the present perfect tense and the past perfect tense. When combined with a form of the auxiliary verb *be*, it forms the passive voice.

Present Perfect and Past Perfect Tenses

Tip For more about using perfect tense verbs, see Chapter 26.

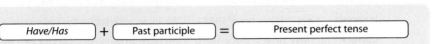

Have/Has + Past participle = Present perfect tense

The **present perfect** tense is used for an action that began in the past and either continues into the present or was completed at some unknown time in the past.

Present tense of *have* (helping verb)
| Past participle

Present perfect tense   My car has stalled several times recently.

[This sentence says that the stalling began in the past and may continue into the present.]

Past tense   My car stalled yesterday.

[This sentence says that the car stalled once and that it's over.]

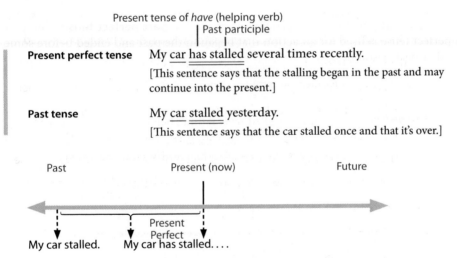

Past   Present (now)   Future

Present
Perfect
My car stalled.   My car has stalled. . . .

Present Perfect Tense

	Singular	Plural
First person	I have laughed.	We have laughed.
Second person	You have laughed.	You have laughed.
Third person	She /he /it has laughed.	They have laughed.
	The baby has laughed.	The babies have laughed.

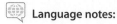 **Language notes:**

1. Be careful not to leave out *have* when it is needed for the present perfect.

2. Time-signal words, such as *since* and *for,* may mean that the present perfect is required.

3. Do not use simple present or present progressive tenses for actions that indicate they started in the past and continue to the present.

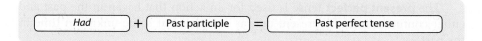

Incorrect	I driven since 1985.	We grown vegetables for two years.
Incorrect	I am driving since 1985.	We grow vegetables for two years.
Correct	I **have** driven since 1985.	We **have** grown vegetables for two years.

Had	+	Past participle	=	Past perfect tense

Use *had* plus the past participle to make the **past perfect tense**. The past perfect tense is used for an action that began in the past and ended before some other past action began.

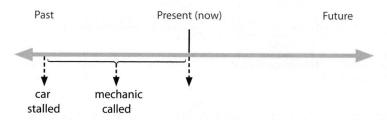

Past perfect tense

Had (helping verb)
|Past participle
|

My car had stalled several times before I called the mechanic.

[This sentence says that both the *stalling* and *calling the mechanic* happened in the past but that the *stalling* happened before the *calling* did.]

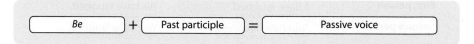

Past   Present (now)   Future

car   mechanic
stalled   called

Passive Voice

Be	+	Past participle	=	Passive voice

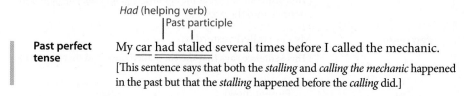

A sentence that is written in the **passive voice** has a subject that does not perform an action. Instead, the subject is acted on. To create the passive voice, combine a form of the verb *be* with a past participle.

Form of *be* (helping verb)
| Past participle
|
Passive   The <u>newspaper</u> <u>was thrown</u> onto the porch.

[The subject, *newspaper*, did not throw itself onto the porch. Some unidentified person threw the newspaper.]

Writers normally use the **active voice**, which means that the subject performs the action, when they know who is doing the action or when they want to emphasize the action.

Active   My <u>neighbor</u>, Mrs. Jenkins, <u>threw</u> the newspaper onto the porch.

[The subject, *my neighbor*, performed the action: she threw the newspaper.]

Use the passive voice when no one person performed the action, when you do not know who performed the action, or when you want to emphasize the receiver of the action (the object of the sentence).

Active   <u>Someone</u> <u>stole</u> my textbook.

Passive   My <u>textbook</u> <u>was stolen</u>.

[Since you do not know who stole the book, the passive makes sense here.]

Active   The <u>bandleader</u> <u>chose</u> Kelly to do a solo.

Passive   <u>Kelly</u> <u>was chosen</u> to do a solo.

[If you wanted to emphasize Kelly's being chosen rather than the bandleader's choice, you might decide to use the passive voice.]

PRACTICE 19–3   **Changing the Passive Voice to the Active Voice**

Rewrite the following sentences, changing them from the passive voice to the active voice.

Example: The legislature cut funding
~~Funding~~ for animal shelters. ~~was cut by the legislature.~~
        ^   ^

1. Some shelters were going to be closed by the owners.

2. What would become of the animals was unknown.

3. A campaign was started by animal lovers.

4. Interviews were given by the owners and volunteers at shelters.

5. The animals were filmed by news teams.

6. The stories were aired on all the local television stations.

7. A protest was staged by animal lovers across the state.

8. Fund-raisers of all sorts were held.

9. Some funds were restored by the legislature.

10. Enough money was raised to keep the shelters open.

Consistency of Verb Tense

Consistency of verb tense means that all actions in a sentence that happen (or happened) at the same time are in the same tense. If all the actions happen in the present or happen all the time, use the present for all verbs in the sentence. If all the actions happened in the past, use the past tense for all verbs.

	Past tense Present tense
	| |
Inconsistent	The <u>movie</u> <u><u>started</u></u> just as <u>we</u> <u><u>take</u></u> our seats.
	[The actions both happened at the same time, but *started* is in the past tense, and *take* is in the present tense.]

	Past tense Present tense
	| |
Consistent, past tense	The <u>movie</u> <u><u>started</u></u> just as <u>we</u> <u><u>took</u></u> our seats.
	[The actions *started* and *took* both happened in the past, and both are in the past tense.]

Use different tenses only when you are referring to different times.

My <u>daughter</u> <u><u>hated</u></u> math as a child, but now <u>she</u> <u><u>loves</u></u> it.
[The sentence uses two tenses because the first verb (*hated*) refers to a past condition, whereas the second verb (*loves*) refers to a present one.]

> **PRACTICE 19–4** **Using Consistent Verb Tense**
>
> In each of the following sentences, double-underline the verbs, and correct any unnecessary shifts in verb tense. Write the correct form of the verb in the blank space provided.

Example: have Although some people <u>dream</u> of having their picture
                 taken by a famous photographer, not many ~~had~~ the chance.

1.   Now, special stores in malls take magazine-quality photographs
   of anyone who wanted one.

2.   The founder of one business got the idea when she hear friends
   complaining about how bad they looked in family photographs.

3.   She decide to open a business to take studio-style photographs
   that did not cost a lot of money.

4.   Her first store included special lighting and offers different sets,
   such as colored backgrounds and outdoor scenes.

5.   Now, her stores even have makeup studios for people who
   wanted a special look for their pictures.

Edit for Verb Problems

Use the chart on page 394, "Finding and Fixing Verb Tense Errors," to help you
complete the practices in this section and edit your own writing.

> **PRACTICE 19–5**   **Correcting Various Verb Problems**
>
> In the following sentences, find and correct any verb problems.
>
> **Example:**   Sheena ~~be~~ *is* tired of the tattoo on her left shoulder.
>
> 1. Sheena had never consider a tattoo until several of her friends got
>   them.
>
> 2. Sheena was twenty-two when she goes to the tattoo parlor.
>
> 3. After looking at many designs, she choose a purple rose design, which
>   she gave to the tattoo artist.
>
> 4. Her sister liked the tattoo, but her mother faints.
>
> 5. Like Sheena, many people who now reached their thirties want to get
>   rid of their old tattoos.
>
> 6. A few years ago, when a person decides to have a tattoo removed,
>   doctors had to cut out the design.
>
> 7. That technique leaved scars.

8. Today, doctors using laser light to break up the ink molecules in the skin.

9. Six months ago, Sheena start to have treatments to remove her tattoo.

10. The procedure hurted every time she saw the doctor, but she hoped it would be worth the pain.

> **PRACTICE 19-6**   **Editing Paragraphs for Verb Problems**

Find and correct seven problems with verb tense in the following paragraphs.

In his essay, "Yes, Money Can Buy Happiness," John Tierney reports on research connecting how we spend money and what makes us happy. In one experiment mentioned in the article, researchers conducted a survey of over six hundred people in the United States. People who reported spending more on charitable giving also seemed to be happier. While I cannot speak for all the students on this campus, the finding makes sense to me. I have found that when I make the effort to share either time or money during an on-campus fund-raiser or volunteer opportunity, I felt better about myself and my studies. During my first semester at college, I am struggling with depression; I even considered dropping out of school. I lived at home and worked 25 hours a week, so I didn't really have time to join in campus events or get to know anyone. My counselor has suggested that I join a club, so at the start of the next term, I got involved with a group that works with senior citizens near campus, and I cutted my hours back at work. We hosted a fund-raiser to raise money to purchase a sound system for the seniors' community center, and I contributed a good bit of my own money. Within a few weeks, I had found myself feeling more energized, confident, and hopeful about the future. Money did not buy my happiness, but spending it helped me recover a positive attitude.

PRACTICE 19–7   Editing Verb Problems and Using Formal English

Your sister has a bad case of laryngitis and wants to bring a note about her condition to her doctor. Help her by correcting the verb problems in the note. Then, edit the informal English.

(1) What's up, Doc Kerrigan? (2) Your assistant ask me to tell you about my symptoms, so I will describe them as well as I can. (3) I becomed sick about a day ago. (4) Now, my throat hurt every time I swallowed, and I cannot speak. (5) Also, I has a high fever, and I be wicked tired. (6) I do not think I has ever feeled so crappy before. (7) I looked forward to seeing you during my appointment.

(8) Thanks mucho,

Corrine Evans

Chapter Review

1. What is verb tense?

2. What are the two present tense endings for regular verbs?

3. How do regular verbs in the past tense end?

4. What is a past participle? How is it used?

5. What are irregular verbs? Give an example.

6. What is present perfect tense? How is it formed?

7. What is past perfect tense? How is it formed?

8. When do writers use passive voice?

Reflect and Apply

1. Has your instructor in this course (or previous instructors) pointed out problems with verb forms in your writing? If so, how have you tried to fix the problem?

2. Different academic areas have different expectations for verb forms and tenses. For example, some science disciplines expect writers to use passive voice to explain experiments and procedures, while writers in other disciplines may prefer active voice. Talk to a professor or student in your major. What kinds of writing is required for that major? What expectations do professors have for verb forms and tenses in that kind of writing?

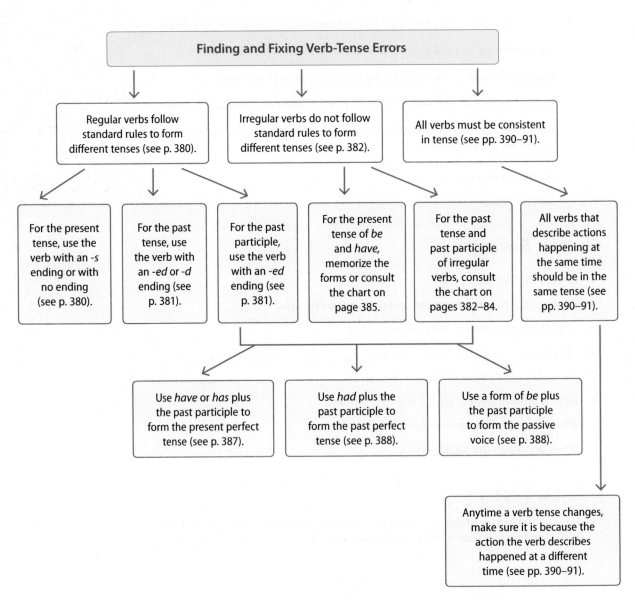

Finding and Fixing Verb-Tense Errors

Regular verbs follow standard rules to form different tenses (see p. 380).

Irregular verbs do not follow standard rules to form different tenses (see p. 382).

All verbs must be consistent in tense (see pp. 390–91).

For the present tense, use the verb with an *-s* ending or with no ending (see p. 380).

For the past tense, use the verb with an *-ed* or *-d* ending (see p. 381).

For the past participle, use the verb with an *-ed* ending (see p. 381).

For the present tense of *be* and *have*, memorize the forms or consult the chart on page 385.

For the past tense and past participle of irregular verbs, consult the chart on pages 382–84.

All verbs that describe actions happening at the same time should be in the same tense (see pp. 390–91).

Use *have* or *has* plus the past participle to form the present perfect tense (see p. 387).

Use *had* plus the past participle to form the past perfect tense (see p. 388).

Use a form of *be* plus the past participle to form the passive voice (see p. 388).

Anytime a verb tense changes, make sure it is because the action the verb describes happened at a different time (see pp. 390–91).

Other Grammar Concerns

20 Pronouns 397

21 Adjectives and
    Adverbs 413

22 Misplaced
    and Dangling
    Modifiers 420

23 Coordination and
    Subordination 426

24 Parallelism 437

25 Sentence
    Variety 444

26 Formal English and
    ESL Concerns 458

Pronouns
Using Substitutes for Nouns

Understand What Pronouns Are

A **pronoun** is used in place of a noun or other pronoun. Pronouns enable you to avoid repeating those nouns or other pronouns mentioned earlier.

Sheryl got into ~~Sheryl's~~ *her* car.

I like Mario. ~~Mario~~ *He* is a good dancer.

The noun or pronoun that a pronoun replaces is called the **antecedent**. In most cases, a pronoun refers to a specific antecedent nearby.

Antecedent

I picked up my new glasses. They are cool.

Pronoun replacing antecedent

> **Writing Note**
> Because pronouns can link a word from one sentence to the antecedent in a previous sentence, pronouns are an important tool for creating **cohesion** in writing—a tight connection between sentences.

Practice Using Pronouns Correctly

Identify Pronouns

Before you practice finding and correcting common pronoun errors, it is helpful to practice identifying pronouns.

Common Pronouns

Personal pronouns	Possessive pronouns	Indefinite pronouns	
I	my	all	much
me	mine	any	neither (of)
you	your/yours	anybody	nobody
she/he	hers/his	anyone	none (of)
her/him	hers/his	anything	no one
it	its	both	nothing
we	our/ours	each (of)	one (of)
us	our/ours	either (of)	some
they	their/theirs	everybody	somebody
them	their/theirs	everyone	someone
		everything	something
		few (of)	

PRACTICE 20–1   **Identifying Pronouns**

In each of the following sentences, circle the pronoun, underline the noun it refers to, and draw an arrow from the pronoun to the noun.

Example: Telling a friend he looks great when he looks like hell can be based on a decision that the friend needs a compliment more than a frank opinion. (Ericsson 212)

1. OneGoal teachers begin work with students during their junior year of high school and bridge the gap between high school and college with a curriculum that continues into each student's first year of college. (Riggs 284)

2. If the climate models that show a dire impact because of global warming aren't reliable—and they're not—then the long-term projections they make are meaningless. (Hawkins 313).

3. This small female crustacean later laid a dozen or so eggs in hopes of doing what Mother Nature intended—that she reproduce. (Sheffers and Watson 315)

4. Simply put, America's culture and dominant ideology give its citizens a lot more freedom of expression compared to Indonesia's. (Rantung 255).

5. A young person with ADHD cannot easily sit still, certainly a problem in the classroom. He or she often leaves his assigned seat, running around and attempting to climb on shelves, desks, and the like. (Vaz 259)

6. By tracking sixteen workers before and after they received profit-sharing bonuses, the researchers found that the workers who gave more of the money to others ended up happier than the ones who spent more of it on themselves. (Tierney 260)

7. Dr. Dunn, in keeping with the results of her experiments, has generously offered to provide some answers free of charge. (Tierney 261)

8. The best way to face your fears is to think about them, visualize the worst-case scenario, and then in your visualization, come up with a way to solve your worst-case scenario. (Maddox 233)

9. My heart was racing, pounding as if it were trying to escape from my chest when we came to a screeching halt. (Healy 162)

10. And while the men of that generation worked a lot of overtime, or a second job, they always had their day or two off. (Hijuelos 167)

Check for Pronoun Agreement

A pronoun must agree with (match) the noun or pronoun it refers to in number. It must be either singular (one) or plural (more than one).

If a pronoun is singular, it must also match the noun or pronoun it refers to in gender (*he, she,* or *it*).

Consistent	Magda sold *her* old television set.
	[*Her* agrees with *Magda* because both are singular and feminine.]
Consistent	The Wilsons sold *their* old television set.
	[*Their* agrees with *the Wilsons* because both are plural.]

> **Language note:** Some languages require possessive pronouns to agree with the noun they describe: *her books*, for example, would require a plural form of *her*. English, however, does not make possessive pronouns agree with the following noun. Instead, they agree with the antecedent only.
>
> **Incorrect**   Janelle spent the afternoon with his boyfriend.
>
> [*Janelle* is a female; the possessive pronoun should agree with *Janelle*, not *boyfriend*].
>
> **Correct**   Janelle spent the afternoon with her boyfriend.

Watch out for singular, general nouns. If a noun is singular, the pronoun that refers to it must be singular as well.

> **Inconsistent** Any student can tell you what *their* least favorite course is.
> [*Student* is singular, but the pronoun *their* is plural.]
>
> **Consistent** Any student can tell you what *his* or *her* least favorite course is.
> [*Student* is singular, and so are the pronouns *his* and *her*.]

To avoid using the awkward phrase *his or her*, make the subject plural when you can.

> **Consistent** Most students can tell you what *their* least favorite course is.

Two types of words often cause errors in pronoun agreement: indefinite pronouns and collective nouns.

Indefinite Pronouns

An **indefinite pronoun** does not refer to a specific person, place, or thing: it is general. Indefinite pronouns often take singular verbs. Whenever a pronoun refers to an indefinite pronoun, check for agreement.

his

The monks got up at dawn. Everybody had ~~their~~ chores for the day.

Indefinite Pronouns

Always singular			May be plural or singular
another	everyone	nothing	all
anybody/anyone	everything	one (of)	any
anything	much	somebody	none
each (of)	neither (of)	someone	some
either (of)	nobody	something	
everybody	no one		

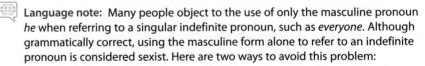 **Language note:** Many people object to the use of only the masculine pronoun *he* when referring to a singular indefinite pronoun, such as *everyone*. Although grammatically correct, using the masculine form alone to refer to an indefinite pronoun is considered sexist. Here are two ways to avoid this problem:

1. Use *his or her.*
   Someone posted *his or her* email address to the Web site.

2. Change the sentence so that the pronoun refers to a plural noun or pronoun.
   Some students posted *their* email addresses to the Web site.

Language note: There is a growing acceptance among linguists and scholars for third-person singular *they* and *their*. In fact, there are examples of third person singular *they/their* in the writing of famous authors ranging from Jane Austen to Oscar Wilde. Prominent linguists, such as Geoff Pullum, have made the case that classifying singular use of *they/their* as error is out of step with linguistic history and usage.

PRACTICE 20–2   **Using Indefinite Pronouns**

Circle the correct pronoun or group of words in parentheses.

(1) Anyone who wants to start (their/his or her) own business had better be prepared to work hard. (2) One may find, for example, that (his or her/their) work is never done. (3) Something is always waiting, with (its/their) own peculiar demands. (4) Nothing gets done on (their/its) own. (5) Anybody who expects to have more freedom now that (he or she no longer works/they no longer work) for a boss may be disappointed. (6) After all, when you work as an employee for a company, someone above you makes decisions as (they see/he or she sees) fit. (7) When you are your own boss, no one else places (themselves/himself or herself) in the position of final responsibility.

(8) Somebody starting a business may also be surprised by how much tax (they/he or she) must pay. (9) Each employee at a company pays only about half as much toward social security as what (they/he or she) would pay if self-employed. (10) Neither medical nor dental coverage can be obtained as inexpensively as (it/they) can when a person is an employee at a corporation.

Collective Nouns

A **collective noun** names a group that acts as a single unit.

Common Collective Nouns

audience	company	group
class	crowd	jury
college	family	society
committee	government	team

Collective nouns are usually singular, so when you use a pronoun to refer to a collective noun, it is also usually singular.

          its

The team had ~~their~~ sixth consecutive win of the season.

If the people in a group are acting as individuals, however, the noun is plural and should be used with a plural pronoun.

The class brought *their* papers to read.

Make Pronoun Reference Clear

In an **ambiguous pronoun reference**, the pronoun could refer to more than one noun.

Ambiguous	Enrico told Jim that *he* needed a better résumé.
	[Did Enrico tell Jim that Enrico himself needed a better résumé? Or did Enrico tell Jim that Jim needed a better résumé?]
Edited	Enrico advised Jim to revise his résumé.

Ambiguous	I put the glass on the shelf, even though it was dirty.
	[Was the glass dirty? Or was the shelf dirty?]
Edited	I put the dirty glass on the shelf.

In a **vague pronoun reference**, the pronoun does not refer clearly to any particular person, place, or thing. To correct a vague pronoun reference, use a more specific noun instead of the pronoun.

Vague	When Tom got to the clinic, they told him it was closed.
	[Who told Tom the clinic was closed?]
Edited	When Tom got to the clinic, the nurse told him it was closed.

Vague	Before I finished printing my report, it ran out of paper.
	[What ran out of paper?]
Edited	Before I finished printing my report, the printer ran out of paper.

> **PRACTICE 20-3**   **Avoiding Ambiguous or Vague Pronoun References**

Edit each sentence to eliminate ambiguous or vague pronoun references. Some sentences may be revised in more than one way.

Example: I am always looking for good advice on controlling my
                                experts
                 weight, but ~~they~~ have provided little help.
                          ^

1. My doctor referred me to a physical therapist, and she said that I needed to exercise more.

2. I joined a workout group and did exercises with the members, but it did not solve my problem.

3. I tried a lower-fat diet along with the exercising, but it did not really work either.

4. They used to say that eliminating carbohydrates is the easiest way to lose weight.

5. Therefore, I started eating fats again and stopped consuming carbs, but this was not a permanent solution.

6. Although I lost weight and loved eating fatty foods, it did not keep me from eventually gaining the weight back.

7. Last week, I overheard my Uncle Kevin talking to my brother, and he explained how he stayed slender even while traveling a lot.

8. Uncle Kevin eats fruit and vegetables instead of junk food while traveling, and it has kept off the pounds.

9. He says that it is not hard to pack carrots or apples for a trip, so anyone can do this.

10. I now try to plan better, eat less at each meal, and ignore all diet books, and I hope it works.

In a **repetitious pronoun reference**, the pronoun repeats a reference to a noun rather than replacing the noun.

The nurse at the clinic ~~he~~ told Tom that it was closed.

The newspaper/ ~~it~~ says that the new diet therapy is promising.

> ### PRACTICE 20-4   Avoiding Repetitious Pronoun References
>
> Correct any repetitious pronoun references in the following sentences.
>
> **Example:**   Car commercials ~~they~~ want viewers to believe that buying a certain brand of car will bring happiness.

1. Young people they sometimes take advertisements too literally.

2. In a beer advertisement, it might suggest that drinking alcohol makes people more attractive and popular.

3. People who see or hear an advertisement they have to think about the message.

4. Parents should help their children understand why advertisements they do not show the real world.

5. A recent study, it said that parents can help kids overcome the influence of advertising.

Use the Right Type of Pronoun

Three important types of pronouns are **subject pronouns**, **object pronouns**, and **possessive pronouns**. Notice their uses in the following sentences.

Object   Subject
pronoun pronoun

The dog barked at *him*, and *he* laughed.

Possessive
pronoun

Tip Never put an apostrophe in a possessive pronoun.

As Josh walked out, *his* phone started ringing.

Pronoun Types

	Subject	**Object**	**Possessive**
First-person singular/plural	I/we	me/us	my, mine/our, ours
Second-person singular/plural	you/you	you/you	your, yours/your, yours
Third-person singular	he, she, it	him, her, it	his, her, hers, its
	who	whom	whose
Third-person plural	they	them	their, theirs
	who	whom	whose

 Language note: Notice that English has different forms for subject and object pronouns, as shown in the previous chart. When using pronouns, pay attention to the gender and number of the antecedent as well as the position of the pronoun in the sentence.

Read the following sentence, and replace the underlined nouns with pronouns. Notice that all the pronouns are different.

When Andreas made an A on <u>Andreas's</u> final exam, <u>Andreas</u> was proud of

himself, and the teacher congratulated <u>Andreas</u>.

Subject Pronouns

Subject pronouns serve as the subject of a verb.

> *You* live next door to a coffee shop.
> *I* opened the door too quickly.

Object Pronouns

Object pronouns either receive the action of a verb or are part of a prepositional phrase.

Tip For a list of common prepositions, see page 339

Object of the verb	Jay gave *me* his watch.
Object of the preposition	Jay gave his watch to *me*.

Possessive Pronouns

Possessive pronouns show ownership. Some possessives come before a noun:

> Dave is *my* uncle.
> *My* new car is blue.

Other possessive pronouns replace both a possessive and the following noun:

> John's new car is red, but *mine* is blue.
> [[Mine = my new car]]

 Language note: The word *hers* is the second type of possessive: it replaces *her + a noun*. Do not use *hers* before plural nouns:

Incorrect	She cannot find hers shoes.
Correct	I found my shoes, but she cannot find hers.

Other Types of Pronouns

Intensive pronouns emphasize a noun or other pronoun. **Reflexive pronouns** are used when the performer of an action is also the receiver of the action. Both types of pronouns end in *-self* or *-selves*.

> Reflexive   He taught *himself* how to play the guitar.
>
> Intensive   The club members *themselves* have offered to support the initiative.

> Language note: The forms of the reflexive/intensive pronouns must be memorized. Note that the following forms are considered nonstandard: *hisself, theirself, theirselves, ourself.*

Relative pronouns refer to a noun already mentioned and introduce a group of words that describe this noun (*who, whom, whose, which, that*).

> Tomatoes, *which* are popular worldwide, were first grown in South America.

Tip Relative pronouns introduced adjective clauses. For more on adjective clauses, see pp. 526–527

Interrogative pronouns are used to begin questions (*who, whom, whose, which, what*).

> *What* did the senator say at the meeting?

Demonstrative pronouns specify which noun is being referred to (*this, these, that, those*).

> Use *this* simple budgeting app, not *that* complicated one.

Reciprocal pronouns refer to individuals when the antecedent is plural (*each other, one another*).

> My friend and I could not see *one another* in the crowd.

Three trouble spots make it difficult to know which type of pronoun to use: compound subjects and objects, comparisons, and sentences that need *who* or *whom*.

Pronouns Used with Compound Subjects and Objects

A **compound subject** has more than one subject joined by *and* or *or*. A **compound object** has more than one object joined by *and* or *or*.

Compound subject	*Chandler and I* worked on the project.
Compound object	My boss gave the assignment to *Chandler and me*.

Tip When you are writing about yourself and someone else, always put yourself after everyone else. *My friends and I went to a club,* not *I and my friends went to a club.*

To decide which type of pronoun to use in a compound construction, try leaving out the other part of the compound and the *and* or *or*. Then, say the sentence aloud to yourself.

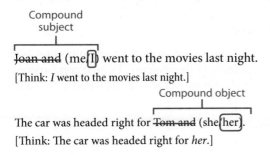

~~Joan and~~ (me/**I**) went to the movies last night.

[Think: *I* went to the movies last night.]

The car was headed right for ~~Tom and~~ (she/**her**).

[Think: The car was headed right for *her*.]

Tip Many people make the mistake of using *I* in the phrase *between you and I.* The correct pronoun with *between* is the object *me.*

If a pronoun is part of a compound object in a prepositional phrase, use an object pronoun.

I will keep that information just between you and (I/**me**).

[*Between you and me* is a prepositional phrase, so an object pronoun, *me*, is required.]

PRACTICE 20-5 **Editing Pronouns in Compound Constructions**

Correct any pronoun errors in the following sentences. If a sentence is already correct, write a "C" next to it.

Example: Marie Curie made several major contributions to science, but
in 1898, ~~her~~ she and her husband, Pierre Curie, announced their greatest achievement: the discovery of radium.

1. Before this discovery, the Curies understood that certain substances gave off rays of energy, but them and other scientists were just beginning to learn why and how.

2. Eventually, the Curies made a discovery that intrigued they and, soon afterward, hundreds of other researchers.

3. Two previously unknown elements, radium and polonium, were responsible for the extra radioactivity; fascinated by this finding, Marie Curie began thinking about the consequences of the work that she and her husband had done.

4. As them and other researchers were to discover, radium was especially valuable because it could be used in X-rays and for other medical purposes.

5. Marie Curie was deeply moved when, in 1903, the scientific community honored she and her husband with the Nobel Prize in physics.

Pronouns Used in Comparisons

Using the right type of pronoun in comparisons is particularly important because using the wrong type changes the meaning of the sentence. Editing comparisons can be tricky because they often imply words that are not actually included in the sentence.

> Bob trusts Donna more than *I*.

[This sentence means that Bob trusts Donna more than I trust her. The implied words are *trust her.*]

Tip To find comparisons, look for the word *than* or *as*.

> Bob trusts Donna more than *me*.

[This sentence means that Bob trusts Donna more than he trusts me. The implied words are *he trusts.*]

To decide whether to use a subject or object pronoun in a comparison, try adding the implied words and saying the sentence aloud.

Tip Add the additional words to the comparison when you speak and write. Then, others will not think you are incorrect.

The registrar is much more efficient than (us/we).
[Think: The registrar is much more efficient than *we are.*]
Susan rides her bicycle more than (he/him).
[Think: Susan rides her bicycle more than *he does.*]

Choosing between Who and Whom

Tip In the examples here, subjects are underlined, and verbs are double-underlined.

Who is always a subject; *whom* is always an object. If a pronoun performs an action, use the subject form *who*. If a pronoun does not perform an action, use the object form *whom*.

Who = **subject**   I would like to know *who* delivered this package.
Whom = **object**   He told me to *whom* I should report.

In sentences other than questions, when the pronoun (*who* or *whom*) is followed by a verb, use *who*. When the pronoun (*who* or *whom*) is followed by a noun or pronoun, use *whom*.

Tip *Whoever* is a subject pronoun; *whomever* is an object pronoun.

The pianist (who/whom) <u>played</u> was excellent.

[The pronoun is followed by the verb *played*. Use *who*.]

The pianist (who/whom) I <u>saw</u> was excellent.

[The pronoun is followed by another pronoun: *I*. Use *whom*.]

Make Pronouns Consistent in Person

Person is the point of view a writer uses—the perspective from which he or she writes. Pronouns may be in first person (*I* or *we*), second person (*you*), or third person (*he, she,* or *it*). (See the chart on p. 404)

Inconsistent	As soon as *a shopper* walks into the store, *you* can tell it is a weird place.
	[The sentence starts with the third person (*a shopper*) but shifts to the second person (*you*).]
Consistent, singular	As soon as *a shopper* walks into the store, *he* or *she* can tell it is a weird place.
Consistent, plural	As soon as *shoppers* walk into the store, *they* can tell it is a weird place.

Edit for Pronouns

> **PRACTICE 20-6** **Correcting Various Pronoun Problems**
>
> In the following sentences, find and correct problems with pronoun use. You may be able to revise some sentences in more than one way, and you may need to rewrite some sentences to correct errors.

Example: ~~Everyone with a busy schedule has~~ Students with busy schedules have probably been tempted to take shortcuts on their coursework.

1. My class received its term paper grades yesterday.

2. My friend Gene and me were shocked to see that he had gotten an F on his paper.

3. I usually get better grades than him, but he does not usually fail.

4. Mr. Padilla, the instructor, who most students consider strict but fair, scheduled an appointment with Gene.

5. When Gene went to the department office, they told him where to find Mr. Padilla.

6. Mr. Padilla told Gene that he did not think he had written the paper.

7. The paper it contained language that was unusual for Gene.

8. The instructor said that you could compare Gene's in-class writing with this paper and see differences.

9. Mr. Padilla, whom had typed some passages from Gene's paper into a search engine, found two online papers containing sentences that were also in Gene's paper.

10. Gene told Mr. Padilla that he had made a terrible mistake.

11. Gene told my girlfriend and I later that he did not realize that borrowing sentences from online sources was plagiarism.

12. We looked at the paper, and you could tell that parts of it did not sound like Gene's writing.

13. Anyone doing Internet research must be especially careful to document their sources, as Gene now knows.

14. The department decided that they would not suspend Gene from school.

15. Mr. Padilla will let Gene take the class again and will help him avoid accidental plagiarism, and Gene said that no one had ever been more relieved than him to hear that news.

Tip For more information on using sources and avoiding plagiarism, see the Appendix.

PRACTICE 20-7 Editing Paragraphs for Pronoun Problems

Find and correct seven errors in pronoun use in the following paragraphs.

    Ask anyone who has moved to a city, and they will tell you: at first, life can feel pretty lonely. Fortunately, it is possible to make friends just about anywhere. One good strategy is to get involved in a group that interests you, such as a sports team or arts club. In many cases, a local baseball team or theater group will open their arms to new talent. Joining in on practices, games, or performances is a great way to build friendships with others whom have interests like yours. Also, most community organizations are always in need of volunteers. It is a great way to form new friendships while doing something positive for society.

Getting a pet or gardening, it is another great way to meet new people. In many cities, you can walk down the street for a long time and never be greeted by another person. If you are walking a dog, though, it is likely that others will say hello. Some may even stop to talk with you and pet your dog. Also, gardeners tend to draw other gardeners. If you are planting flowers and other flower growers stop by to chat, them and you will have plenty to talk about.

To sum up, newcomers to any city do not have to spend all their nights alone in front of the TV. You have plenty of opportunities to get out and feel more connected.

Chapter Review

1. What are pronouns?

2. What is pronoun agreement?

3. What is an ambiguous pronoun reference?

4. What are three types of pronouns?

5. What are three trouble spots in pronoun use?

Reflect and Apply

1. What grammar concepts in this chapter were new to you?

2. Analyze a paragraph from your own writing: identify pronouns and their antecedents, checking for agreement, consistency, and clarity. What problems or patterns do you notice?

3. Suppose you read the following sentence during a peer review exercise. What would you say to the writer? Why?

   After a few weeks, the teacher who we liked the most threw a party for the rest of the students and I.

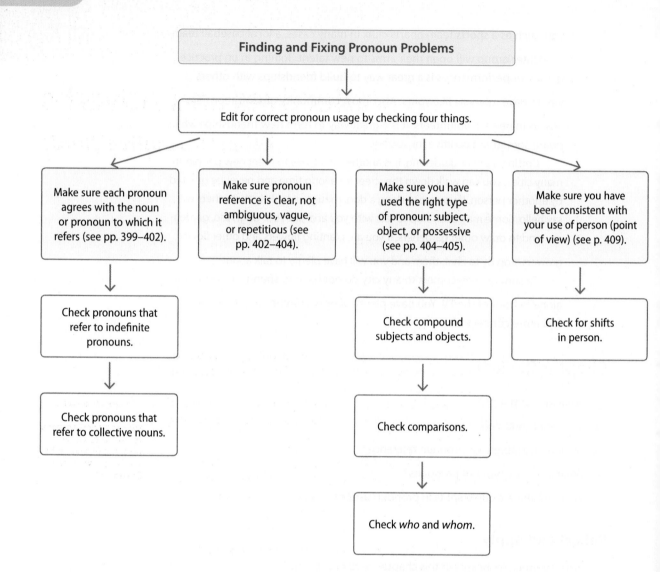

Finding and Fixing Pronoun Problems

↓

Edit for correct pronoun usage by checking four things.

Make sure each pronoun agrees with the noun or pronoun to which it refers (see pp. 399–402).

Make sure pronoun reference is clear, not ambiguous, vague, or repetitious (see pp. 402–404).

Make sure you have used the right type of pronoun: subject, object, or possessive (see pp. 404–405).

Make sure you have been consistent with your use of person (point of view) (see p. 409).

Check pronouns that refer to indefinite pronouns.

Check compound subjects and objects.

Check for shifts in person.

Check pronouns that refer to collective nouns.

Check comparisons.

Check *who* and *whom*.

Adjectives and Adverbs

Using Descriptive Words

Understand What Adjectives and Adverbs Are

Adjectives describe or modify nouns (words that name people, places, things, or ideas) and pronouns (words that replace nouns). They add information about *what kind, which one,* or *how many.*

Consider the following sentences from Amy Tan's narrative "Fish Cheeks" (p. 121). In each sentence, the adjectives are in italics, and the nouns that these adjectives describe are in bold.

> The kitchen was littered with *appalling* **mounds** of *raw* **food**: a *slimy* **rock cod** with *bulging* **eyes** that pleaded not to be thrown into a pan of *hot* **oil**. Tofu, which looked like *stacked* **wedges** of *rubbery white* **sponges**. A bowl soaking *dried* **fungus** back to life.

 Language note: In English, adjectives do not indicate whether the words they describe are singular or plural.

Incorrect	The three babies are *adorables.*
	[The word *adorables* should not end in *-s.*]
Correct	The three babies are *adorable.*

Adverbs describe or modify verbs (words that tell what happens in a sentence), adjectives, or other adverbs. They add information about *how, how much, how often, when, where, why,* or *to what extent.*

Look at the following sentences from Stephanie Ericsson's essay, "The Ways We Lie" (p. 211). The adverbs are underlined.

Tip To understand this chapter on adjectives and adverbs, you need to know what nouns and verbs are. For a review, see Chapter 15.

I discovered that telling the truth all the time is <u>nearly</u> impossible.

As I said <u>earlier</u>, it's not easy to <u>entirely</u> eliminate lies from our lives.

The new diocese was aware of Father Porter's obsession with children, but they needed priests and <u>recklessly</u> believed treatment had cured him.

Adverbs that answer the question "how often" are called adverbs of frequency. Adverbs that answer the question "how" are called adverbs of manner. Pay attention to the placement of these adverbs.

Adverbs of frequency

Verb	Position
Be	After the verb.
	The teacher is usually early.
Other verbs	Before the verb.
	The teacher usually starts class at 9:30.

Special adverbs of frequency

Adverbs	Verb	Position
sometimes usually often	Any verb	Beginning or end of the sentence.
		Sometimes, the teacher is late.
		The teacher forgets her notes sometimes.
never rarely seldom	Any verb	These adverbs can occur at the beginning of the sentence, but they trigger question word order.
		Never have I seen such devastation.
		Rarely do I come home before 11:00 p.m.

Adverb of manner

Verb	Position
Any verb	Before or after the verb.
	Beginning or end of the sentence.
	John quickly ran to the office.
	John ran quickly to the office.
	Quickly, John ran to the office.
	John ran to the office quickly.

Adjectives usually come before the words they modify; adverbs come before or after. You can use more than one adjective or adverb to modify a word.

 Language note: The *-ed* and *-ing* forms of verbs can be used as adjectives. Common examples include *bored/boring, confused/confusing, excited/exciting,* and *interested/interesting*. Sometimes, these forms can cause confusion. Usually, the *-ed* form describes a person's reaction, whereas the *-ing* form describes the thing that causes the reaction.

Incorrect	Some students are interesting in their grammar classes.
Correct	Some students are interested in their grammar classes.
Correct	Grammar classes can be quite interesting for students.
	Some students find their grammar classes interesting.

Use Adjectives and Adverbs Correctly

How and when to use adjectives and adverbs depends on the words you are describing and whether you are making a comparison.

Choosing between Adjectives and Adverbs

Many adverbs are formed by adding *-ly* to the end of an adjective.

Adjective	Adverb
She received a *quick* answer.	Her sister answered *quickly*.
Our *new* neighbors just got married.	The couple is *newly* married.
That is an *honest* answer.	Please answer *honestly*.

To decide whether to use an adjective or an adverb, find the word being described. If that word is a noun or pronoun, use an adjective. If it is a verb, adjective, or another adverb, use an adverb.

PRACTICE 21-1   **Choosing between Adjectives and Adverbs**

In each sentence, underline the word in the sentence that is being described or modified. Then, circle the correct word in parentheses.

Example: People are (common/commonly) aware that smoking causes health risks.

1. Many smokers are (stubborn/stubbornly) about refusing to quit.

2. Others who are thinking about quitting may decide (sudden/suddenly) that the damage from smoking has already been done.

3. In such cases, the (typical/typically) smoker sees no reason to stop.

4. The news about secondhand smoke may have made some smokers stop (quick/quickly) to save the health of their families.

5. Research now shows that pet lovers who smoke can have a (terrible/terribly) effect on their cats.

Using Adjectives and Adverbs in Comparisons

To compare two people, places, or things, use the **comparative** form of adjectives or adverbs. Comparisons often use the word *than*.

> Carol ran *faster* than I did.
>
> Johan is *more intelligent* than his sister.

To compare three or more people, places, or things, use the **superlative** form of adjectives or adverbs.

> Carol ran the *fastest* of all the women runners.
>
> Johan is the *most intelligent* of the five children.

If an adjective or adverb is short (one syllable), add the endings *-er* to form the comparative and *-est* to form the superlative. Also use this pattern for adjectives that end in *-y* (but change the *-y* to *-i* before adding *-er* or *-est*).

For all other adjectives and adverbs, add the word *more* to make the comparative and the word *most* to make the superlative.

Forming Comparatives and Superlatives

Adjective or adverb	Comparative	Superlative
Adjectives and adverbs of one syllable		
tall	taller	tallest
fast	faster	fastest
Adjectives ending in -y		
happy	happier	happiest
silly	sillier	silliest
Other adjectives and adverbs		
graceful	more graceful	most graceful
gracefully	more gracefully	most gracefully
intelligent	more intelligent	most intelligent
intelligently	more intelligently	most intelligently

Use either an ending (*-er* or *-est*) or an extra word (*more* or *most*) to form a comparative or superlative—not both at once.

This park is known for the ~~most~~ greatest hiking trails.

Using Good, Well, Bad, *and* Badly

Four common adjectives and adverbs have irregular forms: *good, well, bad,* and *badly.*

Forming Irregular Comparatives and Superlatives

	Comparative	Superlative
Adjective		
good	better	best
bad	worse	worst
Adverb		
well	better	best
badly	worse	worst

People often get confused about whether to use *good* or *well*. *Good* is an adjective, so use it to describe a noun or pronoun. *Well* is an adverb, so use it to describe a verb or an adjective.

Adjective   She has a *good* job.

Adverb   He works *well* with his colleagues.

Well can also be an adjective to describe someone's health: I am not *well* today.

Edit for Adjectives and Adverbs

PRACTICE 21–2   **Editing Paragraphs for Correct Adjectives and Adverbs**

Find and correct seven adjective and adverb errors in the following paragraphs.

Every day, many people log on to play one of the popularest computer games of all time, *World of Warcraft*. This multiplayer game was first introduced by Blizzard Entertainment in 1994, and it grew quick after that. More than 12 million users played at its height in 2010; over 5 million players still participate, according to the recentest figures.

Computer game experts call *World of Warcraft* a "massively multiplayer online role-playing game," or MMORPG for short. Players of this game select a realm in which to play. They choose from among four differently realms. Each realm has its own set of rules and even its own language. Players also choose if they want to be members of the Alliance or the Horde, which are groups that oppose each other. Each side tends to think that it is gooder than the other one.

In *World of Warcraft,* questing is one of the funnest activities. Questing players undertake special missions or tasks to earn experience and gold. The goal is to trade these earnings for better skills and equipment.

Players must proceed careful to stay in the game and increase their overall power and abilities.

Read to Write
Choose an article from an online newspaper or other source, print it, and find all the adjectives and adverbs, drawing arrows from the modifiers to the words they modify.

Chapter Review

1. What are adjectives?

2. What are adverbs?

3. What is one way to form adverbs from adjectives?

4. What is the comparative form of adjectives and adverbs? How is it used?

5. What is the superlative form of adjectives and adverbs? How is it used?

Reflect and Apply

1. What grammar concepts in this chapter were new to you?

2. Linguist Ben Yagoda wrote a book called *If You Catch an Adjective, Kill It.* The title refers to common writing advice: don't use too many adjectives and adverbs. Instead, use strong nouns and verbs.

   a. Analyze a paragraph from your own writing: identify adjectives and adverbs. Do you notice any patterns of mistakes? How often do you use adjectives and adverbs?

b. You notice the following sentence in a draft during peer review. What would you suggest to the writer?

The kind old gentleman walked cautiously and slowly up the icy, ancient steps towards the city's famous library, ignoring the frightening power of the arctic winds and heavy, wet snow.

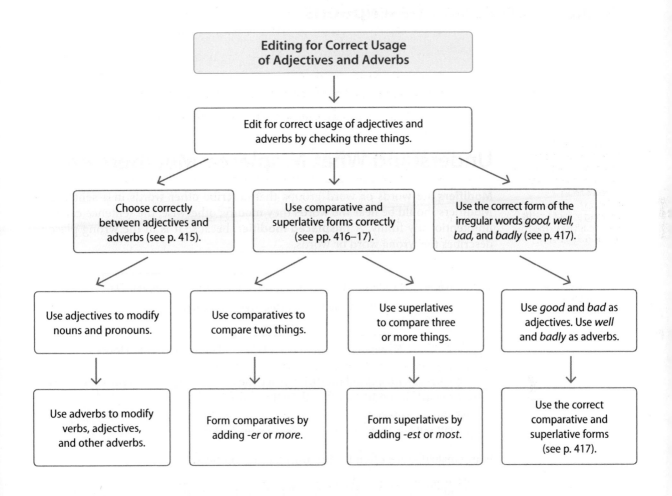

22

Misplaced and Dangling Modifiers

Avoiding Confusing Descriptions

Understand What Misplaced Modifiers Are

Modifiers are words or word groups that describe other words in a sentence. Modifiers should be near the words they modify; otherwise, the sentence can be unintentionally funny. A **misplaced modifier**, because it is in the wrong place, describes the wrong word or words.

Tip For a review of basic sentence elements, see Chapter 15.

Misplaced   Linda saw the White House *flying over Washington, D.C.*

[Was the White House flying over Washington?]

Clear   *Flying over Washington, D.C.,* Linda saw the White House.

To correct a misplaced modifier, place the modifier as close as possible to the word or words it modifies, often directly before it.

Wearing my bathrobe,
I went outside to get the paper. ~~wearing my bathrobe.~~

Four constructions often lead to misplaced modifiers.

1. Modifiers such as *only, almost, hardly, nearly,* and *just.* These words need to be immediately before—not just close to—the words or phrases they modify.

only
I ~~only~~ found two old photos in the drawer.

[The intended meaning is that just two photos were in the drawer.]

almost
Joanne ~~almost~~ ate the whole cake.

[Joanne actually ate; she did not "almost" eat.]

420

nearly
Thomas ~~nearly~~ spent 2 hours waiting for the bus.
^
[Thomas spent close to 2 hours waiting; he did not "nearly" spend them.]

2. Modifiers that are prepositional phrases.

from the cash register
The cashier found money on the floor. ~~from the cash register.~~
^   ^

in plastic cups
Jen served punch to the seniors. ~~in plastic cups.~~
^   ^

3. Modifiers that start with *-ing* verbs.

Using jumper cables,
Darlene started the car. ~~using jumper cables.~~
^   ^
[The car was not using jumper cables; Darlene was.]

Wearing flip-flops,
Javier climbed the mountain. ~~wearing flip-flops.~~
^   ^
[The mountain was not wearing flip-flops; Javier was.]

4. Modifier clauses that start with *who, whose, that,* or *which.*

that was infecting my hard drive
Joel found the computer virus attached to an email message. ~~that was infecting~~
^   ^
~~my hard drive.~~
[The email did not infect the hard drive; the virus did.]

who was crying
The baby on the bus ~~who was crying~~ had curly hair.
^
[The bus was not crying; the baby was.]

Practice Correcting Misplaced Modifiers

PRACTICE 22–1   **Correcting Misplaced Modifiers**

Find and correct misplaced modifiers in the following sentences.

only
Example: I write things in my blog that I used to ~~only~~ tell my best friends.
^

1. I used to write about all kinds of personal things and private observations in a diary.

2. Now, I nearly write the same things in my blog.

3. Any story might show up in my blog that is entertaining.

4. The video I was making was definitely something I wanted to write about in my blog of my cousin Tim's birthday.

5. I had invited to the birthday party my loudest, wildest friends wanting the video to be funny.

6. We jumped off tables, had mock swordfights, and almost used ten cans of whipped cream in a food fight.

7. Unfortunately, the battery in the smartphone died that I was using to make the video.

8. I told my friends that I would write a blog post about the party anyway apologizing to them.

9. I explained how I would include the funny story about the failed video session in the blog post.

10. My friends hardly said that they could wait until we tried again to make the video.

dangle: to swing loosely, not tightly attached

Understand What Dangling Modifiers Are

A **dangling modifier** "dangles" because the word or word group it modifies is not in the sentence. Dangling modifiers usually appear at the beginning of a sentence and seem to modify the noun or pronoun that immediately follows them, but they are really modifying another word or group of words.

Dangling	*Rushing to class,* the books fell out of my bag.
	[The books were not rushing to class.]
Clear	*Rushing to class,* I dropped my books.

There are two basic ways to correct dangling modifiers. Use the one that makes more sense. One way is to add the word being modified immediately after the opening modifier so that the connection between the two is clear.

                             I   on my bike
Trying to eat a hot dog, ~~my bike~~ swerved.
                            ^   ^

Another way is to add the word being modified in the opening modifier itself.

    While I was trying
~~Trying~~ to eat a hot dog, my bike swerved.
    ^

Practice Correcting Dangling Modifiers

> **PRACTICE 22–2**   **Correcting Dangling Modifiers**

Find and correct any dangling modifiers in the following sentences. If a sentence is correct, write a "C" next to it. It may be necessary to add new words or ideas to some sentences.

Example: ~~Inviting~~ *Because I had invited* my whole family to dinner, the kitchen was filled with all kinds of food.

1. Preparing a big family dinner, the oven suddenly stopped working.

2. In a panic, we searched for Carmen, who can solve any problem.

3. Trying to help, the kitchen was crowded.

4. Looking into the oven, the turkey was not done.

5. Discouraged, the dinner was about to be canceled.

6. Staring out the window, a pizza truck went by.

7. Using a credit card, Carmen ordered six pizzas.

8. With one quick phone call, six large pizzas solved our problem.

9. Returning to the crowd in the kitchen, family members still surrounded the oven.

10. Delighted with Carmen's decision, cheers filled the room.

Edit for Misplaced and Dangling Modifiers

> **PRACTICE 23–3**   **Editing Paragraphs for Misplaced and Dangling Modifiers**

Find and correct any misplaced or dangling modifiers in the following paragraphs.

Carrying overfilled backpacks is a common habit, but not necessarily a good one. Bulging with books, water bottles, and sports equipment and weighing an average of fourteen to eighteen pounds, students' backs can gradually become damaged. Because they have to plan ahead for the whole day and often need books, extra clothes, and on-the-go meals, backpacks get heavier and heavier. An increasing number of medical professionals, primarily physical therapists, are seeing young people with chronic back problems.

Researchers have recently invented a new type of backpack from the University of Pennsylvania and the Marine Biological Laboratory. Designed with springs, the backpack moves up and down as a person walks. This new backpack creates energy, which is then collected and transferred to an electrical generator. Experiencing relief from the wear and tear on muscles, the springs make the pack more comfortable.

What is the purpose of the electricity generated by these new backpacks? Needing electricity for their night-vision goggles, the backpacks could solve a problem for soldiers. Soldiers could benefit from such an efficient energy source to power their global positioning systems and other electronic gear. Instead of being battery operated, the soldiers could use the special backpacks and would not have to carry additional batteries. For the average student, these backpacks might one day provide convenient energy for video games, television, and music players, all at the same time. Designed with this technology, kids would just have to look both ways before crossing the street.

Read to Write
Choose a paragraph from a reading. Circle each modifier in the paragraph, and draw an arrow to show what word or words the modifier describes.

Chapter Review

1. What is a modifier?

2. What is a misplaced modifier?

3. What is a dangling modifier?

4. What are four situations that can lead to misplaced modifiers?

Reflect and Apply

1. What grammar concepts in this chapter were new to you?

2. Analyze a paragraph from your own writing: what kinds of modifiers do you use? Which of the four situations described on pages 420–421 is most likely to occur in your writing? Do you have any misplaced or dangling modifiers?

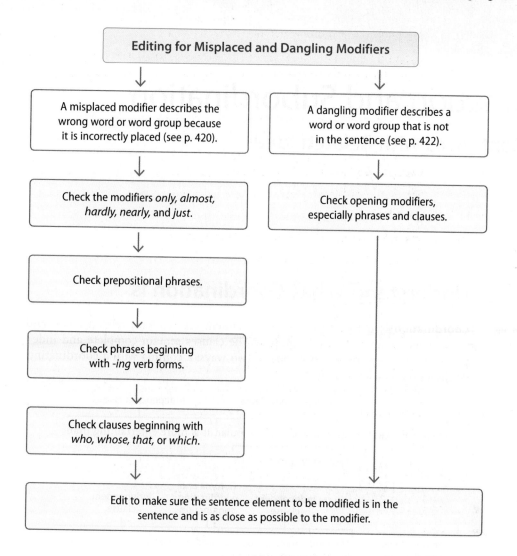

Editing for Misplaced and Dangling Modifiers

A misplaced modifier describes the wrong word or word group because it is incorrectly placed (see p. 420).

A dangling modifier describes a word or word group that is not in the sentence (see p. 422).

Check the modifiers *only, almost, hardly, nearly,* and *just.*

Check opening modifiers, especially phrases and clauses.

Check prepositional phrases.

Check phrases beginning with *-ing* verb forms.

Check clauses beginning with *who, whose, that,* or *which.*

Edit to make sure the sentence element to be modified is in the sentence and is as close as possible to the modifier.

23

Coordination and Subordination
Joining Sentences with Related Ideas

Understand What Coordination Is

Tip To understand this chapter, you need to be familiar with basic sentence elements. For a review, see Chapter 15.

Coordination is used to join two independent clauses with related ideas, and it can make your writing less choppy. The clauses remain complete and independent, but they are joined in one of two ways: a comma with a coordinating conjunction or a semicolon.

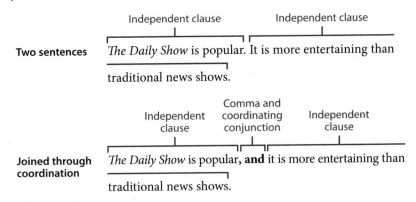

Practice Using Coordination

Using Coordinating Conjunctions

Conjunctions join words, phrases, or clauses. **Coordinating conjunctions** join ideas of equal importance. (You can remember them by thinking of **FANBOYS**—*for, and, nor, but, or, yet, so.*) To join two sentences through coordination, put a comma and one of these conjunctions between the sentences. Choose the conjunction that makes the most sense for the meaning of the two sentences.

Independent clause	, for , and , nor , but , or , yet , so	Independent clause

Tip For more on the use of commas, see Chapter 30.

Wikipedia is a popular encyclopedia	, for [*For* indicates a reason or cause.]	it is easily available online.
The encyclopedia is open to all	, and [*And* simply joins two ideas.]	anyone can add information to it.
Often, inaccurate entries cannot be stopped	, nor [*Nor* indicates addition of another negative idea.]	is there any penalty for them.
People have complained about errors	, but [*But* indicates a contrast.]	the mistakes may or may not be fixed.
Some people delete information	, or [*Or* indicates alternatives.]	they add their own interpretations.
Many people know that Wikipedia is flawed	, yet [*Yet* indicates a contrast or possibility.]	they continue to use it.
Wikipedia now has trustees	, so [*So* indicates a result.]	perhaps it will be monitored more closely.

 Language note: *Nor* has an interesting effect on the independent clause that follows it. In that clause, the word order changes: an auxiliary verb comes before the subject. This is called subject-verb inversion, similar to the word order in questions.

PRACTICE 23–1   **Combining Sentences with Coordinating Conjunctions**

Combine each pair of sentences into a single sentence by using a comma and a coordinating conjunction. In some cases, there may be more than one correct answer.

Example: In business, emails can make a good or bad impression. ~~People~~ *, so people* should mind their email manners.

1. Many professionals use email to keep in touch with clients and contacts. They must be especially careful not to offend anyone with their email messages.

2. However, anyone who uses email should be cautious. It is dangerously easy to send messages to the wrong person.

3. Employees may have time to send personal messages from work. They should remember that employers often have the ability to read their workers' messages.

4. R-rated language and jokes may be deleted automatically by a company's server. They may be read by managers and cause problems for the employee sending or receiving them.

5. No message should be forwarded to everyone in a sender's address book. Senders should ask permission before adding someone to a mass-mailing list.

6. People should check the authenticity of mailings about lost children, dreadful diseases, and terrorist threats before passing them on. Most such messages are hoaxes.

7. Typographical errors and misspellings in email make the message appear less professional. Using all capital letters—a practice known as *shouting*—is usually considered even worse.

8. People who use email for business want to be taken seriously. They should make their emails as professional as possible.

Using Semicolons

A **semicolon** is a punctuation mark that can join two independent clauses through coordination. Use semicolons *only* when the ideas in the two sentences are closely related.

Independent clause	;	Independent clause

Antarctica is a mystery	;	few people know much about it.
Its climate is extreme	;	few people want to endure it.
My cousin went there	;	he loves to explore the unknown.

A semicolon alone does not tell readers much about the relationship between the two ideas. To give more information about the relationship, use a **conjunctive adverb** after the semicolon. Put a comma after the conjunctive adverb.

Tip You may also use a conjunctive adverb at the beginning of a sentence. In this case, it is still followed by a comma.

Independent clause	; also, ; as a result, ; besides, ; furthermore, ; however, ; in addition, ; in fact, ; instead, ; moreover, ; still, ; then, ; therefore,	Independent clause

Antarctica is largely unexplored	; as a result,	it is unpopulated.
It receives little rain	; also,	it is incredibly cold.
It is a huge area	; therefore,	scientists are becoming more interested in it.

PRACTICE 23–2   **Combining Sentences with Semicolons and Conjunctive Adverbs**

Combine each pair of sentences by using a semicolon and a conjunctive adverb. In some cases, there may be more than one correct answer.

Example: More and more people are researching their family history or
                                       ; in *fact, this*
               genealogy. ~~This~~ type of research is now considered one of the
                         ^
               fastest-growing hobbies in North America.

1. Before the Internet, genealogy researchers had to contact public offices to get records of ancestors' births, marriages, occupations, and deaths. Some visited libraries to search for old newspaper articles mentioning the ancestors.

2. There was no quick and easy way to search records or article databases. With the rise of the Internet and new digital tools, genealogy research has become much simpler.

3. These tools allow people to search a wide range of records with key words. Researchers can gather details about their ancestors' lives much more quickly and efficiently.

4. Recently, people have started using social-networking tools to find out about living and dead relatives. Some of them are getting more information even more quickly.

5. One researcher, Lauren Axelrod, used Ancestry.com to gather some information on the birth mother of her husband, who had been adopted. Using this information, she searched for his birth mother on Facebook.

6. The entire search, which ended successfully, took only 2 hours. In less than a week, Axelrod's husband was talking on the phone with his birth mother.

7. Not everyone thinks that genealogy research has to be a purely serious hobby. Some people see it as a great way to have fun.

8. In the online Family Village Game, players create characters, or avatars, representing their ancestors. Using genealogical records, they add background information on these ancestors.

9. Players have a lot of fun creating the characters and their worlds. They get additional genealogical information by following the research suggestions provided by the game.

10. Some parents play Family Village Game with their children. The children see their connection to the past.

Understand What Subordination Is

Like coordination, **subordination** is a way to combine clauses with related ideas into a longer sentence. In fact, writers often use subordination to avoid too many short, choppy sentences. With subordination, you put a dependent word (such as *after*, *although*, *because*, or *when*) in front of one of the clauses, which then becomes a dependent clause.

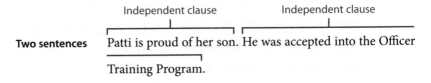

Two sentences   Patti is proud of her son. He was accepted into the Officer Training Program.

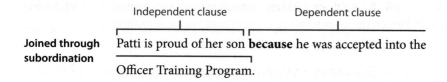

Independent clause   Dependent clause

Joined through   Patti is proud of her son **because** he was accepted into the
subordination   Officer Training Program.

Practice Using Subordination

To join two sentences through subordination, use a **subordinating conjunction**. Choose the conjunction that makes the most sense with the two sentences. Here are some of the most common subordinating conjunctions.

Independent clause		Dependent clause

after	now that
although	once
as	since
as if	so that
because	unless
before	until
even if/	when
though	whenever
if	where
if only	while

I love music   because   it makes me relax.

It is hard to study at home   when   my children want my attention.

When a dependent clause ends a sentence, it usually does not need to be preceded by a comma unless it is showing a contrast.

When the dependent clause begins a sentence, use a comma to separate it from the rest of the sentence.

Subordinating conjunction		Dependent clause		,		Independent Clause

When   I eat out   ,   I usually have steak.

Although   it is harmful   ,   young people still smoke.

Language note: *So that* is a subordinating conjunction that shows a purpose. Writers sometimes omit the word *that*:

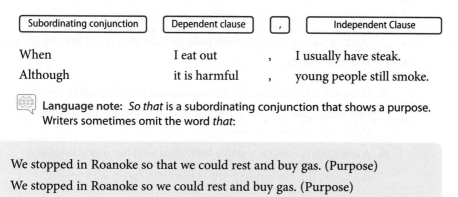

We stopped in Roanoke so that we could rest and buy gas. (Purpose)

We stopped in Roanoke so we could rest and buy gas. (Purpose)

Don't confuse *so (that)* with the coordinating conjunction *so*, which shows a result. Notice the coordinating conjunction requires a comma:

We stopped in Roanoke, so we did not arrive on time. (Result)

> **PRACTICE 23-3** **Combining Sentences through Subordination**

Combine each pair of sentences into a single sentence by using an appropriate subordinating conjunction either at the beginning of or between the two sentences. Use a conjunction that makes sense with the two sentences, and add commas where necessary.

Example: More schools and educators are interested in second language acquisition and teaching techniques. ~~Many~~ *because many* immigrant students are arriving in their classrooms with different levels of English proficiency.

1. A student speaks a language other than English at home. The student is usually classified as an ESL (English as a second language), EAL (English as another language), LEP (limited English proficiency), or ELL (English language learning) student.

2. Some students feel they are treated unfairly. They are given these labels.

3. Other schools place students in "bilingual education" courses. The schools can celebrate the students' ability to speak two languages, not their differences from other students.

4. One important purpose of bilingual education courses is to help students acquire, strong skills in English. English is not the only focus in these courses.

5. Linguists do not know everything about a bilingual mind. They know that a bilingual speaker is not two separate monolingual people in one body.

6. A bilingual speaker is a single individual who has many language resources she can employ. She is communicating with others.

7. In fact, a bilingual person communicates. He is not turning one language off and the other one on.

8. Linguists have data from many studies of language learners. Researchers are focused on the ability of bilingual speakers (or multilingual speakers) to use multiple language resources at one time, an ability they call *translanguaging*.

9. Linguists and teachers did not understand the benefits of translanguaging. They demanded in the past that students use only English in the classroom.

10. Experts believe there are situations that require the use of English. Many educators are looking for ways to encourage translanguaging in their classrooms.

PRACTICE 23–4   **Combining Sentences through Coordination and Subordination**

Join each of the following sentence pairs in two ways, first by coordination and then by subordination.

Example: Rick has many talents. He is still deciding what to do with his life.

Joined by coordination: Rick has many talents, but he is still deciding what to do with his life.

Joined by subordination: Although Rick has many talents, he is still deciding what to do with his life.

1. Rick rides a unicycle. He can juggle four oranges.
   Joined by coordination:

   Joined by subordination:

2. A trapeze school opened in our town. Rick signed up immediately.
   Joined by coordination:

   Joined by subordination:

3. Rick is now at the top of his class. He worked hard practicing trapeze routines.
   Joined by coordination:

   Joined by subordination:

4. Rick asks me for career advice. I try to be encouraging.
   Joined by coordination:

   Joined by subordination:

5. He does not want to join the circus. He could study entertainment management.
   Joined by coordination:

   Joined by subordination:

Edit for Coordination and Subordination

PRACTICE 23–5   **Editing Paragraphs for Coordination and Subordination**

In the following paragraphs, combine the six pairs of underlined sentences. For three of the sentence pairs, use coordination. For the other three sentence pairs, use subordination. Do not forget to punctuate correctly, and keep in mind that there may be more than one way to combine each sentence pair.

Washington, DC, was the first city in the United States to offer a public bicycle-sharing program. The idea has been popular in Europe for years. In fact, Paris has more than twenty thousand bikes available for people to rent and ride around the city. Called Capital Bikeshare, the Washington program costs citizens $8 a day, $28 a month, or $85 a year to join. For that fee, they have access to more than 3,700 bikes available at 440 stations set up all over Washington, as well as Arlington, Alexandria, and Fairfax, Virginia, and Montgomery County, Maryland. After using the bikes, people must return them to one of the stations. Other riders might be waiting for one. Regular users have come to depend on Capital Bikeshare for short trips and errands. The popularity of the program is growing.

Throughout the United States, cycling has become much more popular in recent years. Gasoline prices have fluctuated. A number of other cities are now considering bike-sharing programs. Studies show that these programs can reduce city traffic by 4 to 5 percent. Some companies are already creating similar programs to encourage their employees to exercise more and drive less. Company leaders are aware that fit employees and a healthier environment are important goals to achieve. It means that the company spends a little extra time, money, and effort to start and run a bike-sharing program.

Chapter Review

1. What are the two ways to join independent clauses through coordination?
2. When can a semicolon be used to join independent clauses?
3. What is subordination?
4. Why do writers use coordination and subordination?

Reflect and Apply

1. What grammar concepts in this chapter were new to you?
2. Analyze a paragraph from your own writing: do you use both coordination and subordination?
3. Look at several paragraphs from a textbook from a course in your major. What do you notice about the use of coordination and subordination?

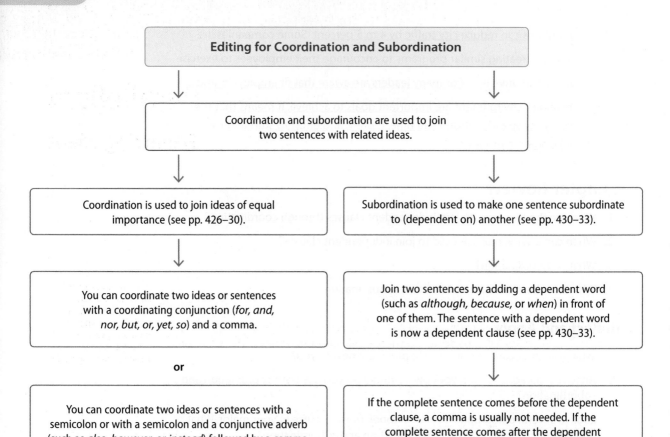

24

Parallelism

Balancing Ideas

Understand What Parallelism Is

Parallelism in writing means that similar parts in a sentence have the same structure: their parts are balanced. Use nouns with nouns, verbs with verbs, and phrases with phrases.

Tip To understand this chapter, you need to be familiar with basic sentence elements, such as nouns and verbs. For a review, see Chapter 15.

Not parallel	I enjoy <u>basketball</u> more than <u>playing video games</u>.
	[*Basketball* is a noun, but *playing video games* is a phrase.]
Parallel	I enjoy <u>basketball</u> more than <u>video games</u>.
Parallel	I enjoy <u>playing basketball</u> more than <u>playing video games</u>.
Not parallel	Last night, I <u>worked</u>, <u>studied</u>, and <u>was watching</u> television.
	[Verbs must be in the same tense to be parallel. *Was watching* has a different structure from *worked* and *studied*.]
Parallel	Last night, I <u>worked</u>, <u>studied</u>, and <u>watched</u> television.
Parallel	Last night, I was <u>working</u>, <u>studying</u>, and <u>watching</u> television.
Not parallel	This weekend, we can go <u>to the beach</u> or <u>walking in the mountains</u>.
	[*To the beach* should be paired with another prepositional phrase: *to the mountains*.]
Parallel	This weekend, we can go <u>to the beach</u> or <u>to the mountains</u>.

Practice Writing Parallel Sentences

Parallelism in Pairs and Lists

When two or more items in a series are joined by *and* or *or,* use a similar form for each item.

Not parallel	The professor assigned <u>readings</u>, <u>practices to do</u>, and <u>a paper</u>.
Parallel	The professor assigned <u>readings</u>, <u>practices</u>, and <u>a paper</u>.

Not parallel	The story was <u>in the newspaper</u>, <u>on the radio</u>, and <u>the television</u>.
	[*In the newspaper* and *on the radio* are prepositional phrases. *The television* is not.]
Parallel	The story was <u>in the newspaper</u>, <u>on the radio</u>, and <u>on the television</u>.

> **PRACTICE 24–1**   **Using Parallelism in Pairs and Lists**

In each sentence, underline the parts of the sentence that should be parallel. Then, edit the sentence to make it parallel.

Example: Coyotes roam the <u>western mountains</u>, the <u>central plains</u>, and
suburbs.
~~they are in the suburbs of~~ the East Coast ~~of the United States.~~

1. Wild predators, such as wolves, are vanishing because people hunt them and are taking over their land.

2. Coyotes are surviving and they do well in the United States.

3. The success of the coyote is due to its varied diet and adapting easily.

4. Coyotes are sometimes vegetarians, sometimes scavengers, and sometimes they hunt.

5. Today, they are spreading and populate the East Coast for the first time.

6. The coyotes' appearance surprises and is worrying many people.

7. The animals have chosen an area that is more populated and it's not as wild as their traditional home.

8. Coyotes can adapt to rural, suburban, and even living in a city.

9. One coyote was identified, tracked, and they captured him in Central Park in New York City.

10. Suburbanites are getting used to the sight of coyotes and hearing them.

Parallelism in Comparisons

Comparisons often use the word *than* or *as*. When you edit for parallelism, make sure the items on either side of those words have parallel structures.

Not parallel	<u>Taking the bus</u> downtown is as fast as <u>the drive</u> there.
Parallel	<u>Taking the bus</u> downtown is as fast as <u>driving</u> there.

Not parallel	<u>To admit a mistake</u> is better than <u>denying it</u>.
Parallel	<u>To admit a mistake</u> is better than <u>to deny it</u>.
	<u>Admitting a mistake</u> is better than <u>denying it</u>.

Sometimes you need to add or delete a word or two to make the parts of a sentence parallel.

Not parallel	<u>A tour package</u> is less expensive than <u>arranging every travel detail yourself</u>.
Parallel, word added	<u>*Buying* a tour package</u> is less expensive than <u>arranging every travel detail yourself</u>.

Not parallel	The <u>sale price</u> of the shoes is as low as <u>paying half of the regular price</u>.
Parallel, words dropped	The <u>sale price</u> of the shoes is as low as <u>half of the regular price</u>.

PRACTICE 24-2   Using Parallelism in Comparisons

In each sentence, underline the parts of the sentence that should be parallel. Then, edit the sentence to make it parallel.

Example: <u>Leasing</u> a new car may be less expensive than <s>to buy</s> ^buying^ one.

1. Car dealers often require less money down for leasing a car than for the purchase of one.

2. The monthly payments for a leased car may be as low as paying for a loan.

3. You should check the terms of leasing to make sure they are as favorable as to buy.

4. You may find that to lease is a safer bet than buying.

5. You will be making less of a financial commitment by leasing a car than to own it.

6. Buying a car may be better than a lease on one if you plan to keep it for several years.

7. A used car can be more economical than getting a new one.

8. However, maintenance of a new car may be easier than taking care of a used car.

9. A used car may not be as impressive as buying a brand-new vehicle.

10. To get a used car from a reputable source can be a better decision than a new vehicle that loses value the moment you drive it home.

Parallelism with Certain Paired Words

Certain paired words, called **correlative conjunctions**, link two equal elements and show the relationship between them. Here are the paired words:

both . . . and	neither . . . nor	rather . . . than
either . . . or	not only . . . but also	

Make sure the items joined by these paired words are parallel.

Not parallel	Bruce wants *both* <u>freedom</u> *and* <u>to be wealthy</u>.
	[*Both* is used with *and*, but the items joined by them are not parallel.]
Parallel	Bruce wants *both* <u>freedom</u> *and* <u>wealth</u>.
Parallel	Bruce wants *both* <u>to have freedom</u> *and* <u>to be wealthy</u>.
Not parallel	He can *neither* <u>fail the course</u> and <u>quitting his job</u> is also impossible.
Parallel	He can *neither* <u>fail the course</u> *nor* <u>quit his job</u>.

> **PRACTICE 24-3**   **Using Parallelism with Certain Paired Words**
>
> In each sentence, circle the paired words, and underline the parts of the sentence that should be parallel. Then, edit the sentence to make it parallel. You may need to change one of the paired elements to make the sentence parallel.

an annoyance
Example: A cell phone can be either <u>a lifesaver</u> or ~~it can be annoying~~.

1. Twenty years ago, most people neither had cell phones nor did they want them.

2. Today, cell phones are not only used by people of all ages but also are carried everywhere.

3. Cell phones are not universally popular: some commuters would rather ban cell phones on buses and trains than being forced to listen to other people's conversations.

4. No one denies that a cell phone can be both useful and convenience is a factor.

5. A motorist stranded on a deserted road would rather have a cell phone than to walk to the nearest gas station.

6. When cell phones were first introduced, some people feared that they either caused brain tumors or they were a dangerous source of radiation.

7. Most Americans today neither worry about radiation from cell phones nor other injuries.

8. The biggest risk of cell phones is either that drivers are distracted by them or people getting angry at someone talking too loudly in public on a cell phone.

9. Cell phones probably do not cause brain tumors, but some experiments on human cells have shown that energy from the phones may both affect people's reflexes and it might alter the brain's blood vessels.

10. Some scientists think that these experiments show that cell-phone use might have not only physical effects on human beings but it also could influence mental processes.

PRACTICE 24–4 **Completing Sentences with Paired Words**

For each sentence, complete the correlative conjunction, and add more information. Make sure the structures on both sides of the correlative conjunction are parallel.

Example: I am both impressed by your company *and enthusiastic to work for you.*

1. I could bring to this job not only youthful enthusiasm

2. I am willing to work either in your main office

3. My current job neither encourages initiative

4. I would rather work in a challenging job

5. In college, I learned a lot both from my classes

Edit for Parallelism

PRACTICE 24-5   **Editing Paragraphs for Parallelism Problems**

Find and correct five parallelism errors in the following paragraphs.

On a mountainous island between Norway and the North Pole is a special underground vault. It contains neither gold and currency. Instead, it is full of a different kind of treasure: seeds. They are being saved for the future in case something happens to the plants that people need to grow for food.

The vault has the capacity to hold 4.5 million types of seed samples. Each sample contains an average of five hundred seeds, which means that up to 2.25 billion seeds can be stored in the vault. To store them is better than planting them. Stored, they are preserved for future generations to plant. On the first day that the vault's storage program began, 268,000 different seeds were deposited, put into sealed packages, and collecting into sealed boxes. Some of the seeds were for maize (corn), and others were for rice, wheat, and barley.

Although some people call it the "Doomsday Vault," many others see it as a type of insurance policy against starvation in the case of a terrible natural disaster. The vault's location keeps it safe from floods, earthquakes, and storming. Carefully storing these seeds will help ensure not only that people have food to eat important crops never go extinct.

Chapter Review

1. What is parallelism in writing?

2. In what three situations do problems with parallelism most often occur?

3. What are two pairs of correlative conjunctions?

Reflect and Apply

1. Was the concept of parallel structure new to you? If not, where have you encountered it before?

2. Analyze a few paragraphs from a paper you are writing. First, find examples of the three situations that require parallel structure. Check to make sure you have used parallel structure in each case. Do you notice a pattern in your own writing? What will you watch for as you edit in the future?

3. Analyze a few paragraphs from a textbook or reading assignment for a course in your major. Can you find examples of parallel structure?

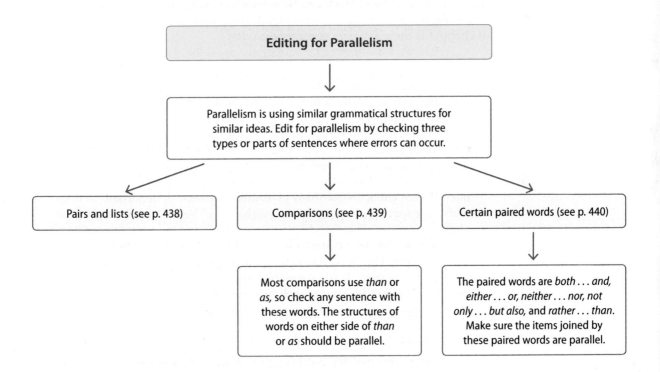

25

Sentence Variety

Putting Rhythm in Your Writing

Understand What Sentence Variety Is

Sentence variety means using different sentence patterns and lengths to give your writing a strong rhythm and flow, allowing your readers to follow you more easily. Read the following example aloud. How does it sound? Does it flow or is it choppy? Is there a variety of sentence styles?

Many people do not realize how important their speaking voice and style are. Speaking style can make a difference, particularly in a job interview. What you say is important. How you say it is nearly as important. Your speaking voice creates an impression. Mumbling is a bad way of speaking. It makes the speaker appear sloppy and lacking in confidence. Mumbling also makes it difficult for the interviewer to hear what is being said. Talking too fast is another bad speech behavior. The speaker runs his or her ideas together. The interviewer cannot follow them or distinguish what is important. A third ineffective speech behavior concerns verbal "tics." Verbal tics are empty filler phrases like "um," "like," and "you know." Practice for an interview. Sit up straight. Look the person to whom you are speaking directly in the eye. Speak up. Slow down. One good way to find out how you sound is to leave yourself a voice-mail message. If you sound bad to yourself, you need practice speaking aloud. Do not let poor speech behavior interfere with creating a good impression.

Now compare the first version with the one that follows. Can you hear a difference as you read it aloud?

Many people do not realize how important their speaking voice and style are, particularly in a job interview. What you say is important, but how you say it is nearly as important in creating a good impression. Mumbling is a bad way of speaking. Not only does it make the speaker appear sloppy and lacking in confidence, but mumbling also makes it difficult for the interviewer to hear what is being said. Talking too fast is another bad speech behavior. The speaker runs his or her ideas together, and the interviewer cannot follow them or distinguish what is important. A third ineffective speech behavior is called verbal "tics," empty filler expressions such as "um," "like," and "you know." When you practice for an interview, sit up straight, look the person to whom you are speaking directly in the eye, speak up, and slow down. One good way to find out how you sound is to leave yourself a voice-mail message. If you sound bad to yourself, you need practice speaking aloud. Do not let poor speech behavior interfere with creating a good impression.

Practice Creating Sentence Variety

Many writers tend to write short sentences that start with the subject, so this chapter focuses on techniques for starting with something other than the subject and for writing a variety of longer sentences. Two additional techniques for achieving sentence variety—coordination and subordination—are covered in Chapter 23.

Start Some Sentences with Adverbs

Adverbs are words that describe verbs, adjectives, or other adverbs; they often end with *-ly*. As long as the meaning is clear, adverbs can be placed at the beginning of a sentence instead of in the middle. Adverbs at the beginning of a sentence are usually followed by a comma.

Adverb in middle	Stories about haunted houses *frequently* surface at Halloween.
Adverb at beginning	*Frequently*, stories about haunted houses surface at Halloween.
Adverb in middle	These stories *often* focus on ship captains lost at sea.
Adverb at beginning	*Often*, these stories focus on ship captains lost at sea.

Tip For more about adverbs, see Chapter 22.

PRACTICE 25–1   **Starting Sentences with an Adverb**

Edit each sentence so that it begins with an adverb.

Example: *Often, student*
~~Student~~ writers are ~~often~~ advised to be original and create
something new.

1. This advice, however, does not match with the habits of experienced writers.

2. Writers and composers today rarely create something that is entirely new.

3. They draw on years of experience with the works of others.

4. Most great writers have typically been reading novels and poems their entire lives.

5. Echoes of the characters and themes of these novels and poems may naturally appear in these writers' works.

Read to Write
Explore the readings in Part 2. Find and annotate examples of adverbs at the beginnings of sentences.

> ### PRACTICE 25-2   Writing Sentences That Start with an Adverb
>
> Write three sentences that start with an adverb. Use commas as necessary. Choose among the following adverbs: *often, sadly, amazingly, luckily, lovingly, aggressively, gently, frequently, stupidly.*

Join Ideas Using an -ing *Verb*

One way to combine sentences is to add -*ing* to the verb in the less important of the two sentences and to delete the subject, creating a phrase.

Two sentences	A pecan roll from our bakery is not a health food. It contains 800 calories.
Joined with verb form	*Containing* 800 calories, a pecan roll from our bakery is not a healthy food.

You can add the -*ing* phrase to the beginning or the end of the other sentence, depending on what makes more sense.

The fat content is also high. It Equals the fat in a huge country breakfast.
                         , equaling

If you add the -*ing* phrase to the beginning of a sentence, you will usually need to put a comma after it. If you add the phrase to the end of a sentence, you will usually need to put a comma before it. A comma should *not* be used only when the -*ing* phrase is essential to the meaning of the sentence.

Two sentences	Experts examined the effects of exercise on arthritis patients. The experts found that walking, jogging, or swimming could reduce pain.
Joined without commas	Experts examining the effects of exercise on arthritis patients found that walking, jogging, or swimming could reduce pain.
	[The phrase *examining the effects of exercise on arthritis patients* identifies the experts, and it is therefore essential to the meaning of the sentence.]

If you put a phrase starting with an *-ing* verb at the beginning of a sentence, be sure the word that the phrase modifies follows immediately. Otherwise, you will create a dangling modifier.

Tip For more on finding and correcting dangling modifiers, see Chapter 22, and for more on joining ideas, see Chapter 23.

Two sentences	I ran through the rain. My raincoat got all wet.
Dangling modifier	Running through the rain, my raincoat got all wet.
Edited	Running through the rain, I got my raincoat all wet.

PRACTICE 25-3   **Joining Ideas Using an *-ing* Verb**

Combine each pair of sentences into a single sentence by using an *-ing* verb. Add or delete words as necessary.

Example: All compositions are connected to other works. ~~Each~~ ~~composition reflects~~ an artist's encounters and responses to other texts or compositions.

, reflecting (inserted above)

1. In academic writing, writers often refer explicitly to other works. They use summaries, paraphrases, and quotes to connect ideas.

2. In literature, writers may employ a strategy called an allusion. They make references to characters, places, or events in other works of literature.

3. Many high school students do not know plays by Shakespeare. They find allusions to Shakespearean characters difficult to understand without footnotes.

4. Some artists today use literary works differently. They adapt them for a different medium, such as film or live theater.

5. These literary adaptations use the characters and plot of the original text. These literary adaptations change the setting or other details about the work.

6. Adaptations are always interpretations. Adaptations change setting, language, characters, or the plot.

7. Lin-Manuel Miranda followed a book by Ron Chernow. Lin-Manuel Miranda wrote the Broadway smash, *Hamilton*, which is an adaptation that includes music and dance.

8. Some adaptations occur across multiple media types. Some adaptations are actually examples of transmediation.

9. For example, the creators connected to social media sites. The creators of the web series *Nothing Much to Do* transmediated Shakespeare's play, *Much Ado About Nothing*.

10. It is clear that artists and writers do not pull all their material from their own imaginations. They borrow instead from all the stories they have experienced.

Join Ideas Using a Past Participle

Another way to combine sentences is to use a past participle (often, a verb ending in -*ed*) to turn the less important of the two sentences into a phrase. Writers often use a past participle phrase to give readers background information.

Two sentences	Henry VIII was a powerful English king. He is *remembered* for his many wives.
Joined with a past participle	*Remembered* for his many wives, Henry VIII was a powerful English king.

Tip For a list of irregular verbs and their past participles, see pages 382–384.

Past participles of irregular verbs do not end in -*ed*; they take different forms.

| Two sentences | Tim Treadwell was *eaten* by a grizzly bear. He showed that wild animals are unpredictable. |
| Joined with a past participle | *Eaten* by a grizzly bear, Tim Treadwell showed that wild animals are unpredictable. |

Notice that sentences can be joined this way when one of them has a form of *be* along with a past participle (*is remembered* in the first Henry VIII example and *was eaten* in the first Tim Treadwell example).

To combine sentences this way, delete the subject and the *be* form from the sentence that has the *be* form and the past participle. You now have a phrase that can be added to the beginning or the end of the other sentence, depending on what makes more sense.

~~Henry VIII was~~ determined to divorce one of his wives. ~~He~~, Henry VIII created the Church of England because Catholicism does not allow divorce.

If you add a phrase that begins with a past participle to the beginning of a sentence, put a comma after it. If you add the phrase to the end of the sentence, put a comma before it.

Language note: How do you know if you need an *-ing* word (also called a present participle) or a past participle when you join two sentences? Use the present participle to replace an **active** verb, where the subject is doing the action. In the following sentence, John (the subject) is doing something: traveling.

Traveling   ,
~~John travels~~ for his job. John had to miss his daughter's recital.

Use the past participle to replace a **passive** verb, where the subject is receiving the action. In the following sentence, John is not doing anything. He is receiving the action of criticizing:

Criticized   ,
~~John was criticized~~ for his performance. John began to look for a new job.

Tip If you put a phrase starting with a past participle at the beginning of a sentence, be sure the word that the phrase modifies follows immediately. Otherwise, you will create a dangling modifier.

Tip For more on active and passive verbs, see Chapter 19.

PRACTICE 25-4   **Joining Ideas Using a Past Participle**

Combine each pair of sentences into a single sentence by using a past participle.

Example:
          Forced
      ~~The oil company was forced~~ to take the local women's
                   , the oil
      objections seriously. ~~The~~ company had to close for ten days
      during their protest.

1. The women of southern Nigeria were angered by British colonial rule in 1929. They organized a protest.

2. Nigeria is now one of the top ten oil-producing countries. The nation is covered with pipelines and oil wells.

3. The oil is pumped by American and other foreign oil companies. The oil often ends up in wealthy Western economies.

4. The money from the oil seldom reaches Nigeria's local people. The cash is stolen by corrupt rulers in many cases.

5. The Nigerian countryside is polluted by the oil industry. The land then becomes a wasteland.

6. Many Nigerians are insulted by the way the oil industry treats them. They want the oil companies to pay attention to their problems.

7. Local Nigerian women were inspired by the 1929 women's protests. They launched a series of protests against the oil industry in the summer of 2002.

8. The women prevented workers from entering or leaving two oil company offices. The offices were located in the port of Warri.

9. Workers at the oil company were concerned about the women's threat to take off their clothes. Many workers told company officials that such a protest would bring a curse on the company and shame to its employees.

10. The company eventually agreed to hire more local people and to invest in local projects. The projects are intended to supply electricity and provide the villagers with a market for fish and poultry.

Join Ideas Using an Appositive

An **appositive** is a noun or noun phrase that renames a noun or pronoun. Appositives can be used to combine two sentences into one.

Two sentences	Brussels sprouts can be roasted for a delicious flavor. They are a commonly disliked food.
Joined with an appositive	Brussels sprouts, a commonly disliked food, can be roasted for a delicious flavor.
	[The phrase *a commonly disliked food* renames the noun *Brussels sprouts*.]

Notice that the sentence that renames the noun was turned into a noun phrase by dropping the subject and the verb (*They* and *are*). Also, commas set off the appositive.

Read to Write
Look at Samantha Levine-Finley's essay, "Isn't It Time You Hit the Books?" on page 187. Annotate this essay, marking the appositives she uses. What is the purpose of the appositives in her essay?

PRACTICE 25–5   Joining Ideas Using an Appositive

Combine each pair of sentences into a single sentence by using an appositive. Be sure to use a comma or commas to set off the appositive.

Example: , perhaps the most famous work clothes in the world,
Levi's jeans have looked the same for well over a century. ~~They~~
~~are perhaps the most famous work clothes in the world.~~

1. Jacob Davis was a Russian immigrant working in Reno, Nevada, He was the inventor of Levi's jeans.

2. Davis came up with an invention that made work clothes last longer.

   The invention was the riveted seam.

3. Davis bought denim from a wholesaler. The wholesaler was Levi Strauss.

4. In 1870, he offered to sell the rights to his invention to Levi Strauss for

   the price of the patent. Patents then cost about $70.

5. Davis joined the firm in 1873 and supervised the final development of

   its product. The product was the famous Levi's jeans.

6. Davis oversaw a crucial design element. The jeans all had orange stitching.

7. The curved stitching on the back pockets was another choice Davis

   made. It also survives in today's Levi's.

8. The stitching on the pockets has been a trademark since 1942. It is very recognizable.

9. During World War II, Levi Strauss temporarily stopped adding the pocket stitches because they wasted thread. It was a valuable resource.

Tip For more about
adjectives, see
Chapter 21.

10. Until the war ended, the pocket design was added with a less valuable material. The company used paint.

Join Ideas Using an Adjective Clause

An **adjective clause** is a group of words with a subject and a verb that describes a noun. In other words, it is a dependent clause that functions like an adjective in the sentence. An adjective clause often begins with the word *who*, *which*, or *that*, and it can be used to combine two sentences into one.

Two sentences	Lauren has won many basketball awards. She is captain of her college team.
Joined with an adjective clause	Lauren, *who is captain of her college team*, has won many basketball awards.

To join sentences this way, use *who*, *which*, or *that* to replace the subject in a sentence that describes a noun in the other sentence. You now have an adjective clause that you can move so that it follows the noun it describes.

Tip Use *who* to refer
to a person, *which*
to refer to places or
things (but not to
people), and *that* for
places or things.

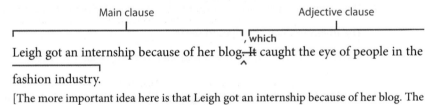

Main clause   Adjective clause

, which
Leigh got an internship because of her blog. It caught the eye of people in the fashion industry.

[The more important idea here is that Leigh got an internship because of her blog. The less important idea is that the blog caught the eye of people in the fashion industry.]

If an adjective clause can be taken out of a sentence without completely changing the meaning of the sentence, put commas around it.

Lauren, *who is captain of her college team*, has won many basketball awards.

[The phrase *who is captain of her college team* adds information about Lauren, but it is not essential to understanding the meaning of the sentence.]

If an adjective clause is an essential part of a sentence, do not put commas around it.

> Lauren is an award-winning basketball player who overcame childhood cancer.
>
> [*Who overcame childhood cancer* is an essential part of this sentence.]

 Language note: Essential adjective clauses are also called restrictive or identifying adjective clauses; these clauses are often needed for readers to identify which noun the sentence is discussing. Nonessential clauses (which require commas) are also called nonrestrictive or non-identifying clauses. Note that a proper name identifies a specific noun; therefore, adjective clauses following proper names are almost always nonessential and require commas:

> Atlanta, *which is the capital of Georgia*, hosted the summer Olympics in 1996. Theresa May, *who is the prime minister of the United Kingdom*, has the difficult job of leading Britain out of the European Union.

The relative pronoun *that* is only used with essential adjective clauses; in other words, don't use commas when the adjective clause begins with *that*:

Incorrect	The exam, that we took last week, required three different essays.
	[*That we took last week* identifies the exam and is essential]
Correct	The exam that we took last week required three different essays.
Incorrect	An entire generation hoped there would be a reunion of the Beatles that were popular in the 1960s, but it never happened.
	[The information here is not needed to identify the Beatles; the clause is nonessential and should have a comma.]
Correct	An entire generation hoped there would be a reunion of the Beatles, who were popular in the 1960s, but it never happened.

PRACTICE 25–6 **Joining Ideas Using an Adjective Clause**

Combine each pair of sentences into a single sentence by using an adjective clause beginning with *who, which,* or *that*.

Example: *, who has been going to college for the past three years,*
My friend Erin ‸ had her first child last June. ~~She has been going to college for the past three years.~~

1. While Erin goes to classes, her baby boy stays at a day-care center. The day-care center costs Erin about $100 a week.

2. Twice when her son was ill, Erin had to miss her geology lab. The lab is an important part of her grade for that course.

3. Occasionally, Erin's parents come up and watch the baby while Erin is studying. They live about 70 miles away.

4. Sometimes Erin feels discouraged by the extra costs. The costs have come from having a child.

5. She believes that some of her professors are not very sympathetic. These professors are the ones who have never been parents themselves.

6. Erin understands that she must take responsibility for both her child and her education. She wants to be a good mother and a good student.

7. Her grades have suffered somewhat since she had her son. They were once straight A's.

8. Erin wants to graduate with honors. She hopes to go to graduate school someday.

9. Her son is more important than an A in geology. He is the most important thing to her.

10. Erin still expects to have a high grade point average. She has simply given up expecting to be perfect.

PRACTICE 25–7   **Joining Ideas Using an Adjective Clause**

Fill in the blank in each of the following sentences with an appropriate adjective clause. Add commas, if necessary.

Example: The firefighters <u>who responded to the alarm</u> entered the
              burning building.

1. A fire _____ began in our house in the middle of the night.

2. The members of my family _____ were all asleep.

3. My father _____ was the first to smell smoke.

4. He ran to our bedrooms _____ and woke us up with his shouting.

5. The house _____ was damaged, but everyone in my family reached safety.

Edit for Sentence Variety

PRACTICE 25–8   **Editing Paragraphs for Sentence Variety**

Create sentence variety in the following paragraphs by joining at least two sentences in each of the paragraphs. Use several of the techniques covered in this chapter. More than one correct answer is possible.

   Few people would associate the famous English poet and playwright William Shakespeare with prison. However, Shakespeare has taken on an important role in the lives of certain inmates. They are serving time at the Luther Luckett Correctional Complex in Kentucky. These inmates were brought together by the Shakespeare Behind Bars program. They spend nine months preparing for a performance of one of the great writer's plays.

   Recently, prisoners at Luckett performed *The Merchant of Venice*. It is one of Shakespeare's most popular plays. Many of the actors identified with Shylock. He is a moneylender who is discriminated against because he is Jewish. When a rival asks Shylock for a loan to help a friend, Shylock drives a hard bargain. He demands a pound of the rival's flesh if the loan is not repaid. One inmate shared his views of this play with a newspaper reporter. The inmate said, "It deals with race. It deals with discrimination. It deals with gambling, debt, cutting people. It deals with it all. And we were all living that someway, somehow."

Through the Shakespeare performances, the inmates form bonds not only with the characters but also with one another. Additionally, they are able to explore their own histories and their responsibility for the crimes they committed. Many feel changed by their experience on the stage.

One actor was affected deeply by his role in *The Merchant of Venice*. He said, "You feel like you're in a theater outside of here. You don't feel the razor wire."

Chapter Review

1. What does it mean to have sentence variety?

2. If you tend to write short, similar-sounding sentences, what five techniques should you try?

3. What is an appositive?

4. What is an adjective clause?

5. When should writers use commas with an adjective clause?

Reflect and Apply

1. What grammar concepts were new to you in this chapter? What concepts are not yet clear to you?

2. Analyze three to four paragraphs from a paper you have written or are currently writing. Can you find examples of the strategies mentioned in this chapter? Is the writing choppy? How could you improve it, using the concepts mentioned in this chapter?

3. Examine a few paragraphs from a textbook from a course in your major (or look at an important document used in your chosen field). Annotate the paragraphs for the strategies in this chapter. Has the writer used all of them? What patterns can you see?

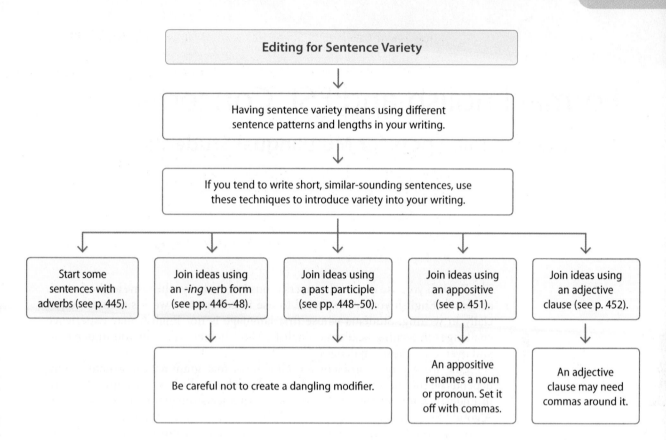

26

Formal English and ESL Concerns
Grammar Trouble Spots for Multilingual Students

The English you use in casual conversations is not always the same as the formal, academic English you are expected to use in college and work situations, especially in writing. Students whose first language is not English may experience challenges in writing academic English. This chapter will help you understand and overcome those challenges.

One troublesome problem for students is that grammatical structure often depends on the specific words used. Even if you know the basic meaning of a word in English, you may not know how that word affects the grammar of a sentence. A good ESL dictionary contains both definitions and information about the way a word is used (and cannot be used); we call this **lexical information**. As you read and write, you may want to keep a vocabulary list that includes lexical information.

Basic Sentence Patterns

Basic sentence patterns include statements, negatives, and questions.

Tip In this chapter, we use the word *English* to refer to formal English. Throughout the chapter, subjects in example sentences are underlined, and verbs are double-underlined.

Statements

Every sentence in English must have at least one subject **(S)** and one verb **(V)** that together express a complete idea. The subject performs the action, and the verb names the action. In English, the word order is fixed; subjects usually come before verbs in statements.

```
         S    V
         |    |
The pitcher throws.
```

Other English sentence patterns build on that structure. One of the most common patterns is subject-verb-object (**S-V-O**).

```
    S      V      O
    |      |      |
The pitcher throws the ball.
```

There are two kinds of objects.

Direct objects receive the action of the verb.

```
    S      V      DO
    |      |      |
The pitcher throws the ball.
```
[The ball directly receives the action of the verb *throws*.]

Indirect objects do not receive the action of the verb. Instead, the action is performed *for* or *to* the person.

```
    S      V    IO     DO
    |      |    |      |
The pitcher throws me the ball.
```

Another common sentence pattern is subject-verb-prepositional phrase (PP). In standard English, the prepositional phrase typically follows the subject and verb.

```
  S    V      (PP)
  |    |    ┌───────┐
Lilah went to the movies.
```

Language note: Not every verb can occur in every pattern. For example, the verbs *give* and *throw* occur in two patterns:

S + V + IO + DO

The instructor gives the students an extra assignment.
The quarterback threw Jason the ball.

S + V + DO + PP (to + IO)

The instructor gives an extra assignment to the students.
The quarterback threw the ball to Jason.

The verb *explain*, however, occurs only with the second pattern:

Incorrect	The teacher explains us the assignment.
Correct	The teacher explains the assignment to us.

The verbs *ask* and cost, in contrast, occur in the first pattern (S + V + IO + DO), but not the second:

Incorrect	The students ask questions to the new teacher.
	The new car cost a lot of money to me.
Correct	The students ask the new teacher questions.
	The new car cost me a lot of money.

Understanding which verbs occur in which patterns requires lexical information. Use a dictionary to help determine which patterns to use with different verbs.

PRACTICE 26–1   **Sentence Patterns**

Label the subject (S), verb (V), direct object (DO), indirect object (IO), and prepositional phrase (PP), if any, in the following sentences.

1. John sent the letter.

2. John sent Beth the letter.

3. John sent the letter to Beth.

4. After the game, John mailed Beth the package.

Tip For more on the parts of sentences, see Chapter 15.

5. Shayla bought an extra ticket for her friend Beth.

PRACTICE 26–2   **Using Correct Word Order**

Read each of the sentences that follow. If the sentence is correct, write "C" in the blank to the left of it. If it is incorrect, write "I"; then, rewrite the sentence to the right, using correct word order.

Example: $\underline{\text{I}}$ My friend to me gave a present. *My friend gave me a present.*

1. ___ Presents I like very much.

2. ___ To parties I go often.

3. ___ To parties, I always bring a present.

4. ___ At my parties, people bring me presents, too.

5. ___ Always write to them a thank-you note.

Negatives

No matter which sentence pattern you use, you can form a negative by adding the word *not* after the auxiliary verb. If a sentence does not have an auxiliary verb, make the verb negative by adding a form of the auxiliary verb *do* and the word *not*.

Sentence	Dina can sing.
Negative	Dina ~~no can~~ sing. [cannot]
Sentence	The store sells cigarettes.
Negative	The store ~~no~~ sells cigarettes. [does not]
Sentence	Bruce will call.
Negative	Bruce ~~no~~ will call. [not]
Sentence	Caroline walked.
Negative	Caroline ~~no~~ did walk. [not]

Tip For more information about auxiliary verbs, see Chapter 15.

Notice in these examples that the word *not* comes *after* the helping verb. The auxiliary verb cannot be omitted in expressions using *not*.

Incorrect	The store *not sell* cigarettes.
Correct	The store *does not sell* cigarettes.
	[*Does*, a form of the verb *do*, must come before *not*.]
Correct	The store *is not selling* cigarettes.
	[*Is*, a form of *be*, must come before *not*.]

A verb can also be made negative with the word *never*. An auxiliary is not required with the word *never*:

> The store never sells cigarettes.
> Caroline never walks.
> She has never walked to work.

Common Auxiliary Verbs

Forms of *be*	Forms of *have*	Forms of *do*	Modal verbs
am	have	do	can
are	has	does	could
is	had	did	may
been			might
being			must
was			should
were			will
			would

You may also make a sentence negative by negating the subject or object with these words: *no, nobody, none, no one,* and *nowhere*. Use only one negative word in a sentence; double negatives are not standard in English.

Incorrect	Shane *does not have no* ride.
Correct	Shane *does not have a* ride.
Correct	Shane *has no* ride.

> **Language note:** When forming a negative in the simple past tense, use the past tense of the helping verb *do* and the base form of the verb:

> [*did*] + [*not*] + [Base verb without an *-ed*] = [Negative past tense]

Sentence	I *talked* to Jairo last night.
	[*Talked* is the past tense.]
Negative	I *did not* talk to Jairo last night.
	[Notice that *talk* in this sentence does not have an *-ed* ending because the helping verb *did* conveys the past tense.]

PRACTICE 26–3   **Forming Negatives**

Rewrite the sentences to make them negative.

                        not
Example: Hassan's son is ^ talking now.

1. He can say several words.

2. Hassan remembers when his daughter started talking.

3. He thinks it was at the same age.

4. His daughter was an early speaker.

5. Hassan expects his son to be a talkative adult.

Questions

To turn a statement into a question, move the auxiliary verb so that it comes before the subject. Add a question mark (**?**) to the end of the question.

Statement	Johan *can go* tonight.
Question	*Can* Johan *go* tonight?

If the only verb in the statement is a form of *be,* it should be moved before the subject.

Statement	Jamie *is* at work.
Question	*Is* Jamie at work?

If the statement does not contain an auxiliary verb or a form of *be,* add a form of *do* and put it before the subject. Be sure to end the question with a question mark (**?**).

Statement	Norah sings in the choir.	Tyrone goes to college.
Question	*Does* Norah sing in the choir?	*Does* Tyrone go to college?
Statement	The building burned.	The plate broke.
Question	*Did* the building burn?	*Did* the plate break?

Tip Sometimes the verb appears before the subject in sentences that are not questions: *Behind the supermarket is the sub shop.* This inversion occurs with linking verbs followed by prepositional phrases.

Notice that the verb changed once the helping verb *did* was added.

Do is used with *I, you, we,* and *they*. *Does* is used with *he, she,* and *it.*

> **Examples**   *Do* [I/you/we/they] practice every day?
> *Does* [he/she/it] sound terrible?

> **PRACTICE 26–4**   **Forming Questions**
>
> Rewrite the sentences to make them into questions.
>
> **Example:**   *Does*
> Brad knows how to cook. ?
>
> 1. He makes dinner every night for his family.
>
> 2. He goes to the grocery store once a week.
>
> 3. He uses coupons to save money.
>
> 4. Brad saves a lot of money using coupons.

There Is and *There Are*

English sentences often include *there is* or *there are* to indicate the existence of something.

> *There is* a man at the door.
> [You could also say, *A man is at the door.*]
> *There are* many men in the class.
> [You could also say, *Many men are in the class.*]

When a sentence includes the words *there is* or *there are*, the verb (*is, are*) comes before the noun it goes with (which is actually the subject of the sentence). The verb must agree with the noun in number. For example, the first sentence above uses the singular verb *is* to agree with the singular noun *man*, and the second sentence uses the plural verb *are* to agree with the plural noun *men*.

In questions, *is* or *are* comes before *there*.

> **Statements**   *There is* plenty to eat.
> *There are* some things to do.
>
> **Questions**   *Is there* plenty to eat?
> *Are there* some things to do?

Pronouns

Pronouns replace nouns or other pronouns in a sentence so that you do not have to repeat them. Three common types of pronouns are subject pronouns, object pronouns, and possessive pronouns.

Tip For more on pronouns, see Chapter 20.

   Subject pronouns serve as the subject of the verb (and remember that every English sentence *must* have a subject).

<u>Rob</u> <u>is</u> my cousin. _{He} <s>Rob</s> <u>lives</u> next to me.

   Object pronouns receive the action of the verb or are part of a prepositional phrase.

<u>Rob</u> <u>asked</u> *me* for a favor.
[The object pronoun *me* receives the action of the verb *asked*.]
<u>Rob</u> <u>lives</u> next door *to me*.
[*To me* is the prepositional phrase; *me* is the object pronoun.]

   Possessive pronouns show ownership.

<u>Rob</u> <u>is</u> *my* cousin.

Use the following chart to check which type of pronoun to use.

Pronoun Types

Subject		Object		Possessive	
Singular	**Plural**	**Singular**	**Plural**	**Singular**	**Plural**
I	we	me	us	my/mine	our/ours
you	you	you	you	your/yours	your/yours
he/she/it	they	him/her/it	them	his/her/hers/its	theirs
Relative pronouns					
who, which, that					

The singular pronouns *he/she*, *him/her*, and *his/hers* show gender. *He, him*, and *his* are masculine pronouns; *she, her*, and *hers* are feminine.
   Here are some examples of common pronoun errors, with corrections.

Confusing Subject and Object Pronouns

Use a subject pronoun for the word that *performs* the action of the verb, and use an object pronoun for the word that *receives* the action.

> She
> Tashia is a good student. ~~Her~~ gets all A's.
>
> [The pronoun performs the action *gets*, so it should be the subject pronoun, *she*.]

> her   him
> Tomas gave the keys to ~~she~~. Banh gave the coat to ~~he~~.
>
> [The pronoun receives the action of *gave*, so it should be the object pronoun, *her* or *him*.]

Confusing Gender

Use masculine pronouns to replace masculine nouns, and use feminine pronouns to replace feminine nouns.

> He
> Nick is sick. ~~She~~ has the flu.
>
> [*Nick* is a masculine noun, so the pronoun must be masculine.]

> her
> The jacket belongs to Jane. Give it to ~~him~~.
>
> [*Jane* is feminine, so the pronoun must be feminine.]

Leaving Out a Pronoun

Some sentences use the pronoun *it* as the subject or object. Do not leave *it* out of the sentence.

> It is
> ~~Is~~ a holiday today.

> It will
> Maria will bring the food. ~~Will~~ be delicious.

> it
> I tried calamari last night and liked very much.

Using a Pronoun to Repeat a Subject

A pronoun *replaces* a noun, so do not use both a subject noun and a pronoun.

> My father ~~he~~ is very strict.
>
> [*Father* is the subject noun, so the sentence should not also have the subject pronoun *he*.]

> The bus ~~it~~ was late.
>
> [*Bus* is the subject noun, so the sentence should not also have the subject pronoun *it*.]

Using Relative Pronouns

The words *who, which,* and *that* are **relative pronouns**. Use relative pronouns in a clause that gives more information about the subject.

- Use *who* to refer to a person or people.

  The man *who* lives next door plays piano.

- Use *which* or *that* to refer to nonliving things.

  The plant, *which* was a gift, died.
  The phone *that* I bought last week is broken.

Verbs

Verbs have different tenses to show when something happened: in the past, present, or future.

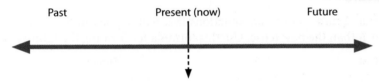

This section contains timelines, examples, and common errors for the simple and perfect tenses; coverage of progressive tenses; and more. See Chapter 19 for full coverage of the simple tenses and the perfect tenses, as well as practice exercises.

The Simple Tenses

The simple tenses include the simple present, simple past, and simple future.

Simple Present

Use the simple present to describe situations that exist now and will continue to exist, including facts, habits, schedules, and preferences.

I like pizza.

I/You/We/They like pizza.

She/He likes pizza.

The third-person singular (*she/he*) of regular verbs ends in *-s* or *-es*. For irregular verb endings, see pages 382–84.

Simple Past

Use the simple past to describe situations that began and ended in the past.

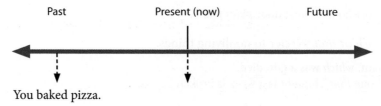

You baked pizza.

I/You/She/He/We/They bak**ed** pizza.

For regular verbs, the simple past is formed by adding either *-d* or *-ed* to the verb. For the past forms of irregular verbs, see the chart on pages 382–84.

Simple Future

Use the simple future to describe situations that will happen in the future. It is easier to form than the past tense. Use this formula for forming the future tense.

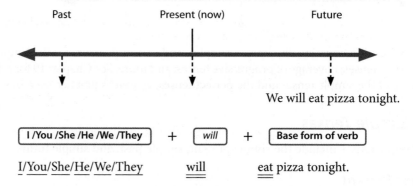

We will eat pizza tonight.

I/You/She/He/We/They   will   eat pizza tonight.

Common Errors in Using Simple Tenses

Following are some common errors in using simple tenses.

Simple present.   Forgetting to add *-s* or *-es* to verbs that go with third-person singular subjects (*she/he/it*)

Incorrect	She know the manager.
Correct	She knows the manager.

Simple past. Forgetting to add *-d* or *-ed* to regular verbs

Incorrect	Gina <u>work</u> late last night.
Correct	Gina <u>work**ed**</u> late last night.

Forgetting to use the correct past forms of irregular verbs (see the chart of irregular verb forms on pages 382–84).

Incorrect	Gerard <u>speaked</u> to her about the problem.
Correct	Gerard **spoke** to her about the problem.

Forgetting to use the base verb without an ending for negative sentences:

Incorrect	She <u>does</u> not <u>wants</u> money for helping.
Correct	She <u>does</u> not **want** money for helping.

Tip Remember that double negatives (*Johnetta will not call no one*) are not standard in English. One negative is enough (*Johnetta will not call anyone*).

 Language note: Do not use the future tense in a dependent clause beginning with a time word, even if the action occurs in the future:

Incorrect	After <u>he</u> <u>will retire</u>, my <u>father</u> <u>will move</u> to Florida. The <u>students</u> <u>are planning</u> to <u>celebrate</u> after <u>they</u> <u>will finish</u> exams.
Correct	After <u>he</u> <u>retires</u>, my <u>father</u> <u>will move</u> to Florida. The <u>students</u> <u>are planning</u> to celebrate after <u>they</u> <u>finish</u> exams.

> ## Common Time Words (Subordinating Conjunctions)
>
> after   as soon as   once   before   when   while

The Perfect Tenses

The present tenses include present perfect, past perfect, and future perfect.

Present Perfect

Use the present perfect to describe situations that started in the past and either continue into the present or were completed at some unknown time in the past.

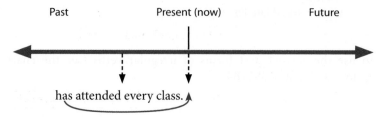

To form the present perfect tense, use this formula:

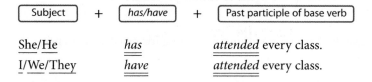

| Subject | + | has/have | + | Past participle of base verb |

| She/He | *has* | *attended* every class. |
| I/We/They | *have* | *attended* every class. |

Notice that *I/we/they* use *have* and that *she/he* use *has.*

Past Perfect

Use the past perfect to describe situations that began and ended before some other situation happened.

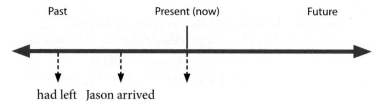

To form the past perfect tense, use this formula:

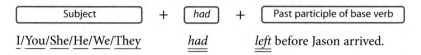

| Subject | + | had | + | Past participle of base verb |

| I/You/She/He/We/They | *had* | *left* before Jason arrived. |

Future Perfect

Use the future perfect to describe situations that begin and end before another situation begins.

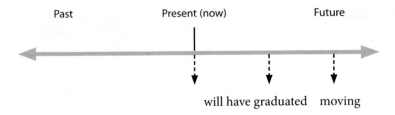

will have graduated   moving

Use this formula to form the future perfect tense:

I/You/She/He/We/They   *will have*   *graduated* before moving.

Common Errors in Forming the Perfect Tense

Using *had* instead of *has* or *have* for the present perfect

Incorrect	We **had** lived here since 2003.
Correct	We **have** lived here since 2003.

Forgetting to use past participles (with -*d* or -*ed* endings for regular verbs)

Incorrect	She has attend every class.
Correct	She has attend**ed** every class.

Using *been* between *have* or *has* and the past participle of a base verb

Incorrect	I have **been** attended every class.
Correct	I have attended every class.
Incorrect	I will have **been** graduated before I move.
Correct	I will have graduated before I move.

The Progressive Tenses

The progressive tenses describe ongoing actions in the present, past, or future. They are formed by using a form of the verb *be* and the -*ing* form of the verb. The following charts show how to use the present, past, and future progressive tenses in regular statements, negative statements, and questions.

THE PROGRESSIVE TENSES

Tense

Present Progressive

Time line: a situation that is happening now but started in the past

I am typing.

STATEMENTS

[Present of *be* (*am/is/are*)] + [Base verb ending in *-ing*]

I **am typing**.   We **are typing**.

You **are typing**.   They **are typing**.

She/he **is typing**.

NEGATIVES

[Present of *be* (*am/is/are*)] + [*not*] + [Base verb ending in *-ing*]

I **am not typing**.   We **are not typing**.

You **are not typing**.   They **are not typing**.

She/He **is not typing**.

QUESTIONS

[Present of *be* (*am/is/are*)] + [Subject] + [Base verb ending in *-ing*]

Am I **typing**?   **Are** we **typing**?

Are you **typing**?   **Are** they typing?

Is she/he **typing**?

Past Progressive

Time line: a situation that was going on in the past

began arrival at
raining restaurant

STATEMENTS

[Past of *be* (*was/were*)] + [Base verb ending in *-ing*]

It **was raining** when I got to the restaurant at 7:00.

The students **were studying** all night.

NEGATIVES

[Past of *be* (*was/were*)] + [*not*] + [Base verb ending in *-ing*]

It **was not raining** when I got to the restaurant at 7:00.

The students **were not studying** all night.

QUESTIONS

[Past of *be* (*was*/*were*)] + [Subject] + [Base verb ending in *-ing*]

Was it **raining** when I got to the restaurant at 7:00?

Were the students **studying** all night?

Future Progressive

Time line: a situation that will be ongoing at some point in the future

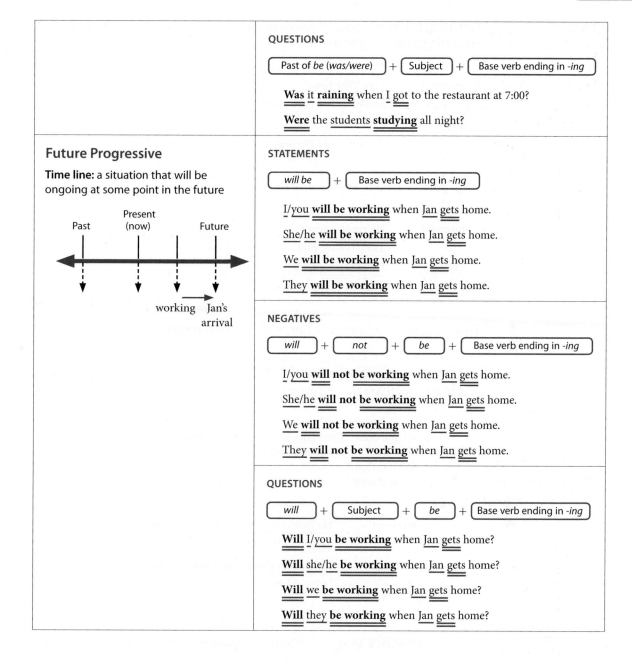

STATEMENTS

[*will be*] + [Base verb ending in *-ing*]

I/you **will be working** when Jan gets home.

She/he **will be working** when Jan gets home.

We **will be working** when Jan gets home.

They **will be working** when Jan gets home.

NEGATIVES

[*will*] + [*not*] + [*be*] + [Base verb ending in *-ing*]

I/you **will not be working** when Jan gets home.

She/he **will not be working** when Jan gets home.

We **will not be working** when Jan gets home.

They **will not be working** when Jan gets home.

QUESTIONS

[*will*] + [Subject] + [*be*] + [Base verb ending in *-ing*]

Will I/you **be working** when Jan gets home?

Will she/he **be working** when Jan gets home?

Will we **be working** when Jan gets home?

Will they **be working** when Jan gets home?

Following are some common errors in using the present progressive tense.
Forgetting to add -*ing* to the verb

Incorrect	I am type now.
	She/he is not type now.
Correct	I am typ**ing** now.
	She/he is not typ**ing** now.

Forgetting to include a form of *be* (*am/is/are*)

Incorrect	He typing now.
	They typing now.
Correct	He **is** typing now.
	They **are** typing now.

Forgetting to use a form of *be* (*am/is/are*) to start questions

| Incorrect | They typing now? |
| Correct | **Are** they typing now? |

Language note: Some English verbs do not generally occur in the progressive tenses. These are nonaction verbs; they usually describe states, possession, or opinion. Common nonaction verbs include *believe, like, need, own, possess, prefer,* and *seem*.

Incorrect	My mother is owning three different cars.
	I am needing a haircut.
Correct	My mother owns three different cars.
	I need a haircut.

PRACTICE 26–5 **Forming Negative Statements and Questions**

Rewrite the following sentences as indicated.

1. Betsy is golfing today. *Make the sentence a question:*
2. It was snowing when we got up. *Make the sentence a negative statement:*

3. You are going to the mall. *Make the sentence a question:*

4. They are losing the game. *Make the sentence a negative statement:*

5. Miriam was eating when you arrived. *Make the sentence into a question:*

Modal (Helping) Verbs

Modal verbs are auxiliary verbs that express the writer's attitude about an action. The following chart lists eight of the most common modal verbs and their uses.

MODAL (HELPING) VERBS	
General Formulas For all modal verbs	STATEMENTS Present: [Subject] + [Modal verb] + [Base verb] Dumbo can fly. Past: Forms vary.
	NEGATIVES Present: [Subject] + [Modal verb + not] + [Base verb] Dumbo cannot fly. Past: Forms vary.
	QUESTIONS Present: [Modal verb] + [Subject] + [Base verb] Can Dumbo fly? Past: Forms vary.

Can
means *ability*
	STATEMENTS
	  Present: Beth **can** work fast.
	  Past: Beth **could** work fast.

	NEGATIVES
	  Present: Beth **cannot** work fast.
	  Past: Beth **could** not work fast.

	QUESTIONS
	  Present: Can Beth work fast?
	  Past: Could Beth work fast?

→

MODAL (HELPING) VERBS	
Could means *possibility*. It can also be the past tense of *can*.	**STATEMENTS** **Present:** Beth **could** work quickly if she had more time. **Past:** Beth **could** have worked quickly if she had had more time.
	NEGATIVES *Can* is used for present negatives. (See above.) **Past:** Beth **could** not have worked quickly.
	QUESTIONS **Present: Could** Beth work quickly? **Past: Could** Beth have worked quickly?
May means *permission*. For past tense forms, see *might*.	**STATEMENTS** **Present:** You **may** borrow my car.
	NEGATIVES **Present:** You **may** not borrow my car.
	QUESTIONS **Present: May** I borrow your car?
Might means *possibility*. It can also be the past tense of *may*.	**STATEMENTS** **Present** (with *be*): Lou **might** be asleep. **Past** (with *have* + past participle of *be*): Lou **might** have been asleep. **Future:** Lou **might** sleep.
	NEGATIVES **Present** (with *be*): Lou **might** not be asleep. **Past** (with *have* + past participle of *be*): Lou **might** not have been asleep. **Future:** Lou **might** not sleep.
	QUESTIONS *Might* in questions is very formal and not often used.

MODAL (HELPING) VERBS

Must means *necessity*	**STATEMENTS** **Present:** We **must** try. **Past** (with *have* + past participle of base verb): We **must** have tried hard enough. (Expresses a logical conclusion about the past) **Past** (with *had* + *to* + base verb): We **had to** try. (Expresses past necessity)
	NEGATIVES **Present:** We **must** not try. **Past** (with *have* + past participle of base verb): We **must** not have tried hard enough. (Expresses a logical conclusion about the past)
	QUESTIONS **Present:** **Must** we try? Past tense questions with *must* are unusual.
Should means *duty, advice,* or *expectation*	**STATEMENTS** **Present:** They **should** call. **Past** (with *have* + past participle of base verb): They **should** have called.
	NEGATIVES **Present:** They **should** not call. **Past** (with *have* + past participle of base verb): They **should** not have called. (Expresses a regret or criticism of past action)
	QUESTIONS **Present:** **Should** they call? **Past** (with *have* + past participle of base verb): **Should** they have called?
Will means *intend to* (future). For past tense forms, see *would*.	**STATEMENTS** **Future:** I **will** succeed.
	NEGATIVES **Future:** I **will** not succeed.
	QUESTIONS **Future:** **Will** I succeed? ➜

MODAL (HELPING) VERBS	
Would means *prefer* or used to start a future request. It can also be the past tense of *will*.	**STATEMENTS** **Present:** I **would** like to travel. **Past** (with *have* + past participle of base verb): I **would** have traveled if I had had the money.
	NEGATIVES **Present:** I **would** not like to travel. **Past** (with *have* + past participle of base verb): I **would** not have traveled if it had not been for you.
	QUESTIONS **Present: Would** you like to travel? Or to start a request: **Would** you help me? **Past** (with *have* + past participle of base verb): **Would** you have traveled with me if I had asked you?

Common Errors with Modal Verbs

Following are some common errors in using modal verbs.

Using more than one auxiliary verb:

Incorrect	They **will can** help.
Correct	They **will** help. (future intention) They **can** help. (are able to)

Using *to* between the modal verb and the main (base) verb:

Incorrect	Emilio **might to** come with us.
Correct	Emilio **might** come with us.

Using *must* instead of *had to* to form the past tense:

Incorrect	She **must** work yesterday.
Correct	She **had to** work yesterday.

Forgetting to change *can* to *could* to form the past negative:

| Incorrect | Last night, I **can**not sleep. |
| Correct | Last night, I **could** not sleep. |

Forgetting to use *have* with *could/should/would* to form the past tense:

| Incorrect | Tara **should** called last night. |
| Correct | Tara **should have** called last night. |

Using *will* instead of *would* to express a preference in the present tense:

| Incorrect | I **will** like to travel. |
| Correct | I **would** like to travel. |

Using -s on verbs that follow modals:

| Incorrect | David can speaks French. |
| Correct | David can speak French. |

PRACTICE 26–6   Using the Correct Tense

Fill in the blanks with the correct form of the verbs in parentheses, adding helping verbs as needed. Refer to the verb charts if you need help.

Example: *Have* you *heard* (hear) of volcano boarding?

In an article in *National Geographic Today*, Zoltan Istvan _____ (report) on a new sport: volcano boarding. Istvan first _____ (get) the idea in 1995, when he _____ (sail) past Mt. Yasur, an active volcano on an island off the coast of Australia. For centuries, Mt. Yasur _____ (have) the reputation of being a dangerous volcano. For example, it regularly _____ (spit) out lava bombs. These large molten rocks _____ often _____ (strike) visitors on the head.

There is a village at the base of Mt. Yasur. When Istvan arrived with his snowboard, the villagers _____ not _____ (know) what to think. He _____ (make) his way to the volcano, _____ (hike) up the highest peak, and rode his board all the way down. After he _____ (reach) the bottom, Istvan admitted that volcano boarding is more difficult than snowboarding. Luckily, no lava bombs _____ (fall) from the sky, although the volcano _____ (erupt) seconds before his descent. Istvan hopes that this new sport _____ (become) popular with snowboarders around the world.

Gerunds and Infinitives

A **gerund** is a verb form that ends in -*ing* and acts as a noun. An **infinitive** is a verb form that is preceded by the word *to*. Gerunds and infinitives cannot be the main verbs in sentences; each sentence must have another word that is the main verb.

Gerund	Mike loves **swimming**.
	[*Loves* is the main verb, and *swimming* is a gerund.]
Infinitive	Mike loves **to run**.
	[*Loves* is the main verb, and *to run* is an infinitive.]

How do you decide whether to use a gerund or an infinitive? The decision often depends on the main verb in a sentence. A good ESL dictionary will include information about using gerunds or infinitives, or you may refer to the charts below.

Some verbs can be followed by either a gerund or an infinitive.

Verbs That Can Be Followed by Either a Gerund or an Infinitive

begin	hate	remember	try
continue	like	start	
forget	love	stop	

Sometimes, using a gerund or an infinitive after one of these verbs results in the same meaning.

Gerund	Joan likes **playing** the piano.
Infinitive	Joan likes **to play** the piano.

Other times, however, the meaning changes depending on whether you use a gerund or an infinitive.

Infinitive	Carla <u>stopped</u> **helping** me.
	[This wording means Carla no longer helps me.]
Gerund	Carla <u>stopped</u> **to help** me.
	[This wording means Carla stopped what she was doing and helped me.]

Some verbs should be followed only by a gerund, while others are followed by an infinitive, and not a gerund.

Verbs That Are Followed by a Gerund

admit	discuss	keep	risk
avoid	enjoy	miss	suggest
consider	finish	practice	
deny	imagine	quit	

The <u>politician</u> <u>risked</u> **losing** her supporters.
<u>Sophia</u> <u>considered</u> **quitting** her job.

Verbs That Are Followed by an Infinitive

agree	decide	need	refuse
ask	expect	offer	want
beg	fail	plan	
choose	hope	pretend	
claim	manage	promise	

<u>Aunt Sally</u> <u>wants</u> **to help**.
<u>Cal</u> <u>hopes</u> **to become** a millionaire.

Do not use the base form of the verb when you need a gerund or an infinitive.

Incorrect, base verb	*Swim* is my favorite activity. [*Swim* is the base form of the verb, not a noun; it cannot be the subject of the sentence.]
Correct, gerund	*Swimming* is my favorite activity. [*Swimming* is a gerund that can be the subject of the sentence.]

Incorrect, base verb	My goal is *graduate* from college.
Correct, gerund	My goal is *graduating* from college.
Correct, infinitive	My goal is *to graduate* from college.

Incorrect, base verb	I need *stop* at the store. [*Need* is the verb, so there cannot be another verb that shows the action of the subject, *I*.]
Correct, infinitive	I need *to stop* at the store.

PRACTICE 26-7   **Using Gerunds and Infinitives**

Read the paragraphs, and fill in the blanks with either a gerund or an infinitive as appropriate.

Example: If you want __*to be*__ (be) an actor, be aware that the profession is not all fun and glamour.

When you were a child, did you pretend _____ (be) famous people? Did you imagine _____ (play) roles in movies or on television? Do you like _____ (take) part in plays? If so, you might want _____ (make) a career out of acting.

Be aware of some drawbacks, however. If you hate _____ (work) with others, acting may not be the career for you. Also, if you do not enjoy _____ (repeat) the same lines over and over, you will find acting dull. You must practice _____ (speak) lines to memorize them. Despite these drawbacks, you will gain nothing if you refuse _____ (try). Anyone who hopes _____ (become) an actor has a chance at succeeding through hard work and determination.

Articles

Articles announce a noun. English uses only three articles—*a, an*, and *the*—and the same articles are used for both masculine and feminine nouns.

Definite and Indefinite Articles

The is a **definite article** and is used before a specific person, place, or thing. *A* and *an* are **indefinite articles** and are used with a person, place, or thing whose specific identity is not known.

Definite article	*The* car crashed into the building. [A specific car crashed into the building.]
Indefinite article	*A* car crashed into the building. [Some car, we don't know which one exactly, crashed into the building.]

When the word following the article begins with a vowel sound (*a, e, i, o, u*), use *an* instead of *a*.

An **old** car crashed into the building.

An **h**our from now, you will be finished with the interview.
[The h in hour is silent, so the word begins with a vowel sound.]

Does the guard have to wear *a* **u**niform?
[Uniform begins with a vowel in spelling, but the first sound (y) is not a vowel.]

Count and Noncount Nouns

To use the correct article, you need to know what count and noncount nouns are. **Count nouns** name things that can be counted, and they can be made plural, usually by adding *-s* or *-es*. **Noncount nouns** name things that cannot be counted, and they are usually singular. They cannot be made plural.

Count noun/singular	I got a **ticket** for the concert.
Count noun/plural	I got two **tickets** for the concert.
Noncount noun	The Internet has all kinds of **information**. [You would not say, *The Internet has all kinds of informations.*]

Here is a brief list of several count and noncount nouns. In English, all nouns are either count or noncount. Use an ESL dictionary to determine if other nouns are count or noncount.

Count	Noncount	
apple/apples	beauty	milk
chair/chairs	flour	money
dollar/dollars	furniture	postage
letter/letters	grass	poverty
smile/smiles	grief	rain
tree/trees	happiness	rice
	health	salt
	homework	sand
	honey	spaghetti
	information	sunlight
	jewelry	thunder
	mail	wealth

Use the chart that follows to determine when to use *a, an, the,* or no article.

Articles with Count and Noncount Nouns

Count nouns		Article used
Singular		
Specific (both the writer and reader know which one)	→	***the*** I want to read **the book** on taxes that you recommended. [The sentence refers to one particular book: the one that was recommended.] I cannot stay in **the sun** very long. [There is only one sun.]
Not specific	→	***a*** or ***an*** I want to read **a book** on taxes. [It could be any book on taxes.]
Plural		
Specific (both the writer and reader know which ones)	→	***the*** I enjoyed **the books** that we read. [The sentence refers to a particular group of books: the ones that we read.]

Not specific	→	no article or *some*
		I usually <u>enjoy</u> **books.**
		[The sentence refers to books in general.]
		<u>She</u> <u>found</u> **some books.**
		[I do not know which books she found.]

Noncount nouns	Article used
Singular	

Specific	→	*the*
(both the		I <u>put</u> away **the food** that we bought.
writer and		[The sentence refers to particular food: the food that we bought.]
reader know		
which specific		
noun)		

Not specific	→	no article or *some*
		There <u>is</u> **food** all over the kitchen.
		[The reader does not know what food the sentence refers to.]
		<u>Give</u> **some food** to the neighbors.
		[The sentence refers to an indefinite quantity of food.]

Prepositions

A **preposition** is a word (such as *of, above, between,* or *about*) that connects a noun, pronoun, or verb with information about it. The correct preposition to use is often determined by common practice rather than by the preposition's actual meaning. Also, many verbs, adjectives, and nouns are followed by particular prepositions. A good ESL dictionary will provide this lexical information.

Prepositions after Adjectives

Adjectives are often followed by prepositions. Here are some common examples.

afraid of	full of	scared of
ashamed of	happy about	sorry about/sorry for
aware of	interested in	tired of
confused by	proud of	
excited about	responsible for	

Tip For more on prepositions, see Chapter 15.

> of
> Peri is afraid ~~to~~ walking alone.
>   ^
>   about
> We are happy ~~of~~ Dino's promotion.
>   ^

Prepositions after Verbs

Many verbs consist of a verb plus a preposition. The meaning of these combinations is not usually the meaning that the verb and the preposition would each have on its own. In an ESL dictionary, these are called phrasal verbs. Often, the meaning of the verb changes completely depending on which preposition is used with it.

> You must **take out** the trash.   [*take out* = bring to a different location]
> You must **take in** the exciting sights of New York City.   [*take in* = observe]

Here are a few common verb/preposition combinations.

call in (telephone)	You can *call in* your order.
call off (cancel)	They *called off* the party.
call on (ask for a response)	The teacher always *calls on* me.
drop by (visit)	*Drop by* the next time you are in town.
drop off (leave behind)	Juan will *drop off* the car for service.
drop out (quit)	Many students *drop out* of school.
fight against (combat)	He tried to *fight against* the proposal.
fight for (defend)	We will *fight for* our rights.
fill out (complete)	Please *fill out* the form.
fill up (make full)	Do not *fill up* with junk food.
find out (discover)	Did you *find out* the answer?
give up (forfeit)	Do not *give up* your chance to succeed.
go by (visit, pass by)	I may *go by* the store on my way home.
go over (review)	Please *go over* your notes before the test.
grow up (mature)	All children *grow up*.
hand in (submit)	Please *hand in* your homework.
lock up (secure)	*Lock up* the apartment before leaving.
look up (check)	*Look up* the meaning in the dictionary.

pick out (choose)	*Pick out* a good apple.
pick up (take or collect)	Please *pick up* some drinks.
put off (postpone)	Do not *put off* starting your paper.
sign in (register)	*Sign in* when you arrive.
sign out (borrow)	You can *sign out* a book from the library.
sign up (register for)	I want to *sign up* for the contest.
think about (consider)	Simon *thinks about* moving.
turn in (submit)	Please *turn in* your homework.

 Language note: Some verb/preposition pairs can be separated by an object. These are called **separable phrasal verbs**:

Correct (verb/preposition not separated)	I must fill out the form.
Correct (verb/preposition separated)	I must fill the form out.

Other verb/preposition pairs cannot be separated by an object. These are called **inseparable phrasal verbs.**

Correct (verb/preposition not separated)	We should go over your notes.
Incorrect (verb/preposition separated)	We should go your notes over.

Use an ESL dictionary to identify the meaning of phrasal verbs and to determine whether the verb and preposition are separable or inseparable.

PRACTICE 26–8   **Editing Paragraphs for Preposition Problems**

Edit the following paragraphs to make sure the correct prepositions are used.

Example: At some point, many people think ~~out~~ having a more flexible
                                 about
           work schedule.

    (1) If they are responsible in child care, they might want to get home from work earlier than usual. (2) Or they might be interested on having one workday a week free for studying or other activities. (3) Employees shouldn't be afraid to asking a supervisor about the possibility of a flexible schedule. (4) For instance, the supervisor might be willing to allow the employee to do 40 hours of work in four days instead of five days. (5) Or a worker who wants to leave a little earlier than usual might give out half of a lunch hour to do so.

(6) The wide use of computers also allows for flexibility. (7) For example, busy parents might use their laptops to work from home a day or two a week. (8) They can stay in touch with the office by emailing supervisors or coworkers, or they might call on.

(9) Often, employers who allow more flexibility find in that they benefit, too.

(10) Workers are happy on having more control over their own time; therefore, they are less stressed out and more productive than they would have been on a fixed schedule.

Chapter Review

1. What is a pronoun?

2. What are the three types of pronouns in English?

3. What are three simple tenses? How is each formed?

4. What are the progressive tenses? How are they formed?

5. Give an example of a modal verb.

6. What is a gerund?

7. What is an infinitive?

8. Give an example of a count noun. Give an example of a noncount noun.

9. What is a preposition?

Reflect and Apply

1. What grammar concepts were new to you in this chapter?

2. Some of the grammar concepts covered in this chapter (such as articles) are difficult for native speakers of English to explain, even though they are able to use these forms correctly. Why do you think this is true?

3. Look at the feedback your instructors have given you about your writing in the past or in this course. Which of the following has been the most troublesome for you: word order, sentence patterns, pronouns, verb tenses, modal verbs, gerunds versus infinitives, articles, or prepositions? What strategies have you learned in this course and this chapter to help you address this troublesome area?

Part 5

Word Use

27 Vocabulary and Word Choice 491

28 Commonly Confused Words 502

29 Spelling 512

ALEXANDER SPATARI/GETTY IMAGES

Vocabulary and Word Choice

Using the Right Words

Understand the Importance of Building Vocabulary and Choosing Words Carefully

In conversation, you show much of your meaning through facial expressions, tone of voice, and gestures. In writing, you have only the words on the page to make your point, so you must choose them carefully. If you use vague or inappropriate words, your readers may not understand you.

Four strategies will help you build your vocabulary and find the best words for your meaning: using context clues, understanding word parts, using a dictionary, and using a thesaurus.

Using Context Clues

The best source for new vocabulary is our reading. While you may need to consult a dictionary to understand some unfamiliar words encountered in a text, you may be able to use context to determine what many words mean—and how they are used. Consider the following passage from Stephanie Ericsson's essay, "The Ways We Lie":

> We all put up façades to one degree or another. When I put on a suit to go to see a client, I feel as though I am putting on another face, obeying the expectation that serious businesspeople wear suits rather than sweatpants. But I'm a writer. Normally, I get up, get the kid off to school, and sit at my computer in my pajamas until four in the afternoon.

A reader who does not know the word façade can guess the meaning of the word by looking at the next sentence, where Ericsson mentions "putting on another face." A façade is a mask or a "false front." Ericsson gives her readers clues to this definition through her description and examples.

Using Word Parts

Another strategy you can use to build vocabulary from reading is understanding word parts. Many words in English can be divided into recognizable parts: a root, which provides the basic meaning of the word, and either a prefix or suffix. A prefix is added to the beginning of a word, changing the meaning of the word, and a suffix is added to the end of the word, changing the meaning or part of speech.

You may already know some common roots, such as *bene* (good), *bio* (life), or *scope* (seeing). You find these roots in words like *beneficial*, *biology*, and *microscope*. You may also recognize common prefixes, such as *un-* (not) and *pre-* (before), and suffixes, such as *–tion* (a noun suffix) and *–ly* (an adverb suffix). Understanding word parts can help you learn new words and select appropriate words for writing.

Using a Dictionary

Dictionaries give you all kinds of useful information about words: spelling, division of words into syllables, pronunciation, parts of speech, other forms of words, definitions, and examples of use. Following is a sample dictionary entry.

Spelling and end-of-line division	Pronunciation	Parts of speech	Other forms

Definition ——————
Example ——————

con • crete (kon´krēt, kong´-, kon-krēt´), *adj., n., v.* **-cret • ed**, **-cret • ing**, *adj.* **1.** constituting an actual thing or instance; real; perceptible; substantial: *concrete proof.* **2.** pertaining to or concerned with realities or actual instances rather than abstractions; particular as opposed to general: *concrete proposals.* **3.** referring to an actual substance or thing, as opposed to an abstract quality: the words *cat*, *water*, and *teacher* are concrete, whereas the words *truth*, *excellence*, and *adulthood* are abstract.

— *Random House Webster's College Dictionary*

Tip A number of good dictionaries are now available free online. An excellent resource is at www.dictionary.com.

🌐 **Language note:** Tips for Using a Dictionary to Learn Vocabulary

- Don't stop at the first definition given for a word; look to see which definition makes the most sense for the context.

- Develop a system for recording, reviewing, and making notes about vocabulary.

  ○ Consider keeping a vocabulary journal or online list of useful words.

  ○ Note the definition and the part of speech of new words.

- ○ If you encounter the word in reading, copy the sentence and the source.
- ○ Create your own sentence with the word.
- ○ Look for ways to include the word in your own writing.

Using a Thesaurus

A thesaurus gives **synonyms** (words that have the same meaning) for the word you look up. Use a thesaurus when you cannot find the right word for what you mean. Be careful, however, to choose a word that has the precise meaning you intend. Following is a sample thesaurus entry.

> **Concrete**, *adj.* 1. Particular, specific, single, certain, special, unique, sole, peculiar, individual, separate, isolated, distinct, exact, precise, direct, strict, minute; definite, plain, evident, obvious; pointed, emphasized; restrictive, limiting, limited, well-defined, clear-cut, fixed, finite; determining, conclusive, decided.
>
> —J. I. Rodale, *The Synonym Finder*

 Language note: What about Translators?

Are online language translators good tools for finding the right word in English? Online translators can be very helpful for students who are more comfortable speaking a language other than English. Translators can help you check new words quickly while reading and find English words to express key words from a different language. But you must use them carefully. Here are some tips for using translators effectively:

- Make sure that the words suggested by the translator make sense in the context of the sentence. Don't accept the first word that appears; check it in a dictionary.

- Check the part of speech of words suggested by the translator. Make sure you know how to use the words in a sentence.

- Do not use translators for phrases or sentences. While translators usually provide reliable translations for individual words, they do not work well for longer expressions, idioms, or sentences.

Practice Avoiding Four Common Word-Choice Problems

Four common problems with word choice may make it hard for readers to understand your point.

Vague and Abstract Words

Vague and abstract words are too general. They do not give your readers a clear idea of what you mean. Here are some common vague and abstract words.

Vague and Abstract Words

a lot	cute	nice	stuff
amazing	dumb	OK (okay)	terrible
awesome	good	old	thing
bad	great	pretty	very
beautiful	happy	sad	whatever
big	huge	small	young

When you see one of these words or another general word in your writing, replace it with a concrete or more specific word or description. A **concrete** word names something that can be seen, heard, felt, tasted, or smelled. A **specific** word names a particular person or quality. Compare these two sentences:

Vague and abstract	An old man crossed the street.
Concrete and specific	An eighty-seven-year-old priest stumbled along Main Street.

The first version is too general to be interesting. The second version creates a clear, strong image. Some words are so vague that it is best to avoid them altogether.

Vague and abstract	It is nice. [This sentence is neither concrete nor specific.]
Concrete and specific	Your poster uses blue, red, and yellow colors to highlight the key points of your presentation, and it follows a clear pattern from left to right. The graphics are clear, and there are no grammar or spelling mistakes.

PRACTICE 27-1   **Avoiding Vague and Abstract Words**

In the following sentences, underline any words that are vague or abstract. Then, edit each sentence by replacing the vague or abstract words with concrete, specific ones. You may invent details or base them on brief online research into physician-assistant careers.

Example: It would be <u>cool</u> to be a physician assistant (PA). *It would be rewarding to be a physician assistant (PA).*

1. I am drawn to this career because it would let me do neat things for others.

2. I know that becoming a PA would require tons of work.

3. Also, each day in the classroom or clinic would be long.

4. Furthermore, I would have to be able to tolerate some rough sights.

5. However, I would learn a lot.

6. And in meetings with patients, I would be able to apply my great listening skills.

7. All this stuff would be interesting.

8. I am confident that my PA education will have a good outcome.

9. Also, my starting salary would be decent.

10. Getting accepted into a PA program would be awesome.

Slang

Slang, informal and casual language, should be used only in informal situations. Avoid it when you write, especially for college classes or at work. Use language that is appropriate for your audience and purpose.

Slang	Edited
S'all good.	Everything is going well.
Dawg, I don't deserve this grade.	Professor, I don't deserve this grade.

| **PRACTICE 27–2** | **Avoiding Slang** |

In the following sentences, underline any slang words. Then, edit the sentences by replacing the slang with language appropriate for a formal audience and purpose. Imagine that you are writing to a boss where you work.

Example: ~~Yo,~~ *Hello,* Randy, I need to talk ~~at~~ *to* you for a minute.

1. That reference letter you wrote for me was really awesome sweet.

2. I am grateful because the one my English instructor did for me sucked.

3. She said that I thought I was all that, but that is not true.

4. I would be down with doing a favor for you in return if you need it.

5. Maybe you and I could hang sometime one of these weekends?

6. I know that we cannot be best buds, but we could shoot some hoops or something.

7. You could let me know whazzup when I see you at work next week.

8. If you are too stressed, do not go all emo on me.

9. Just chill out, and forget about it.

10. Text me when you get a sec.

Wordy Language

People sometimes use too many words to express their ideas. They may think that using more words will make them sound smart, but too many words can weaken a writer's point.

Wordy	I am not interested *at this point in time*.
Edited	I am not interested now.
	[The phrase *at this point in time* uses five words to express what could be said in one word: *now*.]

Common Wordy Expressions

Wordy	Edited
As a result of	Because of
Due to the fact that	Because
In spite of the fact that	Although
It is my opinion that	I think (*or just make the point*)
In the event that	If
The fact of the matter is that	(*Just state the point.*)
A great number of	Many
At that time	Then
In this day and age	Now
At this point in time	Now
In this paper, I will show that . . .	(*Just make the point; do not announce it.*)

PRACTICE 27-3   Avoiding Wordy Language

In the following sentences, underline the wordy or repetitive language. Then, edit each sentence to make it more concise. Some sentences may contain more than one wordy phrase.

Example: Sugar substitutes are a popular diet choice for people ~~of all~~
~~ages~~ when they are searching for ways to ~~cut down on all~~ *reduce* the
calories they ingest ~~on a daily basis~~. *each day*

1. It is a well-known fact that dieting is difficult for most people.

2. Due to the fact that people are trying to cut calories, sugar substitutes are used in sodas, snacks, and other products.

3. The fact of the matter is that these substitutes provide a sweet taste, but without the calories of sugar or honey.

4. A great number of researchers have stated at this time that such substitutes are not necessarily safe or healthy to use in large quantities.

5. Some of the current experts on the matter are of the opinion that sugar substitutes can cause cancer, allergies, and other serious health problems.

6. At this point in time, other experts on the same subject believe that using these substitutes maintains a person's addiction to sugar and leads people to eat more junk food.

7. Despite these warnings, negative evaluations, and critical opinions from the experts, nearly 200 million people consume sugar-free or low-calorie products each year.

8. In this day and age, people are consuming an average of four of these items each day.

9. In spite of the fact that people know sugar is bad for them, their tastes will probably not change anytime in the near future.

10. It is my opinion that it would be better if people just learned to consume foods that do not contain sweeteners of any kind.

Clichés

Clichés are phrases used so often that people no longer pay attention to them. To get your point across and to get your readers' attention, replace clichés with fresh and specific language.

Clichés	Edited
That teacher's bark is worse than his bite.	That teacher is not nearly as strict or inflexible as he appears in class the first day.
My uncle *worked his way up the corporate ladder*.	My uncle started as a shipping clerk but ended up as a regional vice president.
This roll is *as hard as a rock*.	This roll is so hard I could bounce it.

Common Clichés

as big as a house	few and far between	skating on thin ice
as light as a feather	hell on earth	starting from scratch
better late than never	last but not least	sweating blood/bullets
break the ice	no way on earth	the more the merrier
crystal clear	110 percent	too little, too late
a drop in the bucket	playing with fire	tough as nails
easier said than done	quick as a wink	work like a dog

PRACTICE 27–4   **Avoiding Clichés**

In the following sentences, underline the clichés. Then, edit each sentence by replacing the clichés with fresh and specific language.

Example: Riding a bicycle 100 miles a day can be ~~hell on earth~~ *excruciating* unless you are willing to ~~give 110 percent~~ *work extremely hard*.

1. You have to persuade yourself to sweat blood and work like a dog for up to 10 hours.

2. There's no way on earth you can do it without extensive training.

3. Staying on your bike until the bitter end, of course, is easier said than done.

4. It is important to keep the fire in your belly and keep your goal of finishing the race crystal clear in your mind.

5. No matter how long it takes you to cross the finish line, remind yourself that it's better late than never.

6. Even if you are not a champion racer, training for a bike race will keep you fit as a fiddle.

7. It may take discipline to make yourself train, but you should keep your nose to the grindstone.

8. Bike racers should always play it safe by wearing helmets.

9. When you train for road racing, keep an eye peeled for cars.

10. You do not want to end up flat on your back in the hospital, or six feet under!

A final note: Language that favors one gender over another or that assumes that only one gender performs a certain role is called *sexist*. Such language should be avoided.

Tip See Chapter 20 for more advice on using pronouns.

Sexist	A doctor should politely answer *his* patients' questions. [Not all doctors are male, as suggested by the pronoun *his*.]
Revised	A doctor should politely answer *his or her* patients' questions.
	Doctors should politely answer *their* patients' questions. [The first revision changes *his* to *his or her* to avoid sexism. The second revision changes the subject to a plural noun (*doctors*) so that a genderless pronoun (*their*) can be used. Usually, it is preferable to avoid *his or her*.]

Edit for Word Choice

> **PRACTICE 27–5**   **Editing Paragraphs for Word Choice**
>
> Find and edit six examples of vague or abstract language, slang, wordy language, or clichés in the following paragraphs.

Imagine spending almost two weeks living in the coolest home in the world. That is what scientist Lloyd Godson did when he lived at the bottom of a lake in Australia for thirteen days. Although there is no way on earth I would want to do that, it sure sounds fascinating.

Godson's home was an 8-by-11-foot-long yellow steel box that he dubbed the BioSUB. His air supply came from the algae plants growing inside the BioSUB. Divers brought him food, water, and other junk through a manhole built in the bottom of his underwater home. To keep busy, he rode on an exercise bicycle, which created electricity for him to recharge his laptop and run the lights for his plants. He used his computer to talk to students all over the world and to watch movies.

Godson paid for this experiment with money he had won in the "Live Your Dream" contest. At this point in time, I have to say that for most people, the BioSUB home would be less appealing than a regular, aboveground room, apartment, or house. Indeed, by the time his two weeks were over, Godson was ready to come up, feel the sunshine and wind on his face again, and "smell the roses."

Chapter Review

For Reflect and Apply questions for Part 5, please see page 518.

1. What are four strategies that will help you build vocabulary?

2. What are four common word-choice problems?

3. What are vague words? Why are they a problem for writers?

4. When is it appropriate to use slang in college writing or in writing at work?

5. What is a cliché? Give an example.

6. What is a wordy expression? Give an example.

7. What is sexist language? Give an example.

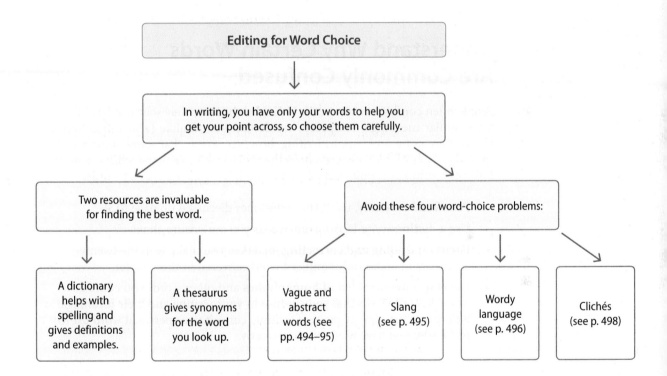

Editing for Word Choice

In writing, you have only your words to help you get your point across, so choose them carefully.

Two resources are invaluable for finding the best word.

Avoid these four word-choice problems:

A dictionary helps with spelling and gives definitions and examples.

A thesaurus gives synonyms for the word you look up.

Vague and abstract words (see pp. 494–95)

Slang (see p. 495)

Wordy language (see p. 496)

Clichés (see p. 498)

Commonly Confused Words

Avoiding Mistakes with Soundalike Words

Understand Why Certain Words Are Commonly Confused

People often confuse certain words in English because they sound alike and may have similar meanings. In speech, words that sound alike (also called homophones) are not a problem. In writing, however, words that sound alike may be spelled differently, and readers rely on the spelling to understand what you mean. Edit your writing carefully to make sure you have used the correct words.

- **Proofread carefully,** using the techniques discussed on page 513.
- **Use a dictionary** to look up any words you are unsure about.
- **Focus on finding and correcting mistakes** you make with the twenty-seven sets of commonly confused words covered in this chapter.
- **Develop a personal list of homophones** and other words you confuse often. Record words that you confuse in your writing and their meanings. Before you turn in any piece of writing, consult your personal word list to make sure you have used words correctly.

Practice Using Commonly Confused Words Correctly

Study the different meanings and spellings of these twenty-seven sets of commonly confused words. Complete the sentence after each set of words, filling in each blank with the correct word.

A/AN/AND

a: used before a word that begins with a consonant sound (article)

A friend of mine just won the lottery.

an: used before a word that begins with a vowel sound (article)

An old friend of mine just won the lottery.

and: used to join two words (conjunction)

My friend *and* I went out to celebrate.

A friend *and* I ate at *an* Italian restaurant.

Other lottery winners were _____ algebra teacher _____ bowling team.

ACCEPT/EXCEPT

accept: to agree to receive or admit (verb)

I will *accept* the job offer.

except: but, other than (preposition)

All the stores are closed *except* the Quik-Stop.

I *accept* all the job conditions *except* the low pay.

Do not _____ gifts from clients, _____ those who are also personal friends.

ADVICE/ADVISE

advice: opinion (noun)

I would like your *advice* before I make a decision.

advise: to give an opinion (verb)

Please *advise* me what to do.

Please *advise* me what to do; you always give me good *advice*.

If you do not like my _____, please _____ me how to proceed.

AFFECT/EFFECT

affect: to make an impact on, to change something (verb)

The whole city was *affected* by the hurricane.

effect: a result (noun)

What *effect* will the hurricane have on the local economy?

Although the storm will have many negative *effects*, it will not *affect* the price of food.

The _____ of the disaster will _____ many people.

Tip Thinking "*the* effect" will help you remember that *effect* is a noun.

Tip In some dialects of American English, these two words are homophones (pronounced the same way). Other dialects pronounce them differently.

ARE/OUR

are: a form of the verb *be*

> The workers *are* about to go on strike.

our: a pronoun showing ownership

> The children played on *our* porch.

My relatives *are* staying at *our* house.

_____ new neighbors _____ moving in today.

BY/BUY/BYE

by: next to, before, or past (preposition)

> Meet me *by* the entrance.
>
> Make sure the bill is paid *by* the fifteenth of the month.
>
> The motorcycle raced *by* me.

buy: to purchase (verb)

> I would like to *buy* a new laptop.

bye: an informal way to say *goodbye*

> "Bye, Grandma!"

I said "_____" from the window as we drove _____ our friends, who were

standing next to the house I wanted to _____.

CONSCIENCE/CONSCIOUS

Tip Remember that one of the words is *con-science*; the other is not.

conscience: a personal sense of right and wrong (noun)

> Jake's *conscience* would not allow him to cheat.

conscious: awake, aware (adjective)

> The coma patient is now *conscious*.
>
> I am *conscious* that it is getting late.

The judge was *conscious* that the accused had acted according to his *conscience* even though he had broken the law.

The man said that he was not _____ that what he had done was illegal, or his _____ would not have let him do it.

FINE/FIND

fine: of high quality (adjective); feeling well (adjective); a penalty for breaking a law (noun)

> This jacket is made of *fine* leather.

After a day in bed, Jacob felt *fine*.

The *fine* for exceeding the speed limit is $50.

find: to locate, to discover (verb)

Did Clara *find* her glasses?

I *find* gardening to be a *fine* pastime.

Were you able to _____ a place to store your _____ jewelry?

ITS/IT'S

its: a pronoun showing ownership

The dog chased *its* tail.

it's: a contraction of the words *it is*

It's about time you got here.

It's very hard for a dog to keep *its* teeth clean.

_____ no surprise that the college raised _____ tuition.

Tip If you are not sure whether to use *its* or *it's* in a sentence, try substituting *it is*. If the sentence does not make sense with *it is*, use *its*.

KNEW/NEW/KNOW/NO

knew: understood; recognized (past tense of the verb *know*)

I *knew* the answer, but I could not think of it.

new: unused, recent, or just introduced (adjective)

The building has a *new* security code.

know: to understand; to have knowledge of (verb)

I *know* how to bake bread.

no: used to form a negative

I have *no* idea what the answer is.

I never *knew* how much a *new* car costs.

The _____ teacher _____ many of her students already.

There is _____ way Tom could _____ where Celia is hiding.

I _____ that there is _____ cake left.

LOOSE/LOSE

loose: baggy; relaxed; not fixed in place (adjective)

In hot weather, people tend to wear *loose* clothing.

lose: to misplace; to forfeit possession of (verb)

Every summer, I *lose* about three pairs of sunglasses.

If the ring is too *loose* on your finger, you might *lose* it.

I _____ my patience with the _____ rules on Wall Street.

MIND/MINE

mind: to object to (verb); the thinking or feeling part of one's brain (noun)

Toby does not *mind* if I borrow his tool chest.

Estela has a good *mind,* but often she does not use it.

mine: belonging to me (pronoun); a source of ore and minerals (noun)

That coat is *mine.*

My uncle worked in a coal *mine* in West Virginia.

That writing problem of *mine* was on my *mind.*

If you do not _____, the gloves you just took are _____.

OF/HAVE

of: coming from; caused by; part of a group; made from (preposition)

The leader *of* the band played bass guitar.

have: to possess (verb; also used as an auxiliary verb)

I *have* one more course to take before I graduate.

I should *have* started studying earlier.

The president *of* the company should *have* resigned.

Sidney could _____ been one _____ the winners.

Note: Do not use *of* after *would, should, could,* and *might.* Use *have* after those words (*would have, should have*).

PASSED/PAST

passed: went by or went ahead (past tense of the verb *pass*)

We *passed* the hospital on the way to the airport.

past: time that has gone by (noun); gone by, over, just beyond (preposition)

In the *past,* I was able to stay up all night and not be tired.

I drove *past* the burning warehouse.

This *past* school year, I *passed* all my exams.

Trish _____ me as we ran _____ the one-mile marker.

PEACE/PIECE

peace: no disagreement; calm (noun)

Could you quiet down and give me a little *peace*?

piece: a part of something larger (noun)

May I have a *piece* of that pie?

The feuding families found *peace* after they sold the *piece* of land.

To keep the _____, give your sister a _____ of candy.

PRINCIPAL/PRINCIPLE

principal: main (adjective); head of a school or leader of an organization (noun)

Brush fires are the *principal* risk in the hills of California.

Ms. Edwards is the *principal* of Memorial Elementary School.

Corinne is a *principal* in the management consulting firm.

principle: a standard of beliefs or behaviors (noun)

Although tempted, she held on to her moral *principles*.

The *principal* questioned the delinquent student's *principles*.

The _____ problem is that you want me to act against my _____.

QUIET/QUITE/QUIT

quiet: soft in sound; not noisy (adjective)

The library was *quiet*.

quite: completely; very (adverb)

After cleaning all the windows, Alex was *quite* tired.

quit: to stop (verb)

She *quit* her job.

After the band *quit* playing, the hall was *quite quiet*.

If you would _____ shouting and be _____, you would find that the

scenery is _____ pleasant.

RIGHT/WRITE

right: correct; in a direction opposite from left (adjective)

You definitely made the *right* choice.

When you get to the stoplight, make a *right* turn.

write: to put words on paper (verb)

Will you *write* your phone number for me?

Please *write* the *right* answer in the space provided.

You were _____ to _____ to the senator.

SET/SIT

set: a collection of something (noun); to place an object somewhere (verb)

Paul has a complete *set* of Johnny Cash records.

Please *set* the package on the table.

sit: to rest in a chair or other seat-like surface; to be located in a particular place (verb)

I need to *sit* on the sofa for a few minutes.

The shed *sits* between the house and the garden.

If I *sit* down now, I will not have time to *set* the plants outside.

Before you _____ on that chair, _____ the magazines on the floor.

SUPPOSE/SUPPOSED

suppose: to imagine or assume to be true (verb)

I *suppose* you would like something to eat.

Suppose you won a million dollars.

supposed: past tense of *suppose*; intended or expected (verb)

Karen *supposed* Thomas was late because of traffic.

I *suppose* you know that Rita was *supposed* to be home by 6:30.

I _____ you want to leave soon because we are _____ to arrive before the guests.

THAN/THEN

than: a word used to compare two or more people, places, or things (conjunction)

It is colder inside *than* outside.

then: at a certain time; next in time (adverb)

I got out of the car and *then* realized the keys were still in it.

Clara ran more miles *than* she ever had before, and *then* she collapsed.

Back _____, I smoked more _____ three packs a day.

THEIR/THERE/THEY'RE

Tip If you are not sure whether to use *their* or *they're*, substitute *they are*. If the sentence does not make sense, use *their*.

Tip If you are not sure whether to use *their* or *there*, remember that *there* has the word *here* in it; *here* and *there* go together.

their: a pronoun showing ownership

I borrowed *their* clippers to trim the hedges.

there: a word indicating location or existence (adverb)

Just put the keys *there* on the desk.

There are too many lawyers.

they're: a contraction of the words *they are*

>   *They're* about to leave.

There is a car in *their* driveway, which indicates that *they're* home.

_____ beach house is empty except for the one week that _____

vacationing _____.

THOUGH/THROUGH/THREW

though: however; nevertheless; in spite of (conjunction)

>   *Though* he is short, he plays great basketball.

through: finished with (adjective); from one side to the other (preposition)

>   I am *through* arguing with you.

>   The baseball went right *through* the window.

threw: hurled; tossed (past tense of the verb *throw*)

>   She *threw* the basketball.

Even *though* it was illegal, she *threw* the empty cup *through* the window onto the road.

_____ she did not really believe it would bring good luck, Jan _____

a penny _____ the air into the fountain.

TO/TOO/TWO

to: a word indicating a direction or movement (preposition); part of the infinitive form of a verb

>   Please give the message *to* Sharon.

>   It is easier *to* ask for forgiveness than *to* get permission.

too: also; more than enough; very (adverb)

>   I am tired *too*.

>   Dan ate *too* much and felt sick.

>   That dream was *too* real.

two: the number between one and three (noun)

>   The lab had only *two* computers.

They went *to* a restaurant and ordered *too* much food for *two* people.

When Marty went _____ pay for his meal, the cashier charged him _____

times, which was _____ bad.

USE/USED

use: to employ or put into service (verb)

How do you plan to *use* that blueprint?

used: past tense of the verb *use*. *Used + infinitive* indicates a past fact or habit. *Be used to* (preposition) means "be familiar with." The preposition *to* may be followed by a noun or a gerund (the *–ing* form of a verb).

He *used* his lunch hour to do errands. [past tense]

He *used* to go for a walk during his lunch hour. [past habit]

She *used* to be a chef [past fact], so she knows how to *use* all kinds of kitchen gadgets.

She *is used* to noise. [familiar with]

She *is* also *used* to improvising in the kitchen. [familiar with]

Tom _____ the prize money to buy a boat; his family hoped he

would _____ the money for his education, but Tom was _____ to getting

his way.

WHO'S/WHOSE

Tip If you are not sure whether to use *whose* or *who's*, substitute *who is*. If the sentence does not make sense, use *whose*.

who's: a contraction of the words *who is*

Who's at the door?

whose: a pronoun showing ownership

Whose car is parked outside?

Who's the person *whose* car sank in the river?

The student _____ name is first on the list is the one _____ in charge.

YOUR/YOU'RE

your: a pronoun showing ownership

Did you bring *your* wallet?

you're: a contraction of the words *you are*

You're not telling me the whole story.

Tip If you are not sure whether to use *your* or *you're*, substitute *you are*. If the sentence does not make sense, use *your*.

You're going to have *your* third exam tomorrow.

_____ teacher says that _____ good with numbers.

Edit for Commonly Confused Words

PRACTICE 28-1   **Editing Paragraphs for Commonly Confused Words**

Edit the following paragraphs to correct eighteen errors in word use.

More and more women are purchasing handguns, against the advise of law enforcement officers. Few of these women are criminals or plan to commit crimes. They no the risks of guns, and they except those risks. They buy weapons primarily because their tired of feeling like victims. They do not want to contribute too the violence in are society, but they also realize that women are the victims of violent attacks far to often. Many women loose they're lives because they cannot fight off there attackers. Some women have made a conscience decision to arm themselves for protection.

But does buying a gun make things worse rather then better? Having a gun in you're house makes it three times more likely that someone will be killed there—and that someone is just as likely to be you or one of your children as a criminal. Most young children cannot tell the difference between a real gun and a toy gun when they fine one. Every year, their are tragic examples of children who accidentally shoot and even kill other youngsters while they are playing with guns. A mother who's children are injured while playing with her gun will never again think that a gun provides piece of mind. Reducing the violence in are society may be a better solution.

Chapter Review

1. What strategies can you use to avoid confusing words that sound alike or have similar meanings?

2. What are the top five commonly confused words on your personal list?

For Reflect and Apply questions for Part 5, please see page 518.

29

Spelling

Using the Right Letters

Finding and Correcting Spelling Mistakes

Some extremely smart people are poor spellers. Unfortunately, spelling errors are easy for readers to spot, and they make a bad impression. Learn to find and correct spelling mistakes in your writing by using the following strategies.

Use a Dictionary

When proofreading your papers, consult a dictionary whenever you are unsure about the spelling of a word. *Checking a dictionary is the single most important thing you can do to improve your spelling.*

Use a Spell Checker—with Caution

Tip Online dictionaries can help you spell because they often allow you to type an incorrectly spelled word and get the correct spelling. Be sure to check the dictionary to make sure you have found the word you need.

Use a spell checker after you have completed a piece of writing but before you print it out. This word-processing tool finds and highlights a word that may be misspelled, suggests other spellings, and gives you the opportunity to change the spelling of the word.

However, you should never rely on a spell checker to do your editing for you. Because a spell checker ignores anything it recognizes as a word, it will not help you find misused words or misspellings that are also words. For example, a spell checker would not highlight any of the problems in these phrases:

Just *to* it.	(Correct: Just *do* it.)
pain in the *nick*	(Correct: pain in the *neck*)
my writing *coarse*	(Correct: my writing *course*)

Use Proofreading Techniques

Use some of the following proofreading techniques to focus on the spelling of one word at a time. Try them all. Then, decide which ones work best for you.

- Print out your paper before proofreading. (Many writers find it easier to detect errors on paper than on a computer screen.)
- Put a piece of paper under the line that you are reading.
- Proofread your paper backward, one word at a time.
- Print out a version of your paper that looks noticeably different: make the words larger, make the margins larger, triple-space the lines, or make all these changes.
- Read your paper aloud. This strategy will help you if you tend to leave out words.
- Have someone else read your paper aloud. You may hear where you have made a mistake or left a word out.
- Exchange papers with a partner and proofread each other's papers, identifying possible misspellings.

Make a Personal Spelling List

Set aside a section of your course notebook for your spelling list. Every time you edit a paper, write down the words that you misspelled. Every couple of weeks, go back to your spelling list to see whether your problem words have changed. Are you misspelling fewer words in each paper?

For each word on your list, create a memory aid to help you remember the correct spelling. For example, if you often misspell *a lot*, you could remember that "*a lot* is a lot of words." You could also sing the spelling to a familiar tune.

Strategies for Becoming a Better Speller

Here are three good strategies for becoming a better speller.

Master Commonly Confused Words

Chapter 28 covers twenty-seven sets of words that are commonly confused because they sound similar, such as *write* and *right*. If you can master these commonly confused words, you will avoid many spelling mistakes.

Learn Six Spelling Rules

If you can remember the following six rules, you can correct many of the spelling errors in your writing.

First, here is a quick review of vowels and consonants.

Vowels:	*a, e, i, o,* and *u*
Consonants:	*b, c, d, f, g, h, j, k, l, m, n, p, q, r, s, t, v, w, x,* and *z*

The letter *y* can be either a vowel or a consonant. It is a vowel when it sounds like the *y* in *fly* or *hungry*. It is a consonant when it sounds like the *y* in *yellow*.

Rule 1. "*I* before *e*, except after *c*, or when sounding like *a*, as in *neighbor* or *weigh*."

Many people repeat this rhyme to themselves as they decide whether a word is spelled with an *ie* or an *ei*.

pie ce (*i* before *e*)

rece ive (except after *c*)

eight (sounds like *a*)

Exceptions: *either, neither, foreign, height, seize, society, their, weird*

Rule 2. Drop the final *e* when adding an ending that begins with a vowel.

hope + ing = hoping

imagine + ation = imagination

Keep the final *e* when adding an ending that begins with a consonant.

achieve + ment = achievement

definite + ly = definitely

Exceptions: *argument, awful, judgment, simply, truly,* and others

Rule 3. When adding an ending to a word that ends in *y*, **change the *y* to *i*** when a consonant comes before the *y*.

lonely + est = loneliest   apology + ize = apologize

happy + er = happier   likely + hood = likelihood

Do not change the *y* when a vowel comes before the *y*.

boy + ish = boyish   survey + or = surveyor
pay + ment = payment   buy + er = buyer

Exceptions:

1. When adding *-ing* to a word ending in *y*, always keep the *y*, even if a consonant comes before it: study + ing = studying.

2. Other exceptions include *daily, dryer, said,* and *paid*.

Rule 4. When adding an ending that starts with a vowel to a one-syllable word, follow these rules.

Double the final consonant only if the word ends with a consonant-vowel-consonant.

trap + ed = trapped   knit + ed = knitted
drip + ed = dripped   fat + er = fatter

Do not double the final consonant if the word ends with some other combination.

Vowel-vowel-consonant	Vowel-consonant-consonant
clean + est = cleanest	slick + er = slicker
poor + er = poorer	teach + er = teacher
clear + ed = cleared	last + ed = lasted

Rule 5. When adding an ending that starts with a vowel to a word with two or more syllables, follow these rules.

Double the final consonant only if the word ends with a consonant-vowel-consonant and the stress is on the last syllable.

submit + ing = submitting

prefer + ed = preferred

Do not double the final consonant in other cases.

understand + ing = understanding

offer + ed = offered

Rule 6. Add *-s* to most nouns to form the plural, including words that end in *o* preceded by a vowel.

Most words	Words that end in vowel plus *o*
book + s = books	video + s = videos
college + s = colleges	stereo + s = stereos

Add -es to words that end in *o* preceded by a consonant and words that end in *s, sh, ch,* or *x.*

Words that end in consonant plus *o*	Words that end in *s, sh, ch,* or *x*
pota**to** + **es** = potato**es** he**ro** + **es** = hero**es**	cla**ss** + **es** = class**es** pu**sh** + **es** = push**es** ben**ch** + **es** = bench**es** fa**x** + **es** = fax**es**

Exceptions When Forming Plurals

A **compound noun** is formed when two nouns are joined with a hyphen (*in-law*), a space (*life vest*), or no space (*keyboard, stockpile*). Plurals of compound nouns are generally formed by adding an *-s* to the end of the last noun (*in-laws, life vests*) or to the end of the combined word (*keyboards, stockpiles*). Some hyphenated compound words such as *mother-in-law* or *hole-in-one* form plurals by adding an *-s* to the chief word (*mothers-in-law, holes-in-one*).

Some words form plurals in different ways, as in the list below.

Different Types of Plurals

Singular	Plural	Singular	Plural
analysis	analyses	loaf	loaves
bacteria	bacterium	louse	lice
bison	bison	man	men
cactus	cacti	medium	media
calf	calves	mouse	mice
child	children	phenomenon	phenomena
deer	deer	roof	roofs
die	dice	sheep	sheep
focus	foci	shelf	shelves
foot	feet	thief	thieves
goose	geese	tooth	teeth
half	halves	vertebra	vertebrae
hoof	hooves	wife	wives
knife	knives	wolf	wolves
leaf	leaves	woman	women

Consult a List of Commonly Misspelled Words

Use a list like the one that follows as an easy reference to check your spelling.

One Hundred Commonly Misspelled Words and Phrases

absence	dollar	ninety
achieve	eighth	noticeable
across	embarrass	occasion
aisle	environment	perform
a lot	especially	physically
already	exaggerate	prejudice
analyze	excellent/excellence	probably
answer	exercise	psychology
appetite	fascinate	receive
argument	February	recognize
athlete	finally	recommend
awful	foreign	restaurant
basically	friend	rhythm
beautiful	government	roommate
beginning	grief	schedule
believe	guidance	scissors
business	harass	secretary
calendar	height	separate
career	humorous	sincerely
category	illegal	sophomore
chief	immediately	succeed
column	independent	successful
coming	interest	surprise
commitment	jewelry	truly
conscious	judgment	until
convenient	knowledge	usually
cruelty	license	vacuum
daughter	lightning	valuable
definite	loneliness	vegetable
describe	marriage	weight
develop	meant	weird
dictionary	muscle	writing
different	necessary	written
disappoint		

Chapter Review

1. What are two important tools for finding and correcting spelling mistakes?

2. What three strategies can you use to become a better speller?

Reflect and Apply

1. Why is it important to use words precisely and accurately in writing?

2. Talk to someone who has taken courses in your major. What challenges did that person face in learning the vocabulary needed for success in the major?

3. What is one strategy from this Part (Chapters 27, 28, and 29) that you can apply in your courses now?

Part 6

Punctuation and Capitalization

30 Commas 521

31 Apostrophes 532

32 Quotation Marks 536

33 Other Punctuation 543

34 Capitalization 548

Commas ,

Understand What Commas Do

Commas (,) are punctuation marks that help readers understand a sentence. Read the following three sentences aloud. How does the use of commas change the meaning?

No comma	When you call Sarah I will start cooking.
One comma	When you call Sarah**,** I will start cooking.
Two commas	When you call**,** Sarah**,** I will start cooking.

To get your intended meaning across to your readers, it is important that you understand when and how to use commas.

Practice Using Commas Correctly

Writers use commas to separate information within sentences to make sure that readers can accurately interpret the meaning of the sentence.

Commas between Items in a Series

Use commas to separate the items in a series (three or more items), including the last item in the series, which usually has *and* before it.

521

To get from South Dakota to Texas, we will drive through *Nebraska*, *Kansas*, and *Oklahoma*.

We can *sleep in the car*, *stay in a motel*, or *camp outside*.

As I drive, I see many beautiful sights, such as *mountains*, *plains*, and *prairies*.

Note: Writers do not always use a comma before the final item in a series (this comma is known as the Oxford comma or serial comma). In college writing, however, it is best to include it.

Commas between Coordinate Adjectives

Coordinate adjectives are two or more adjectives that independently modify the same noun and are separated by commas.

Conor ordered a *big*, *fat*, greasy burger.

The diner food was *cheap*, *unhealthy*, and *delicious*.

Do *not* use a comma between the final adjective and the noun it describes.

Incorrect	Joelle wore a *long*, *clingy*, *red*, dress.
Correct	Joelle wore a *long*, *clingy*, *red* dress.

Cumulative adjectives describe the same noun but are not separated by commas because they form a unit that describes the noun. You can identify cumulative adjectives because separating them by *and* does not make any sense.

The store is having its *last storewide clearance* sale.

[Putting *and* between *last* and *storewide* and between *storewide* and *clearance* would make an odd sentence: The store is having its *last* and *storewide* and *clearance* sale. The adjectives in the sentence are cumulative adjectives and should not be separated by commas.]

In summary:

- **Do** use commas to separate two or more **coordinate adjectives**.
- **Do not** use commas to separate **cumulative adjectives**.

 Language note: When two or more adjectives come before a noun, they usually occur in a specific order. We could say that Joelle wore *a long silk dress*, but we would not say that she wore a *silk long dress*. The second version sounds odd to our ears. If your first language is not English, however, the order of adjectives before nouns may be confusing. Although there may be some variation, the following order is usually

Tip How does a comma change the way you read a sentence aloud? Many readers pause when they come to a comma; they may also change the intonation or pitch of their voices.

acceptable. Based on this list, size (*long*) comes before material (*silk*); therefore, *long silk dress* sounds more natural than *silk long dress*.

1. Quantity (*three*)
2. Opinion (*ridiculous*)
3. Size (*large*)
4. Age (*old*)
5. Shape (*round*)
6. Color (*yellow*)
7. Nationality or material (*German, wooden*)
8. Purpose or noun compound (*grammar* book)

Commas in Compound Sentences

A **compound sentence** contains two independent clauses joined by a coordinating conjunction: *and, but, for, nor, or, so, yet.* Use a comma before the joining word to separate the two independent clauses.

Tip Remember the coordinating conjunctions with *FANBOYS: for, and, nor, but, or, yet,* and *so.* For more information, see Chapter 23.

Independent clause	**,**	and, but, for, nor, or, so, yet	**,**	independent clause.

I called my best friend**,** and she agreed to drive me to work.

I asked my best friend to drive me to work**,** but she was busy.

I can take the bus to work**,** or I can call another friend.

Language note: A comma alone cannot separate two sentences in English. Using a comma between independent clauses creates a comma splice (see Chapter 17).

Commas after Introductory Words

Use a comma after an introductory word, phrase, or clause. The comma lets your readers know when the main part of the sentence is starting.

Introductory word or word group	**,**	Main part of sentence.

Introductory word   *Yesterday*, I went to the game.

Introductory phrase   *By the way*, I do not have a babysitter for tomorrow.

Introductory clause   *While I waited outside*, Susan went backstage.

PRACTICE 30-1   Using Commas after Introductory Word Groups

In each item, underline introductory words or word groups. Then, add commas after introductory word groups where they are needed. If a sentence is already correct, put a "C" next to it.

Example: <u>In the 1960s</u>, John Mackey became famous for his speed and strength as a tight end for the Baltimore Colts football team.

1. In his later years the National Football League Hall-of-Famer was in the news for another reason: he suffered from dementia possibly linked to the head blows he received on the football field.

2. According to medical experts repeated concussions can severely damage the brain over time, and they are especially harmful to young people, whose brains are still developing.

3. Based on these warnings and on stories like John Mackey's athletic associations, coaches, and parents of young athletes are taking new precautions.

4. For example more football coaches are teaching players to tackle and block with their heads up, reducing the chance that they will receive a blow to the top of the head.

5. Also when players show signs of a concussion—such as dizziness, nausea, or confusion—more coaches are taking them out of the game.

6. Ideally coaches then make sure injured players receive immediate medical attention.

7. Once concussion sufferers are back home they should take a break from sports until the symptoms of their injury are gone.

8. During their recovery they should also avoid any activity that puts too much stress on the brain; these activities can include playing video games, studying, and driving.

9. When concussion sufferers feel ready to get back into the game a doctor should confirm that it is safe for them to do so.

10. As a result of these new precautions young athletes may avoid experiencing anything like the long, difficult decline of John Mackey, who died in 2011.

Commas around Appositives and Interrupters

An **appositive** comes directly before or after a noun or pronoun and renames it.

Tip For more on appositives, see Chapter 25.

Lily, *a senior,* will take her nursing exam this summer.

The prices are outrageous at Beans, *the local coffee shop.*

An **interrupter** is an aside or transition that interrupts the flow of a sentence and does not affect its meaning.

My sister, *incidentally,* has good reasons for being late.

Her child had a fever, *for example.*

Putting commas around appositives and interrupters tells readers that these elements give extra information but are not essential to the meaning of a sentence. If an appositive or interrupter is in the middle of a sentence, set it off with a pair of commas, one before and one after. If an appositive or interrupter comes at the end of a sentence, separate it from the rest of the sentence with one comma.

Your proposal, *by the way,* has been accepted.

Your proposal has been accepted, *by the way.*

Note: Sometimes, an appositive is essential to the meaning of a sentence. When a sentence would not have the same meaning without the appositive, the appositive should not be set off with commas.

The actor *Glenn Close* has never won an Oscar.

[The sentence *The actor has never won an Oscar* does not have the same meaning.]

> **PRACTICE 30-2**   **Using Commas to Set Off Appositives and Interrupters**
>
> Underline all the appositives and interrupters in the following sentences. Then, use commas to set them off.
>
> **Example:**   Harry, <u>an attentive student</u>, could not hear his teacher because the radiator in class made a constant rattling.
>
> 1. Some rooms in fact are full of echoes, dead zones, and mechanical noises that make it hard for students to hear.
>
> 2. The American Speech-Language-Hearing Association experts on how noise levels affect learning abilities has set guidelines for how much noise in a classroom is too much.

3. The association recommends that background noise the constant whirring or whining sounds made by radiators, lights, and other machines be no more than thirty-five decibels.

4. That level thirty-five decibels is about as loud as a whispering voice fifteen feet away.

5. One study found a level of sixty-five decibels the volume of a vacuum cleaner in a number of classrooms around the country.

6. Other classroom noises came for example from ancient heating systems, whirring air-conditioning units, rattling windows, humming classroom computers, buzzing clocks, and the honking of traffic on nearby streets.

7. An increasing number of school districts are beginning to pay more attention to acoustics the study of sound when they plan new schools.

8. Some changes such as putting felt pads on the bottoms of chair and desk legs to keep them from scraping against the floor are simple and inexpensive.

9. Other changes however can be costly and controversial; these changes include buying thicker drapes, building thicker walls, or installing specially designed acoustic ceiling tiles.

10. School administrators often parents themselves hope that these improvements will result in a better learning environment for students.

Commas around Adjective Clauses

An **adjective clause** is a group of words that begins with *who, which,* or *that*; has a subject and a verb; and describes a noun right before it in a sentence.

If an adjective clause can be taken out of a sentence without completely changing the meaning of the sentence, put commas around the clause.

Lily, *who is my cousin,* will take her nursing exam this summer.

Beans, *which is the local coffee shop,* charges outrageous prices.

I complained to Mr. Kranz, *who is the shop's manager.*

If an adjective clause is essential to the meaning of a sentence, do not put commas around it. You can tell whether a clause is essential by taking it out and seeing if the meaning of the sentence changes significantly, as it would if you took the clauses out of the following examples.

The only grocery store *that sold good bread* went out of business.

Students *who do internships* often improve their hiring potential.

Salesclerks *who sell liquor to minors* are breaking the law.

| Noun | adjective clause essential to meaning | rest of sentence. |

| Noun | , | adjective clause not essential to meaning | , | rest of sentence. |

Language note: The relative pronoun *that* is only used in essential (also called restrictive) adjective clauses. Therefore, commas are not used with adjective clauses beginning with *that*.

PRACTICE 30–3   Using Commas to Set Off Adjective Clauses

In each item, underline the adjective clauses. Then, put commas around these clauses where they are needed. Remember that if an adjective clause is essential to the meaning of a sentence, commas are not necessary. If a sentence is already correct, put a "C" next to it.

Example: Daniel Kish, who has been blind since the age of one, has changed many people's ideas about what blind people can and cannot do.

1. Kish who runs the organization World Access for the Blind regularly rides his bike down busy streets and goes on long hikes.

2. His system for "seeing" his surroundings which is known as echolocation uses sound waves to create mental pictures of buildings, cars, trees, and other objects.

3. As Kish bikes around his neighborhood or hikes to sites that are deep in the wilderness, he clicks his tongue and listens to the echoes.

4. The echoes which differ depending on the distance and physical features of nearby objects allow him to map his surroundings in his mind.

5. This mental map which he constantly revises as he moves ahead helps him avoid running into cars, trees, and other obstacles.

6. Researchers who recently investigated Kish's echolocation made some interesting discoveries.

7. They found that Kish's visual cortex which is the part of the brain that processes visual information was activated during his sessions of mapping with sound.

8. This finding which received a lot of attention in the scientific community suggests that Kish's way of seeing the world is indeed visual.

9. Other blind people who have been trained in echolocation have learned to be as active and independent as Kish is.

10. The successes that they and Kish have achieved offer additional proof that blindness does not equal helplessness.

Other Uses for Commas

Commas are also used to set off information in the following situations.

Commas with Quotation Marks

Tip For more on quotation marks, see Chapter 32.

Quotation marks are used to show that you are repeating exactly what someone said. Use commas to set off the words inside quotation marks from the rest of the sentence.

"Let me see your license**,**" demanded the police officer.

"Did you realize**,**" she asked**,** "that you were going 80 miles per hour?"

I exclaimed**,** "No!"

Notice that a comma never comes directly after a quotation mark.

When quotations are not attributed to a particular person, commas may not be necessary.

"Pretty is as pretty does" never made sense to me.

Commas in Addresses

Use commas to separate the elements of an address included in a sentence. However, do not use a comma before a zip code.

My address is 2512 Windermere Street**,** Jackson**,** Mississippi 40720.

If a sentence continues after a city-state combination or after a street address, put a comma after the state or the address.

> I moved here from Detroit, Michigan, when I was eighteen.
>
> I've lived at 24 Heener Street, Madison, since 1989.

Commas in Dates

Separate the day from the year with a comma. If you give just the month and year, do not separate them with a comma.

> My daughter was born on November 8, 2004.
>
> The next conference is in August 2014.

If a sentence continues after the date, put a comma after the date.

> On April 21, 2013, the contract will expire.

Commas with Names

Put a comma after (and sometimes before) the name of someone being addressed directly.

> Don, I want you to come look at this.
>
> Unfortunately, Marie, you need to finish the report by next week.

Commas with Yes or No

Put a comma after the word *yes* or *no* in response to a question.

> Yes, I believe that you are right.

 Language note: There are some places in English where a comma is not appropriate.

- Don't separate a verb from its subject or object with commas.

Incorrect	My cousin and her family, are coming to visit for the summer.
	[A comma separates the subject and verb.]
Incorrect	The websites will provide, exercises and other practice materials.
	[A comma separates the verb and the object.]

- Don't separate a compound subject, verb, or object with commas.

Incorrect	Kayleigh**,** and her mother are shopping for the holidays this afternoon.
	[A comma separates two parts of a compound subject.]
Incorrect	After shopping, they will get dinner**,** and go to a movie.
	[A comma separates two parts of a compound verb.]
Incorrect	Kayleigh hopes to find a fitness-tracker**,** and sweatshirt for her dad.
	[A comma separates two parts of a compound object.]

- Don't put a comma before the first item in a list.

Incorrect	Information about**,** diet, fitness, weight reduction, and muscle development can be found at the front of the gym.
	[A comma comes before the first noun in the list.]

- Don't put a comma after a subordinating conjunction.

Incorrect	Although**,** he has changed his diet, he has not yet lost weight.
	[A comma follows the subordinating conjunction *although*.]

Edit for Commas

> **PRACTICE 30-4**   **Editing Paragraphs for Commas**

Edit the following paragraphs by adding commas where they are needed.

By the end of 2011, communities in California Texas Washington and several other states had banned the use of plastic bags. One grocery store chain Whole Foods Market was an early leader in restricting the use of these bags. As of April 22 2008 Whole Foods stopped asking customers if they wanted paper bags or plastic bags. The store which cares about environmental issues now offers only paper bags made from recycled paper.

The president of Whole Foods stated "We estimate we will keep 100 million new plastic grocery bags out of our environment between Earth Day and the end of this year." The company also sells cloth bags, hoping to encourage shoppers to bring their own reusable bags with them when they go shopping.

Experts believe that plastic bags do a great deal of damage to the environment. They clog drains harm wildlife and take up an enormous amount of space in the nation's landfills. According to the experts it takes more than a thousand years for a plastic bag to break down, and Americans use 100 billion of them every single year.

Chapter Review

1. What is the purpose of a comma?

For Reflect and Apply questions for Part 6, please see page 552.

2. How do you use commas in these three situations:

    In a series of items?

    In a compound sentence?

    With introductory words?

3. What is an appositive?

4. What is an interrupter?

5. What are two situations when a comma is not appropriate?

31

Apostrophes '

Understand What Apostrophes Do

An **apostrophe (')** is a punctuation mark that either shows ownership (*Susan's*) or indicates that a letter has been intentionally left out to form a contraction (*I'm, that's, they're*).

Practice Using Apostrophes Correctly

It is important to know when to use an apostrophe and when not to.

Apostrophes to Show Ownership

Add -'s to a singular noun to show ownership even if the noun already ends in -s.

> *Karen's* apartment is on the South Side.
>
> *James's* roommate is looking for him.

If a noun is plural and ends in -s, just add an apostrophe. If it is plural but does not end in -s, add -'s.

> My *books'* covers are falling off.
>
> [More than one book]
>
> The *twins'* father was building them a playhouse.
>
> [More than one twin]

The *children's* toys were broken.

The *men's* locker room is being painted.

The placement of an apostrophe makes a difference in meaning.

My *sister's* six children are at my house for the weekend.

[One sister who has six children]

My *sisters'* six children are at my house for the weekend.

[Two or more sisters who together have six children]

Do not use an apostrophe to form the plural of a noun.

Gina went camping with her *sisters* and their children.

All the *highways* to the airport are under construction.

Do not use an apostrophe with a possessive pronoun. These pronouns already show ownership (possession).

Is that bag *yours*?   No, it is *ours*.

Possessive Pronouns

my	his	its	their
mine	her	our	theirs
your	hers	ours	whose
yours			

The single most common error with apostrophes and pronouns is confusing *its* (a possessive pronoun) with *it's* (a contraction meaning "it is"). Whenever you write *it's*, test correctness by replacing it with *it is* and reading the sentence aloud to hear if it makes sense.

Apostrophes in Contractions

A **contraction** is formed by joining two words and leaving out one or more of the letters. When writing a contraction, put an apostrophe where the letter or letters have been left out.

She's on her way. = *She is* on her way.

I'll see you there. = *I will* see you there.

Tip To shorten the full year to only the final two numbers, replace the first two numbers with an apostrophe: the year 2016 becomes '16.

Be sure to put the apostrophe in the correct place.

It *doesn't* really matter.

Common Contractions

aren't = are not	she'll = she will
can't = cannot	she's = she is, she has
couldn't = could not	there's = there is
didn't = did not	they'd = they would, they had
don't = do not	they'll = they will
he'd = he would, he had	they're = they are
he'll = he will	they've = they have
he's = he is, he has	who'd = who would, who had
I'd = I would, I had	who'll = who will
I'll = I will	who's = who is, who has
I'm = I am	won't = will not
I've = I have	wouldn't = would not
isn't = is not	you'd = you would, you had
it's = it is, it has	you'll = you will
let's = let us	you're = you are
she'd = she would, she had	you've = you have

Apostrophes with Letters, Numbers, and Time

Use -'s to make letters and numbers plural. The apostrophe prevents confusion or misreading.

In Scrabble games, there are more *e's* than any other letter.

In women's shoes, size *8's* are more common than size *10's*.

Use an apostrophe or -'s in certain expressions in which time nouns are treated as if they possess something.

She took four *weeks'* maternity leave after the baby was born.

This *year's* graduating class is huge.

Edit for Apostrophes

PRACTICE 31–1   Editing Paragraphs for Apostrophes

Edit the following paragraphs by adding two apostrophes where needed and crossing out six incorrectly used apostrophes.

Have you noticed many honeybee's when you go outside? If not, it

is'nt surprising. For reasons that scientists still don't quite understand, these bees have been disappearing all across the country. This mass disappearance is a problem because bees are an important part of growing a wide variety of flowers, fruits, vegetables, and nuts as they spread pollen from one place to another.

In the last year, more than one-third, or billions, of the honeybees in the United States' have disappeared. As a consequence, farmers have been forced either to buy or to rent beehives for their crops. Typically, people

who are in the bee business ship hives to farmers fields by truck. The hives often have to travel hundreds of miles.

Scientist's have been trying to find out what happened to the once-thriving bee population. They suspect that either a disease or chemicals harmed the honeybee's.

Chapter Review

For Reflect and Apply questions for Part 6, please see page 552.

1. What are two situations that require the use of an apostrophe?

2. How is ownership indicated on singular nouns? On plural nouns ending with -s?

3. Is an apostrophe needed with possessive pronouns? Explain.

4. What is the difference between *its* and *it's*?

5. What is a contraction?

32

Quotation Marks " "

Understand What Quotation Marks Do

Quotation marks (" ") always appear in pairs. Quotation marks have two common uses in college writing:

- They are used with direct quotations, which exactly repeat, word for word, what someone said or wrote. (Nick said, "You should take the downtown bus.")
- They are used to set off the **titles** of songs, poems, essays, and articles. (My favorite song is "Sophisticated Lady.")

Practice Using Quotation Marks Correctly

It is important to use quotation marks correctly, especially when quoting sources in college papers: using someone else's words without giving them credit is considered plagiarism. Quotation marks are also useful for referring to the titles of short works.

(For more on using quotes in research, see Appendix, pp. 555–561.)

Quotation Marks for Direct Quotations

When you write a direct quotation, use quotation marks around the quoted words. Quotation marks tell readers that the words used are exactly what was said or written.

1. "I do not know what she means," I said to my friend Lina.
2. Lina asked, "Do you think we should ask a question?"

3. "Excuse me, Professor Jones," I called out, "but could you explain that again?"

4. "Yes," said Professor Jones. "Let me make sure you all understand."

5. After further explanation, Professor Jones asked, "Are there any other questions?"

When you are writing a paper that uses outside sources, use quotation marks to indicate where you are quoting the exact words of a source.

> We all need to become more conscientious recyclers. A recent editorial in the *Bolton Common* reported, "When recycling volunteers spot-checked bags that were supposed to contain only newspaper, they found a collection of nonrecyclable items such as plastic candy wrappers, aluminum foil, and birthday cards."

When quoting, writers usually use words that identify who is speaking, such as *I said to my friend Lina* in the first example above. The identifying words can come after the quoted words (example 1), before them (example 2), or in the middle of them (example 3). Here are some guidelines for capitalization and punctuation.

Guidelines for Capitalization and Punctuation

- Capitalize the first letter in a complete sentence that is being quoted, even if it comes after some identifying words (example 2 on page 536).

- Do not capitalize the first letter in a quotation if it is not the first word in a complete sentence (*but* in example 3).

- If it is a complete sentence and it is clear who the speaker is, a quotation can stand on its own (second sentence in example 4).

- Identifying words must be attached to a quotation; they cannot be a sentence on their own.

- Use commas to separate any identifying words from quoted words in the same sentence.

- Always put quotation marks after commas and periods. Put quotation marks after question marks and exclamation points if they are part of the quoted sentence.

Tip For more on commas with quotation marks, see Chapter 30.

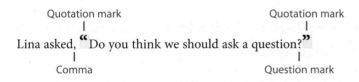

Quotation mark   Quotation mark

Lina asked, "Do you think we should ask a question?"

Comma   Question mark

- If a question mark or exclamation point is part of your own sentence, put it after the quotation mark.

Quotation mark   Quotation mark
| |

What did she mean when she said, "All tests are graded on a curve"?

| |
Comma   Question mark

Setting Off a Quotation within Another Quotation

Sometimes, when you quote someone directly, part of what that person said quotes words that someone else said or wrote. Put single quotation marks (' ') around the quotation within a quotation so that readers understand who said what.

> The student handbook says, "Students must be given the opportunity to make up work missed for legitimate reasons."

> Terry told his instructor, "I am sorry I missed the exam, but that is not a reason to fail me for the term. Our student handbook says, 'Students must be given the opportunity to make up work missed for legitimate reasons,' and I have a good reason."

PRACTICE 32–1   **Punctuating Direct Quotations**

Edit the following sentences by adding quotation marks and commas where needed.

Example: A radio journalist asked a nurse at a critical-care facility, "Do you believe that the medical community needlessly prolongs the lives of the terminally ill?"

1. If I could answer that question quickly, the nurse replied, I would deserve an honorary degree in ethics.

2. She added, But I see it as the greatest dilemma we face today.

3. How would you describe that dilemma? the reporter asked the nurse.

4. The nurse said, It is a choice of when to use our amazing medical technology and when not to.

5. The reporter asked, So there are times when you would favor letting patients die on their own?

6. Yes, the nurse replied, I would.

7. The reporter asked, Under what circumstances should a patient be allowed to die?

8. I cannot really answer that question because so many variables are involved, the nurse replied.

9. Is this a matter of deciding how to allocate scarce resources? the reporter asked.

10. In a sense, it is, the nurse replied. As a colleague of mine says, We should not try to keep everyone alive for as long as possible just because we can.

No Quotation Marks for Indirect (Reported) Speech

When you report what someone said but do not use the person's exact words, you are writing **indirect speech.** Do not use quotation marks for reported speech. Indirect speech often begins with the word *that.*

Reported speech	Direct quotation
Sam said that there was a fire downtown.	Sam said, "There was a fire downtown."
The police told us to move along.	"Move along," directed the police.
Tara told me that she was doing homework.	Tara said, "I am doing homework."

> ### PRACTICE 32–2 Punctuating Direct Quotations and Reported Speech
>
> Edit the following sentences by adding quotation marks where needed and crossing out quotation marks that are used incorrectly. If a sentence is already correct, put a "C" next to it.
>
> **Example:** Three days before her apartment was robbed, Jocelyn told a friend, "I worry about the safety of this building."
>
> 1. Have you complained to the landlord yet? her friend asked.
>
> 2. Not yet, Jocelyn replied, although I know I should.

3. Jocelyn phoned the landlord and asked him to install a more secure lock on the front door.

4. The landlord said that "he believed that the lock was fine the way it was."

5. When Jocelyn phoned the landlord after the burglary, she said, I know this burglary would not have happened if that lock had been installed.

6. I am sorry, the landlord replied, but there is nothing I can do about it now.

7. Jocelyn asked a tenants' rights group whether she had grounds for a lawsuit.

8. The person she spoke to said that "she probably did."

9. If I were you, the person said, I would let your landlord know about your plans.

10. When Jocelyn told her landlord of the possible lawsuit, he said that he would reimburse her for the stolen items.

Quotation Marks for Certain Titles

When you refer to a short work, such as a magazine or newspaper article, a chapter in a book, a short story, an essay, a song, or a poem, put quotation marks around the title of the work.

Newspaper article	"Volunteers Honored for Service"
Short story	"The Awakening"
Essay	"Why Are We So Angry?"

Usually, titles of longer works, such as novels, books, magazines, newspapers, movies, television programs, and albums, are italicized. The titles of sacred books, such as the Bible or the Koran, are neither underlined nor surrounded by quotation marks.

Book	*To Kill a Mockingbird*
Newspaper	*Washington Post*

Do not italicize or capitalize the word *the* before the name of a newspaper or magazine, even if it is part of the title: I saw that article in the *New York Times*.

But do capitalize *The* when it is the first word in titles of books, movies, and other sources.

If you are writing a paper with many outside sources, your instructor will probably refer you to a particular system of citing sources. Follow that system's guidelines when you use titles in your paper.

Note: Do not enclose the title of a paragraph or an essay that you have written in quotation marks when it appears at the beginning of your paper. Do not italicize it either.

Edit for Quotation Marks

PRACTICE 32–3   **Editing Paragraphs for Quotation Marks**

Edit the following paragraphs by adding twelve sets of quotation marks where needed and crossing out the two sets of incorrectly used quotation marks. Correct any errors in punctuation.

When Ruiz first came into my office, he told me that he was a poor student. I asked, What makes you think that?

Ruiz answered, I have always gotten bad grades, and I do not know how to get any better. He shook his head. I have just about given up.

I told him that "there were some resources on campus he could use and that we could work together to help him."

"What kind of things are you talking about?" asked Ruiz. What exactly will I learn?

I said, There are plenty of programs to help you. You really have no excuse to fail.

Can you be a little more specific? he asked.

Certainly, I said. I told him about the survival skills program. I also pulled out folders on study skills, such as managing time, improving memory, taking notes, and having a positive attitude. Take a look at these, I said.

Ruiz said, No, I am not interested in that. And I do not have time.

I replied, "That is your decision, Ruiz, but remember that education is one of the few things that people are willing to pay for and not get." I paused and then added, It sounds to me like you are wasting the money you spent on tuition. Why not try to get what you paid for?

Ruiz thought for a moment while he looked out the window and finally told me that "he would try."

Good, I said. I am glad to hear it.

For Reflect and Apply questions for Part 6, please see page 552.

Chapter Review

1. Why do quotation marks always appear in pairs?

2. What do quotation marks around words indicate?

3. What is reported (indirect) speech? Does it require quotation marks?

4. How are quotations within quotations indicated?

5. When are quotation marks used for titles?

33

Other Punctuation ; : ( ) -- -

Understand What Punctuation Does

Punctuation helps readers understand your writing. If you use punctuation incorrectly, you send readers a confusing—or, even worse, a wrong—message.

Practice Using Punctuation Correctly

This chapter covers five punctuation marks that people sometimes use incorrectly because they are not quite sure what these marks are supposed to do.

Semicolon ;

Semicolons to Join Closely Related Independent Clauses

Use a semicolon to join two closely related independent clauses into one sentence.

> In an interview, hold your head up and do not slouch; it is important to look alert.
>
> Make good eye contact; looking down is not appropriate in an interview.

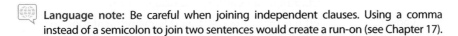 Language note: Be careful when joining independent clauses. Using a comma instead of a semicolon to join two sentences would create a run-on (see Chapter 17).

Semicolons When Items in a List Contain Commas

Use semicolons to separate items in a list that itself contains commas. Otherwise, it is difficult for readers to tell where one item ends and another begins.

For dinner, Bob ate an order of onion rings; a 16-ounce steak; a baked potato with sour cream, bacon bits, and cheese; a green salad; and a huge bowl of ice cream with fudge sauce.

Because one item, *a baked potato with sour cream, bacon bits, and cheese,* contains its own commas, all items need to be separated by semicolons.

Colon :

Colons before Lists

Use a colon after an independent clause to introduce a list. Remember that an independent clause contains a subject and a verb. It can stand on its own as a sentence.

> The software conference fair featured a vast array of products: financial-management applications, games, educational CDs, college-application programs, and so on.

Colons before Explanations or Examples

Use a colon after an independent clause to let readers know that you are about to provide an explanation or example of what you just wrote.

> The conference was overwhelming: too much hype about too many things.

One of the most common misuses of colons is to use them after a phrase instead of an independent clause. Watch out especially for colons following the phrases *such as* and *for example.*

Tip See Chapter 30 (Commas), Chapter 31 (Apostrophes), and Chapter 32 (Quotation Marks) for coverage of these punctuation marks. For more information on using semicolons to join sentences, see Chapter 23.

Incorrect	Tonya enjoys sports that are sometimes dangerous. For example: white-water rafting, wilderness skiing, rock climbing, and motorcycle racing.
Correct	Tonya enjoys sports that are sometimes dangerous: white-water rafting, wilderness skiing, rock climbing, and motorcycle racing.
Incorrect	Jeff has many interests. They are: bicycle racing, sculpting, and building musical instruments.
Correct	Jeff has many interests: bicycle racing, sculpting, and building musical instruments.

Colons before Quotes

If an independent clause introduces a quotation, a colon is used.

> Karla's acceptance showed great humility: "I could never have achieved this on my own."

Do not use a colon if a signal phrase introduces a quote. Use a comma after a phrase.

Incorrect	Karla said**:** "I am so thankful for your help."
Correct	Karla said, "I am so thankful for your help."

Colons in Business Correspondence and before Subtitles

Use a colon after a greeting (called a *salutation*) in a business letter and after the standard heading lines at the beginning of a memorandum.

Dear Mr. Hernandez**:**

To**:** Pat Toney

From**:** Miriam Moore

Colons should also be used before subtitles—for example, "Running a Marathon**:** The Five Most Important Tips."

Parentheses ( )

Use parentheses to set off information that is not essential to the meaning of a sentence. Parentheses can also indicate an aside, when an author directly addresses the audience. In academic writing, parentheses may also be used for citations, which signal information about the source of borrowed words or ideas. Parentheses are always used in pairs.

My grandfather's most successful invention **(** and also his first **)** was the electric blanket.

The implementation of the new health-care policies caused considerable confusion **(** as you can imagine **)**.

As Ericsson has pointed out, "When someone lies, someone loses" **(** 212 **)**.

Dash --

Dashes can be used like parentheses to set off additional information, particularly information that you want to emphasize. Make a dash by writing or typing two hyphens together. Do not put extra spaces around a dash.

The final exam--worth 25 percent of your total grade--will be next Thursday.

A dash can also indicate a pause, much like a comma does.

My uncle went on long fishing trips--without my aunt and cousins.

Hyphen -

Hyphens to Join Words that Form a Single Description

Writers often join two or more words that together form a single description of a person, place, or thing. To join the words, use a hyphen.

> Being a stockbroker is a high-risk career.

> Jill is a lovely three-year-old girl.

When writing out two-word numbers from twenty-one to ninety-nine, put a hyphen between the two words.

> Seventy-five people participated in the demonstration.

> 🌐 **Language note:** When a hyphenated adjective that shows age, size, or measurement precedes a noun, do not use plural forms.

Incorrect	My son is a typical thirteen-years-old boy.
Correct	My son is a typical thirteen-year-old boy.
Incorrect	We need a fifteen-inches screen.
Correct	We need a fifteen-inch screen.

Hyphens to Divide a Word at the End of a Line

Use a hyphen to divide a word when part of the word must continue on the next line.

> Critics accused the tobacco industry of increasing the amounts of nico-
> tine in cigarettes to encourage addiction and boost sales.

Tip Most word-processing programs automatically put an entire word on the next line rather than hyphenating it. When you write by hand, however, you need to hyphenate correctly.

If you are not sure where to break a word, look it up in a dictionary. The word's main entry will show you where you can break the word: *dic • tio • nary.* If you still are not confident that you are putting the hyphen in the correct place, do not break the word; write it all on the next line.

Edit for Other Punctuation Marks

> **PRACTICE 33-1** **Editing Paragraphs for Other Punctuation Marks**
>
> Edit the following paragraphs by adding semicolons, colons, parentheses, dashes, and hyphens when needed. In some places, more than one type of punctuation may be acceptable.

When John Wood was on a backpacking trip to Nepal in 1998, he discovered something he had not expected only a few books in the nation's schools. He knew that if the students did not have the materials they needed, it would be much harder for them to learn. They did not need high tech supplies as much as they needed old fashioned books. Wood decided that he would find a way to get those books.

Two years later, Wood founded Room to Read, an organization dedicated to shipping books to students who needed them. Since then, the group has donated more than three million books. One of Wood's first shipments was carried to students on the back of a yak. Many others arrived in a Cathay Pacific Airlines plane.

Along with the books, Room to Read has also built almost three hundred schools and has opened five thousand libraries. Different companies donate books to the organization Scholastic, Inc., recently sent 400,000 books to Wood's group. Money to fund all these efforts comes through various fund-raisers read-a-thons, auctions, and coin drives.

Chapter Review

For Reflect and Apply questions for Part 6, please see page 552.

1. How are semicolons used?

2. What are three ways to use a colon?

3. What must come before a colon?

4. How are parentheses used?

5. How are dashes used?

6. How are hyphens used?

34

Capitalization

Using Capital Letters

Understand Capitalization

Capital letters (A, B, C, etc.) are generally bigger than lowercase letters (a, b, c, etc.), and they may have a different form.

Practice Three Rules of Capitalization

To avoid the most common errors of capitalization, follow these three rules:

Capitalize the first letter
- of every new sentence.
- in names of specific people, places, dates, and things (also known as proper nouns).
- of important words in titles.

Capitalization of Sentences

Capitalize the first letter of each new sentence, including the first word of quoted sentences.

> The superintendent was surprised.
> He asked, "What is going on here?"

Capitalization of Names of Specific People, Places, Dates, and Things

The general rule is to capitalize the first letter in names of specific people, places, dates, and things. Do not capitalize a generic (common) name, such as *college*, as opposed to the specific name: *Carroll State College*. Look at the examples for each group.

 Language note: Rules for capitalization are not the same in all languages. German, for example, capitalizes all nouns, while English only capitalizes proper (specific) nouns.

People

Capitalize the first letter in names of specific people and in titles used with names of specific people.

Specific	Not specific
Jean Heaton	my neighbor
Professor Fitzgerald	your math professor
Dr. Cornog	the doctor
Aunt Pat, Mother	my aunt, your mother

The name of a family member is capitalized when the family member is being addressed directly: Happy Birthday, *Mother*. In other instances, do not capitalize: It is my *mother's* birthday.

The word *president* is not capitalized unless it comes directly before a name as part of that person's title: *President* Barack Obama.

The only pronoun that is capitalized is *I*; other pronouns are capitalized only if they are the first word in a sentence. *I* is capitalized no matter where it occurs in the sentence.

Places

Capitalize the first letter in names of specific buildings, streets, cities, states, regions, and countries.

Specific	Not specific
Bolton Town Hall	the town hall
Arlington Street	our street
Dearborn Heights	my hometown
Arizona	this state
the South	the southern region
Spain	that country

Do not capitalize directions in a sentence.

Drive *south* for five blocks.

Dates

Capitalize the first letter in the names of days, months, and holidays. Do not capitalize the names of the seasons (winter, spring, summer, fall).

Specific	Not specific
Wednesday	tomorrow
June 25	summer
Thanksgiving	my birthday

 Language note: Some languages, such as Spanish, French, and Italian, do not capitalize the names of days, months, and languages. In English, such words must be capitalized.

Incorrect	I study russian every monday, wednesday, and friday from january through may.
Correct	I study **Russian** every **Monday**, **Wednesday**, and **Friday** from **January** through **May**.

Organizations, Companies, and Groups

Specific	Not specific
Taft Community College	my college
Microsoft	that software company
Alcoholics Anonymous	the self-help group

Languages, Nationalities, and Religions

Specific	Not specific
English, Greek, Spanish	my first language
Christianity, Buddhism	your religion

The names of languages should be capitalized even if you aren't referring to a specific course.

> I am taking psychology and *Spanish*.

Courses

Specific	Not specific
Composition 101	a writing course
Introduction to Psychology	my psychology course

Commercial Products

Specific	Not specific
Diet Pepsi	a diet cola
Skippy peanut butter	peanut butter

Tip For more on punctuating titles, see Chapter 32. For a list of common prepositions, see page 327.

Capitalization of Titles

When you write the title of a book, movie, television program, magazine, newspaper, article, story, song, paper, poem, and so on, capitalize the first word and all important words. The only words that do not need to be capitalized (unless they are the first word) are *the, a, an*, coordinating conjunctions (*and, but, for, nor, or, so, yet*), and prepositions.

> *The X-Files* was a long-running television program.
>
> Both *USA Today* and the *New York Times* are popular newspapers.
>
> "Once More to the Lake" is one of Chuck's favorite essays.

Chapter Review

1. What are three important capitalization rules?

2. When do organizations and places need to be capitalized?

3. Which words in a title do NOT need to have the first letter capitalized?

Reflect and Apply

1. Do we use capitalization and punctuation in speech? Why or why not?

2. Why do you think college instructors emphasize punctuation and capitalization so strongly?

3. Are there writing contexts in which capitalization and punctuation would not be so important? Explain.

4. Talk to a professor who teaches courses in your major or to someone who is working in your future career. Why are punctuation and capitalization important for people studying or working in this area?

Appendix:

Understanding a Writing Prompt

A **writing prompt** is a document (or part of a document) that gives instructions for a writing assignment. Prompts vary in length and the amount of information given; on a timed examination, the prompt may be a single sentence, while a course syllabus may include several pages of instructions and background for a course research project. No matter what kind of prompt an instructor provides, follow these steps to analyze the prompt and develop an effective writing strategy.

1. Read carefully. Many students set themselves up for failure by not read-ing the prompt thoroughly and carefully. Read the prompt multiple times before you begin writing, and refer to it while you are writing to make sure you are following instructions in the prompt.

2. Annotate the prompt. As you make notes, pay attention to the following:

    a. The purpose of the assignment, if it is given. Try to understand why the instructor has asked you to do this.

    b. The specific requirements of the assignment: length, number of pages/words, formatting rules, number of sources needed, and the due date.

    c. The nature of the task. What are you being asked to do? Circle or underline the action verbs (discuss, outline, compare, summarize, etc.). You will find a list of common action verbs for writing prompts below.

3. Make a plan for completing the work. Even if you are writing in an essay exam, taking a few moments to plan the essay helps you to organize your thinking. (For more on planning an essay, see Chapter 5.)

4. Leave time for revision and editing.

Action verb	What you need to do
Agree or Disagree (Take a stand)	Explain your position on a topic, with reasons and evidence (a form of argument).
Analyze	Break something down into parts and show how the parts work together.
Analyze Causes or Effects	Break down the factors that caused an event, or break down the results of an event.
Apply	Use information or knowledge you have learned to solve a problem or interpret data.
Argue (Persuade)	Explain your position on a controversial topic, with reasons and evidence.
Choose (Decide)	Make a choice between given options, and justify the choice.
Classify (Explain Types or Categories)	Organize a complex topic by dividing it into groups.
Compare	Show similarities between two things to make a point (note: some instructors want to see both similarities and differences).
Contrast (Distinguish between)	Show differences between two things to make a point.
Define	Show what something means.
Describe (Identify)	Give the features or characteristics of something.
Discuss	Explain something from different points of view. (This is a broad term, and it often allows students to use any of the approaches on this list as a way of explaining a topic or answering a question.)
Evaluate (Assess, Judge)	Make a judgment about something, providing reasons and evidence (a form of argument).
Explain (Examine)	Show how something works or what it means. (This is a broad term. Explanations may use several of the strategies on this list.)
Explain the steps	Show specifically how something works by listing the steps in a process.
Illustrate	Give examples that explain a concept or support a point.
Outline	Show how a text is organized from beginning to end.
Relate (Connect)	Explain the relationship between two or more things.
Summarize	Provide a condensed version of a longer text, with a focus on the main ideas.
Trace (Show Development)	Present a sequence of events or steps that led to a historical event, a development, an innovation, or a change.

Appendix:
Citing Research Sources in MLA Style

Many assignments in college require that you research a topic before writing about it, using books, articles, websites, or other sources. When you write a paper with research, you will be required to **document**—or show—where you found your information. Different disciplines and majors use different styles of documentation. Humanities and English majors usually use MLA (Modern Language Association) style, while science majors usually document sources in APA (American Psychological Association) style. Always check with your instructor to find out which style is required for a specific course. This appendix presents MLA style.

Beginning Well: Using College Resources and Taking Good Notes

It is always tempting to begin research by going to Google and copying information from the first search results that you find. But searching in this way actually sets you up for problems later. Once you have identified a research task (also called a **research question**), begin with the best resource that your school provides: the library. Talk with a librarian about an effective search strategy, and learn to use research tools in the library, including databases and the card catalog.

As you begin to find sources, it is important to do three things:

1. **Evaluate the credibility of your sources**. Can the source be trusted? How do you know? Whether you are using a search engine (like Google) or a database from the library website, you need to consider the quality and purpose of the information. Use the information in Chapter 14 (Argument) to help you assess the source for bias.

2. **Keep a source trail**. Make a note of what you found, how you found it, who wrote it, the date of publication, and the date you found it. You will need this information later.

3. **Take careful notes to avoid plagiarism.** As you find information for your research essay, do not rely on your memory to recall details about your sources; take good notes from the start. It is usually a good idea to write a short summary of the source (see Chapter 1). You may also paraphrase a writer's words (see Chapter 1). If you copy the writer's exact words, be sure to enclose them in quotation marks (see Chapter 32). If the source you are using has page numbers, be sure to write down the page for any quotes or paraphrases in your notes.

Understanding Documentation: In-Text Citations

In-text citations signal to readers that information comes from a source. These citations may include two parts: a signal phrase (such as *Dr. Leavell says* or *according to Dr. Leavell*) and a parenthetical citation, which includes the author's last name (if it is not given in a signal phrase) and the page number for the quote or paraphrase.

In-text Citation

Signal phrase   Citation

> According to psychologists Don Hockenbury and Sandra Hockenbury, "four key features define anorexia nervosa" (593).

The examples below show in-text citations for different kinds of sources.

One Author

> As David Shipler states, "..." (16).
>
> The number of people who work and fall below the poverty line has increased dramatically (Shipler 16).

Two Authors

Use both authors' last names.

> Quigley and Morrison found that ... (243).
>
> Banks and credit card companies are charging many more fees ... (Quigley and Morrison 243).

Three or More Authors

Use the first author's last name and the words et al. (The term et al. means "and others").

> According to Sen et al., ... (659).
>
> The overuse of antibiotics can result in ... (Sen et al. 659).

Group, Corporation, or Government Agency

Use the name of the group, corporation, or government agency. The source can be abbreviated in the parentheses, as shown in the second example.

> The Texas Parks and Wildlife Department offers guidelines for landscaping … (26).
>
> Texas has more native plants than any other … (Texas Parks and Wildlife Dept. 26).

Author Not Named

Use the article title in quotations, shortened if it is a long title.

> In the article "Texas Wildscapes," … (7).
>
> Many areas of Texas are filled with drought-tolerant native … ("Texas Wildscapes" 7).

Encyclopedia or Other Reference Work

Use the name of the entry you are using as a source.

> In its entry on xeriscaping, the *Landscape Encyclopedia* claims that … ("Xeriscaping").
>
> Xeriscaping is often used in … ("Xeriscaping").

Understanding Documentation: The Works Cited List

A list of works cited is a complete list, alphabetized by author, of the outside sources that you actually use in your essay. This list follows the essay.

The two most basic elements of any works cited entry are the author's name and the title of the work, both of which are followed by a period.

> Lutz, Iva. *The Passenger.* (novel)
>
> Coles, Kimberly Anne. "The Matter of Belief in John Donne's Holy Sonnets."
>
> (periodical)
>
> Levy, Shawn. *Stranger Things.* (TV series)

In MLA style, after noting these two elements, you must indicate the **container** of the information. The container is the larger work in which you found the material you are citing. If you cite a passage from a novel, the novel *is* the container. However, for an essay or article, the container might be a newspaper, magazine, or radio show; for an online article, it could be a podcast, website, or database. Whatever the origin of the container, you should provide as many of the following elements as you can find or that apply to the source you are citing, in the order shown.

- the title of the container
- the names of other contributors (such as editors and translators)
- the version (e.g., revised, expanded, 2nd ed., director's cut, etc.)
- the number (e.g., volume and issue numbers)
- the publisher
- the date of publication (use day-month-year format and abbreviate names of all months longer than four letters, e.g., 6 Feb. 2018 or 17 June 2018)
- the location of the information (a page number, DOI, permalink, or URL)

Note: To indicate the location of an online source, provide a DOI (digital object identifier), a permalink (a stable URL), or at least the current URL for a site. As websites can rapidly become obsolete, you should note the date you accessed a site at the end of your entry *if* the site provides no information about when it was produced or published.

Each of these items is followed by a comma, except the last one, which ends with a period.

Lutz, Iva. *The Passenger.* Simon and Schuster, 2016, p. 26.

Coles, Kimberly Anne. "The Matter of Belief in John Donne's Holy Sonnets." *Renaissance Quarterly,* vol. 68, no. 3, Fall 2015, pp. 899–931.

"Holly Jolly." *Stranger Things*, produced by Shawn Levy, written by Matt and Ross Duffer, Netflix, 2016.

In some cases, the container you cite might itself be part of a larger container. In that case, simply add the same information listed above, in the order shown, after the title of the second container.

Coles, Kimberly Anne. "The Matter of Belief in John Donne's Holy Sonnets." *Renaissance Quarterly*, vol. 68, no. 3, Fall 2015, pp. 899–931. *JSTOR*, doi:10.1086/683855.

Models and Examples

One Author

Author's Last Name, First Name. *Title of Book: Subtitle.* Name of Publisher, Publication Date.

Shipler, David K. *The Working Poor: Invisible in America.* Knopf, 2004.

Two Authors

Author's Last Name, First Name, and Other Authors' First and Last Names. *Title of Book: Subtitle*. Name of Publisher, Publication Date.

Picciotto, Richard, and Daniel Paisner. *Last Man Down: A New York City Fire Chief and the Collapse of the World Trade Center*. Berkeley, 2002.

Three or More Authors

Author's Last Name, First Name, et al. *Title of Book: Subtitle*. Name of Publisher, Publication Date.

Roark, James L., et al. *The American Promise: A History of the United States*. 7th ed. Macmillan, 2017.

Group, Corporation, or Government Agency

Name of Group, Corporation, or Agency. *Title of Book: Subtitle*. Name of Publisher, Publication Date.

Human Rights Watch. *World Report 2017: Events of 2016*. Seven Stories Press, 2017.

Editor

Editor's Last Name, First Name, editor. *Title of Book: Subtitle*. Name of Publisher, Publication Date.

Canellos, Peter S., editor. *The Last Lion: The Fall and Rise of Ted Kennedy*. Simon & Schuster, 2009.

Encyclopedia

Entry Author's Last Name, First Name. "Title of Entry." *Title of Encyclopedia*, Edition Number [1st, 2nd, 3rd] ed, Date of publication. Name of Publisher.

Araya, Yoseph. "Ecology of Water Relations in Plants." *Encyclopedia of Life Sciences*, 8 Aug. 2014. *Wiley Online Library*, doi: 10.1002/9780470015902.a0003201.pub2.

The citation here is for an online encyclopedia and includes the container in which the encyclopedia was found and the DOI.

Magazine Article, Print

Author's Last Name, First Name. "Title of Article." *Title of Magazine*, Date Abbrev. Month Year of Publication, Page Numbers.

Sanneh, Kelefa. "Skin in the Game." *New Yorker*, 24 Mar. 2014, pp. 48–55.

Magazine Article, Online

Author's Last Name, First Name. "Title of Article." *Title of Magazine*, Date Abbrev. Month Year of Publication, URL.

Leonard, Andrew. "The Surveillance State High School." Salon, 27 Nov. 2012, www.salon.com/2012/11/27/the_surveillance_state_high_school/.

Short Work from a Website

Author's Last Name, First Name. "Title of Work." *Title of Website*, Publication Date, DOI or URL. [Include the date of access if there is no publication date on the website.]

Bali, Karan. "Kishore Kumar." Upperstall.com, upperstall.com/profile/ kishore-kumar/. Accessed 2 Mar. 2017.

Newspaper Article, Print

Author's Last Name, First Name. "Title of Article." *Title of Newspaper*, Date Abbrev. Month Year of Publication, Page Numbers.

Barringer, Felicity. "Indians Join Fight for an Oklahoma Lake's Flow." *New York Times*, 12 Apr. 2011, A1+.

Newspaper Article, Online

Author's Last Name, First Name. "Title of Article." *Title of Newspaper*, Date Abbrev. Month Year of Publication, URL.

Wolfers, Justin, et al. "1.5 Million Missing Black Men." *The New York Times*, 20 Apr. 2015, nyti.ms/1P5Gpa7.

Article, Scholarly Journal with Numbered Volumes

Author's Last Name, First Name. "Title of Article." *Title of Journal,* Volume Number, Issue Number, Publication Date, Page Numbers.

> Fountain, Glinda H. "Inverting the Southern Belle: Romance Writers Redefine Gender Myths." *Journal of Popular Culture,* vol. 41, issue 1, Feb. 2008, pp. 37–55.

Work from a Database (Such as InfoTrac)

Author's Last Name, First Name. "Title of Article." *Title of Periodical,* Volume number, Issue number, Publication Date, Page Numbers. *Database Title,* DOI.

> Coles, Kimberly Anne. "The Matter of John Donne's Holy Sonnets." *Renaissance Quarterly,* vol. 68, no. 3, Fall 2015, pp. 899–931. *JSTOR,* doi:10.1086/683855.

Note: Rita Rantung's essay, "Indonesian and U.S. School Systems" in Chapter 12 (pp. 254–57) is an example of a researched essay.

Acknowledgments

Sarah Bigler, "High School Is Not Preparing Us for College." *Daily Eastern News*, October 10, 2010. Reprinted by permission.

Lisa Currie, "Profile of Success: Lisa Currie." Reprinted by permission.

Stephanie Ericsson, "The Ways We Lie." Copyright © 1992 by Stephanie Ericsson. Originally published by the *Utne Reader* in its November/December 1992 issue. Reprinted by permission of Dunham Literary as agents for the author.

Paola Garcia-Muniz, "Profile of Success: Paola Garcia-Muniz, Editorial Assistant." Reprinted by permission.

Juan C. Gonzalez, "Profile of Success: Juan C. Gonzalez, Vice Chancellor for Student Affairs, University of California, San Diego" and "Workplace Essay: Juan C. Gonzalez, Address to New Students." Reprinted by permission of the author.

John Hawkins, "Five Scientific Reasons Climate Change Is Not Happening." *Townhall.com*, February 18, 2014. Reprinted by permission.

Oscar Hijuelos, "Memories of New York City Snow," from *Metropolis Found: New York Is Book Country 25th Anniversary Collection* (New York: New York Is Book Country, 2003). Copyright © 2003 by Oscar Hijuelos. Reprinted with the permission of the Jennifer Lyons Literary Agency, LLC, for the estate of the author.

Katie Horn (student), "A Beginner's Guide to Movie Night." Reprinted by permission.

Kelly Hultgren, "Pick Up the Phone to Call, Not Text." *Dailywildcat .com*, August 31, 2011. Reprinted by permission.

Amanda Jacobowitz, "A Ban on Water Bottles: A Way to Bolster the University's Image." Posted by Amanda Jacobowitz on April 28, 2010. Forum Staff Columnists. Reprinted by permission.

Samantha Levine-Finley, "Isn't It Time You Hit the Books?" Originally published in *U.S. News and World Report's America's Best Colleges 2008*, August 17, 2007. Reprinted by permission. Copyrighted 2007. *U.S. News & World Report*. 277406:0918BC

Adam McCrimmon, University of Calgary, "Does My Child Have Autism or Is This 'Normal' Behavior?" *The Conversation*, January 8, 2018, https://theconversation.com/does-my-child -have-autism-or-is-this-normal-behaviour-88778.Republished under a Creative Commons license.

Rita Rantung (student), "Indonesian and U.S. School Systems." Reprinted by permission.

Liz Riggs, "What It's Like to Be the First Person in Your Family to Go to College." *Atlantic Magazine*, January 13, 2014. Copyright © 2014 The Atlantic Media Company, as first published in the *Atlantic Magazine*. All rights reserved. Distributed by Tribune Content Agency, LLC.

Trevor Riley-Jewell (student), "An Unusual Inspiration." Reprinted by permission.

James Roy, "Profile of Success: James Roy" and "Workplace Essay: James Roy, Police Report." Reprinted by permission.

Brett Scheffers, University of Florida, and James Watson, the University of Queensland, "Climate Change Is Affecting All Life on Earth—and That's Not Good News for Humanity." *The Conversation*, November 11, 2016, https://theconversation. com/climate-change-is-affecting-all-life-on-earth-and-thats -not-good-news-for-humanity-66475. Republished under a Creative Commons license.

Amy Tan, "Fish Cheeks." Copyright © 1987 by Amy Tan. First appeared in *Seventeen Magazine*. Reprinted by permission of the author and the Sandra Dijkstra Literary Agency.

John Tierney, "Yes, Money Can Buy Happiness…." *New York Times*, March 20, 2008, https://tierneylab.blogs.nytimes.com /2008/03/20/yes-money-can-buy-happiness/. © 2008 The New York Times. All rights reserved. Used by permission and protected by the Copyright Laws of the United States. The printing, copying, redistribution, or transmission of this Content without express written permission is prohibited.

Garth Vaz, "Profile of Success and Workplace Comparison and Contrast: Garth Vaz, Physician." Reprinted by permission.

Andrea Whitmer, "When Poor People Have Nice Things." *sooverthis .com*, June 18, 2012. Reprinted by permission.

Index

A

a versus *an/and*, 503
Abbreviations, possessive of, 532–33
Abstract and vague words, 494–95
accept/except, 503
Action verbs, 328, 330–31
Active voice, 389–90
Addresses, commas in, 528–29
Adjective clause
    commas around, 526–28
    joining ideas using, 452–55
Adjectives, 168, 326, 413–19
    comparative form of, 262, 416–17
    coordinate, 522
    correct use of, 415–17
    cumulative, 522
    editing for, 417–18
    joining ideas using, 452–55
    prepositions after, 485–86
    understanding, 413–15
Adoga, Alice, 119
Adverbs, 326–27, 413–19
    in comparisons, 416–17
    conjunctive, 355–57, 429
    correct use of, 415–17
    editing for, 417–18
    starting sentences with, 445–46
    understanding, 413–15
advice/advise, 503
affect/effect, 503
Alaimo, Stephanie and Mark Koester, "The Backdraft
    of Technology," 279–80
"All My Music" (Mattazi), 206–7
Ambiguous pronoun references, 402–3
an versus *a/and*, 503
Analysis
    of argument, 308–17
    of cause and effect, 277–85
    of classification, 206–14
    of comparison and contrast, 253–62
    of definition, 228–37
    of description, 161–68
    of illustration, 137–46
    of narration, 116–23
    of problems, 26
    of process analysis, 182–90
    of reading, 19–20
    of visuals, 25
and
    versus *a/an*, 503
    in compound sentences, 523
    as coordinating conjunction, 426–27
    in coordination, 426–27
    in correlative conjunctions, 440
    used in series with commas, 521–22
And/or rule, 372
Antecedents, 397
Apostrophes, 532–35
    in contractions, 533–34
    editing for, 535
    with letters, numbers, and time, 534
    practice using, 532–34
    to show ownership, 532–33
    understanding, 532
Appositives, 190
    commas around, 525–26
    joining ideas using, 451–52
Appropriate paraphrase, 14–15
are/our, 504
Argument, 291–321
    basics of good, 291–92
    checklist, 320–21
    considering and responding to views, 301–2
    evaluating, 307–8
    identify reasons and question assumptions, 295–96
    main idea in, 292–94
    organization in, 302–6
    paragraphs versus essays in, 304–5
    professional, 311–17
    reading and analyzing, 308–17
    in the real world, 309
    support in, 294–301
    transitions in, 303, 306
    understanding, 291–306
    workplace, 309–10
    writing, 318–21
Arranging ideas in drafting, 73–75
Articles, 483–85
    with count and noncount nouns, 484–85
    definite and indefinite, 483
Assumptions, questioning
    in argument, 295–96
    critical thinking and, 7–8
    topic narrowing, 43–45
Audience, understanding, 29–32
Auxiliary verbs, 329–31, 387
    common errors with, 478–80
    in negative statements, 461–63

B

"Backdraft of Technology, The" (Alaimo and Koester),
    279–80
bad/badly, 417
"Ban on Water Bottles: A Way to Bolster the University's
    Image, A" (Jacobowitz), 15–16

Base form of verbs, 379
be
   past tense of, 385
   present tense of, 385
   subject-verb agreement with, 368–70
"Beginner's Guide to Movie Night, A" (Horn), 183–84
Biases, avoiding, 9–10
Bigler, Sarah, "High School Is Not Preparing Us for
   College," 139–40
"Bird Rescue" (Cepeda), 161
Body of essay
   compared to paragraph, 33
   drafting, 81–82
   purpose of, 34
Body of paragraph
   compared to essay, 34
   purpose of, 33
Boldface words, previewing, 11
Books, quotation marks for titles of, 540–41
both...and, 440
Boyce, Joshua, 281
Brainstorming, 46
Brown, Charlton, "Buying a Car at an Auction," 182–83
Brown, Stacie, 309
Business correspondence, colons in, 545
but
   in compound sentences, 523
   as coordinating conjunction, 426–27
   in correlative conjunctions, 440
"Buying a Car at an Auction" (Brown), 182–83
by/buy/bye, 504

C

can as helping verb, 475
Capitalization, 537–38, 548–52
   of commercial products, 551
   of courses, 551
   of dates, 550
   of languages, nationalities, and religions, 550–51
   of organizations, companies, and groups, 550
   of people, 549
   of places, 549–50
   rules of, 548–51
   of sentences, 548
   of titles, 551
   understanding, 548
Cause and effect, 267–90
   basics of good, 267–68
   checklist, 289
   evaluating, 276–77
   grammar for, 286
   main idea in, 268–69
   organization in, 272–76
   paragraphs versus essays in, 274–75
   primary support in, 270–71
   professional, 282–85
   reading and analyzing, 277–85
   in the real world, 281

   secondary support in, 271–72
   student, 278–80
   transitions in, 273, 276
   understanding, 267–76
   workplace, 281–82
   writing, 286–89
Cepeda, Alessandra, "Bird Rescue," 161
Checklists
   argument writing, 320–21
   cause and effect, 289
   classification, 217–18
   comparison and contrast, 265–66
   definition, 240
   description writing, 171
   drafting, 89
   evaluating draft essay, 89
   evaluating draft paragraph, 87–88
   evaluating revised essays, 102
   illustration writing, 150
   main idea, 64
   narration, 126
   process analysis, 193–94
   revising, 90–91
   student preparedness, 4–5
   support, 71
   for topic, 49
Chronological order, 74
Classification, 195–218
   basics of good, 195–96
   checklist, 217–18
   evaluating, 204–5
   grammar for, 214–15
   main idea in, 196–99
   organization in, 201–4
   paragraphs versus essays in, 202–3
   primary support in, 199–200
   professional, 211–14
   reading and analyzing, 206–14
   in the real world, 209–11
   secondary support in, 200–1
   student, 206–8
   transitions in, 201, 204
   understanding, 195–204
   writing, 215–18
Clause, 328
Clichés, 498–500
"Climate Change Is Affecting All Life on Earth – and
   That's Not Good News for Humanity" (Scheffers and
   Watson), 314–17
Clustering, 47
Coherence, revising for, 95–97
Collective nouns, 401–2
Colons
   in business correspondence and before subtitles, 545
   before explanations or examples, 544
   before lists, 544
   before quotes, 544–45
Commas, 521–31
   in addresses, 528–29

around adjective clauses, 526–28
around appositives and interrupters, 525–26
in compound sentences, 523
between coordinate adjectives, 522–23
correcting run-ons by adding, 355–57
in dates, 529
editing for, 530–31
after introductory words, 523–24
between items in series, 521–22
with names, 529
practice using, 521–30
with quotation marks, 528
splices, 351
understanding, 521
with *yes* or *no*, 529–30
Commercial products, capitalization of names of, 551
Companies, capitalization of names of, 550
Comparative form of adjectives, 416–17
Comparison and contrast, 241–66
    basics of, 241–42
    checklist, 265–66
    evaluating, 252–53
    grammar for, 262
    main idea in, 242–43
    organization in, 246–51
    paragraphs versus essays in, 250–51
    parallelism in, 439–40
    primary support in, 243–46
    professional, 260–62
    pronouns used in, 408
    reading and analyzing, 253–62
    in the real world, 258–60
    secondary support in, 246
    student, 253–57
    transitions in, 248–49
    understanding, 241–51
    using adjectives and adverbs in, 416–17
    workplace, 258–60
    writing, 263–66
Complete verbs, 329–30
Compound nouns, 516
Compound objects, pronouns used with, 407–8
Compound sentences, 523
Compound subjects, 331
    pronouns used with, 407–8
    subject-verb agreement and, 372
Concession, 301
Concluding sentences
    compared to conclusion, 34
    drafting, 79–80
    purpose of, 33
Conclusion of essay
    compared to concluding sentence, 34
    drafting, 84–86
    purpose of, 34
Concrete word, 494
Confused words, commonly, 502–11
    editing for, 511
    mastering, 513

practice using, 502–10
    understanding, 502
Conjunctions, 328
    coordinating, 357–59, 426–28
    correlative, 440
    subordinating, 431, 469
Conjunctive adverbs, 355–57, 429
conscience/conscious, 504
Consistency of verb tense, 390–91
Consonants
    doubling final, 515
    list of, 514
Context clues, 491–92
Contractions, apostrophes in, 533–34
Coordinate adjectives, 522
Coordinating conjunctions, 357–59, 426–28
Coordination
    editing for, 434–35
    practice using, 426–30
    understanding, 426
Corporation, MLA citations style, 557, 559
Corrections, submitting reprint, 185–87
Correlative conjunctions, 440
Costas, Corin, "What Community Involvement
    Means to Me," 228–29
could as helping verb, 476
Counterarguments, 301
Counterclaim, 301
Count nouns, 484–85
Course names, capitalization of, 551
Critical reading, 10–16
Critical thinking
    in argument, 304
    in cause and effect, 274
    in classification, 202
    in comparison and contrast, 250
    defined, 7–10
    in definition, 224
    in description, 158
    in illustration, 134
    in narration, 112
    in process analysis, 178
    questioning assumptions in, 43–44
    support in arguments, 294
Critical writing
    about readings, 17–23
    about problems, 26–27
    about visuals, 23–25
Cumulative adjectives, 522
Currie, Lisa, 209–11
Cut-and-paste paraphrase, 14

D

Dangling modifiers
    correcting, 423
    editing for, 423–24
    understanding, 422–23
Dashes, 545

Dates
  capitalization of, 550
  commas in, 529
Definite articles, 483
Definition, 201, 219–40
  basics of good, 219–20
  checklist, 240
  evaluating, 227–28
  grammar for, 237
  main idea in, 220–21
  organization in, 226
  paragraphs versus essays in, 224–25
  primary support in, 222–23
  professional, 234–37
  reading and analyzing, 228–37
  in the real world, 232–34
  secondary support in, 223–26
  student, 228–31
  of terms, previewing, 10
  transitions in, 226
  understanding, 219–26
  workplace, 232–34
  writing, 237–40
Demonstrative pronouns, 406
Dependent clauses between subject and verb, 371
Dependent words, 340–42
  correcting run-ons by adding, 359–62
Description, 151–71
  basics of good, 151–52
  checklist, 171
  evaluating, 157–60
  grammar for, 168
  main idea in, 152–54
  organization in, 156–57
  paragraphs versus essays in, 158–59
  primary support in, 154–55
  professional, 166–68
  reading and analyzing, 161–68
  in the real world, 164–65
  secondary support in, 155
  student, 161–64
  transitions in, 156–57
  understanding, 151–57
  workplace, 164–65
  writing, 168–71
Detail. *See* Support
Dictionaries, 492–93, 512
"Difficult Decision with a Positive Outcome, A"
  (Prokop), 278–79
Direct quotations, 536–38
Discussing as prewriting technique, 46–47
Dominant elements of visuals, 23
do, subject-verb agreement with, 368–70
Drafting, 73–89
  arranging ideas in, 73–75
  basics of good, 73
  checklist, 87–88, 89
  essay, 80–89
  making plan for, 76–78
  outlining before, 76–78
  paragraph, 78–80, 86–89
  understanding, 73
  in writing process, 35

E
-ed
  form of adjectives, 414–15
  past participle ending, 381–82
  regular past tense ending, 381
Editing
  adjectives and adverbs, 417–18
  apostrophes, 535
  commas, 530–31
  commonly confused words, 511
  compared to revising, 90
  coordination and subordination, 434–35
  fragments, 346–49
  misplaced and dangling modifiers, 423–24
  parallelism, 442
  pronouns, 409–11
  punctuation marks, 546–47
  quotation marks, 541–42
  run-ons, 362–65
  sentence variety, 455–56
  subject-verb agreement, 374–77
  verb problems, 391–93
  word choice, 500
  in writing process, 35
effect/affect, 503
ei versus *ie*, spelling rules for, 514
either...or, 440
Encyclopedia, MLA citations style, 557, 559
-er, adjectives or adverbs ending in, 416–17
Ericsson, Stephanie, "The Ways We Lie," 211–14
Errors, 325
  with modal verbs, 478–79
  in perfect tense formation, 471
  in using simple tenses, 468–69
-es ending, 516
-e, spelling rules for dropping final, 514
Essays. *See also* Essays versus paragraphs
  drafting, 80–89
  outlining, 77–78
  quotation marks for titles of, 540–41
  relationship between paragraphs and, 36–37, 50–51
  revising, 100–2
  support in, 66–67
  titles, 86
  understanding form of, 34
  workplace, 184–87
Essays versus paragraphs. *See also* Essays
  in argument, 304–5
  in cause and effect, 274–75
  in classification, 202–3
  in comparison and contrast, 250–51
  comparison of forms in, 36–37, 50–51
  in definition, 224–25

in description, 158–59
in illustration, 134–35
in narration, 112–13
in process analysis, 178–79
support in, 66–67
Essential adjective clauses, 453
-est
adjectives ending in, 416–17
superlative form of adjectives or adverbs, 416
Evaluation
of argument, 307–8
of cause and effect, 276–77
of classification, 204–5
of comparison and contrast, 252–53
of definition, 227–28
of description, 157–60
evidence, 299–301
of illustration, 136–37
of narration, 114–15
of problems, 27
of process analysis, 180–81
of readings, 22–23
of visuals, 25
Evidence
evaluating, 299–301
types of, 296–99
Examples
colons before, 544
as evidence, 296
fragments that are, 345–46
except/accept, 503
Expert opinions as evidence, 297
Explanations
colons before, 544
fragments that are, 345–46
Explanatory process analysis, 174
Exploring topics, 45–49
"Eyeglasses versus Laser Surgery: Benefits and Drawbacks" (Ibrahim), 253–54

F

Facts
as evidence, 296
opening essay with surprising, 83
FANBOYS, 426
Feedback, 98
Figures in visuals, 23–24
fine/find, 504–5
"First Day in Fallujah" (Healy), 162–64
"Fish Cheeks" (Tan), 121–23
"5 Scientific Reasons That Global Warming Isn't Happening" (Hawkins), 311–14
for
in compound sentences, 523
as coordinating conjunction, 426–27
Fragments, 337–50
editing for, 346–49
finding and correcting, 338–46

importance of correcting, 337–38
that are examples or explanations, 345–46
that start with dependent words, 340–42
that start with *-ing* verb forms, 342–44
that start with prepositions, 339, 341–42
that start with *to* and a verb, 344–45
understanding, 337–38
Freewriting, 45–46
Fused sentences, 351
Future perfect tense, 470–71
Future progressive tense, 473
Future tense, simple, 468

G

Garcia-Muniz, Paola, 185
Gender, confusion of, 466
Generating ideas in writing process, 35
Gerunds, 480–82
"Gifts from the Heart" (Palmer), 138
Gonzalez, Juan C., 141–43
Good, use of, 417
Government agency, MLA citations style, 557, 559
Grading criteria, 38–40
Grammar
for cause and effect, 286
for classification, 214–15
for comparison and contrast, 262
for definition, 237
for description, 168
four most serious errors in, 325
for illustration, 146
for narration, 123
parts of speech, 326–28
for process analysis, 190
Groups
capitalization of names of, 550
MLA citations style, 557, 559

H

have
versus *of*, 506
present tense of, 385
subject-verb agreement with, 368–70
Hawkins, John, "5 Scientific Reasons That Global Warming Isn't Happening," 311–14
Headings, previewing, 11
Headnote, previewing, 11
Healy, Brian, "First Day in Fallujah," 162–64
Helping verbs. *See* Auxiliary verbs
here, sentences that begin with, 373–74
"High School Is Not Preparing Us for College" (Bigler), 139–40
Hijuelos, Oscar, "Memories of New York City Snow," 166–68
Horn, Katie, "A Beginner's Guide to Movie Night," 183–84
Hultgren, Kelly, "Pick Up the Phone to Call, Not Text," 207–8
Hyphens, 546

I

Ibrahim, Said, "Eyeglasses versus Laser Surgery: Benefits and Drawbacks," 253–54
Ideas
  arranging, in essay, 73–75
  in narration, 106–8
  opening essay with surprising, 83
Identifying adjective clauses, 453
Illustration, 128–50
  basics of good, 128–29
  checklist, 150
  evaluating, 136–37
  grammar for, 146
  main idea in, 129–30
  organization in, 133
  paragraphs versus essays in, 134–35
  primary support in, 130–31
  professional, 143–46
  reading and analyzing, 137–46
  in the real world, 141
  secondary support in, 131–32
  student, 138–40
  transitions in, 133
  understanding, 128–33
  workplace, 141–43
  writing, 146–50
Importance, order of, 75
Incomplete thoughts, 333
Indefinite articles, 483
Indefinite pronouns, 372–73, 400–2
Independent clause, 328
  semicolons to join closely related, 543
Indirect speech. *See* Reported speech
"Indonesian and U.S. School Systems" (Rantung), 254–57
Infinitives, 480–82
-ing
  forms of adjectives, 414–15
  joining ideas using, 446–48
  in present progressive tenses, 471–75
  verb forms, 342–44
Inseparable phrasal verbs, 487
Instructional process analysis, 174
Intensive pronouns, 406
Internet, prewriting and, 48
Interrogative pronouns, 406
Interrupters, commas around, 525–26
In-text citations, 556–57
Introduction of essay
  drafting, 82–84
  purpose of, 34
Introductory words, 523–24
Invention strategies, 45–49
Irregular verbs, 368–70, 382–86
"Isn't It Time You Hit the Books?" (Levine-Finley), 187–90
-i, spelling rules for, 514
its/it's, 505

J

Jacobowitz, Amanda, "A Ban on Water Bottles: A Way to Bolster the University's Image," 15–16
Journal, prewriting and, 48–49

K

Key words
  coherence and, 97
  previewing, 11
knew/new/know/no, 505
Kowalski, Mary T., *Textbook of Basic Nursing*, 18–23

L

Languages, capitalization of, 550–51
Letters
  apostrophes with, 534
  capitalizing first, 548
Levine-Finley, Samantha, "Isn't It Time You Hit the Books?", 187–90
Lexical information, 458
Linking verbs, 328–29, 330–31
Lists
  colons before, 544
  parallelism in, 438–39
  as prewriting technique, 46
Logical fallacies, 270
loose/lose, 505
Lynch, Jelani, "My Turnaround," 116–17

M

Maddox, Moses, 232–34
Main idea. *See also* Thesis statement; Topic sentences
  in argument, 292–94
  in cause and effect, 268–69
  in classification, 196–99
  in comparison and contrast, 242–43
  in critical reading and, 11–12
  in definition, 220–21
  in description, 152–54
  direct statement, 61–62
  of essay, 34
  finding while reading, 10–13
  generating support for, 67–68
  as idea to show, explain, or prove, 60–61
  in illustration, 129–30
  in narration, 106–8
  of paragraph, 33
  in process analysis, 174–75
  single versus multiple, 57–58
  specific versus general, 58–59
  topic sentence and thesis statement for expressing, 49–54
Main verbs, 328
Major events, choosing, 108

Mapping, 47
Mattazi, Lorenza, "All My Music," 206–7
may as helping verb, 476
McCrimmon, Adam, 234–37
"Memories of New York City Snow" (Hijuelos), 166–68
might as helping verb, 476
mind/mine, 506
Misplaced modifiers, 420–24
    correcting, 421–22
    editing for, 423–24
    understanding, 420–21
Misspelled words, commonly, 517
MLA citation style, 555–61
    in-text citations, 556–57
    works cited list, 557–58
Modal verbs, 475–78. *See also* Auxiliary verbs
    common errors with, 478–79
    in negative statements, 461–63
Modifiers
    dangling, 422–24
    misplaced, 420–22
Multiple author, in-text citations style, 556, 559
must as helping verb, 477
"My Turnaround" (Lynch), 116–17

N

Names
    capitalization of, 549
    commas with, 529
Narration, 105–27
    basics of good, 105–6
    checklist, 126
    choosing major events for, 108
    evaluating, 114–15
    grammar for, 123
    main idea in, 106–8
    opening essay with, 82
    organization in, 111–14
    paragraphs versus essays in, 112–13
    primary support in, 108
    professional, 121–23
    reading and analyzing, 116–23
    in the real world, 119
    secondary support in, 109–11
    student, 116–18
    transitions in, 111, 114
    understanding, 105–14
    workplace, 120
    writing, 123–26
Narrowing, topic, 42–45
Nationalities, capitalization of, 550–51
Negatives, 461–63
neither...nor, 440
new/knew/no/know, 505
Newspaper articles, quotation marks for titles of, 540–41

no, commas with, 529–30
Noncount nouns, 484–85
Nonessential adjective clauses, 453
nor
    in compound sentences, 523
    as coordinating conjunction, 426–27
    in correlative conjunctions, 440
not only...but also, 440
Noun phrases, 326
Nouns, 326
    articles and, 483–85
    collective, 401–2
    compound, 516
    count and noncount, 483–85
    proper, 131
Numbers, apostrophes with, 534

O

Object of preposition, 331
Object pronouns, 404–5, 466
Objects in visuals, 23–24
of/have, 506
Online translators, 493
Opinions, 296
    opening essay with, 83
"Optimistic Generation, The" (Willey), 229–31
or
    in compound sentences, 523
    as coordinating conjunction, 426–27
    in correlative conjunctions, 440
Order
    of importance, 75, 133, 201, 226, 248
    space, 74–75
    time, 74, 133, 201
Organization
    in argument, 302–6
    capitalization of names of, 550
    in cause and effect, 272–76
    in classification, 201–4
    in comparison and contrast, 246–49
    in definition, 226
    in description, 156–57
    in illustration, 133
    in narration, 111–14
    in process analysis, 177
Organizations, capitalization of names of, 550
Organizing principle, 195
our/are, 504
Outlining, 76–78
Overgeneralizing, 296
Ownership, apostrophes to show, 532–33

P

Paired words, parallelism with, 440
Pairs, parallelism in, 438–39
Palmer, Cassandra, "Gifts from the Heart," 138

Paragraphs. *See also* Paragraphs versus essays
    comparison of forms in, 36–37, 50–51
    drafting, 78–80, 86–89
    outlining, 76
    relationship between essays and, 36–37, 50–51
    revising, 98–100
    support in, 34, 66–67
    understanding form of, 33
Paragraphs versus essays. *See also* Paragraphs
    in argument, 304–5
    in cause and effect, 274–75
    in classification, 202–3
    in comparison and contrast, 250–51
    comparison of forms in, 36–37, 50–51
    in definition, 224–25
    in description, 158–59
    in illustration, 134–35
    in narration, 112–13
    in process analysis, 178–79
    support in, 66–67
Parallelism, 437–43
    in comparisons, 439–40
    editing for, 442
    with paired words, 440–42
    in pairs and lists, 438–39
    understanding, 437
Parallel sentences, 437–42
Parallel structure, 215
Paraphrasing, 13–15
Parentheses, 545
Parts of speech, 326–28
passed/past, 506
Passive voice, 388–90
Past participles, 381–82, 387–90
    joining ideas using, 448–50
Past perfect tense, 388, 470–71
Past progressive tense, 472–73
Past tense, 381
    of *be*, 385
    simple, 468, 469
Patterns, sentence, 334–35, 458–64
peace/piece, 506–7
Peer review, 98
Perfect tenses, 469–71
Periods, correcting run-ons by adding, 354
Person, pronouns consistent in, 409
Phrases, transitional, 95–96
"Pick Up the Phone to Call, Not Text" (Hultgren), 207–8
Places, capitalization of names of, 549–50
Plagiarism, 48
Plan for drafting, 76–78
Plural pronouns, 465
Plurals
    apostrophes not used to form, 533
    types of, 516
Point-by-point organization in comparison and contrast, 246
Point of comparison/contrast, 244–46
Possessive pronouns, 404–5, 465
    apostrophes not used with, 533

Post hoc fallacy, 270
Predictions as evidence, 297
Prefix, 492
Prepositional phrases, 331–33
    between subject and verb, 370
Prepositions, 327, 485–88
    after adjectives, 485–86
    fragments that start with, 339, 341–42
    after verbs, 486–87
Present perfect tense, 387, 470
Present progressive tense, 381, 471–74
Present tense, 380–81
    of *be* and *have*, 385
    simple, 467–68
Previewing before reading, 10–11
Prewriting techniques for exploring topic, 45–49
Primary support. *See also* Support
    in cause and effect, 270–71
    in classification, 199–200
    in comparison and contrast, 243–46
    in definition, 222–23
    in description, 154–55
    in essays, 67
    in illustration, 130–31
    in narration, 108
    in process analysis, 175–76
    selecting best, 68
    understanding, 65
    writing, 69–71
principal/principle, 507
Problems, writing critically about, 26–27
Process analysis, 173–94
    basics of good, 173–74
    checklist, 193–94
    evaluating, 180–81
    grammar for, 190
    main idea in, 174–75
    organization in, 177–79
    paragraphs versus essays in, 178–79
    primary support in, 175–76
    professional, 187–90
    reading and analyzing, 182–90
    secondary support in, 176–77
    student, 182–84
    transitions in, 177
    understanding, 173–79
    workplace, 185
    writing, 190–94
Progressive tenses, 471–75
Prokop, Caitlin, "A Difficult Decision with a Positive Outcome," 278–79
Pronouns, 326, 397–411
    agreement, 399–400
    ambiguous reference, 402–3
    in comparisons, 408
    with compound subjects and objects, 407–8
    confusing gender and, 466
    consistent in person, 409
    correct use of, 397–409
    demonstrative, 406

editing, 409–11
identifying, 397–99
indefinite, 372–73, 400–2
intensive, 406
interrogative, 406
leaving out, 466
object, 404–5, 466
plural, 465
possessive, 404–5, 465, 533
practice using correct, 397–409
reciprocal, 406
reflexive, 406
relative, 406, 467
repetitious reference, 403–4
singular, 465
subject, 404–5, 465
types of, 404–9, 465
understanding, 397
used to repeat subject, 466
vague reference, 402–3
Proofreading techniques, 513
Proper nouns, 131
Punctuation, 543–47
editing for, 546–47
practice using, 543–46
of quotations, 537–38
understanding, 543
Purpose for writing
finding while reading, 13
understanding, 29–32

Q

Questioning assumptions, 43–44
in argument, 295–96
critical thinking and, 7–8
topic narrowing, 43–44
Questions, 373, 463–64
opening essay with, 83–84
quiet/quite/quit, 507
Quotation marks, 536–42
for certain titles, 540–41
commas with, 528
for direct quotations, 536–38
editing for, 541–42
for indirect (reported) speech, 539–40
practice using, 536–41
understanding, 536
Quotations
direct, 536–38
opening essay with, 82
set off within another quotation, 538–39

R

Rantung, Rita, "Indonesian and U.S. School Systems,"
254–57
rather . . . than, 440
Reading

and analysis. *See* Analysis
critically, 10–16
finding main idea and support during, 11–13
on Internet, 48
previewing, 10–11
writing critically about, 17–23
Rebuttal, 301
Reciprocal pronouns, 406
Reflexive pronouns, 406
Regular verbs, 367, 380–82
Relative pronouns, 406, 467
Religions, capitalization of, 550–51
Repetitious pronoun references, 403
Reported speech, 539–40
Restrictive adjective clauses, 453
Revising, 90–102
checklist, 90–91, 100, 102
for coherence, 95–97
for detail and support, 93–94
essays, 100–2
paragraphs, 98–100
understanding, 90–91
for unity, 91–93
in writing process, 35
Rhetorical context, 10–11
Riggs, Liz, "What It's Like to Be the First Person
in Your Family to Go to College," 282–85
right/write, 507
Riley-Jewell, Trevor, "An Unusual Inspiration," 117–18
Rosdahl, Caroline Bunker, *Textbook of Basic Nursing*,
18–23
Roy, James, 164–65
Rubric, 38–40
Run-ons, 351–66
caused by *then*, 362
editing for, 362–65
finding and correcting, 353–62
understanding, 351–53

S

-s
added to nouns to form plural, 515
added to show ownership, 532–33
ending, 380–81
used to make letters and numbers plural, 534
Scheffers, Brett and James Watson, "Climate Change Is
Affecting All Life on Earth – and That's Not Good
News for Humanity," 314–17
Secondary support. *See also* Support
adding, 69
in cause and effect, 271–72
in classification, 200–1
in comparison and contrast, 246
in definition, 223–26
in description, 155
in illustration, 131–32
in narration, 109–11
in process analysis, 176–77
understanding, 65

Semicolons
    in coordination, 428–30
    correcting run-ons by adding, 354–57
    to join closely related independent clauses, 543
    when items in list contain commas, 543–44
Sentences. *See also* Run-ons
    basic, 328–36
    basic patterns, 334–36, 458–64
    begin with *here* or *there*, 373
    capitalization of, 548
    compound, 523
    with compound subjects, 372
    concluding, 33, 79–80
    coordination of, 426–30
    drafting using complete, 78–79
    direct statement, 61–62
    four most serious errors in, 325
    incomplete thought in, 333
    negative statement, 461–63
    neither too broad nor too narrow, 57
    parallelism in, 437–42
    question, 373, 463–64
    short, simple, 444–45
    specific, 58–59
    statement, 458–61
    subjects in, 328, 331–33, 370–74
    subordination of, 430–35
    support, 33
    that fit assignment, 55–56
    there is and *there are* in, 464
    verbs in, 328–31, 467–82
Sentence variety, 444–56
    adjective clauses for, 452–55
    appositives for, 451–52
    creating, 445–55
    editing for, 455–56
    -*ing* verbs for, 446–48
    past participles for, 448–50
    starting sentences with adverbs for, 445–46
    understanding, 444–45
Separable phrasal verbs, 487
Series, commas between items in, 521–22
set/sit, 508
Short stories, quotation marks for titles of, 540–41
should as helping verb, 477
Simple future tense, 468
Simple past tense, 468, 469
Simple present tense, 467–68
Simple tenses, 467–69
Single author, MLA citations style, 556, 558
Singular pronouns, 465
Slang, 495–96
Slippery slope fallacy, 271
so
    in compound sentences, 523
    as coordinating conjunction, 426–27
Space order, 74–75
Specific people, capitalization of names of, 549
Specific word, 494

Speech, parts of, 326–28
Spell checkers, 512
Spelling, 512–18
    finding and correcting mistakes in, 512–13
    list, 513
    rules, 514–16
    strategies for better, 513–17
Statements, 458–61
    negative, 461–63
Story. *See* Narration
Student preparedness, 4–5
Subject pronouns, 404–5, 465
Subjects
    compound, 331, 372
    indefinite pronouns as, 372–73
    in sentences, 331–33
    using pronoun to repeat, 466
    verb coming before, 373–74
    words that come between verb and, 370–71
Subject-verb agreement, 367–77
    editing for, 374–77
    finding and correcting errors in, 368–74
    understanding, 367–68
Subordinating conjunction, 431, 469
Subordination, 430–35
    editing for, 434–35
    practice using, 431–34
    understanding, 430–31
Subtitles, 545
Success, preparing for, 4–7
Suffix, 492
Summary
    previewing, 11
    of problems, 26
    of readings, 18–19
    of visuals, 23–24
Superlative form of adjectives, 416–17
Support, 13, 65–72. *See also* Primary support; Secondary
        support
    in argument, 294–301
    checklist, 71
    in critical reading and, 13
    about events, 110–11
    finding while reading, 13
    good, features of, 65–66
    for main idea, 67–69
    paragraphs, 33
    in paragraphs versus essays, 66–67
    revising for, 93–94
    sentences, 33, 34
    understanding, 65–67
    writing, 69–71
suppose/supposed, 508
Surprise, opening essay with, 83
Synonyms, 493
Synthesis
    of problems, 26
    of readings, 20–22
    of visuals, 25

T

Tan, Amy, "Fish Cheeks," 121–23
Tense. *See* Verb tense
Textbook of Basic Nursing (Rosdahl and Kowalski), 18–23
than
    in correlative conjunctions, 440
    versus *then*, 508
their/there/they're, 508–9
then
    run-ons caused by, 362
    versus *than*, 508
there
    sentences that begin with, 373–74
    versus *they're* and *their*, 508–9
there is and *there are*, 464
Thesaurus, 493
Thesis statement. *See also* Main idea; Topic sentences
    compared to topic sentence, 34, 49–54
    developing, 54–62
    writing, 62–64
they're/their/there, 508–9
Things, capitalization of, 549
Thinking critically. *See* Critical thinking
though/through/threw, 509
Tierney, John, "Yes, Money Can Buy Happiness ...", 260–62
Time
    apostrophes with, 534
    order, 74, 133, 201
    words, 469
Titles
    capitalization of, 551
    essay, 86
    previewing, 11
    set off with quotation marks, 536, 540–41
to
    fragments that start with, 344–45
    versus *too* and *two*, 509
Topic, 41–64
    checklist for, 49
    exploring, 45–49
    narrowing, 42–45
    understanding, 41–42
Topic sentences. *See also* Main idea; Thesis statement
    compared to thesis statement, 34, 49–54
    developing, 54–62
    drafting, 81–82
    of support paragraphs in essay, 33
    writing, 62–64
Transitions, 95–97
    in argument, 303, 306
    in cause and effect, 273, 276
    in classification, 201, 204
    in comparison and contrast, 248–49
    in definition, 226
    in description, 156–57
    in illustration, 133
    in narration, 111, 114
    in process analysis, 177
Translators, 493

U

Unity, revising for, 91–93
"Unusual Inspiration, An" (Riley-Jewell), 117–18
use/used, 510

V

Vague and abstract words, 494–95
Vague pronoun references, 402–3
Vaz, Garth, 258–60
Verbs, 326, 467–82
    action, 328, 330–31
    auxiliary, 329–31, 387, 461–62, 475–80
    base form, 379
    be, have, or *do,* 368–70
    coming before subject, 373–74
    complete, 329
    gerunds and infinitives as, 480–82
    -ing forms, 342–44, 446–48
    irregular, 368–70, 382–86
    linking, 328–29, 330–31
    main, 328
    prepositions after, 486–87
    regular, 367, 380–82
    words that come between subject and, 370–71
Verb tense, 379–94
    consistency of, 390–91
    editing for problems with, 391–93
    perfect, 469–71
    practice using correct, 380–91
    present progressive, 380, 471–73
    simple, 467–69
    understanding, 379–80
Visuals, writing critically about, 23–25
Vocabulary, building, 491–93
    context clues for, 491–92
    dictionary for, 492–93
    thesaurus for, 493
    word parts for, 492
Vowels, list of, 514

W

"Ways We Lie, The" (Ericsson), 211–14
well, use of, 417
"What Community Involvement Means to Me" (Costas), 228–29
"What It's Like to Be the First Person in Your Family to Go to College" (Riggs), 282–85
"When Poor People Have Nice Things" (Whitmer), 143–46
which, adjective clause beginning with, 526–28
Whitmer, Andrea, "When Poor People Have Nice Things," 143–46

who
  adjective clause beginning with, 526–28
  as subject, 408–9
Whole-to-whole organization in comparison and contrast, 246–47
whom as object, 408–9
who's/whose, 510
will as helping verb, 477
Willey, Kevin, "The Optimistic Generation," 229–31
Woodson, Carter G., 281
Word choice, 491–501
  avoiding common problems with, 493–500
  context clues for, 491–92
  dictionary for, 492–93
  editing for, 500–1
  thesaurus for, 493
Word parts, 492
Words
  commonly confused, 502–11, 513
  correct spelling of, 512–18
  divided at end of line, 546
  introductory, 523–24
  joined with hyphens, 546
  order, 460–61
  transitional, 96
  vague and abstract, 494–95
Wordy language, 496–98
Workplace
  argument, 309–10
  cause and effect, 281–82
  comparison and contrast, 258–60
  definition, 232–34
  description, 164–65
  essay, 184–87
  illustration, 141–43
  narration, 120
  process analysis, 185

Works cited list, 557–58
would as helping verb, 478
Writing basics, 29–40
  audience and, 29–32
  grading criteria and, 38–40
  paragraph and essay form, 33–34
  topic sentence and thesis statement, 62–64
  writing process and, 34–35
Writing class, 3
Writing critically
  about readings, 17–23
  about problems, 26–27
  about visuals, 23–25
Writing, pre-, 45–49
Writing process, understanding, 34–35
Writing prompt, 553–54

Y

-y
  adding *-ing* to, 515
  changing to *-i,* spelling rules for, 514
  as vowel or consonant, 514
yes, commas with, 529–30
"Yes, Money Can Buy Happiness . . ." (Tierney), 260–62
yet
  in compound sentences, 523
  as coordinating conjunction, 426–27
your/you're, 510

Z

Z pattern, 23

Useful Editing and Proofreading Marks

The marks and abbreviations below are those typically used by instructors when marking papers (add any alternate marks used by your instructor in the left-hand column), but you can also mark your own work or that of your peers with these helpful symbols.

Alternate symbol	Standard symbol	How to revise or edit (numbers in boldface are chapters where you can find help)
	adj	Use correct adjective form **Ch. 21**
	adv	Use correct adverb form **Ch. 21**
	agr	Correct subject-verb agreement or pronoun agreement **Chs. 18 and 20**
	awk	Awkward expression: edit for clarity **Ch. 5**
	cap or triple underline [example]	Use capital letter correctly **Ch. 34**
	case	Use correct pronoun case **Ch. 20**
	cliché	Replace overused phrase with fresh words **Ch. 27**
	coh	Revise paragraph or essay for coherence **Ch. 5**
	coord	Use coordination correctly **Ch. 23**
	cs	Comma splice: join the sentences correctly **Ch. 17**
	dev	Develop your paragraph or essay more completely **Chs. 2 and 4**
	dm	Revise to avoid a dangling modifier **Ch. 22**
	frag	Attach the fragment to a sentence or make it a sentence **Ch. 16**
	fs	Fused sentence: join the two sentences correctly **Ch. 17**
	ital	Use italics **Ch. 30**
	lc or diagonal slash [Example]	Use lowercase **Ch. 32**
	mm	Revise to avoid a misplaced modifier **Ch. 22**
	pl	Use the correct plural form of the verb **Ch. 18**
	ref	Make pronoun reference clear **Ch. 20**
	ro	Run-on sentence: join the two sentences correctly **Ch. 17**
	sp	Correct the spelling error **Ch. 29**
	sub	Use subordination correctly **Ch. 23**
	sup	Support your point with details, examples, or facts **Ch. 4**
	tense	Correct the problem with verb tense **Ch. 19**
	trans	Add a transition **Ch. 5**
	w	Delete unnecessary words **Ch. 25**
	wc	Reconsider your word choice **Ch. 27**
	?	Make your meaning clearer **Ch. 5**
	⌃ ,	Use comma correctly **Ch. 30**
	; : ( ) - —	Use semicolon / colon / parentheses / hyphen / dash correctly **Ch. 33**
	" " ⌄ ⌄	Use quotation marks correctly **Ch. 32**
	⌃	Insert something
	⸜ [example]	Delete something
	⌣ [(words)(example)]	Change the order of letters or words
	¶	Start a new paragraph
	# [example # words]	Add a space
	⌒ [ex ⌒ample]	Close up a space